Integrations of Data Warehousing, Data Mining and Database Technologies:

Innovative Approaches

David Taniar
Monash University, Australia

Li Chen
LaTrobe University, Australia

Senior Editorial Director:	Kristin Klinger
Director of Book Publications:	Julia Mosemann
Editorial Director:	Lindsay Johnston
Acquisitions Editor:	Erika Carter
Development Editor:	Michael Killian
Production Coordinator:	Jamie Snavely
Typesetters:	Milan Vracarich Jr., Jennifer Romanchak & Michael Brehm
Cover Design:	Nick Newcomer

Published in the United States of America by
      Information Science Reference (an imprint of IGI Global)
      701 E. Chocolate Avenue
      Hershey PA 17033
      Tel: 717-533-8845
      Fax: 717-533-8661
      E-mail: cust@igi-global.com
      Web site: http://www.igi-global.com/reference

Library of Congress Cataloging-in-Publication Data

Integrations of data warehousing, data mining and database technologies :
innovative approaches / David Taniar and Li Chen, editors.
    p. cm.
 Includes bibliographical references and index.
 Summary: "This book provides a comprehensive compilation of knowledge
covering state-of-the-art developments and research, as well as current
innovative activities in data warehousing and mining, focusing on the
integration between the fields of data warehousing and data mining, with
emphasis on the applicability to real world problems"--Provided by publisher.
 ISBN 978-1-60960-537-7 (hardcover) -- ISBN 978-1-60960-538-4 (ebook) 1.
Data warehousing. 2. Data mining. I. Taniar, David. II. Chen, Li, 1982-
 QA76.9.D37I4577 2011
 006.3'12--dc22
               2011009996

British Cataloguing in Publication Data
A Cataloguing in Publication record for this book is available from the British Library.

Table of Contents

Section 1

Detailed Table of Contents

Section 1

Chapter 1

Matteo Golfarelli, DEIS - University of Bologna, Italy
Stefano Rizzi, DEIS - University of Bologna, Italy

Data warehouses are information repositories specialized in supporting decision making. Since the decisional process typically requires an analysis of historical trends, time and its management acquire a huge importance. In this paper we consider the variety of issues, often grouped under term temporal data warehousing, implied by the need for accurately describing how information changes over time in data warehousing systems. We recognize that, with reference to a three-levels architecture, these issues can be classified into some topics, namely: handling data/schema changes in the data warehouse, handling data/schema changes in the data mart, querying temporal data, and designing temporal data warehouses. After introducing the main concepts and terminology of temporal databases, we separately survey these topics. Finally, we discuss the open research issues also in connection with their implementation on commercial tools.

Chapter 2

Rosine Cicchetti, Aix-Marseille Universités, France
Lotfi Lakhal, Aix-Marseille Universités, France
Sébastien Nedjar, Aix-Marseille Universités, France
Noël Novelli, Aix-Marseille Universités, France
Alain Casali, Aix-Marseille Universités, France

Datacubes are especially useful for answering efficiently queries on data warehouses. Nevertheless the amount of generated aggregated data is huge with respect to the initial data which is itself very large. Recent research work has addressed the issue of summarizing Datacubes in order to reduce their size. In this chapter, we present three different approaches. They propose structures which make it possible to reduce the size of the data cube representation. The two former, the closed cube and the quotient cube, are said semantic and discard the redundancies captured within data cubes. The size of the underlying representations is especially reduced but the counterpart is an additional response time when answering the OLAP queries. The latter approach is rather syntactic since it enforces an optimization at the logical level. It is called Partition Cube and based on the concept of partition. We also give an algorithm to compute it. We propose a Relational Partition Cube, a novel R-Olap cubing solution for managing Partition Cubes using the relational technology. An analytical evaluation shows that the storage space of Partition Cubes is smaller than Datacubes. In order to confirm analytical comparison, experiments are performed in order to compare our approach with Datacubes and with two of the best reduction methods, the Quotient Cube and the Closed Cube.

Chapter 3

Vasudha Bhatnagar, University of Delhi, India
Sharanjit Kaur, University of Delhi, India
Laurent Mignet, IBM, Indian Research Lab, India

Clustering of data streams finds important applications in tracking evolution of various phenomena in medical, meteorological, astrophysical, seismic studies. Algorithms designed for this purpose are capable of adapting the discovered clustering model to the changes in data characteristics but are not capable of adapting to the user's requirements themselves. Based on the previous observation, we perform a comparative study of different approaches for existing stream clustering algorithms and present a parameterized architectural framework that exploits nuances of the algorithms. This framework permits the end user to tailor a method to suit his specific application needs. We give a parameterized framework that empowers the end-users of KDD technology to build a clustering model. The framework delivers results as per the user's application requirements. We also present two assembled algorithms G-kMeans and G-dbscan to instantiate the proposed framework and compare the performance with the existing stream clustering algorithms.

Chapter 4

Guangzhu Yu, Donghua University, China
Shihuang Shao, Donghua University, China
Bin Luo, Guangdong University of Technology, China
Xianhui Zeng, Donghua University, China

Existing algorithms for high-utility itemsets mining are column enumeration based, adopting an Apriori-like candidate set generation-and-test approach, and thus are inadequate in datasets with high dimensions or long patterns. To solve the problem, this paper proposed a hybrid model and a row enumeration-based algorithm, i.e., Inter-transaction, to discover high-utility itemsets from two directions: an existing algorithm can be used to seek short high-utility itemsets from the bottom, while Inter-transaction can be used to seek long high-utility itemsets from the top. Inter-transaction makes full use of the characteristic that there are few common items between or among long transactions. By intersecting relevant transactions, the new algorithm can identify long high-utility itemsets, without extending short itemsets step by step. In addition, we also developed new pruning strategies and an optimization technique to improve the performance of Inter-transaction.

Section 2

In the last years, data warehousing systems have gained relevance to support decision making within organizations. The core component of these systems is the data warehouse and nowadays it is widely assumed that the data warehouse design must follow the multidimensional paradigm. Thus, many methods have been presented to support the multidimensional design of the data warehouse. The first methods introduced were requirement-driven but the semantics of the data warehouse (since the data warehouse is the result of homogenizing and integrating relevant data of the organization in a single, detailed view of the organization business) require to also consider the data sources during the design process. Considering the data sources gave rise to several data-driven methods that automate the data warehouse design process, mainly, from relational data sources. Currently, research on multidimensional modeling is still a hot topic and we have two main research lines. On the one hand, new hybrid automatic methods have been introduced proposing to combine data-driven and requirement-driven approaches. These methods focus on automating the whole process and improving the feedback retrieved by each approach to produce better results. On the other hand, some new approaches focus on considering alternative scenarios than relational sources. These methods also consider (semi)-structured data sources, such as ontologies or XML, that have gained relevance in the last years. Thus, they introduce innovative solutions for overcoming the heterogeneity of the data sources. All in all, we discuss the current scenario of multidimensional modeling by carrying out a survey of multidimensional design methods. We present the most relevant methods introduced in the literature and a detailed comparison showing the main features of each approach.

Chapter 6

A data warehouse architecture (DWA) has been developed for the purpose of integrating data from multiple heterogeneous, distributed, and autonomous external data sources (EDSs) as well as for providing means for advanced analysis of integrated data. The major components of this architecture include: an external data source (EDS) layer, and extraction-transformation-loading (ETL) layer, a data warehouse (DW) layer, and an on-line analytical processing (OLAP) layer. Methods of designing a DWA, research developments, and most of the commercially available DW technologies tacitly assumed that a DWA is static. In practice, however, a DWA requires changes among others as the result of the evolution of EDSs, changes of the real world represented in a DW, and new user requirements. Changes in the structures of EDSs impact the ETL, DW, and OLAP layers. Since such changes are frequent, developing a technology for handling them automatically or semi-automatically in a DWA is of high practical importance. This chapter discusses challenges in designing, building, and managing a DWA that supports the evolution of structures of EDSs, evolution of an ETL layer, and evolution of a DW. The challenges and their solutions presented here are based on an experience of building a prototype Evolving-ETL and a prototype Multiversion Data Warehouse (MVDW). In details, this chapter presents the following issues: the concept of the MVDW, an approach to querying the MVDW, an approach to handling the evolution of an ETL layer, a technique for sharing data between multiple DW versions, and two index structures for the MVDW.

Data Warehouses are a crucial technology for current competitive organizations in the globalized world. Size, speed and distributed operation are major challenges concerning those systems. Many data warehouses have huge sizes and the requirement that queries be processed quickly and efficiently, so parallel solutions are deployed to render the necessary efficiency. Distributed operation, on the other hand, concerns global commercial and scientific organizations that need to share their data in a coherent distributed data warehouse. In this article we review the major concepts, systems and research results behind parallel and distributed data warehouses.

The software processes that facilitate the original loading and the periodic refreshment of the data warehouse contents are commonly known as Extraction-Transformation-Loading (ETL) processes. The intention of this survey is to present the research work in the field of ETL technology in a structured way. To this end, we organize the coverage of the field as follows: (a) first, we cover the conceptual and logical modeling of ETL processes, along with some design methods, (b) we visit each stage of the E-T-L triplet, and examine problems that fall within each of these stages, (c) we discuss problems that pertain to the entirety of an ETL process, and, (d) we review some research prototypes of academic origin.

Chapter 9

Geographic Information Systems (GIS) have been extensively used in various application domains, ranging from economical, ecological and demographic analysis, to city and route planning. Nowadays, organizations need sophisticated GIS-based Decision Support System (DSS) to analyze their data with respect to geographic information, represented not only as attribute data, but also in maps. Thus, vendors are increasingly integrating their products, leading to the concept of SOLAP (Spatial OLAP). Also, in the last years, and motivated by the explosive growth in the use of PDA devices, the field of moving object data has been receiving attention from the GIS community, although not much work has been done to provide moving object databases with OLAP capabilities. In the first part of this paper we survey the SOLAP literature. We then address the problem of trajectory analysis, and review recent efforts regarding trajectory data warehousing and mining. We also provide an in-depth comparative study between two proposals: the GeoPKDD project (that makes use of the Hermes system), and Piet, a proposal for SOLAP and moving objects, developed at the University of Buenos Aires, Argentina. Finally, we discuss future directions in the field, including SOLAP analysis over raster data.

Chapter 10

    Christian Thomsen, Aalborg University, Denmark
    Torben Bach Pedersen, Aalborg University, Denmark

The industrial use of open source Business Intelligence (BI) tools is becoming more common, but is still not as widespread as for other types of software. It is therefore of interest to explore which possibilities are available for open source BI and compare the tools. In this survey article, we consider the capabilities of a number of open source tools for BI. In the article, we consider a number of Extract-Transform-Load (ETL) tools, database management systems (DBMSs), On-Line Analytical Processing (OLAP) servers, and OLAP clients. We find that, unlike the situation a few years ago, there now exist mature and powerful tools in all these categories. However, the functionality still falls somewhat short of that found in commercial tools.

Section 4

Chapter 11

    Ladjel Bellatreche, University of Poitiers, France
    Kamel Boukhalfa, University of Poitiers, France
    Pascal Richard, University of Poitiers, France

Horizontal partitioning has evolved significantly in recent years and widely advocated by the academic and industrial communities. Horizontal Partitioning affects positively query performance, database manageability and availability. Two types of horizontal partitioning are supported: primary and referential. Horizontal fragmentation in the context of relational data warehouses is to partition dimension tables by primary fragmentation then fragmenting the fact table by referential fragmentation. This fragmentation can generate a very large number of fragments which may make the maintenance task very complicated. In this paper, we first focus on the evolution of horizontal partitioning in commercial DBMS motivated by decision support applications. Secondly, we give a formalization of the referential fragmentation schema selection problem in the data warehouse and we study its hardness to select an optimal solution. Due to its high complexity, we develop two algorithms: hill climbing and simulated annealing with several variants to select a near optimal partitioning schema. We present ParAdmin, an advisor tool assisting administrators to use primary and referential partitioning during the physical design of their data warehouses. Finally, extensive experimental studies are conducted using the data set of APB1 benchmark to compare the quality the proposed algorithms using a mathematical cost model. Based on these experiments, some recommendations are given to ensure the well use of horizontal partitioning.

Chapter 12

Optimizing decisions has become a vital factor for companies. In order to be able to evaluate beforehand the impact of a decision, managers need reliable provisional systems. Though data warehouses enable analysis of past data, they are not capable of giving anticipations of future trends. What-if analysis fills this gap by enabling users to simulate and inspect the behavior of a complex system under some given hypotheses. A crucial issue in the design of what-if applications is to find an adequate formalism to conceptually express the underlying simulation model. In this paper the authors report on how, within the framework of a comprehensive design methodology, this can be accomplished by extending UML 2 with a set of stereotypes. Their proposal is centered on the use of activity diagrams enriched with object flows, aimed at expressing functional, dynamic, and static aspects in an integrated fashion. The paper is completed by examples taken from a real case study in the commercial area.

Chapter 13

As an unsupervised learning process, document clustering has been used to improve information retrieval performance by grouping similar documents and to help text mining approaches by providing a high-quality input for them. In this article, the authors propose a novel hybrid clustering technique that incorporates semantic smoothing of document models into a neural network framework. Recently, it has been reported that the semantic smoothing model enhances the retrieval quality in Information Retrieval (IR). Inspired by that, the authors developed and applied a context-sensitive semantic smoothing model to boost accuracy of clustering that is generated by a dynamic growing cell structure algorithm, a variation of the neural network technique. They evaluated the proposed technique on biomedical article sets from MEDLINE, the largest biomedical digital library in the world. Their experimental evaluations show that the proposed algorithm significantly improves the clustering quality over the traditional clustering techniques including k-means and self-organizing map (SOM).

Chapter 14

Zoran Bosnic, University of Ljubljana, Slovenia
Igor Kononenko, University of Ljubljana, Slovenia

In machine learning, the reliability estimates for individual predictions provide more information about individual prediction error than the average accuracy of predictive model (e.g. relative mean squared error). Such reliability estimates may represent decisive information in the risk-sensitive applications of machine learning (e.g. medicine, engineering, and business), where they enable the users to distinguish between more and less reliable predictions. In the atuhors' previous work they proposed eight reliability estimates for individual examples in regression and evaluated their performance. The results showed that the performance of each estimate strongly varies depending on the domain and regression model properties. In this paper they empirically analyze the dependence of reliability estimates' performance on the data set and model properties. They present the results which show that the reliability estimates perform better when used with more accurate regression models, in domains with greater number of examples and in domains with less noisy data.

Preface

INTRODUCTION

A data warehouse stores a massive amount of data integrated from data sources, which can reflect the reality of the real world for reporting and analysis purposes, and its tools can be used to discover from the data, the trend or potential direction of developments. Therefore, in application areas such as commerce, health care and monitoring of global changes in the environment and biodiversity, data warehouses are used extensively for the purposes of inquiries, decision making and data mining.

The purpose of this book is to present and disseminate the latest developments in data warehousing. The focus is on the most recent research and discoveries, in particular several interesting issues and trends that have emerged in the last few years. This chapter provides introductory background information leading into the topic of Data Warehouse. It consists of five sections. Figure 1 is a flowchart showing the connection among these sections.

Traditionally, a data warehouse is mainly used as a repository for a massive amount of data. It focuses on the data storage and reflects only the historical static data. However, in the dynamic business environment typical of many organizations, a data warehouse plays an important role in both strategy and tactical decision-making, therefore, users require that the requested data be the most recent, or the 'freshest'. This process includes extracting the new transaction data from the database, transforming, aggregating and then updating it into a data warehouse. Moreover, users usually expect prompt responses to their queries. These fundamental requirements present a challenge to the data warehouse due to the high loads and update complexity of data warehouse refresh mechanisms. Therefore, in the following section, we will present an overview of a data warehouse which includes its components, the

Figure 1. Flowchart

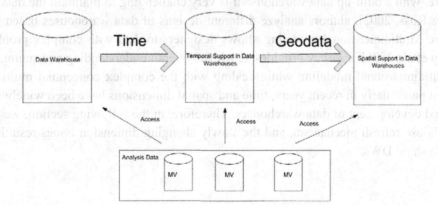

categories of its refresh mechanism and the slowly changing dimension which will lead us to the temporal support in data warehouses. A geospatial domain has been widely developed by the availability of wireless networks and portable devices, so the complexity of the decision making with the spatial and temporal dimension involved will greatly increase. In recent years, it has become increasingly important to extend the data warehouse with spatial and temporal features. Finally, Materialized Views are discussed, since the data warehouse must be increasingly queried effectively for decision making purposes, and the use of materialized views is presumably the most effective and popular means of speeding up query processing.

DATA WAREHOUSING: AN OVERVIEW

W.H. Inmon characterized a Data Warehouse (DW) as a subject-oriented, integrated, non-volatile, time-variant collection of data in support of management's decisions [Inmon, 1996]. A DW is an environment, not a product, in which the user can gain the current or historical data. These data being used for making decision or analyzing are usually difficult or impossible to process from the operational database. Therefore, data warehousing is a technology that aggregates data into the DW for complex analysis, and quick, efficient query response and decision-making. When the data are deposited into the data warehouse, the administrator or other users can easily gain access in order to manipulate the data or obtain useful data information about business performance by using a DW application tool such as online analytical processing (OLAP).

There are several major components of the architecture of a DW (see Figure 2): the source system, the data mart, transformation mechanism, the metadata repository, central data warehouse and end-user decision support tools for data analysis.

The most common data model is multidimensional modeling, in which star schema and snow flake schema are introduced in [Inmon, 1996]. The star schema is a technique used in modeling to map multidimensional decision support data into a relational database. It consists of "fact table" and a number of "dimensional tables". A fact table (e.g., Sales facts) represents a specific business aspect or activity by numeric measurements (values). (e.g. analysis of sales, quantity or Amount representing analysis needs in numeric form.) Dimensions (e.g., Product, Time, Customer and Location) are qualifying characteristics that are used as measures from different analysis perspectives. Further, a dimension may include descriptive attributes (e.g., customer name or sex in the Customer dimension).

The dynamic business environment of many organizations requires high freshness of requested data. Therefore, with a built-up data warehouse it is very challenging to maintain the data warehouse. In [Kimball & Ross, 2002], authors analyze different designs of data warehouses based on different real-life issues. Multidimensional modeling allows designers to deal with complex problems in real life, in [Mazón et al., 2009], a survey provides us with an overall understanding and summary of issues regarding multidimensional modeling while dealing with the complex conceptual multidimensional structure. Most particularly in recent years, time and spatial dimensions have been widely investigated in the advanced development of data warehouses. Therefore, in the following section, we will discuss the data warehouse refresh mechanism, and the slowly changing dimension issues resulting from the process of refreshing DWs.

Figure 2. The major components of the architecture of a data warehouse

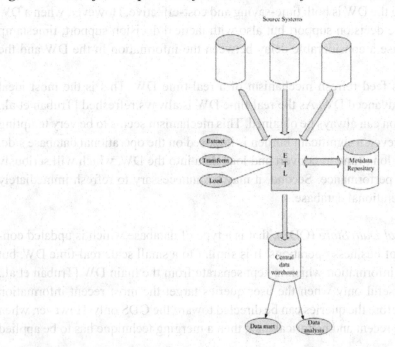

Data Warehouse Refresh Mechanism

In respect to the refreshing of a data warehouse, as changes are made in the operational database, the DW must reflect these changes, which includes the changes made in fact and the slow changes made in dimensions. Since a DW is non-volatile, the refresh of a DW here means that data is uploaded into the DW, while the data that is already in the DW will never be deleted from the DW. This section of the chapter summarizes the categories of existing data warehouse refresh mechanisms and the issue of the slow changes made in dimensions.

In general, DW refresh mechanisms have gradually shifted from traditional DW to real-time DW mechanisms, as outlined in the following four categories:

- The first category is a traditional DW refresh mechanism which consists of traditional batch-based updates. The whole DW is rebuilt from scratch by running the schema, repopulating all the data from the current operational database with a timestamp. Based on the schedule of the business at that time, DW can be refreshed monthly, quarterly, even yearly [Mumick et al., 1997]. The benefit of this is that all the data in the DW remains consistent [Bin et al., 2002], because while batching the data into the DW, the users do not have ready access to the DW, and will not get the data analyzing that is not the current data in the DW [Thiele et al., 2009; Truban et al., 2008]. However, the full refresh mechanism cannot possibly meet users' requirements when the size of the DW is greatly increasing; the data need to be refreshed more frequently and the batch windows for data acquisition need to be increasingly smaller.
- The second category is incremental batch refresh based on a timestamp, which means that instead of redoing the entire old and new data, it recalculates only the data updated since the last refresh,

and it will place only these new data into the DW. Compared with the naive way of rebuilding a DW, incrementally updating the DW is both time-saving and cost-effective. However, when a DW deals not only with strategic decision support but also with tactical decision support, timestamp refresh may potentially cause a considerable delay between the information in the DW and the reality in data sources.

- The third is the continuous feed refresh mechanism of a real-time DW. This is the most ideal refresh mechanism for an advanced DW. As the real-time DW is always refreshed [Truban et al., 2008], up-to-date information can always be obtained. This mechanism seems to be very tempting for the business world; however, a significant burden is imposed on the operational database side. One transaction may take a long time to convert and load data into the DW, which will seriously affect the daily transaction performance. Second, it may be unnecessary to refresh immediately after each change to the operational database.

Another one is the *Operational Data Store* (ODS), that is a type of database which is updated continuously throughout the course of business operations. It is similar to a small scale real-time DW, but it stores only very recent update information which is kept separate from the main DW [Truban et al., 2008]. This ODS technique is useful only when the user queries target the most recent information separately from the DW and therefore the queries can be directed toward the ODS only. However, when the query coverage includes both recent and historical data, then a merging technique has to be applied and this can be very costly.

- The fourth mechanism, an incremental continuous refresh mechanism, is based on investigating a combination of the second and third approaches. This mechanism aggregates only the new insertions and updates from the operational database, when the system accurately identifies that the DW needs to be continuously refreshed or just-in-time [Maurer et al., 2009].

In [Italiano et al., 2006], the authors argue that not all transactional data need to be immediately dealt with despite even a real-time decision making requirement. In the same DW, we should allow different time priorities, such as urgent, which should be in real-time, or just be in time based on the business characteristics. The DW data freshness time interval should always be driven by the business requirements, not the technology itself. It is a challenging and critical goal to enable a DW to provide multiple levels of freshness time intervals. In [Chen et al., 2010], a near real-time refresh DW can reflect the real world requirements by making the interval of the timestamp 'dynamic' or flexible depending on factors such as impact from one update, the number of records affected, and the frequency of requests. It proves that a near real-time DW refresh can be a beneficial extension to the existing DW environment and shows that a near real-time DW could save significant operational costs.

Slowly Changing Dimension (SCD)

When the issue of updating a DW arises, usually the focus is on the changes relating to the attributes in the fact table, such as customer orders or product quantity; there is little concern about the changes needed to support dimension attributes, such as customer name or product description. Compared with changes to facts, the data changes in dimension are comparatively slow and static, so we call this *Slowly Changing Dimensions* (SCD). [Kimball, 1996] suggests three types of SCD [Ross & Kimball, 2005].

- **Type 1** is the most common one; when the data of a dimensional attribute changes, the system updates it directly (overwritten), without recording the old value. Generally, this seems to work. For instance, if the price of a product labeled P0002 is 40 dollars (e.g., in Figure 3), and then the next day the provider changes the price of P0002 to 60 dollars, then the price of P0002 is overwritten. And if a customer bought 10 Products P0002 several days earlier, and now wants to buy the same quantity of Product P0002 the customer will be faced with a different total amount due. Any user will find the pricing of this product confusing since we cannot track back to the old price of the product, because the DW stores only the latest value.

- **Type 2** is when the dimensional attribute changes. We insert a new row with a new surrogate primary key to record the changes, and both rows (old one and new one) will be included. At the same time, there are the most-recent-row flags, the row effective and expiration dates recorded for them. This type can retain all the changing information, but it will not be very appropriate for application to a large dimensional table whose attributes are semi-rapidly changing. In Figure 4, it is obvious that except for the price column changes, the data of the same product contains the same, and if the price of products is frequently changing in a large dimension table containing thousands of products, this method takes up a lot of space and is expensive. Furthermore, it is difficult to implement and query due to the changing nature of the surrogate key. It might be better to have another table to record the old values.

Figure 3. Type 1 SCD Implementation

Surrogate Key	Product ID	Description	Color	Size	Price
10001	P0001	Bag	Black	20	20
10002	P0002	Shoes	White	7	40 → 60
10003	P0003	Coat	Red	9	60

Figure 4. Type 2 SCD Implementation

Surrogate Key	Product ID	Description	Color	Size	Price
10001	P0001	Bag	Black	20	20
10002	P0002	Shoes	White	7	40
10003	P0003	Coat	Red	9	60
10004	P0001	Bag	Black	20	30
10005	P0002	Shoes	White	7	30
...	...	...	...	...	...

- **Type 3** requires putting another attribute into the existing dimension row as either the previous value recorded or new current value. This is the least commonly required technique. Up to a certain point, people can refer only to the latest changes in the dimensional table, but are unable to obtain the historical records. In Figure 5, we can see that we can record only the current value and the previous one. So only partial historical data is recorded using this approach.

SCD is complicated, each type having its own problems, but it is still necessary to consider it when updating a DW. Based on SDC solution, [Nguyen et al., 2007] classify the incoming information into state-oriented data and event-oriented data, and they provide a *Comprehensive enhanced SCD solution* (CSCD) solution to retain the entire historical data of dimensions by combining type2 and type3. [Eder et al., 2004] provide two different approaches called 'Grouping' and 'Fixing' to detect the structure changes in dimensions; the first one performs faster and the second one can provide better results. [Malinowski & Zimányi, 2006; Malinowski & Zimányi, 2008] use object-relational nested table collection types to store the changes of attributes (e.g. Figure 6); Box 1 is a snapshot of object-relational nested table implementation. Note that we can also use array. However, since the number of changes can be huge, the nested table would be a more suitable implementation.

Figure 5. Type 3 SCD Implementation

Product ID	Description	Color	Size	Old Price	Current Price
P0001	Bag	Black	20	20	30
P0002	Shoes	White	7	40	30
P0003	Coat	Red	9	60	60

Figure 6. Nested table collection type

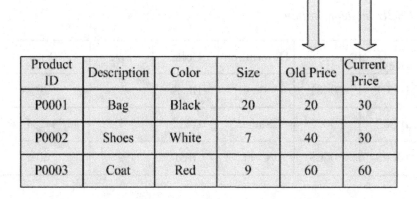

Product ID	Description	Color	Size	Price Value	Price From Date	Price To Date
P0001	Bag	Black	20	20	02/2007	03/2007
				30	04/2007	now
P0002	Shoes	White	7	40	02/2007	03/2007
				30	04/2007	now

Implemented in Figure 7 ·

The solutions provided by SCD either cannot retain the whole history data, or the process is quite complicated. Therefore, based on the development of temporal databases, a temporal data warehouse can address this shortcoming.

TEMPORAL SUPPORT IN DATA WAREHOUSE

Due to dynamic changes of business activities, data consistency in the application of analysis is very important. Clients of the warehouse may be interested not only in fact measurement data, but also in the history showing how the dimension data has evolved. However, currently, the time dimension in data warehouses can track only the changes to measurement values in the fact table; it cannot represent the changes that occur in the dimension tables. These changes have been mentioned previously, and are termed 'slowly changing dimensions'. The solutions of SCD either cannot retain the whole history data or the process is quite complicated.

In an attempt to address this problem, a *Temporal Data Warehouse* (TDW) is a new field of research that adopts the concept of temporal database and is combined with a data warehouse since a temporal database can manage and represent the data that vary over time. A survey on temporal data warehousing is presented in [Golfarelli et al., 2009].

Temporal Databases

A conventional database stores only the current data, and the historical data (updated, deleted) are overwritten by the current data. So the temporal meaning of data is buried. Realizing the importance of modeling time and handling historical data, temporal databases have been extensively investigated dur-

Box 1. example code to create object-relational nested table collection types for price

```
CREATE OR REPLACE TYPE IntervalType as OBJECT
(FromDate          DATE,
ToDate           DATE)/
CREATE OR REPLACE TYPE IntervalType_Table AS TABLE OF IntervalType/
CTEATE OR REPLACE TYPE PriceType AS OBJECT
(Value           Number,
ValueInterval     IntervalType_Table)/
CREATE OR REPLACE TYPE PriceType_Table AS TABLE OF PriceType/
CREATE OR REPLACE TYPE ProductType AS OBJECT
(Product_ID     VARCHAR2(10),
Description     VARCHAR2(20),
Color             VARCHAR2(10),
Size             NUMBER,
Price             PriceType_Table)/
CREATE TABLE Product OF Price_Tab
(NESTED TABLE ValueInterval STORE AS Value_Tab);
```

ing the past two decades. Researching topics covered temporal models, query languages (e.g., [Chau et al., 2008]), and implementation techniques. A Temporal Database System is a system that represents and manages the data with timestamps being integral components (e.g., [Clifford & Tansel, 1993]). There are several ways to represent time in a temporal database [Dyreson et al., 1994; Clifford et al., 1997]:

- **Valid time (VT)** represents the time interval during which the fact is true in the model reality; this can be past, current or even future. It relies on the behavior of the reality, so that if an error is made in the reality, valid time can be corrected by altering the database. Valid time has a wide range of applications such as sales, renting etc. For example, if an employee quits his job on 15th Jan 2010, and his information is deleted from the company's database on 31st Jan 2010, the employee's valid time will be the time from when he began working for the company until 15th Jan 2010; not until 31st Jan 2010. If the finance department calculates his payment, it should be based on the valid time, even though his information was not deleted from the database until later.
- **Transaction time (TT)** records the time when the transaction occurred in the database. Transaction time cannot be altered since it is the timestamp captured by the system. TT does not exist without the database. It plays a very important role in the applications that place particular emphasis on traceability and accountability, such as auction, auditing, billing etc. So if we apply this to the example above, 31st Jan 2010 will be regarded as the transaction time when the employee's information is deleted to show that the employee no longer works at the company.
- **Bitemporal time (BT)** is when data is associated with both valid time and transaction time. Bitemporal time can be used to more accurately review the reality and allow the retroactive and prospective changes. Therefore, in the example of the employee, the system will record both time 15th Jan 2010 and 31st Jan 2010 as BT.

Based on the time dimension(s) within the database, databases can be categorized into four types, as shown in Table 1.

Time Temporality Type and Relationship

The time dimension is ubiquitous and very important in the temporal data warehousing design. Much research work on the modeling of a temporal data warehouse has provided several temporal types to facilitate time manipulations (eg., [Dyreson et al., 1994 ; Ravat & Teste.,2000; Rizzi & Golfarelli, 2006;

Table 1. Types of databases based on the time dimension(s)

Type of Database	Description
Snapshot Database	The state or an instance represents only the current contents and information in the database. If operations (insert/ update/delete) are done to the database, the previous state or instance is thrown completely.
Rollback Database	The database supports the query of selecting a snapshot state by moving along the transaction time axis. The operation of selecting the snapshot is called 'Rollback'. It records the history of database activities rather than the history of the real world.
History Database	The database time axis is changed to valid time, the data corresponds more closely to reality rather than the history of database updating operations.
Bitemporal Database	Both transaction time and valid time are recorded, so that the database is able to store not only the current data, but also the historical data and even future data expected to occur.

Malinowski & Zimányi, 2006]). Some of temporality types are directly derived from the temporal database, such as valid time, transaction time. And other temporality types are widely accepted such as chronons, instant, interval, lifespan, and loading time.

Chronon is defined as a 'non-decomposable time interval of some fixed, minimal duration' [Dyreson et al., 1994]. This means a chronon is the finest unit in the dimension time. In reality, the time dimension is linear, but in data warehousing, we treat time as a discrete entity, so the time axis is defined as a series of chronons.

Instant is like an instance of chronons. It is used to describe when an event happened or will happen. For example, instant is used to record a patient's time of death.

Interval implies a period duration which includes a set of chronons between two instant limits. For example, during 10/01/2010 and 31/01/2010, the patient stayed in the hospital. It includes a start time and an end time. And **duration** is just the length of an interval. There are thirteen possible ways in which an ordered pair of intervals can be related [Allen, 1983]. Figure 7 shows the 13 distinct relationships between two intervals X and Y with X being described in relation to Y. The right column can be viewed as the inverse relationship of the left column. For example, X before Y is the same as Y after X. It depends only on which time interval is regarded as the comparison object.

In [Rizzi & Golfarelli, 2006], the authors maintain that transaction time and valid time are not sufficient to ensure the correctness of meaningful historical analysis. Delayed registration should be considered as well. Here the delayed registration means the delay occurring in real life. For example, when students enroll in their university subjects, the validation date will be the day they pay their tuition fee, but there might be a delay in the bank transactions (sometimes even a week for international transactions). In [Malinowski & Zimányi, 2008], the authors defined lifespan (LS) or existence time and loading time. Lifespan implies the duration of an object's existance. It can be the duration of the valid time of the related fact, or relationships between two objects, or a transaction time indicating the time when the object or relationship is currently in the database. Once data is inserted into a data warehouse, it will

Figure 7. Time interval relations

Relation			Relation	
	X before Y			X after Y
	X meets Y			X met-by Y
	X overlaps Y			X overlapped-by Y
	X starts Y			X started-by Y
	X during Y			X contains Y
	X finishes Y			X finished-by Y
	X equal Y			

Interval X: ▨   Interval Y: ▭

neither be modified nor deleted, so loading time is used to record when the data is loaded into the data warehouse since there is likely to be a delay between the data source and the data warehouse. These features are very helpful in the application of data analysis and decision-making.

[Larsen et al., 2006] presented an approach to deal with ill-known temporal data by supporting fuzzy time intervals. In [Winarko & Roddick, 2007], the authors propose an algorithm for discovering richer relative temporal association rules from interval-based data. [Moreno et al., 2010] specifically tackle season queries on a temporal multidimensional model for OLAP, and they propose a new operator to make the query for season simple and concise.

For many observations regarding time, temporal information interacts with it. An efficient exploitation of the time dimension may provide users with a more compact visualization of the temporal data and the temporal relationships that exist between the data and the time. We may be able to further explore the temporal data warehouse and gain more insights. Here, we present two different methods for analyzing time.

Based on the Temporality of Time Type

According to the temporality of the time, we can define the time as either Temporal or Permanent. Here the temporality of time is different from the temporality types we mentioned above.

The temporal time point/interval means the data associated with the time is temporal. When we insert/update/delete it with the temporal time, we know that when the time point/interval has expired, the data will no longer be valid. For example, in the supermarket, when we update one item's price from 100 dollars to 50 dollars in a promotion for one week, we know that after one week, the cheaper price will expire.

The permanent time point/interval means the data associated with the time is permanent. When we insert/update/delete it with the permanent time, at that time we know the data is potentially valid forever. So, when one data associated with a permanent time interval is replaced by a data with temporal time, after the temporal time expires, the data with permanent time will continue. For example, after one week's promotion, the item's price will still be 100 dollars. Obviously, one data with permanent time can be replaced by another data with permanent time; when this happens, the previous one will no longer be permanent.

Based on Regularity of Time

We can divide the regularity of time into four categories:

1. **Regular Time Interval** means the different events carry on for the same length of duration, such as every week, every month, and the relevant data may change significantly based on this. For example, a 5% discount on one product for one week, compared with 50% discount on one product for one week, will affect the sales figure very differently.
2. **Irregular Time Interval** means the same data repeats for the different lengths of duration. Then, the relevant data may change significantly based on this. For example, a 20% discount on one product may last one day or one week, so the sales figure will be affected very differently.
3. **Regular Time Instant** means a different event happened at the same time instant; the relevant data may change significantly based on this. For example, if a car accident occurs at 8:00 a.m. on

a particular morning, the traffic would be totally different compared with 8.00 a.m. traffic on a morning when no accident occurs.

4. **Irregular Time Instant** means the same data is repeats for a different instant; the relevant data may change significantly based on this. For example, if a car accident occurs at midnight, the traffic situation will be significantly different from traffic conditions caused by an accident occurring at 8:00 a.m.

Based on Temporality Level

No matter what time temporal types are applied, they are all used to timestamp the temporal changes to the database. The temporality level of changes simply relates to two types of changes. One is a type of change that occurs as a whole member; we term this temporal instance level (for example, inserting or deleting an employer from a list of employers of a company). The other one is a type of change that occurs within the whole member; we term this temporal attribute level (for example, updating an employee's address within the list of company employees).

Being able to record both types of changes is very important for analytical purposes. For example, the allocation of employees to different departments or the addition of more labor may influence the company's budget.

Design for Temporal Data Warehouses

The conventional data warehouse systems can effectively manage the changes in the fact table, but not the data in dimension members. Many temporal data warehouse design models (eg., [Chamoni & Stock, 1999; Eder & Koncilia, 2001; Malinowski & Zimányi, 2008]) have been proposed to overcome these limitations. These designs have made a considerable contribution to the development of advanced data warehouse systems.

An object-oriented paradigm has been proven applicable to complex data modeling [Bukhres, 1995]. Furthermore, [Ravat & Teste, 2000] present an object-oriented data warehouse model to manage and present the temporal data. Their model is not based on a multidimensional model concept. They introduced the two concepts of temporal filter and archive filter to define the past states and the archive states. Some mapping functions are specified. But a query language based on temporal extension of OQL needs to be specified to handle their DW elements. However, the multidimensional model is accepted widely and applied in various areas.

Malinowski and Zimanyi, leading temporary data warehouse experts, have proposed a temporal extension for the multidimensional model. [Malinowski & Zimányi, 2008] refer to different temporality types supported by the model, describe different temporal level, hierarchies and measures needing to be considered, and finally, they provide the mapping of the constructs of the MultiDim model to the ER and OR models. They provide a formal basis which can lead to better understanding of issues, alternatives and techniques.

[Eder et al., 2002] adopt the COMET Metamodel for temporal warehouse. This model is able to represent and manage all temporary changes including data and structure changes for both fact and dimensions. Based on this model, [Eder et al, 2004; Eder & Wiggisser, 2008] focused on the data transformation, analyze the transformation functions' impact and their efficient representation. They present six transformation operations and elaborate on two different representations (matrix-based and graph-based) for them. Further optimization techniques are needed.

SPATIAL SUPPORT IN DATA WAREHOUSE

Worldwide globalization has significantly increased the complexity of the problems. The geo-spatial domain has been widely developed due to the availability of wireless networks and portable devices, so the complexity of the decision-making process, with the spatial and temporal dimension involved, will greatly increase. Therefore, our community requires an enhanced and more knowledgeable data management system to solve the complex problems in many areas including economic and social environments. DW plays a significant role in *Decision Support Systems* (DSS). If DSS can deal with both spatial and non-spatial dimensions and measures, the functionality of DSS will be widely enhanced. Within a spatial data warehouse model, it is natural to extend existing spatial data models with time. Since all these spatial data are constantly changing, a great deal of spatial data will exist between the spatial database and DW. Therefore, in the last years, extending data warehouse with spatial and temporal features has attracted the attention of the GIS and database communities (e.g. [Lopez et al., 2005; Rivest et al., 2005; Viqueira & Lorentzos, 2007]).

There are two features that the data warehouse house system intends to cover: one is the capability to manage a more accurate and complete analysis to the underlying data, process and events. The data does not represent only the current status, but also the past and future status; second, thanks to the availability of sensor networks and mobile devices (e.g. [Deligiannakis & Kotidis, 2006; Medeiros et al., 2010]), many business processes contain geo-spatial information, so there is increasing demand for a system which is able to include the spatial information [Bertino & Damiani, 2005]. A spatial database system (SDBS) is a fully-fledge database system with extra capabilities for handling spatial data [Güting, 1994]. *Geographic Information System (GIS)* is able to capture, manipulate, analyze and display all forms of spatial data. Moreover, it is extensively used for geographical applications such as choosing sites, targeting market segments, planning distribution networks, responding to emergencies, or re-drawing country boundaries. Therefore, another research area based on both solid techniques has appeared: *Spatial Data Warehousing (SDW)*[Bimonte et al., 2005]. *Spatial temporal data warehouse* (STDW) combines both temporal and spatial features, both being included in the data warehouse.

Recent Work

In recent years, much work has been conducted in the area of spatial temporary data warehousing. Several works (e.g. [Šaltenis & Jensen, 2002; Choi et al., 2006]) focus on indexing structures and search structures. Other works (e.g. [Orlando et al., 2007]) concentrate on the Trajectory Data Warehouse since moving objects are typical examples of spatial-temporal objects. Others focus on the conceptual models of a spatial temporal data warehouse. [Spaccapietra et al., 2008] apply a concept model called MADS model to show how time and spatial data are represented and provide the data to be analyzed from different perspectives. It is worth noting that [Malinowski & Zimányi, 2008] the dimension level as spatial based on the multi-dimension design. In [Vaisman & Zimányi, 2009], the authors maintain that there is still no clearly defined meaning of spatial data warehouses among these efforts, and existing works do not clearly specify the kinds of queries that are made. So it is hard to compare the different proposals and approaches. In this paper, the authors reviewed the conceptual models proposed in order to improve our understanding about the spatial and temporal characteristics of real-world phenomena and the recent implementations. They also defined a conceptual framework supported by a spatial-temporal data warehouse.

Spatial Dimension Types in Spatial Temporal Data Warehouse

When we talk about time issues in reference to STDW, most works focus on the different time granularities. [Camossi et al., 2009] emphasized that it is crucial to base the selection of the appropriate on what is required from the system; factors such as efficient performance vs. data reduction must be considered. The data stored at the finest granularity, might cause waste of space and additional increase in query cost. However, storing data at coarser granularity will improve the efficiency of the system, but the detailed information might be ignored. Therefore, authors provide ST^2_ODMGe, a spatio-temporal data model to be able to define multi-granular spatial temporal data. For example, according to whether the information is current or old, we might store the current data at a finer granularity, and the older data at a coarser granularity.

Here, we can also distinguish three types of spatial dimensions based on time lines:

- **Static spatial type:** It can be used to describe a fixed location, such as the location of a building. A building does not move and its location is therefore static.
- **Semi-static spatial type:** It is used to describe the activities of something that can change from static to active. For example, let us consider a volcano. When the volcano is dormant, the magma remains almost static; its state does not change too much for a period of time. But once the volcano becomes active, the level of magma, the temperature, the dimensions are changing constantly; its state then becomes active. So the state of an object referring to a semi-static spatial dimension can change from static to active.
- **Dynamic/Active spatial type:** It can describe a dynamic environment. The state of the environment is changing all the time (e.g. moving cars, bushfires). These objects' spatial dimension is not static but changing greatly all the time.

From the above, we can see that for the first category, maintaining spatial dimension in real time is unnecessary; it can be maintained by the old batch window method. However, for the second and third categories, the maintenance of spatio-temporal DW in real time is very impractical due to the complexity of the transformation process and the large size of spatial data. The cost is extremely high. Therefore, near real-time temporary DW is most applicable in the spatial temporary data environment. It can accurately detect the right time to refresh spatial DW, offering a significant benefit in terms of refresh operation cost, while simultaneously maintaining a high freshness level of the data warehouse. The spatio-temporal data warehouse is still a young research area compared with the conventional data warehouse. In the current work, further research is needed to tackle the near-real time spatial temporal data warehouse which remains an open research problem.

MATERIALIZED VIEW

In conjunction with the data warehouse refresh, since the DW is required to be queried very effectively for decision-making, increasingly the use of materialized views is becoming the most effective and popular means of speeding up query processing efficiently [Rizzi & Saltarelli, 2003; Goldstein & Larson, 2001; Mistry et al., 2001; Mumick et al., 1997]. Hence, the concept of materialized view must also be considered. This section gives an overview and discussion of existing research regarding materialized views and how they are maintained.

In the database, a view is a virtual table that is derived from other existing tables. These other tables can be ordinary tables or another previously-defined view. It does not exist in physical form, as opposed to an ordinary base table whose records are actually stored in the database. We usually create a view for specifying a table that we need to reference frequently.

A *materialized view* (MV) is similar to a view but the difference is that the data in an MV is actually stored on disk (that is "materialized") and it must be refreshed from the original base tables from time to time. Moreover, in some ways, we can treat a MV as a real table, since anything that we do to a table can be done to an MV as well. Therefore, we can build indexes on any column with the advantage that this improves the system's performance by speeding up query time. So, a materialized view is used in order to decrease the cost of expensive joins or aggregations for an important and large class of queries.

A DW contains a large amount of information aggregated from diverse and independent data sources. One of the main reasons for designing a DW relates to queries and analysis, such as *on-line analytical processing* (OLAP), where hundreds of complex aggregations of queries have evolved over large volumes of data. It is not feasible to compute these queries by connecting the data source each time. For example, perhaps some data source is not always able to be accessed for it might be located at different places. So in order to speed up the queries in such an environment, many summary tables stored in the DW can be pre-computed including aggregated data such as the sum of sales. These tables represent materialized views. When users query a DW, frequent queries of the actual base tables is extremely expensive so the MV will be queried instead of the DW, which enables much more efficient access and saves cost [Samtani et al., 1999; Mumick et al., 1997] (e.g., Figure 8).

Maintenance of Materialized View Based on Data Warehousing

DW maintenance can be seen, in a somewhat simplified way, as a generalization of view maintenance used in relational databases. When a warehouse is updated, the MV must also be updated to reflect the changes in the operational database. In the dynamic environment business world, two types of changes should be considered:

Data changes. As data changes, a naive method of maintaining a MV is to re-compute the MV from scratch [Mumick et al., 1997]. However, this is impractical because it is extremely costly.

A number of algorithms have been proposed for batch incremental view. [Mumick et al., 1997; Samtani et al., 1999] use auxiliary tables (ATR) to keep some additional information in the DW. Auxiliary tables contain two kinds of attributes: primary key, which is in a select group and used for finding the corresponding actual values and actually attributes, which are the attributes we aggregate; they are usually the main things to be analyzed. Usually, there are more than one ATR in the DW, because each auxiliary table represents one individual data source.

Figure 8. MV in Data Warehouse

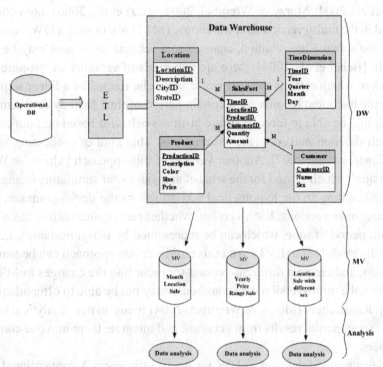

This approach handles the problem of making MV self-maintainable, because data sources could be located anywhere in the world; therefore, accessing them in order to keep MVs up to date could be very time consuming. Moreover, it minimizes the batch time needed for maintenance by splitting the maintenance process into two parts, propagation which occurs outside of the batch window and refresh which occurs inside of the batch window. This method considers the situation where the changes in the data source are only the content changes, i.e., insert/update/delete records; however, it does not consider schema changes, i.e., add/modify/drop an attribute or a table, that are very common operations occurring in the data source. In this case, MVs cannot be self-maintained.

Schema changes. In order to maintain MVs and enable them to handle both schema and relationships, certain approaches have been proposed to solve the problem. They fall into two categories:

- **Schema evolution** (e.g., [Rundensteiner et al., 1999; Lee et al., 2002; Bébel et al., 2004]). A naive approach to solving the problem of schema changes is to isolate the changes from a data warehouse, which means that once schema changes occur, the attributes relating to the changes in the DW are restricted to be queried. This approach might be used for a limited period of time only, but is not an ultimate appropriate solution for it is not practical in business decision-making and analysis. Once the schema changes in the sources, it is impossible to query that part; hence, the DW function becomes incomplete.
- **Another better approach** [Rundensteiner et al., 1999; Lee et al., 2002, Bébel et al., 2004] is to transfer the schema changes related to the old view schema in MV and rewrite the schema. This approach considers only the rename attributes or relations at sources, drop attributes or relations.

Versioning (e.g., [Bébel et al., 2004; Morzy & Wrembel, 2004; Golfarelli et al., 2006; Rizzi et al., 2006]). In [Bébel et al., 2004; Morzy & Wrembel, 2004; Rizzi et al., 2006], both content and schema changes are tracked in the multi-version data warehouse (MVDW). In such a DW, versioning of schema, where histories of the schema are retained, changes to a schema or content may be applied to a new version of a DW. In [Bébel et al., 2004], there are two kinds of versions are proposed in the DW, one is called 'real version' which reflects the real world, it can be treated as a linear sequence of different versions to record the historical records for a certain period of time [Morzy & Wrembel, 2004]. Good decision making should be able to forecast future business behavior based on both current and historical data from which decision makers make assumptions. This kind of processing is termed 'What-if analysis' [Papastefanatos et al., 2007]. Another version of this approach [Morzy & Wrembel, 2004] is the 'alternative version', which is used for the what-if analysis or for simulating changes in the structure of a DW schema. According to the hypothetical scenario from the decision maker, a DW can create alternative data warehouse versions. Each version, whether real or alternative, has a valid time which is valid for a certain period of time, which can be represented by two timestamps, i.e. beginning valid time (BVT) and ending valid time (EVT). And this multi-version approach can be similarly adopted by the materialized view, and create a different version for recording the changes in MV. Compared with the schema evolution, the multi-version data warehouse may not be able to offer adequate functionality [Rizzi et al., 2006]. Researchers [Morzy & Wrembel, 2004] focus on new analytical tools and extended query language to extract partial results from versions, and integrate them into one consistent and meaningful result for users.

Materialized views are widely used in DW for query efficiency. A conventional database usually contains non-temporal data; i.e., only the current state of the data is available in the database. Thus, temporal materialized views can significantly benefit the query over the history of the source data. For example, a company's database might contain only current employees' information, and the previous employees' information might be removed once they quit their job or are fired. Nevertheless, the company analysts might want an overview of all the employees who have ever worked in the company [Yang & Widom, 2000]. The problem of maintaining materialized views is highly challenging. On the one hand, a temporal materialized view does not only relate to the content and schema changes of operational database, but also to changes as time advances. When the data is removed or updated in the operational database, the replaced information might not be lost forever; it might be just temporally removed or invalid for a certain period. And the interaction between the data and time two dimension of change is evolved as well. [Yang and Widom, 2000] introduce a framework for maintaining temporal views over the non-temporal data sources. They present a temporal model that can be applied directly to the temporal support. The maintenance of temporal materialized views becomes more challenging than the non-temporal materialized views.

Little research has been conducted in temporal materialized views due to the problem of complex maintenance and view adaptation. And due to the large size of SDWs, the performance of spatial multidimensional queries and the efficient creation of a geographic materialized view without causing the problem termed 'explosion of aggregates' also present challenges.

CONCLUSION

The purpose of this preface was to highlight some of the trends and advancements made by the research work in data warehousing. We showed that attention to data warehouses has shifted from textual DWs to temporal and spatial DWs due to the requirements from the business world and diverse application contexts. Within this chapter, we focused on the time issues including DW refresh mechanisms, temporal time dimensions and the spatial feature in data warehousing. We categorized different types of time dimension and spatial dimension to broaden our perspective and gain a better insight into the field of data warehousing development.

Certainly, research has not been limited to the issues mentioned in this preface. The chapters of this book will give more details and techniques pertaining to various modern areas of data warehousing and data mining.

David Taniar
Monash University, Australia

Li Chen
LaTrobe University, Australia

REFERENCES

Allen, J. (1983). Maintaining knowledge about temporal intervals. *Communications of the ACM*, 832–843. doi:10.1145/182.358434

Bébel, B., Eder, J., Koncilia, C., Morzy, T., & Wrembel, R. (2004). Creation and management of versions in multiversion data warehouse. *SAC '04: Proceedings of the 2004 ACM symposium on Applied computing* (pp. 717-723). New York, NY, USA: ACM.

Bertino, E., & Damiani, M. L. (2005). *Spatial Knowledge-Based Applications and Technologies: Research Issues* (pp. 324–328). Knowledge-Based Intelligent Information and Engineering Systems.

Bimonte, S., Tchounikine, A., & Miquel, M. (2005). Towards a spatial multidimensional model. *Dolap '05: Proceedings of the Eighth ACM International Workshop on Data Warehousing and OLAP: November 4-5, 2005, Bremen, Germany* (pp. 39-46). New York: Association For Computing Machinery (Acm).

Bin, L., Chen, S., & Rundensteiner, E. *(2002). Batch data warehouse maintenance in dynamic environments. CIKM '02:* Proceedings of the eleventh international conference on Information and knowledge management (pp. 68-75). *New York, NY, USA: ACM.*

Bukhres, A. E. (1995). *Object-Oriented Multidatabase Systems: A Solution for Advanced Applications --1995 publication.* New Delhi: Prentice Hall.

Camossi, E., Bertino, E., Guerrini, G., & Bertolotto, M. (2009). Adaptive Management of Multigranular Spatio-Temporal Object Attributes. *Advances in Spatial and Temporal Databases: 11th International Symposium, SSTD 2009 Aalborg, Denmark, July 8-10, 2009 Proceedings (Lecture Notes in Computer... Applications, incl. Internet/Web, and HCI)* (1 ed., pp. 320-337). New York: Springer.

Chamoni, P., & Stock, S. (1999). Temporal Structures in Data Warehousing. *Data Warehousing and Knowledge Discovery: First International Conference, DaWaK '99 Florence, Italy, August 30 - September 1, 1999 Proceedings (Lecture Notes in Computer Science)* (1 ed., pp. 353-358). New York: Springer.

Chau, V. T., & Chittayasothorn, S. (2008). A temporal object relational SQL language with attribute timestamping in a temporal transparency environment. *Data & Knowledge Engineering, 67*(3), 331–361. doi:10.1016/j.datak.2008.06.008

Chen, L., Rahayu, W., & Taniar, D. (2010). Towards Near Real-Time Data Warehousing. *Advanced Information Networking and Applications (AINA), 2010 24th IEEE International Conference on* (pp. 1150-1157). Los Alamitos, CA, USA: IEEE Computer Society Press.

Choi, W., Kwon, D., & Lee, S. (2006). Spatio-temporal data warehouses using an adaptive cell-based approach. *Data & Knowledge Engineering, 59*(1), 189–207. doi:10.1016/j.datak.2005.08.001

Clifford, J., Dyreson, C., Isakowitz, T., Jensen, C. S., & Snodgrass, R. T. (1997). On the semantics of "now" in databases. *ACM Transactions on Database Systems, 22*(2), 171–214. doi:10.1145/249978.249980

Clifford, J., & Tansel, S. G. (1993). *Temporal Databases: Theory, Design, and Implementation --1993 publication.* San Francisco: Benjamincummings Pub Co.

Deligiannakis, A., & Kotidis, Y. (2006). Exploiting Spatio-temporal Correlations for Data Processing in Sensor Networks. *GeoSensor Networks: Second International Conference, GSN 2006, Boston, MA, USA, October 1-3, 2006, Revised Selected and Invited Papers (Lecture Notes in... Applications, incl. Internet/Web, and HCI)* (1 ed., pp. 45-65). New York: Springer.

Dyreson, C., Grandi, F., Roddick, J. F., Sarda, N. L., Scalas, M. R., & Segev, A. (1994). A consensus glossary of temporal database concepts. *SIGMOD Record, 23*(1), 52–64. doi:10.1145/181550.181560

Eder, J., & Koncilia, C. (2001). Changes of Dimension Data in Temporal Data Warehouses. *Data Warehousing and Knowledge Discovery: Third International Conference, DaWaK 2001 Munich, Germany September 5-7, 2001 Proceedings (Lecture Notes in Computer Science)* (1 ed., pp. 284-293). New York: Springer.

Eder, J., Koncilia, C., & Mitsche, D. (2004). Analysing Slices of Data Warehouses to Detect Structural Modifications. *Advanced Information Systems Engineering: 16th International Conference, CAiSE 2004, Riga, Latvia, June 7-11, 2004, Proceedings (Lecture Notes in Computer Science)* (1 ed., pp. 123-227). New York: Springer.

Eder, J., Koncilia, C., & Morzy, T. (2002). The COMET Metamodel for Temporal Data Warehouses. *CAiSE '02: Proceedings of the 14th International Conference on Advanced Information Systems Engineering* (pp. 83-99). London, UK: Springer-Verlag.

Eder, J., & Wiggisser, K. (2008). Modeling Transformations between Versions of a Temporal Data Warehouse. *Advances in Conceptual Modeling - Challenges and Opportunities: ER 2008 Workshops CMLSA, ECDM, FP-UML, M2AS, RIGiM, SeCoGIS, WISM, Barcelona, Spain, October... (Lecture Notes in Computer Science)* (1 ed., pp. 68-77). New York: Springer.

Goldstein, J., & Larson, P. (2001). Optimizing queries using materialized views: a practical, scalable solution. *Proceedings of the 2001 ACM SIGMOD International Conference on Management of Data: Santa Barbara, California, May 21-24, 2001 (SIGMOD record)* (pp. 331-342). New York: Association for Computing Machinery.

Golfarelli, M., Lechtenbörger, J., Rizzi, S., & Vossen, G. (2006). Schema versioning in data warehouses: Enabling cross-version querying via schema augmentation. *Data & Knowledge Engineering, 59*(2), 435–459. doi:10.1016/j.datak.2005.09.004

Golfarelli, M., & Rizzi, S. (2009). A Survey on Temporal Data Warehousing. *International Journal of Data Warehousing and Mining, 5*(1), 1–17. doi:10.4018/jdwm.2009010101

Güting, R. H. (1994). An introduction to spatial database systems. *The VLDB Journal, 3*(4), 357–399. doi:10.1007/BF01231602

Inmon, W. H. (1996). The data warehouse and data mining. *Communications of the ACM, 39*(11), 49–50. doi:10.1145/240455.240470

Italiano, I. C., & Ferreira, J. E. (2006). Synchronization Options for Data Warehouse Designs. *Computer, 39*(3), 53–57. doi:10.1109/MC.2006.104

Kimball, R. (1996). *The Data Warehouse Toolkit: Practical Techniques for Building Dimensional Data Warehouses*. New York: John Wiley & Sons.

Kimball, R., & Ross, M. (2002). *The Data Warehouse Toolkit: The Complete Guide to Dimensional Modeling (Second Edition)* (2 Sub ed.). New York, NY: Wiley.

Larsen, H. L., Pasi, G., Arroyo, D. O., Andreasen, T., & Christiansen, H. (2006). *Flexible Query Answering Systems: 7th International Conference, FQAS 2006, Milan, Italy, June 7-10, 2006 (Lecture Notes in Computer Science / Lecture Notes in Artificial Intelligence)* (1 ed.). New York: Springer.

Lee, A. J., Nica, A., & Rundensteiner, E. A. (2002). The EVE Approach: View Synchronization in Dynamic Distributed Environments. []. Piscataway, NJ, USA: IEEE Educational Activities Department.]. *IEEE Transactions on Knowledge and Data Engineering, 14*, 931–954. doi:10.1109/TKDE.2002.1033766

Lopez, I. F., Snodgrass, R. T., & Moon, B. (2005). Spatiotemporal Aggregate Computation: A Survey. *IEEE Transactions on Knowledge and Data Engineering, 17*(2), 271–286. doi:10.1109/TKDE.2005.34

Malinowski, E., & Zimányi, E. (2006). A conceptual solution for representing time in data warehouse dimensions. In *APCCM '06: Proceedings of the 3rd Asia-Pacific Conference on Conceptual Modelling* (Vol. 53, pp. 45-54). Darlinghurst, Australia, Australia: Australian Computer Society, Inc.

Malinowski, E., & Zimányi, E. (2008). A conceptual model for temporal data warehouses and its transformation to the ER and the object-relational models. *Data & Knowledge Engineering, 64*(1), 101–133. doi:10.1016/j.datak.2007.06.020

Malinowski, E., & Zimányi, E. (2008). *Advanced Data Warehouse Design*. New York: Springer-Verlag New York Inc.

Maurer, D., Rahayu, W., Rusu, L., & Taniar, D. (2009). A Right-Time Refresh for XML Data Warehouses. *Database Systems for Advanced Applications: 14th International Conference, DASFAA 2009, Brisbane, Australia, April 21-23, 2009, Proceedings (Lecture Notes... Applications, incl. Internet/Web, and HCI)* (1 ed., pp. 745-749). New York: Springer.

Mazón, J., Lechtenbörger, J., & Trujillo, J. (2009). A survey on summarizability issues in multidimensional modeling. *Data & Knowledge Engineering, 68*(12), 1452–1469. doi:10.1016/j.datak.2009.07.010

Medeiros, C. B., Joliveau, M., Jomier, G., & Vuyst, F. D. (2010). Managing sensor traffic data and forecasting unusual behaviour propagation. *GeoInformatica, 14*(3), 279–305. doi:10.1007/s10707-010-0102-7

Mistry, H., Roy, P., Sudarshan, S., & Ramamritham, K. (2001). Materialized view selection and maintenance using multi-query optimization. *Proceedings of the 2001 ACM SIGMOD International Conference on Management of Data: Santa Barbara, California, May 21-24, 2001 (SIGMOD record)* (pp. 307-318). New York: Association for Computing Machinery.

Moreno, F., Fileto, R., & Arango, F. (2010, February 18). ScienceDirect - Mathematical and Computer Modelling: Season queries on a temporal multidimensional model for OLAP. *ScienceDirect - Home*. Retrieved July 13, 2010, from http://www.sciencedirect.com/science/article/B6V0V-4YDT3WX-1/2/d94179199e48dfd1dce56fe5b8

Morzy, T., & Wrembel, R. (2004). On querying versions of multiversion data warehouse. *Dolap 2004: Proceedings of the Seventh ACM International Workshop on Data Warehousing and OLAP Co-Located with CIKM 2004: November* (pp. 92-101). New York: Association for Computing Machinery (Acm).

Mumick, I. S., Quass, D., & Mumick, B. S. (1997). Maintenance of data cubes and summary tables in a warehouse. in M. Peckman, S. Ram, & M. Franklin (Eds.). *SIGMOD '97: Proceedings of the 1997 ACM SIGMOD International Conference on Management of Data*(pp. 100-111.). Tucson, Arizona, United States: ACM.

Nguyen, T. M., Tjoa, A. M., Nemec, J., & Windisch, M. (2007). An approach towards an event-fed solution for slowly changing dimensions in data warehouses with a detailed case study. *Data & Knowledge Engineering, 63*(1), 26–43. doi:10.1016/j.datak.2006.10.004

Orlando, S., Orsini, R., Raffaetà, A., Roncato, A., & Silvestri, C. (2007). Spatio-temporal Aggregations in Trajectory Data Warehouses.*Data Warehousing and Knowledge Discovery: 9th International Conference, DaWaK 2007, Regensburg, Germany, September 3-7, 2007, Proceedings (Lecture Notes in Computer Science)* (1 ed., pp. 66-77). New York: Springer.

Papastefanatos, G., Vassiliadis, P., Simitsis, A., & Vassiliou, Y. (2007). What-If Analysis for Data Warehouse Evolution. *Data Warehousing and Knowledge Discovery: 9th International Conference, DaWaK 2007, Regensburg, Germany, September 3-7, 2007, Proceedings (Lecture Notes in Computer Science)* (1 ed., pp. 23-33). New York: Springer.

Ravat, F., & Teste, O. (2000). A Temporal Object-Oriented Data Warehouse Model. *Database and Expert Systems Applications: 11th International Conference, DEXA 2000 London, UK, September 4-8, 2000 Proceedings (Lecture Notes in Computer Science)* (1 ed., pp. 583-592). New York: Springer.

Rivest, S., Bédard, Y., Proulx, M., Nadeau, M., Hubert, F., & Pastor, J. (2005). SOLAP technology: Merging business intelligence with geospatial technology for interactive spatio-temporal exploration and analysis of data. *ISPRS Journal of Photogrammetry and Remote Sensing, 60*(1), 17–33. doi:10.1016/j.isprsjprs.2005.10.002

Rizzi, S., Abelló, A., Lechtenbörger, J., & Trujillo, J. (2006). Research in data warehouse modeling and design: dead or alive? *DOLAP '06: Proceedings of the 9th ACM International Workshop on Data warehousing and OLAP* (pp. 3-10). New York, NY, USA: ACM.

Rizzi, S., & Golfarelli, M. (2006). What Time Is It in the Data Warehouse? *Data Warehousing and Knowledge Discovery: 8th International Conference, DaWaK 2006, Krakow, Poland, September 4-8, 2006, Proceedings (Lecture Notes in Computer Science)* (1 ed., pp. 134-144). New York: Springer.

Rizzi, S., & Saltarelli, E. (2003). View Materialization vs. Indexing: Balancing Space Constraints in Data Warehouse Design. *Advanced Information Systems Engineering: 15th International Conference, CAiSE 2003, Klagenfurt, Austria, June 16-18, 2003, Proceedings (Lecture Notes in Computer Science)* (1 ed., p. 1030). New York: Springer.

Ross, M., & Kimball, R. (2005, March 1). Slowly Changing Dimensions Are Not Always as Easy as 1, 2, 3 > Data Warehousing > Intelligent Enterprise: Better Insight for Business Decisions. *Intelligent Enterprise -- Better Insight for Business Decisions*. Retrieved July 13, 2010, from http://intelligent-enterprise.informationweek.com/ info_centers/ data_warehousing/ showArticle.jhtml; jsessionid= P4 GY55YC2FJINQE1GHPCKH4ATMY32JVN?articleID =59301280

Rundensteiner, E., Koeller, A., Zhang, X., Lee, A., Nica, A., Wyk, A., et al. (1999). *Sigmod 1999: Proceedings from Sigmod Conference*. New York: Assn for Computing Machinery.

Šaltenis, S., & Jensen, C. S. (2002). Indexing of now-relative spatio-bitemporal data. *The VLDB Journal, 11*(1), 1–16. doi:10.1007/s007780100058

Samtani, S., Kumar, V., & Mohania, M. *(1999). Self-maintenance of multiple views in data warehousing.* Cikm 99 Conference Proceedings: Conference on Information Knowledge Management (CIKM) *(pp. 292-299). New York: Assn for Computing Machinery.*

Spaccapietra, S., Parent, C., & Zimányi, E. (2008). Spatio-temporal and Multi-representation Modeling: A Contribution to Active Conceptual Modeling. *Active Conceptual Modeling of Learning: Next Generation Learning-Base System Development (Lecture Notes in Computer Science)* (1 ed., pp. 194-205). New York: Springer.

Thiele, M., Fischer, U., & Lehner, W. (2009). Partition-based workload scheduling in living data warehouse environments. []. Oxford, UK, UK: Elsevier Science Ltd.]. *Information Systems, 34*, 382–399. doi:10.1016/j.is.2008.06.001

Truban, E., Sharda, R., Aronson, J., & King, D. (2008). *Business Intelligence: A Managerial Approach.* Upper Saddle River, N.J.

Vaisman, A., & Zimányi, E. (2009). What Is Spatio-Temporal Data Warehousing? *Data Warehousing and Knowledge Discovery: 11th International Conference, DaWaK 2009 Linz, Austria, August 31-September 2, 2009 Proceedings (Lecture Notes... Applications, incl. Internet/Web, and HCI)* (1 ed., pp. 9-23). New York: Springer.

Viqueira, J. R., & Lorentzos, N. A. (2007). SQL extension for spatio-temporal data. *The VLDB Journal, 16*(2), 179–200. doi:10.1007/s00778-005-0161-9

Winarko, E., & Roddick, J. F. (2007). An algorithm for discovering richer relative temporal association rules from interval-based data. *Data & Knowledge Engineering, 63*(1), 76–90. doi:10.1016/j.datak.2006.10.009

Yang, J., & Widom, J. (2000). Temporal View Self-Maintenance. *Advances in Database Technology - EDBT 2000: 7th International Conference on Extending Database Technology Konstanz, Germany, March 27-31, 2000 Proceedings (Lecture Notes in Computer Science)* (1 ed., pp. 395-412). New York: Springer.

Section 1

Chapter 1
Temporal Data Warehousing:
Approaches and Techniques

Matteo Golfarelli
DEIS - University of Bologna, Italy

Stefano Rizzi
DEIS - University of Bologna, Italy

ABSTRACT

Data warehouses are information repositories specialized in supporting decision making. Since the decisional process typically requires an analysis of historical trends, time and its management acquire a huge importance. In this paper we consider the variety of issues, often grouped under term temporal data warehousing, implied by the need for accurately describing how information changes over time in data warehousing systems. We recognize that, with reference to a three-levels architecture, these issues can be classified into some topics, namely: handling data/schema changes in the data warehouse, handling data/schema changes in the data mart, querying temporal data, and designing temporal data warehouses. After introducing the main concepts and terminology of temporal databases, we separately survey these topics. Finally, we discuss the open research issues also in connection with their implementation on commercial tools.

INTRODUCTION

At the core of most business intelligence applications, *data warehousing systems* are specialized in supporting decision making. They have been rapidly spreading within the industrial world over the last decade, due to their undeniable contribu-

tion to increasing the effectiveness and efficiency of the decisional processes within business and scientific domains. This wide diffusion was supported by remarkable research results aimed at improving querying performance, at refining the quality of data, and at outlining the design process, as well as by the quick advancement of commercial tools.

DOI: 10.4018/978-1-60960-537-7.ch001

In the remainder of the paper, for the sake of terminological consistency, we will refer to a classic architecture for data warehousing systems, illustrated in Figure 1, that relies on three levels:

1. The *data sources*, that store the data used for feeding the data warehousing systems. They are mainly corporate operational databases, hosted by either relational or legacy platforms, but in some cases they may also include external web data, flat files, spreadsheet files, etc.
2. The *data warehouse* (also called *reconciled data level*, *operational data store* or *enterprise data warehouse*), a normalized operational database that stores detailed, integrated, clean and consistent data extracted from data sources and properly processed by means of ETL tools.

Figure 1. Three-levels architecture for a data warehousing system

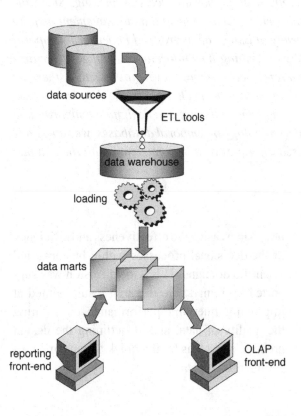

3. The *data marts*, where data taken from the data warehouse are summarized into relevant information for decision making, in the form of *multidimensional cubes*, to be typically queried by OLAP and reporting front-ends.

Cubes are structured according to the *multidimensional model*, whose key concepts are fact, measure and dimension. A *fact* is a focus of interest for the decisional process; its occurrences correspond to *events* that dynamically occur within the business world. Each event is quantitatively described by a set of numerical *measures*. In the multidimensional model, events are arranged within an n-dimensional space whose axes, called *dimensions* of analysis, define different perspectives for their identification. Dimensions commonly are discrete, alphanumerical attributes that determine the minimum granularity for analyzing facts. Each dimension is the root of a *(roll-up) hierarchy* that includes a set of *levels*, each providing a way of selecting and aggregating events. Each level can be described by a set of *properties*.

As a consequence of the fact that the decisional process typically relies on computing historical trends and on comparing snapshots of the enterprise taken at different moments, one of the main characterizations of data warehousing systems is that of storing historical, non volatile data. Thus, time and its management acquire a huge importance. In this paper we discuss the variety of issues, often grouped under term *temporal data warehousing*, implied by the need for accurately describing *how information changes over time*. These issues, arising by the never ending evolution of the application domains, are even more pressing today, as several mature implementations of data warehousing systems are fully operational within medium to large business contexts. Note that, in comparison with operational databases, temporal issues are more critical in data warehousing systems since queries frequently span long periods of time; thus, it is very common that they are required to cross the boundaries of different versions of data and/or schema. Besides, the criticality of the problem is obviously higher for systems that have been established for a long time, since unhandled evolutions will determine a stronger gap between the reality and its representation within the database, which will soon become obsolete and useless (Golfarelli et al, 2006).

So, not surprisingly, there has been a lot of research so far regarding temporal issues in data warehousing systems. Basically, the approaches devised in the literature can be accommodated in the following (sometimes overlapping) categories:

- *Handling changes in the data warehouse* (discussed in the third section). This mainly has to do with maintaining the data warehouse in sync with the data sources when changes on either of these two levels occur.
- *Handling data changes in the data mart* (fourth section). Events are continuously added to data marts; while recorded events are typically not subject to further changes, in some cases they can be modified to accommodate errors or late notifications of up-to-date values for measures. Besides, the instances of dimensions and hierarchies are not entirely static.
- *Handling schema changes in the data mart* (fifth section). The data mart structure may change in response to the evolving business requirements. New levels and measures may become necessary, while others may become obsolete. Even the set of dimensions characterizing a fact may be required to change.
- *Querying temporal data* (sixth section). Querying in presence of data and schema changes require specific attention, especially if the user is interested in formulating queries whose temporal range covers different versions of data and/or schema.
- *Designing temporal data warehouses* (seventh section). The specific characteristics

of temporal data warehouses may require ad hoc approaches for their design, especially from the conceptual point of view.

The paper outline is completed by the second section, that introduces the main concepts and terminology of temporal databases, and by the eighth section, that summarizes some open issues and draws the conclusions.

TEMPORAL DATABASES

Databases where time is not represented are often called *transient databases*. Within a transient database, only the current representation of real-world objects is stored and no track of changes is kept, so it is impossible to reconstruct how the object was in the past. Conversely, *temporal databases* focus on representing the inherent temporal nature of objects through the time-dependent recording of their structure and state. Two different time dimensions are normally considered in temporal databases, namely *valid time* and *transaction time* (Jensen et al., 1994). Valid time is the "real-world time", i.e., it expresses the time when a fact is true in the business domain. Transaction time is the "database system time", i.e., it expresses the time when facts are registered in the database. Temporal database systems are called *valid-time databases*, *transaction-time databases* or *bi-temporal databases* depending on their capacity to handle either or both of these two time dimensions (Tansel et al., 1993). The main benefit of using a bi-temporal database is that not only the history of the changes an object is subject to is recorded, but it is also possible to obtain the same result from a query independently of the time when it is formulated (which might not happen if transaction time is not properly represented).

In the real world, objects change in both their state and their structure. This means that, within a database, both the values of data and their schema may change. Obviously, values of data are constantly modified by databases applications. On the other hand, modifying the database schema is a less frequent, though still common, occurrence in database administration. With reference to changes in the database schema, the literature commonly distinguishes three possibilities (Roddick, 1995):

- *Schema modification* is supported when a database system allows changes to the schema definition of a populated database, which may lead to loss of data.
- *Schema evolution* is supported when a database system enables the modification of the database schema without loss of existing data.
- *Schema versioning* is supported when a database system allows the accessing of all data, both retrospectively and prospectively, through user-definable version interfaces.

The significant difference between evolution and versioning is that the former does not require the maintenance of a schema history, while in the latter all past schema versions are retained. Note that, in the context of schema evolution and versioning, most authors agree that there is no need to distinguish valid time from transaction time (McKenzie & Snodgrass, 1990).

On the language side, TSQL2 (Snodgrass, 1995) is the most noticeable attempt to devise a query language for relational temporal databases. TSQL2 is a temporal extension to the SQL-92 language standard, augmented to enable users to specify valid-time and transaction-time expressions for data retrieval. As to querying in presence of schema versioning, while TSQL2 only allows users to punctually specify the schema version according to which data are queried, other approaches also support queries spanning multiple schema versions (Grandi, 2002).

The concepts introduced in this section were originally devised for operational databases, and in particular for relational databases. While in prin-

ciple they can also be applied to data warehousing systems, that in a ROLAP implementations are based on relational databases, the peculiarities of the multidimensional model and the strong relevance of time in the OLAP world call for more specific approaches.

HANDLING CHANGES IN THE DATA WAREHOUSE

When considering temporal data, it is first of all necessary to understand how time is reflected in the database, and how a new piece of information affects existing data. From this point of view, Devlin (1997) proposes the following classification:

- *Transient data*: alterations and deletions of existing records physically destroy the previous data content.
- *Periodic data*: once a record is added to a database, it is never physically deleted, nor is its content ever modified. Rather, new records are added to reflect updates or deletions. Periodic data thus represent a complete record of the changes that have occurred in the data.
- *Semi-periodic data*: in some situations, due to performance and/or storage constraints, only the more recent history of data changes is kept.
- *Snapshot data*: a data snapshot is a stable view of data as it exists at some point in time, not containing any record of the changes that determined it. A series of snapshots can provide an overall view of the history of an organization.

Data sources normally adopt either a transient or a (semi-)periodic approach, depending on whether the application domains requires keeping history of past data or not. The historical depth of a data warehouse is typically not less than the one of its data sources, thus data warehouses more often contain periodic data. Conversely, data marts normally conform to the snapshot model.

In order to model historical data in the data warehouse, Abello and Martín (2003) propose a bi-temporal storage structure where each attribute is associated to two couples of timestamps, so as to track the history of its values according to both valid and transaction time. Each attribute, or each set of attributes having the same behaviour with reference to changes (i.e., such that whenever an attribute in the set changes its value, all the others change too), is stored in a separate table so that a change occurred to one concept does not affect the other concepts. Obviously, such normalized and time-oriented structure is not suited for querying, that will take place on denormalized data marts fed from the data warehouse.

Since the data warehouse can be thought of as a set of derived, materialized views defined over a set of source schemata, the problem of evolving the content and the schema of derived views in connection to the source changes is highly relevant in the context of temporal data warehouses. Bellahsene (2002) distinguishes two subproblems: view maintenance and view adaptation.

View maintenance consists in maintaining a materialized view in response to data modifications of the source relations. Considering the width of the problem, we refer the reader to Gupta & Mumick (1995) for a taxonomy of view maintenance problems and a description of the main techniques proposed in the literature. A specific issue in view maintenance is how to provide temporal views over the history of source data, that may be non-temporal. We mention two approaches in this direction. Yang & Widom (1998) describe an architecture that uses incremental techniques to automatically maintain temporal views over non-temporal source relations, allowing users to ask temporal queries on these views. De Amo & Halfeld Ferrari Alves (2000) present a self-maintainable temporal data warehouse that, besides a set of temporal views, includes a set of auxiliary relations containing only temporal information.

Such auxiliary relations are used to maintain the data warehouse without consulting the source databases and to avoid storing the entire history of source databases in the warehouse.

View adaptation consists in recomputing a materialized view in response to changes either in the schema of the source relations or in the definition of the view itself. Changes in the source schemata may be due to an evolution of the application domain they represent, or to a new physical location for them. Changes in the definition of the view (i.e., in the data warehouse schema) may also be due to new requirements of the business users who query the data marts fed by the data warehouse. Among the approaches in this direction we mention the one by Bellahsene (1998), who proposes an extended relational view model to support view adaptation, aimed at maintaining data coherence and preserving the validity of the existing application programs. Performing a schema change leads to creating a new view, by means of an extended view definition language that incorporates two clauses: *hide*, which specifies a set of attributes to be hidden, and *add*, that allows a view to own additional attributes that do not belong to source relations. In the EVE framework (Lee, Nica, & Rundensteiner, 2002), in order to automate the redefinition of a view in response to schema changes in the data sources, the database administrator is allowed to embed her preferences about view evolution into the view definition itself. The preference-based view rewriting process, called *view synchronization*, identifies and extracts appropriate information from other data sources as replacements of the affected components of the original view definition, in order to produce an alternative view that somehow preserves the original one. Finally, the DyDa framework (Chen, Zhang, & Rundensteiner, 2006) supports compensating queries, that cope with erroneous results in view maintenance due to concurrent updates in data source, in presence of data and schema changes.

The key idea of adaptation techniques is to avoid recomputing the materialized view from scratch by relying on the previous materialization and on the source relations. For instance, Bellahsene (2002) focuses on the adaptation of the data warehouse in response to schema changes arising on source relations located on multiple sites. To adapt the extent of the data warehouse in response to these changes, she adopts rewriting algorithms that make use of containment checking, so that only the part of the new view that is not contained in the old view will be recomputed. In the same context, a distinctive feature of the *AutoMed* system (Fan & Poulovassilis, 2004) is the capability of handling not only schema evolutions in materialized data integration scenarios, but also changes in the data model in which the schema is expressed (e.g., XML vs. relational). This is achieved by applying sequences of primitive transformations to a low-level hypergraph-based data model, in whose terms higher-level modeling languages are defined.

With reference to the problem of keeping the data warehouse in sync with the sources, Wrembel (2009) proposes a metamodel for handling changes in the operational data sources, which supports the automatic detection of structural and content changes in the sources and their automatic propagation to the data warehouse. Similarly, Papastefanos et al. (2009) propose a graph-based technique for detecting evolution changes in the source schemata and semi-automatically carrying out changes in ETL procedures through a set of predefined polices.

Finally, Combi & Oliboni (2007) focus on the management of time-variant semi-structured XML data within the data warehouse. In particular, they propose a representation based on graphs whose nodes denote objects or values and are labeled with their validity interval; the constraints related to correct management of time are then discussed.

HANDLING DATA CHANGES IN THE DATA MART

Content changes result from user activities that perform their day-to-day work on data sources by means of different applications (Wrembel & Bebel, 2007). These changes are reflected in the data warehouse and then in the data marts fed from it.

The multidimensional model provides direct support for representing the sequence of events that constitute the history of a fact: by including a temporal dimension (say, with date granularity) in the fact, each event is associated to its date. For instance, if we consider an ORDER fact representing the quantities in the lines of orders received by a company selling PC consumables, the dimensions would probably be product, orderNumber, and orderDate. Thus, each event (i.e., each line of order) would be associated to the ordered product, to the number of the order it belongs to, and to the order date.

On the other hand, the multidimensional model implicitly assumes that the dimensions and the related levels are entirely static. This assumption is clearly unrealistic in most cases; for instance, considering again the order domain, a company may add new categories of products to its catalog while others can be dropped, or the category of a product may change in response to the marketing policy.

Another common assumption is that, once an event has been registered in a data mart, it is never modified so that the only possible writing operation consists in appending new events as they occur. While this is acceptable for a wide variety of domains, some applications call for a different behavior; for example the quantity of a product ordered in a given day could be wrongly registered or could be communicated after the ETL process has run.

These few examples emphasize the need for a correct handling of changes in the data mart content. Differently from the problem of handling schema changes, the issues related to data changes have been widely addressed by researchers and practitioners, even because in several cases they can be directly managed in commercial DBMSs. In the following subsections we separately discuss the issues related to changes in dimensional data and factual data, i.e., events.

Changes in Dimensional Data

By this term we mean any content change that may occur within an instance of a hierarchy, involving either the dimension itself, or a level, or a property. For instance, considering a product hierarchy featuring levels type and category, the name of a product may change, or a new category may be introduced so that the existing types have to be reassigned to categories.

The study of changes in dimensional data has been pioneered by Kimball (1996), who coined the term *slowly-changing dimension* to point out that, differently from data in fact tables, changes within the dimension tables occur less frequently. He proposed three basic modeling solutions for a ROLAP implementation of the multidimensional model, each inducing a different capability of tracking the history of data. In the *Type I* solution he simply proposes to overwrite old tuples in dimension tables with new data: in this case, tracking history is not possible but changes in the hierarchy data keep the data mart up-to-date. Conversely, in the *Type II* solution, each change produces a new record in the dimension table: old events stay related to the old versions of hierarchies, while new events are related to the current version. In order to allow two or more tuples representing the same hierarchy instance to be included in the dimension table, surrogate keys must necessarily be adopted. Finally, the *Type III* solution is based on augmenting the schema of the dimension table by representing both the current and the previous value for each level or attribute subject to change.

Other solutions, based on these basic ones, have been proposed over time. In particular, a complete historicization of the dimension tables

determines higher expressivity. This can be obtained for instance as an extension of Type II, by adding to the dimension table schema a couple of timestamps storing the validity interval for each tuple, plus an attribute storing the surrogate key of the first version of the tuple. This solution is sometimes called *Type VI* (I+II+III) since it covers all the previous ones.

The solutions discussed so far have different querying capabilities; with reference to the terminology proposed by SAP (2000), three main querying scenarios can be distinguished:

- *Today is yesterday*: all events are related to the current value of the hierarchy. This scenario is supported by all the discussed solutions.
- *Today or Yesterday*: each event is related to the hierarchy value that was valid when the event occurred. This scenario, that reconstructs the historical truth, is supported by Type II and VI solutions.
- *Yesterday is Today*: each event is related to the hierarchy value that was valid at a given time in the past. This scenario is supported by Type VI solution only.

Other solutions for handling changes in dimensional data have been devised thereafter. Two relevant proposals, that study the problem from a more conceptual point of view, are by Bliujute et al. (1998) and Pedersen and Jensen (1999). The first one proposes a temporal star schema that, differently from the traditional one, omits the time dimension table and timestamps each row in every table instead, treating the fact table and the dimension tables equally with respect to time. Similarly, the second one proposes to handle changes by adding timestamps to all the components of a multidimensional schema: the values of both dimensions and facts, the inter-level partial order that shapes hierarchy instances and the fact-dimension relationships. Another model that supports changes in data by timestamping

7

dimensional data is COMET (Eder, Koncilia, & Morzy, 2002), that also supports schema versioning using a fully historicized meta-model. Finally, Chamoni and Stock (1999) suggest to couple the multidimensional cube with meta-cubes that store dimension structures together with their timestamps.

A model supporting data changes should be coupled with meaningful operators to carry them out. An interesting proposal in this direction comes from Hurtado, Mendelzon, & Vaisman (1999b), who introduces a set of high-level operators based on sequences of elemental operators (Hurtado, Mendelzon, & Vaisman, 1999a) for both schema and data changes. The operators for data changes are *reclassify*, that changes the roll-up partial order between levels, *split*, that reorganizes a hierarchy after one instance has been replaced by two or more ones, *merge*, that merges two instances of a hierarchy into a single one, and update, that simply changes the value of an instance without affecting the roll-up partial order. More recently, Moreno, Fileto, & Arango (2010) proposed the *season* idea to effectively query cubes when reclassification took place. Informally, a season is a continuous interval during which a member of a level is associated with the same member of a higher level, e.g., a season of a player with a team, a season of a team in a division. The authors propose the season operator to transform the multidimensional schema by adding a season dimension. Such a dimension determines the historicization of data and allows queries such as "*Return the total number of goals scored by each player in each season with each team*" to be easily answered.

Since changes to hierarchy instances could affect summarizability, the definition of models and operators is usually coupled with a set of constraints aimed at enforcing data consistency (Hurtado, Mendelzon, & Vaisman, 1999b; Eder, Koncilia, & Morzy, 2002; Letz, Henn, & Vossen, 2002).

Changes in Factual Data

We start this section by preliminarily mentioning the two basic paradigms introduced by Kimball (1996) for representing inventory-like information in a data mart: the *transactional model*, where each increase and decrease in the inventory level is recorded as an event, and the *snapshot model*, where the current inventory level is periodically recorded. A similar characterization is proposed by Bliujute et al. (1998), who distinguish between *event-oriented data*, like sales, inventory transfers, and financial transactions, and *state-oriented data*, like unit prices, account balances, and inventory levels. This has been later generalized to define a classification of facts based on the conceptual role given to events (Golfarelli & Rizzi, 2007b):

- *Flow facts* (*flow measures* in Lenz & Shoshani, 1997) record a single transaction or summarize a set of transactions that occur during the same time interval; they are monitored by collecting their occurrences during a time interval and are cumulatively measured at the end of that period. Examples of flow facts are orders and enrollments.
- *Stock facts* (*stock measures* in Lenz & Shoshani, 1997) refer to an instant in time and are evaluated at that instant; they are monitored by periodically sampling and measuring their state. Examples are the price of a share and the level of a river.

By the term *changes in factual data* we mean any content change an event may be subject to, involving either the values of its measures or the dimensional elements it is connected to. Changes in factual data are a relevant issue in all those cases where the values measured for a given event may change over a period of time, to be consolidated only after the event has been for the first time registered in the data mart. These *late measurements* typically happens when the early measurements made for events are subject to errors (e.g., the amount of an order may be corrected after the order has been registered) or when events inherently evolve over time (e.g., notifications of university enrollments may be received and registered several days after they were issued). This problem becomes even more evident as the timeliness requirement takes more importance (Jarke, Jeusfeld, Quix, & Vassiliadis, 1999). This is the case for *zero-latency* data warehousing systems (Bruckner & Tjoa, 2002), whose goal is to allow organizations to deliver relevant information as fast as possible to knowledge workers or decision systems that need to react in near real-time to new information.

In these contexts, if the up-to-date state is to be made timely visible to the decision makers, past events must be continuously updated to reflect the incoming late measurements. Unfortunately, if updates are carried out by physically overwriting past registrations of events, some problems may arise. In fact, accountability and traceability require the capability of preserving the exact information the analyst based her decision upon. If the old registration for an event is replaced by its latest version, past decisions can no longer be justified. Besides, in some applications, accessing only up-to-date versions of information is not sufficient to ensure the correctness of analysis. A typical case is that of queries requiring to compare the progress of an ongoing phenomenon with past occurrences of the same phenomenon: since the data recorded for the ongoing phenomenon are not consolidated yet, comparing them with past consolidated data may not be meaningful (Golfarelli & Rizzi, 2007b).

Supporting accountability and traceability in presence of late measurements requires the adoption of a bi-temporal solution where both valid and transaction time are represented by means of timestamps. Only few approaches in the literature are specifically focused on studying this specific topic. Kimball (2000) states that a bi-temporal solution may be useful to cope with late mea-

surements. Bruckner & Tjoa (2002) discuss the problem of temporal consistency in consequence of delayed discovery of real-world changes and propose a solution based on valid time, revelation time and loading time. Loading time is the point in time when a new piece of information is loaded in the data mart, while revelation time is the point in time when that piece of information was realized by at least one data source. Finally, Golfarelli & Rizzi (2007b) propose to couple valid time and transaction time and distinguish two different solutions for managing late measurements: *delta solution*, where each new measurement for an event is represented as a delta with respect to the previous measurement, and transaction time is modeled by adding to the schema a new temporal dimension to represent when each registration was made in the data mart; and *consolidated solution*, where late measurements are represented by recording the consolidated value for the event, and transaction time is modeled by two temporal dimensions that delimit the time interval during which each registration is current.

HANDLING SCHEMA CHANGES IN THE DATA MART

According to (Wrembel & Bebel, 2007), schema changes in the data mart may be caused by different factors:

- Subsequent design iterations in the context of an incremental approach to data mart design.
- Changes in the user requirements, triggered for instance by the need for producing more sophisticated reports, or by new categories of users that subscribe to the data mart.
- Changes in the application domain, i.e., arising from modifications in the business world, such as a change in the way a busi-

ness is done, or a changing in the organizational structure of the company.

- New versions of software components being installed.
- System tuning activities.

For instance, it may be necessary to add a subcategory level to the product hierarchy to allow more detailed analysis, or to add a measure revenueInEuro due to the introduction of a new currency.

As stated in the second section, depending on how previous schema versions are managed, two main classes of approaches may be distinguished: *schema evolution*, that allows modifications of the schema without loss of data but does not maintain the schema history, and *schema versioning*, where past schema definitions are retained so that all data may be accessed through a version specified by the user. In the two following subsection these two classes of approaches will be separately surveyed.

Evolution

The main problem here is to support a set of operators for changing the data mart schema, while enabling lossless migration of existing data from the past schema version to the new one.

In this context, FIESTA is a methodology where the evolution of multidimensional schemata is supported on a conceptual level, thus for both ROLAP and MOLAP implementations (Blaschka, Sapia, & Höfling, 1999; Blaschka, 2000). Core of the approach is a schema evolution algebra which includes a formal multidimensional data model together with a wide set of schema evolution operations, whose effects on both schema and instances are described. Essentially, the operations allow dimensions, hierarchy levels, properties and measures to be added and deleted from the multidimensional schema. Since OLAP systems are often implemented on top of relational DBMSs, the approach also shows how a multidimensional schema can be mapped to a relational schema by

means of a meta-schema that extends the catalogue of the underlying DBMS. Each sequence of evolution operations is then transformed into a sequence of relational evolution commands that adapt the relational database schema together with its instances, and update the contents of the meta-schema accordingly.

Conversely, in (Kaas, Pedersen, & Rasmussen, 2004) the evolution problem is investigated with particular reference to its impact on the logical level for ROLAP implementations, namely, on star and snowflake schemata. Eight basic evolution operators are defined (insert/delete dimension, level, property, and measure). For each of them, the changes implied on star and snowflake schemata are described and their impact on existing SQL queries in reporting tools is discussed. Remarkably, an in-depth comparison reveals that the star schema is generally more robust than the snowflake schema against schema changes.

A comprehensive approach to evolution is the one jointly devised at the Universities of Toronto and Buenos Aires. The fundamentals are laid by Hurtado, Mendelzon, & Vaisman (1999a), who propose a formal model for updating dimensions at both the schema and instance level, based on a set of modification operators (generalize, specialize, relate/unrelated/delete level are those defined at the schema level). An incremental algorithm for efficiently maintaining a set of materialized views in the presence of dimension updates is also presented. This work is then extended by Vaisman, Mendelzon, Ruaro, & Cymerman (2004) by introducing *TSOLAP*, an OLAP server supporting dimension updates and view maintenance, built following the OLE DB for OLAP proposal. The approach is completed by *MDDLX*, an extension of MDX (Microsoft's language for OLAP) with a set of statements supporting dimension update operators at both schema and instance levels.

A relevant aspect related to evolution is how changes in schema affect the data mart quality, which is discussed in (Quix, 1999). A set of schema evolution operators is adapted from those for object-oriented databases; for each operator, its impact on the quality factors (such as completeness, correctness, and consistency between the conceptual and logical schema) as emerged in the context of the *DWQ Project - Foundations of Data Warehouse Quality* (Jarke, Jeusfeld, Quix, & Vassiliadis, 1999) is discussed. The tracking of the history of changes and the consistency rules to enforce when a quality factor has to be re-evaluated due to evolution is supported by an ad hoc meta-model.

Versioning

According to the frequently cited definition by Inmon (1996), one of the characteristic features of a data warehouse is its non-volatility, which means that data is integrated into the data warehousing system once and remains unchanged afterwards. Importantly, this feature implies that the re-execution of a single query will always produce the same result. In other words, past analysis results can be verified and then inspected by means of more detailed OLAP sessions at any point in time. While non-volatility in the presence of changes at the data level can be achieved by adopting one of the solutions discussed in the third section, non-volatility in the presence of changes at the schema level requires some versioning approach to be undertaken. In fact, it is easy to see that the ability to re-execute previous queries in the presence of schema changes requires access to past schema versions, which cannot be achieved with an evolution approach.

The first work in this direction is COMET (Eder, Koncilia, & Morzy, 2002), a metamodel that supports schema and instance versioning. All classes in the metamodel are timestamped with a validity interval, so multiple, subsequent versions of cubes can be stored and queried. Transformation of data from one version into the (immediate) succeeding or preceding one is supported; though the paper reports no details on how a new version can be obtained from the

previous one, a comprehensive set of constraints that the versions have to fulfill in order to ensure the integrity of the temporal model is proposed.

The peculiarity of the timestamp-based versioning model proposed by Body, Miquel, Bédard, and Tchounikine (2003) is that hierarchies are deduced from the dimensions instances, so that explicitly defining the multidimensional schema is not necessary. In this way, schema changes are implicitly managed as a result of handling changes in instances. On the other hand, the versioning approach proposed by Ravat, Teste, & Zurfluh (2006) uses a constellation of star schemata to model different versions of the same fact, and populates versions by means of mapping functions.

A comprehensive approach to versioning is presented by Wrembel and Bebel (2007). Essentially, they propose two metamodels: one for managing a multi-version data mart and one for detecting changes in the operational sources. A multi-version data mart is a sequence of versions, each composed of a schema version and an instance version. Remarkably, besides "real" versions determined by changes in the application domain or in users' requirements, also "alternative" versions are introduced, to be used for simulating and managing hypothetical business scenarios within what-if analysis settings.

Another approach to versioning specifically oriented to supporting cross-version queries is the one by Golfarelli, Lechtenbörger, Rizzi and Vossen (2006). Here, multidimensional schemata are represented as graphs of simple functional dependencies, and an algebra of graph operations to define new versions is defined. Data migration from the old to the new version is semi-automated, i.e., based on the differences between the two versions the system suggests a set of migration actions and gives support for their execution. The key idea of this approach is to support flexible cross-version querying by allowing the designer to enrich previous versions using the knowledge of current schema modifications. For this purpose, when creating a new schema version the designer may choose to create *augmented schemata* that extend previous schema versions to reflect the current schema extension, both at the schema and the instance level. In a nutshell, the augmented schema associated with a version is the most general schema describing the data that are actually recorded for that version and thus are available for querying purposes. Like for migration, a set of possible augmentation actions is proposed to the designer (e.g., the designer may choose to manually insert values of a newly added attribute for hierarchy instances whose validity was limited to previous versions).

To the best of our knowledge, only two approaches use both valid and transaction time in the context of versioning. Koncilia (2003) presents a bi-temporal extension of the COMET metamodel, aimed at representing not only the valid time of schema modifications, but also the transaction time. Rechy-Ramírez and Benítez-Guerrero (2006) introduce a conceptual model for bi-temporal versioning of multidimensional schemata, aimed at enabling modifications in the data mart schema without affecting the existing applications. Each version has a temporal pertinence composed by a valid time and a transaction time, thus enabling the existence of two or more versions with the same valid time, but different transaction times. Associated to this model, there are 16 operators for schema changing and a SQL-like language to create and modify versions.

QUERYING TEMPORAL DATA

The development of a model for temporal data warehousing is of little use without an appropriate query language capable of effectively handling time. In principle, a temporal query could be directly formulated on a relational schema using standard SQL, but this would be exceedingly long and complex even for a skilled user.

In this direction, Bliujute, Saltenis, Slivinskas, & Jensen (1998) discuss the performance of their temporal star schema considering five types of temporal queries. Golfarelli & Rizzi (2007b) distinguish three querying scenarios in presence of late measurements:

- *Up-to-date queries*, that require the most recent measurement for each event;
- *Rollback queries*, that require a past version measurement for each event;
- *Historical queries*, that require multiple measurements for events, i.e., are aimed at reconstructing the history of event changes.

To cope with schema changes, Mendelzon and Vaisman (2000) proposed the *Temporal OLAP* (TOLAP) query language. TOLAP, based on the temporal multidimensional model proposed by Hurtado et al. (1999b), fully supports schema evolution and versioning, differently from best-known temporal query languages such as TSQL2 (Snodgrass, 1995), that supports versioning in a limited way only. TOLAP combines the temporal features of TSQL2 with some high-order features of SchemaLog in order to support querying multidimensional data with reference to different instants in time in a concise and elegant way. All three querying scenarios (today is yesterday, yesterday is today, and today or yesterday) are supported. Also meta-queries, e.g. concerning the instant changes to data took place, can be expressed.

Several approaches face the problem of formulating cross-version querying, i.e., formulating queries that span different schema versions. For instance, Morzy and Wrembel (2004) propose a SQL extension aimed at expressing queries on multiple (either real or alternative) schema versions. Each query is decomposed into a set of partial queries, one for each schema version involved. The results of partial queries are separately presented, annotated with version and metadata information; in some cases, partial queries results can be merged into a common set of data. In (Wrembel & Bebel, 2007), the problem of cross-version queries is addressed by allowing users to specify either implicitly (by specifying a time interval for the query) or explicitly (by specifying a set of version identifiers) the set of versions for querying. Similarly, in (Golfarelli & Rizzi, 2007a) the relevant versions for answering a query are either chosen explicitly by the user or implicitly by the system based on the time interval spanned by the query, as shown in the prototype implementation X-Time.

In the context of querying, a number of works are related to the so-called *temporal aggregation problem*, that was studied mainly in the context of MOLAP systems and consists in efficiently computing and maintaining temporal aggregates. In fact, time dimensions typically lead to a high degree of sparseness in traditional array-based MOLAP cubes because of their large cardinality, and to significant overhead to answer time-parameterized range queries. For instance, the work by Tao, Papadias, & Faloutsos (2004) focuses on approximate temporal aggregate processing. Specifically, for count queries, its goal is to provide answers guaranteed to deviate from the exact ones within a given threshold. Riedewald, Agrawal, & El Abbadi (2002) proposed efficient range aggregation in temporal data warehouses by exploiting the append-only property of the time-related dimension. Their framework allows large amounts of new data to be integrated into the warehouse and historical summaries to be efficiently generated, independently of the extent of the data set in the time dimension. Feng, Li, Agrawal, & El Abbadi (2005) proposed a general approach to improve the efficiency of range aggregate queries on MOLAP data cubes in a temporal data warehouse by separately handling time-related dimensions to take advantage of their monotonic trend over time. Yang & Widom (2001) introduce a new index structure called the SB-tree, which supports fast lookup of aggregate results based on time, and can be maintained efficiently when the data changes along the time line. In the same direction, Chmiel, Morzy, & Wrembel (2010)

propose a multiversion join index characterized by a a two-level structure, where an upper level is used for indexing attributes and a lower level is used for indexing data warehouse versions. This index joins multiple versions of a fact table with versions of a dimension table that are physically stored in separate data warehouse versions, and is designed for optimizing star queries addressing multiple versions.

DESIGNING TEMPORAL DATA WAREHOUSES

It is widely recognized that designing a data warehousing system requires techniques that are radically different from those normally adopted for designing operational databases (Golfarelli & Rizzi, 1999). On the other hand, though the literature reports several attempts to devise design methodologies for data warehouses, very few attention has been posed on the specific design issues related to time. Indeed, as stated by Rizzi et al. (2006), devising design techniques capable of taking time and changes into account is one of the open issues in data warehouse research.

Pedersen and Jensen (1999) recognize that properly handling time and changes is a must-have for multidimensional models. Sarda (1999) summarizes the distinguishing characteristics of time dimensions: they are continuously valued and constantly increasing, they can be associated with multiple user-defined calendars, they express the validity of both facts and other dimensions (either in the form of time instants or validity intervals). Sarda also proposes a design methodology for temporal data warehouses featuring two phases: logical design, that produces relations characterized by a temporal validity, and physical design, that addresses efficient storage and access.

Considering the leading role played by temporal hierarchies within data marts and OLAP queries, it is worth adopting ad hoc approaches for their modeling not only from the logical, but also from the conceptual point of view. While all conceptual models for data marts allow for temporal hierarchies to be represented like any other hierarchies, to the best of our knowledge the only approach that provides ad hoc concepts for modeling time is the one by Malinowski & Zimányi (2008), based on a temporal extensions of the MultiDim conceptual model. Different temporality types are allowed (namely, valid time, transaction time, lifespan, and loading time), and temporal support for levels, properties, hierarchies, and measures is granted.

Finally, Golfarelli & Rizzi (2007b) discuss the different design solutions that can be adopted in presence of late measurements, depending on the flow or stock nature of the events and on the types of queries to be executed.

OPEN ISSUES AND CONCLUSION

In this survey we classified and discussed the issues related to temporal data warehousing. An in-depth analysis of the literature revealed that the research community not always devoted a comprehensive attention to all these aspects. As a matter of fact, a wide agreement on the possible design solutions has been reached only with reference to changes in dimensional data. As to changes in factual data and changes in schema, though some interesting solutions have been proposed, no broad and shared framework has been devised yet.

Similarly, on the commercial side, changes in data have been supported since almost a decade ago. Already in year 2000, systems such as Business Warehouse by SAP (2000) were allowing to track changes in data and to effectively query cubes based on different temporal scenarios by letting users choose which version of the hierarchies to adopt for querying. On the other hand, today there still is very marginal support to changes in schema by commercial tools. For instance, *SQL Compare* compares and synchronizes SQL Server database schemata, and can be used when changes

made to the schema of a local database need to be pushed to a central database on a remote server. Also, the *Oracle Change Management Pack* is aimed to report and track the evolving state of meta-data, thus allowing to compare database schemata, and to generate and execute scripts to carry out the changes. In both cases, formulating a single query spanning multiple databases with different schemata is not possible.

We believe that, considering the maturity of the field and the wide diffusion of data warehousing systems, in the near future decision makers will be more and more demanding for advanced temporal support. Thus, it is essential that both vendors and researchers be ready to deliver effective solutions. In this direction we envision two main open issues. On the one hand, some research aspects indeed require further investigation. For instance, support for cross-version queries is not satisfactory yet, and its impact on performance has not been completely investigated; similarly, the effectiveness of view adaptation approaches is still limited. On the other hand, in order to encourage vendors to add full temporal support to commercial platforms, the solutions proposed in the literature should be better harmonized to converge into a complete, flexible approach that could be effortlessly accepted by the market.

REFERENCES

Abelló, A., & Martín, C. (2003). A Bi-temporal Storage Structure for a Corporate Data Warehouse. *Proceedings International Conference on Enterprise Information Systems*, Angers, France, 177-183.

Bellahsene, Z. (1998). View Adaptation in Data Warehousing Systems. *Proceedings International Conference on Database and Expert Systems Applications*, Vienna, Austria, 300-309.

Bellahsene, Z. (2002). Schema Evolution in Data Warehouses. *Knowledge and Information Systems*, *4*(3), 283–304. doi:10.1007/s101150200008

Blaschka, M. (2000). *FIESTA - A Framework for Schema Evolution in Multidimensional Databases*. PhD Thesis, Technische Universitat Munchen, Germany.

Blaschka, M., Sapia, C., & Höfling, G. (1999). On Schema Evolution in Multidimensional Databases. *Proceedings International Conference on Data Warehousing and Knowledge Discovery*, Florence, Italy, 153-164.

Bliujute, R., Saltenis, S., Slivinskas, G., & Jensen, C. S. (1998). Systematic Change Management in Dimensional Data Warehousing. *Proceedings International Baltic Workshop on Databases and Information Systems*, Riga, Latvia, 27–41.

Body, M., Miquel, M., Bédard, Y., & Tchounikine, A. (2003). Handling Evolutions in Multidimensional Structures. *Proceedings International Conference on Data Engineering*, Bangalore, India, 581-591.

Bruckner, R., & Tjoa, A. (2002). Capturing Delays and Valid Times in Data Warehouses - Towards Timely Consistent Analyses. *Journal of Intelligent Information Systems*, *19*(2), 169–190. doi:10.1023/A:1016555410197

Chamoni, P., & Stock, S. (1999). Temporal Structures in Data Warehousing. *Proceedings International Conference on Data Warehousing and Knowledge Discovery*, Florence, Italy, 353-358.

Chen, S., Zhang, X., & Rundensteiner, E. (2006). A Compensation-Based Approach for View Maintenance in Distributed Environments. *IEEE Transactions on Knowledge and Data Engineering*, *18*(8), 1068–1081. doi:10.1109/TKDE.2006.117

Chmiel, J., Morzy, T., & Wrembel, R. (2009). Multiversion join index for multiversion data warehouse. *Information and Software Technology*, *51*(1), 98–108. doi:10.1016/j.infsof.2008.01.003

Combi, C., & Oliboni, B. (2007). Temporal semi-structured data models and data warehouses. In *Data Warehouses and OLAP: Concepts, Architectures and Solutions*, Wrembel & Koncilia (Eds.), IRM Press, 277-297.

De Amo, S., & Halfeld Ferrari Alves, M. (2000). Efficient Maintenance of Temporal Data Warehouses. *Proceedings International Database Engineering and Applications Symposium*, Yokohoma, Japan 188-196.

Devlin, B. (1997). Managing Time In The Data Warehouse. *InfoDB*, *11*(1), 7–12.

Eder, J., & Koncilia, C. (2001). Changes of Dimension Data in Temporal Data Warehouses. *Proceedings International Conference on Data Warehousing and Knowledge Discovery*, Munich, Germany, 284-293.

Eder, J., Koncilia, C., & Morzy, T. (2002). The COMET Metamodel For Temporal Data Warehouses. *Proceedings International Conference on Advanced Information Systems Engineering*, Toronto, Canada, 83-99.

Fan, H., & Poulovassilis, A. (2004). Schema Evolution in Data Warehousing Environments - A Schema Transformation-Based Approach. *Proceedings International Conference on Conceptual Modeling*, Shanghai, China, 639-653.

Feng, Y., Li, H.-G., Agrawal, D., & El Abbadi, A. (2005). Exploiting Temporal Correlation in Temporal Data Warehouses. *Proceedings International Conference on Database Systems for Advanced Applications*, Beijing, China, 662-674.

Golfarelli, M., Lechtenbörger, J., Rizzi, S., & Vossen, G. (2006). Schema Versioning in Data Warehouses: Enabling Cross-Version Querying via Schema Augmentation. *Data & Knowledge Engineering*, *59*(2), 435–459. doi:10.1016/j.datak.2005.09.004

Golfarelli, M., & Rizzi, S. (1999). Designing the data warehouse: key steps and crucial issues. *Journal of Computer Science and Information Management*, *2*(1), 1–14.

Golfarelli, M., & Rizzi, S. (2007a). X-Time: Schema Versioning and Cross-Version Querying in Data Warehouses. *Proceedings International Conference on Data Engineering*, Istanbul, Turkey, 1471-147.

Golfarelli, M., & Rizzi, S. (2007b). Managing late measurements in data warehouses. *International Journal of Data Warehousing and Mining*, *3*(4), 51–67. doi:10.4018/jdwm.2007100103

Grandi, F. (2002). A Relational Multi-Schema Data Model and Query Language for full Support of Schema Versioning. *Proceedings SEBD*, Portoferraio, Italy, 323-336.

Gupta, A., & Mumick, I. S. (1995). Maintenance of materialized views: problems, techniques, and applications. *Data Engineering Bulletin*, *18*(2), 3–18.

Hurtado, C., Mendelzon, A., & Vaisman, A. (1999a). Maintaining Data Cubes under Dimension Updates. *Proceedings International Conference on Data Engineering*, Sydney, Austrialia, 346-355.

Hurtado, C., Mendelzon, A., & Vaisman, A. (1999b). Updating OLAP Dimensions. *Proceedings International Workshop on Data Warehousing and OLAP*, Kansas City, USA, 60-66.

Inmon, W. (1996). *Building the data warehouse*. John Wiley & Sons.

Institute, S. A. P. (2000). *Multi-dimensional Modeling with SAP BW*. SAP America Inc. and SAP AG.

Jarke, M., Jeusfeld, M., Quix, C., & Vassiliadis, P. (1999). Architecture and Quality in Data Warehouses: An Extended Repository Approach. *Information Systems*, *24*(3), 229–253. doi:10.1016/S0306-4379(99)00017-4

Jensen, C., Clifford, J., Elmasri, R., Gadia, S. K., Hayes, P. J., & Jajodia, S. (1994). A Consensus Glossary of Temporal Database Concepts. *SIGMOD Record*, *23*(1), 52–64. doi:10.1145/181550.181560

Kaas, C., Pedersen, T. B., & Rasmussen, B. (2004). Schema Evolution for Stars and Snowflakes. *Proceedings International Conference on Enterprise Information Systems*, Porto, Portugal, 425-433.

Kimball, R. (1996). *The Data Warehouse Toolkit*. Wiley Computer Publishing.

Kimball, R. (2000). Backward in Time. *Intelligent Enterprise Magazine*, *3*(15).

Koncilia, C. (2003). A Bi-Temporal Data Warehouse Model. *Short Paper Proceedings Conference on Advanced Information Systems Engineering*, Klagenfurt/Velden, Austria.

Lee, A., Nica, A., & Rundensteiner, E. (2002). The EVE Approach: View Synchronization in Dynamic Distributed Environments. *IEEE Transactions on Knowledge and Data Engineering*, *14*(5), 931–954. doi:10.1109/TKDE.2002.1033766

Lenz, H. J., & Shoshani, A. (1997). Summarizability in OLAP and Statistical Databases. *Proceedings Statistical and Scientific Database Management Conference*, Olympia, US, 132-143.

Letz, C., Henn, E., & Vossen, G. (2002). Consistency in Data Warehouse Dimensions. *Proceedings International Database Engineering and Application Symposium*, Edmonton, Canada, 224-232.

Malinowski, E., & Zimányi, E. (2008). A conceptual model for temporal data warehouses and its transformation to the ER and the object-relational models. *Data & Knowledge Engineering, 64*, 101–133. doi:10.1016/j.datak.2007.06.020

McKenzie, E., & Snodgrass, R. (1990). Schema Evolution and the Relational Algebra. *Information Systems, 15*(2), 207–232. doi:10.1016/0306-4379(90)90036-O

Mendelzon, A., & Vaisman, A. (2000). Temporal queries in OLAP. *Proceedings Conference on Very Large Data Bases*, Cairo, Egypt, 242-253.

Moreno, F., Fileto, R., & Arango, F. (2010). Season queries on a temporal multidimensional model for OLAP. *Mathematical and Computer Modelling, 52*(7-8), 1103–1109. doi:10.1016/j.mcm.2010.02.007

Morzy, T., & Wrembel, R. (2004). On querying versions of multiversion data warehouse. *Proceedings International Workshop on Data Warehousing and OLAP*, Washington, DC, 92-101.

Papastefanatos, G., Vassiliadis, P., Simitsis, A., Sellis, T., & Vassiliou, Y. (2009). HECATAEUS: Regulating schema evolution. Proceedings 26th International Conference on Data Engineering, Long Beach, California, 1181-1184.

Pedersen, T. B., & Jensen, C. (1998). Research Issues in Clinical Data Warehousing. *Proceedings Statistical and Scientific Database Management Conference*, Capri, Italy, 43-52.

Pedersen, T. B., & Jensen, C. (1999). Multidimensional Data Modeling for Complex Data. *Proceedings International Conference on Data Engineering*, Sydney, Austrialia, 336-345.

Quix, C. (1999). Repository Support for Data Warehouse Evolution. *Proceedings International Workshop on Design and Management of Data Warehouses*, Heidelberg, Germany.

Ravat, F., Teste, O., & Zurfluh, G. (2006). A Multiversion-Based Multidimensional Model. *Proceedings International Conference on Data Warehousing and Knowledge Discovery*, 65-74.

Rechy-Ramírez, E.-J., & Benítez-Guerrero, E. (2006). A Model and Language for Bi-temporal Schema Versioning in Data Warehouses. *Proceedings International Conference on Computing*, Mexico City, Mexico.

Riedewald, M., Agrawal, D., & El Abbadi, A. (2002). Efficient integration and aggregation of historical information. *Proceedings SIGMOD Conference*, Madison, Wisconsin, 13-24.

Rizzi, S., Abelló, A., Lechtenbörger, J., & Trujillo, J. (2006). Research in Data Warehouse Modeling and Design: Dead or Alive? *Proceedings International Workshop on Data Warehousing and OLAP*, Arlington, USA, 3-10.

Roddick, J. (1995). A Survey of Schema Versioning Issues for Database Systems. *Information and Software Technology, 37*(7), 383–393. doi:10.1016/0950-5849(95)91494-K

Sarda, N. L. (1999). Temporal Issues in Data Warehouse Systems. *Proceedings International Symposium on Database Applications in Non-Traditional Environments*, Kyoto, Japan, 27-34.

Snodgrass, R. T. (1995). *The TSQL2 Temporal Query Language*. Kluwer Academic Publishers.

Tansel, A. U., Clifford, J., Gadia, S. K., Jajodia, S., Segev, A., & Snodgrass, R. T. (1993). *Temporal databases: theory, design and implementation*. Benjamin Cummings.

Tao, Y., Papadias, D., & Faloutsos, C. (2004). Approximate Temporal Aggregation. *Proceedings International Conference on Data Engineering*, Boston, Massachusetts, 190-201.

Vaisman, A., & Mendelzon, A. (2001). A Temporal Query Language for OLAP: Implementation and a Case Study. *Proceedings DBPL*.

Vaisman, A., Mendelzon, A., Ruaro, W., & Cymerman, S. (2004). Supporting Dimension Updates in an OLAP Server. *Information Systems, 29*, 165–185. doi:10.1016/S0306-4379(03)00049-8

Wrembel, R. (2009). A Survey of Managing the Evolution of Data Warehouses. *International Journal of Data Warehousing and Mining, 5*(2), 24–56. doi:10.4018/jdwm.2009040102

Yang, J., & Widom, J. (1998). Maintaining Temporal Views over Non-Temporal Information Sources for Data Warehousing. *Proceedings International Conference on Extending Database Technology*, Valencia, Spain, 389-403.

Yang, J., & Widom, J. (2001). Incremental Computation and Maintenance of Temporal Aggregates. *Proceedings International Conference on Data Engineering*, Heidelberg, Germany, 51-60.

Chapter 2
Summarizing Datacubes:
Semantic and Syntactic Approaches

Rosine Cicchetti
Aix-Marseille Universités, France

Lotfi Lakhal
Aix-Marseille Universités, France

Sébastien Nedjar
Aix-Marseille Universités, France

Noël Novelli
Aix-Marseille Universités, France

Alain Casali
Aix-Marseille Universités, France

ABSTRACT

Datacubes are especially useful for answering efficiently queries on data warehouses. Nevertheless the amount of generated aggregated data is huge with respect to the initial data which is itself very large. Recent research work has addressed the issue of summarizing Datacubes in order to reduce their size. In this chapter, we present three different approaches. They propose structures which make it possible to reduce the size of the data cube representation. The two former, the closed cube and the quotient cube, are said semantic and discard the redundancies captured within data cubes. The size of the underlying representations is especially reduced but the counterpart is an additional response time when answering the OLAP queries. The latter approach is rather syntactic since it enforces an optimization at the logical level. It is called Partition Cube and based on the concept of partition. We also give an algorithm to compute it. We propose a Relational Partition Cube, a novel R-Olap cubing solution for managing Partition Cubes using the relational technology. An analytical evaluation shows that the storage space of Partition Cubes is smaller than Datacubes. In order to confirm analytical comparison, experiments are performed in order to compare our approach with Datacubes and with two of the best reduction methods, the Quotient Cube and the Closed Cube.

DOI: 10.4018/978-1-60960-537-7.ch002

INTRODUCTION

In order to efficiently answer OLAP queries (Chaudhuri and Dayal, 1997), a widely adopted solution is to compute and materialize Datacubes (Gray et al., 1997). For example, given a relation r over the schema $\mathcal{R}$, a set of dimensions $\mathcal{D} = \{D_1, D_2, D_3\}$, $\mathcal{D} \subseteq \mathcal{R}$, a measure $\mathcal{M} \in \mathcal{R}$, an aggregate function f, the cube operator is expressed as follows:

```
SELECT D_1, D_2, D_3, f(M)
FROM r
GROUP BY CUBE(D_1, D_2, D_3)
```

Dimensions are also called categorical attributes and r a categorical database relation. The given query achieves all the possible *group-by* according to any attribute combination belonging to the power set of $\mathcal{D}$. It results in what is called a Datacube, and each sub-query performing a single *group-by* yields a cuboid. Computing Datacubes is exponential in the number of dimensions (the dimension powerset lattice must be explored), and the problem worsens when very large data sets are to be aggregated.

Datacubes are considerably larger than the input relation. Ross and Srivastava (1997) exemplify the problem by achieving a full Datacube encompassing more than 210 millions of tuples from an input relation having 1 million of tuples. The problem is originated by a twofold reason: on one hand the exponential number of dimensional combinations to be dealt, and on the other hand the cardinality of dimensions. The larger dimension domains are, the more aggregated results there are (according to each real value combination). Unfortunately, it is widely recognized that in OLAP databases, data can be very sparse (Ross and Srivastava, 1997; Beyer and Ramakrishnan, 1999) thus scarce value combinations are likely to be numerous and, when computing entirely the Datacubes (full Datacubes), each exception must be preserved. In such a context, (1) approaches favor the efficiency of OLAP queries to the detriment of storage space or (2) they favor an optimal representation of cubes but OLAP query performances are likely to be debased (Morfonios et al., 2007).

Related Work

The approaches addressing the issue of Datacube computation and storage attempt to reduce at least one of the quoted drawbacks. The algorithms BUC (Beyer and Ramakrishnan, 1999) and HCUBING (Han et al., 2001) enforce anti-monotone constraints and partially compute Datacubes (iceberg cubes) to reduce both execution time and disk storage requirements. The underlying argument is that OLAP users are only interested in general trends (and not in atypical behaviors). With a similar argumentation, other methods use the statistic structure of data to compute density distributions and give approximate answers to OLAP queries (see for details (Morfonios et al., 2007)).

The above mentioned approaches are efficient and meet their twofold objective (reduction of execution time and space storage). However, they are not able to answer whatever query (although OLAP queries are, by their very nature, ad hoc queries).

Another category of approaches is the so-called "information lossless". They aim to find the best compromise between OLAP query efficiency and storage requirements without discarding any possible query (even infrequent). Their main idea is to pre-compute and store frequently used aggregates while preserving all the data (possibly at various aggregation levels) needed to compute on line the result of a not foreseen query. They are mostly found in view materialization research.

The following five methods also fit in the information lossless trend:

- the Dwarf Cube (Sismanis et al., 2002),
- the Condensed Cube (Wei et al., 2002),

- the CURE for Cubes (Morfonios and Ioannidis, 2006),
- the Quotient Cube (Lakshmanan et al., 2002),
- the Closed Cube (Casali et al., 2009a, 2003b; Xin et al., 2007).

They favor the optimization of storage space while preserving the capability to answer whatever query. The two latter compute the two smallest representations of a Datacube and thus are the most efficient for both saving storage space and answering queries like "Is this behavior frequent or not?". From these two representations, the exact data of a whole Datacube can be retrieved by performing a computation on line, because all the results of queries are not precomputed and preserved.

Contribution

In this chapter we propose an overview of information lossless approaches which introduce reduced representations for data cubes. More precisely, we present three different structures which make it possible to reduce the size of the data cube representation. The two former, the closed cube and the quotient cube, are said semantic and discard the redundancies captured within data cubes. The size of the underlying representations is especially reduced but the counterpart is an additional response time when answering the OLAP queries. The latter approach, called Partition Cube, is rather syntactic since it enforces an optimization at the logical level.

- we investigate the construction of Quotient Cube and Closed Cube. The choice of these two structures is motivated by their small size (Xin et al., 2007) and theoretical foundation: lattices and closure systems (Ganter and Wille, 1999).
- we propose a new concise representation of Datacubes: the Partition Cube, based

on simple concepts which extend the ones of the partitional model (Spyratos, 1987). Unlike the other information lossless methods, our approach can answer any query without additional execution time. Moreover, our representation provides a simple mechanism reducing significantly the size of aggregates to be stored.

- we introduce a depth-first search algorithm called PCUBE in order to build up the Partition Cube. PCUBE enumerates the aggregates to be computed according to the lectic order. We show that PCUBE minimizes main memory requirements (and avoids swaps);
- by considering the most used environment when managing data warehouses (ROLAP), we propose a relational implementation of our solution (which can be easily achieved).
- finally, a detailed analytical and experimental comparison is made between our representation and the Datacube, the Quotient Cube and the Closed Cube. We show that our representation provides an important reduction of storage space when compared to the Datacube. Meanwhile, as expected the Quotient Cube and the Closed Cube are smaller than the Partition Cube (even if, in theory and for extreme cases, the two former can be equal to the size of the Datacube itself which is never the case for the Partition Cube when $|\mathcal{D}| > 2$). As an additional benefit of our method, once the Relational Partition Cube is stored, any query can be answered on line with no additional computation time.

The remainder of this chapter is organized as follows. The following Section focuses on the two approaches chosen as references. Our proposal is detailed in Section *Partition Cubes*. We define the concepts of our representation, the algorithm

PCUBE along with a relational implementation of our representation. We relate analytical and experimental evaluations in the following Sections. In conclusion, we resume the strengths of our contribution.

MATHEMATICAL FOUNDATION: THE CUBE LATTICE FRAMEWORK

When computing data cubes, the cuboid lattice is frequently considered. By organizing all the possible dimension combinations within a lattice, it can be used for choosing navigation and computation strategies. However it is not the search space for cube computation.

In this section, we recall the concept of the cube lattice (Casali et al., 2003a) proposed as a general and soundly founded framework to state and solve several OLAP mining problems, including the Emerging Cube characterization (Nedjar et al., 2009).

Throughout the chapter, we make the following assumptions and use the following introduced notations. Let r be a relation over the schema $\mathcal{R}$. Attributes of $\mathcal{R}$ are divided in two sets (*i*) $\mathcal{D}$ the set of dimensions, also called categorical or nominal attributes, which correspond to analysis criteria and (*ii*) $\mathcal{M}$ the set of measures.

The multidimensional space of the categorical database relation r groups all the valid combinations built up by considering the value sets of attributes in $\mathcal{D}$, which are enriched with the symbolic value ALL. The latter, introduced in (Gray et al., 1997) when defining the operator Cube-By, is a generalization of all the possible values for any dimension.

The multidimensional space of r is noted and defined as follows:

$$space(r) = \times \{(\varnothing, \ldots, \varnothing)\} \cup_{A \in \mathcal{D}} (r(A) \cup ALL)$$

Where $\times$ symbolizes the Cartesian product, $r(A)$ is the projection of r on the attribute A and the tuple $(\varnothing, \ldots, \varnothing)$ stands for the combination of empty values. Any combination belonging to the multidimensional space is a tuple and represents a multidimensional pattern.

The multidimensional space of r is structured by the generalization / specialization order between tuples, denoted by $\preceq_s$.

Definition 2.1 (Generalization / Specialization order) - Let u, v be two tuples of the multidimensional space of r:

$$u \preceq_s v \Leftrightarrow \begin{cases} \forall A \in \mathcal{D} \text{ such that } u[A] \neq ALL, u[A] = v[A] \\ \text{or } v = (\varnothing, \ldots, \varnothing) \end{cases}$$

The ordered set $(space(r), \preceq_s)$ is denoted by $CL(r)$.

If $u \preceq_s v$, we say that u is less specific (more general) than v in $CL(r)$. In other words, u captures similar information than v but at a rougher granularity level.

Example 2.1 - Let us consider the sale relation r (*cf.* Table 1) which contains the attributes City (C), Day (D), Product (P) and Quantity (Q) yielding the quantity of products sold in a city for a given day. Figure 1 gives the representation as a lattice of the Datacube of r. For reason of space, ALL is replaced by '*' in all figures. Let us consider the sales of Sweet in Marseilles for all Days. It is represented by the tuple (Marseilles, Sweet, ALL). This tuple is specialized by the two following tuples of the relation: (Marseilles, Sweet, d_1) and (Marseilles, Sweet, d_2). Furthermore, (Marseilles, Sweet, ALL) $\preceq_s$ (Marseilles, Sweet, d_1) exemplifies the generalization/specialization order between tuples.

The two basic operators provided for tuple construction are: Sum (denoted by +) and Product (noted ·). The Sum of two tuples yields the most specific tuple which generalizes the two operands.

Table 1. Sale relation r

RowId	City	Product	Day	Quantity
1	Marseilles	Flower	d_1	2
2	Paris	Sweet	d_2	5
3	Marseilles	Sweet	d_1	8
4	Marseilles	Sweet	d_2	12

Definition 2.2 (Sum operator) - Let u and v be two tuples in $CL(r)$,

$$t = u + v \Leftrightarrow \forall A \in \mathcal{D}, t[A] = \begin{cases} u[A] \text{ if } u[A] = v[A] \\ ALL \text{ otherwise.} \end{cases}$$

We say that t is the Sum of the tuples u and v.

Example 2.2 - In our example, we have (Marseilles, Sweet, d_1) + (Marseilles, Sweet, d_2) = (Marseilles, Sweet, ALL). This means that the tuple (Marseilles, Sweet, ALL) is built up from the tuples (Marseilles, Sweet, d_1) and (Marseilles, Sweet, d_2).

The Product of two tuples yields the most general tuple which specializes the two operands. If for these two tuples a dimension A, provided with distinct and real world values, exists, then the only tuple specializing them is the tuple $(\varnothing, \dots, \varnothing)$ (apart from it, the tuple sets which can be used to retrieve them are disjoined).

Definition 2.3 (Product operator) - Let u and v be two tuples in $CL(r)$, then:

$$t = u \bullet v \Leftrightarrow \begin{cases} t = (\varnothing, \dots, \varnothing) \text{ if } \exists A \in \mathcal{D} \text{ such that } u[A] \neq v[A] \neq ALL, \\ \text{otherwise } \forall A \in \mathcal{D} \begin{cases} t[A] = u[A] \text{ if } v[A] = ALL \\ t[A] = v[A] \text{ if } u[A] = ALL. \end{cases} \end{cases}$$

We say that t is the Product of the tuples u and v.

Figure 1. Hasse diagram of the Datacube of r for the aggregate function SUM

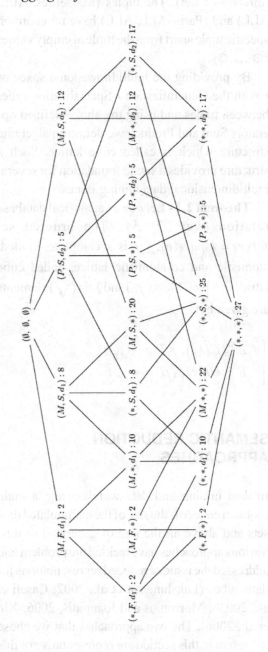

Example 2.3 - In our example, we have (Marseilles, ALL, ALL) • (ALL, Flower, ALL) = (Marseilles, Flower, ALL). This means that (Marseilles, ALL, ALL) and (ALL, Flower, ALL) are less specific than (Marseilles, Flower, ALL) and this latter tuple participates in the construction of

(Marseilles, ALL, ALL) and (ALL, Flower, ALL) (directly or not). The tuples (Marseilles, ALL, ALL) and (Paris, ALL, ALL) have no common specific tuple apart from the tuple of empty values $(\varnothing, \ldots, \varnothing)$.

By providing the multidimensional space of r with the Generalization / Specialization order between tuples and using the above-defined operators Sum and Product, we define an algebraic structure which is called cube lattice. Such a structure provides a sound foundation for several multidimensional data mining issues.

Theorem 2.1 - Let r be a categorical database relation over $\mathcal{D} \cup \mathcal{M}$. The ordered set $CL(r) = (space(r), \preceq_s)$ is a complete, graded, atomistic and co-atomistic lattice, called cube lattice in which Meet ($\wedge$) and Join ($\vee$) elements are given by:

$$\begin{cases} \forall\, T \subseteq CL(r), \bigwedge T = +_{t \in T}\, t \\ \forall\, T \subseteq CL(r), \bigvee T = \bullet_{t \in T}\, t \end{cases}$$

SEMANTIC REDUCTION APPROACHES

In data mining and data warehousing, a main problem concerns the size of the manipulated data sets and above all the size of generated results. Various approaches have tackled the problem and addressed the issue of reduced representations for data cubes (Lakshmanan et al., 2002; Casali et al., 2003b; Morfonios and Ioannidis, 2006; Xin et al., 2006). The two approaches that we chose to present in this section are representative of this reduction trend. They are the closed cube and the quotient cube.

Closed Cube

When computing data cubes, the combinatorial explosion of results is a well known phenomenon

(Han and Kamber, 2006). The approach proposing the closed cube aims to represent data cubes in information lossless way and with a significant reduction of the required storage space.

The idea behind our representation is to remove redundancies existing within Datacubes. In fact certain multidimensional tuples are built up by aggregating the very same tuples of the original relation but at different granularity levels. Thus a single tuple, the most specific of them, can stand for the whole set. The Cube Closure operator is intended for computing this representative tuple.

The cube connection (Casali et al., 2009a) is a couple of functions $cc = (f, g)$, such that f is defined from the cube lattice of r to the power set lattice of tuple identifier set and g is the dual function of f. We show that cc is a special case of Galois connection between two lattices (Ganter and Wille, 1999). Hence, we obtain a closure operator over $CL(r)$ under r.

Definition 3.1 (Cube Connection) - Let $Rowid : r \to \mathbb{N}^*$ be a mapping which associates each tuple with a single positive integer and $Tid(r) = \{Rowid(t) \mid t \in r\}$ (i.e. the set of the tuple identifiers of the relation r). Let f and g be two functions defined as follows:

$$\begin{aligned} f : \quad CL(r) &\to \langle \mathcal{P}(Tid(r)), \subseteq \rangle \\ t &\mapsto \bigcup_{t \preceq_s t',\, t' \in r} Rowid(t') \\ g : \quad \langle \mathcal{P}(Tid(r)), \subseteq \rangle &\to CL(r) \\ P &\mapsto +_{Rowid(t) \in P}\, t \end{aligned}$$

Where $\mathcal{P}(Tid(r))$ $(Tid(r))$ stands for the power set of the tuple identifiers of the relation r $(Tid(r))$.

The function f associates any tuple t of the cube lattice with the set of identifiers of all the tuples which specialize t. The function g applies on the set of tuple identifiers and yields the sum (*cf.* definition 2.2) of tuples provided with these identifiers. In other words, it returns the most general tuple specializing these tuples.

Proposition 3.1 - The cube connection $cc = (f,g)$ is a Galois connection between the cube lattice of r and the power set lattice of $Tid(r)$.

The cube connection being a particular case of the Galois connection, the composition of the two functions $g \circ f$ is a closure operator (Ganter and Wille, 1999) and can be defined as follows.

Definition 3.2 (Cube Closure) - Let $T \subseteq CL(r)$ be a set of tuples, the Cube Closure operator $\mathbb{C} : CL(r) \to CL(r)$ according to T can be defined as follows:

$$\mathbb{C}(t,T) = g \circ f(t) = \sum_{\substack{t' \in T \\ t \preceq_s t'}} t' + (\varnothing, ..., \varnothing)$$

Let us consider all the tuples t' in T. Let us aggregate them together by using the operator $+$. We obtain a new tuple which generalizes all the tuples t' and which is the most specific one. This new tuple is the closure of t.

Example 3.1- Let us consider the relation r (*cf.* Table 1). We achieve the closure of the tuple (ALL, ALL, d_1) in the relation r by aggregating all the tuples which specialize it by using the operator $+$.

$\mathbb{C}((ALL,ALL,d_1))$ $= (Marseilles, Flower, d_1) + (Marseilles, Sweet, d_1)$
$= (Marseilles, ALL, d_1)$
$\mathbb{C}((Paris,ALL,ALL))$ $= (Paris, Sweet, d_2)$

Definition 3.3 (Measure function compatible with the cube closure) - A measure function, f_{val}, relative to an aggregate function f, from $CL(r) \to \mathbb{R}$ is compatible with the closure operator $\mathbb{C}$ over T if and only if $\forall t, u \in CL(r)$, it satisfies the three following properties:

$t \preceq_s u \Rightarrow$ $\quad f_{val}(t,T) \geq f_{val}(u,T)$
$\quad\quad\quad\quad\quad$ or$f_{val}(t,T) \leq f_{val}(u,T)$,
$\mathbb{C}(t,T) = \mathbb{C}(u,T) \Rightarrow$ $\quad f_{val}(t,T) = f_{val}(u,T)$,
$t \preceq_s u$ and$f_{val}(t,T) = f_{val}(u,T) \Rightarrow$ $\quad \mathbb{C}(t,T) = \mathbb{C}(u,T)$.

This function is an adaptation of the weight function introduced in (Stumme et al., 2002) for any closure system of the power set. For example the measure functions COUNT and SUM are compatible with the Cube Closure operator.

Thus in the same spirit as in (Stumme et al., 2002), we can give another definition of the cube closure operator using the previous measure functions. Let us recall that atoms in the cube lattice (their set is noted $Atom(CL(r))$ are the tuples provided with a single real value (all the others are equal to ALL). The Cube Closure operator according to T can be defined as follows:

$$\mathbb{C}(t,T) = t \bullet \{t' \in Atom(CL(r)) : f_{val}(t,T) = f_{val}(t \bullet t',T)\}$$

Proposition 3.2- $\mathbb{C}$ is a closure operator over $CL(r)$ under r and thus it satisfies the following properties (Birkhoff, 1970):

$t \preceq_s t' \Rightarrow \mathbb{C}(t) \preceq_s \mathbb{C}(t')$(monotony)
$t \preceq_s \mathbb{C}(t)$(extensity)
$\mathbb{C}(t) = \mathbb{C}(\mathbb{C}(t))$(idempotency)

The closure of each tuple is computed and results are gathered within a closure system. Each result is called a closed cube tuple. The property of extensity guarantees that any closed cube tuple is more general than all the tuples which generate it. Moreover, it is equal to its own closure because of the idempotency property. The monotony property ensures that the order of closed tuples compared with the order of tuples which have generated them is respected.

Definition 3.4 (Closure System) - Let us assume that $\mathbb{C}(r) = \{t \in CL(r) \mid \mathbb{C}(t) = t\}$. $\mathbb{C}(r)$ is a closure system over r and its related closure operator is $\mathbb{C}$. Any tuple belonging to $\mathbb{C}(r)$ is a closed tuple.

Example 3.2- Considering the multidimensional space of our example relation, we have:

$$\mathbb{C}(r) = \begin{Bmatrix} ALL, ALL, ALL, & Marseilles, ALL, ALL \\ ALL, Sweet, ALL, & Marseilles, ALL, d_1 \\ Marseilles, Sweet, ALL, & ALL, Sweet, d_2 \\ Marseilles, Flower, d_1, & Marseilles, Sweet, d_1 \\ Marseilles, Sweet, d_2, & Paris, Sweet, d_2 \end{Bmatrix}$$

By applying the theorem of G. Birkhoff (Birkhoff, 1970) on the cube lattice using $\mathbb{C}$ as the closure operator, it is possible to build up a lattice gathering all the closed tuples. The order relation in such a lattice is the generalization order. However, in contrast with other closed lattices (Ganter and Wille, 1999), this lattice is co-atomistic.

Theorem 3.3 (Casali et al. (2009a)) - The poset $CCL(r) = \langle \{(t, f(t) \mid t \in \mathbb{C}(r), \preceq_s \rangle$ is a complete and coatomistic lattice called the Closed Cube. Moreover, we have:

$$\begin{cases} \forall\, T \subseteq CCL(r), \bigwedge T = {}_{t \in T}\, t \\ \forall\, T \subseteq CCL(r), \bigvee T = \mathbb{C}({}_{t \in T}\, t, r) \end{cases}$$

where $\bigwedge$ stands for the meet operator and $\bigvee$ for the join operator.

Example 3.3- Figure 2 illustrates the Closed Cube of the relation r.

All the tuples sharing the very same closure generalize the same tuples of the original relation and thus they are provided with the same aggregated value of the measure (property of the GROUP-BY operator). In order to retrieve the measure value of any tuple in the cube lattice, it is enough to compute its closure. Thus the closed cube is a cover for the data cube.

Quotient Cube

In this section, we propose another vision of the structure of the Quotient Cube by providing it with a semantics based on the closure operator.

A Quotient Cube (Lakshmanan et al., 2002) provides a summary of a data cube for certain aggregate functions like COUNT, SUM,... Moreover the Quotient Cube preserves the semantics of the operators ROLL-UP/DRILL-DOWN over the data cube (Gray et al., 1997). Let us underline that we revisit the original definitions of the Quotient Cube in the Cube Lattice environment. The idea under the representation in question is to discard redundancies by gathering together tuples sharing an equivalent information. This results in a set of equivalence classes partitioning the tuples of the data cube. Such a partitioning can be performed in various ways. But, in order to preserve navi-

Figure 2. Hasse diagram of the Closed Cube of r

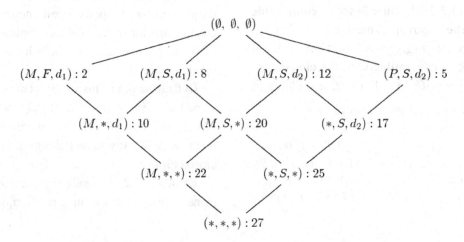

gation capabilities, it is necessary to deal with convex classes.

Definition 3.5 (Convex equivalence class) - Let $\mathcal{C} \subseteq CL(r)$ be an equivalence class. We say $\mathcal{C}$ is convex if and only if:

$$\forall t \in CL(r) \text{ if } \exists t', t'' \in \mathcal{C} \text{ such that } t' \preceq_s t \preceq_s t'' \text{ then } t \in \mathcal{C}$$

A partition $\mathcal{P}$ of $CL(r)$ which encompasses only convex equivalence classes is called a convex partition.

The convexity property makes it possible to represent each equivalence class through its maximal and minimal tuples. Intermediary tuples are no longer useful and the underlying representation is reduced. To ensure that the partition is convex, the following equivalence relation is used.

Definition 3.6 (Quotient equivalence relation) - Let f_{val} be a measure function. We define the equivalence relation $\equiv_f$ as the reflexive transitive closure of the following relation τ: let t, t' be two tuples, $t \, \tau \, t'$ holds if and only if $f_{val}(t, r) = f_{val}(t', r)$ and t is either a parent or a child of t'.

The equivalence relation $\equiv_f$ is said a *quotient equivalence relation* if and only if it satisfies the property of weak congruence: $\forall t, t', u, u' \in CL(r)$ if $t \equiv_f t', u \equiv_f u', t \preceq_s u$ and $u' \preceq_s t'$ then $t \equiv_f u$

We denote by $[t]_{\equiv_f}$ the equivalence class of t ($[t]_{\equiv_f} = \{t' \in CL(r)$ such that $t \equiv_f t'\}$). Then the Quotient Cube is defined as the set of equivalence classes, each one being provided by the value of the measure.

Definition 3.7 (Quotient Cube) - Let $CL(r)$ be the cube lattice of the relation r and $\equiv_f$ a quotient equivalence relation. The Quotient Cube of r, denoted by $QuotientCube(r, \equiv_f)$, is defined as follows:

$$QuotientCube(r, \equiv_f) = \{([t]_{\equiv_f}, f_{val}(t, r)) \text{ such that } t \in CL(r)\}$$

The Quotient Cube of r is a convex partition of $CL(r)$. For two equivalence classes $\mathcal{C}, \mathcal{C}' \in QuotientCube(r, \equiv_f)$, $\mathcal{C} \preceq_{QC} \mathcal{C}'$ when $\exists t \in \mathcal{C}$ and $\exists t' \in \mathcal{C}'$ such that $t \preceq_s t'$.

The construction of a Quotient Cube depends on the chosen quotient equivalence relation. As a consequence for two quotient equivalence relations, their related quotient cube can be different. Moreover, the most useful quotient equivalence relation is the cover equivalence relation. The cover of any tuple t is the set of all tuples aggregated together to achieve t.

Definition 3.8 (Cover) - Let $t \in CL(r)$, the cover of t is the set of tuples of r that are generalized by

t (*i.e.* $cov(t, r) = \{t' \in CL(r) \text{ such that } t \preceq_s t'\}$).

Two tuples $t, t' \in CL(r)$ are cover equivalent over r, $t \equiv_{cov} t'$, if they have the same cover, *i.e.* $cov(t, r) = cov(t', r)$. Using the cover equivalence relation as an instance of $\equiv_f$ in definition 3.2, we can define the *cover quotient cube*.

Now we show that the cover quotient cube is strongly related to the cube closure. Two tuples $t, t' \in CL(r)$ are Cube Closure equivalent, $t \equiv_{\mathbb{C}} t'$, if and only if $\mathbb{C}(t, r) = \mathbb{C}(t', r)$.

Proposition 3.4 - Let $t, t' \in CL(r)$, t is cover equivalent to t' over r if and only if t is Cube Closure equivalent to t'.

The above proposition states the relationship between the Quotient Cube and the concepts related with the cube closure. Moreover it shows that it is possible to define a cover quotient cube by using any aggregate function compatible with the cube closure.

Example 3.4 - With the relation r (*cf.* Table 1), Table 2 gives the Quotient Cube. The two first columns correspond to the maximal tuple of the equivalence class and to its minimal tuples respectively. The last column represents the measure for the considered equivalence class. The Figure 3 illustrates the Quotient Cube of the relation r.

SYNTACTIC REDUCTION APPROACH: THE RELATIONAL PARTITION CUBE

Like the two approaches previously presented, the partition cube (Casali et al., 2009b; Laporte et al., 2002) proposes a representation more concise than the data cube itself. However, it does not take advantage of redundancies captured within data cubes unlike the closed and quotient cubes. In fact, it enforces an optimization at the logical level, this is why we say that it is a syntactic approach. The idea behind this syntactic reduction is mere: for any tuple t of the data cube, it is not necessary to store the values of all the attributes dimensions but it is only required to know on the one hand the dimensions which do not have the value ALL for t and on the other one the identifier of a tuple in the original relation sharing with t the very same values for this set of dimensions. Provided with such an information, the values of

all the dimensions can be retrieved. The approach is based on the partitional model (Spyratos, 1987).

We start this section by presenting the concepts of our approach. Then we present an algorithm for computing such a representation. Finally, by considering the most used environment when managing data warehouses, we propose a relational implementation of our solution (which can be easily achieved).

Partition Cube

In this section, we introduce a new characterization of Datacube based on simple concepts using partitions. The following definition uses the concept of agree sets (Mannila and Toivonen, 1996; Lopes et al., 2002).

Definition 4.1 (DM-Class) - Let r be a categorical database relation and X a set of dimension attributes. A dimension-measure class (DM-Class), of a tuple t according to X, $[t]_X$, is defined by the set of couples (identifier(u), measure(u)) of all the tuples u which agree with t according to a set of attributes X (*i.e.* the set of tuples u having the same values as t for X). Thus, we have:

Table 2. QuotientCube($r, \equiv_{Sum}$)

Minimal Tuples	Maximal Tuples	Sum$_{val}$
(ALL, ALL, ALL)	(ALL, ALL, ALL)	27
(Marseilles, ALL, ALL)	(Marseilles, ALL, ALL)	22
(ALL, Sweet, ALL)	(ALL, Sweet, ALL)	25
(ALL, ALL, d_1)	(Marseilles, ALL, d_1)	10
(Marseilles, Sweet, ALL)	(Marseilles, Sweet, ALL)	20
(ALL, ALL, d_2)	(ALL, Sweet, d_2)	17
(ALL, Flower, ALL)	(Marseilles, Flower, d_1)	2
(ALL, Sweet, d_1)	(Marseilles, Sweet, d_1)	8
(Marseilles, ALL, d_2)	(Marseilles, Sweet, d_2)	12
(Paris, ALL, ALL)	(Paris, Sweet, d_2)	5

Figure 3. Quotient Cube of relation r for the aggregate function SUM

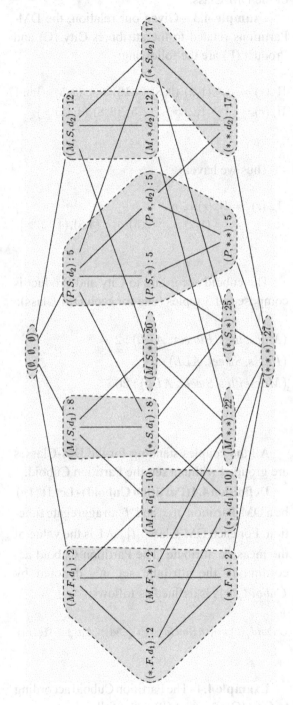

$$[t]_X = \{(u[RowId], u[\mathcal{M}]) \text{ such that } u[X] = t[X], \forall u \in r\}$$

The DM-classes are built up in order to be aggregated when computing the data cube by applying the aggregation function on the attribute measure. In fact, it is not necessary to preserve all the couples in DM-classes. To capture the whole information enclosed in a DM-class, we only need to know the result of the aggregation function applied on all the measure values and the values of the concerned dimensions. The latter values are common to all the tuples in the DM-class which agree on these dimensions. The idea to retrieve the dimension values is to reference the identifier of a tuple which has exactly these dimension values. Such a tuple is representative of the DM-class.

Each DM-Class is represented by a couple of numbers: the former is one of the identifiers of the original tuples gathered within the considered class, and the latter is the computed measure for the class.

Example 4.1- With our relation example, the DM-Class associated to the first tuple according to the dimension attribute *City* groups all the couples (identifier, measure) for tuples satisfying, like t_1, the constraint (*City*=`Marseilles'):

$$[t_1]_{City} = \{(1,2),(3,8),(4,12)\}$$

In a multidimensional context, it is possible to associate each DM-class with a multidimensional tuple. For instance, the class $[t_1]_{City}$ corresponds to the tuple (*Marseilles, ALL, ALL*) : 22 .

All the DM-Classes for a dimension attribute set X are gathered within a single set: the Dimension-Measure Partition (DM-Partition).

Definition 4.2 (DM-Partition) - Let r be a categorical database relation and X a set of dimension attributes, the DM-Partition of r according to X, is defined as:

$$\Pi_X(r) = \{[t]_X, \forall\ t \in r\}$$

Example 4.2 - In our examples, for a better readability, the DM-Classes are delimited by the symbols ' $<$ ' and ' $>$ ' when writing the DM-Partitions. Thus, in our example, the DM-Partition associated to the attribute *City* is:

$$\Pi_{City}(r) = \{< (1,2), (3,8), (4,12) >, < (2,5) >\}$$

The one associated to the attribute *Product* is:

$$\Pi_{Product}(r) = \{< (1,2) >, < (2,5), (3,8), (4,12) >\}$$

Let us consider two DM-Partitions computed according to the attribute sets X and Y. Their product yields the DM-Partition according to $X \cup Y$. Such a product is performed by intersecting DM-classes of the two DM-Partitions and preserving only not empty classes (their cardinality greater than or equal to 1).

Definition 4.3 (Product of DM-Partitions) - Let r be a categorical database relation, X and Y two sets of dimension attributes, $\Pi_X(r)$ and $\Pi_Y(r)$ their DM-Partitions respectively. The product of the DM-partitions $\Pi_X(r)$ and $\Pi_Y(r)$, noted by $\Pi_X(r)\Pi_Y(r)$, returns the DM-Partition over $X \cup Y$ and is obtained as follows:

$$
\begin{aligned}
\Pi_X(r)\Pi_Y(r) &= \Pi_{X \cup Y}(r) \\
&= \{[t]_{X \cup Y} \\
&= [t]_X \cap [t]_Y : [t]_{X \cup Y} \\
&\neq \varnothing, [t]_X \in \Pi_X(r) \text{ and } [t]_Y \in \Pi_Y(r)\}
\end{aligned}
$$

Once the DM-Partitions are computed, the cuboids of the Datacube can be easily obtained. Any DM-Class originates a tuple of a cuboid and the measure value is achieved by applying the

aggregate function on the set of measure values of the DM-Class.

Example 4.3 - Given our relation, the DM-Partitions related to the attributes City (C) and Product (P) are the following:

$$
\begin{aligned}
\Pi_C(r) &= \{< (1,2), (3,8), (4,12) >, < (2,5) >\} \text{and} \\
\Pi_P(r) &= \{< (1,2) >, < (2,5), (3,8), (4,12) >\}
\end{aligned}
$$

Thus we have:

$$
\begin{aligned}
\Pi_{CP}(r) &= \Pi_C(r)\Pi_P(r) \\
&= \{< (1,2) >, < (2,5) >, < (3,8), (4,12) >\}.
\end{aligned}
$$

The cuboid according to City and Product is composed of 3 tuples (one for each DM-Class):

$(Marseilles, Flower, ALL) : 2$
$(Paris, Sweet, ALL) : 5$
$(Marseilles, Sweet, ALL) : 20$

All the couples standing for the DM-Classes are grouped within a set: the Partition Cuboid.

Definition 4.4 (Partition Cuboid) - Let $\Pi_X(r)$ be a DM-Partition of r and f an aggregate function. For each DM-Class, $[t]_X . \mathcal{M}$ is the value of the measure attribute. The Partition Cuboid according to the attribute set X, denoted by $Cuboid_X(r)$, is defined as follows:

$$Cuboid_X(r) = \{(t[RowId], f([t]_X.\mathcal{M})), \forall\ [t]_X \in \Pi_X(r)\}$$

Example 4.4 - The Partition Cuboid according to City (C), Product (P) is the following:

$$Cuboid_{CP}(r) = \{(1,2), (2,5), (3,20)\}$$

Our representation of the Datacube can be defined as the whole set of Partition Cuboids according to any dimension combination.

Definition 4.5 (Partition Cube) - Let r be a categorical database relation. The Partition Cube associated to r is defined as:

$$PartitionCube(r) = \{Cuboid_X(r), \forall\, X \in \mathcal{P}(\mathcal{D})\},$$

where $\mathcal{P}(\mathcal{D})$ stands for the powerset lattice of dimension attributes.

Example 4.5- The Partition Cube for the aggregate function Sum is given in Table 3. It contains $2^3 = 8$ cuboids (because there are 3 dimensions), each of which corresponding to a dimension combination (used as an index to identify cuboids).

The Pcube algorithm

In this section, we describe the principles of our algorithmic solution. First, we give a simple definition of the lectic order (Ganter and Wille, 1999). Then, we propose a new recursive algorithm for enumerating, according to the lectic order, the subsets of $\mathcal{P}(\mathcal{D})$

Definition 4.6 (Lectic Order) - Let $(\mathcal{D}, <_{\mathcal{D}})$ be a finite set totally ordered. We assume, by simplicity, that $\mathcal{D}$ can be defined as follows: $\mathcal{D} = \{A_1, A_2, \ldots A_n\}$. $\mathcal{D}$ is provided with the following operator:

$Max : \mathcal{P}(\mathcal{D}) \to \mathcal{D}$
$X \qquad\qquad \mapsto$ the last element of X according to $<_{\mathcal{D}}$

The lectic order, denoted by $<_l$, is defined as follows:

$\forall\, X, Y \in \mathcal{P}(\mathcal{D}), X <_l Y \Leftrightarrow Max(X \setminus Y) <_{\mathcal{D}} Max(Y \setminus X)$

This order is a strict linear order over the set of all subsets of a set.

Example 4.6 - Let us consider the following totally order set $\mathcal{D} = \{C, D, P\}$. Enumerating the combinations of $\mathcal{P}(\mathcal{D})$, with respect to the lectic order, provides the following results:

$$\varnothing <_l C <_l D <_l CD <_l P <_l CP <_l DP <_l CDP$$

Proposition 4.1- (Ganter and Wille, 1999) $\forall\, X, Y \in \mathcal{P}(\mathcal{D}), X \subset Y \Rightarrow X <_l Y$

We firstly present the new algorithm Ls (Lectic Subsets) which gives the general algorithmic schema used by Pcube (the algorithm building the Partition Cube).

Recursive Algorithmic Schema for Enumerating the Subsets in Lectic Order

The algorithm Ls has as parameters two dimensional attribute subsets X and Y. The algorithm is

Table 3. Partition Cube for the aggregate function Sum.

$Cuboid_\varnothing =$	$\{(1, 27)\}$
$Cuboid_C =$	$\{(1, 22),(2, 5)\}$
$Cuboid_D =$	$\{(1, 10),(2, 17)\}$
$Cuboid_P =$	$\{(1, 2),(2, 25)\}$
$Cuboid_{CD} =$	$\{(1, 10),(2, 5)(4, 12)\}$
$Cuboid_{CP} =$	$\{(1, 2),(2, 5)(3, 20)\}$
$Cuboid_{DP} =$	$\{(1, 2),(2, 17)(3, 8)\}$
$Cuboid_{CDP} =$	$\{(1, 2),(2, 5)(3, 8)(4, 12)\}$

based on a twofold recursion. The recursive calls form a binary balanced tree in which each execution branch returns a dimensional subset. The general strategy for enumerating dimensional attribute combinations consists in considering firstly all the subsets not encompassing a dimensional attribute, and then all the subsets which encompass it. More precisely, the maximal attribute, according to the lectic order, is discarded from Y and added to X in the variable Z. The algorithm is recursively applied with (*i*) X and a new subset Y (from which the maximal attribute is pruned), then (*ii*) Z and Y. The first call of Ls is provided with two parameters $X = \varnothing$ and $Y = \mathcal{D}$.

The correctness of the algorithm Ls is based on proposition 4.1 and the distributive property of the dimension attribute powerset lattice:

$$\forall\, A \in \mathcal{D}, \forall\, X \subseteq \mathcal{D}, \mathcal{P}(X \cup A) \cap \mathcal{P}(\mathcal{D} \setminus (X \cup A)) = \varnothing.$$

Thus, each subset of dimension attributes is enumerated exactly once.

Example 4.7 - Let us consider our relation r. In this context, the binary tree of recursive calls when running our algorithm is depicted in Figure 4. The leaves in the tree correspond to outputs which are, from left to right, ordered in a lectic way. In any left subtree, all subsets not encompassing the maximal attribute (according to the lectic order) of the subtree root are considered while in right subtrees, the maximal attribute is preserved.

Now, we can introduce our algorithm, called PCUBE, for computing Partition Datacubes. As previously mentioned, PCUBE fits in the theoretical framework previously presented. A pre-processing step is required in order to build DM-Partitions according to each single attribute from the input relation. Performing this initial step also computes the empty set based cuboid ($Cuboid_\varnothing$) and its result is yielded. If the original partitions ($\cup_{A \in \mathcal{D}} \Pi_A(r)$) cannot fit in main memory, then the fragmentation strategy proposed in (Ross and Srivastava, 1997) and used in (Beyer and Ramakrishnan, 1999) is applied. Its main idea is to divide the input relation in fragments according to an attribute until the original associated DM-partitions can be loaded. PCUBE adopts the general algorithm schema of Ls but it is intended to compute all desired aggregates and thus it yields the condensed representation of all possible cuboids. PCUBE deals with DM-partitions and enforces product of DM-partitions. Like Ls, its input parameters are the subsets of dimensions X and Y. The DM-Partition associated to Z is computed by applying the product over the two partitions in memory: $\Pi_X(r)$ and $\Pi_A(r)$. The second recursive

Algorithm 1. Algorithm Ls

Input : X and Y two sets of dimensions (first call $X = \emptyset$ and $Y = \mathcal{D}$)
Output : $\mathcal{P}(Y)$
1: **if** $Y = \emptyset$ **then**
2:     **return** X
3: **else**
4:     $A := max(Y)$
5:     $Y := Y \setminus \{A\}$
6:     $LS(X, Y)$
7:     $Z := X \cup \{A\}$
8:     $LS(Z, Y)$
9: **end if**

Figure 4. Execution tree of Ls

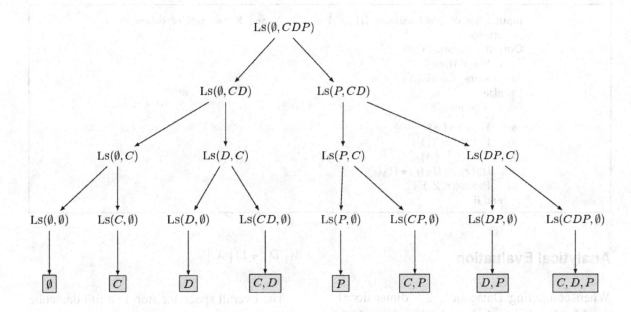

call is performed. The pseudo-code of the algorithm PCUBE is given in the Algorithm 2.

Relational Partition Cubes

When the OLAP application is managed by a relational system, the Partition Cube can be stored through a relation (called Cube) in which each tuple describes a DM-Class of a cuboid according to X. More precisely, for each DM-Class, are known the identifier of its representative tuple, the measure value and the dimension combination (*DimId*). Like in the other approaches computing cubes, real values of dimensions are encoded with integers (Ross and Srivastava, 1997; Beyer and Ramakrishnan, 1999; Han et al., 2001). We propose the following schema called relational Partition Cubes:

$r(\underline{RowId}, \mathcal{D}, \mathcal{M})$

$Dimension(\underline{DimId}, \mathcal{D})$

$Cube(\underline{RowId, DimId}, f(\mathcal{M}))$

To compute Relational Partition Cubes from Datacubes using the algorithm Ls, PL/SQL procedures can be downloaded at http://infodoc.iut. univ-aix.fr/casali/PL-RPC.zip. The relation *Dimension* is intended for storing all the dimension combinations. Their value are binary and for any attribute A, A has the value 0 if it does not belong to the considered combination, else its value is 1. Finally the original relation makes it possible to retrieve the real values of dimensions for various representing elements of the DM-Classes.

Example 4.8 - For our example, the two latter relations of the schema implementing our concise representation are given in Tables 4 and 5 respectively.

EVALUATIONS

In this section, we propose an analytical evaluation of the size of the partition cube and compare it with the size of the data cube. Then we present the results of experiments in which we compare the size reductions offered by the semantic approaches and the syntactic one.

Algorithm 2. Algorithm PCUBE

```
Input : Set of DM-Partitions {Π_A, A ∈ D}, X and Y two sets of dimension
        attributes
Output : Partition Cube
 1: if Y = ∅ then
 2:    Write_Cuboid(X)
 3: else
 4:    A := max(Y)
           <p
 5:    Y := Y\{A}
 6:    PCUBE(r, X, Y)
 7:    Z := X ∪ {A}
 8:    Π_Z(r) := Π_X(r) • Π_A(r)
 9:    PCUBE(r, Z, Y)
10: end if
```

Analytical Evaluation

When computing Datacubes, $2^{|D|}$ dimensional combinations have to be examined, each of which originates a cuboid. For each cuboid, the number of output tuples depends on the domain cardinality of the considered combination (Shoshani, 1997), which is denoted by $|X|$

As previously mentioned, all approaches do not deal with original data but instead with coded data (for obvious optimization reasons). Actually each value of a dimensional attribute A_i is replaced by an integer in the range $[0...|A_{i-1}|]$ during a preprocessing step. Under this assumption, the storage space required for preserving a cuboid according to X is:

$$4(|D|+1)|X|$$

The overall space for storing a full datacube is bounded by:

$$2^{|D|}4(|D|+1)Max(|X|), \forall X \in \mathcal{P}(D)$$

In contrast, PCUBE generates concise representations of Datacubes. For each cuboid according to a dimensional combination X, $|X|$ tuples are to be computed but each one only requires to store three values (an identifier, the associated aggregated value and the corresponding dimensional combination), each one needing 4 bytes. Thus the storage requirement for a cuboid is:

$$12|X|$$

Table 4. Relation Dimension.

DimId	C	P	D
1	0	0	0
2	1	0	0
3	0	1	0
4	0	0	1
5	1	1	0
6	1	0	1
7	0	1	1
8	1	1	1

Table 5. Relation Cube.

RowId	DimId	Sum(Q)
1	1	27
1	2	22
2	2	5
1	3	2
2	3	25
...		

When compared to the classical representation (used by BUC for example (Beyer and Ramakrishnan, 1999)), the latter result is really significant because as soon as the number of dimensions is higher than 2, our concise representation is more compact. Of course this advantage is increased as the set of dimensions is enlarged because PCUBE storage requirement, for any cuboid, is independent of the number of dimensions. The latter remark explains results reported in Table 6. They give, according to the number of considered dimensions, the percentage of space occupied by our concise representation when compared to classical datacube storage. When the number of dimensions is equal to 10, our condensed representation requires 27.2% of the space needed by classical representation to store a full datacube, and only 14.2%, for 20 dimensions.

In order to confirm this analytical comparison, it remains to provide experimental results.

Experimental Evaluations

We choose to compare our syntactic approach with the two most concise semantics lossless representations. Through these experiments, our aim is to compare the underlying main memory requirements and the size of the Datacube to be stored. In order to compute the Quotient Cube and Closed Cube, we use the algorithm CLOSE Pasquier et al. (1999), proved to be very efficient for mining frequent closed patterns, because we have its sources. The computer has a Pentium 4 to 3 GHz with 1 Gb of RAM and runs under Windows XP.

Table 7 gives the datasets used for experiments. The columns #Attributes and #Tuples stand for the number of attributes and tuples respectively. In the last column, the size in bytes of the dataset is reported (each dimension or attribute is encoded as an integer requiring 4 bytes for any value).

Mushroom and Death are datasets widely known in frequent pattern mining. Mushroom provides various characteristics of mushrooms. Death is dataset gathering information about patient decease with the date and cause. Tomb-Necropolis and TombObjects are issued from archaeological excavation. They encompass a list of necropolises, their tombs and other properties like: the country, the funeral rite, the objects discovered in the tombs and their description. Finally, Joint_Objects_Tombs results from the natural join between TombObjects and TombNecropolis according to the identifiers of necropolises and tombs. These private datasets are provided by an archaeological laboratory of Aix-Marseilles University.

Remark: The two datasets Mushroom and Joint_Objects_Tombs require too much main memory (> 4Go) when computing the Quotient Cube and the Closed Cube with a minimum threshold equal to 1 (all the possible patterns), thus we have to state a minimum threshold equal to 5% and 1%.

Tables 8 and 9 present the results obtained for the algorithms CLOSE and PCUBE for the various datasets. The column Max Memory shows in MB the maximal used memory.

PCUBE memory requirements are incomparably lower than the ones of CLOSE. Concerning the size

Table 6. percentage of storage space for PCUBE versus classical representation

C	1	2	3	4	5	6
% of space condensed vs. classical storages	150%	100%	75%	60%	50%	42.8%
Y	7	9	10	12	20	25
% of space condensed vs. classical storages	37.5%	33.3%	27.2%	23%	14.2%	11.5%

of Datacube representations, the best results are obtained for the Closed Cube and then the Quotient Cube. Although more voluminous, the Partition Cube reduces significantly the size of the Datacube. For instance, the Partition Cube computed for the dataset Mushroom only needs 12% of the space necessary to store the Datacube. In the worst case (few attributes) the gain is about 50%.

The counterpart of storage saving for the Quotient and Closed Cubes is efficiency deterioration when evaluating OLAP queries. Actually, with these two representations, only a cover of a Datacube is preserved and additional computations are necessary to answer OLAP queries.

- PCUBE computes a concise representation of the Datacube which is based on its characterization (DM-Classes, DM-Partitions and their product). In such a representation, a row of the cube (as exemplified in Table 5) contains three elements: *RowId*, *DimId* and *f*(M). Moreover, *DimId* can be encoded as a bit field to avoid the join

Table 7. Datasets.

Tables	# Attributes	# Tuples	Size
mushroom	23	81 240	7 474 080
death	5	389 000	7 780 000
TombNecropolis	7	184 600	5 168 800
TombObjects	12	827 800	39 734 400
Joint_Objects_Tombs	17	764 300	51 972 400

Table 8. Use of memory of CLOSE.

Tables	Max Memory (MB)
mushroom 5%	354,1
death	8,1
TombNecropolis	12,8
TombObjects	721,0
Joint_Objects_Tombs 1%	36,3

operation with the relation Dimension (*cf.* Table 4) when evaluating OLAP queries. In a similar way, the link with the original relation (through *RowId*) does not require a join operation but a direct index. When the number of dimensions is less than 32, each attribute value needs 4 bytes and thus each row 12 bytes. The representation includes the original relation. Thus its size is equal to: $NbRows \times 12 + RelationSize$.

- For the Quotient Cubes and Closed Cubes, the size of any row is obtained by the product of the number of dimensions and the measure in the original relation by 4 bytes (dimensions are encoded as integers). The obtained size is: $NbRows' \times 4(|Dim|+1)$, where $NbRows'$ is the number of tuples

Table 9. Use of memory of PCUBE.

Tables	Max Memory (MB)
mushroom	4,8
mushroom 5%	4,7
death	2,5
TombNecropolis	2,6
TombObjects	3,7
Joint_Objects_Tombs	4,1
Joint_Objects_Tombs 1%	4,0

Table 10. Size of the Datacubes.

2-5	Size of the Datacube (byte)			
	``Classical''	Partition	Closed	Quotient
TombNecropolis	3 639 072	1 416 340	189 728	543 232
TombObjects	903 611 124	208 922 988	8 032 648	25 806 404
Joint_Objects_Tombs (1%)	58 848 264	10 327 768	4 485 168	9 720 576
Death	220 152	117 856	24 984	73 656
Mushroom (5%)	436 823 808	55 350 384	1 233 984	3 265 344

required for the Quotient Cube or Closed Cube. Let us underline that $NbRows' \leq NbRows$.

Table 10 illustrates the size of the three studied representations for the various datasets. These results are resumed in Figure 5.

CONCLUSION

Addressing the issue of Datacube computation and storage is challenging because such a computation needs costly execution time and large main memory space. Datacube yields huge volume of results, and its storage requires enormous space on disk. In this chapter, we focus on the lossless information approaches emphazing the two ones which propose the most concise representations, namely the Quotient Cube and Closed Cube. We propose an alternative method also providing a storage reduction for the Datacube. Even if the cube reduction is less important than in the two previous ones, all the data is stored. Thus, OLAP queries can be answered very efficiently (simple selections in a table) while other approaches require additional computations for yielding results. In the worse scenario, when data is very sparse, the size of the Closed and the Quotient Cubes can be as voluminous as the Datacube itself. On the contrary, when there are more than 2 dimensions, the Partition Cube is always smaller than the data cube. So our approach is a compromise between Datacube storage reduction and efficient execution of OLAP queries.

Research perspectives of the presented work are to investigate new issues: *(i)* Taking into account the dimension hierarchies (Hurtado and Mendelzon, 2002) in the very same spirit as Cure for Cubes (Morfonios and Ioannidis, 2006). *(ii)* The reduction of Convex Cubes (Nedjar et al., 2010) and Emerging Cube (Nedjar et al., 2009) using partitions.

REFERENCES

Beyer, K. S., & Ramakrishnan, R. (1999). Bottom-up computation of sparse and iceberg cubes. In Delis, A., Faloutsos, C., and Ghandeharizadeh, S., editors, *SIGMOD Conference*, pages 359–370. ACM Press.

Birkhoff, G. (1970). *Lattice Theory*, volume XXV of *AMS Colloquium Publications*. American Mathematical Society, third (new) edition.

Casali, A., Cicchetti, R., & Lakhal, L. (2003a). Cube lattices: A framework for multidimensional data mining. In Barbará, D., & Kamath, C. (Eds.), *SDM. SIAM*.

Casali, A., Cicchetti, R., & Lakhal, L. (2003b). Extracting semantics from data cubes using cube transversals and closures. In Getoor, L., Senator, T. E., Domingos, P., & Faloutsos, C. (Eds.), *KDD* (pp. 69–78). ACM.

Casali, A., Nedjar, S., Cicchetti, R., & Lakhal, L. (2009a). Closed cube lattices. [New Trends in Data Warehousing and Data Analysis.]. *Annals of Information Systems*, *3*(1), 145–164.

Casali, A., Nedjar, S., Cicchetti, R., Lakhal, L., & Novelli, N. (2009b). Lossless reduction of datacubes using partitions. *International Journal of Data Warehousing and Mining*, *5*(1), 18–35. doi:10.4018/jdwm.2009010102

Chaudhuri, S., & Dayal, U. (1997). An overview of data warehousing and olap technology. *SIGMOD Record*, *26*(1), 65–74. doi:10.1145/248603.248616

Ganter, B., & Wille, R. (1999). *Formal Concept Analysis: Mathematical Foundations*. Springer.

Gray, J., Chaudhuri, S., Bosworth, A., Layman, A., Reichart, D., & Venkatrao, M. (1997). Data cube: A relational aggregation operator generalizing group-by, cross-tab, and sub totals. *Data Mining and Knowledge Discovery*, *1*(1), 29–53. doi:10.1023/A:1009726021843

Han, J., & Kamber, M. (2006). *Data Mining: Concepts and Techniques*. Morgan Kaufmann.

Han, J., Pei, J., Dong, G., & Wang, K. (2001). Efficient computation of iceberg cubes with complex measures. In *SIGMOD Conference*, pages 1–12.

Hurtado, C. A., & Mendelzon, A. O. (2002). Olap dimension constraints. In Popa, L. (Ed.), *PODS* (pp. 169–179). ACM.

Lakshmanan, L. V. S., Pei, J., & Han, J. (2002). Quotient cube: How to summarize the semantics of a data cube. In Lochovsky, F. H. and Shan, W., editors, *VLDB*, pages 778–789. Morgan Kaufmann.

Laporte, M., Novelli, N., Cicchetti, R., & Lakhal, L. (2002). Computing full and iceberg datacubes using partitions. In Hacid, M.-S., Ras, Z. W., Zighed, D. A., and Kodratoff, Y., editors, *ISMIS*, volume 2366 of *Lecture Notes in Computer Science*, pages 244–254. Springer.

Lopes, S., Petit, J.-M., & Lakhal, L. (2002). Functional and approximate dependency mining: database and fca points of view. *Journal of Experimental & Theoretical Artificial Intelligence*, *14*(2-3), 93–114. doi:10.1080/09528130210164143

Mannila, H., & Toivonen, H. (1996). *Multiple uses of frequent sets and condensed representations (extended abstract)* (pp. 189–194). KDD.

Morfonios, K., & Ioannidis, Y. E. (2006). Cure for cubes: Cubing using a rolap engine. In Dayal, U., Whang, K.-Y., Lomet, D. B., Alonso, G., Lohman, G. M., & Kersten, M. L. (Eds.), *VLDB* (pp. 379–390). ACM.

Morfonios, K., Konakas, S., Ioannidis, Y. E., & Kotsis, N. (2007). Rolap implementations of the data cube. *ACM Computing Surveys*, *39*(4). doi:10.1145/1287620.1287623

Nedjar, S., Casali, A., Cicchetti, R., & Lakhal, L. (2009). Emerging cubes: Borders, size estimations and lossless reductions. *Information Systems*, *34*(6), 536–550. doi:10.1016/j.is.2009.03.001

Nedjar, S., Cicchetti, R., & Lakhal, L. (2010). *Constrained Closed and Quotient Cubes*, volume 2 of *Studies in Computational Intelligence*, chapter 5. Springer-Verlag.

Pasquier, N., Bastide, Y., Taouil, R., & Lakhal, L. (1999). Efficient mining of association rules using closed itemset lattices. *Information Systems*, *24*(1), 25–46. doi:10.1016/S0306-4379(99)00003-4

Ross, K. A., & Srivastava, D. (1997). Fast computation of sparse datacubes. In Jarke, M., Carey, M. J., Dittrich, K. R., Lochovsky, F. H., Loucopoulos, P., & Jeusfeld, M. A. (Eds.), *VLDB* (pp. 116–125). Morgan Kaufmann.

Shoshani, A. (1997). Olap and statistical databases: Similarities and differences. In Mendelzon, A. and Özsoyoglu, Z. M., editors, *PODS*, pages 185–196, New York, NY, USA. ACM. Chairman-Mendelzon, Alberto and Chairman-Özsoyoglu, Z. Meral.

Sismanis, Y., Deligiannakis, A., Roussopoulos, N., & Kotidis, Y. (2002). Dwarf: shrinking the petacube. In *SIGMOD Conference*, pages 464–475.

Spyratos, N. (1987). The partition model: A deductive database model. *ACM Transactions on Database Systems*, *12*(1), 1–37. doi:10.1145/12047.22718

Stumme, G., Taouil, R., Bastide, Y., Pasquier, N., & Lakhal, L. (2002). Computing iceberg concept lattices with titanic. *Data & Knowledge Engineering*, *42*(2), 189–222. doi:10.1016/S0169-023X(02)00057-5

Wei, W., Lu, H., Feng, J., & Yu, J. X. (2002). *Condensed cube: An efficient approach to reducing data cube size* (pp. 155–165). ICDE.

Xin, D., Han, J., Li, X., Shao, Z., & Wah, B. W. (2007). Computing iceberg cubes by top-down and bottom-up integration: The starcubing approach. *IEEE Transactions on Knowledge and Data Engineering*, *19*(1), 111–126. doi:10.1109/TKDE.2007.250589

Xin, D., Shao, Z., Han, J., & Liu, H. (2006). C-cubing: Efficient computation of closed cubes by aggregation-based checking. In Liu, L., Reuter, A., Whang, K.-Y., & Zhang, J. (Eds.), *ICDE* (p. 4). IEEE Computer Society.

Chapter 3
A Parameterized Framework for Clustering Streams

Vasudha Bhatnagar
University of Delhi, India

Sharanjit Kaur
University of Delhi, India

Laurent Mignet
IBM, Indian Research Lab, India

ABSTRACT

Clustering of data streams finds important applications in tracking evolution of various phenomena in medical, meteorological, astrophysical, seismic studies. Algorithms designed for this purpose are capable of adapting the discovered clustering model to the changes in data characteristics but are not capable of adapting to the user's requirements themselves. Based on the previous observation, we perform a comparative study of different approaches for existing stream clustering algorithms and present a parameterized architectural framework that exploits nuances of the algorithms. This framework permits the end user to tailor a method to suit his specific application needs. We give a parameterized framework that empowers the end-users of KDD technology to build a clustering model. The framework delivers results as per the user's application requirements. We also present two assembled algorithms G-kMeans and G-dbscan to instantiate the proposed framework and compare the performance with the existing stream clustering algorithms.

INTRODUCTION

Data streams pose special challenges to mining algorithms, not only because of the huge volume of on-line data streams and its computation (Henz-inger, Raghavan & Rajagopalan, 1998; Babcock, Babu, Datar, Motwani & Widom, 2002; Carney, Cetintemel, Cherniack, Convey, Lee, Seidman et al., 2002; Domingos and Hulten, 2000), but also because of the fact that data in streams may show temporal correlations. Such temporal correlations help in disclosing important data trends in XML document clustering (Rusu, Rahayu & Taniar, 2008), multimedia communication and programming support for ubiquitous distributed computing environment (Aggarwal, 2007).

Clustering is considered as one of the most popular and effective techniques for discovering similarity trends in data streams. Compactness of representation, fast incremental processing of new data points, insensitivity to order of input records have been identified as basic requirements in stream clustering algorithms (Henzinger, Raghavan & Rajagopalan, 1998; Barb´ara, 2002; Orlowska, Sun & Li, 2006).

The problem of incremental clustering is addressed in Zhang, Ramakrishnan & Livny (1996) and inspired clustering of data streams. The importance of the problem is evident from the large body of work (Aggarwal, Han, Wang & Yu, 2003; Motoyoshi, Miura & Shioya, 2004; Park & Lee, 2004) that has evolved over a relatively short period of time since the earliest attempt to address the problem of stream clustering (Guha, Mishra, Motwani & O'Callaghan, 2000).

The algorithms that have been developed for stream clustering have either an on-line or a batch component for processing incoming data, to maintain synopsis. A mechanism is used to highlight the evolving nature of data in stream. Clustering is done using varied approaches based on distance (*k-means* or *k-median*), density estimation, statistical methods (e.g. co-variance, skewness etc.) and connected component analysis.

Motivation

One of the reasons for the fallen-short-of-anticipated growth curve of KDD technology is that the end-user is forced to use the mining algorithms provided by the data mining packages and has no say in designing the algorithm. The current KDD technology is limited by the adhoc approach for solving individual problems (Yang & Wu, 2006). The need for a unified framework for integrating

different data mining tasks has been recognized recently (Yang & Wu, 2006).

Motivated by the above observation, we propose a parameterized framework for stream clustering. The framework empowers the end-user to choose the features of the algorithm to suit their business requirements in terms of nature of inputs, outputs, availability of resources etc.. The proposed component-based architecture of stream clustering algorithms advocates development of a data-mining environment where the user can match the application needs with the features of the components and assemble the algorithm. The approach overcomes the rigidity prevalent in the use of data mining environments, where the match between the available algorithmic features and desired functionality is sometime less than satisfactory. This work lays the theoretical foundation for the unified framework by parameterizing an algorithm based on application requirements.

Outline of the Paper

The paper is divided into five sections. Section "Comparison of Stream Clustering Algorithms" studies different approaches used in stream clustering algorithms, and a systematic comparison vis-à-vis the nature of input, output, processing and functionality is presented. The study leads to a component based architectural framework underlying all stream clustering algorithms, which is discussed in Section "Generic Architecture for Stream Clustering Algorithms". Based on this framework, subsection "Architectural Framework" proposes a scheme to assemble designer algorithms by selecting appropriate components to suit the user's specific needs. Section "Realization of the Framework" instantiates the proposed framework by laying down hypothetical user requirements and assembling two algorithms *G-kMeans* and *G-dbscan*. Experimental evaluation of the two algorithms is also presented in the same section.

Figure 1. Categorization of stream clustering algorithms

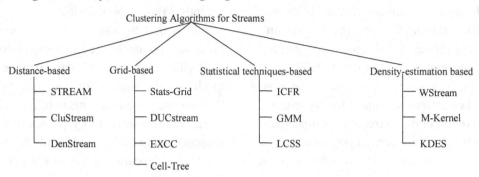

COMPARISON OF STREAM CLUSTERING ALGORITHMS

In this section, we describe some of the recent stream clustering algorithms and categorize them based on the underlying approach for clustering (Figure 1).

A closer look reveals that some algorithms qualify for more than one category (e.g. *DenStream*), but for the sake of clarity, each algorithm has been placed in the most appropriate category. The salient features of some representative stream clustering algorithms from each category are described in the following section and a comparison of these features are given at the end of the section. Algorithms for handling noisy and high dimensional data streams have been consciously omitted, since such features are add-ons to the basic problem of clustering data streams.

Distance-Based Algorithms

In this approach, initially a set of points is selected to represent the center of clusters. Subsequently a distance metric is used to place points in appropriate clusters. Some well-known stream clustering algorithms that use this approach are described below.

a.   *STREAM* algorithm (Guha, Mishra, Motwani & O'Callaghan, 2002), uses the landmark window model that processes stream in batches and generates *k* optimal clusters using an approximation approach. Stream is treated as a sequence of chunks (batches), and for each chunk frequency of each distinct point is computed leading to weighted chunks. An approximation algorithm (LOCALSEARCH), which is a *Lagrangian relaxation* of *k-Median* problem is applied on each weighted chunk to retain *k* weighted cluster centers. The weight of each cluster center is the sum of the weights of the members in the cluster. Subsequently the same algorithm is applied on retained weighted cluster centers to get optimal number of clusters for the entire stream. The algorithm is memory efficient and has $O(nm + nklogk)$ running time where *n* is data size, *m* is the number of centers used in computation in a batch, and *k* is number of centers retained in each chunk.

b.   *CluStream* (Aggarwal, Han, Wang & Yu, 2003) handles evolving stream using an on-line and an off-line component. The algorithm generates clusters over different portions of stream using pyramidal time frame.

It summarizes information about incoming points in micro-clusters (μCs), which maintain summary information similar to cluster feature vector of Zhang, Ramakrishnan & Livny (1996), except for the additional information about time stamp.

k-Means algorithm is applied to a set of first few points in the stream to generate k micro-clusters (μCs), which form the synopsis. Subsequently, the on-line component absorbs incoming data points into micro-clusters based on distance. If the new incoming point cannot be absorbed in one of the existing μCs, then a new μC is created. It is imperative to ensure that the size of the synopsis remains constant. Thus, either a cluster with few points or least relevance time stamp is deleted, or two clusters with which that are close to each other are merged. The deleted μC is treated as an outlier from the current point of view. Pyramidal time frame is used to store snapshots of the synopsis at different time instances so that clusters can be discovered in user specified time horizon h with desired granularity.

The off-line component of the algorithm discovers convex clusters by applying *k-Means* algorithm on all μCs generated in time horizon h. Subtractive properties of μCs are exploited to generate higher-level clusters from the stored synopsis at different time horizons.

c. *DenStream* handles the dynamic nature of evolving data streams using a damped window model (Cao, Ester, Qian & Zhou, 2006). This algorithm also has an on-line and an off-line component. The on-line component is used for micro-cluster maintenance and off-line component generates clusters on demand. Potential-microclusters ($P\text{-}\mu Cs$) and Outlier-microclusters ($O\text{-}\mu Cs$) are used for incremental computation by the on-line component for handling dynamics of an evolving data stream. The definitions of $P\text{-}\mu C$ and $O\text{-}\mu C$ are extended definitions of μC used in Aggarwal, Han, Wang & Yu (2003) wherein, summarized information is also weighted with respect to time.

During initialization phase, *dbscan* algorithm (Ester, Kriegel, Sander & Xu, 1996) is applied to initial n points to generate potential-microclusters ($P\text{-}\mu Cs$). New data points arriving in stream are added to the nearest $P\text{-}\mu C$, provided, addition does not cause increase in the radius of the $P\text{-}\mu C$ beyond a pre-defined threshold. Otherwise, either a new outlier-microcluster ($O\text{-}\mu C$) is created or the incoming point is merged into its nearest existing outlier microcluster ($O\text{-}\mu C$). In the latter case, the weight of each $O\text{-}\mu C$ is computed. If the weight is greater than some threshold θ, then $O\text{-}\mu C$ is converted into $P\text{-}\mu C$. Similarly, the weight of each $P\text{-}\mu C$ is checked periodically to ensure that it is still a valid potential microcluster, else it is deleted. The algorithm uses a fading mechanism to reduce impact of older data on current trends.

As the number of $O\text{-}\mu Cs$ may continuously increase with time, *pruning* strategy is used to delete real outliers after reporting them to the user. When clustering is demanded , the offline component applies a variant of *dbscan* algorithm on the set of $P\text{-}\mu Cs$. Use of density-based approach for clustering discovers arbitrary shape clusters and makes the algorithm robust.

The major drawback of distance-based approach is that the number of clusters to be generated needs to be defined in advance. Further, clustering results also depend on data ordering. Distance-based algorithms like *CluStream, DenStream* do not generate exclusive clusters. Thus, a point that is originally placed in one cluster as per its features may be merged with another cluster due to memory constraint later.

Grid-Based Algorithms

Grid-based algorithms for stream divide multidimensional data space into a set of mutually exclusive equal-size cells to maintain detailed data distribution. While distance-based methods work with numerical attributes, grid-based methods work with attributes of mixed types (Berkhin,

2003). Some of the recent algorithms using this approach are described below:

a. *Stats-Grid* algorithm (Park & Lee, 2004) generates arbitrary-shape clusters with high processing speed. Incoming data points in stream are inserted in the cells of grid on the basis of distribution statistics. The number of data points in a cell constitutes its support. When the support of a cell becomes greater than a pre-defined threshold, it is partitioned into two cells on the selected dimension. Cell partitioning is done on a dimension having maximum mean or standard deviation, depending on distribution statistics. Cell partitioning helps maintain information about current trends at appropriate granularity levels. To reduce the impact of historical data on current trend, cells are pruned based on support of the cell and its statistics are added back to its parent cell. Clustering is done on demand using connected component analysis.

b. *DUCStream* is a grid-based algorithm that treats the stream as a sequence of chunks of the same size and uses connected component analysis for clustering (Gao, Li, Zhang & Tan, 2005). Distribution statistics of incoming data points are maintained in the grid and initial clusters are created using dense cells of the first chunk. At any time, relative density of a cell (rd_c) is computed as $N_c/(m * t)$, where N_c is number of points in the cell c, m is size of chunk and t is the number of chunks accessed so far. A cell is dense if $rd_c > \delta$ where δ is a user-defined threshold. Connected component analysis is used to create initial clusters using dense cells. For subsequent chunks, newly formed cell are merged with one of the existing cluster if possible. Else a new cluster is generated. Clusters are updated by removing or merging existing clusters to incorporate new cells after each chunk. The clustering result is set of all clusters found in t chunks of data seen so far. The algorithm misses emerging clusters because it does not consider recent non-dense cells for clustering.

c. *ExCC* algorithm (Bhatnagar & Kaur, 2007) addresses two important features of clustering viz. exclusiveness and completeness. The on-line component of the algorithm summarizes the incoming data stream in a grid. Each cell in the grid stores the number of points and the average inter-arrival time of data points in the cell. This information is used during grid pruning which needs to be performed either when clustering is demanded or when the grid outgrows the memory. The second component performs on-demand clustering using connected component analysis and may be run either on-line or off-line, depending on the requirement of the application/user. Prior to clustering, outdated cells are pruned in order to get a current clustering model. This is accomplished while ensuring that even a small cluster that showed up in the stream after last clustering, is detected. This feature ensures complete clustering. Exclusive clustering means that at any time, a point belongs to a unique cluster to which it genuinely belongs (Orlowska, Sun & Li, 2006). This algorithm delivers a precise description of the discovered clusters in terms of their boundaries, signatures of seeds etc.

d. *Cell-Tree* algorithm (Park & Lee, 2007) is an extension of *Stats-Grid* algorithm and aims to overcome the limitation of the latter's scalability. This is achieved by employing two data structures: sibling-list and cell-tree. Initially the multi-dimensional data space is partitioned into fixed number of mutually exclusive equi-sized cells termed as grid cells. The distribution statistics maintained in each cell is diminished by a pre-defined decay rate as time elapses, to reduce the impact of old information on the current clustering scheme.

A sibling-list is used to manage the set of all grid cells in a one dimensional data space. It acts as an index for locating a specific grid cell. After a dense unit cell on one dimensional data space is created, a new sibling list for another dimension is created as a child of the grid cell. This process is recursively repeated for each dimension and it leads to a cell-tree with maximum depth of d. A unique path in the cell-tree identifies each dense unit grid cell. While clustering, connected component analysis is applied on d-dimensional dense unit grid cell whose current support is greater than a pre-defined threshold. Although the algorithm is computationally more expensive, it generates arbitrary-shaped clusters with current trends.

Accumulation of data in a grid structure makes grid-based clustering techniques independent of data ordering (Berkhin, 2003). Hence, the clusters generated are not effected by the input order of incoming data points. The main drawback of grid-based clustering techniques is their degraded performance for high dimensional data. In such situations, the number of cells becomes very large and the grid may not fit in the memory. The pruning strategies are used to accommodate the grid in memory. However, frequent and aggressive pruning of grid may result into the loss of patterns.

Statistical Methods Based Algorithms

Clustering methods based on statistical techniques rely on initial samples to estimate the unknown probabilities and probability densities. These resulting estimates are then used as an approximation of true values for future computations (Duda, Hart & Stork, 2000).

a. ICFR (Incremental Clustering using F-value by Regression Analysis) proposed in Motoyoshi, Miura & Shioya (2004),

claims to give a more accurate clustering for stream, with constraint of treating stream as a sequence of chunks. Each chunk has a constant size ($t2 - t1$) over time axis. In the initialization phase, clusters are generated using similarity function applied on initial ($h - 1$) chunks. For each cluster, the center of gravity, variance, regression-coefficient and F-value is maintained. To reduce the number of clusters, close clusters are combined iteratively if F-value of newly merged cluster is bigger than the F-value of each of the candidate cluster. This procedure is repeated till no more clusters can be combined. New incoming points are collected in a chunk referred to as *recent chunk*. Initial clusters in *recent chunk* are discovered and combined with existing clusters. Else clustering is done from scratch using all clusters formed so far using new F-value. While clustering, only last ($h - 1$) chunks are used to get recent and current clusters.

b. The algorithm proposed in Song & Wang (2004), detects clusters using *Gaussian Mixture Model* (*GMM*). This algorithm incrementally updates the density estimates, taking into account only the newly arrived data and previously estimated density. This algorithm is based on *Expectation Maximization* technique and uses a cluster merging strategy based on multivariate statistical tests for equality of covariance and mean. Covariance and mean are used as representations for clusters. The benefit of using a covariance matrix is that it is translation invariant and is used for determining the orientation of a cluster.

c. Algorithm for detecting low complexity clusters by *skewness* and *kurtosis* was proposed by Song & Wang (2006). *Skewness* and *kurtosis* are employed in addition to mean and covariance, to capture underlying distribution. Multivariate skewness is a single non-negative number, which characterizes the asymmetry of a probability distribution (*PD*) and hence represents asymmetry of clusters. Multivariate kurtosis is also a single non-negative number, which is used to measure the peakedness of a *PD* and indicates the concentration of a cluster. Clusters are generated using *Expectation Maximization* (*EM*) algorithm and for each cluster, all required statistics are computed. The algorithm generates low complexity clusters and provides an accurate description of the shape of a cluster.

In order to reduce the number of clusters, merging is done in two phases. In the first phase, two clusters with comparable mean and covariance are merged. Otherwise, skewness and kurtosis of the entire data in both clusters are tested against multivariate normality. If the normality is acceptable, then these two clusters are merged despite inequalities in their mean and covariance. This merging process is repeated till no more clusters can be merged.

Statistical approaches for clustering are efficient if data dimensionality is low and data belongs to single distribution. A major limitation of these approaches is that stream is always processed in batches. Thus net clustering results is influenced by the initial model generated using the initial sample. Since real life applications, data may belong to different distributions or may evolve with time, these approaches have limited utility.

Density Estimation Based Algorithms

Given a sequence of independent random variables, identically drawn from a specific distribution, the general *Density Estimation* (*DE*) problem is to reveal a density function of underlying distribution. This probability distribution is then used to identify dense and sparse regions in data set with local maxima of the probability distribution function taken as cluster centers (Sain, 1994).

Kernel-Density Estimation (*KDE*) is a widely studied nonparametric *DE* method and is suited to data mining applications because it does not make any assumption about the underlying distribution. Most of the algorithms in this category use window-based model.

a. Zhou, Cai, Wei & Qian (2003) propose *M-Kernel* algorithm for estimating probability density function on line with limited memory and in linear time. The basic idea is to group similar data points and estimate the kernel function for the group. This strategy is instrumental in keeping the memory requirement in control because if *N* data points have arrived in the stream so far, then number of kernels, *m* is very less i.e. $m \ll N$. Each *M-Kernel* has three parameters weight, mean and bandwidth. The algorithm works for both landmark and window models, although in the latter case, only an approximation is delivered. The computed kernels are then ranked to identify clusters. The algorithm has been tested for one dimensional data using *Gaussian Kernel*. The major limitation of this approach is that it processes one dimensional data streams and the memory used is very sensitive to the distribution of the data set.

b. Heinz &Seeger (2006) extend the idea of merging kernels and propose a resource aware algorithm for *KDE* over streaming data. This algorithm uses *Epanechnikow Kernel*, which has a simple form and bounded support, thereby reducing the computational cost (Gray & Moore, 2003). Bandwidth is dynamically computed based on standard deviation in amortized constant time. For each kernel, a counter (for the incorporated points) and min-max value of all points is maintained. Whenever the number of kernels maintained exceeds a threshold, a merging

Table 1. Comparison of Features of some Clustering Algorithms for Streams, DS*: Distance based, CCA*: Connected Component Analysis, RA*: Regression Analysis, DN*: Density based, C*: Convex, A*: Arbitrary, E*: Elliptical

Features	STREAM	CluStream	Stat-Grid	ICFR	DUC-Stream	Den-Stream	ExCC
Year	2002	2003	2004	2004	2005	2006	2007
Nature of Processing	Batch	Online	Online	Batch	Batch	Online	Online
Pre-defined Number of Clusters	No	Yes	No	No	No	No	No
Initial Phase	Yes	Yes	No	Yes	No	Yes	No
Support for On-demand Clustering	No	Yes	Yes	No	No	Yes	Yes
Evolution Mechanism	No	Yes	No	Yes	No	Yes	Yes
Clustering Technique	DS*	DS*	CCA*	RA*	CCA*	DN*	CCA*
Shape of Cluster	C*	C*	A*	E*	A*	A*	A*
Outlier Detection	No	No	No	No	No	Yes	Yes
Exclusive Clustering	Yes	No	Yes	Yes	Yes	No	Yes

technique, similar to merging technique given in Zhou, Cai, Wei & Qian (2003), is used.

c. *WStream* algorithm (Tasoulis, Adams & Hand, 2006) extends conventional *KDE* clustering to spatio-temporal data in stream environment, using *Epanechnikow Kernel*. This algorithm maintains a list of windows, each capturing a cluster. The windows are moved, expanded and contracted incrementally depending on the values of the data points that join the clusters. These operations inherently take into account the fading of older data by periodically computing the weight of windows and using it in kernel function. In case a new data point arrives, which does not belong to any of the existing windows (clusters), a new window is created with suitably initialized kernel parameters. Two windows that overlap considerably, are merged. A major drawback of this approach is that with increase in points more windows

need to be maintained where each cluster is represented by at least one window. Hence, with increase in the number of clusters more memory is required.

The major drawback of Kernel Density Estimation based approach is that it is computationally very expensive.

Comparison of Algorithms

In this section we consolidate the strengths and weaknesses of the algorithms mentioned earlier. Table 1 shows a feature wise comparative analysis of algorithms described in previous subsections.

CluStream and *DenStream* process incoming data in an on-line manner and are capable of handling evolving data whereas *STREAM* processes incoming data in batches. *STREAM* works on the approximation of entire data stream from the beginning to the end without distinguishing between old and new data. *CluStream* discards outdated

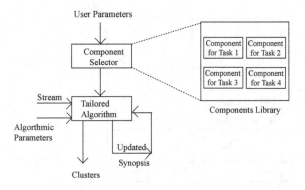

Figure 2. Architectural framework for assembling stream clustering algorithms

GENERIC ARCHITECTURE FOR STREAM CLUSTERING ALGORITHMS

This section presents the parameterized framework for stream clustering. Section "Architectural Framework" presents a generic architecture in which the user specifies the requirements of the application, and the framework selects the appropriate components to assemble the algorithm. The later sub-sections describe the tasks in detail and the issues involved in the selection of the components.

Architectural Framework

Figure 2 shows the architectural framework for assembling a stream clustering algorithm. The framework exploits the task-based generic architecture of stream clustering algorithms that emerges from the comparative study presented in Section "Comparison of Stream Clustering Algorithms". In the proposed framework, the end user specifies parameters at two levels. The first set of parameters (user parameters) reflects the specific user needs and is used for assembling the algorithm. This provides flexibility to the user to set goals for each of the tasks. The second set of parameters (algorithmic parameters) is specific to the tailored algorithm.

The component selector selects the components for accomplishing tasks involved in stream clustering. The selection is based on the user parameters. The output of the component selector is a tailored algorithm that accomplishes tasks summarized in Figure 3. Each of the tasks is accomplished using a strategy from some existing algorithm, to meet the user's requirements in totality.

The user parameters include output needs like shape of the clusters, on-demand/periodic clustering requirement, outlier handling; resources availability in terms of memory and computational power; the nature of the stream in terms of speed, smoothness etc. The 'Feature' column of Table 1 is

data by using relevance time stamp, whereas *DenStream* fades away synopsis on the basis of the arrival rate of data points in it. Convex-shaped clusters are generated by *STREAM* and *CluStream* whereas arbitrary-shaped clusters are generated by *DenStream*.

Stats-Grid, *DUCstream* and *ExCC* use grid structure for summarizing incoming points and require less processing time per point as compared with distance-based algorithms. They use connected component analysis for connecting adjacent cells in grid and hence generate arbitrary shaped clusters. *Stats-Grid* and *DUCstream* do not handle evolving stream because they prune cells on the basis of density, whereas *ExCC* prunes cells on the basis of arrival rate of points in each cell. Hence *ExCC* is capable of generating clusters that depict current trends.

Statistical and *Density Estimation* based approaches are computationally more expensive than the previous two approaches and cannot handle high speed stream. *Statistical* approaches are suitable for data belonging to single distribution, while *Density Estimation* based approaches are more flexible. Density Estimation based approaches are capable of handling evolving stream. However, both approaches give efficient results for low dimensional data only and the final clustering result is influenced by the initial model generated.

Figure 3. Tasks in a Stream Clustering Algorithm (* required in some synopsis structures)

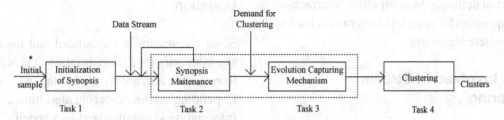

Table 2. Sample set of user parameters

Requirement	Type	Candidate Algorithms
Initialization	No	STREAM, Stat-Grid, ICFR, ExCC
	Yes	CluStream, DenStream, DUCStream
Data processing	Batch	STREAM, DUCStream, ICFR
	Online	CluStream, DenStream, Stat-Grid, ExCC
Speed of Stream	Low	STREAM, ICFR
	High	CluStream, DenStream, Stat-Grid, DUCStream, ExCC
Dimensions of data	Low/Moderate	STREAM, CluStream, DenStream, ICFR
	High	Stat-Grid, DUCStream, ExCC
Number of clusters	Known	CluStream
	Unknown	STREAM, DenStream, Stat-Grid, ICFR, DUCStream, ExCC
Shape of Clusters	Convex	STREAM, CluStream
	Arbitrary	DenStream, Stat-Grid, DUCStream, ExCC
	Elliptical	ICFR
Type of clusters	Exclusive	STREAM, Stat-Grid, ICFR, DUCStream, ExCC
	Non-exclusive	CluStream, DenStream
Evolution handling	No	STREAM, Stat-Grid, DUCStream
	Yes	CluStream, DenStream, ICFR, ExCC
Computational requirements	Low	CluStream, DenStream, DUCStream, ExCC
	High	High & STREAM, Stat-Grid, ICFR

a sample of user requirements that are interpreted as user parameters for component selection. These are the inputs for the selector mechanism to select suitable components from the library. The selected components are subsequently bound to create a tailored stream clustering algorithm.

Table 2 gives the possible alternatives for picking up the candidates (parents) for assembling,

depending on user level parameters. Once the algorithm has been assembled, the user gives relevant algorithmic parameters, for instance density threshold, number of clusters, intervals, in order to get the desired results.

A wide variety of programming technologies are available for the rapid development of an environment for assembling algorithms in order to implement the framework. Major effort is required in defining the compatible interfaces of the components for seamless integration, leading to a complete algorithm.

Tasks Involved in Stream Clustering

Figure 3 shows the sequence of the tasks that need to be performed for clustering of data stream. The formulation is based on the comparative study of available stream clustering algorithms. The figure illustrates a generic stream clustering algorithm consisting of four components, each performing one of the tasks mentioned below.

a.   Selecting the synopsis structure and initializing it (if required)
b.   Processing the incoming data and updating the synopsis
c.   Capturing evolution of stream (i.e. detection of evolving and fading clusters)
d.   Clustering on the synopsis

Initialization of the synopsis structure (task 1) is optional and depends on the clustering algorithm used in task 4. The second component updates synopsis (task 2) while processing incoming points in the stream. To capture changes in data trends, a fading or pruning mechanism is applied on synopsis highlighting the evolution of the new clusters and disappearance of older ones. For some algorithms, the on-line component integrates both these tasks (as indicated by the dotted box). The final component accomplishes the last task using the up-to-date synopsis and delivers the clustering scheme.

We now discuss the issues involved in each of these tasks and their handling in different algorithms. The discussion helps in understanding the issues that arise while interfacing of the components during the assembly.

Synopsis Structure and its Updation

Since the stream is unbounded and the data is available only for a short duration, it is necessary to maintain a synopsis of the data as it comes. Depending on the clustering algorithm used, the information is summarized in a specific format and is stored as synopsis for future reference. The structure of the synopsis and the clustering algorithm intended to be used, are closely inter-related. In some situations, the synopsis needs to be initialized.

The incoming data points of the stream can be incorporated into the synopsis structure either in batch mode or in an on-line fashion. The on-line approach requires constant time complexity so that there is no data loss, whereas batch processing does not face this constraint. Batch processing uses the landmark window model to compute clusters over the complete stream received so far. The usage of the landmark window model in clustering makes batch processing unsuitable for capturing evolutionary trends (Aggarwal, Han, Wang & Yu, 2003).

Two commonly used synopsis structures in stream clustering algorithms are i) Set of micro-clusters and ii) Grid.

The algorithms using the set of micro-clusters as synopses or those using Kernel density estimation (Heinz & Seeger, 2006) need an initialization phase for determining the initial set of clusters. In case of both, the micro-clusters (μCs) and fading micro-clusters ($P\text{-}\mu Cs$ and $O\text{-}\mu Cs$) (Table 3), new incoming points are absorbed within the closest micro-cluster either in batch or on-line mode. This results into updated synopsis. Time required for maintaining synopsis depends on its size and is an important consideration in the design of the on-line component.

Grid-based synopsis structure maintains detailed data distribution in the data space. The structure does not need initialization and takes constant time for insertion of a new data point

Table 3. Synopsis data structures of some stream clustering algorithms

Features	CluStream	Stats-Grid	ICFR	ExCC	DenStream
Name of Synopsis	Set of Micro-clusters (μC)	Statistical Grid	Set of Initial Clusters	Grid	Set of P-μCs and O-μCs
Structure of Synopsis	$\overline{CF2^x}, \overline{CF1^x},$ $\overline{CF2^t}, \overline{CF1^t}, n$	$(RS_i, C_i, \mu_i, \sigma_i)$	$(\mu, \sigma, fval, RC, DM)$	n, ts, aat	$\overline{(CF2^x, CF1^x, wt)}$ $\overline{(CF2^x, CF1^x, wt, ts)}$
Storage Complexity	$O(2d+3)*N$	$\Omega(K^d)$	$O(N^2)$	$\Omega(K^d)$	$O(2d+1)*N$
Time Complexity	$O(Nd)$	$\Omega(d)$	$O(N^2)$	$O(d)$	$O(Nd)$
Remarks	N: no. of Microclusters, n: no. of points in each Microcluster x: data value t: time stamp	RS_i:range C_i: count μ_i: mean σ_i: Std. dev. For each dim i	DM: distance matrix RC: Regression Coefficient	ts: time stamp K: no. of intervals aat: average arrival time	N: no. of P-μCs and O-μCs ts: time stamp of O-μCs tw: weight

(Park & Lee, 2004). This characteristic makes it attractive for handling high speed data stream. The incoming points are absorbed in the synopsis based on data values along different dimensions. Grid-based synopsis handles high dimensional sparse data more efficiently compared to distance function (Agrawal, Gehrke, Dimitrious & Raghavan, 1998).

Mechanism to Capture Evolving Data

In order to capture data evolution over time, algorithms employ a recency criterion to highlight current patterns in the stream, and fade out or reduce the impact of older data. Pruning (Aggarwal, Han, Wang & Yu, 2003; Bhatnagar & Kaur, 2007; Park and Lee, 2004) and fading (Cao, Ester, Qian & Zhou, 2006; Motoyoshi, Miura & Shioya, 2004) are two commonly used mechanisms for determining recency.

Pruning can be performed either using time-stamp or data volume, or both. In time-based pruning, the unit of information (e.g. micro-cluster, cell) that has not been updated for a specified period of time is permanently deleted from synopsis structure. The period may either be explicitly defined as in the sliding window model or may be some pre-defined function of time (Aggarwal, Han, Wang & Yu, 2003). Pruning done on the basis of data volume may miss detection of a slight change in current trend or data distribution (Gao, Li, Zhang & Tan, 2005; Park & Lee, 2004). Data volume-based pruning is thus desirable in applications where only significant distribution changes need to be captured. Some algorithms also use the time of creation of the unit of information in addition to data volume for pruning information, which is not updated for a specified period of time (Bhatnagar & Kaur, 2007).

Fading mechanism dynamically computes the weight of the information in synopsis, based on arrival of conforming data points, as in damped-window model (Cao, Ester, Qian & Zhou, 2006). The importance of historical data is gradually reduced by using a fading function that is typically of the form $2^{-\lambda t}$ (Cao, Ester, Qian & Zhou, 2006). This mechanism is preferred when even a slight change in distribution needs to be captured.

Clustering Technique

Clustering the synopsis is the final task that needs to be performed. Importance of the choice of a clustering technique cannot be undermined since

Table 4. Comparison of clustering components of selected algorithms

Algorithm	STREAM	CluStream	DenStream	Stat-Grid & ExCC	ICFR
Technique Used	*k*-Median	*k*-Means	*db*scan	CCA	RA
Complexity	$O(NM+Nk\log k)$	$O(Nkt)$	$O(N^2)$	$O(N!)$	$O(N^2)$
Remarks	N: Data size M: No. of Outliers k: No. of Centers	N: No. of μCs t: No. of iterations k: No. of centers	N: No. of core-μCs	N: No. of cells	N: No. of initial clusters

it has a direct impact on the nature of the output (e.g. shape of the cluster), resource requirement (size and structure of the synopsis) and the efficiency of the overall algorithm (design of the on-line/batch component). There is a wide variety of clustering techniques available in literature (Hartigan, 1975; Jain, Murty & Flynn, 1999). Many of these techniques have been suitably modified for clustering data streams.

k-Median, k-Means and neighborhood density search are commonly used approaches for clustering streams. The *k-Median* based *LOCASEARCH* algorithm is used in *STREAM* (Guha, Mishra, Motwani & O'Callaghan, 2002) at two stages. It initially maintains weighted cluster centers for each chunk and subsequently generates optimal number of clusters from these weighted centers.

CluStream uses *weighted k-Means* algorithm for discovering (macro-)clusters when demanded by the user. *DenStream* applies a variant of *db-scan* (Ester, Kriegel, Sander & Xu, 1996) on the synopsis to get arbitrary shaped clusters. Unlike *CluStream,* it does not require pre-defined number of clusters to be generated and reports all density-connected and density-reachable core-μCs as clusters.

In the grid based approach for clustering, connected component analysis is performed on selected cells to deliver arbitrary shaped clusters. Cells to be clustered are selected based on pruning/fading criteria, as applicable. *Stats-Grid* algorithm selects cells based on points whereas

ExCC algorithm uses points as well as time for selection. *DUCStream* does clustering on dense cells formed in the first chunk. This algorithm uses an incremental approach and keeps on updating existing clusters by merging all new dense cells formed in subsequent chunks. A new cluster is formed only when a cell cannot be merged within existing clusters.

Statistical approaches use various statistical measures like mean, median, variance, covariance, regression co-efficient etc. to generate a mathematical model for clustering. This mathematical model is subsequently updated to incorporate new trends. Because of extensive computation, this approach always clusters offline and gives efficient results for a low dimensional data set. *ICFR* uses regression analysis for capturing clusters with local trends. It delivers non-convex shaped and exclusive clusters.

Table 4 summarizes the clustering techniques used in the chosen set of algorithms, along with their respective time complexities.

REALIZATION OF THE FRAMEWORK

To demonstrate the application of the framework, we assemble two stream clustering algorithms as per two different sets of user requirements. The rationale for selecting the components is outlined and experimental evaluation is reported. Experiments reveal that both the assembled algorithms perform comparably with the parent algorithms, from which components have been drawn.

G-kMeans Algorithm: Example 1

Table 5 lists the requirements of a user. Table 2 helps in determining that *CluStream* satisfies requirements (1), (2), (5), (6) and (9) while *ExCC* satisfies requirements (2), (3), (4), (7), (8) and (9).

Since *CluStream* is a distance based algorithm with on-line component of complexity $O(Nd)$ (Table 3), it may not be able to handle high speed, high dimensional data stream. Further, *CluStream* also does not lead to exclusive and complete clustering. Both these requirements are met by *ExCC* algorithm, which also delivers arbitrary shaped large number of clusters. To overcome this situation, we assemble an algorithm *G-kMeans* that uses grid structure for synopsis and *k-means* algorithm for clustering. The choice is made due to the following reasons :

a. Per point processing time in grid is lesser than that in micro-cluster approach.
b. A complete and desired number of exclusive clusters need to be generated.

When user demands clustering in *G-kMeans*, the grid is pruned to remove the effect of old data

Table 5. First set of user'requirement for clustering streams

1.	Initialization	Yes
2.	Clustering Requirements	On Demand
3.	Speed of Stream	High
4.	Dimensionality of Data	High
5.	Number of Clusters	Known
6.	Shape of Clusters	Convex
7.	Type of Clusters	Exclusive
8.	Type of Clustering	Complete
9.	Evolution Handling	Yes

on current trends. Each cell in grid is then used by the clustering component, which uses *k-Means* as in *CluStream*.

G-dbscan Algorithm: Example 2

Considering the user requirements given in Table 6 with reference to Table 2, it was found that *DenStream* satisfies all requirements except (3), (4) and (7).

DenStream is also a distance based algorithm with the on-line component of complexity $O(Nd)$ (Table 3) and may not be able to handle high speed, high dimensional data stream. *DenStream* generates non-exclusive clusters on demand because potential micro-clusters are merged to compute real clusters.

As discussed in previous section, these requirements are met by *ExCC*. We assemble an algorithm *G-dbscan* that uses grid structure as synopsis and *dbscan* algorithm for clustering as used in *DenStream*.

G-dbscan uses grid for storing summarized information about incoming data points. The grid is pruned just before clustering as done in *ExCC*. Each cell in the grid is used as a pseudo point, represented by its signature, while clustering using *dbscan*.

Table 6. Second set of user'requirement for clustering streams

1.	Initialization	Yes
2.	Clustering Requirements	On Demand
3.	Speed of Stream	High
4.	Dimensionality of Data	High
5.	Number of Clusters	Unknown
6.	Shape of Clusters	Arbitrary
7.	Type of Clusters	Exclusive
8.	Evolution Handling	Yes
9.	Type of Clustering	Complete
10.	Reporting Outliers	Yes

Experimental Analysis of *G-kMeans* and *G-dbscan*

In this section, we describe the experiments to demonstrate two important features of the assembled algorithms. We show that the quality delivered by the assembled algorithm and time taken are comparable to those of the clustering schemes delivered by the parent algorithms. If both scalability and quality requirements are comparable, meeting the requirements of the user by the assembled algorithm, is certainly an added advantage. The results give us the confidence that the components used for assembling the algorithm do not lead to any deterioration.

All experiments are performed on the Intel Centrino processor with 256 MB RAM, running stand-alone Linux (kernel 2.4.22-1). The algorithm is implemented in ANSI C with no optimizations, and compiled using a g++ compiler (3.3.2-2). In the experiments with streaming data, the results are averaged over multiple runs with total number of data points remaining the same. The following data sets are used:

a. Network Intrusion Detection Data used in kdd cup, 1999, is available at UCI KDD archive. The data consists of 494,021 records, each having 42 attributes (34 continuous and 8 categorical). Each record corresponds to either normal class or an attack class. The experiments were performed with 23 classes using 34 continuous attributes.
b. Forest Cover type Data, acquired from UCI KDD archive, has been widely used in clustering experiments. This data has 581,012 observations, each with 54 attributes. There are seven classes in this data set and all ten quantitative attributes are used in the reported experiments.
c. Synthetic Data generated by *Enclus* data generator (Cheng, Fu & Zhang, 1999) has been used in some experiments. The generated data sets are denoted as *ENdDcCrR*

indicating that there are *d* dimensions (*D*), *c* clusters (*C*) and r * 1000 records (*R*) and are used for verification of proposed assembly approach.

Evaluation of Cluster Quality of G-kMeans

Two measures viz. cluster purity and squared sum of distance (SSQ), were used to evaluate the quality of clusters delivered by *G-kMeans*. The results were compared with those of *CluStream* and *ExCC*. Synthetic data (EN8D10C100R) generated by *Enclus* and Network intrusion data was used for these experiments.

All the three algorithms gave cluster purity above 99.8% on synthetic data establishing the feasibility and comparable quality of stream clustering algorithm tailored using the proposed framework. Average cluster purity of *G-kMeans* with *CluStream* and *ExCC* was compared by recreating the experiment reported in Aggarwal, Han, Wang & Yu (2004), and using the results reported therein. Figure 4 shows that cluster purity of *G-kMeans* is better than *CluStream* but lower than *ExCC*. Marginal lowering of cluster purity of *G-kMeans* can be attributed to the use of distance function for clustering, which is generally not recommended for high-dimensional data set.

The cluster quality of *k-Means* and *G-kMeans* was compared with respect to SSQ, as shown in

Figure 4. Cluster purity comparison (Network Intrusion Data)

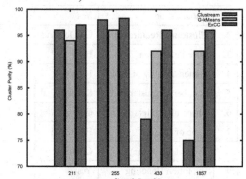

Figure 5. Comparison of cluster quality (SSQ) of EN8D10C100R, Interval = 14

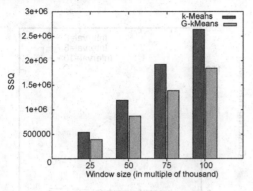

Table 7. Comparison of cluster quality (SSQ) of network intrusion data

Points (in thousands)	*CluStream*	*G-kMeans*
150	1E+13	1E+12
250	1E+5	1E+8
350	1E+12	1E+9
450	1E+8	1E+8

Figure 6. Increase in grid cells with number of points (EN5D10C200R)

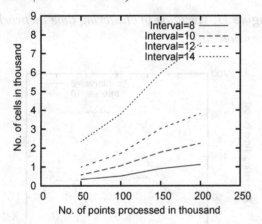

Figure 7. Clustering time (EN5D10C200R)

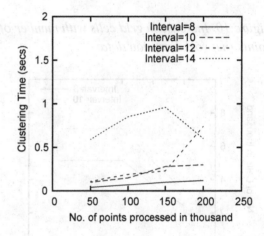

Figure 5. All records were used in the experiment without treating them as stream in this experiment. The high quality of *G-kMeans* is attributed to the detailed data distribution information summarized in grid. Table 7 shows the comparison of SSQ of the clustering schemes delivered by *G-kMeans* and *CluStream,* using the results reported in Aggarwal, Han, Wang & Yu (2003). We get mixed results, though we appreciate better compactness achieved by *CluStream* because of the micro-cluster based approach.

Testing Scalability of G-kMeans

The scalability of a stream clustering algorithm needs to be examined with respect to both time and memory requirement. Time complexity is crucial for the on-line component to avoid loss of data in a high speed stream. High scalability is desirable for the offline component so that clustering results are delivered in reasonable time, when demanded by the user. Scalability of the on-line component of *G-kMeans* is not an issue since incoming points are processed in constant time. Therefore, the scalability of the offline component is tested for different granularity levels (Interval) of the grid.

Time required by the component is influenced by the number of cells in the grid, which are used as data points in *G-kMeans*. Figures 6, 8, 10 show the increasing number of grid cells with data points, while Figures 7, 9, 11 show the corresponding clustering times. Though the theoretical time

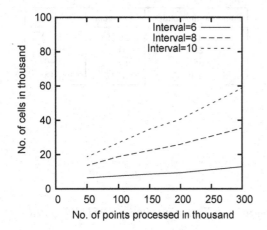

Figure 8. Increase in grid cells with number of points (forest cover data)

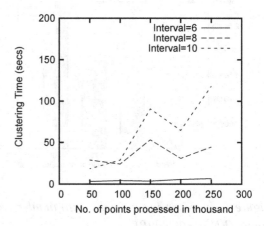

Figure 9. Variation in clustering time (forest cover data)

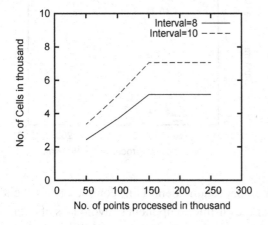

Figure 10. Increase in grid cells with number of points (network intrusion data)

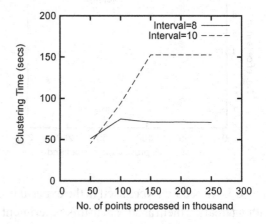

Figure 11. Variation in clustering time (network intrusion data)

complexity of *k-Means* is $O(nkt)$, the actual times are influenced by the data distribution. As seen in Figure 7, the time taken by the *G-kMeans* at finer granularity (Interval=14) decreases at 200,000 data points. This dip is explained by change in data distribution leading to pruning of large number of cells and consequent reduction in the iterations required by *k-Means* to generate cluster.

In case of Forest Cover data, though the number of cells in the grid show a constant increase for different grid granularities (Figure 8), the clustering timings do not show a regular pattern

(Figure 9). This can be explained by changing data distribution leading to unpredictable pruning and consequent reduction in clustering time. Figures 10, 11 show the observation on Network intrusion data.

Scalability of clustering component of *G-kMeans* algorithm was tested by varying number of input clusters in synthetic data. Figure 12 shows that the clustering time is linear with respect to increase in the number of clusters.

Figure 12. Scalability of cluster component using synthetic data (Interval = 8)

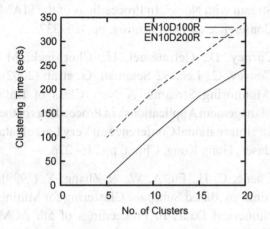

Figure 13. Cluster purity comparison

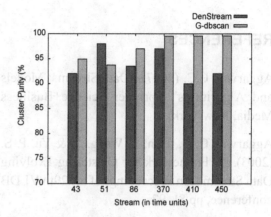

Evaluation of Cluster Quality in G-dbscan

Cluster purity was used as the measure to evaluate the quality of clusters generated by *G-dbscan*. Synthetic data was used to compare *G-dbscan* with *dbscan*. Both algorithms gave approximately 99.8% purity on this data.

The experiment reported in Cao, Ester, Qian & Zhou (2006) was recreated to compare cluster quality of *DenStream* and *G-dbscan* on Network Intrusion data. Figure 13 shows that *G-dbscan* outperforms *DenStream* at every time unit.

Figure 14. Execution time vs. stream length (network intrusion detection data, interval =12)

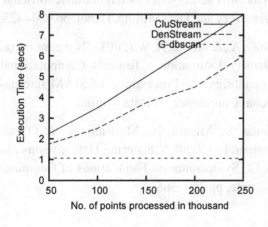

Testing Scalability of G-dbscan

The results of the experiment on Network Intrusion data for comparing the scalability of *CluStream*, *DenStream* and *G-dbscan* are shown in Figure 14. The execution times of *CluStream* and *DenStream* grow linearly as stream proceeds, whereas *G-dbscan* executes stream in constant time because of grid structure.

CONCLUSION

This paper presents a parameterized framework for assembling a stream clustering algorithm. The framework is based on the generic architecture underlying the existing algorithms and is motivated by the need to overcome the adhoc approach for designing algorithms to solve individual problems. The proposed framework enhances the user involvement in the use of the KDD technology, by accepting the business requirements as high level parameters, and tailoring the algorithm best suited for the application needs.

The two algorithms *G-kMeans* and *G-dbscan* are presented to instantiate the proposed framework based on two different user requirements sets. Experimental evaluation of the two algorithms with respect to the quality of clustering and scalability indicate viability of the proposal.

REFERENCES

Aggarwal, C.C. (2007). 'Data Streams: Models and Algorithms', Springer Science+Business Media, New York.

Aggarwal, C. C., Han, J., Wang, J., & Yu, P. S. (2003). 'A Framework for Clustering Evolving Data Streams', In Proceedings of the 29th VLDB conference, pp.81–92.

Aggarwal, C. C., Han, J., & Yu, P. S. (2004). 'A Framework for Projected Clustering of High Dimensional Data Streams', In Proceedings of International Conference on Very Large Data Bases, Toronto, Canada, pp.852–863.

Agrawal, R., Gehrke, J., Dimitrious, G., & Raghavan, P. (1998). 'Automatic Subspace Clustering of High Dimensional data for Data Mining application', ACM SIGMOD Record, pp.94–105.

Babcock, B., Babu, S., Datar, M., Motwani, R., & Widom, J. (2002). 'Models and Issues in Data Stream Systems', In Proceedings of the ACM Symposium on Principles of Database Systems (PODS), pp.1–16.

Barb´ara, D. (2002). 'Requirements of Clustering Data Streams', ACM SIGKDD Explorations Newsletter, Vol. 3, pp.23–27.

Berkhin, P. (2003). 'Survey of Clustering Data Mining Techniques', Accure Software Inc.

Bhatnagar, V., & Kaur, S. (2007). 'Exclusive and Complete Clustering of Streams', In Proceedings of the International Conference on Database and Expert Systems Applications, Germany, pp.629–638.

Cao, F., Ester, M., Qian, W., & Zhou, A. (2006) 'Density-Based Clustering over an Evolving Data Stream with Noise', In Proceedings of the SIAM Conference on Data Mining, pp.326–337.

Carney, D., Cetintemel, U., Cherniack, M., Convey, C., Lee, S., Seidman, G. et al. (2002). 'Monitoring Streams: A New Class of Data Management Applications', In Proceedings of the 28th International Conference on Very Large Data Bases, Hong Kong, China, pp.215–226.

Cheng, C. H., Fu, A. W., & Zhang, Y. (1999). 'Entropy Based Subspace Clustering for Mining Numerical Data', In Proceedings of 5th ACM SIGKDD International Conference on Knowledge Discovery and Data Mining, pp.84–93.

Domingos, P., & Hulten, G. (2000). 'Mining High-Speed Data Streams', In Proceedings of 6th International Conference on Knowledge Discovery and Data Mining, pp.71–80.

Duda, R. O., Hart, P. E., & Stork, D. G. (2000). 'Pattern Classification', John Wiley and Sons.

Ester, M., Kriegel, H. P., Sander, J., & Xu, X. (1996). 'A Density-based Algorithm for Discovering Clusters in Large Spatial DBs with Noise', In Proceedings of 2nd International Conference on Knowledge Discovery and Data Mining.

Gao, J., Li, J., Zhang, Z., & Tan, P. (2005). 'An Incremental Data Stream Clustering Algorithm Based on Dense Units Detection', In Proceedings of the 9th Pacific-Asia Conference on Knowledge Discovery and Data Mining, Hanoi, pp.420–425.

Gray, A., & Moore, A. W. (2003). 'Nonparametric Density Estimation : Towards Computational Tractability', In Proceedings of SIAM International Conference on Data Mining.

Guha, S., Mishra, N., Motwani, R., & O'Callaghan, L. (2000). 'Clustering Data Streams', In IEEE Symposium on Foundations of Computer Science, pp.259–366.

Guha, S., Mishra, N., Motwani, R., & O'Callaghan, L. (2002). 'Streaming-Data Algorithms for High-Quality Clustering', In Proceedings of IEEE International Conference on Data Engineering.

Hartigan, J. A. (1975). 'Clustering Algorithms', John Wiley & Sons Inc.

Heinz, C., & Seeger, B. (2006). 'Towards Kernel Density Estimation Over Streaming Data', In Proceedings of 13th International Conference on Management of Data(COMAD), Delhi, India.

Henzinger, M. R., Raghavan, P., & Rajagopalan, S. (1998). 'Computing on Data Streams', Technical Note 1998-011, Digital Systems Research Center, Palo Alto, California.

Jain, A. K., Murty, M. N., & Flynn, P. L. (1999). 'Data Clustering : A Review', ACM Computing Survey, pp.264–323.

Motoyoshi, M., Miura, T., & Shioya, I. (2004). 'Clustering Stream Data by Regression Analysis', In Proceedings of the 2nd workshop on Australasian Information security, Data Mining and Web Intelligence, and Software Internationalization, Dunedin, New Zealand, pp.115–120.

Orlowska, M. E., Sun, X., & Li, X. (2006). 'Can Exclusive Clustering on Streaming Data be Achieved', ACM SIGKDD Explorations Newsletter, Vol 8, pp.102–108.

Park, N. H., & Lee, W. S. (2004). 'Statistical Grid-based Clustering over Data streams', ACM SIGMOD Record, Volume 33, pp.32–37.

Park, N. H., & Lee, W. S. (2007). 'Cell trees: An Adaptive Synopsis Structure for Clustering Multi-dimensional On-line Data Streams', Data and Knowledge Engineering, Vol 63, pp.528–549.

Rusu, L. I., Rahayu, W., & Taniar, D. (2008). 'Intelligent Dynamic XML Documents Clustering', In Proceedings of the 22nd International Conference on Advanced Information Networking and Applications, Japan, pp 449-456.

Sain, S. R. (1994). 'Adaptive Kernel Density Estimation', PhD Thesis, Rice University.

Song, M., & Wang, H. (2004). 'Incremental Estimation of Gaussian Mixture Models for Online Data Stream Clustering', In International Conference on Bioinformatics and its Applications, Hong Kong.

Song, M., & Wang, H. (2006). 'Detecting Low Complexity Clusters by Skewness and Kurtosis in Data Stream Clustering', In 9th International Symposium on AI and Maths, Florida.

Tasoulis, D. K., Adams, N. M., & Hand, D. J. (2006). 'Unsupervised Clustering in Streaming Data', In Proceedings of 6th IEEE International Conference on Data Mining -Workshops, pp.638–642.

UCI KDD Archive, http://kdd.ics.uci.edu.

Yang, Q., & Wu, X. (2006). '10 Challenging Problems in Data Mining Research', International Journal of Information Technology & Decision, Vol 5, pp.597–604.

Zhang, T., Ramakrishnan, R., & Livny, M. (1996). 'BIRCH: An Efficient Data Clustering Method for Very Large Databases', In Proceedings of the ACM SIGMOD International Conference on Management of Data, Quebec, Canada, pp.103–114.

Zhou, A., Cai, Z., Wei, L., & Qian, W. (2003). 'M-Kernel Merging : Towards Density Estimation Over Data Streams', In Proceedings of 8th International Conference on Database Systems for Advanced Applications (DASFAA), pp.285–292.

This work was previously published in the International Journal of Data Warehousing & Mining 5(1), edited by David Taniar, pp. 36-56, copyright 2009 by IGI Publishing (an imprint of IGI Global).

Chapter 4
A Hybrid Method for High–Utility Itemsets Mining in Large High–Dimensional Data

Guangzhu Yu
Donghua University, China

Shihuang Shao
Donghua University, China

Bin Luo
Guangdong University of Technology, China

Xianhui Zeng
Donghua University, China

ABSTRACT

Existing algorithms for high-utility itemsets mining are column enumeration based, adopting an Apriori-like candidate set generation-and-test approach, and thus are inadequate in datasets with high dimensions or long patterns. To solve the problem, this paper proposed a hybrid model and a row enumeration-based algorithm, i.e., Inter-transaction, to discover high-utility itemsets from two directions: an existing algorithm can be used to seek short high-utility itemsets from the bottom, while Inter-transaction can be used to seek long high-utility itemsets from the top. Inter-transaction makes full use of the characteristic that there are few common items between or among long transactions. By intersecting relevant transactions, the new algorithm can identify long high-utility itemsets, without extending short itemsets step by step. In addition, we also developed new pruning strategies and an optimization technique to improve the performance of Inter-transaction.

INTRODUCTION

Traditional association rule mining (ARM) assumes that the important must be frequent and aims at discovering frequent itemsets. However, in the real world, the frequent is not necessarily important; some infrequent itemsets may have high utility values and thus are important to users. For example, in a transaction database, there are 1000 sale records of milk which occupy 10% of the total transaction number, contributing 1% of the total profit. In the meantime, there are 600 sale records of birthday cake that occupy 6% of the total transaction number, contributing 5% of the total profit. If the support threshold is 8%, according to traditional algorithms for frequent itemset mining, milk will be reported as a frequent itemset and birthday cake will be ignored. But in fact, market professionals must be more interested in birthday cake because it contributes a larger portion to total profit than milk. The example shows that support is not sufficient to reflect users' interests and such mining results might not be satisfactory.

According to Expectancy Theory (Vroom, 1964), we have the well-known equation "motivation = probability * utility", which says that motivation is determined by the utility of making a decision and the probability of success. In retailing field, users are not only interested in the frequency of occurrence of an itemset (support), but also its utility. So a decision-oriented ARM algorithm should output both the support and the utility of interesting patterns. For this reason, utility-based ARM (or utility mining for short) has been proposed to discover all the itemsets in a database with utility values higher than a user-specified threshold.

Utility of an item is a subjective term, depending on users and applications; it could be measured in terms of profit, cost, risk, aesthetic value or other expressions of user preference. For easy understanding, in this paper, "utility" is viewed as economic utility such as sales profit, and all

databases are regarded as transaction databases, so that we can define the utility of an item as the product of quantity sold and the unit profit of the item. Table 1 is an example of a simplified transaction database where the total utility value is 162. The number in each transaction in Table 1 is the sales profit of each item. If $s(X)$ and $u(X)$ represent the support and utility of itemset X respectively (for details, refer to definition 4 in Section 2), then $u(A,B)=43$, $s(A,B)=5$, $u(A,B,C)=54$, $s(A,B,C)=3$, $u(A,B,C,D)=45$, $s(A,B,C,D)=2$, $u(A,B,C,D,E)=57$, and $s(A,B,C,D,E)=2$.

If the support threshold is 3 and the utility threshold is 50, $\{A, B\}$ is a frequent but not a high-utility itemset. On the other hand, $\{A,B,C\}$ is both a frequent and high-utility itemset, $\{A,B,C,D\}$ is neither a frequent nor a high-utility itemset and $\{A,B,C,D,E\}$ is a high-utility but non-frequent itemset.

From the above example, we can draw a conclusion: downward closure property, which states that if an itemset is frequent by support, all its nonempty subsets must also be frequent by support, does not apply to utility mining. Relevant studies have shown that utility constraint is neither anti-monotone, monotone, succinct, nor convertible (Shen, Zhang, & Yang, 2000; Yao, Hamilton, & Geng, 2006). Because of this property, most algorithms for frequent pattern mining

Table 1. A transaction database

	A	B	C	D	E
T1	0	0	5	0	1
T2	2	3	0	0	0
T3	3	5	15	7	4
T4	0	0	4	7	2
T5	4	5	8	0	0
T6	9	4	0	0	2
T7	6	0	8	3	6
T8	0	0	0	6	3
T9	3	0	0	9	5
T10	3	5	6	1	8

such as FP-Tree (Han, Pei, Yin, & Mao, 2004), CARPENTER (Pang, Cong, Tung, Yang, & Zaki, 2003), Tree-projection (Agarwal, Aggarwal, & Prasad, 2000) and so on can not be used to find high-utility itemsets.

Lots of researches have been conducted to improve the usefulness of traditional ARM. Ngan, Lam, Wong, and Fu (2005) proposed an algorithm called COFI+BOMO to mine N-most interesting itemsets, but the interestingness measure still depends on the support. Value added association rule (Wang, Zhou, & Han, 2002; Lin, Yao, & Louie, 2002) extends traditional association rule by taking the semantics of data into consideration. The difference between Wang et al. (2002) and Lin et al. (2002) is that price and quantity of supermarket sales are considered in the former, while the latter tries to attach a value to every item in the database and use the added values to rank the association rule. Weighted association rule gives up treating all the items and all the transactions uniformly by assigning different weights to items (Cai, Fu, Cheng, & Kong, 1998) or transactions (Lu, Hu, & Li, 2001). These weights essentially reflect the users' preferences. Quantitative association rule mining (Aumann & Lindell, 2003; Webb, 2001) introduces statistical inference theory into the data mining field to find extraordinary phenomena in the database. In order to provide efficient data initialization for mining association rules in data warehouse, Tjioe and Taniar (2005) proposed four algorithms, which focus on quantitative attributes.

To find frequent high-utility itemsets, Shen et al. (2002) proposed an objective-oriented Apriori (OOApriori) model by putting utility constraint into the Apriori algorithm. Chan, Yang, and Shen (2003) proposed an algorithm to mine top-k frequent high-utility closed patterns. To reduce search space, Chan et al. (2003) developed a new pruning strategy based on a weaker but anti-monotonic condition to prune low-utility itemsets. Barber and Hamilton (2003) use itemset share as a measure to overcome the lack of support. Item share is defined as a fraction of some numerical values.

It can reflect the impact of the sales quantities of items on the cost or profit of an itemset, and thus it should be regarded as a utility.

All the algorithms mentioned above are utility-related, but none of them are utility-based. To the best of our knowledge, only UMining (Yao & Hamilton, 2006) and Two-phase (Liu, Liao, & Choudhary, 2005) can be used to find high-utility itemsets. In UMining algorithm, the utility upper bound property is used to reduce the size of the candidate set. In addition, the support upper bound property is used in a heuristics model to predict whether an itemset should be added into the candidate set. Unfortunately, the heuristics model can not guarantee an accurate prediction. In Two-phase algorithm, transaction weighted downward closure property is used to reduce search space. The algorithm often overestimates the utility of a candidate itemset, especially in long transaction databases.

Both the UMining and Two-phase are Apriori-like algorithms, they are inadequate in datasets with long patterns or high dimensions. To solve the problem, we proposed a hybrid top-down/bottom-up search model and a row enumeration-based algorithm, Inter-transaction, to discover all high-utility itemsets from two directions. Under the hybrid model, an existing algorithm such as Two-phase can be used to seek the short high-utility itemsets by starting from the bottom, while Inter-transaction seeks long high-utility itemsets by starting from the top, they complement each other.

Different from inter-transaction association rule (Feng, Li, & Wong, 2001; Feng, Yu, Lu, & Han, 2002; Liu, Feng, & Han, 2000), which aims at discovering correlation between transactions, our Inter-transaction algorithm aims at discovering long high-utility itemsets. It is based on the characteristic that there are few common items between or among long transactions, which means that the intersection of multiple long transactions is usually very short. In a high-dimensional data environment, the characteristic is especially obvious. By intersecting relevant transactions, Inter-transaction can identify long itemsets directly, without extending short itemsets step by step. In addition, new pruning strategies were developed to cut down the search space and an optimization technique was adopted to improve the performance of the intersection of transactions. This paper emphasizes on the introduction of Inter-transaction algorithm.

The remainder of the paper is organized as follows: Section 2 formally defines relevant terms and notations; Section 3 presents the new algorithm; Section 4 introduces an optimization technique. Experimental results are presented in Section 5 and we summarize our work in Section 6.

DEFINITIONS

This section presents definitions and terminology used in the description of the algorithm. Let $I = \{i_1, i_2 \ldots i_m\}$ be a set of items, $T = \{T_1, T_2 \ldots T_n\}$ be a transaction database. Each transaction T_q in database T ($T_q \in T$) is a subset of I, i.e., $T_q \subseteq I$. To simplify a notation, we sometimes write a set $\{i_1, i_2 \ldots i_k\}$ as $i_1 i_2 \ldots i_k$. Adapting from the notations described in (Yao et al., 2006; Liu et al., 2005; Savasere, Omiecinsky, & Navathe, 1995), we have following definitions:

Definition 1. The transaction utility of item x **in transaction** T_q, denoted $u(x, T_q)$, is the utility brought on by item x when transaction T_q occurs. Take the example from Table 1, $u(A, T_1) = 0$, $u(A, T_2) = 2$.

Definition 2. The transaction utility of itemset X **in transaction** T_q, denoted $u(X, T_q)$, is the sum of the transaction utility of item x contained in X, i.e.,

$$u(X, T_q) = \sum_{x \in X} u(x, T_q) \tag{1}$$

For example, in Table 1, $u(AB, T_2) = u(A, T_2) + u(B, T_2) = 2 + 3 = 5$, $u(ABC, T_5) =$

$u(A, T_5) + u(B, T_5) + u(C, T_5) = 4 + 5 + 8 = 17$. When $X = T_q$, we refer to $u(X, T_q)$ as **the utility of transaction** T_q, denoted $u(T_q, T_q)$.

Definition 3. The partition utility of itemset X **in partition** P_i, denoted $u(X, P_i)$, is the sum of the transaction utility of itemset X in partition P_i, i.e.,

$$u(X, P_i) = \sum_{T_q \in P_i \wedge X \subseteq T_q} u(X, T_q) \tag{2}$$

For more details about partitions, refer to (Savasere et al., 1995).

Definition 4. The utility of X **in database** T, denoted $u(X)$, is the sum of the transaction utility of itemset X in database T, i.e.,

$$u(X) = \sum_{X \subseteq T_q \wedge T_q \in P_i \wedge P_i \subseteq T} u(X, P_i) = \sum_{T_q \in T \wedge X \subseteq T_q} u(X, T_q) \tag{3}$$

Examples can be seen in Section 1.

Definition 5. Transaction identifier list, denoted *tidlist*, is a set of transaction identifiers.

We define an **intersection transaction**, denoted $T_{tidlist}$, as an itemset obtained from the intersection of transactions listed in a *tidlist*. For example, let $T_1 = ABDFHILM$, $T_2 = ADFGJKOP$, $T_3 = ADFMNOQP$, then one of the *tidlists* is $\{1,2,3\}$, and the corresponding intersection transaction $T_{\{1,2,3\}} = T_1 \cap T_2 \cap T_3 = ADF$. If $|tidlist| = k$ ($1 \leq k \leq n$, n is the number of transactions), we refer to the $T_{tidlist}$ as a k-intersection transaction. A k-intersection transaction is the intersection of k individual transactions. It can also be regarded as the intersection of two other intersection transactions. For example, the 4-intersection transaction $T_{\{1,3,5,6\}} = T_1 \cap T_3 \cap T_5 \cap T_6 = T_{\{1,3\}} \cap T_{\{5,6\}} = T_{\{1,5\}} \cap T_{\{3,6\}}$, and so on. When $k=1$, $T_{tidlist}$ is an individual transaction.

Both k-intersection transaction and k-itemset are a set of items, but there are some differences between them. For example, a k-itemset is an itemset with k items. The term does not tell us any information about its support $s(T_{tidlist})$ (i.e., the number of transactions containing the itemset); on the contrary, a k-intersection transaction does not tell us how many items the itemset has, but it tells us that the itemset stems from the intersection of k transactions, with support no less than k. To distinguish the difference between k and $s(T_{tidlist})$, we refer to k as the **current support** of k-intersection transaction $T_{tidlist}$. Obviously, $k \leq s(T_{tidlist})$.

For any $T_{tidlist}$, we can regard the transactions listed in the *tidlist* as a partition, denoted $P_{tidlist}$. According to definitions, the current support of k-intersection transaction $T_{tidlist}$ should be the number of transactions contained in $P_{tidlist}$, denoted $s(T_{tidlist}, P_{tidlist})$. We also refer to the corresponding partition utility of the $T_{tidlist}$ as the **current utility** of $T_{tidlist}$ under current support (or under current *tidlist*). If $u(T_{tidlist})$ stands for the utility of $T_{tidlist}$ and $u(T_{tidlist}, P_{tidlist})$ for the current utility of $T_{tidlist}$, according to equation (2) and equation (3), $u(T_{tidlist}, P_{tidlist})$ should be less than $u(T_{tidlist})$. If $s(T_{tidlist}, P_{tidlist}) = s(T_{tidlist})$, the corresponding *tidlist* is called **maximal *tidlist***, and $u(T_{tidlist}, P_{tidlist}) = u(T_{tidlist})$ holds. Actually, the meaning of the term "maximal *tidlist*" corresponds to the feature support set in (Pang et al., 2003).

We define a long transaction/itemset/pattern as the transaction/itemset/pattern that includes more than *minlen* items. *Minlen* is a user-defined value. Otherwise, it is called a short transaction/itemset/pattern. Likewise, we define a **high-utility itemset** as the itemset with a utility value higher than a user-specified threshold, i.e., *minutil*. If an itemset is a high-utility itemset, we say the itemset is high, otherwise, the itemset is low. The goal of utility-based ARM is to find all high-utility itemsets. We also define a **long high-utility itemset** as the high-utility itemset with more than *minlen* items.

A local (long) high-utility itemset is a (long) itemset in partition p_i with partition utility value higher than the **local utility threshold** *minutil*/N, N is the partition number. A (long) high-utility itemset is also called a global (long) high-utility itemset.

INTER-TRANSACTION ALGORITHM

This section describes Inter-transaction algorithm. As we know, each itemset is determined either by a transaction or by a group of transactions listed in a *tidlist*. If we let any two transactions intersect each other ($|tidlist|=2$), we can obtain all itemsets (2-intersection transaction) with support no less than two. Likewise, we can obtain all itemsets (k-intersection transaction) with support no less than k by intersecting any k transactions ($|tidlist|=k$, $1 \leq k \leq n$, n is the number of transactions). Theoretically, by intersecting transactions, we can obtain all itemsets along with corresponding supports and utility values. Like CARPENTER, Inter-transaction is based on row enumeration.

Partition Method

This subsection presents the necessity and correctness of partition method. Suppose n is the number of transactions, there will be 2^n combinations of transactions at the worst situation. As the number of rows grows, the explosive growth of the combination of rows causes the performance of row-enumeration methods decrease dramatically. In a real database, n can easily reach to several millions, and enumerating all the 2^n intersection transactions is not feasible. To solve the problem, Inter-transaction adopts a partition method to divide a database into multiple partitions, with each partition containing a fitting number of transactions. In the first scan of a database, Inter-transaction finds all local long high-utility itemsets from every partition, and then these local long high-utility itemsets are merged to generate a set of potential long high-utility itemsets. In the second scan of the database, the actual utility and support for these itemsets are computed and global high-utility itemsets are identified. The whole process is just like the one described in (Savasere et al., 1995). The correctness of the partition method is guaranteed by Theorem 1:

Theorem 1. *Suppose T is a transaction database,* $P = \{P_1, P_2, ..., P_N\}$ *is a set of partitions of*

$$T \left(\bigcup_{i=1}^{N} P_i = T, P_u \cap P_v = \varphi, u \neq v \right).$$

If $X \subseteq I$ is a high-utility itemset, it will appear as a local high-utility itemset in at least one of the partitions.

Proof. *Let X be a high-utility itemset, then $u(X) \geq minutil$. Divide database T into N partitions, then X may fall into M partitions $(1 \leq M \leq N)$. Assume $B = Max [u(X, P_i)]$ denotes the biggest partition utility value of X in all partitions, By definition 4, we have:*

$$u(X) = \sum_{X \subseteq T_q \wedge T_q \in P_i \wedge P_i \subseteq T} u(X, P_i) \leq MB \tag{4}$$

If $B \leq minutil/N$, then $u(X) \leq M*minutil/N \leq minutil$. This is a contradiction. □

Let u be total utility value, and coefficient a be the minimum acceptable ratio of the utility value of an itemset to the total utility value in the database. That is to say, $minutil = \alpha * u$. Suppose we divide the database T into N partitions, the local utility threshold $(minutil/N = a*u/N)$ should be far larger than the average transaction utility (u/n), denoted as $a*u/N >> u/n$. Otherwise, a large number of local high-utility itemsets would be generated. Let S be the size of partitions, we have:

$$S = n/N >> 1/a \tag{5}$$

Inequation (5) contradicts the goal of the partition method (reducing the number of transactions in a partition). Experiments (in Figure 8) show that it is applicable for S to be between $5/a$ and $10/a$ in the context of our datasets.

Task Decomposing

This subsection explains why we decompose the mining task. If the partition number is N, the average size of partitions will be n/N (a positive integer), and the total number of potential intersec-

tion transactions becomes $N2^{n/N}$. When n is too large, enumerating $N2^{n/N}$ intersection transactions is still not feasible. The partition method is insufficient in reducing the search space.

Given a proper length threshold *minlen*, most of the patterns in a database belong to the category of short itemsets. In other words, long patterns are relatively "sparse" compared with short patterns. Although the number of long patterns is usually much smaller than that of short patterns, it is usually true for these long patterns to cost most of the resources in finding all high-utility (or frequent) itemsets when a down-top method is adopted, since a long pattern always means a lot of short patterns have to be handled ahead. On the other hand, there are few common items between or among long transactions, which means the intersection of multiple long transactions, i.e., intersection transaction is usually very short. By intersecting transactions, we can obtain long itemsets directly, without extending short itemsets step by step. On the contrary, short itemsets are relatively dense; the overhead of enumerating all short intersection transactions is too high. Based on the different features, it is reasonable for us to decompose the mining task into two subtasks (discovering long patterns and short patterns), so that we can choose proper algorithms to solve them separately.

In the process of identifying long high-utility itemsets, we can filter out all short (intersection) transactions. The rationale behind this method is that short transactions have no effect on the support or utility of long patterns/itemsets, and the intersection of a short transaction with another transaction must be short. Now that the intersection of two long transactions is usually very short, a large number of intersection transactions can be pruned out in time.

The Algorithm

The subsection describes the Inter-transaction algorithm. Based on above discussions, the new algorithm can be described in Figure 1.

Figure 1. The inter-transaction algorithm

Name: Inter-transaction
Input: A database *T*, *minutil*, *minlen*
Output: All long high-utility itemsets.
1.   Divide *T* into *N* equal partitions;   //*N*=number of partitions
2.   For (*i*=1; ι≤*N*, *i*++) {
3.   Read in partition P_i ;
4.   Call subroutine Gen-LHU-Itemsets to obtain all local long high-utility
            itemsets in P_i, generating a set of potential long high-utility itemsets
            C^G;
5.   }
6.   For (*i*=1; ι≤*N*, *i*++) {
7.   Read in partition P_i ; // second scan of the data
8.   For each candidate $c \in C^G$, compute the utility of *c* in terms of equation
            (3), along with its support;
9.   }
10.   If itemset *c* is high, output its utility and support.

The algorithm is very similar to the partition algorithm (Savasere et al., 1995), but there are two important differences between them. One is that in the partition algorithm, the size of partitions is chosen in terms of the main memory size, such that at least those itemsets and other information that is used for generating candidates can fit in the main memory, whereas Inter-transaction seeks balance between keeping a higher local utility threshold and reducing the number of transactions in a partition: given transaction number *n* and *minutil*, if partition number *N* is small, the local utility threshold (*minutil*/*N*) will be large (we hope so), but the number of transactions in a partition (*n* /*N*) will also be large (we want to avoid), and vice versa. The other difference is that in the partition algorithm a certain algorithm such as Apriori is used to generate local frequent itemsets of all length, whereas Inter-transaction discovers only local long high-utility itemsets via enumerating intersection transactions.

In order to compute the current support and current utility of an intersection transaction, a *tidlist* is used to record which transactions are involved in the intersection transaction. If $T_{tidlist}$. *tidlist* represents the transaction identifier list associated with $T_{tidlist}$, let *tidlist*= *tidlist1*∪*tidlist2* *(tidlist1≠tidlist2)*, according to relevant definitions, we have:

$$T_{tidlist} = T_{tidlist1} \cup {}_{tidlist2}$$
$$= T_{tidlist1} \cap T_{tidlist2} \tag{6}$$

$$T_{tidlist}.\, tidlist = tidlist$$
$$= tidlist1 \cup tidlist2 \tag{7}$$

$$s(T_{tidlist}, P_{tidlist}) = |T_{tidlist}.\, tidlist|$$
$$= |tidlist1 \cup tidlist2| \tag{8}$$

$$u(T_{tidlist}, P_{tidlist}) = \sum_{T_q \in P_{tidlist} \wedge T_{tidlist} \subseteq T_q} u(T_{tidlist}, T_q)$$
$$= \sum_{T_q \in P_{tidlist}} (u\ T_{tidlist}, T_q) \tag{9}$$

In equation (9), the condition $T_{tidlist} \subseteq T_q$ is always met in partition $P_{tidlist}$. If *X* is a sub-itemset of $T_{tidlist}$ ($X \subseteq T_{tidlist}$), we can use equation (10) to compute the current utility of *X* under the current *tidlist*:

$$u(X, P_{tidlist}) = \sum_{T_q \in P_{tidlist} \wedge X \subseteq T_q} u(X, T_q)$$
$$= \sum_{T_q \in P_{tidlist}} u(X, T_q) \tag{10}$$

Both equation (9) and equation (10) stem from equation (2). When the number of transactions in $P_{tidlist}$ is one, i.e., $|P_{tidlist}|$=1, $T_{tidlist}$ denotes an individual transaction, and equation (1) can be regarded as a special form of equation (10). Likewise, when $|P_{tidlist}|$=n, i.e., $P_{tidlist}$=*T*, equation (3) is

Figure 2. The Gen-LHU-itemsets subroutine

Name: Gen-LHU-Itemsets
Input: A partition P_i, *minutil*, *minlen*
Output: All local long high-utility itemsets in P_i
1. Take a partition P_i and calculate the current utility of each long (intersection) transaction $T_{tidlist}$ ($T_{tidlist}$ can also be an individual transaction, i.e., $|P_{tidlist}|=1$) independently according to equation (10). If $u(T_{tidlist}, P_{tidlist}) \geq minutil/N$, put $T_{tidlist}$ into the set of potential long high-utility itemsets: $C^G = C^G \cup T_{tidlist}$, and then call subroutine Mine-Single-Trans to identify all local long high-utility itemsets that $T_{tidlist}$ contains;
2. Perform all the intersections of any two long (intersection) transactions;
3. If the number of long (intersection) transactions is not larger than one, the subroutine ends;
4. Filter out all the short intersection transactions;
5. Check all the long intersection transactions. If $T_{tidlist1} = T_{tidlist2}$, merge the repetitious intersection transactions into a single one, i.e., $T_{tidlist}$ such that $T_{tidlist} = T_{tidlist1} = T_{tidlist2}$, $tidlist = tidlist1 \cup tidlist2$. All the long intersection transactions can form a new partition, go to step 1;

Figure 3. The mine-single-trans subroutine

Name: Mine-Single-Trans
Input: $T_{tidlist}$, *minutil*, *minlen*   // $T_{tidlist}$ can also be an individual transaction
Output: All local long high-utility itemsets in $T_{tidlist}$
Method:
1. Sort the (intersection) transaction $T_{tidlist}$ decreasingly by its utility value: $T_{tidlist} = t_0 t_1 t_2 \dots, t_{k-1} t_k \dots t_{L-1}$, such that $u(t_i, P_{tidlist}) \geq u(t_j, P_{tidlist})(i \leq j)$;
2. For ($k=L-1$; $k \geq minlen$; $k--$) {   // L is the length of $T_{tidlist}$
3.   Select the top left k items to build a k-itemset X, i.e., $X = t_0 t_1 t_2 \dots t_{k-1}$. The utility of X is the largest among all k-itemsets. Compute $u(X, P_{tidlist})$ in terms of equation (10), if $u(X, P_{tidlist}) \geq minutil/N$, add X into C^G, go to next step. Otherwise, the subroutine ends;
4.   For ($j=1$; $j \leq k$; $j++$) {
5.   For ($r=k$; $r \leq L-1$; $r++$) {
6.   Replace t_{k-j} $(1 \leq j \leq k)$ in X with t_r, obtaining $X' = t_0 t_1, \dots, t_{k-j-1} t_{k-j+1} \dots t_{k-2} t_{k-1} t_r$. If X' is high, add X' into C^G, otherwise, exit the loop;
7.   }
8.   For any $j \in [1, k]$, if $X' = t_0 t_1 t_2, \dots, t_{k-j-1} t_{k-j+1} \dots t_{k-2} t_{k-1} t_k$ (replacing t_{k-j} with t_k) is low, stop building and testing all k-itemsets that $T_{tidlist}$ contains;
9.   }
10. }

also a special form of equation (2). For simplicity, in later sections of the paper, we use equation (10) to compute the current utility of an itemset.

Gen-LHU-Itemsets is responsible for generating all local long high-utility itemsets in a partition. To achieve the goal, the subroutine computes the intersection of any two long (intersection) transactions, and then decides whether to call subroutine Mine-Single-Trans to mine every long intersection transaction obtained. The process is repeated until no long intersection transaction is generated. This method guarantees that all the maximal *tidlist*s of all long intersection transactions can be discovered and finally all local long high-utility itemsets in the partition can be identified. Since the intersection of two transactions is not longer than any of the two transactions, the method has a good convergence. Gen-LHU-Itemsets can be described in Figure 2.

Subroutine Mine-Single-Trans (described in Figure 3) tries to discover all local long high-utility itemsets that an intersection transaction $T_{tidlist}$ contains. First, the subroutine chooses a sorting algorithm to sort the items in descending order by utility values so that we can build multiple monotone decreasing sequences of itemsets. Then, in each monotone decreasing sequence, we build and test long high-utility itemsets by utility values from top to bottom. In this way, a large number of low-utility itemsets can be pruned off.

By replacing t_{k-j} with t_r, we can obtain a monotone decreasing sequence of k-itemsets (from step

5 to step 7). For example, if $j=1$, by replacing t_{k-1} with t_k, t_{k+1}, ..., t_{L-1} respectively, we can obtain following monotone decreasing sequence of k-itemsets:

$$t_0 t_1 t_2 \dots t_{k-2} t_k;$$
$$t_0 t_1 t_2 \dots t_{k-2} t_{k+1};$$
$$t_0 t_1 t_2 \dots t_{k-2} t_{k+2};$$
$$\dots$$
$$t_0 t_1 t_2 \dots t_{k-2} t_{L-1}.$$

Obviously, $u(t_0 t_1 t_2 \dots t_{k-2} t_{k+u}, T_{tidlist}) \geq u(t_0 t_1 t_2 \dots t_{k-2} t_{k+v}, T_{tidlist})$ $(u \leq v)$. When j varies from one to k, multiple monotone decreasing sequences can be generated (step 4 to step 9). For example, let $j=2$, by replacing t_{k-2} with t_k, t_{k+1}, ..., t_{L-1} respectively, we can obtain another monotone decreasing sequence:

$$t_0 t_1 t_2 \dots t_{k-3} t_{k-1} t_k;$$
$$t_0 t_1 t_2 \dots t_{k-3} t_{k-1} t_{k+1};$$
$$t_0 t_1 t_2 \dots t_{k-3} t_{k-1} t_{k+2};$$
$$\dots$$
$$t_0 t_1 t_2 \dots t_{k-3} t_{k-1} t_{L-1}.$$

In subroutine Mine-Single-Trans, the following pruning strategies are used:

Strategy 1: if no k-itemset is high, all (k-j)-itemsets must be low and thus can be pruned off ($1 \leq j \leq k$), subroutine ends (step 3).

Strategy 2: in each monotone decreasing sequence, if a certain k-itemset is low, subsequent k-itemsets in the same monotone decreasing sequence must be low (step 6).

Strategy 3: if $X' = t_0 t_1 t_2, \dots, t_{k-j-1} t_{k-j+1} \dots t_{k-2} t_{k-1} t_k$ is low, all the k-itemsets in subsequent monotone decreasing sequences must be low (step 8).

In a monotone decreasing sequence, strategy 2 is easy to understand. To understand strategy 3, consider $X'' = t_0 t_1 t_2, \dots, t_{k-i-1} t_{k-i+1} \dots t_{k-2} t_{k-1} t_k$, which is obtained by replacing t_{k-i} with t_k, the first (and thus the largest) one in a monotone decreasing sequence. When $i > j$, $u(X') \geq u(X'')$. So if X' is low, X'' must be low. For strategy 1, we have following theorem:

Theorem 2. (Current Utility Upward Closure Property) *Given an intersection transaction $T_{tidlist}$, if an itemset $X \subseteq T_{tidlist}$ is high, all superset of X must be high. In other words, under the same current support, if an itemset is low, all its subsets must be low.*

Proof. *Suppose I' and I'' are two itemset, satisfying $I' \subset I'' \subseteq T_{tidlist}$. All the transactions listed in tidlist form a partition $P_{tidlist}$, and every transaction in $P_{tidlist}$ contains both I' and I''. That's to say, I' and I'' have the same current support. Suppose the current support is r, let $I'' = I' + X$ ($X \neq \phi$), and tidlist $= \{1, 2, \dots, r\}$, by definition 3, we have:*

$$u(I', P_{tidlist}) = \sum_{T_q \in P_{tidlist} \wedge I' \subseteq T_q} u(I', T_q) \left(= \sum_{q=1}^{r} u\ I', T_q \right)$$

Likewise, we have

$$u(I'', P_{tidlist}) = \sum_{T_q \in P_{tidlist} \wedge I' \subseteq T_q} u(I'', T_q) = \sum_{q=1}^{r} u(I'', T_q)$$

$$= \sum_{q=1}^{r} u((I' + X), T_q) = \sum_{q=1}^{r} u(I', T_q) + \sum_{q=1}^{r} u(X, T_q)$$

Since $\sum_{q=1}^{r} u(X, T_q) > 0$, then we have:

$$u(I'', P_{tidlist}) > u(I', P_{tidlist}).$$

So if I' is high, I'' must be high. □

The following example can show how the subroutine works. Suppose there are three transactions T_1, T_3, and T_7, their intersection is equal to $ABCDEF$, i.e., $T_{\{1,3,7\}} = ABCDEF$, and the corresponding utility values can be seen in Table 2.

After sorting, $T_{\{1,3,7\}}$ can be expressed as $ACBEFD$, with item utility values decreasing gradually. Here the length of $T_{\{1,3,7\}}$ is six, i.e., $L=6$. If $minutil=18$, $minlen=3$, itemsets will be examined in the order shown in Table 3.

Four-itemsets $ACBE$, $ACBF$ and $ACBD$ are in the same monotone decreasing sequence, which can be generated by replacing E of $ACBE$ with F

Table 2. Three transactions and the utility value of each item

	A	B	C	D	E	F
T_1	2	1	1	0.3	1	0.5
T_3	3	1	2	0.3	1	0.5
T_7	1	2	2	0.4	1	1
Partition utility	6	4	5	1	3	2

and *D* respectively. Since *ACBF* is low, there is no need to build and test *ACBD*.

Although sorting an (intersection) transaction is costly, according to step 1 of subroutine Gen-LHU-Itemsets, only a small number of (intersection) transactions need to call the subroutine Mine-Single-Trans. So this method will not cause high computational cost.

OPTIMIZATION TECHNIQUE

Generally, a database can usually be implemented in HIV, HIL, VTV and VTL format (Shenoy, Haritsa, Sundarshan, Bhalotia, Bawa, & Shah 2000; Zaki & Gouda, 2003). If we express each transaction in HIV format, an intersection transaction can be obtained from the intersection of bit-vectors. Although the bitwise logical (And) operation is well supported by computer hardware and very efficient, the overall performance

of the intersection of two transactions decreases dramatically with the increase of the number of items. For example, if the number of items is eight kilos, we have to use one kilo bytes (8K bits) to express each transaction. In order to perform the intersection of two transactions, eight kilo bit operations are needed and this is not acceptable.

Some optimization techniques such as run-length encoding (RLE), VIPER (Shenoy et al., 2000) and DIFFSET (Zaki & Gouda, 2003) have been proposed to enhance the performance of the intersection of two bit-vectors in vertical mining algorithms. These existing optimizations adopt various compressed formats to store databases. Since data compressing and uncompressing is costly, these methods have limited effect on increasing the speed of the intersection of long bit-vectors. So in our algorithm, we not only refrain from compressing each row in main memory, but also use redundant information to reduce the number of bitwise logical operations.

Besides the HIV format, we also store each transaction in HIL format. Although this method wastes lots of memory, the cost is affordable because the partition method can save lots of memory (every time we read only a partition into a continuous memory address space). HIV format is used to perform the intersection of bit-vectors, while HIL format is used to store redundant information which guide us to choose only necessary bits in a bit-vector to perform bitwise logical

Table 3. The process of calculating utility values of itemsets

Itemset Utility	Results	Comments
$u(ACBEF, P_{(1,3,7)})= 20$	*ACBEF* is high	The largest 5-itemset consisting of the top left 5-items
$u(ACBED, P_{(1,3,7)})= 19$	*ACBED* is high	obtained by replacing *F* of *ACBEF* with *D*
$u(ACBFD, P_{(1,3,7)})= 18$	*ACBFD* is high	obtained by replacing *E* of *ACBEF* with *D*
$u(ACEFD, P_{(1,3,7)})= 17$	stop finding 5-itemsets	obtained by replacing *B* of *ACBEF* with *D*
$u(ACBE, P_{(1,3,7)}) =18$	*ACBE* is high	The largest 4-itemset consisting of the top left 4-items
$u(ACBF, P_{(1,3,7)}) =17$	stop finding 4-itemsets	obtained by replacing *E* of *ACBE* with *F*
$u(ACB, P_{(1,3,7)}) =15$	Algorithm end	The largest 3-itemset consisting of the top left 3-items

Table 4. Three transactions and the process of computing $T_{\{1,2,3\}}$

	HIV format	HIL format
T_1	1011,0000,1100,001	1,3,4,9,10,15
T_2	*1*000,0000,0000,0*11*	1,14,15
$T_{\{1,2\}}$	*1*000,0000,0000,00*1*	1,15
T_3	1011,1100,0001,001	1,3,4,5,6,12,15
$T_{\{1,2,3\}}$	1000,0000,0000,001	1,15

(And) operation. If the length of transaction T_1 in HIL format is longer than that of T_2, we choose T_2 (the shorter transaction) as the benchmark to determine on what bits the bitwise logical operation should be performed: if the k-th bit in T_2 is one, "And" operation should be performed on the k-th bit, and the other bits should be set zero directly in the result.

For example, there are three transactions T_1, T_2 and T_3, and the corresponding data can be seen in Table 4. If we want to compute $T_{\{1,2,3\}}$, we can firstly compute $T_{\{1,2\}}$ by intersecting T_1 with T_2, and then we compute $T_{\{1,2,3\}}$ by intersecting $T_{\{1,2\}}$ with T_3. In step one, we choose the shorter transaction T_2 as the benchmark and decide bitwise logical (And) operation should be performed only on the first bit, the fourteenth bit and the fifteenth bit (written in bold Italic in Table 4), other bits should be set at zero. As an intermediate result, we obtain $T_{\{1,2\}}=\{1,15\}$ (in HIL format). In step two, we choose $T_{\{1,2\}}$ as the benchmark and decide that bitwise logical (And) operation should be performed only on the first bit and the last bit. We get the final result $T_{\{1,2,3\}}= \{1,15\}$. As shown in Table 4, only five bit operations are needed for the whole process.

In this way, the number of bit operations linearly depends only on the length of the short transaction in HIL format. Experiment shows this optimization technique is a key to the success of Inter-transaction.

EXPERIMENTAL RESULTS

All the experiments were performed on a 2GHz Legend server with 4GB of memory, running windows 2003. The program was coded in Delphi 7.

Seven datasets were used in our experiments; all were generated by IBM quest data generator (retrieved from the web May 10, 2007. http://www.almaden.ibm.com/cs/projects/ iis/hdb/Projects/data_mining/datasets/syndata.html). Six of them are T40.I30.D8000K with 0.5K, 1K, 2K, 4K, 8K and 16K items respectively, the seventh is T20.I6.D8000K with 4K items, where T# stands for the average length of transactions, I# for the average length of maximal potentially large itemsets and D# for the number of transactions. Because the generator only generates the quantity of zero or one for each item in a transaction, we use Delphi function "RandG" to generate random numbers with Gaussian distribution, which mimic the quantity sold of an item in each transaction. The unit profit of each item is defined as item ID%100, where % is a modulus operator. The utility threshold *minutil* is defined as the minimum acceptable ratio of the utility value of an itemset to the total utility value in the database.

Figure 4 presents the scalability of Inter-transaction by increasing the number of transactions from 0.25M (million) to 8M. Experimental results show that our algorithm scales linearly with the number of transactions.

Figure 5 shows the performance when the number of items varies. Different from other algorithms, the performance of Inter-transaction improves as the number of items increases. The reason is that the number of items is directly related to the sparseness of a dataset. The more items there are, the sparser the dataset is, and the shorter the intersection of two transactions may be. That means Inter-transaction can enumerate all long intersection transactions easily in a sparse dataset. From Figure 5 we can observe that Inter-transaction is suitable for those datasets with more than one kilo (1K) items.

Figure 4. Scalability with the number of transactions

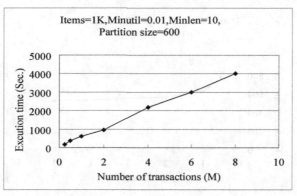

Figure 5. Scalability with the number of items

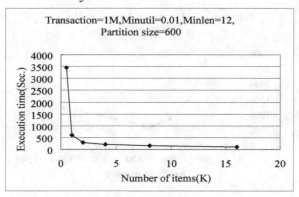

Figure 6. The effect of the number of items on minlen

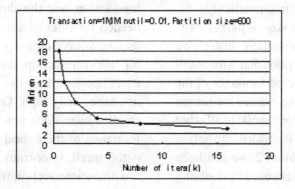

In Figure 6, *minlen* (a positive integer) is the minimum length of itemsets that the Inter-transaction can discover within a reasonable time (within 2 hours). It actually determines the task assigned to Inter-transaction. Figure 6 shows that *minlen* decreases as the number of items increases,

which means Inter-transaction can complete more mining tasks in a sparse database. The reason is just the same as mentioned above.

Figure 7 shows the execution time of Inter-transaction when the utility threshold varies. Since the number of candidate itemsets decreases

Figure 7. Scalability with utility threshold

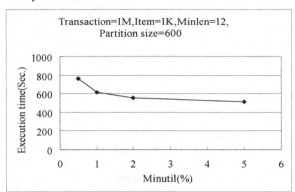

Figure 8. The effect of size of partitions on performance

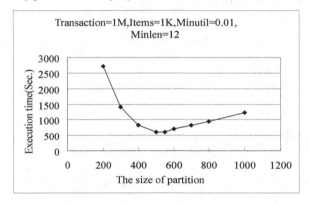

as the minimum utility threshold increases, the execution time decreases, correspondingly.

Figure 8 shows that the size of partitions is very important to Inter-transaction. Just as we have mentioned above, a partition that is too small or too large will degrade the performance of the algorithm. From Figure 8, we can see the reason why we set the size of partitions to 600 in all other experiments. When *minutil* is divided into half of the initial value, that is, *minutil*/2, we can keep the local utility threshold unchanged by doubling the size of partitions. In this way, large amounts of candidate itemsets can be avoided. This is why our method can work well under a small *minutil*.

Figure 9 shows the effect of *minlen* on the performance of Inter-transaction. As we have mentioned, *minlen* actually assigns mining tasks between Inter-transaction and its cooperator, such as Umining or Two-phase. The larger the

minlen, the fewer the tasks assigned to Inter-transaction, and the shorter the execution time needed for Inter-transaction. Although a larger *minlen* always means a shorter execution time for Inter-transaction, more tasks will be left for its cooperator, and the overall performance is not necessarily high. On the other hand, a too small *minlen* does not benefit the overall performance of the hybrid model either. If *minlen* is too small, Inter-transaction has to enumerate too many intersection transactions, the running time increases dramatically. So a proper *minlen* is a key parameter for the hybrid model. Figure 6 indicates that we should choose different *minlen* in terms of the number of items.

To test the total performance of the hybrid model, we choose Two-phase to mine short high-utility itemsets, then compare the performance of the hybrid method (here hybrid method

Figure 9. The effect of minlen on performance

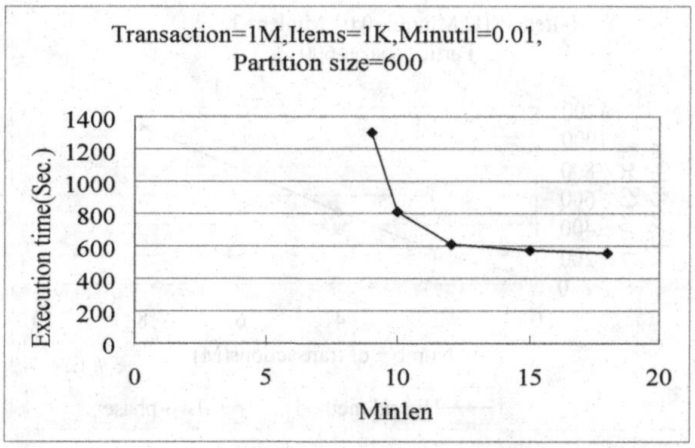

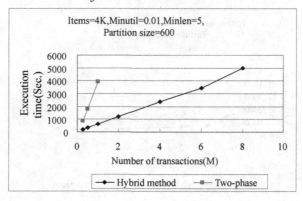

Figure 10. Scalability with the number of transactions on T40I30D8000

means Inter-transaction + Two-phase) with that of Two-phase. That is, the total running time of the hybrid method is equal to the running time of Inter-transaction (used to find long high-utility itemsets) plus the running time of Two-phase (used to find short high-utility itemsets). The reason for choosing Two-phase is that we are certain that it is the best approach for utility mining by now. Experiments were performed on T20I6D8000K and T40I30D8000K, with one kilo and four kilo items, respectively. *Minlen* is set three for T20I6D8000K and five for T40I30D8000K, corresponding performance curves are illustrated in Figures 10, 11, 12 and 13.

From Figures 10 and 11 we can observe that the hybrid model does not suit datasets with only short patterns. The reason is that Inter-transaction can not take obvious effect on these datasets. As for those datasets with lots of long patterns or

high dimensions, Two-phase has to extend short itemsets step by step to obtain long itemsets, while Inter-transaction can obtain long itemsets directly by intersecting relevant transactions. In this situation, the hybrid method has great advantages over the Two-phase algorithm. Figures 12 and 13 show the hybrid method is not sensitive to utility threshold *minutil*. With *minutil* growing down, the performance of Two-phase decreases rapidly. When *minutil* is less than 0.25, our hybrid method outperform Two-phase even on the datasets with only short patterns.

CONCLUSION

The paper proposes a hybrid model to discover high-utility itemsets from two directions. The intention of the hybrid model is to decompose

Figure 11. Scalability with the number of transactions on T20I6D8000

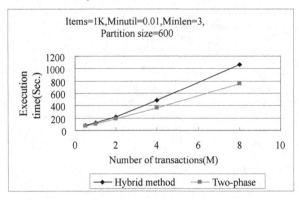

Figure 12. Scalability with utility threshold on T40I30D8000

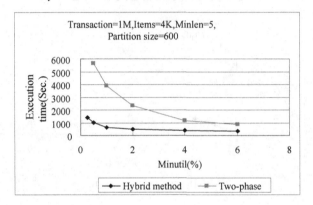

Figure 13. Scalability with utility threshold on T20I6D8000

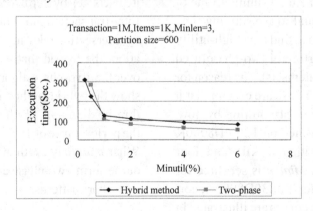

a complex problem into two easy subtasks, and then use proper methods to solve them separately.

By integrating the advantages of the partition algorithm and row enumeration algorithms, Inter-transaction can handle large high-dimensional databases efficiently. It scans a database at most twice, and is ideally suited for parallelization. Since inter-transaction is based on the sparseness of long patterns, its performance is affected by the characteristics of the database, including data skew and the number of items. Parameters such as minimum length threshold *minlen* and the size of partitions also affect its performance. In our next plan, we will make an intensive study of how to choose minimum length threshold *minlen* to achieve the best performance for the hybrid model.

REFERENCES

Agarwal, R. C., Aggarwal, C. C., & Prasad, V.V.V. (2000). A tree projection algorithm for generation of frequent itemsets, *Journal of Parallel and Distributed Computing*, 61(3), 350-371.

Aumann, Y., & Lindell, Y. (2003). A Statistical Theory for Quantitative Association Rules. *Journal of Intelligent Information Systems*, 20(3), 255–283

Barber, B., & Hamilton, H. J. (2003). Extracting Share Frequent Itemsets with Infrequent Subsets. *Data Mining and Knowledge Discovery*, 7, 153-185.

Cai, C. H., Fu, A. W. C., Cheng, C. H., & Kong, W.W. (1998). Mining Association Rules with Weighted Items. *Proceedings of the International Database Engineering and Applications Symposium*. Cardiff, UK, (pp. 68-77).

Chan, R., Yang, Q., & Shen, Y. D. (2003). Mining high utility itemsets. *Proceedings of the 3rd IEEE International Conference on Data Mining*, (pp. 19-26).

Feng, L., Li, Q., & Wong, A. (2001). Mining Inter-Transactional Association Rules: Generalization and Empirical Evaluation. *Proc. of the 3rd International Conference on Data Warehousing and Knowledge Discovery*, Lecture Notes in Computer Science, Germany, (pp. 31-40).

Feng, L., Yu, J. X., Lu, H. J., & Han, J. W. (2002). A Template Model for Multidimensional Inter-Transactional Association Rules. *International Journal of Very Large Data Bases*, 11(2), 153-175.

Han, J. W., Pei, J., Yin, Y., & Mao, R. (2004). Mining Frequent Patterns without Candidate Generation: A Frequent pattern Tree Approach, *Data Mining and Knowledge Discovery*, 8 (1), 53-87.

Lin, T. Y., Yao, Y. Y., & Louie, E. (2002). Mining Value Added Association rules. *Proceedings of PAKDD*, (pp. 328-333)

Liu, H., Feng, L., & Han, J. (2000). Beyond intra-transactional association analysis: Mining multi-dimensional inter-transaction association rules. *ACM Transactions on Information Systems*, 18(4), 423-454.

Liu, Y., Liao, W. K., & Choudhary, A. (2005). A fast high-utility itemsets mining algorithm. *Proceedings of the First International Workshop on Utility-based Data Mining*. Chicago, Illinois, (pp. 90-99).

Lu, S. F., Hu, H. P., & Li, F. (2001). Mining weighted association rules. *Intelligent Data Analysis*, 5(3), 211-225. IOS Press.

Ngan, S. C., Lam, T., Wong, R. C. W., & Fu, A. W.C. (2005). Mining N-most interesting itemsets without support threshold by the COFI-tree. *Journal of Business Intelligence and Data Mining*, 1, 88-106

Pang, F., Cong, G., Tung, A., Yang, J., & Zaki, M. (2003). Carpenter: Finding closed patterns in long biological datasets. *Proceedings of the SIGKDD'03*. (pp. 637-642).

Savasere, A., Omiecinsky, E. & Navathe, S. (1995). An efficient algorithm for mining association rules in large databases. *Proceedings of 21st Int'l Conf. on Very Large Databases.* Zurich, Switzerland, (pp. 432-444).

Shen, Y. D., Zhang, Z., & Yang, Q. (2002). Objective-oriented utility-based association mining. *Proceedings of the 2002 IEEE International Conference on Data Mining.* Maebashi City, Japan, (pp. 426-433).

Shenoy, P., Haritsa, J. R., Sundarshan, S., Bhalotia, G., Bawa, M., & Shah, D. (2000). Turbo-charging Vertical Mining of Large Databases. *Proceedings of ACM SIGMOD International Conference on Management of Data.* Dallas, Texas, (pp. 22-33).

Tjioe, H.C., & Taniar, D. (2005). Mining association rules in data warehouses. *Journal of Data Warehousing and Mining,* 1(3), 28-62.

Vroom, V. H. (1964). *Work and Motivation.* New York, John Wiley & Sons.

Wang, K., Zhou, S., & Han, J. (2002). Profit mining: from patterns to action. *Proceedings of International Conference on Extending Database Technology.* (pp. 70-87).

Webb, G. I. (2001). Discovering associations with numeric variables. *Proceedings of the Seventh ACM SIGKDD International Conference on Knowledge Discovery and Data Mining.* San Francisco, California, (pp. 383-388).

Yao, H., Hamilton, H. J., & Geng, L. (2006). A Unified Framework for Utility Based Measures for Mining Itemsets. *Proceedings of the 2006 International Workshop on Utility-Based Data Mining.* Philadelphia, USA, (pp. 28-37).

Yao, H., & Hamilton, H. J. (2006). Mining itemset utilities from transaction databases. *Data & Knowledge Engineering,* 59, 603 – 626.

Zaki, M. J., & Gouda, K. (2003). Fast vertical mining using diffsets. In *Proc. of ACM SIGKDD.* Washington DC, (pp. 326-335).

This work was previously published in the International Journal of Data Warehousing & Mining 5(1), edited by David Taniar, pp. 57-73, copyright 2009 by IGI Publishing (an imprint of IGI Global).

Section 2

Chapter 5
Multidimensional Design Methods for Data Warehousing

Oscar Romero
Universitat Politècnica de Catalunya, Spain

Alberto Abelló
Universitat Politècnica de Catalunya, Spain

ABSTRACT

In the last years, data warehousing systems have gained relevance to support decision making within organizations. The core component of these systems is the data warehouse and nowadays it is widely assumed that the data warehouse design must follow the multidimensional paradigm. Thus, many methods have been presented to support the multidimensional design of the data warehouse. The first methods introduced were requirement-driven but the semantics of the data warehouse (since the data warehouse is the result of homogenizing and integrating relevant data of the organization in a single, detailed view of the organization business) require to also consider the data sources during the design process. Considering the data sources gave rise to several data-driven methods that automate the data warehouse design process, mainly, from relational data sources. Currently, research on multidimensional modeling is still a hot topic and we have two main research lines. On the one hand, new hybrid automatic methods have been introduced proposing to combine data-driven and requirement-driven approaches. These methods focus on automating the whole process and improving the feedback retrieved by each approach to produce better results. On the other hand, some new approaches focus on considering alternative scenarios than relational sources. These methods also consider (semi)-structured data sources, such as ontologies or XML, that have gained relevance in the last years. Thus, they introduce innovative solutions for overcoming the heterogeneity of the data sources. All in all, we discuss the current scenario of multidimensional modeling by carrying out a survey of multidimensional design methods. We present the most relevant methods introduced in the literature and a detailed comparison showing the main features of each approach.

DOI: 10.4018/978-1-60960-537-7.ch005

INTRODUCTION

Data warehousing systems were conceived to support decision making within organizations. These systems homogenize and integrate data of organizations in a huge repository of data (the data warehouse) in order to exploit this single and detailed representation of the organization and extract relevant knowledge for the organization decision making. The data warehouse is a huge repository of data that does not tell us much by itself; like in the operational databases, we need auxiliary tools to query and analyze data stored. Without the appropriate exploitation tools, we will not be able to extract valuable knowledge of the organization from the data warehouse, and the whole system will fail in its aim of providing information for giving support to decision making. OLAP (On-line Analytical Processing) tools were introduced to ease information analysis and navigation all through the data warehouse in order to extract relevant knowledge of the organization. This term was coined by E.F. Codd in (Codd, 1993), but it was more precisely defined by means of the FASMI test that stands for *fast analysis* of *shared* business *information* from a *multidimensional* point of view. This last feature is the most important one since OLAP tools are conceived to exploit the data warehouse for analysis tasks based on *multidimensionality*.

The multidimensional conceptual view of data is distinguished by the *fact / dimension* dichotomy, and it is characterized by representing data as if placed in an n-dimensional space, allowing us to easily understand and analyze data in terms of facts (the subjects of analysis) and dimensions showing the different points of view where a subject can be analyzed from. One fact and several dimensions to analyze it produce what is known as *data cube*. Multidimensionality provides a friendly, easy-to-understand and intuitive visualization of data for non-expert end-users. These characteristics are desirable since OLAP tools are aimed to enable analysts, managers, executives, and in general

those people involved in decision making, to gain insight into data through fast queries and analytical tasks, allowing them to make better decisions.

Developing a data warehousing system is never an easy job, and raises up some interesting challenges. One of these challenges focus on modeling multidimensionality. Nowadays, despite we still lack a standard multidimensional model, it is widely assumed that the data warehouse design must follow the multidimensional paradigm and it must be derived from the data sources, since a data warehouse is the result of homogenizing and integrating relevant data of the organization in a single and detailed view.

Terminology and Notation

Lots of efforts have been devoted to multidimensional modeling, and several models and methods have been developed and presented in the literature to support the multidimensional design of the data warehouse. However, since we lack a standard multidimensional terminology, terms used to describe the multidimensional concepts may vary among current design methods. To avoid misunderstandings, in this section we detail a specific terminology to establish a common framework where to map and compare current multidimensional design methods.

Multidimensionality is based on the fact/dimension dichotomy. Dimensional concepts produce the multidimensional space in which the fact is placed. Dimensional concepts are those concepts likely to be used as an analytical perspective, which have traditionally been classified as dimensions, levels and descriptors. Thus, we consider that a dimension consists of a hierarchy of levels representing different granularities (or levels of detail) for studying data, and a level containing descriptors (i.e., level attributes). In contrast, a fact contains measures of analysis. One fact and several dimensions for its analysis produce a multidimensional schema. Finally, we denote by base a *minimal* set of levels functionally determining the fact. Thus, the base concept guarantees that two different instances of data cannot be placed at the same point of the multidimensional space.

For example, consider Figure 1. There, one fact (sales) containing two measures (price and discount) is depicted. This fact has four different dimensions of analysis (buyer, seller, time and item sold). Two of these dimensions have just one level of detail, whereas the other two have an aggregation hierarchy with more than one level. For example, the time dimension has three levels of detail that, in turn, contain some descriptors (for example, the holiday attribute). Finally, if we consider {item X day X buyer X seller} to be the multidimensional base of sales it would mean that a value of each of these levels identify one, and just one, instance of factual data (i.e., a specific sale and its price and discount).

A Piece of History

In this section we introduce the background of multidimensional modeling. Our objective here is to provide an insightful view of how this area evolved with time.

Multidimensional modeling as it is known today was first introduced by Kimball in (Kimball, 1996). Kimball's approach was well received by the community and a deeper and advanced view of multidimensional modeling was presented in

(Kimball et al., 1998). In these books the authors introduced the first method to derive the data warehouse logical schema. Like in most information systems, this method is requirement-driven: it starts eliciting business requirements of an organization and through a step-by-step guide we are able to derive the multidimensional schema from them. Only at the end of the process data sources are considered to map data from sources to target.

Shortly after Kimball introduced his ad hoc modeling method for data warehouses, some other methods were presented in the literature. Like Kimball's method, these methods are step-by-step guides to be followed by a data warehouse expert that start gathering the end-user requirements. However, these approaches gave more relevance to the data sources. According to the data warehouse definition, the data warehouse is the result of homogenizing and integrating relevant data of the organization (stored in the organization data sources) in a single and detailed view and consequently, data sources must be considered somehow during the design process. Involving the data sources in these approaches means that it is compulsory to have well-documented data sources (for example, with up-to-date conceptual schemas) at the expert's disposal but it also entailed two main benefits. On the one hand, the user may not know all the potential analysis contained in the data sources and analyzing them we may find unexpected potential analysis of interest for the

Figure 1. Multidimensional concepts

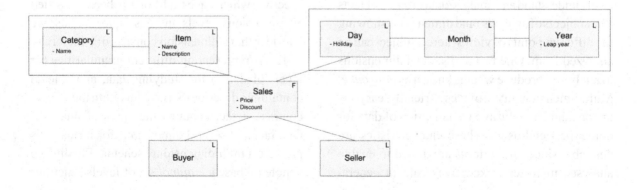

user. On the other hand, we should guarantee that the data warehouse will be able to be populated with data available within the organization.

To carry out the design task manually it is compulsory to have well-documented data sources. However, in a real organization the data sources documentation may be incomplete, incorrect or may not even exist and, in any case, it would be rather difficult for a non-expert designer to follow these guidelines. Indeed, when automating this process is essential not to depend on the expert's ability to properly apply the method chosen and to avoid the tedious and time-consuming task (even unfeasible when working over large databases) of analyzing the data sources.

In order to solve these problems several methods automating the data warehouse design were introduced in the literature. These approaches work directly over relational (i.e., logical) database schemas. Thus, despite they are restricted to relational data sources, they get up-to-date data that can be queried and managed by computers. Furthermore, they argued that restricting to relational technology made sense, since it was / is de facto standard for operational databases. About the process carried out, these methods follow a data-driven process focusing on a thorough analysis of the data sources to derive the data warehouse schema in a reengineering process. This reengineering process consists of techniques and design patterns that must be applied over the relational schema of the data sources to identify data likely to be analyzed from a multidimensional perspective.

Nevertheless, a requirement analysis phase is crucial to meet the user needs and expectations. Otherwise, the user may find himself frustrated since he / she would not be able to analyze data of his / her interest, entailing the failure of the whole system. Today, it is assumed that the ideal scenario to derive the data warehouse conceptual schema would entail a hybrid approach (i.e., a combined data-driven and requirement-driven approach). Therefore, the resulting multidimensional schema would satisfy the end-user requirements and it

would have been conciliated with the data sources simultaneously (i.e., capturing the analysis potential depicted in the data sources and being able to be populated with data within the organization).

Another interesting trend worth to remark, is the level of abstraction used for the methods' output. The first methods introduced (such as Kimball's method) produced multidimensional star schemas (i.e., logical schemas), but soon the community realized it was as important as in any other system to differentiate the conceptual and logical layer in the data warehouse design task (for example, it was obvious when MOLAP tools gained relevance regarding ROLAP ones). As result, newest approaches generate conceptual schemas and it is up to the user to implement them with any of the logical design (either relational or ad hoc multidimensional) alternatives. The fact that logical design was first addressed in data warehousing gave rise to a spread language abuse when referring to multidimensional conceptual schemas, which are also denoted as star schemas. Originally, star schemas were logical design models introduced in (Kimball et al., 1998). The reason is that multidimensional conceptual schemas also are *star-shaped* (with the fact in the center and the dimensions around it), and the star schema nomenclature was reused for conceptual design.

About the last research efforts in this area, we can identify two main addressed issues. On one hand, most recent works aim to automate the process considering both the organization data sources and the user multidimensional requirements. However, automating the requirement management is not an easy job, as it is compulsory to formalize the end-user requirements (i.e., translate them to a language understandable by computers) and nowadays, most of the current methods handle requirements stated in languages (such as natural language) lacking any kind of formalization. On the other hand, some new approaches have been introduced to automate the multidimensional design of data warehouses from other sources that have gained relevance in the last years, such as the semantic web (Berners-Lee, Hendler & Lassila, 2001). In the recent past, the multidimensional analysis of data has been restricted to the well structured information sources within the company (which mainly were relational). Nevertheless, (Inmon, Strauss & Neushloss, 2008) outlines the opportunity and importance of using unstructured and semi-structured data (either textual or not) in the decision making process. These data could still come from the sources in the company, but also from the web. Accordingly, some new approaches consider data sources based on web-related technologies such as ontologies or XML.

A COMPREHENSIVE SURVEY

This section presents an insight into current multidimensional design methods. Methods here discussed were selected according to three factors: reference papers with a high number of citations according to Google Scholar (Google, 2008) and Publish or Perish (Harzing, 2010), papers with novelty contributions and in case of papers of the same authors, we have included the latest version of their works. As general rule, each method is described using the terminology presented in the *Terminology and Notation* section. Finally, we follow a chronological order when introducing the design methods surveyed. As an exception, when a method publications span over several different papers, we place them at the chronological point occupied by their first paper but we quote them by means of the most relevant paper.

All in all, this section provides a comprehensive framework of the evolution of multidimensional design methods.

(Kimball et al., 1998) introduced multidimensional modeling as known today. In addition, they also introduced the first method to produce the multidimensional schema. Being the first approach, it does not introduce a formal design procedure, but a detailed guide of tips to identify the multidimensional concepts and then, give rise

to the multidimensional schema. The presentation is quite informal and it relies on examples rather than on formal rules. Kimball's approach follows a demand-driven framework to derive the data warehouse relational schema (i.e., logical), as follows.

First, the designer must identify all the data marts we could possibly build. Data marts are essentially defined as pragmatic collections of related facts. Although data sources are not considered, they already suggest to take a look at the data sources to find which data marts may be of our interest.

Next step aims to list all conceivable dimensions for each data mart. At this point it is suggested to build an ad hoc matrix to capture our multidimensional requirements. Rows represent the data marts, whereas columns represent the dimensions. A given cell is marked whether that dimension must be considered for a data mart.

This matrix is also used to show the associations between data marts by looking at dimensions shared. This process is supposed to be incremental. First, it is suggested to focus on single-source data marts, since it will facilitate our work and later, in a second iteration, look for multiple-sources data marts combining the single-source designs.

The method's third step designs the fact tables of each data mart:

- First, we must declare the *grain* of detail (i.e., the data granularity of interest). It is suggested to be defined by the design team at the beginning, although it can be reconsidered during the process. Normally, it must be determined by primary dimensions.
- Next, we choose the analysis dimensions for each fact table. Dimensions selected must be tested against the grain selected. This must be a creative step. We need to look for the dimension *pieces* (i.e., levels and descriptors) in different (and potentially heterogeneous) models and through different documents, which, in the end, results

in a time-consuming task. At this point, it is also suggested to choose a large number of descriptors to populate dimensions.

• Finally, the last stage adds as many measures as possible within the context of the declared grain.

(Cabibbo & Torlone, 1998) present one of the most cited multidimensional design methods. This approach generates a logical schema from *Entity-Relationship* (ER) diagrams, and it might produce multidimensional schemas in terms of relational databases or multidimensional arrays.

At first sight, this method may be thought to follow a supply-driven paradigm, as it performs an in-depth analysis of the data sources. However, no formal rules to identify the multidimensional concepts from the data sources are given. In fact, multidimensional concepts must be manually identified by the user (i.e., from requirements).

For this reason, we consider it to follow a hybrid framework. In general, like Kimball's approach, this approach is rather informal but they set up the foundations that were later used by the rest of methods.

This method consists of four steps. First and second steps aim to identify facts and dimensions and restructure the ER diagram. Both steps may be performed simultaneously and benefit from the feedback retrieved by each step. Indeed the authors suggest to perform them in an iterative way to refine results obtained. However, no clue about how to identify facts, measures and dimensions are given and they must be identified from the end-user requirements. Once identified, each fact is represented as an entity. Next, we add dimensions of interest that may be missing in the schema but could be derived from external sources or metadata associated to our data sources. At this point, it is also compulsory to refine the levels of each dimension by means of the following transformations: (i) replacing many-to-many relationships, (ii) adding new concepts to represent new levels of interest, (iii) selecting a simple

identifier for each level entity and (iv) removing irrelevant concepts. Finally, two last steps aim to derive the multidimensional schema. Some clues are given to derive a multidimensional graph that will be directly mapped into the multidimensional schema.

(Golfarelli & Rizzi, 2009) present one of the reference methods in this area. This work present a detailed view of the multidimensional design process proposed, which subsumes their previous works such as (Golfarelli, Maio & Rizzi, 1998a; Golfarelli & Rizzi, 1998b). This approach presents a formal and structured method (partially automatable) that consists of six well-defined steps. However, the fourth step aims to estimate the data warehouse workload which goes beyond the scope of this study:

• First step analyzes the underlying information system and produces a conceptual schema (i.e., a ER diagram) or a logical schema (i.e., a relational schema).

• Second step collects and filters requirements. In this step it is important to identify facts. The authors give some tips to identify them from ER diagrams (entities or n-ary relationships) or relational schemas (tables frequently updated are good candidates).

• Next step derives the multidimensional conceptual schema from requirements and facts identified in previous steps. This step may be carried out semi-automatically as follows:

  ◦ Building the attribute tree: From the primary key of the fact we create a tree by means of functional ependencies. Thus, a given node (i.e., an attribute) of the tree functionally determines its descendants.

  ◦ Pruning and grafting the attribute tree: The tree attribute must be pruned and grafted in order to eliminate unnecessary levels of detail.

○ Defining dimensions: Dimensions must be chosen in the attribute tree among the root vertices.

○ Defining measures: Measures are defined by applying aggregation functions, at root level, to numerical attributes of the tree.

○ Defining hierarchies: The attribute tree shows a plausible organization for hierarchies. Hierarchies must be derived from to-one relationships that hold between each node and its descendants.

• Finally, the last two steps derive the logical (by translating each fact and dimension into one relational table) and physical schemas (the authors give some tips regarding indexes to implement the logical schema in a ROLAP tool).

The fourth step of this method aims to estimate the workload of the data warehouse. The authors argue that this process may be used to validate the conceptual schema produced in the third step, as queries could only be expressed if measures and hierarchies have been properly defined. However, no further information is provided.

(Böehnlein & Ulbrich-vom Ende, 1999) present a hybrid approach to derive logical schemas from SER (Structured Entity Relationship) diagrams. SER is an extension of ER that visualizes existency dependencies between objects. For this reason, the authors argue that SER is a better alternative to identify multidimensional structures. This approach has three main stages:

• Pre-process: First, we must transform the ER diagram into a SER diagram. A detailed explanation is provided.

• Step 1: Business measures must be identified from goals. For example, the authors suggest to look for business events to discover interesting measures. Once business measures have been identified, they are mapped to one or more objects in the SER diagram. Eventually, these measures will give rise to facts.

• Step 2: The hierarchical structure of the SER diagrams is helpful to identify potential aggregation hierarchies. Dimensions and aggregation hierarchies are identified by means of direct and transitive functional dependencies. The authors argue that discovering dimensions is a creative task that must be complemented with a good knowledge of the application domain.

• Step 3: Finally, a star or snowflake schema is derived as follows: each fact table is created by using the set of primary keys of their analysis dimensions as its compound primary key, and denormalizing or normalizing the aggregation hierarchies accordingly.

(Hüsemann, Lechtenbörger & Vossen, 2000) present a requirement-driven method to derive multidimensional schemas in *multidimensional normal form* (MNF). This work introduces a set of restrictions that any multidimensional schema produced by this method will satisfy. Furthermore, although this approach produces conceptual schemas, they also argue that the design process must comprise four sequential phases (requirements elicitation and conceptual, logical and physical design) like any classical database design process:

• Requirement analysis and specification: Despite it is argued that the operational ER schema should deliver basic information to determine the multidimensional analysis potential, no clue about how to identify the multidimensional concepts from the the data sources is given. Business domain experts must select strategically relevant operational database attributes and specify the purpose to use them as dimensions or measures. The resulting requirements specification contains a tabular list of attributes together with their multidimensional purpose, similar to Kimball's proposal. Supplementary informal information may be added such as standard multidimensional queries that the user would like to pose.

- Conceptual design: This step transforms the semi-formal business requirements into a formalized conceptual schema. This process is divided in three sequential stages:
  - Context definition of measures: This approach requires to determine a base for each measure (i.e., a minimal set of dimension levels functionally determining the measure values). Furthermore, measures sharing bases are grouped into the same fact, as they share the same dimensional context.
  - Dimensional hierarchy design: From each atomic level identified, this step gradually develops the dimension hierarchies by means of functional dependencies. Descriptors and levels are distinguished from requirements. In this approach, the authors distinguish between simple and multiple (containing, at least, two different aggregation path) hierarchies. Moreover, specialization of dimensions must be considered to avoid structural NULL values when aggregating data.
  - Definition of summarizability constraints: The authors argue that some aggregations of measures over certain dimensions do not make sense. Therefore, they propose to distinguish meaningful aggregations from meaningless ones and include this information in an appendix of the conceptual schema.

Finally, the authors argue that a multidimensional schema derived by means of this method is in *dimensional normal form* (MNF) (Lehner, Albrecht & Wedekind, 1998) and therefore it fully

makes multidimensional sense. Consequently, we can form a data cube (i.e., a multidimensional space) free of summarizability problems. In short, it is achieved by means of five constraints: measures must be fully functionally identified by the multidimensional base, each dimension hierarchy must have an atomic level, each dimension level must be represented by identifier attribute(s), every descriptor must be associated to a dimension level and dimensions generated must be orthogonal. By following their method, all these constraints are guaranteed.

(Moody & Kortink, 2000) present a method to develop multidimensional schemas from ER models. It was one of the first supply-driven approaches introduced in the literature, and one of the most cited papers in this area. Although it is not the first approach working over ER schemas, they present a structured and formal method to derive multidimensional logical schemas. Their method is divided into four steps:

- Pre-process: This step develops the enterprise data model if it does not exist yet.
- First step: This step classifies the ER entities into three main groups:
  - Transactional entities: These entities record details about particular events that occur in the business (orders, sales, etc). They argue that these are the most important entities in a data warehouse and form the basis of fact tables in star schemas, as these are the events that decision makers want to analyze. Although the authors do not consider requirements, they underline the relevance of requirements to identify facts, because not all the transactional entities will be of interest to the user. Moreover, they provide the key features to look for this kind of entities: the entity must describe an event that happens at a point in time, and

it must contain measures or quantities summarizable.

○ Component entities: These entities are directly related to a transaction entity via a one-to-many relationship and they define details or components of each business event. These entities will give rise to dimension tables in star schemas.

○ Classification entities: These entities are related to component entities by a chain of one-to-many relationships. Roughly speaking, they are functionally dependent on a component entity directly or by transitivity. They will represent dimension hierarchies in the multidimensional schema.

The authors assume that a given entity may fit into multiple categories. Therefore, they define a precedence hierarchy for resolving ambiguities: *Transaction > Classification > Component*. Thus, if an entity may play a transaction entity role, it is not considered neither as a classification nor a component entity. The rest of entities in the ER schema will not be included in the multidimensional schema.

• Second step: Next step aims to shape dimension hierarchies. The authors provide some formal rules to identify them. Specifically, a dimension hierarchy is defined as a sequence of entities joined together by one-to-many relationships all aligned in the same direction. Moreover, they introduce the concept of minimal entity (i.e., atomic level) and maximal entity (i.e., that with a coarser granularity data). Some formal rules to identify minimal and maximal entities are given. For example, minimal entities are those without one-to-many relationships, and maximal are those without many-to-one relationships.

• Third step: Transactional entities will give rise to facts, whereas dimension hierarchies will give rise to their analysis perspectives. The authors introduce two different operators to produce logical schemas:

○ Collapse hierarchy: Higher levels in hierarchies can be collapsed into lower levels. Indeed, the authors propose to denormalize the hierarchies according to our needs, as typically performed in data warehousing to improve query performance.

○ Aggregation: Can be applied to a transaction entity to create a new entity containing summarized data. To do so, some attributes are chosen to be aggregated (i.e., measures) and others to aggregate by (i.e., dimensional concepts).

By these operators, this approach introduces five different dimensional design alternatives. According to the resulting schema level of denormalization and the granularity of data, they introduce rules to derive *flat schemas, terraced schemas, star schemas, snowflake schemas* or *star cluster schemas*. They also introduce the notion of constellation schema that denotes a set of star schemas with hierarchically linked fact tables.

(Bonifati et al., 2001) present a hybrid semi-automatic approach consisting of three basic steps: a demand-driven, a supply-driven and a third stage to conciliate the two first steps (i.e., it introduces a sequential hybrid approach). The final step aims to integrate and conciliate both paradigms and generate a feasible solution that best reflects the user's necessities. This method generates a logical multidimensional schema and it was the first to introduce a formal hybrid approach with a final step conciliating both paradigms. Moreover, this method has been applied and validated in a real case study:

- We start collecting the end-user requirements through interviews and expressing user expectations through the *Goal / Question / Metrics* (GQM) paradigm. GQM is composed of a set of forms and guidelines developed in four stages: (i) a first vague approach to formulate the goals in abstract terms, (ii) a second approach using forms and a detailed guide to identify goals by means of interviews, (iii) a stage to integrate and reduce the number of goals identified by collapsing those with similarities and finally, (iv) a deeper analysis and a detailed description of each goal. Next, the authors present an informal guideline to derive a logical multidimensional schema from requirements. Some clues and tips to identify facts dimensions and measures from the forms and sheets used in this process are given.
- Second step aims to carry out a supply-driven approach from ER diagrams capturing the operational sources. This step may be automated, and it performs an exhaustive analysis of the data-sources. From the ER diagram, a set of graphs that will eventually produce star schemas are created as follows:
  - Potential fact entities are labeled according to the number of additive attributes they have. Each identified fact is taken as the center node of a graph.
  - Dimensions are identified by means of many-to-one and one-to-one relationships from the center node. Moreover, many-to-many relationships are transformed into one-to-many relationships. Finally, each generalization / specialization taxonomy is also included in the graphs.

Next, they introduce an algorithm to derive snowflake schemas from each graph. This transformation is immediate and once done, they transform the snowflake schemas into star schemas by flattening the dimension hierarchies (i.e., denormalizing dimensions).

- Third step aims to integrate star schemas derived from the first step with those identified from the second step. In short, they try to map demand-driven schemas into supply-driven schemas by means of three steps:
  - Terminology analysis: Before integration, demand-driven and supply-driven schemas must be converted to a common terminological idiom. A mapping between GQM and ER concepts must be provided.
  - Schema matching: Supply-driven schemas are compared, one-by-one, to demand-driven schemas. A match occurs if both have the same fact. Some metrics, with regard to the number of measures and dimensions, are calculated.
  - Ranking and selection: Supply-driven schemas are ranked according to the metrics calculated in the previous step and presented to the user.

As final remark, this method does not introduce the concept of descriptor in any moment. However, since they map relational entities into levels, we may consider attributes contained in the entities as the multidimensional descriptors.

(Phipps & Davis, 2002) introduced one of the first methods automating part of the design process. This approach proposes a supply-driven stage to be validated, a posteriori, by a demand-driven stage. It is assumed to work over relational schemas (i.e., at the logical level) and a conceptual multidimensional schema is produced. In this approach, their main objective is the automation of the supply-driven process with two basics premises: numerical fields represent measures and the more numerical fields a relational table has, the more likely it is to play a fact role. Furthermore, any table related with a to-many relationship is likely to play a relevant dimensional role. In general, they go one step beyond in the formalization of their approach since a detailed pseudo-algorithm is presented in this paper (and therefore, automation is immediate). However, this approach generates too many results and a demand-driven stage is needed to filter results according to the end-user requirements. Thus, the demand-driven stage in this approach is rather different from the rest of demand-driven approaches, because they do not derive the multidimensional schema from requirements but they use requirements to filter results. This method consists of five steps:

- First step finds tables with numerical fields and create a fact node for each table identified. Tables with numerical fields are sorted in descending order of number of numeric fields. Tables will be processed in this order.
- Second step creates measures based on numerical fields within fact tables.
- Third step creates date and / or time dimension levels with any date / time fields per fact node.
- Fourth step creates dimensions (consisting of just one level) for each remaining table attribute that is non-numerical, non-key and non date field. Although this may be considered as a controversial decision (any other attribute would give rise to a dimension of analysis), it was the first method handling partially denormalized data sources.
- Fifth step recursively examines the relationships of the tables to add additional levels in a hierarchical manner. To do so, it looks for many-to-one relationships (according to foreign keys and candidate keys) all over the schema.

The heuristics used to find facts and determine dimensional concepts within a fact table are rather generic, and they generate results containing too much noise. Consequently, the authors propose a final requirement-driven step to filter results obtained. This step presents a step-by-step guide to analyze the end-user requirements expressed as MDX queries and guide the selection of candidate schemas most likely to meet user needs. This last step must be manually performed.

(Winter & Strauch, 2003) present a detailed demand-driven approach. This is a reference paper because it presents a detailed discussion between different multidimensional design paradigms. Furthermore, they present a method developed from the analysis of several data warehouse projects in participating companies. However, their approach is rather different from the rest of methods. They do not assume the multidimensional modeling introduced by Kimball like the rest of methods do, and they present a high-level step-by-step guideline.

In short, they identify the best practices that a data warehouse design project must consider, according to their analysis task. The design process must be iterative and it is divided into four stages:

- First step embraces the analysis of the information supply (i.e., from the sources) and the analysis of the information needed.
- Next, we must match requirements demanded with current information supply and order requirements accordingly.
- In a third step, information supply and information demand must be synchronized on a full level of detail (i.e., considering data granularity selected).
- Finally, we must develop the multidimensional schema. This schema must be evaluated and if needed, reformulate the process from the first step to develop the multidimensional schema in an iterative way.

Although this approach gives relevance to the data sources and demands to synchronize data demanded with the sources, we consider it to be a demand-driven approach since no clue about how to analyze the data sources is given.

(Vrdoljak, Banek & Rizzi, 2003) present a semi-automatic supply-driven approach to derive logical schemas from XML schemas. This approach considers XML schemas as data sources. Therefore, the authors propose to integrate XML data in the data warehouse, as XML is now a *de facto* standard for the exchange of semi-structured data. Their approach works as follows:

- Preprocessing the XML schema: The schema is simplified to avoid complex and redundant specifications of relationships.
- Creating and transforming the schema graph: Every XML schema can be represented as a graph. Two transformations are carried out at this point; functional dependencies are explicitly stated (by means of key attributes) and nodes not storing any value are discarded.
- Choosing facts: Facts must be chosen among all *vertexes* (i.e., nodes) and *arcs* (i.e., edges) of the graph. An arc can be chosen only if it represents a many-to-many relationship.
- Building the dependency graph: For each fact, a dependency graph is built. The graphical representation of the XML schema facilitates finding the functional dependencies. The graph must be examined in the direction expressed by arcs and according to cardinalities included in the dependency graph. It may happen that no cardinality is provided. In this case, XML documents are queried by means of XQueries to look for to-one relationships. The authors also consider many-to-many relationships to be of interest in some cases. However, these cases must be manually identified by the

user. Finally, the dependency graph will give rise to aggregation hierarchies.
- Creating the logical schema: Facts and measures are directly depicted from vertexes and arcs chosen, whereas dimensions are derived from the aggregation hierarchies identified.

(Jensen, Holmgren & Pedersen, 2004) present a supply-driven method from relational databases. They present data-mining techniques to be applied over the intensional data to discover functional and inclusion dependencies and, eventually, derive snowflake schemas.

Their method starts collecting metadata such as table and attribute names, cardinality of attributes, frequency, etc. Later, data is divided into three groups according to its potential multidimensional role: measure, keys and descriptive data. Next, integrity constraints such as functional and inclusion dependencies are identified between attributes and finally, the snowflake schema is produced.

First two steps are performed consulting the database catalog. The role of each attribute is derived with a bayesian network that takes as input metadata collected for each attribute. The third step discovers the database structure by identifying functional and inclusion dependencies that represent many-to-one relationships that will give rise to dimensions. Candidate keys and foreign keys are identified assuming that there are no composite keys in the database. Furthermore, inclusion dependencies among foreign keys and candidate keys are identified in this step. These dependencies will be mainly used to identify dimensions. This step is critical, since all permutations of candidate keys and foreign keys are constructed with the consequent computational cost. To pair two keys, both must have the same attribute type and the candidate key must have, at least, as many distinct values for the attribute as the table containing the foreign key. If these constraints hold, a SQL statement is issued to check if the join of both tables (by means of these attributes) has the same cardinality as the table containing the candidate foreign key. If so, an inclusion dependency is identified between both keys. Next, they propose an algorithm to derive snowflake schema from this metadata:

- Fact tables are identified in a semi-automatic process involving the user. First, facts are proposed by means of the table cardinality and the number of measures identified by a bayesian network. Then, the user chooses those of his / her interest.
- Inclusion dependencies discovered form different connected graphs. A connected graph is considered to be a dimension if exists a inclusion dependency between a fact table and a graph node. In this case, that node will play the atomic level role of the dimension. The authors propose an algorithm to break potential cycles and give rise to the aggregation hierarchy from the graph. When shaping the aggregation hierarchy, two consecutive levels are analyzed to avoid aggregation problems (i.e., duplicated or lost values).

(Giorgini, Rizzi & Garzetti, 2005) present a hybrid approach to derive the conceptual multidimensional schema. They propose to gather multidimensional requirements and later map them onto the data sources in a conciliation process. However, they also suggest that their approach could be considered a pure demand-driven if the user do not want to consider the data sources. The authors introduce an agent-oriented method based on the *i** framework. They argue that it is important to model the organization setting in which the data warehouse will operate (organization modeling) and capture the functional and non-functional requirements of the data warehouse (what authors call the decisional modeling). If we consider their hybrid approach, the next step is to match requirements with the schema of the operational sources. In this approach both ER

diagrams and relational schemas are allowed as inputs describing the data sources. This matching stage consists of three steps:

- Requirement mapping: Facts, dimensions and measures identified during the requirement analysis are now mapped over the data sources. According to the kind of data sources considered, the authors introduce a set of hints to map each concept. For example, facts are mapped onto entities or n-ary associations in ER diagrams and onto relations in relational schemas.
- Hierarchy construction: For each fact identified, the data sources are analyzed looking for functional dependencies based on the algorithm already discussed in (Golfarelli & Rizzi, 2009).
- Refinement: This step aims to rearrange the fact schema in order to better fit the user's needs. In this process, we may distinguish among concepts available (mapped from requirements), unavailable (demanded in the requirements but not mappable to the data sources) and what is available and not needed. The authors propose to use this information to reorder dimensions (grafting and pruning the aggregation hierarchies) and / or try to find new directions of analysis.

(Annoni et al., 2006) present a demand-driven approach to derive a multidimensional conceptual schema that meets the end-user requirements. In order to provide a comprehensive framework for the end-user, they propose to distinguish between strategic and tactical requirements. The formers correspond to key performance indicators used for decision making, whereas the lasts represent functional objectives expressed by the end-user. In this paper, both how to collect and formalize each kind of requirements is detailed:

- Tactical and strategic requirements are suggested to be collected in a tabular representation, which in turn, must produce a *decisional dictionary* (i.e., a general view of requirements regarding the information and processes –aimed at modeling the ETL process- involved). At this level, strategic requirements differ from tactical requirements as they are expressed as measures whose only analysis perspective is the time dimension. On the contrary, tactical requirements correspond to the traditional multidimensional queries. To facilitate its collection and the creation of the decisional dictionary, the authors propose a pseudo-language, derived from natural language, to express requirements in a higher abstraction level and easily derive the tabular shape demanded a posteriori.

- Finally, requirements gathered are formalized using *decisional diagrams* by means of transformation rules. These diagrams are closer to how people involved in decision making think and reason and, simultaneously, captures all the information and processes involved to meet them.

Finally, the multidimensional schema must be derived from the decisional diagrams defined.

(Prat, Akoka & Comyn-Wattiau, 2006) present a method to derive the conceptual, logical and physical schema of the data warehouse according to the three abstraction levels recommended by ANSI / X3 / SPARC. Starting from end-user requirements, the conceptual phase leads to a *Unified Modeling Language* (UML) model. To this end, UML is enriched with concepts relevant to multidimensionality that will facilitate the generation of the logical schema. The logical phase maps the enriched UML model into a multidimensional schema and finally, the physical phase maps the multidimensional schema into a physical database schema depending on the target implementation tool (in this case Oracle MOLAP).

At each phase, they introduce a metamodel and a set of transformations to perform the mapping between metamodels. In this study, we will focus on the method to produce the conceptual and logical schemas and we will avoid to discuss the transformations to be performed to derive the physical schema.

- Conceptual phase: In this first step, the authors embrace requirements elicitation and the conceptual representation of requirements. First, requirements should be captured by means of a UML-compliant system analysis method. Requirements engineering techniques used in transactional design processes may be considered, and for example, they mention interviews, joint sessions, study of existing reports and prototyping of future reports as potential techniques to be used. Next, requirements are represented in a UML class diagram that needs to be enriched to capture multidimensional semantics. To do so, they present an extension of the UML metamodel.

  ∘ Classes which are not association classes are denoted as ordinary classes. Similarly, associations which are not association classes are denoted as ordinary associations.

  ∘ Each attribute of an ordinary class must be identified as an attribute or not. According to authors, it must be decided by the end-user and designers jointly.

  ∘ Each attribute belonging to one-to-one or many-to-one relationships is transferred to the to-many side.

  ∘ Generalizations are transformed to facilitate their mapping to the logical level. Each specialization is mapped to a new class that is related to the superclass by means of an aggregation relationship.

91

- Logical phase: Creating the logical schema from the enriched conceptual model produced in the first phase is immediate and a set of transformations expressed in *Object Contraint Language* (OCL) are presented. They also introduce an ad hoc multidimensional metamodel to represent the logical schema as follows:

  ○ Every many-to-many association of the conceptual model is identified as a fact of interest and their attributes (if any) are mapped into measures of the fact. This fact would be dimensioned by mapping the ordinary classes directly or indirectly involved in the association. Similarly, every ordinary class containing numerical values of interest is also identified as a fact. In this case, the fact is dimensioned by one dimension level defined by mapping the class (similar to the approach presented in (Phipps & Davis, 2002)).

  ○ Next, following many-to-one relationships between ordinary classes we give rise to aggregation hierarchies for each dimension level identified in the previous step.

  ○ Descriptors are defined from those non-identifier attributes from the classes involved in the dimension hierarchy that have not been chosen as measures of interest.

  ○ Finally, for each measure and for each dimension related to the fact where the measure is defined, it is compulsory to define which aggregation functions preserve a meaningful aggregation.

(Romero & Abelló, 2010a) present a method to derive conceptual multidimensional schemas from requirements expressed in SQL queries. Thus, it assumes relational data sources. This approach is fully automatic and follows a hybrid paradigm, which was firstly introduced in (Romero & Abelló, 2006). On the one hand, unlike other hybrid approaches, it does not carry out two well-differentiated phases (i.e., data-driven and requirement-driven) that need to be conciliated a posteriori, but carry out both phases simultaneously. In this way, both paradigms benefit from feedback returned by each other and eventually, it is able to derive more valuable information than carrying out both phases sequentially. On the other hand, this is the first method automating its demand-driven stage. In other words, automating the analysis of the end-user requirements. This method produces constellation schemas from the requirements (i.e., the SQL queries) and the data sources logical schema (i.e., relational schemas). Moreover, it is able to cope with denormalization in the input relational schemas and get equivalent outputs when applied over normalized (up-to third normal form) or denormalized relational sources. The multidimensional schema is derived along two different stages:

- For each input query, first stage extracts the multidimensional knowledge contained in the query (i.e., the multidimensional role played by each concept in the query as well as the conceptual relationships among concepts), that is properly stored in a graph. In this stage, the role played by the data sources logical schema will be crucial to infer the conceptual relationships among concepts.

- Second stage validates each multidimensional graph according to multidimensionality. To do so, this method defines a set of constraints that must be preserved in order to place data in a multidimensional space and produce a data cube free of summarizability problems. This step main objective is to guarantee that concepts and relationships captured in the graph give rise, as a whole, to a data cube. If the validation process fails, the method ends since data demanded could not be analyzed from a multidimensional point of view. Otherwise, the resulting multidimensional schema is directly derived form the multidimensional graph.

Unlike data-driven methods, this approach focuses on data of interest for the end-user (by considering the end-user requirements by means of the SQL queries). However, the user may not know all the potential analysis contained in the data sources and, unlike requirement-driven approaches, it is able to propose new interesting multidimensional knowledge related to concepts already queried by the user. To do so, it does not analyze the whole data sources but those concepts closely related to the end-user requirements. Finally, multidimensional schemas are derived from a validation process are proposed. Therefore, like in (Hüsemann, Lechtenbörger & Vossen, 2000) and (Mazón, Trujillo & Lechtenbörger, 2007), schemas proposed are sound and meaningful.

(Mazón, Trujillo & Lechtenbörger, 2007) present a semi-automatic hybrid approach that obtains the conceptual schema from user requirements and then, verifies and enforces its correctness against the data sources by means of *Query / View / Transformation* (QVT) relations. Their approach work over relational sources and requirements expressed in the *i** framework. The modus operandi of this approach shares many common points with (Bonifati et al., 2001), but in this case, they also provide mechanisms for validating the output schema.

This approach starts with a requirement analysis phase. They introduce a detailed demand-driven stage in which the user should state his / her requirements at high level by means of business goals. Then, the information requirements are derived from the information business goals. Both, goals and information requirements must be modeled by an adaptation of the *i** framework and eventually, the multidimensional conceptual schema must be derived from this formalization.

Finally, the authors propose to express the resulting multidimensional schema by using an ad hoc UML extension (i.e., their own data structure) provided in the paper. Recently, the authors improved their deman-driven stage initially presented. In (Pardillo, Mazón & Trujillo, 2008) and (Carmè, Mazón & Rizzi, 2010) they propose two new approaches to detect facts and multidimensional metadata by exploiting the data source schemas. Yet, the demand-driven stage within this approach must be manually performed.

Next, they propose a final step to check the conceptual multidimensional model correctness. The objective of this step is twofold: they present a set of QVT relations based on the *multidimensional normal forms* (MNF) to align the conceptual schema derived from requirements with the relational schema of the data sources. Thus, output schemas will capture the analysis potential of the sources and at the same time, they will be validated according to the MNF. The MNF used in this paper are an evolution of those used in (Hüsemann, Lechtenbörger & Vossen, 2000), and they share the same objective. By means of five QVT relations, in a semi-automatic way, this paper describes how the conceptual multidimensional schema should be aligned to the underlying relational schema:

- 1MNF (a): A functional dependency in the conceptual schema must have a corresponding functional dependency in the relational schema.
- 1MNF (b): Functional dependencies among dimension levels contained in the source databases must be represented as aggregation relationships in the conceptual schema. Therefore, they complement the conceptual schema with additional aggregation hierarchies contained in the sources.
- 1MNF (c): Summarized measures that can be derived from regular measures must be identified in the conceptual schema. Therefore, they support derived measures.

- 1MNF (d): Measures must be assigned to facts in such a way that the atomic levels of the fact form a key. In other words, they demand to place the measure in a fact with the correct base (and thus, preserve the proper data granularity).
- 2MNF and 3MNF: These constraints demand to use specializations of concepts when structural NULLs in the data sources do not guarantee completeness.

(Song, Khare & Dai, 2007) present an automatic supply-driven method that derives logical schemas from ER models. This novel approach automatically identifies facts from ER diagrams by means of the *connection topology value* (CTV). The main idea underlying this approach is that facts and dimensions are usually related by means of many-to-one relationships. Concepts at the many-side are fact candidates and concepts in the one-side are dimension candidates. Moreover, it distinguishes between direct and transitive many-to-one relationships:

- First, the authors demand a preprocess to transform ER diagrams into binary (i.e., without ternary nor many-to-many relationships) ER diagrams.
- The CTV value of an entity is a composite function of the topology value of direct and indirect many-to-one relationships. In this formula, direct relationships have a higher weighting factor with regard to transitive ones. Thus, all those entities with a CTV value higher than a threshold are proposed as facts. Note that facts are identified by their CTV and therefore, it would be possible to consider factless facts.
- For each fact entity, its analysis dimensions are identified by means of many-to-one relationships. Moreover, the authors propose to use *Wordnet* and annotated dimensions (which represent commonly used dimen-

sions in business processes) to enrich aggregation hierarchies depicted.

This approach does not introduce any clue to identify measures, levels and descriptors. However, working over ER diagrams, it would be rather easy to assume that measures are identified by means of numerical attributes once a concept has been identified as a fact, whereas descriptors can be identified from those entities identified as dimensions. Furthermore, no clue about how to identify levels is given and indeed, in the examplification provided in the paper, every dimension identified contains just one level (i.e., they do not identify aggregation hierarchies).

(Romero & Abelló, 2010b) present a semi-automated supply-driven approach. This approach derives conceptual schemas from OWL ontologies that may represent different and potentially heterogeneous data sources. Thus, this method will derive multidimensional schemas from data sources of our domain that do not have anything in common but that they are all described by the same domain ontology. This approach consists of three well-differentiated tasks. In each step it automatically looks for a given multidimensional concept (facts, bases and aggregation hierarchies) by means of a fully supply-driven stage. A formal pattern expressed in Description Logics (DL) is presented at each step. Finally, at the end of each step the user selects results of his / her interest and this will trigger next steps:

- The first task looks for potential facts. Those concepts related to most potential dimensional concepts and measures are good candidates. At the end of this task, the user chooses his / her subjects of interest among those concepts proposed by the method. The rest of the tasks will be carried out once for each fact identified in this step (i.e., each fact will give rise to a multidimensional schema).

- The second task points out sets of concepts likely to be used as bases for each fact identified. Candidate bases giving rise to denser data cubes will be presented first to the user. Finally, it would be up to the user to select those bases making more sense to him / her. Although this step is not discussed in (Romero & Abelló, 2010b), it was introduced in the original paper (Romero & Abelló, 2007). Later, it has been studied in depth in (Abelló & Romero, 2010).
- The third task gives rise to dimension hierarchies. For every concept identified as a dimension its hierarchy of levels is conformed from those concepts related to it by typical part-whole relationships. In this step, this approach builds up graphs giving shape to each dimension hierarchy and again, it will be up to the user to modify them to fit his / her needs.

Finally, this approach uses the same criteria as (Romero & Abelló, 2010a) to validate the multidimensional schema.

Nebot et al. (2009) present an innovative approach based on the semantic web technologies. This work has its origin in the biomedicine field, where data warehouses play a relevant role as analytical tools. Nevertheless, as the authors shown in some of their publications, this approach can be generalized and used in alternative scenarios.

First of all, it is important to remark that the nature of this approach differs from the other works introduced in this section in the sense that it provides a solution for a wider scenario: the data warehouse modeling task (discussed in here) and the ETL process design.

In this work they distinguish between domain ontologies (containing the agreed terminology about the domain) and application ontologies (containing the detailed knowledge needed for a specific application). This method aims at developing *Multidimensional Integrated Ontologies* (MIOs), which gather only the relevant knowledge

from the application ontologies aligned together with the domain ontologies. Next, they aim at extracting the ontological instances from the applications and populate the data warehouse, which is based on the MIOs defined. According to their definitions, we can see the MIOs as the data warehouse schema from where to extract multidimensional cubes (i.e., perform OLAP analysis) or any other kind of analysis tasks. Mappings between the domain ontologies and the application ontologies, as well as between the overlapped part of the application ontologies are needed in advance. From here on, we will focus on the modeling task proposed within this approach and thus, in defining and validating the MIOs and the eventual multidimensional cubes of interest. Relevantly, the authors argue that a MIO is a filtered, multidimensional compliant (i.e., with orthogonal dimensions and free of summarizability problems) ontology, derived from the available domain and application ontologies, from where to extract the multidimensional cubes. As this framework was thought for biomedicine scenarios (i.e., very large, distributed ontologies), the authors propose to carry out the multidimensional design task (i.e., what previous approaches surveyed do) from the MIOs. According to this, this work can be thought as a complementary approach rather than an alternative to previous works introduced.

The definition and generation of the MIOs is done as follows:

- By analyzing the available ontologies we must first select those concepts being the focus of analysis (i.e., the facts). Then, dimensions and measures of interest must be specified, as well as roll-up relationships. All this process, however, must be done manually.
- Concepts demanded in the previous step are expressed as Description Logics axioms and hence, the MIO generation is largely automatic.

- Finally, the authors introduce a step to validate the MIO generated. The aim is to guarantee that the eventual multidimensional cubes produced from it are sound. To do so, they check desirable properties such as if the MIO is free of summarizability problems or the orthogonality of dimensions. In this step, they distinguish between properties that can already be checked at MIO level (e.g., concept satisfiability) and those that can only be considered once the multidimensional cube is demanded (e.g., compatibility of the dimension, measure and aggregation function).

COMPARISON CRITERIA

In order to provide a comprehensive framework of the multidimensional design methods, we aim to provide a detailed comparison of the methods discussed in the previous section. Setting a basis for discussion will facilitate the mapping of the surveyed methods to a common framework from which compare each approach, detect trends such as features in common or analyze the evolution of assumptions made by the modeling methods.

These criteria were defined in an incremental analysis of the methods surveyed. For each method we captured its main features that were mapped onto different criteria. If a method introduced a new criterion, the rest of works were analyzed to know their assumptions with regard to this criterion. Therefore, criteria presented below were defined in an iterative process during the analysis of the multidimensional design methods.

We have summarized these criteria in three main categories: general aspects, dimensional data and factual data. A graphical representation of these features is found in Figure 2. Next to each criterion, the values it may take are provided (in brackets, the acronyms). For example, the values that we may assign for the *paradigm* criterion are *demand-driven* (DD), *supply-driven* (SD),

interleaved hybrid (IH) or *sequential hybrid* (SH). General aspects refer to those criteria regarding general assumptions made in the method, whereas dimensional and factual data criteria refer to how dimensional data and factual data are identified and mapped onto multidimensional concepts.

General Aspects

The general criteria are summarized into nine different items:

- Paradigm: According to (Winter & Strauch, 2003), multidimensional modeling methods may be classified as *supply-driven*, *demand-driven* or *hybrid* approaches. The reader may found a slightly different classification in (List et al., 2002). Furthermore, we distinguish between sequential and interleaved hybrid approaches (depending if their supply-driven and demand-driven approaches are performed either sequentially or simultaneously or sequentially).

- Application: Most methods are semi-automatic. Thus, some stages of these methods must be performed manually by an expert (normally those stages aimed to identify factual data) and some others may be performed automatically (normally those aimed to identify dimensional data). In general, only a few methods fully automate the whole process. On the contrary, some others present a detailed step-by-step guide that is assumed to be manually carried out by an expert.

- Pre-process: Some methods demand to adapt the input data into a specific format that facilitates their work. For example, these processes may ask to enrich a conceptual model with additional semantics or perform data mining over data instances to discover hidden relationships.

- Input abstraction level: Most methods (mainly those automatable) work with in-

Figure 2. Graphical view of the criteria used in the survey

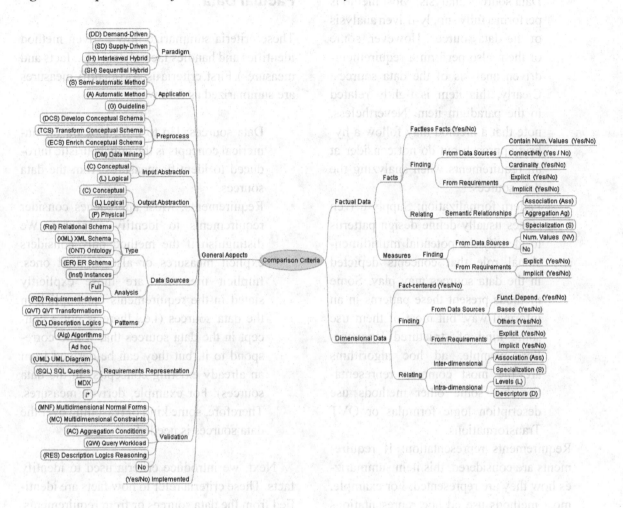

puts expressed at the logical level (e.g., relational schemas), whereas some others work with inputs at the conceptual level (e.g., from conceptual formalizations such as ER diagrams or from requirements in natural language).

• Output abstraction level: Several methods choose to directly generate a star or snowflake schema, whereas some others produce multidimensional conceptual schemas. Although many approaches argue that the data warehouse method should span the three abstraction levels, only a few of them produce the conceptual, logical and physical schema of the data warehouse.

• Data sources: There are three items summarizing the main features about how data sources are considered in the method.

  ○ Type of data sources: The input abstraction item informs about the abstraction level of the input, whereas this item specifies the kind of technology of the data sources supported by the method. For example, if the method works at the conceptual level it may work from UML, ER conceptual schemas or ontologies, and if it works at the logical level it may work from relational schemas or XML schemas.

○   Data sources analysis: Most methods perform a fully supply-driven analysis of the data sources. However, some of them also perform a requirement-driven analysis of the data sources. Clearly, this item is tightly related to the paradigm item. Nevertheless, note that a method may follow a hybrid approach but do not consider at all requirements when analyzing the data sources.

○   Pattern formalization: Supply-driven stages usually define design patterns to identify the potential multidimensional role that concepts depicted in the data sources may play. Some methods present these patterns in an informal way, but most of them use some kind of structured language. For example, ad hoc algorithms are the most common representation but some other methods use description logic formulas or QVT Transformations.

•   Requirements representation: If requirements are considered, this item summarizes how they are represented. For example, most methods use ad hoc representations (like forms, sheets, tables or matrixes), whereas some others use UML diagrams or the *i** framework. Finally, some of them lower the level of abstraction of requirements to a logical level by means of SQL queries or MDX queries.

•   Validation: Some methods integrate a validation process to derive meaningful multidimensional schemas. For example, restricting summarization of data to those dimensions and functions that preserve data semantics or forming multidimensional spaces by means of orthogonal dimensions.

•   Implementation: Some methods have been implemented in CASE tools or prototypes.

Factual Data

These criteria summarize how a given method identifies and handles factual data (i.e., facts and measures). First, criteria used to identify measures are summarized as follows:

•   Data sources: Up to now, looking for numerical concepts is the only heuristic introduced to identify measures from the data sources.

•   Requirements: Most approaches consider requirements to identify measures. We distinguish if the method only considers explicit measures or also implicit ones. Implicit measures are those explicitly stated in the requirements but implicit in the data sources (i.e., there is not a concept in the data sources that would correspond to it, but they can be derived from an already existing concept(s) in the data sources). For example, derived measures. Therefore, some kind of reasoning over the data sources is needed.

Next, we introduce criteria used to identify facts. These criteria refer to how facts are identified from the data sources or from requirements, and how they may be semantically related in the resulting schema:

•   Factless facts: This kind of facts were introduced by Kimball in (Kimball et al., 1998). they are also known as empty facts and they are very useful to describe events and coverage, and a lot of interesting questions may be asked from them.

•   Data sources: Most of the methods demand to explicitly identify facts by means of the requirements, but some others use heuristics to identify them from the data sources. For example, in case of relational sources, most use heuristics such as table cardinalities and the number of numerical attributes that a table contains. Furthermore, some works also look for concepts with high to-one connectivity (i.e., with many potential dimensional concepts).

- Requirements: Similar to measures, if requirements are considered, we distinguish among explicit and implicit facts. We denote by implicit facts those that have not been explicitly stated in the requirements but can be identified from a requirement-driven analysis of the sources.
- Semantic relationships: In case of producing a conceptual schema, some methods are able to identify semantic relationships between facts. We distinguish among associations, aggregations (also called roll-up / drill-down relationships) and generalizations. In the multidimensional model, it means that we may perform multidimensional operators such as drill-across or drill-down over them.

Dimensional Data

These criteria analyze how the method identifies and handles dimensional data (i.e., dimensions, levels and descriptors). We have two main groups of items. Those referring to how dimensional data is identified (either from the data sources or from requirements), and how they are semantically related in the resulting schema. The process to identify dimensions, levels and descriptors must be understood as a whole and, unlike criteria used to identify factual data, we do not distinguish among criteria to look for different dimensional concepts. Roughly speaking, most approaches start looking for concepts representing interesting perspectives of analysis and from these concepts they look for aggregation hierarchies (i.e., levels). The whole hierarchy is then identified as a dimension and level attributes are considered to play a descriptor role:

- Fact-centered: Most methods look for dimensional data once they have identified facts. From each fact, dimensional concepts are identified using a wide variety of techniques according to the method inputs, but always looking for functional dependencies starting from the fact.
- Data sources: There are several techniques to identify dimensional concepts from data sources. We classify these techniques in three main groups: discovering functional dependencies, discovering bases and others. At the conceptual level, functional dependencies are modeled as to-one relationships, and at the logical level it depends on the technology. For example, in the relational model, dimensional concepts are identified by means of foreign keys and candidate keys. Bases (see Section *Terminology and Notation* for further information) are used to identify dimensional concepts as well. In this case, the method looks for candidate multidimensional bases in order to identify interesting perspectives of analysis (i.e., levels).
- Requirements: Dimensional concepts are mostly identified from the data sources once facts and measures have been identified. However, demand-driven approaches rely on requirements to identify dimensional concepts and some hybrid approaches also enrich their supply-driven stages with requirements. Like facts, we distinguish between explicit dimensional concepts and implicit ones.
- Intra-dimensional: Most of the methods distinguish between descriptors and levels, but some others do not.
- Inter-dimensional: Some approaches are able to identify semantic relationships between dimensions. In this case, we consider associations and generalizations as potential relationships.

METHODS COMPARISON

In this section we present a detailed summarization of the main features of each method regarding the criteria introduced in previous section, which provides a common framework to compare and discuss methods surveyed. Results are shown in Figures 3 and 4. Methods surveyed are distributed in these tables according to the chronological order. There, rows correspond to criteria introduced in the previous section and columns correspond to each method. A given cell contains information for a method and a specific criterion (we address the reader to Figure 2 to remind the meaning of each acronym). Some criteria are evaluated as *yes/no*, but most of them have alternative values. Two general values can be found for any criterion: - means that this criterion does not make sense for the method (for example, if it does not consider the data sources then, any of the criteria related to them cannot be evaluated for this method), whereas *none* means that, despite this criterion could be considered for this method, none of the alternatives are considered (i.e., it is overlooked). Therefore, *none* is the equivalent to the *no* value but for criteria having several values.

Analyzing these tables we can find some interesting trends as well as assumptions that have been considered in most of the methods surveyed. First approaches tried to contextualize the multidimensional modeling task by providing tips and informal rules about how to proceed. In other words, they presented the first guidelines to support multidimensional design. Later, when main features with regard to multidimensional modeling were set up, new formal and powerful methods were developed. These new methods focused on formalizing and automating the process. Automation is an important feature along the whole data warehouse lifecycle and multidimensional design has not been an exception. Indeed, first methods were step-by-step guidelines, but in the course of time many semi-automatic and automatic approaches have been presented. This evolution also conditioned the type of inputs used, and logical schemas were considered instead of conceptual schemas. Nowadays, last methods introduced present a high degree of automation. Moreover, we may say that this trend also motivated a change of paradigm. At the beginning, most methods where demand-driven or, in case of being hybrid approaches, they gave much more weight to requirements than to data sources. However, eventually, data sources gained relevance. This makes sense because automation has been tightly related to focusing on data sources instead of requirements. Consequently, first methods introduced gave way to others largely automatable and mostly following a supply-driven framework.

Nevertheless, today, it is assumed that the ideal approach to design multidimensional data warehouses must be a hybrid approach. In this line, last works introduced are mainly hybrid approaches.

In these tables we can also note the evolution of how the multidimensional model has been considered. First approaches used to produce logical multidimensional schemas but later, most of them generate conceptual schemas. One reason for this situation could be that Kimball introduced multidimensional modeling at the logical level (i.e., as a specific relational implementation). With the course of time, it has been argued that it is necessary to generate schemas at a platform-independent level and in fact, the multidimensional design should span the three abstraction levels (conceptual, logical and physical) like in the relational databases field.

About the kind of data sources handled, most of the first approaches choose conceptual entity-relationships diagrams describing the data sources. ER diagrams were the most spread way to represent operational databases (the most common type of data source to populate the data warehouse) but the necessity to automate this process and the need to provide up-to-date conceptual schemas to the data warehouse designer motivated that many methods worked over relational schemas instead

Figure 3. Summary of the comparison of multidimensional design methods

	[KRTR98]	[CT98]	[GR09]	[BvE99]	[HLV00]	[MK00]	[BCC+01]	[PD02]	[WS03]
General Aspects									
Paradigm	DD	IH	SH	SH	DD	SD	SH	SH	DD
Application	G	G	S	G	G	G	S	S	G
Pre-process	-	DCS	-	ECS	-	DCS	-	-	-
Input Abstr.	C	C	C/L	C	C	C	C/L	L	C
Output Abstr.	L	L	C/L/P	L	C	L	L	C	C
Data Sources									
↪ Type	-	ER	ER/Rel	SER	-	ER	ER	Rel	-
↪ Analysis	-	RD	Full	Full	-	Full	Full	Full	-
↪ Patterns F.	-	None	Alg	None	-	None	Alg	Alg	-
Req. Expr.	ad hoc	ad hoc	ad hoc	ad hoc	ad hoc	-	ad hoc	MDX	ad hoc
Validation	No	No	No	No	MNF	No	No	No	No
Tool	No	No	Yes	Yes	No	No	No	No	No
Factual Data									
Facts									
Factless Facts	Yes	No	No	No	No	No	No	No	No
Requirements	Expl	Expl	Expl	Expl	Expl	-	Expl	No	Expl
Data Sources									
↪ C.Num.Val.	-	No	No	No	-	Yes	Yes	Yes	-
↪ Connectivity	-	No	No	No	-	No	No	No	-
↪ Cardinality	-	No	No	No	-	No	No	Yes	-
Semantic Rels.	-	-	Ass	-	Ag	-	-	None	None
Measures									
Requirements	Impl	Expl	Expl	Impl	Expl	-	Expl	No	Expl
Data Sources	-	No	NV	No	-	NV	NV	NV	-
Dimensional Data									
Fact-centered	No	No	Yes	Yes	No	No	Yes	Yes	No
Requirements	Expl	Expl	Expl	Expl	Expl	-	Expl	No	Expl
Data Sources									
↪ FDs	-	No	Yes	Yes	-	Yes	Yes	Yes	-
↪ Bases	-	No	No	No	-	No	No	No	-
↪ Others	-	No	No	No	-	No	No	Yes	-
Related									
Interdim.	None	-	None	-	None	-	-	None	None
Intradim.	L/D	L/D	L/D	L	L/D	L/D	L/D	L	-

of conceptual schemas. Almost every method either considers ER diagrams or relational schemas to describe the data sources. Lately, with the relevance gained by the semantic web area, some other works automating the process from XML schemas or OWL ontologies have been presented. About requirements, their representation have varied considerably. At the beginning, ad hoc representations such as forms, tables, sheets or matrixes were proposed but lately, many methods propose to formalize requirements representation with frameworks such as UML diagrams or *i**. Moreover, some works have also proposed to lower the level of abstraction of requirements to the logical level by means of SQL or MDX queries, which opens new possibilities for automating the process.

Finally, we can also identify a trend to validate the resulting multidimensional schema as well as the importance to provide a tool supporting the method.

About how to identify factual data, there are some trends that most approaches follow. Looking at the data sources, numerical concepts are likely to play a measure role, whereas concepts containing numerical attributes or those with a high table cardinality are likely to play a fact role. First methods were mainly demand-driven but later, most of them used these heuristics to identify factual concepts within supply-driven stages. However, these heuristics do not identify facts or measures but concepts likely to play that role. Thus, requirements must be considered to filter the (vast) amount of results obtained, and in the last

Figure 4. Summary of the comparison of multidimensional design methods

	[VBR03]	[JHP04]	[GRG05]	[ARTZ06]	[PACW06]	[RA10a]	[MTL07]	[SKD07]	[RA10b]	[NBPM+09]
General Aspects										
Paradigm	SH	SD	SH	DD	DD	IH	SH	SD	SH	IH
Application	S	A	S	G	G	A	S	A	S	S
Pre-process	TCS	DM	-	-	ECS	-	-	TCS	-	-
Input Abstr.	L	L	C	C	C	L	C/L	C	C	C/L
Output Abstr.	L	L	C	C	C/L/P	C	C	L	C	C/L
Data Sources										
↪ Type	XML	Inst	ER/Rel	-	-	Rel	Rel	Rel	Ont	Ont
↪ Analysis	Full	Full	RD	-	-	RD	RD	Full	Full	Full
↪ Patterns F.	None	Alg	None	-	-	Alg	QVT	None	DL	DL
Req. Expr.	ad hoc	-	i*	ad hoc	UML	SQL	i*	-	-	ad hoc
Validation	No	AC	No	No	AC	MC	MNF	No	MC	Res
Tool	Yes	Yes	Yes	No	Yes	Yes	Yes	Yes	Yes	Yes
Factual Data										
Facts										
Factless Facts	No	No	No	No	Yes	Yes	No	Yes	No	No
Requirements	Expl	-	Expl	Expl	Expl	Impl	Expl	-	-	Expl
Data Sources										
↪ C.Num.Val.	No	Yes	No	-	-	No	No	No	Yes	No
↪ Connectivity	No	No	No	-	-	No	No	Yes	Yes	No
↪ Cardinality	No	Yes	No	-	-	No	No	No	No	No
Semantic Rels.	-	-	None	None	None	Ass/S	Ass/S	None	Ass/Ag	None
Measures										
Requirements	Expl	-	Expl	Expl	Expl	Impl	Impl	-	-	Expl
Data Sources	No	NV	No	-	-	No	No	No	NV	No
Dimensional Data										
Fact-centered	Yes	Yes	Yes	No	No	No	No	Yes	Yes	No
Requirements	No	-	Expl	Expl	Expl	Impl	Impl	-	-	Expl
Data Sources										
↪ FDs	Yes	Yes	Yes	-	-	Yes	Yes	Yes	Yes	No
↪ Bases	No	No	No	-	-	No	No	No	Yes	No
↪ Others	No	No	No	-	-	No	No	No	No	No
Related										
Interdim.	-	-	None	None	None	Ass/S	S	None	Ass	None
Intradim.	L/D	L/D	L/D	L	L/D	L/D	L/D	L	L/D	L/D

years requirements have gained relevance again. Capturing inter-relationships between schemas (i.e., facts) have also gained relevance lately, as they open new analysis perspectives when considering multidimensional algebras. Finally, the reader may note that although Kimball introduced the concept of factless facts from the very beginning, it has been traditionally overlooked. Lately, some methods considered them again. One of the reasons could be that it is difficult to automate the identification of facts that do not have measures.

According to our study, dimensional concepts have been traditionally identified by means of functional dependencies. From the very beginning, some methods proposed to automate the identification of aggregation hierarchies. In fact, many methods use requirements to identify factual data and later they analyze the data sources looking for functional dependencies to identify dimensional data. Maybe for this reason, the use of requirements to identify dimensional concepts has not been that relevant as to identify factual data. Another clear trend with regard to dimensional concepts is that, in general, the more automatable a method is, the more fact-centered it is. About relationships among dimensional concepts, inter-dimensional relationships (like relationships between facts) open new perspectives of analysis when considering multidimensional algebras. However, in this case they have been traditionally overlooked; even more than this kind of relationships between facts. On the contrary, intra-dimensional relationships gained more and more relevance from the very beginning. Most methods agree that distinguishing among dimensions, levels and descriptors is relevant for analysis purposes.

CONCLUSION

In this paper we provide an insight to the most relevant multidimensional design methods. Specifically, we have surveyed 19 works that have been selected according to three factors: reference papers with a high number of citations, papers with novelty contributions and in case of papers of the same authors we have discussed the latest version of their works.

Since we still lack a standard multidimensional terminology and terms used among methods to describe the multidimensional concepts may vary, we have introduced a common multidimensional notation to avoid misunderstandings and facilitate the mapping of the surveyed methods to a common framework where to compare each approach.

We have also introduced a set of criteria to set a basis for discussion and detect trends such as features in common or the evolution of assumptions made along the way. These criteria were defined in an incremental analysis of the methods surveyed in this paper. For each method we captured its main features that were mapped onto different criteria. If a method introduced a new criterion, the rest of works were analyzed to know their assumptions with regard to this criterion. Therefore, criteria presented were defined along an iterative process during the analysis of the multidimensional design methods. We have summarized these criteria in three main categories: general aspects, dimensional data and factual data. General aspects refer to those criteria regarding general assumptions made in the method and dimensional and factual data criteria refer to how dimensional data and factual data are identified and mapped onto multidimensional concepts.

All in all, we have provided a comprehensive framework to better understand the current state of the area as well as its evolution.

ACKNOWLEDGMENT

This work has been partly supported by the Ministerio de Ciencia e Innovación under project TIN 2008-03863.

REFERENCES

Abelló, A., & Romero, O. (2010). Using Ontologies to Discover Fact IDs. In I. Song, C. Ordoñez (Eds.), *Proceedings of ACM 13th International Workshop on Data Warehousing and OLAP;* pp 1-8, Toronto, Canada: ACM Press.

Annoni, E., Ravat, F., Teste, O., & Zurfluh, G. (2006). Towards Multidimensional Requirements Design. *Proceedings of 8th International Conference on Data Warehousing and Knowledge Discovery; Vol. 4081, Lecture Notes of Computer Science* (pp. 75-84). Krakow, Poland: Springer.

Berners-Lee, T., Hendler, J. & Lassila, O. (2001). The Semantic Web. *Scientific American.*

Böehnlein, M., & Ulbrich-vom Ende, A. (1999). Deriving Initial Data Warehouse Structures from the Conceptual Data Models of the Underlying Operational Information Systems. In I. Song, T. J. Teorey (Eds.), *Proceedings of 2nd International Workshop on Data Warehousing and OLAP;* pp, 15-21. Kansas City, USA: ACM Press.

Bonifati, A., Cattaneo, F., Ceri, S., Fuggetta, A., & Paraboschi, S. (2001). Designing Data Marts for Data Warehouses. *ACM Transactions on Software Engineering and Methodology, 10*(4), 452–483. doi:10.1145/384189.384190

Cabibbo, L., & Torlone, R. (1998). A Logical Approach to Multidimensional Databases. In H. Schek, F. Saltor, I. Ramos, G. Alonso (Eds.), *Proceedings of 6th International Conference on Extending Database Technology; Vol. 1377, Lecture Notes of Computer Science* (pp. 183-197). Valencia, Spain: Springer.

Carmè, A., Mazón, J. N., & Rizzi, S. (2010). A Model-Driven Heuristic Approach for Detecting Multidimensional Facts in Relational Data Sources. *Proceedings of 12th International Conference on Data Warehousing and Knowledge Discovery; Vol. 6263, Lecture Notes of Computer Science* (pp, 13-24). Bilbao, Spain: Springer.

Codd, E. F., Codd, S. B., & Salley, C. T. (1993). *Providing OLAP (On Line Analytical Processing) to Users-Analysts: an IT Mandate*. E. F. Codd and Associates.

Giorgini, P., Rizzi, S., & Garzetti, M. (2005). Goal-oriented Requirement Analysis for Data Warehouse Design. In I. Song, J. Trujillo (Eds.), *Proceedings of 8th International Workshop on Data Warehousing and OLAP*; pp, 47-56. Bremen, Germany: ACM Press.

Golfarelli, M., Maio, D., & Rizzi, S. (1998a). The Dimensional Fact Model: A Conceptual Model for Data Warehouses. *International Journal of Co-operative Information Systems*, 7(2-3), 215–247. doi:10.1142/S0218843098000118

Golfarelli, M., & Rizzi, S. (1998b). Methodological Framework for Data Warehouse Design. In In I. Song, T. J. Teorey (Eds.), *Proceedings of 1st ACM International Workshop on Data Warehousing and OLAP;* pp, 3-9. Bethesda, USA: ACM Press.

Golfarelli, M., & Rizzi, S. (2009). *Data Warehouse Design. Modern Principles and Methodologies*. McGraw Hill.

Google. (2010). Google Scholar. Retrieved October, 15th, 2010, from http://scholar.google.com/.

Harzing (2010). Publish or Perish. Retrieved October, 15th, 2010, from http://www.harzing.com/pop.htm

Hüsemann, B., Lechtenbörger, J., & Vossen, G. (2000). Conceptual Data Warehouse Modeling. In M. A. Jeusfeld, H. Shu, M. Staudt, G. Vossen (Eds.), *Proceedings of 2nd International Workshop on Design and Management of Data Warehouses*; pp 6. Stockholm, Sweden: CEUR-WS.org.

Inmon, W. H., Strauss, D., & Neushloss, G. (2008). *DW 2.0: The Architecture for the Next Generation of Data Warehousing*. Morgan Kauffman.

Jensen, M. R., Holmgren, T., & Pedersen, T. B. (2004). Discovering Multidimensional Structure in Relational Data. In Y. Kambayashi, M. K. Mohania, W. Wöß (Eds.), Proceedings of 6th International Conference on Data Warehousing and Knowledge Discovery; Vol. 3181, Lecture Notes of Computer Science (pp 138-148). Zaragoza, Spain: Springer.

Kimball, R. (1996). *The Data Warehouse Toolkit: Practical Techniques for Building Dimensional Data Warehouses*. John Wiley & Sons, Inc.

Kimball, R., Reeves, L., Thornthwaite, W., & Ross, M. (1998). *The Data Warehouse Lifecycle Toolkit: Expert Methods for Designing, Developing and Deploying Data Warehouses*. John Wiley & Sons, Inc.

Lehner, W., Albrecht, J., & Wedekind, H. (1998). Normal Forms for Multidimensional Databases. In M. Rafanelli, M. Jarke (Eds.), *Proceedings of 10th International Conference on Statistical and Scientific Database Management*; pp 63-72, Capri, Italy: IEEE.

List, B., Bruckner, R. M., Machaczek, K., & Schiefer, J. (2002). A Comparison of Data Warehouse Development Methods Case Study of the Process Warehouse. In A. Hameurlain, R. Cicchetti, R. Traunmüller (Eds.) *Proceedings of 13th International Conference on Database and Expert Systems Applications; Vol. 2453, Lecture Notes in Computer Science (pp 203-215)*. Aix-en-Provence, France: Springer.

Mazón, J. N., Trujillo, J., & Lechtenborger, J. (2007). Reconciling Requirement-Driven Data Warehouses with Data Sources Via Multidimensional Normal Forms. *Data & Knowledge Engineering*, *23*(3), 725–751. doi:10.1016/j. datak.2007.04.004

Moody, D. L., & Kortink, M. A. (2000). From Enterprise Models to Dimensional Models: A Method for Data Warehouse and Data Mart Design. In M. A. Jeusfeld, H. Shu, M. Staudt, G. Vossen (Eds.), *Proceedings of 2nd International Workshop on Design and Management of Data Warehouses*; pp 6. Stockholm, Sweden: CEUR-WS.org.

Nebot, V., Berlanga, R., Pérez-Martínez, J.M., Aramburu, M.J. & Pedersen, T.B. (2009). Multidimensional Integrated Ontologies: A Framework for Designing Semantic Data Warehouses. *Journal of Data Semantics XIII, Vol. 5530, Lecture Notes of Computer Science* (pp, 1-36). Springer.

Pardillo, J., Mazón, J. N., & Trujillo, J. (2008). Model-Driven Metadata for OLAP Cubes from the Conceptual Modelling of Data Warehouses. *Proceedings of 10th International Conference on Data Warehousing and Knowledge Discovery; Vol. 5182, Lecture Notes of Computer Science* (pp, 13-22). Turin, Italy: Springer.

Phipps, C., & Davis, K. C. (2002). Automating Data Warehouse Conceptual Schema Design and Evaluation. In L. V. S. Lakshmanan (Ed.), *Proceedings of 4th International Workshop on Design and Management of Data Warehouses*; pp 23-32, Toronto, Canada: CEUR-WS.org.

Prat, N., Akoka, J., & Comyn-Wattiau, I. (2006). A UML-based Data Warehouse Design Method. *Decision Support Systems*, *42*(3), 1449–1473. doi:10.1016/j.dss.2005.12.001

Romero, O., & Abelló, A. (2006). Multidimensional Design by Examples. In A. M. Tjoa, J. Trujillo (Eds.), *Proceedings of 8th International Conference on Data Warehousing and Knowledge Discovery; Vol. Lecture Notes of Computer Science (pp* 85-94). Krakow, Poland: Springer.

Romero, O., & Abelló, A. (2007). Automating Multidimensional Design from Ontologies. In I. Song, T. B. Pedersen (Eds.), *Proceedings of ACM 10th International Workshop on Data Warehousing and OLAP*; pp 1-8, Lisbon, Portugal: ACM Press.

Romero, O., & Abelló, A. (2010a). Automatic Validation of Requirements to Support Multidimensional Design. *Data & Knowledge Engineering*, *69*(9), 917–942. doi:10.1016/j.datak.2010.03.006

Romero, O., & Abelló, A. (2010b). A Framework for Multidimensional Design of Data Warehouses from Ontologies. *Data & Knowledge Engineering*, *69*(11), 1138–1157. doi:10.1016/j. datak.2010.07.007

Song, I., Khare, R., & Dai, B. (2007). SAMSTAR: A Semi-Automated Lexical Method for Generating STAR Schemas from an ER Diagram In I. Song, T. B. Pedersen (Eds.), *Proceedings of ACM 10th International Workshop on Data Warehousing and OLAP;* pp 9-16, Lisbon, Portugal: ACM Press.

Vrdoljak, B., Banek, M., & Rizzi, S. (2003). Designing Web Warehouses from XML Schemas. In In Y. Kambayashi, M. K. Mohania, W. Wöß (Eds.), *Proceedings of 5th International Conference on Data Warehousing and Knowledge Discovery; Vol. 2737, Lecture Notes of Computer Science* (pp 89-98). Prague, Czech Republic: Springer.

Winter, R., & Strauch, B. (2003). A Method for Demand-Driven Information Requirements Analysis in DW Projects. *In Proceedings of 36th Annual Hawaii International Conference on System Sciences*; pp 231-239. Hawaii, USA: IEEE.

Chapter 6
On Handling the Evolution of External Data Sources in a Data Warehouse Architecture

Robert Wrembel
Poznan University of Technology, Poland

ABSTRACT

A data warehouse architecture (DWA) has been developed for the purpose of integrating data from multiple heterogeneous, distributed, and autonomous external data sources (EDSs) as well as for providing means for advanced analysis of integrated data. The major components of this architecture include: an external data source (EDS) layer, and extraction-transformation-loading (ETL) layer, a data warehouse (DW) layer, and an on-line analytical processing (OLAP) layer. Methods of designing a DWA, research developments, and most of the commercially available DW technologies tacitly assumed that a DWA is static. In practice, however, a DWA requires changes among others as the result of the evolution of EDSs, changes of the real world represented in a DW, and new user requirements. Changes in the structures of EDSs impact the ETL, DW, and OLAP layers. Since such changes are frequent, developing a technology for handling them automatically or semi-automatically in a DWA is of high practical importance. This chapter discusses challenges in designing, building, and managing a DWA that supports the evolution of structures of EDSs, evolution of an ETL layer, and evolution of a DW. The challenges and their solutions presented here are based on an experience of building a prototype Evolving-ETL and a prototype Multiversion Data Warehouse (MVDW). In details, this chapter presents the following issues: the concept of the MVDW, an approach to querying the MVDW, an approach to handling the evolution of an ETL layer, a technique for sharing data between multiple DW versions, and two index structures for the MVDW.

DOI: 10.4018/978-1-60960-537-7.ch006

INTRODUCTION

Contemporary model of managing enterprises, institutions, and organizations is based on decision support systems. In these systems, knowledge is gained from data analysis. Nowadays, core components of the majority of decision support systems include data warehouses (Kimball & Ross, 2002).

A data warehouse architecture has been developed for the purpose of: (1) providing a framework for the integration of multiple heterogeneous, distributed, and autonomous external data sources spread across a company and (2) providing means for advanced analysis of integrated data. A data warehouse architecture is typically composed of four layers, as shown in Figure 1. The first one - an external data sources (EDSs) layer represents heterogeneous and distributed production systems that are integrated. EDSs can include various fully functional databases as well as non-database storage systems. The second layer - an extraction-translation-loading (ETL) layer is responsible for executing multiple tasks, including: extracting data from EDSs, transforming data into a common data model, cleaning data, removing missing and inconsistent values, integrating data, removing duplicates, computing aggregates as well as loading data into a central repository (Kimball & Caserta, 2004). In practice, an ETL layer is modeled as a directed graph whose nodes represent the aforementioned tasks and arcs represent the execution order of these tasks, cf. (Vassiliadis et al., 2005).

The third layer includes a large central repository (database), called a data warehouse (DW), that stores integrated and summarized data. The fourth layer, called an on-line analytical processing (OLAP) layer, is responsible for various types of data analysis and visualizations. In this layer, OLAP applications, which execute complex queries, are used for the purpose of discovering trends, patterns of behavior, and anomalies as well as for finding hidden dependencies between data.

An inherent feature of EDSs is their evolution in time with respect to not only their contents (data) but also their structures (schemas). Content changes result from a day-to-day usage of EDSs. Structure changes result mainly from changes of the real world being modeled in EDSs and new user requirements. Both types of changes must be propagated into a DW architecture. In practice, content changes are handled and propagated by materialized views and standard DW refreshing techniques, cf. (Gupta, Mumick, 1999). Structure changes are more difficult to handle and manage since they have an impact on multiple layers of a DW architecture. First, structural changes have an impact on an ETL layer that must be redesigned and redeployed. Second, they have an impact on a data warehouse schema that must be modified in order to follow changes in EDSs (Rundensteiner, Koeller, & Zhang, 2000). DW schema changes result, in turn, in changes in OLAP applications. Additionally, new requirements of a DW users and creating various simulation scenarios (often called a 'what-if' analysis) may require changes in a DW schema.

As reported in (Sjøberg, 1993; Moon et al., 2008), structures of data sources change frequently. For example, the Wikipedia schema changed on average every 9-10 days during the last 4 years. Also our experience reveals that schemas of EDSs may change very frequently. For example, telecommunication data sources changed their schemas every 7-13 days, on average. Banking data sources are more stable but they changed their schemas every 2-4 weeks, on average. The most frequent changes concerned increasing the length of a column, changing a data type of a column, and adding a new column.

For a long period of time the existing DW technologies and research contributions have tacitly assumed that the structure of a DW is time invariant. As a consequence, many of the research developments and most of the commercially available DW technologies offer functionalities for managing data warehouses of static (time in-

Figure 1. A basic data warehouse architecture

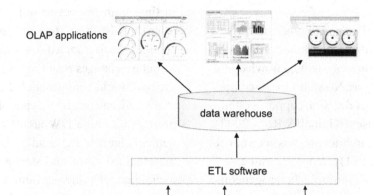

variant) structures. For these reasons, developing a technology for handling structural changes of EDSs and managing them in a DW architecture is of high practical importance.

Managing the evolution of a DW architecture is challenging from a research and technological point of view. The basic issues that should be solved include: (1) a DW model and metadata capable of representing and storing the history of evolution that concerns not only data but also data structures, (2) a query language capable of querying possibly heterogeneous DW states and capable of analyzing metadata on an evolving DW, (3) techniques for detecting changes in EDSs that have an impact on the structure of a DW, (4) techniques of automatic or semi-automatic adjustment of ETL graphs to new structures of EDSs, and (5) physical data structures supporting storage and efficient access to evolving data.

The research and technological developments of handling structural changes of EDSs in a DW architecture so far have mainly focused on managing changes in a DW schema. In this field, the following approaches can be distinguished: (1) materialized view adaptation, (2) schema and data evolution, (3) simulation, (4) temporal schema and data extensions, and (5) versioning of a schema

and data. All of the approaches are outlined in this chapter. Handling and incorporating structural changes to ETL and OLAP layers received so far little attention from the research community.

This chapter discusses challenges in designing, building, and managing a data warehouse architecture that supports the evolution of structures of EDSs, evolution of an ETL layer, and evolution of a DW. The challenges and their solutions presented in this chapter are based on an experience gained by the author and his team while building a prototype *Evolving-ETL* and a prototype *Multiversion Data Warehouse* (MVDW). The chapter is organized as follows. First, we discuss real world examples illustrating DW evolution and motivating our work. Second, we present the concept of the MVDW. Third, we overview an approach to querying the MVDW. Fourth, we overview our approach (currently being developed) to handling the evolution of an ETL layer. Next, we describe a technique for sharing data between multiple DW versions. Next, we present solutions for indexing data in the MVDW. Finally, we summarize the chapter and discuss possible areas for future work.

Figure 2. An example Location dimension and its dimension instance

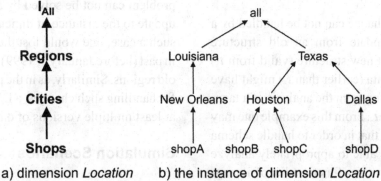

a) dimension *Location*   b) the instance of dimension *Location*

MOTIVATING EXAMPLES

In this section we present some real world examples illustrating the evolution of a DW. Other examples can be found in (Bębel et al., 2004; Mendelzon & Vaisman, 2000). The examples are preceded by basic definitions used in this chapter.

Basic Definitions

Data in a DW are organized according to a dedicated model (Gyssens & Lakshmanan, 1997; Letz, Henn, & Vossen, 2002). In this model, an elementary information being the subject of analysis is called a *fact*. It contains numerical features, called *measures* (e.g., quantity, income, duration time) that quantify the fact and allow to compare different facts. Values of measures depend on a context set up by *dimensions*. A dimension is composed of *levels* that form a hierarchy. A lower level is connected to its direct parent level by a relation, further denoted as →. A dimension contains a distinguished top level, denoted as l_{All}, and a terminal/bottom level. Every level l_i has associated a domain of values. The finite subset of domain values constitutes the set of *level instances*. The instances of levels in a given dimension are related to each other, so that they form a hierarchy, called a *dimension instance*.

A typical example of a dimension, called *Location*, is shown in Fig.2a. It is composed

of four hierarchically connected levels, i.e., *Shops→Cities→Regions→l_{All}*. An example instance of dimension *Location* is shown in Fig.2b. It is composed of 10 related level instances.

This model of a DW can be implemented either in multidimensional OLAP servers (further called MOLAP) or in relational OLAP servers (further called ROLAP). In a MOLAP implementation, data are stored in specialized data structures, e.g., multidimensional arrays, hash tables (e.g., SQL Server), binary large objects (e.g., Oracle), index structures based on a B-tree, Quad-tree, or K-D-tree. In a ROLAP implementation, data are stored in relational tables. Some of the tables represent levels and are called *level tables*, while others store values of measures, and are called *fact tables*. Two basic types of ROLAP logical schemas are used, i.e., a star schema and a snowflake schema (Chaudhuri & Dayal, 1997).

DW Schema Changes

This example comes from gambling machines business (Czejdo et al., 2000). Let us assume that until time t_1 taxes from gambling machines have been collected per every single machine. A simplified logical schema of a DW used for income analysis from this business is shown in Figure 3a. Since time t_2 taxes have been collected per location, regardless the number of machines installed there. As we can observe, the way of collecting taxes has impact on the logical schema of a DW, cf. Figure 3b.

Such schema change can not be handled by a simple schema update from an old structure (valid until t_1) to a new structure (valid from t_2) since some past data (earlier than t_2) might have been lost, preventing from the analysis of a taxation history before t_2. From this example one may draw a conclusion that in order to handle schema changes and to be able to appropriately analyze data, a DW should offer a functionality of managing multiple DW states (versions) including versions of a schema and versions of data.

Dimension Instance Changes

This example comes from Poland and it illustrates how changes to the administrative division of the country could impact analytical results. The administrative division of Poland until 1998 included 49 regions (voivodships). A new division that was set up in 1999 included only 16 regions. Let us now consider a data warehouse allowing to analyze yearly sales of products in regions. The results of this analysis would show a remarkable increase in sales in 1999 as compared to 1998. Actually, this increase would be caused by the changes in the structure of the *Location* dimension instance rather than by real higher sales.

In such and many other cases of changing the structure of dimension instances, in order to appropriately interpret the obtained results a decision maker must be aware of real changes that were

applied to dimension instances. The presented problem can not be solved by applying a simple update to the instance of dimension *Location*. In such a case, one would lost the information that in past (before January 1, 1999) cities belonged to old regions. Similarly, as in the previous example, for handling such changes, a DW should manage at least multiple versions of data.

Simulation Scenarios

An example illustrating the need for the 'what-if' analysis comes from the electricity supply business in Poland. In order to lower taxes, companies apply depreciation of their fixed assets. There are different types of depreciation with different depreciation rates, resulting in higher or lower taxes paid in a given year. In order to chose the best depreciation type for a company, multiple alternative business simulation scenarios may be created, one scenario for one depreciation type. Notice that creating simulation scenarios may require changes to a DW schema and/or data. Such simulation scenarios should be represented by separate DW versions.

CONCEPT OF MULTIVERSION DATA WAREHOUSE

Having analyzed real world examples of a DW evolution, we may draw a conclusion that there is evident need for comprehensive solutions allowing

Figure 3. Example logical schemas of a DW for gambling machines business

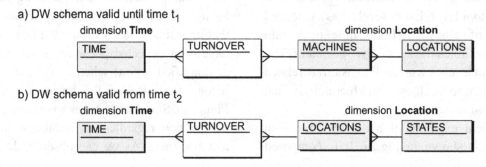

to handle the evolution of DWs. A solution that we proposed is based on the so-called *Multiverison Data Warehouse* (MVDW).

DW Versions

The Multiversion Data Warehouse is composed of the sequence of DW versions. A *DW version* is composed of a DW schema version and a DW instance version. The *DW schema version* describes the structure of a DW within a given time period, whereas the *DW instance version* represents the set of data described by its schema version.

We distinguish two types of DW versions, namely real and alternative ones (Bębel et al., 2004). Real versions are created in order to reflect changes in a real business environment. *Real versions* are linearly ordered by the time they are valid within. *Alternative versions* are created mainly for simulation purposes, as part of the 'what-if' analysis. Such versions represent virtual business scenarios.

Figure 4 schematically shows real and alternative DW versions. R_1 represents an initial real version. Based on R_1, new real version R_2 was derived. Similarly, R_3 was derived from R_2. $A_{2.1}$ and $A_{2.2}$ are alternative versions derived from R_2. $A_{2.1.1}$ is another child alternative version derived from $A_{2.1}$.

Every DW version is valid within certain period of time represented by two timestamps, i.e., *begin validity time* (BVT) and *end validity time* (EVT) (Bębel et al., 2004; Wrembel & Bębel, 2007), as shown in Figure 4. For example, real version R_1 is valid within time t_1 (BVT) and t_2 (EVT).

DW Version Change Operations

After being explicitly derived, a DW version may be modified by means of 15 elementary operations on a schema, further called *schema change operations* and by means of 7 elementary operations on dimension instances, further called *instance change operations*. These operations allow to handle all typical changes that may appear in practice. Notice that multiple schema change operations and instance change operations may be applied to the same DW version.

Schema change operations include: creating a new dimension, creating a new level, connecting a level into a dimension hierarchy, disconnecting a level from a dimension hierarchy, removing a level, removing a dimension, creating a new attribute for a level, removing an attribute from a level, changing the domain of a level or a fact attribute, creating a new fact, creating a new attribute for a fact, removing an attribute from a

Figure 4. An example derivation of real and alternative DW versions

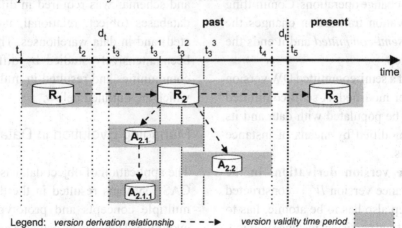

Legend: *version derivation relationship* - - - ▶   *version validity time period*

fact, creating an association between a fact and a level, removing an association between a fact and a level, removing a fact.

Instance change operations include: inserting a new level instance, associating a level instance with its parent level instance, associating a fact instance with a bottom level instance, deleting a level instance, reclassifying a level instance, merging n instances of a given level into a new instance of the same level, splitting an instance of a given level into n new instances of the same level.

DW Version Derivation

DW version derivation is a two-step process including: (1) the derivation of a DW schema version and (2) the derivation of a DW instance version.

DW schema version derivation. In this step, schema version SV_j is derived from its parent schema version SV_i. This step has to be atomic, has to create a consistent and persistent schema version. Moreover, SV_j has to be inaccessible to users until the derivation step is completed. For these reasons, this step is executed transactionally by the so-called *schema derivation transaction* (Bębel, Królikowski, & Wrembel, 2006). While executing this transaction, the newly created DW version V_j containing schema version SV_j obtains status *new*, meaning that only its schema can be modified. Within this transaction, schema objects from SV_i are derived into SV_j and are modified by means of schema change operations. Committing the schema derivation transaction changes the status of V_j into *semi-committed* and it ends the first derivation step.

The schema of a semi-committed DW version can not be further modified. A semi-committed DW version can be populated with data and its content can be modified by means of instance change operations.

DW instance version derivation. In the second step, instance version IV_j is constructed from IV_i. This step also has to be atomic, has to create a consistent and persistent instance version.

Moreover, IV_j has to be inaccessible to users until the derivation step is completed. For these reasons, this step is executed transactionally by the so-called *instance derivation transaction*. While executing this transaction, instance version IV_j is modified by means of instance change operations. Committing the transaction changes the status of DW version V_j containing IV_j into *committed* and it ends the DW version derivation process. A committed DW version is invariant, i.e. neither its schema version nor instance version can be further modified.

Metadata Management

In order to provide the support for schema and data versioning as well as for querying the MVDW, the set of well defined metadata is required. In our approach we developed a metaschema of the MVDW that allows to store data on: (1) the structure and content of every DW version, (2) changes applied to DW versions, (3) data conversion methods, which are required for querying, (4) transactions run in the system. For the reason of space limitations the metaschema is not discussed in this chapter but more information can be found in (Wrembel & Bębel, 2005, 2007).

Related Work

The support for handling the evolution of data and schemas was required in different kinds of databases (object, relational, mediated, federated) and in data warehouses. The problem has been intensively studied by different research communities and resulted in multiple solutions, which are outlined below.

Managing Evolution in Databases

The application of object databases to CAD and CASE systems resulted in the development of multiple concepts and prototypes supporting evolution. They can be categorized as supporting schema and data evolution as well as supporting versioning. In the first category, e.g., (Ferrandina et al., 1995; Liu et al., 1997; Tresh, 1991), a database evolution is implemented by schema updates and transformations of objects according to the definition of a new schema. In versioning approaches a database manages and stores: (1) multiple versions of objects, e.g., (Cellary & Jomier, 1990; Abdessalem & Jomier, 1997; Gançarski & Jomier, 2001; Agrawal et al., 1991; Sciore, 1994), (2) multiple versions of data structures (classes or schemas), e.g., (Abiteboul & Santos, 1995; Grandi, 2004; Liu et al., 2005), and (3) versions of both classes and objects, e.g., (Andonoff et al., 1995; Bellosta, Wrembel, & Jomier, 1995; Cellary, Jomier, & Koszlajda, 1991; Kim & Chou, 1988; Matos Galante et al., 2005; Peters & Özsu, 1997).

Handling schema changes was required also in traditional relational databases as well as in data integration architectures (mediated and federated database systems). In (Curino et al., 2008a; Curino et al. 2008b, and Moon et al., 2008) the authors proposed the *PRISM* framework for expressing schema changes by means of a dedicated language, translating data to conform to a modified schema, and supporting legacy queries on a new schema by applying a query rewriting mechanism or views. In the second area, research has focused on: (1) handling schema changes and propagating them into a global schema, e.g., (Lakshmanan, Sadri, & Subramanian, 1993; McBrien & Poulovassilis, 2002), and (2) maintaining mappings between local schemas and an integrated schema under the evolution of any of these schemas, e.g., (Velegrakis, Miller, & Popa, 2003).

The application of temporal extensions, mainly to relational databases, resulted in the development of temporal databases where temporal versions of data, e.g., (Etzion, Jajoda, & Sripada, 1998; Tansel et al., 1993) or schema, e.g., (Castro, Grandi, & Scalas, 1997; Jensen & Böhlen, 2004; McKenzie & Snodgrass, 1990; Roddick, 1992; Snodgrass, 1995), are created by means of time stamping them with a valid time and/or a transaction time.

Temporal databases allow to store data versions that are linearly ordered by time.

Recently, the need for versioning turned up as an important functionality for XML documents, e.g., (Chien, Tsotras, & Zaniolo, 2001; Combi & Oliboni, 2007). Such versioning is based on time stamping of XML nodes and edges.

Managing Evolution in Data Warehouses

Four eligible approaches for handling changes in data warehouses have been proposed in the literature. The solutions can be categorized as follows: (1) *schema and data evolution* (Blaschka, Sapia, & Hofling, 1999; Fan & Poulovassilis, 2004; Hurtado, Mendelzon, & Vaisman, 1999a, 1999b; Kaas, Pedersen, & Rasmussen, 2004; Favre et al., 2007), (2) *simulation* (Balmin, Papadimitriou, & Papakonstanitnou, 2000a, 2000b; Bellahsene, 1998), (3) *temporal extensions* (Bliujute et al., 1998; Bruckner & Tjoa, 2002; Chamoni & Stock, 1999; Eder & Koncilia, 2001; Eder, Koncilia, & Morzy, 2002; Letz et al., 2002; Malinowski & Zimányi, 2008; Schlesinger et al., 2001), and (4) *versioning extensions* (Body et al., 2002, 2003; Golfarelli et al., 2004; Mendelzon & Vaisman, 2000; Ravat, Teste, & Zurfluh, 2006; Rizzi & Golfarelli, 2007; Vaisman & Mendelzon, 2001; Shahzad, 2010).

In *schema and data evolution* approaches a system maintains only one DW schema and one set of data that evolve in time. Schema modifications, like for example dropping an attribute or a table, cause that these schema elements and their data are persistently removed form a system. Other modifications, like for example changing the domain of an attribute, splitting a table, or changing a dimension hierarchy, require data conversions from a previous state into a new state. These conversions are necessary for assuring the consistency of data with respect to a DW schema. As the result of data conversions, previous DW states are lost. Modifications of the structure of dimension instances are implemented by simple updates of attribute values that also causes the loss of old values. Thus, evolutionary approaches are not able to represent the history of a DW evolution.

Simulation approaches use virtual data structures in order to simulate or to screen a DW evolution. In the approach proposed in (Balmin et al., 2000a, 2000b) a virtual DW structure, called *scenario*, is constructed for hypothetical queries run within the 'what-if' analysis. A scenario is an ordered set of hypothetical modifications to fact tables or derived views. A hypothetical query is expressed by a user in terms of a selected scenario. Such a query is transformed by a system (using substitution and query rewriting techniques) into an equivalent query that is run on a real DW. As this technique computes new values of data for every hypothetical query, based on virtual structures, performance problems may appear for scenarios that provide large data volumes. The approach proposed in (Bellahsene, 1998) simulates changes in a DW schema by means of views. A schema change is handled by creating a new view that reflects the semantics of the schema change. This approach supports only simple changes in tables (add, drop, modify an attribute) and it does not deal either with typical logical schemas of a DW or with the evolution of facts and dimensions.

Temporal extensions use timestamps on modified data in order to create temporal versions. Most of the approaches focus mainly on handling changes in the structure of dimension instances, cf. (Chamoni & Stock, 1999; Eder & Koncilia, 2001; Eder, Koncilia, & Morzy, 2002; Eder & Wigisser, 2010; Kimball & Caserta, 2004; Kimball & Ross, 2002; Letz et al., 2002; Malinowski & Zimányi, 2008; Schlesinger et al., 2001). (Chamoni & Stock, 1999) propose to time stamp hierarchical assignments between level instances. At the implementation level, the assignments are represented as a matrix whose rows and columns store level instances whereas cells store validity times of hierarchical assignments between level instances. Similar concept

was presented in (Eder & Koncilia, 2001; Eder, Koncilia, & Morzy, 2002; Eder & Wigisser, 2010;). It extends a data warehouse model with temporal features allowing to time stamp level instances, their hierarchical assignments, and fact instances with valid time. Timestamps allow to distinguish different consistent versions of dimension and fact instances, called *structure versions*. For the purpose of comparing different structure versions, transformation functions are used that transform data from one structure version into another. A transformation function is expressed by means of a matrix that maps a given fact instance in structure version V_i into another fact instance in structure version V_j. In (Malinowski & Zimányi, 2008) the authors proposed the *MultiDim* model that supports temporal measures, levels, relationships, and hierarchies. Extending these schema objects with temporal support allows to store the change history of instances of these objects. In (Schlesinger et al., 2001), dimension instances are also time stamped, but in this technique, the time stamped history of changes to dimension instances is stored in an additional separate data structure. (Letz et al., 2002) propose consistency criteria that every evolving dimension has to fulfill. It gives an overview how the criteria can be applied to a temporal DW.

R. Kimball proposed the technique called *Slowly Changing Dimensions* (SCDs) of *Type 2* and *Type 3* (Kimball & Caserta, 2004; Kimball & Ross, 2002). In *Type 2 SCD*, every time data record r_i in table T is changed, an old and a new record are stored in T. Although, the whole history of record changes is stored in a database, *Type 2 SCD* has the following limitations. Firstly, all versions of records (coming from different time periods) are stored in the same table that may cause a decrease in query processing efficiency. Secondly, sharing versions of records between multiple DW states requires further extensions to the *Type 2 SCD* technique. In *Type 3 SCD*, for each column c_i whose value changes are to be tracked, there is a corresponding column $c_{i-current}$.

c_i stores an initial value, whereas $c_{i\text{-}current}$ stores a current value. Additionally, for each pair of attributes c_i and $c_{i\text{-}current}$ there exists also a column $t_{i\text{-}active}$ that stores the date when the current value becomes active. Main limitations of *Type 3 SCD* are as follows. Firstly, it does not allow to store the whole history of data changes since only the initial and the last value of an attribute are stored. Secondly, a DW designer has to know in advance which attributes will change their values and he/she has to create for every such an attribute two additional attributes, namely $c_{i\text{-}current}$ and $t_{i\text{-}active}$. As a consequence, any evolving table need to store numerous additional attributes, even if some of them may not be used at all. Neither of the two techniques is capable of handling level instance splitting or level instance merging.

All the discussed approaches from the category of temporal extensions are suitable for representing historical versions of data, but not versions of a schema. Moreover, the linear semantics of time results in total ordering of all temporal versions. As a consequence, temporal extensions are not suitable for simulating business scenarios (the 'what-if' analysis).

In *versioning extensions*, depending on the technique, a DW evolution is managed partially by means of schema versions and partially by data versions. The versioning mechanism presented in (Body et al., 2002, 2003) supports explicit, time stamped persistent versions of data. The proposed technique also uses timestamps on fact instances as well as on level instances and their hierarchical assignments. The version of a fact table that is valid within a given time period is conceptually represented by the so-called *Temporally Consistent Fact Table*. At the implementation level, one central fact table is used for storing all versions of data. As a consequence, only structural changes to dimensions and dimension instances are supported.

In (Golfarelli et al., 2004; Rizzi & Golfarelli, 2007) an explicit DW schema versioning mechanism is presented. Before applying schema changes, a new persistent schema version S_j is derived from S_i. The approach supports only four basic schema change operators, namely adding/deleting an attribute as well as adding/deleting a functional dependency. After deriving S_j, an *augmented schema* S_i^{AUG} is created for S_i. The purpose of creating augmented schemas is to support queries that span multiple DW versions. S_i^{AUG} is always an extension of S_i and the instance of S_i can be computed as a projection of the instance of S_i^{AUG}. For example, if in S_j an attribute is deleted from a table, this attribute remains in S_i^{AUG}; if an attribute is added to a table in S_j then this attribute is added to S_i^{AUG}. S_i^{AUG} has to be populated with data coming from S_i but this issue was not addressed in the publications.

The mechanism described in (Mendelzon & Vaisman, 2000; Vaisman & Mendelzon, 2001) supports versioning a DW schema and data. To this end, the structures of levels as well as fact tables are time stamped. All schema elements within the same range of their timestamps constitute a temporal schema version. Similar concept is used for versioning dimension and fact instances that are stored in a temporal dimension schema and a temporal fact table, respectively. The proposed language (TOLAP) is able to query multiple temporal versions that differ with respect to their structures. Due to a total ordering of temporal versions, this approach is not suitable for the 'what-if' analysis.

The versioning mechanism described in (Ravat, Teste, & Zurfluh, 2006) allows to manage the so-called *constellations*. A constellation is composed of selected versions of fact and level tables. The same version of a fact or level table can belong to multiple constellations. Data and schema versions are distinguished by timestamps. This mechanism is limited by the lack of a query language capable of addressing constellations. Moreover, no solution was provided for assuring the consistency of data versions with respect to their schema versions. In (Shahzad et al., 2007) the authors proposed an algebra for creating and managing schema versions, but no details were given on how to manage data versions. The versioning mechanism outlined in (Shahzad, 2010) follows the approach developed by the author of this chapter and his team.

Implicit versioning of data was proposed in (Kang & Chung, 2002; Kulkarni & Mohania, 1999; Quass & Widom, 1997; Rundensteiner et al., 2000; Teschke & Ulbrich, 1998). In all of these techniques, system managed versions are used for avoiding conflicts and mutual locking between OLAP queries and transactions refreshing a data warehouse.

Commercial DW systems existing on the market (e.g., Oracle, IBM DB2, Sybase IQ, Computer Associates CleverPath OLAP, NCR Teradata Database, Hyperion Essbase OLAP Server, MS SQL Server, SAP Business Warehouse, SAS Enterprise BI Server) do not offer advanced mechanisms for managing DW evolution or handling multiple DW states. Some functionality supporting a DW evolution is offered by: (1) SAP Business Warehouse - it is capable of handling only simple changes (value updates) in dimension instances, (2) Oracle Database 10g/11g - it supports flashback queries; this mechanism can only be used for managing data versions provided that a database schema remains unchanged; moreover, it supports querying data from a specific point in time, (3) SQL Server 2005 - it supports dimension instances updates (Lomet & Barga, 2005; Microsoft BOL, 2007); the updates are implemented by the mechanism of Slowly Changing Dimensions of Type 1 and/or Type 2; in this server, dimension schema changes are not supported.

QUERYING MULTIVERSION DATA WAREHOUSE

In the MVDW, data of user interest are usually distributed among several DW versions and a user may not be aware of the location of the particular set of data. Moreover, DW versions being addressed in queries may differ with respect to their schemas and the structure of dimension instances. Such DW versions will further be called *heterogeneous*. In our approach we developed a query language, called *MVDWQL*, capable of querying the content of multiple heterogeneous DW versions as well as metadata describing DW versions (Morzy & Wrembel, 2004; Wrembel & Bębel, 2007; Wrembel & Morzy, 2006, Leja, Wrembel, Ziembicki, 2010).

Querying the Content of DW Versions

With the support of the MVDWQL a user can query either a single DW version or multiple DW versions, real and alternative ones. A query that addresses a single DW version will be further called a *singleversion query* (SVQ), whereas a query that addresses multiple DW versions will be further called a *multiversion query* (MVQ). A unique feature of the MVDWQL is that it augments query results with metadata. The metadata describe changes in schema versions and dimension instances in queried DW versions. Thanks to these metadata a user is provided with additional information allowing to better interpret the results obtained from heterogeneous DW versions.

Querying Real and Alternative DW Versions

The set of real DW versions addressed in a MVQ is indicated by a user either by specifying a time interval, represented by version begin and version end validity times or by specifying the set of version identifiers $VID_1,..., VID_n$. To this end, the select command was extended with the version from 'beg_date' to 'end_date' and version in ($VID_1,..., VID_n$) clauses, respectively. If the version selection criteria point to one DW version, then a MVQ transforms into a SVQ. If clauses version from and version in are omitted in a MVQ, then the query will address all real DW versions.

Merging Results of SVQs

During the process of executing a MVQ it is decomposed into the set of SVQs, cf. Section "Processing Multiversion Queries". Every SVQ is then executed in its proper DW version. By default, every result of a SVQ is presented to a user separately. In order to provide an overall view on data returned by a MVQ, if possible, results of SVQs may be merged (integrated) into one consistent set. It must be stressed that in many cases merging will not be possible since DW versions may differ with respect to their schemas and structures of dimension instances (Morzy & Wrembel, 2004). In other cases, some results of SVQs will need to be converted into a common representation. To this end, conversion methods have to exist in the MVDW metaschema. These methods, defined by a DW administrator, are responsible for transforming data between adjacent DW versions.

Merging results obtained by SVQs is defined by including the merge into VID_i clause, where VID_i denotes the identifier of a DW version whose schema version will be used as a destination schema for all the obtained results of SVQs. When this clause is omitted, then by default, results of SVQs are converted to the representation as if they were stored in a current real DW version.

Processing Multiversion Queries

Parsing and executing a MVQ is performed in the five following steps (Wrembel & Bębel, 2007).

1. **Constructing the set of DW versions.** The set $S^V = \{V_1, V_2, ..., V_n\}$ of versions (either real or alternative ones) that is to be addressed in a MVQ is constructed taking into account version begin and end validity times, if a user specified a time interval in his/her query. Otherwise, explicitly provided version identifiers are used.

2. **Decomposing MVQ.** Next, for every DW version V_i belonging to S^V, the system constructs an appropriate singleversion query SVQ_i. In this process, the differences in schema versions are taken into consideration. If some tables and attributes changed their names from one version to another, then their names are found in an appropriate dictionary table (in the metaschema) and are used in SVQ_i.

3. **Executing SVQs.** Every SVQ_i constructed in step 2 is executed in its own DW version V_i.

4. **Returning SVQ results.** Results of singleversion queries obtained in step 3 are returned and presented to a user separately. Additionally, every result is annotated with: (1) an information about a DW version the result was obtained from, (2) metadata about schema (e.g., attribute/table renaming, attribute domain modification) and dimension instance changes (e.g., reclassifying, splitting, or merging level instances) between adjacent DW versions addressed by the MVQ.

5. **Integrating SVQ results.** Results of singleversion queries obtained in step 3 may be in some cases integrated into one consistent set that is represented as if it was stored in a DW version specified by a user. The integration of SVQ results will be possible if the MVQ addresses attributes that are present (or have corresponding attributes) in all queried DW versions and if there exist conversion methods between adjacent DW versions (if such conversions are needed).

In order to illustrate querying heterogeneous DW versions, let us consider a DW composed of a real DW version from April 2004, denoted as R_{APR}. Its schema version is composed of fact table *Sales* as well as dimensions *Location* (*Shops→Cities*) and *Product* (*Products→VAT_Categories*). In this version there existed 3 shops, namely *ShopA*,

ShopB, and *ShopC*. These shops were selling bricks with 7% of VAT. Let us further assume that in May, bricks were reclassified to 22% VAT category (which is a real case of Poland after joining the European Union). This reclassification was reflected in a new real DW version, denoted as R_{MAY}. Notice that brick reclassification is an example of changing the instance of dimension *Product*. This reclassification is registered in metadata. Now, let us consider the MVQ that computes gross total sales of products in DW versions from April till May (see Box 1).

As the result of parsing, the query is decomposed into two SVQs: one for version R_{APR} and one for R_{MAY}. Next, the SVQs are executed in their proper DW versions. The result of the SVQ addressing version R_{MAY} is augmented with metadata describing changes in the structure of the *Product* dimension instance between versions R_{APR} and R_{MAY}, as shown in Box 2. This way, a sales analyst will know that a gross sales increase from April to May was at least partially caused by VAT increase.

Querying Metadata

With the support of the *MVDWQL* a user can explicitly query metadata for the purpose of analyzing the change history of either the whole *MVDW* or some DW versions. The functionality of the language allows to execute two types of queries, namely: (1) a query searching for DW versions that include an indicated schema object or a dimension instance, and (2) a query retrieving the evolution history of an indicated schema object or a dimension instance. A query of the first type will be called a *version query* and a query of the second type will be called an *object evolution query*.

Version Query

In particular, a version query allows to search for DW versions that include:

- an attribute of a given name and a type or an equivalent attribute (in the case of changing attribute names in DW versions) in a fact or a level table;
- a table (either fact or level) of a given name or an equivalent table (in the case of changing table names in DW versions);
- a table (either fact or level) that has a given exact or partial structure;
- a dimension that has a given exact or partial structure;

Box 1.

```
select sum(s.amount * pr.item_price * vc.vat_value), pr.name
from sales s, products pr, vat_categories vc
where s.prod_id=pr.prod_id and pr.cat_id=vc.cat_id
group by pr.name
version from '01-04-2004' to '31-05-2004'
```

Box 2.

```
Version R_MAY Reclassified key [br1(brick)->vc7(VAT 7%)] to
                            [br1(brick))->vc22(VAT 22%)]
                    in table PRODUCTS
```

• a dimension instance that has a given exact or partial structure.

The result of a version query is a DW version derivation tree that allows to track the existence of a specified DW object in the DW versions of interest. A version query is expressed by means of the SHOW VERSIONS HAVING clause, followed by keywords specifying the type of an object being searched. The set of keywords includes: ATTRIBUTE, LEVEL TABLE, FACT TABLE, DIMENSION, DIMENSION... INSTANCE. In each of these five types of a version query a user specifies the definition of a searched object. This object definition is valid for an indicated DW version. The DW version where the specified object exists will be called a *base version*. A base version is selected by means of the IN VERSION version_name clause.

A version query can address either all or some DW versions. The set of DW versions being queried is constrained by means of the VERSION FROM start_date [TO end_date] clause, similarly as in content queries. Notice that the TO end_date clause is optional. If it is not specified in a query, then the query addresses all DW versions whose BVT is greater or equal to start_date. If the whole VERSION FROM clause is omitted, then all existing DW versions are queried.

For example, in Box 3, the query searches for DW versions in which in base version *R_June*: (1) dimension *Location* is composed of three hierarchically connected levels *Shops→Cities→Regions*, as specified in the INSTANCE OF EXACT STRUCTURE clause, (2) the instance of dimen-

Box 3.

```
SHOW VERSIONS HAVING DIMENSION Location
INSTANCE OF EXACT STRUCTURE
                      (Shops.shop_name('Auchan') →
                       Cities.city_name('Warsaw') →
                       Regions.reg_name('Central'))
IN VERSION 'R_June'
```

sion *Location* is defined on attributes *Shops.shop_name*, *Cities.city_name*, and *Regions.reg_name*, and (3) the dimension instance has the following structure *Auchan→Warsaw→Central*. Keyword EXACT causes that only dimension instances whose structure is exactly as specified in the query are considered. Since the VERSION FROM clause was omitted, the query will address all existing DW versions. Notice that the dimension, the level tables and their attributes could change their names in other DW versions. In this case their equivalents in other DW versions will also be considered by the query.

Object Evolution Query

An object evolution query allows to retrieve the evolution of:

• an indicated attribute of a fact or a level table;
• an indicated fact or level table;
• an indicated dimension;
• an indicated dimension instance.

The result of an object evolution query is the history of the evolution of a specified object. This history includes a DW version derivation tree and metadata describing the structure of the object in each of the retrieved DW versions.

An object evolution query is expressed by means of the SHOW EVOLUTION OF clause, followed by keywords specifying the type of an object whose evolution is to be retrieved. Similarly as for a version query, the set of keywords includes:

ATTRIBUTE, LEVEL TABLE, FACT TABLE, DIMENSION, DIMENSION... INSTANCE. An object evolution query can address either all existing DW versions or some versions. The set of DW versions being queried can be constrained by means of the VERSION FROM start_date [TO end_date] clause. Its meaning is exactly the same as for a version query.

For example, the below query retrieves the evolution of hierarchy *H_product* belonging to dimension *Product* in base version *R_March*. The evolution history is retrieved from these DW versions that are valid in the interval given in the VERSION FROM clause. Dimensions and hierarchies that changed their names in some DW versions and that are equivalent to *H_product* and *Product* are also considered by the query.

```
SHOW EVOLUTION OF DIMENSION Product
HIERARCHY H_product
IN VERSION 'R_March'
VERSION FROM '1-JAN-2009' TO '31-DEC-
2009'
```

Related Work

Multiple languages for querying evolving databases (object and relational ones) and data warehouses have been developed over the last 20 years.

Querying Evolving Databases

The development of versioning techniques in object databases was followed by numerous proposals of languages capable of querying such databases, e.g., (Abdessalem & Jomier, 1997; Abiteboul & Santos, 1995; Andonoff, Hubert, & Le Parc, 1998; Machado, Moreira, & Matos Galante, 2006; Rose & Segev, 1993; Sciore, 1994; Wuu & Dayal, 1992).

(Wuu & Dayal, 1992) proposed a language called *OODAPLEX*, based on a functional data model where functions are applied to modeling object properties, relationships, and operations.

Queries addressing temporal objects are expressed by means of functions, variables, loops, and quantifiers that range over time. (Rose & Segev, 1993) propose a language called *TOOSQL* based on SQL syntax. The supported constructs allow among others to access objects that are valid within a specified time period and aggregate over temporal data. The *EXCESS-V* language (Sciore, 1994) is based on object data model. *EXCESS-V* allows to iterate in a query over all object versions. The work presented in (Abiteboul & Santos, 1995) formally describes a query language, called *IQL(2)*, based on the notion of a *context*. The context, combined with timestamps can represent historical versions of data. The constructs of *IQL(2)* allow to iterate over multiple data versions. Objects keep their identity in multiple contexts, thus one can track value changes of objects. The language assumes data conversion between contexts but without discussing any details on it. The *VQL* language (Abdessalem & Jomier, 1997) is capable of querying a multiversion database (Cellary & Jomier, 1990). VQL contributes two constructs that allow to: (1) specify a single database version or the set of database versions for querying, (2) keep track of an object through multiple database versions, similarly as *IQL(2)*. (Andonoff, Hubert, & Le Parc, 1998) propose a graphical query language *VOHQL* allowing to query versions of objects and present query results. The language constructs allow to query multiple versions independently, search through multiple versions of the same object as well as query versions organized into forests or trees. The *VOQL* language (Machado, Moreira, & Matos Galante, 2006), extends ODMG OQL with the support for object versioning. The authors propose operators for quantifying over all versions of an object and for testing the position of an object version in its version derivation tree.

In the area of evolving relational databases a few query languages have been developed, e.g., (Etzion et al., 1998; Roddick, 1992; Snodgrass, 1995). *SQL/SE* (Roddick, 1992) allows to query a database under an evolving schema, but only one database version at a time. *SQL/SE* requires that every relation in an evolving schema contains every attribute that has ever been defined for the relation. A query construct allows to view data as if they belonged to another version of a relation, but techniques for converting data between versions are not detailed. The *TSQL2* language (Snodgrass, 1995) adds a temporal extension to the SQL-92 standard. Temporal query constructs allow to query either current data or historic versions of data by means of predicates on their valid times. Schema versioning is implemented with transaction time support. Previous data are stored under their old schema, while newly inserted or updated data are stored with their current schema. In *TSQL2* a query can address only one schema version at a time. A work on adding temporal support to SQL3 based on *TSQL2* is discussed in (Etzion et al., 1998).

From commercially available DBMSs only *Oracle* supports accessing historical data by means of the so-called *flash back* mechanism. If applied in a query, it allows to: (1) query the content of a table with reference to a specific point in time, (2) track versions of a specific row during a specified time period. When applied to a table, the flash back mechanism allows to recover the whole table into a specified point in time. A user is able to access past data as long as they are kept in the so-called *undo tablespace*. This tablespace retains past data only within a limited time period.

Querying Evolving Data Warehouses

In the area of querying temporal or multiversion data warehouses, to the best of our knowledge, only three contributions exist (Mendelzon & Vaisman, 2000; Vaisman & Mendelzon, 2001), (Eder & Koncilia, 2001; Eder, Koncilia, & Morzy, 2001; Eder et al., 2002), and (Rizzi & Golfarelli, 2007).

(Mendelzon & Vaisman, 2000; Vaisman & Mendelzon, 2001) discuss a language called *TOLAP*. It allows to query either a DW version valid at a certain point in time or to query the latest DW version. It can provide consistent query results

under changes to the structure of dimensions (adding a level) and dimension instances (adding a level instance, reclassifying a level instance). Additionally, *TOLAP* allows to explicitly query metadata on DW changes. The support for handling missing fact or level attributes or domain changes between schema versions was not addressed in the publications.

(Eder & Koncilia, 2001; Eder, Koncilia, & Morzy, 2001; Eder et al., 2002) propose a language called *COMET*. In this language a user can express a query that either addresses a single temporal DW version or the set of temporal versions, either contiguous or not. The selection of DW versions is done based on a time interval provided by a user. Since queried DW versions may differ with respect to the structure of their dimension instances, in order to allow query result comparison, data coming from queried versions must be converted into the structure of a selected *base version*. To this end, conversion matrices are applied. The query mechanism was only briefly overviewed without providing details either on a query language syntax or on query processing. Moreover, this contribution does not take into consideration querying tables that differ with respect to their structures.

(Rizzi & Golfarelli, 2007) present a concept, called *X-Time*, for querying multiple DW versions. For the purpose of executing multiversion queries, the concept of the so-called *augmented schema* was introduced (Golfarelli et al., 2004). The augmented schema is associated with each schema version, say SV_i. Moreover, it is the most general schema describing data that are actually recorded for SV_i and are available for querying. When an original user query spans two or more DW versions, the so-called *query execution context*, is determined. The query execution context represents a common schema for the queried versions. It is constructed as the intersection of all the augmented schemas whose validity times are within a given (queried) interval. The query execution context is visualized as the so-called *schema graph*. A user re-formulates his/her original query on the schema graph. Then the query is transparently rewritten into partial queries on every augmented schema involved in the multiversion query. Next, partial queries are executed. Finally, an integrated result is computed as the union of results of partial queries. Unfortunately, the paper does not address problems of constructing an integrated result. Moreover, it does not explain how to handle queries that address tables and dimensions that differ with their structures.

A common limitation of the three discussed contributions is that the results of queries addressing heterogeneous versions return only data, without providing any information on changes made in queried versions. We argue that such information is essential to appropriately understand the obtained results. Only *TOLAP* allows to explicitly query metadata but a user can not query data and metadata in the same query. Moreover, the three contributions do not clearly describe how to integrate results of partial queries. This issue is only signalized in the available publications.

EVOLVING ETL LAYER

Detecting structural changes in external data sources and propagating them into a DW architecture is a difficult task. Research efforts in this area focused mainly on materialized view maintenance under structural changes of EDSs, e.g., (Rundensteiner et al., 1999, Bellahsene, 2002). Few solutions exists for adjusting ETL graphs to evolving structures of EDSs, e.g., (Papastefanos et al, 2007; Papastefanos et al., 2009).

This section outlines a project that we currently run at the Institute of Computing Science, at the Poznań University of Technology. The project aims at designing and developing an ETL framework that will allow a semi-automatic evolution of its ETL graph in order to follow the structural changes of EDSs. The framework is called Evolving-ETL (*E-ETL*).

Structural Changes of EDSs

As mentioned before, the most common structural changes of EDSs include increasing the length or changing a data type of a column, or adding a new column. Other changes that may occur include: renaming a column, deleting a column, renaming a table, deleting a table, splitting a table. All of these changes are handled by the E-ETL framework. To this end, we defined the set of the so-called structural change events (SCE) that may occur at EDSs. Each SCE has associated an action, which is implemented by the so-called evolution algorithm. The purpose of this algorithm is to adjust an ETL graph in order to handle changes in EDSs (for short we will further call this task ETL graph adjustment).

We distinguish 4 general actions, applicable to all SCEs and 8 specific actions applicable only to specific SCEs. The 3 general actions include: (1) DISABLE - an SCE is ignored and an ETL graph adjustment does not produce any outcome, (2) PROMPT - an ETL administrator is informed about an SCE and then a manual modification of an ETL graph is required, (3) MODIFY - an ETL graph is adjusted to handle the EDS change, and (4) VERSION - a new version of an ETL graph and a new version of a DW are derived and then modified in order to handle a schema change. This action is only possible when the E-ETL works with the multiversion data warehouse (cf. Section "Concept of Multiversion Data Warehouse").

The 8 specific actions are associated with the below 8 specific SCEs.

- The ADD_COLUMN event: it signalizes that a column was added to a data structure in an EDS. Two actions are possible, namely IGNORE or ADD. IGNORE causes that the added column is not included in the adjusted ETL graph. ADD causes that the added column is included in the adjusted ETL graph. In this case, the column is also added to a corresponding table in a DW, according to a mapping that relates the EDS data structure an the DW table (mappings between EDSs objects and DW objects are stored in an ETL metadata dictionary).

- The DROP_COLUMN event: it signalizes that a column was dropped from an EDS data structure. Two actions are possible, namely ETL_EXCLUDE or NEW_TABLE. ETL_EXCLUDE causes that the column is excluded from the adjusted ETL graph but it remains in its original table at a DW. The column retains its old values and new values are set to null. NEW_TABLE causes that a new version of the table is created without the dropped column. The ETL graph is adjusted accordingly in order to load data into this version.
- The CHANGE_COLUMN event: it signalizes that either the type or length of a column was changed. Two actions are possible, namely NEW_COLUMN or NEW_TABLE. NEW_COLUMN causes that a new column is added to a table at a DW with a new type and/or length. An ETL graph is adjusted accordingly in order to include the added column. NEW_TABLE causes that a new version of the table is created containing the changed column. The ETL graph is adjusted accordingly in order to load data into this version.
- The RENAME_COLUMN event: it signalizes that a column was renamed. Two actions are possible, namely CHANGE_ETL and CHANGE_BOTH. CHANGE_ETL causes that the name of the column is changed only in an ETL graph. CHANGE_BOTH causes that the name of the column is changed in an ETL graph and in a DW table.
- The RENAME_STRUCTURE event: it signalizes that a data structure at an EDS was renamed. Two actions are possible, namely CHANGE_ETL and CHANGE_BOTH. CHANGE_ETL causes that the

name of the data structure is changed only in an ETL graph. CHANGE_BOTH denotes that the name of the data structure is changed in an ETL graph and in a DW.

- The DROP_STRUCTURE event: it signalizes that a data structure was dropped at an EDS. One action IGNORE is executed. It causes that the dropped data structure is not included in the adjusted ETL graph.. Its corresponding table remains in a DW but is no longer being loaded.
- The VERTICAL_SPLIT event: it signalizes that an EDS data structure T was split vertically into multiple structures $T_1, T_2,...,$ T_n, each of which stores the subset of columns of the original data structure T. One action INTEGRATE_VERT is executed. It modifies an ETL graph in such a way that a new node is added to the graph. This node joins the content of $T_1, T_2,..., T_n$ before further processing.
- The HORIZONTAL_SPLIT event: it signalizes that an EDS data structure T was split horizontally into multiple structures $T_1, T_2,..., T_n$, each of which stores the subset of rows from T. One action INTEGRATE_HORIZ is executed. It modifies an ETL graph in such a way that a new node is added to the graph. This node merges the content of $T_1, T_2,..., T_n$ before further processing.

Notice that an EDS may undergo more complex structural changes. For example, a data structure may be split vertically and some columns may be removed from the split data structures. In this case, the VERTICAL_SPLIT event will be followed by one or more DROP_COLUMN events. As a consequence, a sequence of events will be associated with such a complex change. In this example, the INTEGRATE_VERT action will be followed by a sequence of ETL_EXCLUDE or/and NEW_TABLE actions, depending on a user's needs.

The sequence of SCEs detected during a given time period is stored in an E-ETL metadata dictionary (cf. Figure 5) together with their corresponding actions. An ETL graph adjustment is run before the whole ETL process is run. In some cases, EDSs may change its structure when an ETL process has already been run. In such a case, the ETL process signalizes an execution error that is handled by E-ETL. As the result of this error, a structural change that caused the error is detected and an ETL graph adjustment is executed. After that the ETL process is re-executed.

Prototype System Architecture

The E-ETL framework is currently being implemented. Its technical architecture, shown in Figure 5, includes 4 main components, namely: (1) an EDSs layer, (2) a standard ETL layer, (3) a DW layer, and (4) an E-ETL layer.

EDSs are connected to the standard ETL by means of standard drivers (gateways, ODBC/JDBC/OLEDB) that are supported by EDS and an ETL engine. EDSs are connected to the E-ETL layer by means of a change monitors. A dedicated change monitor (CMon) is deployed for every EDS. Change monitors are responsible for detecting structural changes of EDSs. At the implementation level, structural changes are detected either by triggers or by consecutive metadata snapshots comparison. If an EDS supports triggers defined on a database schema (like for example in Oracle11g) and if installing such triggers is possible in an EDS, then this method is preferable. Otherwise, structural changes are detected by comparing two consecutive metadata snapshots. To this end, metadata snapshots must be maintained and stored in an E-ETL metadata dictionary together with a comparison algorithm.

The standard ETL layer typically includes: (1) an ETL graphical development environment for designing ETL graphs based on predefined components, (2) an ETL metadata and data stor-

age for storing metadata and data loaded and processed from EDSs, (3) an ETL engine that is responsible for executing ETL processes, and (4) an ETL API that allows to access programmatically ETL graphs and metadata by software components external to this layer.

The DW layer includes a data warehouse that is either standard one multiversion.

The E-ETL layer is complementary to the standard ETL layer and potentially can work with any ETL engine that provides its ETL API. The E-ETL layer includes: (1) an E-ETL metadata dictionary (MDD) for storing metadata on EDSs evolution (detected SCEs and corresponding actions), original and adjusted ETL graphs, ETL execution errors, versions of ETL graphs, and evolution algorithms, (2) an E-ETL manager for managing change detection processes, ETL graphs adjustments, and communication with the standard ETL engine as well as (3) an E-ETL API that supports the communication interface between the standard ETL and the E-ETL layers.

In the current implementation, as the standard ETL layer we use Microsoft SQL Server Integration Services since it provides a well documented ETL API. Moreover, ETL graphs are encoded in

Figure 5. The E-ETL framework

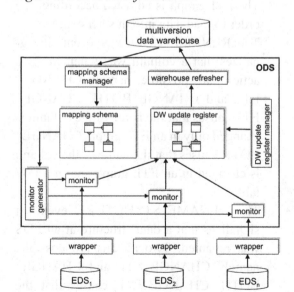

XML that can be downloaded into the E-ETL layer, adjusted there by the E-ETL manager, and uploaded back into the standard ETL layer for execution.

Interaction with E-ETL

An interaction with the E-ETL is realized twofold, depending on the structural change detection method (a schema trigger or metadata snapshot comparison). If a schema trigger is installed at an EDS, it constantly monitors structural changes. If a change is detected, then the trigger inserts metadata describing the change into the MDD and the E-ETL manager associates with the change appropriate evolution algorithm. If a metadata snapshot comparison is used for detecting changes, then a metadata snapshot is loaded into the MDD before an ETL process is executed. Detected changes are stored in the MDD and appropriate evolution algorithms are associated with the changes. Thus, in both cases, the MDD stores the whole history of structural changes of the monitored EDS. In both cases, an ETL graph is adjusted before an ETL process is executed. To this end, the E-ETL manager reads the definition of an ETL graph by means of the ETL API. The graph is then adjusted according to evolution algorithms associated with detected structural change events. The modified ETL graph is uploaded into the ETL metadata storage for execution.

As mentioned before, an execution error of an ETL process may occur when an EDS is being modified when an ETL process is run. In this case, an ETL engine signalizes an error to the E-ETL framework and sends data describing the error (e.g., error code, error message, source SQL, target SQL). The data are inserted into the MDD. After this, the E-ETL manager, based on the content of the MDD, modifies appropriate graph nodes (e.g., SQL commands) according to an indicated evolution algorithm. Adjusted graph nodes are stored in the MDD and are also uploaded via the E-ETL API to the ETL metadata storage. If a metadata snapshot comparison method is used for detecting structural changes, then a metadata snapshot is loaded into the MDD after the ETL engine signalized an execution error. Structural changes are detected and the procedure continues as described above.

Currently the E-ETL framework supports implementation of an ETL graph nodes by means of SQL commands (e.g., data fetching operations from EDSs that are expressed by the select SQL command and data loading commands that are expressed by the insert and merge SQL commands).

As mentioned before, the E-ETL framework is an ongoing project. Currently we are implementing a graphical user interface for visualizing the content of the E-ETL metadata dictionary and for managing ETL graphs adjustments. The project will further be extended with a few features. First, a language will be developed for defining structural changes that are to be detected and propagated and for defining evolution algorithms. Based on these definitions executable codes of change monitors and change detection algorithms will be automatically generated. A pilot basic implementation of this functionality was presented in (Wrembel et al., 2005). Second, the E-ETL manager will be extended towards a self-managing/self-learning module that will be capable of adjusting ETL graphs automatically based on the historical adjustments. Third, methods will be developed for adjusting ETL graph nodes that are implemented by other constructs than SQL. Finally, as reported in (Rundensteiner et al, 2000; Eder et al., 2002) even ordinary data changes in an EDS may cause structural changes at a DW or changes to structures of dimension instances in a DW. Neither of the existing solutions nor E-ETL supports handling appropriately such content changes. In future we will focus on handling such kinds of content changes by the E-ETL layer and on correctly propagating them into a DW.

Related Work

As mentioned in Section "Introduction", structural changes in EDSs have strong impact on the ETL layer. Research development in the ETL area so far focused mainly on: (1) data cleaning techniques, e.g., (Galhardas et al., 2000; Rahm & Hai Do, 2000; Raman & Hellerstein, 2001) and assuring high quality of data, e.g., (Jarke et al., 1999; Rodic & Baranovic, 2009), (2) designing and modeling ETL development environments and architectures, e.g., (El Akkaoui & Zimányi, 2009; Muñoz et al., 2009; Thomsen & Pedersen, 2009; Trujillo & Luján-Mora, 2003; Vassiliadis et al., 2002; Vassiliadis et al., 2005), (3) optimizing ETL executions, e.g., (Andzic et al., 2007; Simitsis et al, 2005a; Simitsis et al., 2005b), and (4) designing ETL processes for near-real-time DWs, e.g., (Thiele et al., 2009; Vassiliadis & Simitsis, 2009). Detecting structural changes in EDSs and propagating them into the ETL layer received less attention from the research community.

The problem of detecting schema changes in EDSs was originally investigated in the context of adjusting materialized view definitions after changing structures of their base tables. A few concepts in this area have been proposed, e.g., (Rundensteiner, Lee, & Nica, 1997; Chen et al., 1998; Chen, Chen, & Rundensteiner, 2002; Zhang & Rundensteiner, 2002; Chen et al., 2004; Bellahsene, 2002).

The *Evolvable View Environment* (EVE) framework (Rundensteiner, Lee, & Nica, 1997; Chen et al., 1998) represents a pioneering work in this area. It allows to include in a materialized view definition rules for its evolution/changes. To this end, a query language, called *E-SQL*, was developed. It extends standard SQL with constructs allowing to specify which materialized view attributes are invariant, which may evolve, and which data may be obtained from EDSs. The language uses metadata for the purpose of rewriting a materialized view as the result of changes in an EDS. The metadata are organized as the so-called *View Knowledge Base* (VKB) and *Meta Knowledge Base* (MKB). The VKB stores materialized view definitions and the MKB stores metadata describing abilities of data sources to co-operate with the EVE framework. The concept presented in (Chen, Chen, & Rundensteiner, 2002) uses a metarelation whose content describes an EDS schema and its changes. The metarelation is stored in a wrapper associated with a data source. This mechanism is capable of handling only basic schema changes, i.e. the creation, deletion, and renaming of an attribute.

(Zhang & Rundensteiner, 2002) discuss the *SDCC* system that is used for synchronizing the maintenance process of materialized views caused by EDS changes. *SDCC* collects and timestamps messages sent by an EDS to a DW when the source needs to change its schema or data. In this system, every change in an EDS has to be approved by a DW before being applied.

(Chen et al., 2004) propose an algorithm, called *Dyno*, that allows to detect the so-called dangerous dependencies among EDS updates, i.e. updates that cause a broken query anomaly. *Dyno* tries to find such an order of data source updates that eliminates dangerous dependencies. To this end, it constructs a dependency graph with vertices representing update operations. The graph is next topologically sorted in order to detect cycles that signalize dangerous dependencies. If there is a cycle in the graph then every update is executed atomically. Otherwise, multiple updates are executed as a transaction.

The work presented in (Bellahsene, 2002) focuses on an incremental adaptation of materialized views after structural changes in EDSs. A structural change is handled in a DW by creating a new version of a materialized view that replaces the old one. The framework allows to handle only 4 basic changes in the structure of an EDS, namely: adding or deleting a table attribute, modifying attribute domain, and deleting a table.

Another technique, described in (Eder, Koncilia, & Mitsche, 2003, 2004), focuses on detecting structural changes in dimension instances. To this end, the authors propose to analyze the so-called *data slices*. A data slice represents fact data coming from consecutive time periods. Data slice analysis applies various data mining techniques. The drawback of this solution is that the discovered changes not always represent real changes made applied to a DW.

Recent developments in handling evolution of an ETL layer include a framework called *Hecateus* (Papastefanos et al, 2007; Papastefanos et al., 2009). In *Hecateus*, all ETL activities and EDSs are modeled as a graph whose nodes are relations, attributes, queries, conditions, views, functions, and ETL steps. Nodes are connected with arcs that represent relationships between different nodes. The graph is annotated with rules that define the behavior of a graph in response to a certain EDS change event. In response to an event, *Hecateus* can either propagate the event, i.e. modify the graph according to a predefined policy, or prompt an administrator, or block the event propagation. This concept was also extended on managing the evolution of a data warehouse, cf. (Papastefanos et al., 2008).

E-ETL versus *Hecateus*. The E-ETL framework, presented in this chapter, is related to *Hecateus*. However, the E-ETL differs from *Hecateus* with respect to:

- the E-ETL detects structural changes in EDSs either by means of schema triggers (if such triggers are available and allowed to be installed in EDSs) or by comparing two consecutive snapshots of EDS metadata (no information was provided how *Hecateus* detects structural changes);
- the E-ETL can work with the Multiversion Data Warehouse and it allows to handle structural changes by means of ETL versions and DW versions, whereas *Hecateus* supports a schema evolution approach;
- the E-ETL can be connected to any ETL engine and development environment that

offers API, whereas *Hecateus* needs a specific ETL engine that models ETL tasks by means of graphs;
- the set of structural changes handled by the E-ETL is extensible by means of implementing new evolution algorithms and storing them in the E-ETL metadata dictionary (no information was provided on the extendibility of *Hecateus*).

DATA SHARING

Versioning techniques have to solve an important problem of making the same set of data available for multiple database versions. There are two typical solutions to this problem. In the first one, the same set of data used by multiple database versions is physically copied into each of these versions. This solution, apart from data redundancy, causes insert, update, and delete anomalies, similarly as for denormalized tables (Elmasri & Navathe, 2000). The second solution is based on physical sharing the same set of data by multiple database versions.

Two typical data sharing cases may take place in the MVDW, namely: (1) sharing dimension instances by multiple versions of fact instances and (2) sharing fact instances by multiple versions of dimension instances. Sharing dimension instances is applicable when, for example, the schema of a fact table is changed in new DW version V_j (some attributes are added/dropped, the domain of some attributes is changed) but the relationships with some or all dimensions remain unchanged. In this case, dimension instances remain unchanged, thus can be used (shared) by V_j. Sharing fact instances is applicable when, for example, for the purpose of the 'what-if' analysis, a user derives a new DW version and changes the structure of some dimension instances, leaving original fact instances for the analysis in a modified scenario.

BitmapSharing Technique

In the MVDW we apply a data sharing technique, called *BitmapSharing*. This technique consists in storing with every record, in a fact and a dimension level table, information about all DW versions this record is shared by (Chmiel & Wrembel, 2007). At the implementation level, the sharing information is stored in the set of bitmaps attached to shared table T. One bitmap in the set represents one DW version. The number of bits in a bitmap equals to the number of records in shared table T. Let V_m denote a real or an alternative DW version and let B_m denote a bitmap in T, describing version V_m. The i-th bit in B_m is set to 1 if the i-th record in T is shared by V_m. Otherwise the bit is set to 0. Additionally, the association between a given DW version and its corresponding bitmap is stored in a separate data structure called a *bitmap directory*. A separate bitmap directory is maintained for every shared table.

In order to illustrate the *BitmapSharing* technique let us consider level table *Items(R₁)* whose structure and content is shown in Table 1. For the simplicity reason this table has only one user-defined attribute *itemID*. Initially, this table exists in real version R_1 and it stores three following records: *ProdA, ProdB,* and *ProdC*. Let *BitmapNo* denote the attribute used for storing bitmaps describing data sharing. Since no data have been shared so far, no bitmap is allocated. Therefore, this attribute stores *null*, which is marked in Table 1 as *BitmapNo=null*

In the next step, the second real DW version R_2 is derived from R_1. R_2 contains its own level table *Items(R₂)*. This table stores its own records, namely *prodD* and *prodE*. These two records are not shared by any other DW version, and therefore no bitmap is allocated in *Items(R₂)*, i.e., *BitmapNo=null*.

Let us further assume that *Items(R₁)* shares all its records with *Items(R₂)*. In order to represent this sharing, bitmap number 1 is allocated in table *Items(R₁)*, i.e., attribute *BitmapNo=1* in *Items(R₁)*,

as shown in Table 2. Since all records in this table are shared, all bits in this bitmap (i.e., for every record) are set to 1.

The fact that bitmap number 1 stores information about sharing data between DW version R_1 and R_2 is represented by record $< R_1, R_2, 1>$ in the bitmap directory, called *BitmapDir(Items)*, as shown in Table 2. This record denotes that: (1) version R_2 shares data with its parent version R_1 and (2) the sharing information between these two versions is stored as bitmap number 1, which is physically stored in table *Items(R₁)*. Notice that a bitmap describing sharing is allocated in the table were shared records are physically stored.

In the next step, the first alternative DW version $A_{2.1}$ is derived from R_2. This version shares *prodA* and *prodB* with version *Items(R₁)* as well

Table 1. An example content of the Items table in version R₁

Items(R_1)	
itemID	BitmapNo=null
prodA	null
prodB	null
prodC	null

Table 2. An example content of tables Items(R₁), Items(R₂), and BitmapDir(Items) after driving real DW version R₂ from R₁ with full data sharing

Items(R_1)			Items(R_2)	
itemID	BitmapNo=1		itemID	BitmapNo=null
prodA	1		prodD	null
prodB	1		prodE	null
prodC	1			

	BitmapDir(Items)		
	VerParent	VerChild	BitmapNo
	R_1	R_2	1

as *prodE* with *Items(R₂)*. In order to represent this sharing: (1) bitmap number 2 (i.e. *BitmapNo=2*) is allocated in table *Items(R₁)* and (2) bitmap number 1 (i.e. *BitmapNo=1*) is allocated in table *Items(R₂)*, as shown in Table 3.

For shared records *prodA* and *prodB* in *Items(R₁)* their bits are set to 1 in bitmap number 2. For shared record *prodE* in *Items(R₂)*, its bit is set to 1 in bitmap number 1.

The two newly allocated bitmaps are described by two new records in *BitmapDir(Items)*, as shown in Table 3. The first record, i.e. $< R_2, A_{2.1}, 1>$, denotes that: (1) version $A_{2.1}$ shares data with its parent version R_2 and (2) the sharing information between these two versions is stored in bitmap number 1, in *Items(R₂)*. The second record, i.e. $< R_1, A_{2.1}, 2>$, denotes that: (1) version $A_{2.1}$ shares data with its transitive parent version R_1 and (2) the sharing information between these two versions is stored in bitmap number 2, in *Items(R₁)*.

In order to reduce the number of allocated bitmaps for tables sharing all their records by the sequence of consecutive DW versions, say $V_i, V_{i+1}, V_{i+2}, ..., V_{i+m}$, we register only the bitmap describing sharing by the last version in the version derivation sequence, i.e. V_{i+m}. While composing a common set of data belonging to a given DW version the system infers the set of data assuming that: if for a given table, say T, bitmap B_{i+m} describes sharing information for a given version, say V_{i+m}, then the content of T is shared by V_{i+m} and all its parent versions transitively reached from V_{i+m}.

This policy allows us to minimize version derivation time overhead caused by bitmap allocations. Moreover, it allows to minimize the amount of data on sharing that has to be maintained and it reduces the amount of data that has to be scanned while finding the set of data belonging to a given DW version.

In order to illustrate the policy, let us assume that alternative DW version $A_{2.2}$ was derived from $A_{2.1}$ and let $A_{2.1}$ share all its data with $A_{2.2}$. In this case, the system does not allocate any new bitmap but it only updates appropriate records

in *BitmapDir(Items)*, i.e., record $<R_2, A_{2.1}, 1>$ is updated to $< R_2, A_{2.2}, 1>$ and record $< R_1, A_{2.1}, 2>$ is updated to $< R_1, A_{2.2}, 2>$. $< R_2, A_{2.2}, 1>$ denotes that: (1) version $A_{2.2}$ shares data with its transitive parent version R_2 (via $A_{2.1}$) and (2) the sharing information between these two versions is stored in bitmap number 1, in *Items(R₂)*. $< R_1, A_{2.2}, 2>$ denotes that: (1) version $A_{2.2}$ shares data with its transitive parent version R_1 (via $A_{2.1}$ and R_2) and (2) the sharing information between these two versions is stored in bitmap number 2, in *Items(R₁)*.

The performance of *BitmapSharing* was evaluated experimentally and compared to the performance of two alternative approaches, namely *DBVA* (Cellary & Jomier, 1990) and *Framework* (Salzberg et al., 2004) outlined in the below Section "Related Work". As the experimental results show, *BitmapSharing* outperforms *DBVA* and *Framework* for operations that include: (1) inserting data into a DW version, (2) deriving a new DW version that shares data with its parent version, and (3) constructing the set of data for a

Table 3. An example content of Items(R₁), Items(R₂), Items(A₂.₁), and BitmapDir(Items) after deriving alternative DW version $A_{2.1}$ from R_2 (shared records in the alternative version are proceeded with sign "*")

Items(R₁)			Items(R₂)	
prodID	Bitmap-No=2	Bitmap-No=1	prodID	Bitmap-No=1
prodA	1	1	prodD	0
prodB	1	1	prodE	1
prodC	0	1		

Items(A₂.₁)		BitmapDir(Items)		
prodID	Bitmap No=null	VerParent	VerChild	BitmapNo
*prodA	null	R_1	R_2	1
*prodB	null	R_2	$A_{2.1}$	1
*prodC	null	R_1	$A_{2.1}$	2

selected DW version in the case of sharing data between DW versions. These characteristics are independent of the number of DW versions and the number of records in each version. Detailed analysis of the obtained results can be found in (Chmiel & Wrembel, 2007).

Related Work

The support for sharing data between multiple database states turned out to be important in multiversion object databases. In this area, the contributions include (Cellary & Jomier, 1990; Chou & Kim, 1988; Kim & Chou, 1988; Talens, Oussalah, & Colinas, 1993). The technique described in (Talens, Oussalah, & Colinas, 1993) supports sharing the version of a component class by several versions of composite classes. To this end, a shared class version is referenced explicitly in versions of composite classes. In *ORION* (Chou & Kim, 1988; Kim & Chou, 1988), the same version of a class may be shared by several versions of a DB schema. For this purpose, a collection of schema version identifiers (in which a version of a class exists) is associated with each version of a class. (Cellary & Jomier, 1990) proposed the so-called *Database Version Approach* (DBVA). *DBVA* uses the concept of a multiversion object. Each multiversion object contains a unique object identifier and the set of its versions. An object version can be either physical or logical. A physical version stores an object value whereas a logical version represents an existence of a physical version in a given database version. Thus, multiple logical versions of an object may share the same physical version. In order to represent sharing, a physical version of object o_i has attached the set of database version identifiers that share o_i.

In the area of relational databases and data warehouses, temporal extensions (cf. Section "Related Work" in "CONCEPT of MULTIVERSION DATA WAREHOUSE") naturally support sharing the same data item by multiple temporal versions. In temporal approaches, a table that shares its records has to be extended with two attributes. These two attributes store a begin validity time and end validity time for all records stored in the table. A given record r_i is shared by these DB/DW versions whose validity times are within the range of begin and end validity times of r_i. Temporal extensions allow to represent versions linearly ordered by time.

(Salzberg et al., 2004) proposed a technique for sharing data between versions that may branch. To this end, records have associated sets of the so-called version ranges. A *version range* describes versions a given record is valid within. The version range contains a start version identifier and the set of end version identifiers. Each end version identifier points to the first version (in a version derivation graph) where a given record does not exist. The set of end version identifiers includes one identifier for one version derivation branch. In a database, records are stored as triples containing: sets of version ranges, unique key, and data. Physically, records are partitioned in disk pages by version identifiers and keys. Access to pages is supported by a B-tree like index.

INDEXING MULTIVERSION DATA

One of the important research and technological issues in the field of data warehousing is the optimization of analytical queries. In a ROLAP implementation, such queries are often implemented as the so-called *star queries*. Star queries typically join a fact table with multiple level tables. In order to reduce the execution time of star queries, join indexes are applied. A *join index* (Valduriez, 1987) can be perceived as the materialized join of a level table and a fact table. The index is typically organized as a B-tree and it is created on a join attribute of a level table. The leaves of the join index store physical addresses of records from joined tables.

OLAP applications also frequently filter data by means of query predicates. Efficient filtering of large data volumes is supported by the so-called bitmap indexes. Conceptually, a *bitmap index* (O'Neil, 1987; Stockinger & Wu, 2007) created on attribute A of table T is organized as the collection of bitmaps. For each value val_i of A, a separate bitmap is created. A bitmap is a vector of bits, where the number of bits equals to the number of records in table T. The values of bits in a bitmap for val_i are set as follows. The n-th bit is set to 1 if the value of attribute A for the n-th record equals to val_i. Otherwise the bit is set to 0.

In the MVDW, the optimization of analytical queries is even more challenging, first, because fact and dimension instances are physically distributed among multiple DW versions. Second, in the MVDW multiple DW versions are queried by the same query, which further will be called a *multiversion query*. For these reasons, standard join indexes need extensions. In the MVDW we propose two different multiversion join index structures for optimizing multiversion star queries. The first one is based on a 2-level B$^+$-tree and the second one is based on a bitmap index.

Joining Multiversion Data

In the MVDW data have the following characteristic with respect to their storage. On the one hand, they are distributed among multiple versions of the same table (e.g., *Sales* in version $V_1, V_2,..., V_n$). On the other hand, they are shared by multiple DW versions. Such a characteristics makes difficult the processing of multiversion queries, since data searching has to be routed to multiple DW versions. The problem of indexing and searching multiversion data is illustrated with the below example.

Let us consider the MVDW composed of three versions (either real or alternative ones), denoted as V_1, V_2, and V_3, as shown in Figure 6. Each of these DW versions is composed of its schema version SV_i and an instance version IV_i. Initial schema version SV_1 is composed of the *Sales* fact table (denoted as S^{SV1}) and three following

level tables: *Time* (denoted as T^{V1}) in dimension *Time*, *Locations* (denoted as L^{V1}) in dimension *Location*, and *Products* (denoted as P^{V1}) in dimension *Product*. In DW version V_2, the *Product* dimension is extended by new level table C^{V2} for storing product categories. As a consequence, a new version of the *Products* level table is also created, i.e. P^{V2}. The *Location* dimension is not changed and its instance is shared by V_1 and V_2. In DW version V_3, new dimension *Promotion* is added. The dimension includes one level table, denoted as Pr^{V3}. In DW version V_3 the *Location* dimension has not changed either and its instance is shared by V_3.

Let us now assume that a user executes a multiversion query that computes turnover from selling pencils (the *Sales* fact table) in Warsaw (the *Locations* level table) based on data stored in all available DW versions. The query addresses three DW versions and it accesses data from: (1) the *Sales* tables S^{V1}, S^{V2}, and S^{V3}, (2) the *Products* level tables P^{V1} and P^{V2}, and (3) the *Locations* table L^{V1}.

The query could be optimized by two following join indexes: one created on *Locations-Sales* and one created on *Products-Sales* tables. The first index stores the result of joining tables *Locations* and *Sales*, and the second index stores the result of joining tables *Products* and *Sales*. Thus, results of the above query can be retrieved without performing expensive joins.

Notice that in the above example, some of the joined tables exist in multiple versions (e.g. *Sales*) and some versions of these tables (e.g. L^{V1}) are shared by several DW versions. In this case, the join index on *Locations-Sales* in fact should join table L^{V1} with three versions of table *Sales*, i.e. S^{V1}, S^{V2}, and S^{V3}. Similarly, the join index on *Products-Sales* should join P^{V1} with S^{V1} as well as P^{V2} with S^{V2} and S^{V3}.

Straightforward Technique

A straightforward technique of supporting the discussed example star query would require the creation of a separate join index, in each of these three DW versions. In particular, six separate join indexes would be created, i.e. L^{V1}-S^{V1} and P^{V1}-S^{V1} in DW version V_1; L^{V1}-S^{V2} and P^{V2}-S^{V2} in DW version V_2; L^{V1}-S^{V3} and P^{V2}-S^{V3} in DW version V_3.

ROWID-Based Multiversion Join Index

In order to optimize multiversion star queries in the MVDW, we propose a ROWID-based Mul-

tiversion Join Index (R-MVJI) (Chmiel, Morzy, & Wrembel, 2009; Chmiel, 2010). Its internal structure is composed of 2 levels and it combines two B$^+$-tree indexes, namely a *value index* (denoted as VaII) and a *version index* (denoted as VerI), cf. Figure 7. The VaII is created on a join attribute, similarly as in a traditional join index. Its leaves store both: (1) values of an indexed attribute and (2) pointers to the VerI. The VerI is used for indexing DW versions. Its leaves store lists of ROWIDs, where ROWIDs in one list point to rows (of a fact and a level table) in one DW version. This way, for a searched value v of a join attribute A, VaII

Figure 6. A schematic view on the MVDW composed of three DW versions

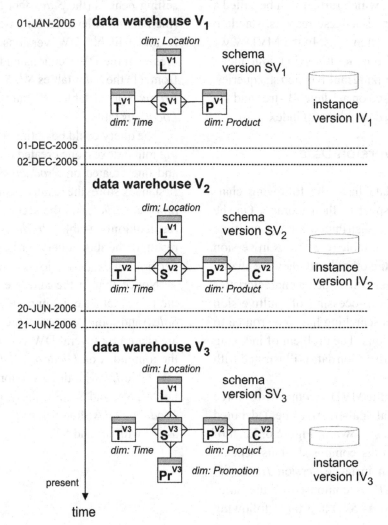

points to all DW versions that store versions of joined records having value v of A.

With the support of the R-MVJI, a multiversion star query can be answered as follows. In the first step, the ValI is accessed and searched for the value of a join attribute specified in a multiversion query. In the second step, being routed from leaves of the ValI, the VerI is searched in order to fetch data records from DW versions specified in the multiversion query.

Bitmap-Based Multiversion Join Index

The second index, called Bitmap-based Multiversion Join Index (BMVJI) that we apply in the MVDW is composed of two bitmap indexes, namely a *value bitmap index* (ValBI) and a *version bitmap index* (VerBI), cf. Figure 8. Similarly as in the R-MVJI, the ValBI is created on a join attribute. Its bitmaps describe records in all DW versions having a given value of an indexed attribute. The VerBI is used for indexing DW versions. Its bitmaps describe records belonging to a given DW version. Bitmaps of the ValBI and VerBI are accessed by means of a B^+-tree.

With the support of the BMVJI a multiversion star query can be answered as follows. In the first step, with the support of the ValBI, bitmaps describing records that fulfill search criteria on a

joined attribute are fetched and OR-ed in order to compute a common bitmap B_i^{ValBI}. In the second step, with the support of the VerBI, bitmaps describing records that belong to searched versions are fetched and OR-ed in order to compute a common bitmap B_i^{VerBI}. In the third step, bitmaps B_i^{ValBI} and B_i^{VerBI} are AND-ed in order to retrieve the final set of records fulfilling the criteria of a multiversion star query.

The performance of the R-MVJI was evaluated experimentally and compared to the performance of the straightforward technique. As the experimental results show, the R-MVJI outperforms its competitor for queries addressing more than one DW version with exact match and range predicates. This behavior is independent of: the number of versions addressed in a multiversion query, orders of the indexes, selectivities of indexed attributes, and the number of records read from each of the queried DW versions. Detailed analysis of the obtained results can be found in (Chmiel, Morzy, & Wrembel, 2009). Recently we have run experiments comparing the R-MVJI and BMVJI (Chmiel, 2010). The results show that the two indexes are complementary, i.e., they offer a good query performance for different ranges of experimental parameters, like a B^+-tree order, the selectivity of an indexed attribute, and the number of DW versions queried.

Figure 7. A schematic view on the structure of the R-MVJI

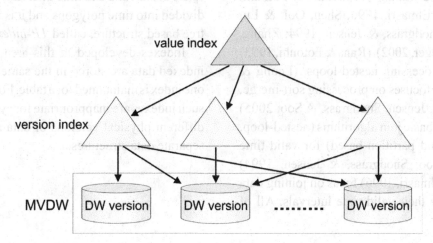

Figure 8. A schematic view on the structure of the BMVJI

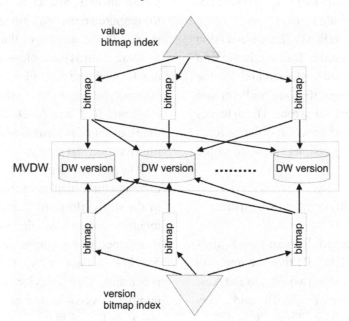

Related Work

There are two research areas that are related to storing and processing temporal and multiversion data, namely (1) join processing in temporal databases and (2) multiversion indexes in databases.

Optimizing Temporal Joins

Multiple techniques were developed in the area of optimizing temporal joins, e.g., (Gao et al., 2005; Leung & Muntz, 1993; Rana & Fotouhi, 1993; Son & Elmasri, 1996; Shen, Ooi, & Lu, 1994; Soo, Snodgrass, & Jensen, 1994; Zhang, Tsotras, & Seeger, 2002). (Rana & Fotouhi, 1993) focuses on processing nested-loops, (Leung & Muntz, 1993) focuses on processing sort-merge, whereas (Gao, Jensen, Snodgrass, & Soo, 2005) propose three basic join algorithms (nested-loop, sort-merge, and partition-based) for valid-time databases. (Soo, Snodgrass, & Jensen, 1994) and (Son & Elmasri, 1996) focus on joining data partitioned by their valid time intervals. All of these approaches do not use indexes in their join execution plans.

(Zhang, Tsotras, & Seeger, 2002) present the evaluation of temporal join efficiency with the support of B[+]-tree and R*-tree indexes on temporal data as well as with the support of the so-called *multiversion B-tree* (MVBT). In the MVBT, every index record contains a key range, a time interval, and a page pointer. In (Lu, Ooi, & Tan, 1994; Shen, Ooi, & Lu, 1994) temporal data are mapped into a two-dimensional temporal space of start and end time intervals. The space is divided into time polygons and it is indexed by a tree based structure, called *TP-index*.

Indexes developed in this area assume that indexed data are stored in the same table. Thus, one index is maintained for a table. For this reason, such indexes are inappropriate for systems where different physical versions of data are stored in separate data structures.

Indexing Multiversion Data

Several structures for indexing data versions were proposed in the research literature, e.g., (Becker et al., 1996; Easton, 1986; Elmasri, Wuu, & Kim, 1991; Kolovson & Stonebreaker, 1989; Lanka & Mays, 1991; Lomet & Salzberg, 1989). All of the techniques but (Kolovson & Stonebreaker, 1989) use B-tree based structures whose leaves store versions of data records. (Easton, 1986) proposes a write-once B-tree (WOBT) for indexing data stored on media of type write-once read-many (WORM). All versions of data records, i.e., modified or deleted ones, are stored on a WORM medium forever. The extension of WOBT, called a *time-split B-tree* (TSBT), was proposed in (Lomet & Salzberg, 1989). In the TSBT, current data records (versions) are stored on a magnetic disc, whereas old data records (versions) are moved to a WORM. In (Kolovson & Stonebreaker, 1989) the authors also aimed at managing data partially on magnetic storage and partially on a WORM medium. To this end, they applied R-tree based structures.

(Elmasri, Wuu, & Kim, 1991) propose the so-called *time index* (TI) for managing temporal versions of data. The TI is based on a B^+-tree that holds versions of data records indexed by time. For every temporal version, the index stores the set of references to data records valid in that version. In this approach only the latest (current) version of a data record can be updated. In contrast, (Lanka & Mays, 1991) proposed, the so-called *fully persistent B^+-tree*, where any version of a data record can be updated, resulting in its new version. Three different storage techniques for data versions were proposed. The first technique is based on the assumption that every internal and leaf node is large enough to store all versions of data records. In the second technique, every leaf stores data records and their insertion version and deletion versions. In the third technique, all versions of data records are treated as if they were non-versioned and they are indexed by a

standard B^+-tree index. In (Becker et al., 1996), information on version a data record belongs to is stored in leaves. Access to leaves is supported by a B-tree like structure. Every indexed data record has attached a creation timestamp and a deletion timestamp. In (Varman & Verma, 1997), the authors apply similar technique as in (Becker et al., 1996) but their technique reduces the storage size of index structures.

(Nascimento & Dunham, 1999) propose an indexing technique where time intervals (either valid or transaction time) $[T_{start}, T_{end}]$ are mapped into a single value which is indexed by a B^+-tree. All open-ended ranges, i.e. valid until present, are indexed by another B^+-tree, called OET. Entry points to the OET are start times. Additionally, time ranges may be partitioned and for each partition an index on $[T_{start}, T_{end}]$ is created. The authors also suggest creating additional index on key values. Its leaves point to current temporal versions of data records.

(Nascimento & Dunham, 1996, 1997) propose index structures for indexing bi-temporal databases. (Nascimento & Dunham, 1996) present the so-called *TDT-tree* that is B^+-tree based. It indexes time points that can be both transaction times and decision times, i.e. there is one TDT-tree for all time points. Leaves of the TDT-tree include: a key, which is a time point, say $t(i)$, and two pointers $T_{t(i)}$ and $D_{t(i)}$. $T_{t(i)}$ points to the list of data records committed at $t(i)$ (transaction time), whereas $D_{t(i)}$ points to the list of data records that were decided upon time $t(i)$ (decision time). (Nascimento & Dunham, 1997) present the so-called *Cooperative Trees* (CT). The CT is composed of B^+-tree based structures, called *VTT* and *TTT* as well as of a *multi list*. The VTT indexes valid start times of data records. Its leaves store pointers to linked lists of pointers to data records that started to be valid at given time points. The TTT indexes transaction times of data records. Its leaves store pointers to linked lists of pointers to data records that were committed before a given time. Finally, the multi list is a pool of the aforementioned linked lists that are shared by the VTT and TTT.

(Manolopoulos & Kapetanakis, 1990; Tzouramanis, Manolopoulos, & Lorentzos, 1999) propose an index for the support of indexing data records in a 2-dimensional space of transaction time - data value. In this indexing scheme, key values are indexed by the so-called *OB⁺-tree*. Additionally, every transaction time slice is indexed by the so-called *Transaction Time Tree* that points to an appropriate OB⁺-tree. Data records that remain unchanged in multiple transaction time slices are shared by multiple OB⁺-trees.

(Jiang et al., 2000; Salzberg et al., 2004) present index structures for indexing temporal versions of data records whose versions may branch. To this end, in (Jiang et al., 2000) a B-tree like structure, called *BT-tree* is used for indexing both data values and database versions. To this end, entries in index pages include: a key value and a database version. In order to support searching derived versions, an index page p_i additionally stores references to other pages describing versions of data records derived from a data record stored in p_i. In (Salzberg et al., 2004), data records have associated sets of the so-called version ranges. A version range describes versions a given data record is valid within. The version range contains a start version identifier and the set of end version identifiers. Each end version identifier points to the first version (in a version derivation graph) where a given data record does not exist. The set of end version identifiers includes one identifier for one version derivation branch. In a database, data records are stored as triples containing: sets of version ranges, unique key, and data. Physically, data records are partitioned in disk pages by version identifiers and keys. Access to pages is supported by a B-tree like index.

The comprehensive analysis of multiple techniques of indexing multiversion data and their cost model evaluations can be found in (Salzberg & Tsotras, 1999) and (Tao, Papadias, & Zhang, 2002), respectively.

Recently, in (Jouini & Jomier, 2007, 2008), three different B⁺-tree based index structures for multiversion data were compared analytically and experimentally. The first index, called *B⁺V-tree* is the extension of the index presented in (Nascimento & Dunham, 1999) with respect to handling branched versions of data records. B⁺V-tree is used for indexing versions of data records by their unique identifiers. Versions of data records are further clustered by database versions. The second index, is the extension of OB⁺-tree (Manolopoulos & Kapetanakis, 1990; Tzouramanis, Manolopoulos, & Lorentzos, 1999) with the support for indexing branching database versions. To this end, each node includes the range of database versions. The third index being compared is the one presented in (Salzberg et al., 2004).

Some achievements have also been made in developing R-tree based structures for indexing historical data in spatial databases (Nascimento & Silva, 1998; Tao & Papadias, 2001a; Tzouramanis, Vassilakopoulos, & Manolopoulos, 1998; Xu, Han, & Lu, 1990). The techniques are based on an idea of the so-called *multiversion R-tree*. It maintains a separate R-tree for each time slice. Common index branches are shared by multiple R-trees. New index branches are created for the purpose of handling changes from a previous temporal version. In (Tao & Papadias, 2001b) the authors extended the concept of (Tao & Papadias, 2001a) by proposing the so-called *MV3R-tree* that is composed of: (1) a multiversion R-tree applied to 3-dimensional data, where the third dimension is time and (2) a small auxiliary 3D R-tree built on leaf nodes of the multiversion R-tree.

The development of the XML technology resulted in techniques for managing temporal and multiversion XML documents as well as in techniques of indexing such documents, e.g., (Chien et al., 2002; Mendelzon, Rizzolo, & Vaisman, 2004). In (Chien et al., 2002) the authors analyze three indexing techniques: (1) a multiversion B-tree, cf. (Becker et al., 1996), (2) clustering of objects valid in a given version combined with the multiversion B-tree, and (3) clustering combined with a multiversion R-tree, cf. (Tao & Papadias, 2001b). Both types of multiversion indexes cluster XML data by node identifiers and node versions. The index proposed in (Mendelzon, Rizzolo, & Vaisman, 2004) supports searching paths in the XML documents that are valid during a given time period. The index is implemented by means of two tables, namely cp and δ_k.. cp is built for a given path label in an XML document and it stores the begin and end validity times of a given path. δ_k stores nodes that are valid during a given time period.

To sum up, the techniques focusing on multiversion indexes in databases, described above, have the following characteristics. Firstly, they are designed for indexing and searching versions of data that are stored in one data storage structure. Secondly, they are not aiming at optimizing queries that join multiple tables. As a consequence, these indexing techniques can not be directly applied to multiversion data warehouses.

SUMMARY

The work presented in this chapter was motivated by the observation that in practice external data sources change their structures often. The changes must be propagated into a data warehouse architecture and must be handled appropriately in this architecture. Unfortunately, most of the existing commercial and open source DW technologies and research contributions have been developed for a static environment. As a consequence, they offer functionalities for managing data warehouse architectures that either are not able to handle or can handle simple changes of EDSs structures. For these reasons, developing a technology for handling structural changes of EDSs and managing them in a DW architecture is of high practical importance.

In our approach to this problem, we developed, implemented as different prototype systems, and tested the *Evolving-ETL* framework and the *Multiversion Data Warehouse*. The main functionalities of the E-ETL include:

1. the support for detecting structural changes of EDSs by means of triggers defined on a database schema or by comparing metadata snapshots;
2. automatic adjustment of an ETL graph by means of evolution algorithms, according to detected structural changes, for a list of predefined structural changes;
3. plug-in architecture, that allows to access from the E-ETL a standard ETL engine and ETL graphs by means of an ETL API.

The main functionalities of the MVDW include:

1. the support for handling the evolution of a DW schema and dimension instances by means of real DW versions;
2. the support for managing alternative simulation scenarios by means of alternative DW versions;
3. a query language and the execution environment for querying the content of the MVDW by means of multiversion queries;
4. a query language and the execution environment for querying metadata describing the history of changes of the MVDW;
5. a technique of sharing common sets of data between multiple DW versions;
6. two basic index structures for indexing multiversion data and supporting multiversion star queries, namely the ROWID-based Multiversion Join Index and the Bitmap-based Multiversion Join Index.

We believe that the techniques developed for the E-ETL and the MVDW may serve as a foundation for just emerging DW and OLAP technologies applied to complex data like XML, spatio-temporal, and multimedia data. Such DWs will also suffer from structural and content changes in data sources and will face the same problems as traditional data warehouses. The contribution presented in this chapter can be further extended towards the development of transaction models, consistency models, and integrity constraints for multiversion data warehouses.

ACKNOWLEDGMENT

The author would like to thank the following colleagues and graduate students from the Poznań University of Technology that have been involved in the MVDW project: prof. Tadeusz Morzy - for discussions on indexing multiversion data, dr. Bartosz Bębel - for discussions on the MVDW metadata, my PhD student Jan Chmiel - for running multiple performance experiments, my master students Tomasz Majchrzak and Robert Guzewicz - for developing the MVDW prototype, Wojciech Leja and Robert Ziembicki - for developing the MVDWQL query language as well as Przemysław Hanicki - for developing the first draft of an evolving ETL layer.

REFERENCES

Abdessalem, T., & Jomier, G. (1997). VQL: A query language for multiversion databases. In *Proc. of Int. Workshop on Database Programming Languages (DBPL)* (pp. 103-122). LNCS 1369.

Abiteboul, S., & Santos, C. S. (1995). IQL(2): A model with ubiquitous objects. In *Proc. of Int. Workshop on Database Programming Languages (DBPL)* (p. 10).

Agrawal, R., Buroff, S., Gehani, N., & Shasha, D. (1991). Object versioning in ODE. In *Proc. of Int. Conference on Data Engineering (ICDE)* (pp. 446-455).

Andonoff, E., Hubert, G., & Le Parc, A. (1998). A database interface integrating a querying language for versions. In *Proc. of East European Conference Advances in Databases and Information Systems (ADBIS)* (pp. 200-211). LNCS 1475.

Andonoff, E., Hubert, G., Le Parc, A., & Zurfluh, G. (1995). Modelling inheritance, composition and relationship links between objects, object versions and class versions. In *Proc. of Conference on Advanced Information Systems Engineering (CAiSE)* (pp. 96-111). LNCS 932.

Andzic, J., Fiore, V., & Sisto, L. (2007). Extraction, transformation, and loading processes. In Wrembel, R., & Koncilia, C. (Eds.), *Data Warehouses and OLAP: Concepts, Architectures and Solutions* (pp. 88–110). Idea Group Inc.

Balmin, A., Papadimitriou, T., & Papakonstantinou, Y. (2000a). Hypothetical queries in an OLAP environment. In *Proc. of Int. Conference on Very Large Data Bases (VLDB)* (pp. 220-231).

Balmin, A., Papadimitriou, T., & Papakonstantinou, Y. (2000b). Optimization of hypothetical queries in an OLAP environment. In *Proc. of Int. Conference on Data Engineering (ICDE)* (p. 311).

Bębel, B., Eder, J., Koncilia, C., Morzy, T., & Wrembel, R. (2004). Creation and management of versions in multiversion data warehouse. In *Proc. of ACM Symposium on Applied Computing (SAC)* (pp. 717-723).

Bębel, B., Królikowski, Z., & Wrembel, R. (2006). Managing evolution of data warehouses by means of nested transactions. In *Proc. of Int. Conference on Advances in Information Systems (ADVIS)* (pp. 119-128). LNCS 4243.

Becker, B., Gschwind, S., Ohler, T., Seeger, B., & Widmayer, P. (1996). An asymptotically optimal multiversion B-tree. *The VLDB Journal, 5*(4), 264–275. doi:10.1007/s007780050028

Bellahsene, Z. (1998). View adaptation in data warehousing systems. In *Proc. of Int. Conference on Database and Expert Systems Applications (DEXA)* (pp. 300-309). LNCS 1460.

Bellahsene, Z. (2002). Schema evolution in data warehouses. [KAIS]. *Knowledge and Information Systems, 4*(3), 283–304. doi:10.1007/s101150200008

Bellosta, M. J., Wrembel, R., & Jomier, G. (1995). *Management of schema versions and versions of a schema instance in a multiversion database. Research report. Project VERSO.* Paris, France: INRIA Rocquencourt.

Blaschka, M., Sapia, C., & Höfling, G. (1999). On schema evolution in multidimensional databases. In *Proc. of Int. Conference on Data Warehousing and Knowledge Discovery (DaWaK)* (pp. 153-164). LNCS 1676.

Bliujute, R., Saltenis, S., Slivinskas, G., & Jensen, C. (1998). Systematic change management in dimensional data warehousing. In *Proc. of Int. Baltic Workshop on Databases and Information Systems (DB&IS)* (pp. 27-41).

Body, M., Miquel, M., Bédard, Y., & Tchounikine, A. (2002). A multidimensional and multiversion structure for OLAP applications. In *Proc. of ACM Int. Workshop on Data Warehousing and OLAP (DOLAP)* (pp. 1-6).

Body, M., Miquel, M., Bédard, Y., & Tchounikine, A. (2003). Handling evolutions in multidimensional structures. In *Proc. of Int. Conference on Data Engineering (ICDE)* (p. 581).

Bruckner, R., & Tjoa, A. M. (2002). Capturing delays and valid times in data warehouses - towards timely consistent analyses. [JIIS]. *Journal of Intelligent Information Systems, 19*(2), 169–190. doi:10.1023/A:1016555410197

Castro, C. D., Grandi, F., & Scalas, R. R. (1997). Schema versioning for multitemporal relational databases. *Information Systems, 22*(5), 249–290. doi:10.1016/S0306-4379(97)00017-3

Cellary, W., & Jomier, G. (1990). Consistency of versions in object-oriented databases. In *Proc. of Int. Conference on Very Large Data Bases (VLDB)* (pp. 432-441).

Cellary, W., Jomier, G., & Koszlajda, T. (1991). Formal model of an object-oriented database with versioned objects and schema. In *Proc. of Int. Conference on Database and Expert Systems Applications (DEXA)* (pp. 239-244).

Chamoni, P., & Stock, S. (1999). Temporal structures in data warehousing. In Proc. of *Int. Conference on Data Warehousing and Knowledge Discovery (DaWaK)* (pp. 353-358). LNCS 1676.

Chaudhuri, S., & Dayal, U. (1997). An overview of data warehousing and OLAP technology. *SIGMOD Record, 26*(1), 65–74. doi:10.1145/248603.248616

Chen, J., Chen, S., & Rundensteiner, E. (2002). A transactional model for data warehouse maintenance. In *Proc. of Int. Conference on Conceptual Modeling (ER)* (pp. 247-262). LNCS 2503.

Chen, J., Chen, S., Zhang, X., & Rundensteiner, E. (2004). Detection and correction of conflicting source updates for view maintenance. In *Proc. of Int. Conference on Data Engineering (ICDE)* (pp. 436-448).

Chien, S. Y., Tsotras, V., & Zaniolo, C. (2001). XML document versioning. *SIGMOD Record Web Edition, 30* (3). (Retrieved November 29, 2006 from http://www.sigmod.org/record/issues/0109/).

Chien, S. Y., Tsotras, V. J., Zaniolo, C., & Zhang, D. (2002). Efficient complex query support for multiversion XML documents. In *Proc. of Int. Conference on Extending Database Technology (EDBT)* (pp. 161-178). LNCS 2287.

Chmiel, J. (2010). Indexing Multiversion Data Warehouse: From ROWID-Based Multiversion Join Index to Bitmap-Based Multiversion Join Index. In Proc. of ADBIS Workshops (pp. 71-78). LNCS 5968.

Chmiel, J., Morzy, T., & Wrembel, R. (2009). Multiversion join index for multiversion data warehouse. *Information and Software Technology, 51*(1), 98–108. doi:10.1016/j.infsof.2008.01.003

Chmiel, J., & Wrembel, R. (2007). Storing and sharing versions of data in multiversion data warehouse - implementation and experimental evaluation. *Foundations of Computing and Decision Sciences Journal, 32*(2), 87–109.

Chou, H. T., & Kim, W. (1988). Versions and Change Notification in an Object-Oriented Database System. In proc. of *ACM/IEEE Design Automation Conference* (pp. 275-281).

Combi, C., & Oliboni, B. (2007). Temporal semistructured data models and data warehouses. In Wrembel, R., & Koncilia, C. (Eds.), *Data Warehouses and OLAP: Concepts, Architectures and Solutions* (pp. 277–297). Idea Group Inc.

Curino, C. A., Moon, H. J., & Zaniolo, C. (2008a). Graceful database schema evolution: the PRISM workbench. In *Proc. of Int. Conference on Very Large Data Bases (VLDB)* (pp.761-772).

Curino, C. A., Moon, H. J., & Zaniolo, C. (2008b). Managing the history of metadata in support for DB archiving and schema evolution. *In Proc. of the ER 2008 Workshops* (pp. 78-88). LNCS 5232.

Czejdo, B., Messa, K., Morzy, T., & Putonti, C. (2000). Design of data warehouses with dynamically changing data sources. In *Proc. of Southern Conference on Computing* (pp. 1-15).

de Matos Galante, R., dos Santos, C. S., Edelweiss, N., & Moreira, A. F. (2005). Temporal and versioning model for schema evolution in object-oriented databases. [DKE]. *Data & Knowledge Engineering, 53*(2), 99–128. doi:10.1016/j.datak.2004.07.001

Easton, M. (1986). Key-sequence data sets on indelible storage. *IBM Journal of Research and Development, 30*(3), 230–241. doi:10.1147/rd.303.0230

Eder, J., & Koncilia, C. (2001). Changes of dimension data in temporal data warehouses. In *Proc. of Int. Conference on Data Warehousing and Knowledge Discovery (DaWaK)* (pp. 284-293). LNCS 2114.

Eder, J., Koncilia, C., & Mitsche, D. (2003). Automatic detection of structural changes in data warehouses. In *Proc. of Int. Conference on Data Warehousing and Knowledge Discovery (DaWaK)* (pp. 119-128). LNCS 2737.

Eder, J., Koncilia, C., & Mitsche, D. (2004). Analysing slices of data warehouses to detect structural modifications. In *Proc. of Conference on Advanced Information Systems Engineering (CAiSE)* (pp. 492-505). LNCS 3084.

Eder, J., Koncilia, C., & Morzy, T. (2001). A model for a temporal data warehouse. In *Int. Workshop on Open Enterprise Solutions: Systems, Experiences, and Organizations (OESSEO)*. (Electronic edition. Retrieved December 20, 2006, from http://cersi.luiss.it/oesseo2001/ papers/papers.htm).

Eder, J., Koncilia, C., & Morzy, T. (2002). The COMET metamodel for temporal data warehouses. In *Proc. of Conference on Advanced Information Systems Engineering (CAiSE)* (pp. 83-99). LNCS 2348.

Eder, J., & Wiggisser, K. (2010). Data Warehouse Maintenance, Evolution and Versioning. In *Bellatreche, L. (2010). Data Warehousing Design and Advanced Engineering Applications*. IGI Global. doi:10.4018/978-1-60566-756-0.ch010

El Akkaoui, Z., & Zimányi, E. (2009). Defining ETL workflows using BPMN and BPEL. In *Proc. of the ACM Int. Workshop on Data Warehousing and OLAP (DOLAP)* (pp. 41-48).

Elmasri, R., & Navathe, S. B. (2000). *Fundamentals of Database Systems* (3rd ed.). Addison-Wesley.

Elmasri, R., Wuu, G., & Kim, Y. J. (1991). Efficient implementation of techniques for the time index. In *Proc. of Int. Conference on Data Engineering (ICDE)* (pp. 102-111).

Etzion, O., Jajoda, S., & Sripada, S. (Eds.). (1998). *Temporal databases: Research and practice*. Springer Verlag, LNCS 1399.

Fan, H., & Poulovassilis, A. (2004). Schema evolution in data warehousing environments - a schema transformation-based approach. In *Proc. of Conference on Advanced Information Systems Engineering (CAiSE)* (pp. 639-653). LNCS 3288.

Favre, C., Bentayeb, F., & Boussaid, O. (2007). Evolution of Data Warehouses' Optimization: A Workload Perspective. In Proc. of Int. Conference on Data Warehousing and Knowledge Discovery (*DaWaK*) (pp. 13-22). LNCS 4654.

Ferrandina, F., Meyer, T., Zicari, R., Ferran, G., & Madec, J. (1995). Schema and database evolution in the O2 object database system. In *Proc. of Int. Conference on Very Large Data Bases (VLDB)* (pp. 170-181).

Galhardas, H., Florescu, D., Shasha, D., & Simon, E. (2000). Ajax: An extensible data cleaning tool. In *Proc. of ACM SIGMOD Int. Conference on Management of Data* (p. 590).

Gançarski, S., & Jomier, G. (2001). A framework for programming multiversion databases. *Data & Knowledge Engineering, 1*(27), 29–53. doi:10.1016/S0169-023X(00)00033-1

Gao, D., Jensen, C. S., Snodgrass, R. T., & Soo, D. M. (2005). Join operations in temporal databases. *The VLDB Journal, 14*(1), 2–29. doi:10.1007/s00778-003-0111-3

Golfarelli, M., Lechtenbörger, J., Rizzi, S., & Vossen, G. (2004). Schema versioning in data warehouses. In *Proc. of ER Workshops* (pp. 415-428). LNCS 3289.

Grandi, F. (2004). Svmgr: A tool for the management of schema versioning. In *Proc. of Int. Conference on Conceptual Modeling (ER)* (pp. 860-861). LNCS 3288.

Gupta, A., & Mumick, I. S. (Eds.). (1999). *Materialized Views: Techniques, Implementations, and Applications*. MIT Press.

Gyssens, M., & Lakshmanan, L. V. S. (1997). A foundation for multidimensional databases. In Proc. of *Int. Conference on Very Large Data Bases (VLDB)* (pp. 106-115).

Hurtado, C. A., Mendelzon, A. O., & Vaisman, A. A. (1999a). Maintaining data cubes under dimension updates. In *Proc. of Int. Conference on Data Engineering (ICDE)* (pp. 346-355).

Hurtado, C. A., Mendelzon, A. O., & Vaisman, A. A. (1999b). Updating OLAP dimensions. In *Proc. of ACM Int. Workshop on Data Warehousing and OLAP (DOLAP)* (pp. 60-66).

Jarke, M., Quix, C., Blees, G., Lehmann, D., Michalk, G., & Stierl, S. (1999). Improving OLTP data quality using data warehouse mechanisms. In *Proc. of ACM SIGMOD Int. Conference on Management of Data* (pp. 536-537).

Jensen, O. G., & Böhlen, M. H. (2004). Multitemporal conditional schema evolution. In *Int. Workshop on Evolution and Change in Data Management (ECDM)* (pp. 441-456). LNCS 3289.

Jiang, L., Salzberg, B., Lomet, D. B., & Barrena, M. (2000). The BT-tree: a branched and temporal access method. In *Proc. of Int. Conference on Very Large Data Bases (VLDB)* (pp. 451-460).

Jouini, K., & Jomier, G. (2007). Indexing multiversion databases. In *Proc. of ACM Conference on Information and Knowledge Management (CIKM)* (pp. 915-918).

Jouini, K., & Jomier, G. (2008). Design and analysis of index structures in multiversion data warehouses. In Kozielski, S., & Wrembel, R. (Eds.), *New trends in data warehousing and data analysis* (pp. 169–185). Springer Verlag.

Kaas, C. K., Pedersen, T. B., & Rasmussen, B. D. (2004). Schema evolution for stars and snowflakes. In *Proc. of Int. Conference on Enterprise Information Systems (ICEIS)* (pp. 425-433).

Kang, H. G., & Chung, C. W. (2002). Exploiting versions for on-line data warehouse maintenance in MOLAP servers. In *Proc. of Int. Conference on Very Large Data Bases (VLDB)* (pp. 742-753).

Kim, W., & Chou, H. T. (1988). Versions of schema for object-oriented databases. In Proc. of *Int. Conference on Very Large Data Bases (VLDB)* (pp. 148-159).

Kimball, R., & Caserta, J. (2004). *The data warehouse ETL toolkit*. John Wiley & Sons Inc.

Kimball, R., & Ross, M. (2002). *The data warehouse toolkit*. John Wiley & Sons Inc.

Kolovson, C., & Stonebreaker, M. (1989). Indexing techniques for historical databases. In *Proc. of Int. Conference on Data Engineering (ICDE)* (pp. 127-137).

Kulkarni, S., & Mohania, M. (1999). Concurrent maintenance of views using multiple versions. In *Proc. of Int. Database Engineering and Application Symposium (IDEAS)* (pp. 254-259).

Lakshmanan, L. V. S., Sadri, F., & Subramanian, I. N. (1993). On the logical foundation of schema integration and evolution in heterogeneous database systems. In *Proc. of Int. Conference on Deductive and Object-Oriented Databases (DOOD)* (pp. 81-100). LNCS 760.

Lanka, S., & Mays, E. (1991). Fully persistent B$^+$-trees. In *Proc. of ACM SIGMOD Int. Conference on Management of Data* (pp. 426-435).

Leja, W., Wrembel, R., & Ziembicki, R. (2010). On Querying Data and Metadata in Multiversion Data Warehouse. In *Bellatreche, L. (2010). Data Warehousing Design and Advanced Engineering Applications*. IGI Global. doi:10.4018/978-1-60566-756-0.ch012

Letz, C., Henn, E. T., & Vossen, G. (2002). Consistency in data warehouse dimensions. In *Proc. of Int. Database Engineering and Application Symposium (IDEAS)* (pp. 224-232).

Leung, T., & Muntz, R. (1993). Stream processing: Temporal query processing and optimization. In Tansel, A., Clifford, J., Gadia, S., Jajodia, S., Segev, A., & Snodgrass, R. (Eds.), *Temporal databases: Theory, design, and implementation* (pp. 329–355). Benjamin/Cummings.

Liu, L., Zicari, R., Hürsch, W. L., & Lieberherr, K. J. (1997). The role of polymorphic reuse mechanisms in schema evolution in an object-oriented database. [TKDE]. *IEEE Transactions on Knowledge and Data Engineering*, *9*(1), 50–67. doi:10.1109/69.567047

Liu, X., Nelson, D., Stobart, S., & Stirk, S. (2005). Managing schema versions in object-oriented databases. In *Proc. of East European Conference Advances in Databases and Information Systems (ADBIS)* (pp. 97-108). LNCS 3631.

Lomet, D., & Barga, R. (2005). *Microsoft ImmortalDB*. (Retrieved November 25, 2005, from http://research.microsoft.com /db/ImmortalDB/).

Lomet, D., & Salzberg, B. (1989). Access methods for multiversion data. In *Proc. of ACM SIGMOD Int. Conference on Management of Data* (pp. 315-324).

Lu, H., Ooi, B. C., & Tan, K. L. (1994). On Spatially Partitioned Temporal Join. In *Proc. of Int. Conference on Very Large Data Bases (VLDB)* (pp. 546-557).

Machado, R., Moreira, A. F., & de Matos Galante, R. (2006). Type-safe versioned object query language. *Journal of Universal Computer Science*, 12 (7). (Retrieved January 3, 2007, from http://www.jucs.org/jucs 12 7).

Malinowski, E., & Zimányi, E. (2008). *Advanced data warehouse design: from conventional to spatial and temporal applications*. Springer Publishing Company, Inc.

Manolopoulos, Y., & Kapetanakis, G. (1990). Overlapping B$^+$-trees for temporal data. In *Proc. of Jerusalem Conference on Information Technology (JCIT)* (pp. 491–498).

McBrien, P., & Poulovassilis, A. (2002). Schema evolution in heterogeneous database architectures, a schema transformation approach. In *Proc. of Conference on Advanced Information Systems Engineering (CAiSE)* (pp. 484-499). LNCS 2348.

McKenzie, L. E., & Snodgrass, R. T. (1990). Schema evolution and the relational algebra. *Information Systems, 15*(2), 207–232. doi:10.1016/0306-4379(90)90036-O

Mendelzon, A. O., Rizzolo, F., & Vaisman, A. (2004). Indexing temporal XML documents. In *Proc. of Int. Conference on Very Large Data Bases (VLDB)* (pp. 216-227).

Mendelzon, A. O., & Vaisman, A. A. (2000). Temporal queries in OLAP. In *Proc. of Int. Conference on Very Large Data Bases (VLDB)* (pp. 242-253).

Microsoft, B. O. L. (2007). *Slowly changing dimension*. (Retrieved February 25, 2007, from http://msdn2.microsoft.com/ enus/library/ms141715.aspx).

Moon, H. J., Curino, C. A., Deutsch, A., Hou, C.-Y., & Zaniolo, C. (2008). Managing and querying transaction-time databases under schema evolution. In *Proc. of Int. Conference on Very Large Data Bases (VLDB)* (pp. 882-895).

Morzy, T., & Wrembel, R. (2004). On querying versions of multiversion data warehouse. In *Proc. of ACM Int. Workshop on Data Warehousing and OLAP (DOLAP)* (pp. 92-101).

Muñoz, L., Mazón, J.-N., & Trujillo, J. (2009). Automatic generation of ETL processes from conceptual models. *In Proc. of the ACM Int. Workshop on Data Warehousing and OLAP (DOLAP)* (pp. 33-40).

Nascimento, M. A., & Dunham, M. H. (1996). Indexing a transaction decision time database. In *Proc. of ACM Symposium on Applied Computing (SAC)* (pp. 166-172).

Nascimento, M. A., & Dunham, M. H. (1997). A proposal for indexing bitemporal databases via cooperative B$^+$-trees. In *Proc. of Int. Database Engineering and Application Symposium (IDEAS)* (p. 349).

Nascimento, M. A., & Dunham, M. H. (1999). Indexing valid time databases via B$^+$-trees. [TKDE]. *IEEE Transactions on Knowledge and Data Engineering, 11*(6), 929–947. doi:10.1109/69.824609

Nascimento, M. A., & Silva, J. R. O. (1998). Towards historical R-trees. In *Proc. of ACM Symposium on Applied Computing (SAC)* (pp. 235-240).

Nica, A., Lee, A. J., & Rundensteiner, E. (1998). The CVS algorithm for view synchronization in evolvable large-scale information systems. In *Proc. of Int. Conference on Extending Database Technology (EDBT)* (pp. 359-373). LNCS 1377.

O'Neil, P. (1987). Model 204 architecture and performance. In *Int. Workshop on High Performance Transactions Systems* (pp. 40-59). LNCS 359.

Papastefanatos, G., Vassiliadis, P., Simitsis, A., Sellis, T., & Vassiliou, Y. (2009). Rule-based management of schema changes at ETL sources. In *ADBIS Workshop on Managing Evolution of Data Warehouses (MEDWa)* (pp. 55-62). LNCS 5968.

Papastefanatos, G., Vassiliadis, P., Simitsis, A., & Vassiliou, Y. (2007). What-if analysis for data warehouse evolution. In *Proc. of Int. Conference on Data Warehousing and Knowledge Discovery (DaWaK)* (pp. 23-33). LNCS 4654.

Papastefanatos, G., Vassiliadis, P., Simitsis, A., & Vassiliou, Y. (2008). Design Metrics for Data Warehouse Evolution. In Proc. of Int. Conference on Conceptual Modeling (*ER*) (pp. 440-454). LNCS 5231.

Peters, R. J., & Özsu, M. T. (1997). An axiomatic model of dynamic schema evolution in object base systems. *ACM Transactions on Database Systems*, *22*(1), 75–114. doi:10.1145/244810.244813

Quass, D., & Widom, J. (1997). On-line warehouse view maintenance. In *Proc. of ACM SIGMOD Int. Conference on Management of Data* (pp. 393-404).

Rahm, E., & Hai Do, H. (2000). Data cleaning: Problems and current approaches. *IEEE Technical Bulletin on Data Engineering*, *23*(4), 3–13.

Raman, V., & Hellerstein, J. M. (2001). Potter's wheel: An interactive data cleaning system. In *Proc. of Int. Conference on Very Large Data Bases (VLDB)* (pp. 381-390).

Rana, S. P., & Fotouhi, F. (1993). Efficient processing of time-joins in temporal data bases. In *Proc. of Int. Conference on Database Systems for Advanced Applications (DASFAA)* (pp. 427-432).

Ravat, F., Teste, O., & Zurfluh, G. (2006). A multiversion-based multidimensional model. In *Proc. of Int. Conference on Data Warehousing and Knowledge Discovery (DaWaK)* (pp. 65-74). LNCS 4081.

Rizzi, S., & Golfarelli, M. (2007). X-time: Schema versioning and cross-version querying in data warehouses. In *Proc. of Int. Conference on Data Engineering (ICDE)* (pp. 1471-1472).

Roddick, J. F. (1992). SQL/SE - a query language extension for databases supporting schema evolution. *SIGMOD Record*, *21*(3), 10–16. doi:10.1145/140979.140985

Rodic, J., & Baranovic, M. (2009). Generating data quality rules and integration into ETL process. In *Proc. of the ACM Int. Workshop on Data warehousing and OLAP (DOLAP)* (pp. 65-72).

Rose, R., & Segev, A. (1993). TOOSQL - A Temporal Object-Oriented Query Language. In Proc. of Int. Conference on Conceptual Modeling (ER) (pp. 122-136). LNCS 823.

Rundensteiner, E., Koeller, A., & Zhang, X. (2000). Maintaining data warehouses over changing information sources. *Communications of the ACM*, *43*(6), 57–62. doi:10.1145/336460.336475

Rundensteiner, E. A., Koeller, A., Zhang, X., Lee, A. J., Nica, A., Van Wyk, A., & Lee, Y. (1999). Evolvable view environment (EVE): non-equivalent view maintenance under schema changes. In *Proc. of ACM SIGMOD Int. Conference on Management of Data* (pp. 553-555).

Rundensteiner, E. A., Lee, A. J., & Nica, A. (1997). On preserving views in evolving environments. In *Proc. of Int. Workshop on Knowledge Representation Meets Databases* (pp. 1-11).

Salzberg, B., Jiang, L., Lomet, D., Barrena, M., Shan, J., & Kanoulas, E. (2004). A framework for access methods for versioned data. In *Proc. of Int. Conference on Extending Database Technology (EDBT)* (pp. 730-747). LNCS 2992.

Salzberg, B., & Tsotras, V. J. (1999). Comparison of access methods for time-evolving data. *ACM Computing Surveys, 31*(2), 158–221. doi:10.1145/319806.319816

Schlesinger, L., Bauer, A., Lehner, W., Ediberidze, G., & Gutzman, M. (2001). Efficiently synchronizing multidimensional schema data. In *Proc. of ACM Int. Workshop on Data Warehousing and OLAP (DOLAP)* (pp. 69-76).

Sciore, E. (1994). Versioning and configuration management in an object-oriented data model. *The VLDB Journal, 3*(1), 77–106. doi:10.1007/BF01231359

Shahzad, K., Nasir, J. A., & Pasha, M. A. (2007). Intermingling evolutionary and versioning approach for data warehouse by Versioning Algebra. In Sobh, T. (Ed.), *Innovations and Advanced Techniques in Computer and Information Sciences and Engineering* (pp. 295–300). Springer Verlag. doi:10.1007/978-1-4020-6268-1_53

Shahzad, M. K. (2010). From Conventional to Multiversion Data Warehouse: Practical Issues. In Furtado, P. (Ed.), *Evolving Application Domains of Data Warehousing and Mining*. IGI Global. doi:10.4018/978-1-60566-816-1.ch003

Shen, H., Ooi, B. C., & Lu, H. (1994). The TP-index: A dynamic and efficient indexing mechanism for temporal databases. In *Proc. of Int. Conference on Data Engineering (ICDE)* (pp. 274-281).

Simitsis, A., Vassiliadis, P., & Sellis, T. (2005a). Optimizing ETL processes in data warehouses. In *Proc. of Int. Conference on Data Engineering (ICDE)* (pp. 564-575).

Simitsis, A., Vassiliadis, P., & Sellis, T. (2005b). State-space optimization of ETL workflows. [TKDE]. *IEEE Transactions on Knowledge and Data Engineering, 17*(10), 1404–1419. doi:10.1109/TKDE.2005.169

Sjøberg, D. (1993). Quantifying schema evolution. *Information and Software Technology, 35*(1), 35–54. doi:10.1016/0950-5849(93)90027-Z

Snodgrass, R. (Ed.). (1995). *The TSQL2 temporal query language*. Kluwer Academic Publishers.

Son, D., & Elmasri, R. (1996). Efficient temporal join processing using time index. In *Proc. of Int. Conference on Scientific and Statistical Database Management (SSDBM)* (pp. 252-261).

Soo, M. D., Snodgrass, R. T., & Jensen, C. J. (1994). Efficient evaluation of the valid-time natural join. In *Proc. of Int. Conference on Data Engineering (ICDE)* (pp. 282-292).

Stockinger, K., & Wu, K. (2007). Bitmap Indices for Data Warehouses. In Wrembel, R., & Koncilia, C. (Eds.), *Data Warehouses and OLAP: Concepts, Architectures and Solutions* (pp. 157–178). Idea Group Inc.

Talens, G., Oussalah, C., & Colinas, M. F. (1993). Versions of simple and composite objects. In *Proc. of Int. Conference on Very Large Data Bases (VLDB)* (pp. 62-72).

Tansel, A., Clifford, J., Gadia, S., Jajodia, S., Segev, A., & Snodgrass, R. (Eds.). (1993). *Temporal databases: Theory, design, and implementation*. Benjamin/Cummings.

Tao, Y., & Papadias, D. (2001a). Efficient historical R-trees. In *Proc. of Int. Conference on Scientific and Statistical Database Management (SSDBM)* (pp. 223-232).

Tao, Y., & Papadias, D. (2001b). MV3R-tree: A spatio-temporal access method for timestamp and interval queries. In *Proc. of Int. Conference on Very Large Data Bases (VLDB)* (pp. 431-440).

Tao, Y., Papadias, D., & Zhang, J. (2002). Cost models for overlapping and multi-version structures. [TODS]. *ACM Transactions on Database Systems, 27*(3), 299–342. doi:10.1145/581751.581754

Teschke, M., & Ulbrich, A. (1998). Concurrent warehouse maintenance without compromising session consistency. In *Proc. of Int. Conference on Database and Expert Systems Applications (DEXA)* (pp. 776-785). LNCS 1460.

Thiele, M., Fischer, U., & Lehner, W. (2009). Partition-based workload scheduling in living data warehouse environments. *Information Systems, 34*(4-5), 382–399. doi:10.1016/j.is.2008.06.001

Thomsen, C., & Pedersen, T. B. (2009). pygrametl: a powerful programming framework for extract-transform-load programmers. In *Proc. of the ACM Int. Workshop on Data Warehousing and OLAP (DOLAP)* (pp. 49-56).

Tresh, M. T. (1991). A framework for schema evolution by meta object manipulation. In *Int. Workshop on Foundations of Models and Languages for Data and Objects* (pp. 1-13).

Trujillo, J., & Luján-Mora, S. (2003). A UML based approach for modeling ETL processes in data warehouses. In *Proc. of Int. Conference on Conceptual Modeling (ER)* (pp. 307-320). LNCS 2813.

Tzouramanis, T., Manolopoulos, Y., & Lorentzos, N. A. (1999). Overlapping B$^+$-trees: an implementation of a transaction time access method. [DKE]. *Data & Knowledge Engineering, 29*(3), 381–404. doi:10.1016/S0169-023X(98)00046-9

Tzouramanis, T., Vassilakopoulos, M., & Manolopoulos, Y. (1998). Overlapping linear quadtrees: a spatio-temporal access method. In *Proc. of ACM Int. Symposium on Advances in Geographic Information Systems* (pp. 1-7).

Vaisman, A., & Mendelzon, A. (2001). A temporal query language for OLAP: implementation and case study. In *Proc. of Int. Workshop on Database Programming Languages (DBPL)* (pp. 78-96). LNCS 2397.

Valduriez, P. (1987). Join indices. [TODS]. *ACM Transactions on Database Systems, 12*(2), 218–246. doi:10.1145/22952.22955

Varman, P., & Verma, R. (1997). An efficient multiversion access structure. [TKDE]. *IEEE Transactions on Knowledge and Data Engineering, 3*(9), 391–409. doi:10.1109/69.599929

Vassiliadis, P., & Simitsis, A. (2009). Near real time ETL. In Kozielski, S., & Wrembel, R. (Eds.), *New Trends in Data Warehousing and Data Analysis* (pp. 19–49). Springer Verlag. doi:10.1007/978-0-387-87431-9_2

Vassiliadis, P., Simitsis, A., Georgantas, P., Terrovitis, M., & Skiadopoulos, S. (2005). A generic and customizable framework for the design of ETL scenarios. *Information Systems, 30*(7), 492–525. doi:10.1016/j.is.2004.11.002

Vassiliadis, P., Simitsis, A., & Skiadopoulos, S. (2002). Conceptual modeling for ETL processes. In *Proc. of ACM Int. Workshop on Data Warehousing and OLAP (DOLAP)* (pp. 14-21).

Velegrakis, Y., Miller, R. J., & Popa, L. (2003). Mapping adaptation under evolving schemas. In *Proc. of Int. Conference on Very Large Data Bases (VLDB)* (pp. 584-595).

Wrembel, R., & Bębel, B. (2005). Metadata management in a multiversion data warehouse. In *Proc. of Ontologies, Databases, and Applications of Semantics (ODBASE)*, (pp. 1347-1364). LNCS 3761.

Wrembel, R., & Bębel, B. (2007). Metadata management in a multiversion data warehouse. *Journal on Data Semantics (JODS)*, 8, 118-157. LNCS 4380.

Wrembel, R., Bębel, B., & Królikowski, Z. (2005). The framework for detecting and propagating changes from data sources structure into a data warehouse. *Foundations of Computing and Decision Sciences Journal, 30*(4), 361–372.

Wrembel, R., & Morzy, T. (2006). Managing and querying versions of multiversion data warehouse. In *Proc. of Int. Conference on Extending Database Technology (EDBT)* (pp. 1121-1124). LNCS 3896.

Wuu, G. T. J., & Dayal, U. (1992). A Uniform Model for Temporal Object-Oriented Databases. In Proc. of Int. Conference on Data Engineering (ICDE) (pp. 584-593).

Xu, X., Han, J., & Lu, W. (1990). RT-tree: An improved R-tree index structure for spatiotemporal databases. In *Proc. of Int. Symposium on Spatial Data Handling* (pp. 1040-1049).

Zhang, D., Tsotras, V., & Seeger, B. (2002). Efficient temporal join processing using indices. In *Proc. of Int. Conference on Data Engineering (ICDE)* (pp. 103-116).

Zhang, X., & Rundensteiner, E. (2002). Integrating the maintenance and synchronization of data warehouses using a cooperative framework. *Information Systems, 27*, 219–243. doi:10.1016/S0306-4379(01)00049-7

Chapter 7
A Survey of Parallel and Distributed Data Warehouses

Pedro Furtado
Universidade Coimbra, Portugal

ABSTRACT

Data Warehouses are a crucial technology for current competitive organizations in the globalized world. Size, speed and distributed operation are major challenges concerning those systems. Many data warehouses have huge sizes and the requirement that queries be processed quickly and efficiently, so parallel solutions are deployed to render the necessary efficiency. Distributed operation, on the other hand, concerns global commercial and scientific organizations that need to share their data in a coherent distributed data warehouse. In this article we review the major concepts, systems and research results behind parallel and distributed data warehouses.

INTRODUCTION

Decision support systems are important tools in the hands of today's competitive and knowledgeable organizations, and data warehouses (DW) are at the core of such systems. They store huge detailed and summarized historical data for decision makers to generate queries, make reports and perform analysis and mining that are the basis for their decisions and deeper knowledge. Users also need fast response times on complex queries in data warehousing, OLAP and data mining operations. Two major forces have contributed to the importance of parallel and distributed data warehousing: On one hand, the fact that data warehouses can be extremely large and highly resource demanding, while queries and analyses must be answered within acceptable time limits has led to a series of specialized techniques that were developed specifically for them, including view and cube materialization (Rousopoulos 1998), specialized indexing structures (O'Neil and Graefe 1995) and implementations on parallel systems, which we review along this article. While all these specialized techniques and structures play an important role in the performing data warehouse, we focus on parallel systems in particular, which can provide top performance and scalability. Parallel processing answers satisfactorily the need to handle huge data sets efficiently, in both query processing and other concerns such as loading or creation of auxiliary structures; On the other hand, the evolution of the data warehouse concept from a centralized local repository into a broader context of sharing and analyzing data in an internet-connected world has given birth to distributed approaches and systems.

In this chapter we review important research and trends on these parallel and distributed approaches. Our approach is to introduce and illustrate the major issues first, and then to review some of the most relevant systems and research results on the field. Our first discussion is on parallel architectures, the physical infrastructure over which to store and process the data, with crucial implications on performance and scalability of the solutions. With this in mind, we then discuss types of parallelism and architectural issues in parallel database management systems. Then we discuss partitioning and allocation, one of the most fundamental enablers of intra-query horizontal parallelism. After discussing architecture and partitioning, we then turn our attention to parallel processing and optimization, including an illustration on how to process in horizontal intra-query parallelism. After reviewing the architectural, partitioning and processing basics of parallel data warehousing, we devote a section to the discussion of systems and research results on the subject of parallel data warehouses and another one on distributed data warehouses. Distributed data warehouse systems are a most relevant subject, since WAN-connected geographically distributed organizations share both data and analysis, and

networking technology currently enables long distance collaboration.

Parallel and distributed data warehousing is an exciting field, and research in these issues is far from being exhausted. In a few words, autonomy, scalability, ubiquity and application contexts are some of the most fundamental issues that will certainly deserve a lot of attention in the future. We end the article with conclusions and a brief discussion on these future trends.

PARALLEL ARCHITECTURES FOR DATA WAREHOUSING

Due to their high-demand on storage and performance, large DWs frequently reside within some sort of parallel system. In this section we review different base architectures that can be used to store and process the parallel data.

There is a whole range of architectures for parallelization, from shared-nothing to shared-disk and hybrid ones, as current state-of-the-art servers come with multiple processors. There are different nomenclatures for the basic models by which a parallel system can be designed, and the details of each model vary as well. Consider three basic elements in a parallel system: the processing unit (PU), the storage device (S) and memory (M). The simplest taxonomy defines three models, as described in (DeWitt and Gray 1992):

- Shared Memory (SM): the shared memory or shared everything architecture, illustrated in Figure 1, is a system where all existing processors share a global memory address space as well as peripheral devices. Only one DBMS is present, which can be executed in multiple processes or threads, in order to utilize all processors;

- Shared Nothing (SN): the shared nothing architecture, illustrated in Figure 2, is composed of multiple autonomous Processing Nodes (PN), each owning its own persistent

Figure 1. Shared memory Architecture

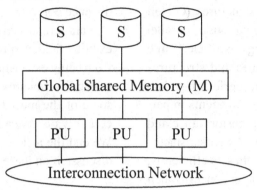

Figure 2. Shared nothing Architecture

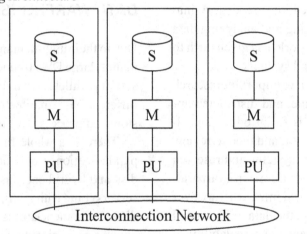

storage devices and running separate copies of the Database Management System (DBMS). Communication between the PNs is done by message passing through the network. A PN can be composed of one or more processors and/or storage devices.

- Shared Disk (SD): the shared disk architecture, illustrated in Figure 3, is characterized by possessing multiple loosely coupled PNs, similar to SN. However, in this case, the architecture possesses a global disk subsystem that is accessible to the DBMS of any PN.

Another typical taxonomy for parallel system architectures categorizes them as multiprocessor systems, then further categorizes these into shared memory and distributed memory alterna-

tives. In shared-memory (typically symmetric multiprocessors - SMP) systems, a number of processors – the processing units (PU) – share common memory and I/O. Distributed memory multiprocessor systems are systems that have multiple processors, but these do not all shared the same memory. This definition is so broad that it encompasses the shared nothing and shared disk models, depending on whether the storage subsystem or a significant part of it is shared or not, and it includes both Massively Parallel Processors, clusters of uni-processors and SMP processors.

One important aspect of any parallel architecture is that the slowest components dictate performance. For this reason, when analyzing the advantages and disadvantages of each model, it is most important to identify the major bottlenecks that each architecture possesses:

Figure 3. Shared disk Architecture

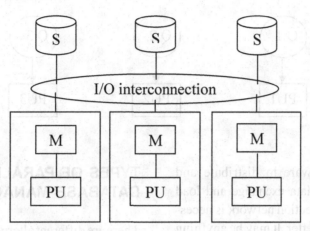

- Shared memory or SMP systems: these machines typically have a small number of processors, and the main advantage of this architecture is that the programming paradigm is the same as in uni-processor machines, and it is the responsibility of the operating system to handle the concurrency issues that result from the multiple parallel executions. These issues are typically shared memory concurrency and dynamic load balancing, which refers to dynamically distributing the tasks among the PUs. SMPs have a major drawback in their limited scalability, since there is a physical by-design limit on the number of processors, which is associated with limitations of the shared system bus and also I/O typical bottlenecks;
- Shared nothing systems: from a hardware perspective, very cost-effective SN systems can be setup, since it is possible to make an SN with commodity computers connected by an ordinary switched network. Furthermore, a large number of PNs can be interconnected in this manner because, other than the network, no other resources are shared. On the other hand, the main disadvantages of SN architectures are the specialized software programming model, since it must take into account the architecture, and the fact that

interconnections between processing units may become a bottleneck, since data needs to be exchanged between nodes. For this reason, data allocation, query processing optimizations and load-balancing issues are most relevant in SN. It is also important to note that SN systems are a very large family, since they range from the lowest-end cluster, built with commodity computing nodes and a standard switched network, to highly sophisticated top-performing clusters, possibly with high-end SM machines in some or all of the nodes;

- Shared disk systems: in shared disk systems, the disk storage is shared. This has the advantage over shared nothing systems of avoiding the need to assign and store specific parts of the data in each node, as the data is all stored in the shared disk subsystem. However, it has the disadvantage of creating a possibly critical bottleneck and scalability limitations in the storage subsystem and interconnections, as all processing units share the same storage system;

One major advantage of shared memory systems over shared nothing ones is that, while they share the same memory, database and data sources in general, shared nothing systems need

Figure 4. Inter-query Parallelism

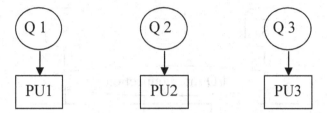

interconnecting middleware to distribute and synchronize tasks, for data exchange and load balancing. An interconnection network is necessary, and the faster the better. It may be anything from an external LAN to a high-speed internal switch. While this is a disadvantage of shared nothing systems, the degree of multiprocessors in shared memory systems is limited by design and by physical hardware limitations, while the degree of shared nothing nodes is theoretically unlimited and in practice can be adjusted to factors such as the data size and application needs.

In practice, hybrid architectures are usual: on one hand, dual and quad-processor computers are already becoming a commodity, and many such computers can be organized in a shared nothing environment with shared memory nodes; On the other hand, optimized software can take advantage of both centralized storage sub-systems and local storage units that may be used as very large disk caches for retrieved data. In practice, solutions range from high-end to low-cost ones. High-end, expensive solutions use proprietary, specialized and highly optimized software on high-end servers with powerful multiprocessor machines, high-end storage and I/O systems; Low-end inexpensive systems build a shared nothing environment with commodity low-end multiprocessors, open-source software and some middleware software.

These architectures are the infrastructure over which parallelism is implemented. In the next section we review types of parallelism and how the parallel architecture influences the design of a Relational Database Management System.

TYPES OF PARALLELISM AND DATABASE MANAGEMENT SYSTEM

There are different alternatives concerning parallel processing in database management systems. In this section we review those alternatives and also how the parallel architecture influences the design of the relational database management system (RDBMS).

Parallel processing refers to executing multiple threads (or processes) concurrently, with three main parallel processing approaches: inter-query, intra-query and hybrid parallelism alternatives.

- Inter-query: in inter-query parallelism, which is illustrated in Figure 4, different threads/processing units handle different queries simultaneously. This has the potential of increasing throughput; On the other hand, it does not account for parallelizing operations such as a join, a sort and a selection, within a single query. This means that such an approach has the potential of producing significant speedups in contexts where multiple concurrent queries are submitted simultaneously;
- Intra-query: intra-query parallelism parallelizes operations within a query, and it can be further decomposed into horizontal, vertical and hybrid parallelism: In horizontal parallelism, the data is divided into multiple pieces and the query is decomposed into a number of smaller sub-queries that will act on those pieces independently. If the data partitions

Figure 5. Intra-query Parallelism

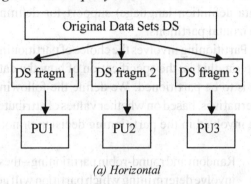

(a) Horizontal

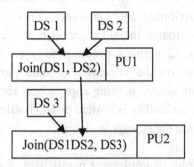

(b) Vertical or pipelined parallelism

are allocated different I/O devices, this can result in a significant speedup. Figure 5(a) illustrate this approach, whereby an original data set is partitioned into what is denoted as fragments or partitions, and each fragment is processed by a processing unit (PU); Vertical or pipelined parallelism assigns query operators to different processing units and feeds the results from one operator into the next one as soon as possible. Figure 5(b) illustrates this kind of parallelism. In that example three datasets are joined. The first two ones are joined in processing unit PU1, while the resulting intermediate data set is then joined with DS3 in PU2.

Hybrid parallelism combines both horizontal and vertical parallelism.

Another relevant issue in parallelism is how a parallel architecture influences the design of a Relational Database Management System (RDBMS) that is to run on that architecture. Depending on the hardware architecture, the RDBMS has certain specialized features.

- RDBMS in shared memory architectures: since in this architecture all processors have access to all the data, the RDBMS design paradigm can be the same as in uni-processor machines. DBMS components in PUs executing SQL statements communicate with each other by exchanging messages and

data through shared memory. Individual processing units may be processes or threads (threads incur in less overhead associated with context switches and achieve better resource utilization). Given the heavy data access characteristics of data warehousing contexts, this approach has hardware architecture inherent scalability limitations, since bottlenecks such as the system bus and I/O are crucial;

- RDBMS in shared nothing architectures: in this context, the data must be partitioned into all disks and the parallel DBMS server is composed by a set of node DBMS components and a global component. The global component must parallelize the SQL queries and send the resulting subqueries to execute locally at each node. Nodes exchange data and messages through the interconnection network. This system offers scalability and significant speedup, but it raises two major issues: the RDBMS design paradigm is different from uni-processor machines, the software is complex and must implement added functionality such as repartitioning (on-the-fly data exchange for join processing); Problems such as data imbalance and excessive data transfer needs are latent in these systems and must be handled by all kinds of optimization features;

- RDBMS in shared disk architectures – the database storage is shared by all RDBMS, and concurrency issues are handled by a distributed lock manager. This solution eliminates memory access bottlenecks of shared memory systems and is less dependent on the allocation of data partitions then shared nothing approaches. However, its scalability is limited by I/O bottlenecks, since the storage is shared.

In order to implement parallelism, it is necessary to divide data or processing into pieces that are to be executed in parallel. In the next section we discuss how data can be partitioned for parallelism.

PARTITIONING AND ALLOCATION

Data Partitioning refers to splitting huge data sets, such as data warehouse fact tables, into much smaller pieces that can be handled efficiently and enables horizontal parallelism. One of the objectives of partitioning is to reduce the amount of data that must be handled in order to answer a query. For instance, if the data is partitioned on an yearly basis, a query requesting the sales of the last year needs only process a partition that corresponds to last years' data.

Data partitioning is also a pre-condition for horizontal (and hybrid) intra-query parallel processing. The data sets are divided into fragments or partitions, and the parallel processing software assigns different fragments to different processing units. Two main types of data partitioning are available (Ozsu and Valduriez 1999): Vertical and Horizontal partitioning. Vertical partitioning allows tables and materialized views to be decomposed into disjoint sets of columns. Note that the key columns are duplicated in each vertical fragment to allow "reconstruction" of an original table; Horizontal partitioning allows tables, materialized views and indexes to be divided into disjoint sets of rows (called fragments), physically stored and accessed separately. Most of today's commercial database systems offer native DDL (data definition language) support for defining horizontal partitions.

Partitioning involves the choice of partitioning criteria, that is, the specification of how the data set is to be partitioned. We define the following alternatives, based on whether values of attributes are involved in the partitioning decision or not:

- Random and round-robin partitioning – these involve determining which partition will get each row randomly (random partitioning) or in a sequential round-the-table manner (round-robin). These are the simplest forms of partitioning, and typically lead to data-balanced placement. However, since the data was placed randomly, a search needs to go to all partitions, even if only a small portion of the data is to be accessed or if only rows with specific values, hash or ranges need to be accessed;

- Value-wise (Hash, range, attribute-value wise) partitioning - a partitioning that is determined by the value, hash or range of one or a combination of attributes. With value-wise partitioning it is possible to locate a partition in a specific node if the search is based on the partitioning key(s). On the other hand, for this kind of partitioning criteria, the allocation algorithm must take data skew into consideration to avoid or decrease data unbalance;

- For many query processing objectives, value-wise partitioning has a significant advantage over random or round-robin in that the database server can identify where a piece of data lies and therefore spare a lot of accesses: for instance, if sales data is partitioned by shop and product and a query requests a specific shop and product, only a partition needs to be processed to answer the query. Parallel hash-join algorithms also benefit immensely from hash-partitioning large relations into nodes in order to minimize data exchange requirements (Kitsuregawa, Tanaka and Motooka, 1983; DeWitt and Gerber, 1985). These strategies typically allocate a hash range to each node, so that joins can proceed in parallel in all nodes.

Given alternative partitioning options and the need to optimize the partitioning approach to handle huge data warehouses efficiently, many authors have investigated this optimization subject in different contexts. Early works include Hua and Lee (1990), which uses variable partitioning (size and access frequency-based) and concludes that partitioning increases throughput for short transactions, but complex transactions involving several large joins result in reduced throughput with increased partitioning. Williams and Zhou (1998) review five major data placement strategies (size-based, access frequency-based and network traffic based) and conclude experimentally that the way data is placed in a shared nothing environment can have considerable effect on performance. Some of the most promising partitioning and placement approaches focus on query workload-based partitioning choices (Zilio, Jhingram and Padmanabhan, 1994; Rao, Zhang and Megiddo, 2002). These strategies use the query workload to determine the most appropriate partitioning attributes, which should be related to typical query access patterns. Generic data partitioning that is independent of the underlying database server and targeted at node partitioned (shared nothing) data warehouses was discussed in (Furtado, 2004; Furtado, 2004b; Furtado 2004c ; Furtado, 2005). This approach allows most queries to be processed in parallel very efficiently, based on hash-based partitioning of large relations and copies of smaller ones. In the work on Multidimensional Hierarchical fragmentation (Stohr 2000) the authors considered star schemas and used workload-based value-wise derived partitioning of facts and in-memory retention of dimensions for efficient processing. They also introduced the use of join-bitmap indexes together with attribute-wise

derived partitioning and hierarchy-aware processing for very efficient partition-wise processing over star schemas. The approach in (Bellatreche 2008) proposes a genetic algorithm for schema partitioning selection, whereby the fact table is fragmented based on the partitioning schemas of dimension tables.

We end this section by describing a typical partitioning and allocation scenario, to help illustrate how it works. In relational databases, Data Warehouses are frequently organized as star schemas (Chaudhuri and Dayal 1997), with a huge fact table that is related to several dimension tables, as represented in Figure 6. In such schema, the facts table (Sales fact in the Figure) stores data to be analyzed and pointers to dimensions, while dimension information is stored in dimension tables (the remaining relations).

It is frequent for dimension tables to be orders of magnitude smaller than the fact table. When considering a parallel environment, this means that it is worth to partition the central fact table into multiple pieces that can be processed in parallel, while the dimension tables are left complete. In a shared nothing environment, this means copying dimension relations into all nodes and dividing the fact throughout the nodes. This approach is very useful in what concerns parallel processing, since most operations can proceed in parallel (Furtado 2005), including processing of joins in parallel. More complex schemas may include bigger dimensions and multiple interconnected big relations that, for best performance, need to be partitioned, and it may happen that it is impossible to partition all for co-location, then a workload-based partitioning solution as the ones referenced above can be adopted, which tries to co-locate the relations that result in highest query processing gain.

Having discussed parallel architectures, types of parallelism and partitioning issues, we now turn our attention to parallel query processing. In the next section we discuss a parallel processing approach.

Figure 6. DW Sample Star Schema

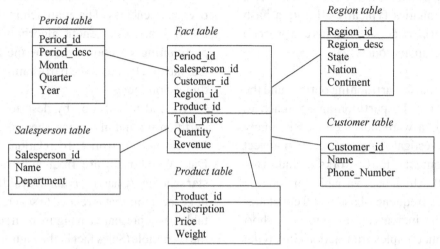

PARALLEL HORIZONTAL INTRA-QUERY PROCESSING

While in inter-query parallelization it is trivial to understand how a query is parallelized, for intra-query parallelism it is interesting to describe how individual queries are parallelized, in particular in the context of data warehouse schemas. In this section we illustrate how queries can be decomposed into a number of smaller sub-queries that will act on fragments independently, with significant speedup. This subject has been discussed in several works, which include (Akinde et al. 2003, Furtado 2005, Stohr 2000). Our illustration is based on the parallel query processing approach followed by the Data Warehouse Parallel Architecture (Furtado 2005, Furtado 2007), while we also discuss other works on the next section.

Figure 7 illustrates the basic architecture of DWPA for the shared nothing, node partitioned data warehouse, which can run in any number of computers interconnected by a LAN. It includes three major entities implemented as services: Submitter, Executor and the DWPA Manager. Submitters are simple services that may reside in any computer, do not require an underlying database server and submit queries to the system.

The query may be submitted from a Submitter Console application or from other applications through an API. Once submitted, the query is parsed and transformed into high-level actions by a query planner. These actions are then transformed into Command Lists for each Executor service. Executors are services that maintain local database sessions and control the execution of commands locally and the data exchange with other nodes. Finally, the DWPA manager is a node which controls the whole system (it can be replicated for fault tolerance reasons), maintaining registries with necessary information for the whole system. When nodes enter the system, they contact the DWPA manager to register themselves and to obtain all the necessary information. In DWPA, any computer can assume any role as long as it runs the corresponding service.

We will now describe basic query processing functionality. For simplicity, we start with the simplest possible example. Consider a single very large relation R partitioned into n nodes and a sum query over some attribute x of the relation. Formula (1) states that the sum of attribute x over all nodes is simply the sum of the sums of x in each node:

Figure 7. The DWPA Architecture

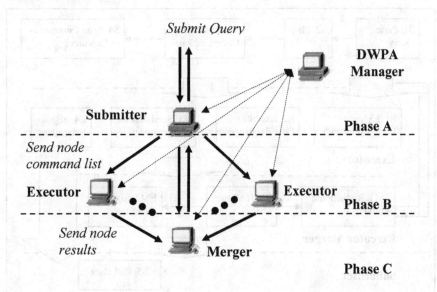

$$\sum x = \sum_{\text{all nodes}}\sum_{\text{over node } i}(x) \qquad (1)$$

The implementation of this very basic operation in DWPA involves the submitter parsing the initial query *sum(x) from R* and producing command lists for every node with the following operations:

1. a local query: *sum(x) as sumx from R_{local}*
2. data transfer commands for every executor node: send *sumx* to merger node
3. a merge query for the merger node: *sum(sumx) from partial_results*
4. signal the submitter to pull the results

The Merger node is an Executor that is chosen for merging the partial results if necessary. The query processing steps depend heavily on the placement layout of the data on the nodes. For instance, if relation *R* is replicated into all nodes or placed in a single node, the commands will be (executed in a single node):

1. a local query: *sum(x) as sumx from R_{local}*
2. signal the submitter to pull the results

Figure 8 shows a set of query processing steps that may be necessary in the processing of each query using DWPA (some queries may not require all these steps). Steps S1 to S4 represent the parsing and planning of queries, the generation of lists of commands for the executor nodes and the sending of those commands to Executors. Steps E1 to E4 represent the processing of the local queries within executor nodes, data exchanges between them and either sending the results to a merger node or signalling to the submitter that he can get the results. The merger node steps include a redistribution step EM3, which may be necessary for processing nested queries (for some queries containing subqueries, in which case more than one processing cycle may be required).

For instance, the following SQL query is from the TPC-H performance benchmark in (TPCC 2008) and computes the sales of each brand per month:

SELECT   p_brand, year_month, sum(l_
              quantity), count(*)
FROM   JOIN lineitem LI, part P, time T,
              supplier S

Figure 8. Query Processing Architecture (QPA) within DWPA

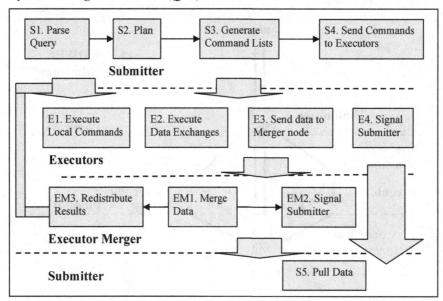

WHERE   year_month>= '1997' AND
    supplier = 'X'
GROUP BY   to_char(l_shipdate,'yyyy-mm'),
    p_brand, year_month;

This typical query contains group-by attributes that allow the aggregation to be determined for each group. This aggregation can be handled using the following scheme, which adheres to the diagram of Figure 7: each node needs to apply an only slightly modified query on its partial data, and the results are merged by applying the same query again at the merging node with the partial results coming from the processing nodes. Figure 9 illustrates this process for a simple sum query:

While the sum operation was unchanged in the query rewrite step of Figure 9, other aggregation operators need slight modifications. In practice simple additive aggregation primitives are computed in each node, from which the final aggregation function is derived. The most common primitives are: (LS, SS, N, MAX, MIN: linear sum LS = sum(x); sum of squares SS = sum(x^2); number of elements N, extremes MAX and MIN). Examples of final aggregation functions are:

$$COUNT = N = \sum\nolimits_{all\_nodes} N_{nodei} \qquad (1)$$

$$SUM = LS = \sum\nolimits_{all\_nodes} LS_{nodei} \qquad (2)$$

$$AVERAGE =$$
$$\sum\nolimits_{all\_nodes} LS_{nodei} / \sum\nolimits_{all\_nodes} N_{nodei} \qquad (3)$$

$$STDDEV =$$
$$\sqrt{\frac{(\sum SS_{node_i} - \sum LS_{node_i}^{2} / N)}{N}} \qquad (4)$$

This means that the query transformation step needs to replace each AVERAGE and STDDEV (or variance) expression in the SQL query by a SUM and a COUNT in the first case and by a SUM, a COUNT and a SUM_OF_SQUARES in the second case to determine the local query for each node. Figure 10 shows an example of aggregation query processing steps, indicating the corresponding steps from Figure 8.

The query processing steps described above are not the only possibility for processing this query using intra-query horizontal parallelism. For instance, it would be possible to assign each

Figure 9. Typical SUM Query over DWPA

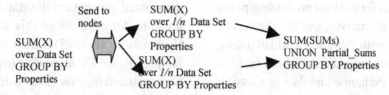

Figure 10. Basic Aggregation Query Steps

```
S1. Query submission:
Select sum(a), count(a),
average(a), max(a), min(a),
stddev(a), group_attributes
From data set
Group by group_attributes;
```

```
E3. Results sending/collecting:
Create cached table
PRqueryX(node, suma, counta, ssuma,
maxa, mina,
group_attributes)
as <insert received results>;
```

```
S3,S4. Query rewriting and distribu-
tion to each node:
Select sum(a), count(a), sum(a x a),
max(a), min(a),  group_attributes
From data set
Group by group_attributes;
```

```
EM1. Results merging:
Select sum(suma), sum(counta),
sum(suma)/ sum(counta), max(maxa),
min(mina)
(sum(ssuma)-sum(suma)²)/sum(counta),
ga
From UNION_ALL(PRqueryX)
Group by group_attributes;
```

group of the group-by clause of the example in Figure 10 to a specific node. Nodes would then have to exchange data so that each node would get the data pertaining to the groups that it should process. Given these and other query processing alternatives, the query optimizer must evaluate the costs of each one, including processing and data exchange costs, and determine the best alternative for each query.

While most SQL operations are readily parallelizable in a way that may allow nodes to process data with minimum data exchange requirements, the parallel join operator may incur in considerable data exchange overheads if the rows to be joined are not co-located or equi-partitioned (located in the same node). This is because the join must match rows from two data sets with the same value for a specific attribute. With careful hash-partitioning, it is possible that the two data sets are already placed in a co-located manner, that is, rows with matching attribute value may

be co-located, but for schemas involving multiple large partitioned relations it is often impossible to co-locate all relations. In those cases some form of data exchange will be required. The following lists the parallel join alternatives:

- Co-located or equi-partitioned join: the data is already partitioned according to the join hash values, so the join can occur in parallel with no data exchange requirements between nodes;

- Redirected join: the data is not co-located but it is enough to re-locate the rows from one of the source data sets in order to co-locate them and proceed with a co-located join;

- Repartitioned join: both source data sets need to be re-located in order to become co-located;

- Broadcast join: one of the source data is broadcasted into all nodes to enable parallel joining with the other partitioned data set;

Once more, it is the task of a global query optimization to search for the best processing plans form a myriad of alternatives, and it is the task of a query processor with dynamic load balancing to counter potential imbalances, which include data storage, data exchange and data processing imbalances. In the next section we review work on parallel query optimizers.

THE PARALLEL OPTIMIZER

The parallel optimizer is a crucial element in any parallel database management system. In this section we review its concept and work on parallel query optimizers along time.

As database systems evolve, the need to develop query optimizers that are able to interpret their new features also arises. The evolution process has not been simple, as query optimizers have to conjugate database feature compatibility with reasonable search times.

The first globally accepted standalone query optimizer was presented by (Selinger et al. 1979) for the System R database engine. The optimizer was based on Dynamic Programming (DP), and tried to obtain the best execution plan by successively joining relations using the cheapest access paths and join methods. After each join iteration, the costliest plans were pruned leaving only the most eligible for the next phase. The exceptions to the previous rule were costlier plans considered to be interesting because they could benefit future join plans or database operations that had yet to be accounted for. The System R query optimizer had a major disadvantage, its space and time complexities are exponential, which limited the join cardinality of a submitted query.

In the early 1980's researchers began to tackle query optimization in parallel/distributed environments with communication costs. At the time standalone query optimizers were not equipped to handle features inherent to distribution, such as query segment node attribution or communi-

cation costs. Extensive work was done to adapt distributed concepts to the standalone optimizer domain. An example of this attempt is the R* (Lohman et al. 1985) which adds distribution features to the DP algorithm (discussed earlier). Kossman and Stocker (2000), develop a series of algorithms that adapt standalone DP to distributed environments. They reduce the inherent complexity, of such an adaptation, by introducing greedy algorithms that lessen the overall search space of a distributed query.

As discussed before, parallel architectures can exploit two types of parallel features, i.e. inter-query and intra-query. The first tries to simultaneously execute independent queries by assigning them to different sets of processors. Intra-query parallelism breaks down the operators that compose a query, conveying them to different processors for concurrent execution. We can further subdivide intra-query parallelism into inter-operator and intra-operator parallelism. The latter promotes the division of a specific operator into fragments, and subsequent concurrent execution of each fragment by a separate processor. Inter-operator parallelism allows two or more operators to be simultaneously executed by different sets of processors. The introduction of these features augments the search space of a parallel system. Thus it is important that parallel optimizers be able to reduce the search space without compromising plan generation.

One of the first parallel query optimizers to appear, the XPRS (Hong and Stonebraker 1993), created effective parallel plans using a two-phase technique. The first generated a traditional single processor execution plan, which was then scheduled for parallelization in the second phase. However the authors did not study the effects of processor communication, which limited its applicability on architectures that heavily rely on this resource, i.e. SN. The Join Ordering and Query Rewrite (JOQR) algorithm proposed in (Hasan 1996) also employed a two phase approach. However the first phase was different from that of the XPRS. JOQR rewrote the queries, submitted to it, by using a set of heuristics to diminish the search space, and took into account processor communication by using node colouring (Hasan and Motwani 1995). Node colouring applies a colour to represent PNs with relations partitioned by the same attribute. Joining relations with the same colour would account for less communication costs, and thus diminish the global response time. In (Shasha and Wang 1991), the authors propose a one-phase search algorithm that uses graph theory to solve the best order by which to join a set of relations. In their approach they apply a CHAIN algorithm to try and minimize the response times of the execution plans. CHAIN is based on DP, yet it can eliminate more plans if Kruskal's (1956) or Primm's (1957) spanning trees are used as a greedy heuristic. The authors focus on equi-join scenarios leaving out the rest of the join types, this limits the applicability of the algorithm.

With the ever-growing complexity of today's queries, researchers are focusing on methods that try to diminish the margin of error of current query optimizers. Special interest has arisen in the usage Robust Query Optimization (Babcock and Chaudhuri 2005, Chu, Halpern and Gehrke 2002) techniques. The methodology allows an optimizer to decide whether it wants to pursue a conservative or more aggressive plan to resolve a query. The conservative plan is likely to perform reasonably well in most situations, whilst the aggressive plan (traditional method) can do better, if the estimations are reliable, or much worse if these are rough approximations. Other researchers have studied Parametric Query Optimization (Ganguly 1998, Hulgeri et al. 2003, Ioannidis et al. 1997), which is based on the finding of a small set of plans that are suitable for different situations. The method postpones some of its decisions until runtime, using a subset of plans to decide how best to proceed to the next execution phase. Parametric query optimization does particularly well in scenarios where queries are compiled once

and executed repeatedly, with possible minor parameter changes. However the subject that has captivated most of the recent interest is that of Adaptive Query Processing. The term classifies algorithms that use execution feedback as a means of resolving execution and optimization problems related to missing statistics, unexpected correlations, unpredictable costs and dynamic data. In (Deshpande et al. 2007) the authors conduct a reasonably complete survey on the issue.

Having discussed most aspects of interest to parallel data warehouse architectures and systems, we devote the next section to reviewing related work on parallel data warehouse systems and solutions.

PARALLEL DATA WAREHOUSE SYSTEMS

In this section we review works on parallel data warehouse systems, including both commercial systems and some of the most relevant research work on parallel data warehouses.

On the commercial side, one of the most popular commercial SN parallel database solutions is the IBM DB2 Parallel Edition (Baru and Fecteau 1995). Its partitioning strategy is based on hashing and nodegroups (NG), which allow a table to span multiple nodes. The relations are hash-partitioned, so as to form collocated data whenever possible. The application is very flexible, as it allows database administrators to introduce or remove processing nodes (PNs) into the system, without having to spend a lot of time reconfiguring the DW. It supports shipping of sub-queries and parallel joins. SQL statements are broken into fragments for each node, executing low-level operations. A cost-based optimizer takes the parallel settings, data partitioning and data exchange costs to optimize the execution plan. On the other hand, DB2 is by no means specialized for data warehouses or data warehouse schemas and workloads, and although it has an advanced cost-based optimizer, it is not specifically adapted to heterogeneous and non-dedicated environments. As with most proprietary application, it requires the acquisition of the entire software bundle together with a fast hardware architecture, which are both usually costly.

Rao (Rao et al. 2002) seeks to automate the process of data partitioning in the IBM DB2 shared nothing architecture. Given a workload of SQL statements, the objective is to determine automatically how to partition the base data across multiple nodes to achieve overall optimal performance for that workload. Instead of using only heuristics as previous approaches did, their solution is tightly integrated with the optimizer and uses it both to recommend candidate partitions for each table that will benefit each query in the workload, and to evaluate various combinations of these candidates.

Another popular commercial solution is Oracles' Real Application Cluster (RAC 2008). The RAC assumes a hybrid parallel architecture. The PNs get their data from a high-end disk arrays such as a Network Attached Storage (NAS) or a Storage Area Network (SAN), meaning that the application is partially built on SD. Once the data is loaded onto the PNs, a cache fusion technology is activated, which basically allows the PNs to query each others' cache so as to obtain needed data without resorting to the disk array. Oracle classifies the cache fusion as a form of shared everything. The main disadvantages of the RAC are its necessity for high-end hardware such as a disk array and a fast network interconnect for inter-node and disk array communication. Thus, a fair amount of expenditure is needed to acquire both the hardware and software to build this system.

Research work and prototypes have proposed relevant solutions to speedup processing over both SN and SD architectures. We review some of those next.

Akal (Akal et al. 2002) investigates processing OLAP queries in parallel, where a coordination infrastructure decomposes a query into subqueries and ships them to appropriate cluster nodes. In the second phase, each cluster node optimizes and evaluates its subquery locally. Their proposal involves efficient data processing in a database cluster by means of full mirroring and creating multiple node-bound sub-queries for a query by adding predicates. This way, each node receives a sub-query and is forced to execute over a subset of the data, called a virtual partition. The advantage of virtual partitions is that they are more flexible than physical ones, since only the ranges need to be changed. The authors of (Lima et al. 2004) further improve the previous solution. They claim that the solution is slow because it does not prevent full table scans when the range is not small, and propose multiple small sub-queries by node instead of just one (Lima et al. 2004b), and an adaptive partition size tuning approach.

The Data Warehouse Parallel Architecture (DWPA) (Furtado 2004, Furtado 2005, Furtado 2007) is an environment adaptable and cost-effective middleware for parallel DWs, which places no requirements in either RDBMS software or hardware. Its services are aimed at SN and mixed SN-Grid environments mostly, because these are very scalable and their cost acquisition is relatively low. In SN environments, the DW is partitioned amongst the PNs so that each DBMS instance can directly access data from its local partition. Partitioning is justified by the fact that PNs do not have enough storage space to accommodate the entirety of the DW, and that by subdividing the relations into various PNs the system is able to parallelize query execution. The DWPA architecture partitions a schema by using a partitioning strategy called Workload Based Placement (WBP) (Furtado 2004). In short, WBP hash-partitions large relations based on the schema and workload characteristics of the DW, whilst small relations are replicated throughout the PNs. A relation is considered to be small if it can fit comfortably in physical memory, and the operations involving that relation are not significantly slower than those of a partitioned alternative. WBP tries to equi-partition relations whenever possible, so as to maximize query throughput. To equi-partition or co-locate relations is to divide two or more relations using the same attribute and hash function. In doing so each PN is able to access locally and join the equi-partitioned relations, which avoids any unnecessary data exchange among the PNs. DWPA can be organized into a set of node groups (NG) (Furtado 2007). Each NG is composed of a set of PNs. NGs are usually created for reasons related to availability, performance enhancement or geographic locality. The usage of NGs benefits parallel query execution in various manners as they may contain any subset of the data warehouse data. The creation of multiple NGs, each containing the entirety of the DW, can also allow the execution of simultaneous queries in local or networked contexts, without these interfering with each others response times. Another application of NGs is to foment the use of bushy trees in query processing: if the DW is subdivided into two or more NGs then it is possible to segment a query and execute portions of it in separate NGs. Replication for dynamic load-balancing and availability is also considered in (Furtado 2005b, Furtado 2007), where instead of node partitions the data set is divided into a much larger set of chunks and those are divided into the nodes in alternative ways that confer the desired load and availability balancing characteristics.

The Multidimensional Hierarchical Fragmentation approach (Stohr et al. 2000) proposes a data allocation solution for parallel data warehouses that takes into account the data warehouse structure, including its multidimensional and hierarchical characteristics. The idea is that a multi-dimensional hierarchical fragmentation of the fact table with in-memory copies of all dimensions supports well queries referencing different subsets of the schema dimensions. Fragments are determined based on dimension attribute values, once a specific combination of attributes is chosen as partitioning criteria. The system then uses hierarchy information to determine which fragments should be accessed to answer a specific

query. Bitmap indexes are also added to speedup processing when small parts need to be accessed from specific fragments.

Stöhr (Stöhr et al. 2002) investigates dynamic load-balancing for parallel data warehouses focused on shared disk systems, proposing a scheduling strategy that simultaneously considers both processors and disks, while utilizing the load balancing potential of a shared disk architecture, also catering for skew.

Aguilar-Saborit et al. 2005 looks at the problem of ad-hoc star join query processing in cluster architectures, and propose the Star Hash Join (SHJ), a generalization of Pushed Down Bit Filters (Aguilar-Saborit et al. 2003) for clusters. The objectives of the technique are to reduce the amount of data communicated, the amount of data spilled to disk during the execution of intermediate joins in the query plan, and the amount of memory used by auxiliary data structures such as bit filters.

In (Raman, Han and Narang 2005), the authors argued for the advantages of a shared disk solution (SD) with no pre-partitioning, with the argument that it allows a completely dynamic allocation of processing to the processing units. They presented DITN, an approach where partitioning is not the means of parallelism. In their approach, data layout decisions are taken outside the scope of the DBMS and handled within the storage software. Query processors see a "Data In The Network" image. The authors argue that repartitioning (on-the-fly data exchange between nodes that is sometimes necessary during the processing of partitioned data sets) is unsuitable for non-dedicated machines because it poorly addresses node heterogeneity, and is vulnerable to failures or load spikes during query execution. DITN uses an alternate intra-fragment parallelism, where each node executes an independent select-project-join-aggregate-group by block, with no tuple exchange between nodes. This method handles heterogeneous nodes cleanly, and adapts during execution to node failures or load spikes.

Initial experiments suggest that DITN performs competitively with a traditional configuration of dedicated machines and well-partitioned data for up to 10 processors at least, while at the same time giving significant flexibility in terms of gradual scale-out and handling of heterogeneity, load bursts, and failures.

Chen (Chen et al. 2004) discusses parallel solutions for handling the data cube, arguing that pre-computation of data cubes is critical to improving the response time of On-Line Analytical Processing (OLAP) systems and can be instrumental in accelerating data mining tasks in large data warehouses. They present a parallel method for generating ROLAP data cubes on a shared nothing multiprocessor. Since no (expensive) shared disk is required, their method can be used on low cost clusters consisting of standard PCs with local disks connected via a data switch.

These research works have shown how allocation and query processing can be optimized in different ways for handling data warehouses and cubes effectively in both shared nothing and shared disk parallel architectures. In the next section we briefly discuss distributed data warehouses.

DISTRIBUTED DATA WAREHOUSES

Many organizations have physically distributed databases with extremely large amounts of data. Traditionally the data warehouse would be seen as a centralized repository, whereby data from all sources would be imported into that large centralized repository for analysis. Nowadays the speed and bandwidth of wide-area computer networks enables a distributed approach, whereby parts of the data may reside in different places, parts being cached and/or replicated for performance reasons, and the system functions to the outside world as a single global access-transparent repository. As the amount of data and number of sites grow, this distributed approach becomes crucial, as a single centralized data warehouse importing data from all the sources has obvious scalability limitations.

Grid technology is another useful element in distributed computing platforms, and naturally also for distributed data warehouses. The computational grid offers services for efficiently scheduling jobs on the grid, and for grid-enabled applications where data handling is a most relevant part, the data grid becomes a crucial element. It typically builds on the concept of files, sites and file transfers between sites. These use services such as GRID-ftp, plus a Replica Manager to keep track of where replicas are located. The multi-site, grid-aware data warehouse is a large distributed repository sharing a schema and data concerning scientific or business domains. However, differently from typical grid scenarios, the data warehouse is not simply a set of files and accesses to individual files, it is a single distributed schema and both localized and distributed computations must be managed over that schema.

Some authors have dealt with allocation and processing of data warehouses in distributed and grid environments. In (Akinde et al. 2003) the authors discuss query processing in a distributed data warehouse, consisting of local data warehouses at each collection point and a coordinator site, with most of the processing being performed at the local sites. In that paper they consider the problem of efficient evaluation of OLAP queries over the distributed data warehouse, and propose the Skalla system for this task. Skalla translates OLAP queries, specified as certain algebraic expressions, into distributed evaluation plans which are shipped to individual sites, and the approach operates in a manner that reduces the amount of data that needs to be shipped among sites.

In (Costa and Furtado 2006) the authors investigate Grid-Dwpa, an efficient architecture to deploy large data warehouses in grids with high availability and good load balancing. They propose both efficient data allocation, partial replication strategies and scheduling solutions that maximize performance and throughput of the grid-enabled architecture for OLAP. The replication strategies provide adequate guarantees that site availability problems do not impair the system and result in only small system slowdown. In (Costa and Furtado 2008) the authors propose scheduling for efficient query processing in the Grid-Dwpa environment. The system generates site and node tasks, forecasts the necessary time to execute the task at each local site, estimates total execution times, and assigns task execution to sites accordingly.

Another work on grid-aware data warehouses is presented in (Lawrence Rau-Chaplin 2006). The OLAP-Enabled Grid considers the scenario where the data of a single organization is distributed across a number of operational databases at remote locations. Each operational database has capabilities for answering OLAP queries, and access to a possible variety of other computational and storage resources which are located close by. Users who are interested in doing OLAP on these databases are distributed over the network. Their proposal considers the following entities:

- OLAP Server - A machine which has sole control over an operational database. It may maintain some materialized views and may also act as a computational or storage resource. The OLAP servers all have the same schema, but each maintains a partition of the total data available to the users;
- Computational Resource - A machine which offers cycles for performing tasks on the behalf of other entities in the Grid;
- Storage Resource - A machine which offers disk space for storing data on behalf of other entities in the Grid;
- Resource Optimizer - There is exactly one resource optimizer for each site. A resource optimizer has the information necessary to perform scheduling and allocation of computational and storage resources, and to carry out queries. It may also have some

cache space for storing common query results for queries generated in its site;
- User - Users submit ad-hoc queries to resource optimizers and may enter and leave the network at will. Each user has an amount of cache space for caching query results.

The proposal itself is for a two-tiered grid-based data warehouse. The first tier is composed by local (cached) data. Remote database servers are in the second tier. Each submitted query is evaluated in order to verify if it can be answered with data from the local site. Then, if it cannot be entirely answered locally, the query is re-written into a set of queries. Some of those are executed locally (with the existent data) and the others, which access the data that is missing at the first tier, are executed at the second tier (database servers). The use of cached data is also considered at the database server level.

Wehrle et al (2007) also deal with a distributed, grid-aware environment. They apply the Globus Toolkit together with a set of specialized services for grid based data warehouses. Fact table data is partitioned and distributed across participant nodes. Dimension tables data is replicated. A *local data index service* provides local information about data stored at each node. A *communication service* uses the *local data index* service from the participant grid's nodes to enable that remote data is accessed. The first step in query execution is to search for data at the local node (using the local index service). Missing data is located by the use of the communication service and accessed remotely.

The distributed and grid-aware data warehouse context is still an evolving one, as community data warehouses come into play in current and future systems and concerning different application scenarios.

CONCLUSION AND FUTURE TRENDS

There has been a significant amount of work during the last two decades related to parallel and distributed data warehouses, and those works have contributed to increasing significantly our knowledge of those systems, issues and solutions, and it has also brought some maturity to the field. In this article we reviewed the main concepts, works and trends on parallel and distributed data warehouse architectures and systems. We first described parallel architectures, types of parallelism, partitioning and allocation. Then we described how parallel horizontal intra-query processing works and we also reviewed the parallel optimizer. We then turned our attention to some of the most relevant works on parallel and distributed data warehouse systems.

Work in parallel and distributed data warehouses in the future is expected to advance the concepts and systems to new levels of autonomy, scalability and ubiquity. It will answer questions such as how the systems will be able to adapt automatically to very heterogeneous environments, in either parallel or wide-area distributed environments. It will provide answers to the issue of how to completely automate and optimize allocation and mixes of base data, materialized views, cubes and indexes in either parallel or distributed settings for optimal performance. We will also increasingly see applications of data warehouse and grid technologies to distributed and collaborative applications and problems.

REFERENCES

Akal F., Böhm K., Schek H.-J.(2002). OLAP Query Evaluation in a Database Cluster: a Performance Study on Intra-Query Parallelism, East-European Conf. on Advances in Databases and Information Systems (ADBIS), Bratislava, Slovakia, 2002.

Akinde, M. O., Bhlen, M. H., Johnson, T., Lakshmanan, L. V. S. and Srivastava, D. (2003) " Efficient OLAP query processing in distributed data warehouses", Information Systems 28, pp. 111-135, Elsevier, 2003.

Babcock B. and Chaudhuri S. (2001). Towards a robust query optimizer: a principled and practical approach. In SIGMOD '05: Proceedings of the 2005 ACM SIGMOD international conference on Management of data, pages 119–130, New York, NY, USA, 2005.

Baru C. and G. Fecteau (1995). An overview of db2 parallel edition. In SIGMOD '95: Proceedings of the 1995 ACM SIGMOD international conference on Management of data, pages 460–462, New York, NY, USA, 1995.

Bellatreche L. (2008). A Genetic Algorithm for Selecting Horizontal Fragments, Encyclopedia of Data Warehousing and Mining - 2nd Edition, John Wang, 2008

Bellatreche L. (2008). Bitmap join indexes vs. Data Partitioning, Encyclopedia of Data Warehousing and Mining - 2nd Edition , 2008.

Chan C.-Y. and Ioannidis Y. E. (1998). Bitmap index design and evaluation. Proceedings of the International Conference on the Management of Data, pages 355-366, 1998.

Chaudhuri, S. and Dayal, U. (1997). An overview of data warehousing and OLAP technology. SIGMOD Rec. 26, 1 (Mar. 1997), 65-74.

Chen Y., Dehne F., Eavis T., Rau-Chaplin A. (2004). Parallel ROLAP Data Cube Construction On Shared-Nothing Multiprocessors. In Distributed and Parallel Databases, Volume 15, Number 3, May 2004, pages 219-236.

Chu F., Halpern J., and Gehrke J. (2002). Least expected cost query optimization: what can we expect? In PODS '02: Proceedings of the twenty-first ACM SIGMOD-SIGACT-SIGART symposium on Principles of database systems, pages 293–302, New York, NY, USA, 2002.

Costa R. and Furtado P (2008). Optimizer and QoS for the Community Data Warehouse Architecture, in New Trends in Database Systems: Methods, Tools, Applications", Eds. D. Zakrzewska, E. Menasalvas, L. Byczkowska-Lipińska1, Springer-Verlag, 2008.

Costa R. and Furtado P. (2006). Data Warehouses in Grids with High QoS. In A. M. Tjoa and J. Trujillo, editors, DaWaK, volume 4081 of Lecture Notes in Computer Science, pages 207–217. Springer, 2006.

Deshpande A., Z. Ives, and V. Raman. (2007). Adaptive query processing. Foundations and Trends in Databases, 1(1):1–140, 2007.

DeWitt D. J. and Gray J. (1992). Parallel database systems: The future of high performance database systems. Commun. ACM, 35(6):85–98, 1992.

Furtado P. (2004). Workload-based Placement and Join Processing in Node-Partitioned Data Warehouses. In proceedings of the International Conference on Data Warehousing and Knowledge Discovery, 38-47, Zaragoza, Spain, September 2004.

Furtado P. (2004). Experimental Evidence on Partitioning in Parallel Data Warehouses. Proceedings of the ACM DOLAP 04 - Workshop of the International Conference on Information and Knowledge Management, Washington USA, Nov. 2004.

Furtado P. (2005). Hierarchical aggregation in networked data management. In Euro-Par, volume 3648 of Lecture Notes in Computer Science, pages 360–369. Springer, 2005.

Furtado P. (2005). Replication in Node-Partitioned Data Warehouses. DDIDR2005 Workshop of International Conference on Very Large Databases, 2005.

Furtado, P. (2005). "Efficiently Processing Query-Intensive Databases over a Non-dedicated Local Network". Proceedings of the 19th International Parallel and Distributed Processing Symposium, Denver, Colorado, USA, May 2005.

Furtado P. (2007). Efficient and Robust Node-Partitioned Data Warehouses", in "Data Warehouses and OLAP: Concepts, Architectures and Solutions, ISBN 1-59904365-3 eds. R. Wrembel and C. Koncilia, Ideas Group, Inc, chapter IX, pp. 203-229, 2007.

Ganguly S. (1998). Design and analysis of parametric query optimization algorithms. Proceedings of the 24rd International Conference on Very Large Data Bases, pages 228–238, San Francisco, CA, USA, 1998. Morgan Kaufmann Publishers Inc.

Golfarelli M., Maniezzo V., and Rizzi S. (2004). Materialization of fragmented views in multidimensional databases. Data & Knowledge Engineering, 49(3):325–351, June 2004.

Hasan W. (1996). Optimization of SQL queries for parallel machines. PhD thesis, Stanford, CA, USA, 1996.

Hasan W. and Motwani R. (1995). Coloring away communication in parallel query optimization. In VLDB '95: Proceedings of the 21th International Conference on Very Large Data Bases, pages 239–250, San Francisco, CA, USA, 1995. Morgan Kaufmann Publishers Inc.

Hong W. and Stonebraker M (1993). Optimization of parallel query execution plans in xprs. Distributed and Parallel Databases, 1(1):9–32, 1993.

Hulgeri A. and Sudarshan S. (2003). Anipqo: almost non-intrusive parametric query optimization for nonlinear cost functions. In Proceedings of the 29th international conference on Very large data bases, pages 766–777.

Ioannidis Y., R. T. Ng, K. Shim, and T. K. Sellis (1997). Parametric query optimization. VLDB J., 6(2):132–151, 1997.

Kossmann D. and Stocker K. (2000). Iterative dynamic programming: a new class of query optimization algorithms. ACM Trans. Database Syst., 25(1):43–82, 2000.

Kruskal J. (1956). On the shortest spanning subtree of a graph and the traveling salesman problem. Proceedings of the American Mathematical Society, 7(1):48–50, Feb. 1956.

Lawrence M. and Rau-Chaplin A. (2006). The OLAP-Enabled Grid: Model and Query Processing Algorithms" in Proceedings of the 20th International Symposium on High Performance Computing Systems and Applications (HPCS'06), IEEE, Eds. R. Deupree, St. Johns, Canada, May 2006.

Lima, A. A. B., Mattoso, M., Valduriez, P. (2004). OLAP Query Processing in a Database Cluster, Proc. 10th Euro-Par Conf., Pisa, Italy, 2004.

Lima, A. A., Mattoso, M., Valduriez (2004). P. Adaptive Virtual Partitioning for OLAP Query Processing in a Database Cluster", 19th Brasilian Simposium on Databases SBBD, 18-20 October 2004, Brasília, Brasil.

Lohman G., Mohan C., Haas L., Daniels D., Lindsay B., Selinger P., and Wilms P. (1985). Query processing in r*. In Query Processing in Database Systems, pages 31–47. Springer, 1985.

O'Neil P. and Graefe G. (1995). Multi-Table Joins Through Bitmapped Join Indices. SIGMOD Record, 24(3):8-11, 1995.

Ozsu M. T. and Valduriez P. (1999). Principles of Distributed Database Systems : Second Edition. Prentice Hall, 1999.

P. Furtado. Replication in node partitioned data warehouses. In VLDB Workshop on Design, Implementation, and Deployment of Database Replication (DIDDR), 2005.

Prim R. (1957) Shortest connection networks and some generalizations. The Bell System Technical Journal, 3:1389–1401, 1957.

Raman V., Han W., Narang I. (2005). Parallel querying with non-dedicated computers, in Proceedings of the 31st international conference on Very large databases, Trondheim, Norway, 2005.

Rao, J., Zhang c., Megiddo n., Lohman G. (2002). "Automating Physical Database Design in a Parallel Database". Proceedings of the ACM International Conference on Management of Data, 558-569, Madison, Wisconsin, USA, June 2002.

Rousopoulos R. (1998). Materialized Views and Data Warehouses. SIGMOD Record, 27(1):21-26, 1998.

Saborit J., Muntés-Mulero V., Larriba-Pey J (2003). Pushing Down Bit Filters in the Pipelined Execution of Large Queries. Euro-Par 2003: 328-337.

Saborit J., Muntés-Mulero V., Zuzarte C, Larriba-Pey J. (2005). Ad Hoc Star Join Query Processing in Cluster Architectures. DaWaK 2005: 200-209.

Sanjay A., Narasayya V. R., and Yang B. (2004). Integrating vertical and horizontal partitioning into automated physical database design. Proceedings of the ACM SIGMOD International Conference on Management of Data, pages 359–370, June 2004.

Sanjay A., Surajit C., and Narasayya V. R. (2000). Automated selection of materialized views and indexes in microsoft sql server. Proceedings of the International Conference on Very Large Databases, pages 496–505, September 2000.

Selinger P., Astrahan M., Chamberlin D., Lorie R., and Price T. (1979). Access path selection in a relational database management system. In SIGMOD '79: Proceedings of the 1979 ACM SIGMOD international conference on Management of data, pages 23–34, New York, NY, USA, 1979.

Shasha D. and Wang T.-L. (1991). Optimizing equijoin queries in distributed databases where relations are hash partitioned. ACM Trans. Database Syst., 16(2):279–308, 1991.

Stöhr, T, Märtens, H.; Rahm E. (2000). Multi-Dimensional Database Allocation for Parallel Data Warehouses, Proc. 26th Intl. Conf. on Very Large Databases (VLDB), Cairo, Egypt, 2000.

Stöhr, Märtens T, Rahm H., Erhard (2002). Dynamic Query Scheduling in Parallel Data Warehouses Proceedings of Euro-Par 2002 Conference, Paderborn, August 2002.

Yu, C. T. and Meng W. (1998). Principles of Database Query Processing for Advanced Applications. Morgan Kaufmann, 1998.

TPC (2008). Transaction processing council benchmarks - http://www.tpc.org/.

RAC (2008) - Oracle real application clusters, http://www.oracle.com/technology /products/ database/clustering/index.html.

Section 3

Chapter 8
A Survey of Extract–Transform–Load Technology

Panos Vassiliadis
University of Ioannina, Greece

ABSTRACT

The software processes that facilitate the original loading and the periodic refreshment of the data warehouse contents are commonly known as Extraction-Transformation-Loading (ETL) processes. The intention of this survey is to present the research work in the field of ETL technology in a structured way. To this end, we organize the coverage of the field as follows: (a) first, we cover the conceptual and logical modeling of ETL processes, along with some design methods, (b) we visit each stage of the E-T-L triplet, and examine problems that fall within each of these stages, (c) we discuss problems that pertain to the entirety of an ETL process, and, (d) we review some research prototypes of academic origin.

INTRODUCTION

A data warehouse typically collects data from several operational or external systems (also known as the *sources* of the data warehouse) in order to provide its end-users with access to integrated and manageable information. In practice, this task of data collection (also known as *data warehouse population*) has to overcome several inherent problems, which can be shortly summarized as follows. First, since the different sources structure information in completely different schemata the need to transform the incoming source data to a common, "global" data warehouse schema that will eventually be used by end user applications for querying is imperative. Second, the data coming from the operational sources suffer from quality problems, ranging from simple misspellings in textual attributes to value inconsistencies, database constraint violations and conflicting or missing information; consequently, this kind of "noise" from the data must be removed so that end-users are provided data that are as clean, complete and truthful as possible. Third, since the information is constantly updated in the production systems that populate the warehouse, it is necessary to refresh the data warehouse contents regularly, in order to provide the users with up-to-date information. All these problems require that the respective software processes are constructed by the data warehouse development team (either manually, or via specialized tools) and executed in appropriate time intervals for the correct and complete population of the data warehouse.

The software processes that facilitate the population of the data warehouse are commonly known as Extraction-Transformation-Loading (ETL) processes. ETL processes are responsible for (i) the extraction of the appropriate data from the sources, (ii) their transportation to a special-purpose area of the data warehouse where they will be processed, (iii) the transformation of the source data and the computation of new values (and, possibly records) in order to obey the structure of the data warehouse relation to which they are targeted, (iv) the isolation and cleansing of problematic tuples, in order to guarantee that business rules and database constraints are respected and (v) the loading of the cleansed, transformed data to the appropriate relation in the warehouse, along with the refreshment of its accompanying indexes and materialized views.

A naïve, exemplary ETL scenario implemented in MS SQL Server Integration Services is depicted in Figure 1. The scenario is organized in two parts. The first part, named *Extraction task* (Figure 1a), is responsible for the identification of the new and the updated rows in the source table *LINEITEM*. The idea is that we have an older snapshot for line items, stored in table *LINEITEM* which is compared to the new snapshot coming from the sources of the warehouse (depicted as *NEW_LIN-*

EITEM) in Figure 1b. Depending on whether a row is (a) newly inserted, or, (b) an existing tuple that has been updated, it is routed to the table *LINEITEM*, via the appropriate transformation (remember that insertions and updates cannot be uniformly handled by the DBMS). Once the table *LINEITEM* is populated, the second part of the scenario, named *Transform & Load task* (Figure 1a) is executed. This task is depicted in Figure 1c and its purpose is to populate with the update information several tables in the warehouse that act as materialized views. The scenario first computes the value for the attribute *Profit* for each tuple and then sends the transformed rows towards four "materialized" views that compute the following aggregated measures (keep in mind that *ExtendedPrice* refers to the money clients pay per line item, *PartKey* is the primary key for items and *SuppKey* is the primary key for suppliers):

- *View A*: aggregate profit and average discount grouped by *PartKey* and *SuppKey*
- *View B*: average profit and extended price grouped by *PartKey* and *LineStatus*
- *View C*: aggregate profit and extended price grouped by *LineStatus* and *PartKey*
- *View D*: aggregate profit and extended price grouped by *LineStatus*

As one can observe, an ETL process is the synthesis of individual tasks that perform extraction, transformation, cleaning or loading of data in an execution graph – also referred to as a workflow. Also, due to the nature of the design artifact and the user interface of ETL tools, an ETL process is accompanied by a plan that is to be executed. For these reasons, in the rest of this survey we will use the terms *ETL process*, *ETL workflow* and *ETL scenario* interchangeably.

The historical background for ETL processes goes all the way back to the birth of information processing software. Software for transforming and filtering information from one (structured, semi-structured, or even unstructured) file to

Figure 1. The environment of Extraction-Transformation-Loading processes

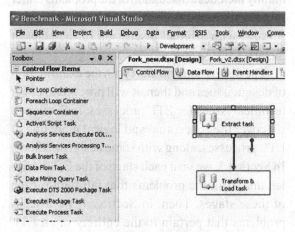

(a) Control flow of an ETL scenario

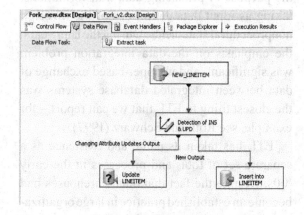

(b) Simple extraction part of an ETL scenario

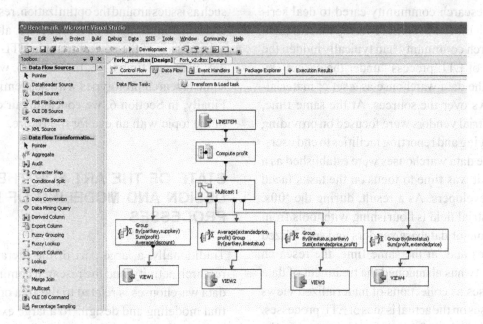

(c) Computation of extra values and multiple aggregations as part of an ETL scenario

another has been constructed since the early years of data banks, where the relational model and declarative database querying were not invented. Data and software were considered an inseparable duo for data management by that time and thus, this software was not treated as a stand-alone, special purpose module of the information system's architecture. As Vassiliadis and Simitsis (2009) mention "since then, any kind of data processing software that reshapes or filters records, calculates new values, and populates another data store than the original one is a form of an ETL program."

After the relational model had been born and the declarative nature of relational database querying had started to gain ground, it was quite natural that the research community would try to apply the declarative paradigm to data transformations. The EXPRESS system (Shu, Housel, Taylor, Ghosh, &

Lum, 1977) is the first attempt that we know with the purpose of producing data transformations, taking as input data definitions or the involved nonprocedural statements. During the later years, the emphasis on the data integration problem was significant, and wrapper-based exchange of data between integrated database systems was the closest thing to ETL that we can report – for example, see Roth and Schwarz (1997).

ETL has taken its name and existence as a separate set of tools and processes in the early '00s. Despite the fact that data warehouses had become an established practice in large organizations since the latest part of the '90s, it was only in the early '00s that both the industrial vendors and the research community cared to deal seriously with the field. It is noteworthy that till then, the research community had typically hidden the internals of ETL process "under the carpet" by treating the data warehouse as a set of materialized views over the sources. At the same time, the industrial vendors were focused on providing fast querying and reporting facilities to end users. Still, once data warehouses were established as a practice, it was time to focus on the tasks faced by the developers. As a result, during the '00s, the industrial field is flourishing with tools from both the major database vendors and specialized companies and, at the same time, the research community has abandoned the treatment of data warehouses as collections of materialized views and focuses on the actual issues of ETL processes.

The intention of this survey is to present the research work in the field of ETL in a structured way. The reader is assumed to be familiar with the fundamental concepts of databases and data warehousing. Since the focus is on ETL processes, we will avoid the detailed coverage of research topics like materialized view refreshment and data cleaning that are close to ETL processes (in fact, in practical situations, these tasks can be important constituents of an ETL workflow) but have an existence of their own in the research literature. Therefore, the coverage of these topics mainly includes a discussion of the problems under investigation and refers the reader to dedicated surveys with a broad discussion of the state of the art.

The discussion will start with the examination of design issues and then, it will proceed to cover technical issues for ETL processes. In Section 2, we cover the conceptual and logical modeling of ETL processes, along with some design methods. In Section 3, we visit each stage of the E-T-L triplet, and examine problems that fall within each of these stages. Then, in Section 4, we discuss problems that pertain to the entirety of an ETL process (and not just in one of its components), such as issues around the optimization, resumption and benchmarking of ETL processes, along with a discussion of the newest trend in ETL technology, near-real time ETL. In Section 5, we review some research prototypes with academic origin. Finally, in Section 6, we conclude our coverage of the topic with an eye for the future.

STATE OF THE ART FOR THE DESIGN AND MODELING OF ETL PROCESSES

Traditionally, a large part of the literature, the research activity, and the research community of data warehouses is related to the area of conceptual modeling and design. To a large extent, this is due to the fact that data warehouse projects are highly costly and highly risky endeavors; therefore, careful design and preparation are necessary. Moreover, due to their complexity, data warehouse environments should be carefully documented for maintenance purposes. ETL processes could not escape the above rule and, therefore, they have attracted the attention of the research community. A typical reason for this attention is also the fact that mainstream industrial approaches –see for example Kimbal, Reeves, Ross & Thornthwaite (1998), or Kimball & Caserta (2004)– focus on the physical-level details and lack a principled approach towards the problem of designing a data warehouse refreshment process. In this section, we will discuss the appearance of research efforts for the conceptual modeling of ETL processes with a chronological perspective and also cover some efforts concerning the logical modeling and design methods for this task.

UML Meta Modeling for Data Warehouses

The first approaches that are related to the conceptual design of data warehouses were hidden in discussions pertaining to data warehouse metadata. Stöhr, Müller, & Rahm (1999) propose an UML-based metamodel for data warehouses that covers both the back stage and the front-end of the data warehouse. Concerning the back stage of the data warehouse, which is the part of the paper that falls in the scope of this survey, the authors cover the workflow from the sources towards the target data stores with entities like *Mapping* (among entities) and *Transformation* (further classified to aggregations, filters, etc.) that are used to trace the inter-concept relationships in this workflow environment. The overall approach is a coherent, UML-based framework for data warehouse metadata, defined at a high-level of abstraction. The main contribution of the authors is that they provide a framework where specialized ETL activities (e.g., aggregations, cleanings, pivots, etc) can be plugged in easily via some kind of specialization.

First Attempts towards a Conceptual Model

The first attempt towards a conceptual model dedicated to the design and documentation of the data warehouse refreshment was presented by Vassiliadis, Simitsis & Skiadopoulos (DOLAP 2002). The main motivation for the model was the observation that during the earliest stages of the

data warehouse design, the designer is concerned with the analysis of the structure and content of the existing data sources and their mapping to the common data warehouse model. Therefore, a formal model for this task was necessary at the time.

The model of Vassiliadis et al (DOLAP 2002) involves concepts (standing for source and warehouse data holders) and their attributes, which define their internal structure. Part-of relationships correlate concepts and their constituent attributes. Attributes of source and warehouse concepts are related to each other with provider relationships. If a transformation takes place during the population of a target attribute, then the provider relationship passes through a transformation node in the model. Multiple transformations are connected via serial composition relationships. The model allows the definition of ETL constraints that signify the need for certain checks at the data (e.g., a certain field must be not null or within a certain range value, etc). Finally, multiple source candidates for the population of a warehouse concept are also tracked via candidate relationships. This is particularly useful for the early stages of the design, where more than one sources can be chosen for the population of a warehouse fact table. If one of them is eventually chosen (e.g., due to its higher data quality), then this source concept is characterized as the active candidate for the model.

A second observation of Vassiliadis et al (DOLAP 2002) was that is practically impossible to forecast all the transformations and cleanings that a designer might ever need. So, instead of proposing a closed set of transformations, the authors discuss the extensibility of the model with template transformations that are defined by the designer.

UML Revisited for ETL Processes

Trujillo & Luján-Mora (2003) revisit the conceptual modeling of ETL workflows from the view point of UML with the basic argument that the previous modeling by Vassiliadis et al is done via an ad-hoc model. So, the authors try to facilitate the modeling effort for ETL workflows with standard methods and they employ UML for this purpose.

It is interesting that the authors employ class diagrams and not activity diagrams for their modeling. The participating entities are UML packages; this is a powerful feature of the model, since it allows the arbitrary nesting of tasks. This nesting mechanism, quite common to UML, alleviates the complexity of the model of Vassiliadis et al., since it allows a gradual zooming in and out of tasks at different levels of detail. The main reason for dealing with class diagrams is that the focus of the modeling is on the interconnection of activities and data stores and not on the actual sequence of steps that each activity performs. Under this prism, whenever an activity A_1 populates an activity A_2, then A_2 is connected to A_1 with a dependency association.

Then, Trujillo & Luján-Mora (2003) provide a short description for a set of commonly encountered activities. Each such template activity is graphically depicted as an icon. The activities covered by the authors are: aggregation, conversion, logging, filtering, join, and loading of data, as well as checks for incorrect data, merging of data coming from different sources, wrapping of various kinds of external data sources and surrogate key assignment.

The authors build their approach on a generic structure for the design process for ETL workflows. So, they structure their generic design process in six stages, specifically, (i) source selection, (ii) source data transformation, (iii) source data join, (iv) target selection, (v) attribute mappings between source and target data and (vi) data loading.

UML and Attribute Mappings

One of the main assumptions of the approach of Trujillo & Luján-Mora (2003) was that the user must not be overwhelmed with the multitude of attribute mappings between sources, ETL activities and target warehouse tables. Still, as already mentioned, such detail is important for the backstage of the data warehouse. Without capturing the details of the inter-attribute mappings, important transformations, checks and contingency actions are not present in the documentation of the process and can be ignored at the construction/generation of code. Despite the effort needed, this documentation can be useful at the early stages of the project, where the designer is familiarized with the internal structure and contents of the sources (which include data quality problems, cryptic codes, conventions made by the administrators and the programmers of the sources and so on). Moreover, this documentation can also be useful during later stages of the project where the data schemata as well as the ETL tasks evolve and sensitive parts of the ETL workflow, both at the data and the activities, need to be highlighted and protected.

It is interesting that no standard formalism like the ER model or the UML treats attributes as *first-class citizens* –and as such, they are unable to participate in relationships. Therefore, Luján-Mora, Vassiliadis & Trujillo (2004) stress the need to devise a mechanism for capturing the relationships of attributes in a way that is (a) as standard as possible and (b) allows different levels of zooming, in order to avoid overloading the designer with the large amount of attribute relationships that are present in a data warehouse setting.

To this end, the authors devise a mechanism for capturing these relationships, via a UML *data mapping* diagram. UML is employed as a standard notation and its extensibility mechanism is exploited, in order to provide a standard model to the designers. Data mapping diagrams treat relations as classes (like the UML relational profile does). Attributes are represented via proxy classes, connected to the relation classes via stereotyped "Contain" relationships. Attributes can be related to each other via stereotyped "Map" relationships.

A particular point of emphasis made by Luján-Mora et al. (2004) is the requirement for multiple, complementary diagrams at different levels of detail. The authors propose four different layers of data mappings, specifically, (a) the database level, where the involved databases are represented as UML packages, (b) the dataflow level, where the relationships among source and target relations are captured, each in a single UML package, (c) the table level, where the dataflow diagram is zoomed in and each individual transformation is captured as a package, and (d) the attribute level, which offers a zoom-in to a table-level data mapping diagram, with all the attributes and the individual attribute level mappings captured.

State-of-the-Art at the Logical Level

Apart from the conceptual modeling process that constructs a first design of the ETL process, once the process has been implemented, there is a need to organize and document the meta-information around it. The organization of the metadata for the ETL process constitutes its *logical level* description – much like the system's catalog acts as the logical level description of a relational database.

Davidson & Kosky (1999) present WOL, a Horn-clause language, to specify transformations between complex types. The transformations are specified as rules in a Horn-clause language. An interesting idea behind this approach is that a transformation of an element can be decomposed to a set of rules for its elements, thus avoiding the difficulty of employing complex definitions.

As already mentioned, the first attempt towards a systematic description for the metadata of the ETL process go back to the works by Stöhr et al. (1999) and Vassiliadis, Quix, Vassiliou & Jarke (2001). This research has been complemented by the approach of Vassiliadis, Simitsis & Skiadopoulos (DMDW 2002) where a formal logical model for ETL process is proposed. The main idea around this model concerns the capturing of the data flow from the sources to the warehouse. This means that meta-information concerning relations or files and their schemata is kept, along with the meta-information on the activities involved and their semantics. Naturally, the interconnection of all these components in a workflow graph that implements the ETL process is also captured. The proposal of Vassiliadis et al (DMDW 2002) models the ETL workflow as a graph. The nodes of the graph are activities, recordsets (uniformly modeling files and relations) and attributes; note that recordsets have a schema in the typical way and activities have input schemata, as well as an output and a rejection schema (the latter serving the routing of offending rows to quarantine). Part-of edges connect the attributes with their encompassing nodes and provider relationships show how the values are propagated among schemata (in other words, provider relationships trace the dependencies in terms of data provision between one or more data provider attributes and a populated, data consumer attribute). Derived relationships also capture the transitive dependency of attributes that are populated with values that are computed via functions and parameters. An ETL workflow is a serializable combination of ETL activities, provider relationships and data stores. The overall modeling of the environment is called *Architecture Graph*; in other words, an architecture graph is the logical level description of the data flow of an ETL process.

The above mentioned model suffered from the lack of concrete modelling of the semantics of the activities as part of the graph. In other words, the provider relationships capture only the dependencies of a consumer attribute to its data providers, without incorporating the actual filterings and transformations that take place on the way from the provider to the consumer. This shortcoming was complemented by the work of Vassiliadis, Simitsis, Georgantas, Terrovitis, & Skiadopoulos (CAiSE 2003, IS 2005, DaWaK 2005, ER 2005). Due to the complicated nature of the internal semantics of the activities, the fundamental idea of these papers is to describe the meta-information via a series of intermediate schemata. Coarsely speaking, the semantics of the activity are related to this graph of internal, intermediate schemata via a simple convention that a schema corresponds to a predicate in rule-based language. LDL, a Datalog variant is the chosen language for this line of papers. Then, each rule of the form

```
OUTPUT<-INPUT, filters, functions, input-to-
output mappings
```

practically stands for a combination of inputs, outputs, comparison nodes and functions that connect the respective schemata via provider edges (see the long version of Vassiliadis et al, ER 2005 for a detailed description).

The works by Vassiliadis et al. (CAiSE 2003, IS 2005) also present a template language that allows ETL designers to define reusable templates of LDL programs via the appropriate macros (see also the discussion in the section "Systems" for the ARKTOS tool).

From the very beginning, this line of work was concerned with the exploitation of the meta-information for ETL processes. The papers by Vassiliadis et al. (DMDW 2002; ER 2005) are concerned with metrics for the identification of important properties of an ETL design. The metrics proposed by Vassiliadis et al. (DMDW 2002) are simple but quite powerful and capture the degree of dependence of a node to other nodes and vice versa. The metrics proposed by Vassiliadis et al. (ER 2005) are based on a rigorous framework for metrics of graph-based software constructs and show the size, cohesion, coupling, and complexity of a constructed ETL process.

Semantics-Aware Design Methods for ETL

A semi-automatic transition from the conceptual to the logical model for ETL processes has been proposed first by Simitsis (2005) and later by Simitsis & Vassiliadis (DSS 2008). Simple mappings involve the mapping of concepts to relations, and the mapping of transformations and constraint checks to the respective activities. The hardest problem that is dealt with is the mapping of the declarative requirements for transformations and checks at the conceptual level to a sequence of activities at the logical level. The paper proposes an algorithm that groups transformations and checks in *stages*, with each stage being a set of activities whose execution order can be transposed. Stage derivation is based on the idea of dependency: if the input attributes of a certain activity *a* depend on the (output) attributes of another activity or recordset *b*, then *a* should be on a higher order stage than *b*. Binary activities and persistent record sets typically act as boundaries for stages. Since the presented algorithms start with simple cases of single source – single target pairs, binary activities used as pivotal points of the scenario for the derivation of common sub-paths (after the output of the binary activity). Overall, since the ordering of stages is quite simple, the determination of the execution orders for all the activities is greatly simplified.

Skoutas & Simitsis (DOLAP 2006, IJSWIS 2007) use ontologies to construct the conceptual model of an ETL process. Based on domain knowledge of the designer and user requirements about the data sources and the data warehouse, an appropriate OWL ontology is constructed and used to annotate the schemas of these data stores. Then, according to the ontology and these annotations, an OWL reasoner is employed to infer correspondences and conflicts between the sources and the target, and to propose conceptual ETL operations for transferring data between them. Skoutas and Simitsis (NLDB 2007) use ontologies to document the requirements of an ETL process. The proposed method takes a formal, OWL description of the semantic descriptions of (a) the data sources, (b) the data warehouse, as well as (c) the conceptual specification of an ETL process and translates them to a textual format that resembles natural language. This is facilitated via a template-based approach for the constructs of the formal description.

INDIVIDUAL OPERATORS AND TASKS IN ETL SCENARIOS

In this section, we organize the review of the literature based on the constituents of the ETL process, specifically, the extraction, transformation (&cleaning), and loading phases. For each phase, we discuss practical problems and solutions proposed by the research community.

Research Efforts Concerning Data Extraction Tasks

The extraction is the hardest part of the refreshment of the data warehouse. This is due to two facts. First, the extraction software must incur minimum overheads to the source system both at runtime and at the nightly time window that is dedicated to the refreshment of the warehouse. Second, the extraction software must be installed at the source side with minimum effect to the source's software configuration. Typical techniques for the task include taking the difference of consecutive snapshots, the usage of timestamps (acting as transaction time) in source relations, or the "replaying" the source's log file at the warehouse side. Non-traditional, rarely used techniques require the modification of the source applications to inform the warehouse on the performed alterations at the source, or, the usage of triggers at the source side.

Snapshot difference between a newer and an older snapshot of a relation seems straightforward: In principle, the identification of records that are present in one snapshot and not in the other gives us the insertions and deletions performed; updates refer to two tuples that are present in the two snapshots and share the same primary key, but different non-key values. Despite this theoretical simplicity, performance considerations are very important and pose a research problem.

The research community has dealt with the problem from the mid '80s. Lindsay, Haas, Mohan, Pirahesh, & Wilms (1986) propose a timestamp based algorithm for detecting insertions, deletions and updates in two snapshots. A simple algorithm annotating changes with timestamps and comparing the values for tuples changed after the last comparison is proposed. Improvements concerning the identification of "empty areas" in the table speed up the process further. Labio & Garcia-Molina (1996) have presented the state of the art method on the topic of snapshot difference. The paper assumes two snapshots as input and produces a sequence of insertion, deletion and update actions to tuples, with each tuple being identified by its key. Several algorithms are discussed in the paper, including sort-merge outerjoins and partitioned hash joins. These algorithms can be extended with compression techniques in order to reduce the size of the processed data and the incurred I/Os as well as in order to exploit the opportunity of fitting one of the two snapshots in main memory. Compression is applied to each tuple individually (or to a whole block) and interestingly, the employed compression function is orthogonal to the algorithm of choice, with the extra observation that lossy compression methods might introduce erroneously identified modifications with very small probability. Overall, the investigated compression techniques include two methods, (a) simple tuple compression and (b) simple tuple compression with a pointer to the original uncompressed record. Then, the authors propose several algorithms for the identification of modifications. The first algorithm performs a sort-merge outer-join. Due to the anticipated periodic execution of the algorithm it is safe to assume that the previous snapshot is sorted. The algorithm sorts the new snapshot into runs and proceeds as the typical sort-merge join with the extra fundamental checks that are mentioned above, concerning the characterization of a tuple as an insertion (deletion), update, or existing entry. A variant of the algorithm involves the usage of compressed snapshot. In this case, the pointer to the original tuple can help with the identification of updates. Another variant of the algorithm concerning the hash join is also discussed. The main proposal of the paper, though, is the so-called window algorithm, which exploits the idea that the tuples that are present in both snapshots are found in approximately the same place in the two snapshots. The algorithm uses an input buffer and a buffer for candidate modified tuples (*ageing buffer* in the paper's terminology) per snapshot. The algorithm fills the input buffers and compares their contents. Tuples found identical in the two buffers are no longer considered. Misses are tested over the ageing buffer of the other snapshot. If a match occurs, the tuples are further ignored. The tuples that remain in the input buffers after these tests are candidates to be insertions or deletions and they are pushed to the ageing buffer of their snapshot. Due to space requirements, if an ageing buffer is full, it must be emptied. To this end, a queue of pointers is maintained, keeping track of the order in which the tuples entered the buffer; if the buffer is full, the oldest tuples are emptied. The algorithm is quite efficient and safe if the same records are physically placed in nearby areas in the two snapshots and the experimental results have proved that this is a realistic assumption.

Research Efforts Concerning Data Transformation Tasks

Although naïve data transformations are inherently built inside SQL and relational algebra, transformations that are used in ETL scenarios have not really found their way in the research literature. The main reason for this is probably due to the fact that transformations of this kind are typically ad-hoc and rather straightforward if studied individually; the complexity arises when their combination in a workflow is introduced.

Nevertheless, there are some approaches that try to deal with the way to transform input to output data efficiently, and elegantly in terms of semantics.

The Pivoting Problem

Pivoting refers to a common spreadsheet operation for the tabular presentation of data to the end user, which is also quite common in ETL processes. Assume that a user wants to represent information about employees' revenues, with the revenues of each employee split into categories like salary, tax, work bonus, and family bonus. There are two possible organizations for this kind of data. First, a row-oriented organization is based on a table with the above categories represented as attributes -- e.g., consider a relation of the form $EMP_r(EID, ESAL, ETAX, EWBonus, EFBonus)$. A second, attribute-value representation splits the revenues of each employee into different rows – e.g., consider a relation of the form $EMP_{av}(EID, RID, Amount)$ with RID being a foreign key to a table $REVENUE\_CATEGORIES(RID, RDescr)$ that contains values $\{(10, Sal), (20, Tax), ...\}$. Pivoting is the operation that transforms relation EMP_{av} to EMP_r; unpivot is the inverse operation. Cunningham, Galindo-Legaria & Graefe (2004) discuss efficient ways to implement these two operations in a DBMS environment. The authors start by suggesting compact extensions of SQL to allow the end user to directly express the fact that this is the requested operation (as opposed to asking the user perform pivot/unpivot through complicated expressions that the optimizer will fail to recognize as one operation). Special treatment is taken for data collisions and NULL values. The authors build upon the fact that pivot is a special case of aggregation, whereas unpivot is a special case of a correlated nested loop self join and explore query processing and execution strategies, as well as query optimization transformations, including the possibilities of pushing projections and selections down in execution plans that directly involve them.

Data Mappers

A sequence of papers by Carreira et al. (DaWaK 2005, DKE 2007, ICEIS 2007) explore the possibilities imposed by data transformations that require one-to-many mappings, i.e., transformations that produce several output tuples for each input tuple. This kind of operations is typically encountered in ETL scenarios. Since relational algebra is not equipped with an operator that performs this kind of input-output mapping, Carreira et al. extend it by proposing a new operator called *data mapper* and explore its semantics and properties. In this discussion, we mainly focus on the work of Carreira et al (DKE, 2007) which is a long version of a previous work (DaWaK 2005). The authors define the data mapper operator as a computable function mapping the space of values of an input schema to the space of values of an output schema. Mappers are characterized as single or multi-value mappers, depending on whether one or more tuples occur at the output given an arbitrary tuple at the input of the operator. Mappers under investigation are minimalistic operators and should be highly cohesive (i.e., they should do exactly one job); to this end, a mapper is defined to be in normal form if it cannot be expressed as the composition of two other mappers. Carreira et al. propose algebraic rewritings to speed up the execution of composite expressions of the extended relation algebra. Specifically, a data mapper can be combined with a (originally subsequent) selection condition, if the condition operates on a parameter of a mapper function. A second rule directs how a selection condition that uses attributes of the output of a data mapper can be translated to the attributes that generate them and thus be pushed through the mapper. A third rule deals with how projection can help avoid unnecessary computations of mappers that will be subsequently projected-out later. Finally, Carreira et al (ICEIS 2007) report some first results on their experimentation with implementing the data mappers in a real RD-BMS. A more detailed description of alternative implementations is given by Carreira et al (QDB 2007) concerning unions, recursive queries, table functions, stored procedures and pivoting operations as candidates for the implementation of the data mapper operator. The first four alternatives where used for experimentation in two different DBMSs and table functions appear to provide the highest throughput for data mappers.

The Data Lineage Problem

Apart from efficiently performing the transformations in an ETL process, it is also important to be able to deal with the inverse problem. Given a certain warehouse tuple (or, set of tuples), the *data lineage problems* involves the identification of the input data that are the originators of the given tuple (or, tuples).

Cui and Widom have investigated the problem of data lineage in a set of papers (Cui & Widom, 2001 & 2003). Here, we mostly focus on Cui & Widom (2003) that describes the authors' method in more detail. This approach treats each transformation as a procedure that can be applied to one or more datasets and produces one or more datasets as output. Cui and Widom present a set of properties that a transformation can have, specifically (a) stability, if it never produces datasets as output without taking any datasets as input, (b) determinism and (c) completeness, if each input data item always contributes to some output data item. The authors assume that all transformations employed in their work are stable and deterministic and proceed to define three major transformation classes of interest: dispatchers, aggregators and black-boxes.

- A transformation is a *dispatcher*, if each input data item produces zero or more output items (with each output item possibly being derived by more than one input data items). A special category of dispatchers are *filters*. A dispatcher is a *filter* if each input item produces either itself or nothing.

- A transformation is an *aggregator,* if it is complete and there exists a unique disjoint partition of the input data set that contributes to some output data item. An aggregator is *context-free* if the output group to which an input data item is mapped can be found by observing the value of this data item alone, independently of the rest of the data items of the input. An aggregator is *key preserving* if all the input originators of an output tuple have the same key value.

- A transformation is a *black-box,* if it is neither a dispatcher nor an aggregator.

Several other sub-categories concerning the mapping of input to output values on the basis of the keys of the input and the output are also defined. The main idea is that if a certain value of an output (input) tuple can directly lead to its respective input (output) tuple(s), then this can be exploited during lineage determination. For example, *backward key transformations* have the property that given an output tuple, one can determine the key of the input tuples that produced it; in this case, lineage is straightforward. In the general case, the lineage determination for dispatchers requires one pass of the input; the lineage determination of aggregators requires several full scans of the input, whereas black boxes have the entire input as their lineage. Given a sequence of transformations in an ETL scenario, it is necessary to keep a set of intermediate results between transformations, in order to be able to determine the data lineage of the output. Appropriate indexes may be used to relate each output to its input. To avoid storing all the intermediate results, the authors propose a *normalization* process that allows the reordering of the transformations in such a way that adjacent transformations share similar properties. Assuming two adjacent transformations *a* and *b*, the idea is that their grouping is beneficial if one can determine the lineage of a tuple in the output of *b* at the input of *a*, without storing any intermediate results. To this end, Cui

and Widom propose a greedy algorithm, called *Normalize,* which repeatedly discovers beneficial combinations of adjacent transformations and combines the best pair of transformations.

Theoretical Foundations for ETL Processes

The theoretical underpinnings concerning the internal complexity of simple ETL transformations are investigated by research that concerns the *data exchange* problem. Assume a source and a target schema, a set of mappings that specify the relationship between the source and the target schema and a set of constraints at the target schema. The problem of data exchange studies whether we can materialize an instance at the target, given an instance at the source, such that all mappings and constraints are respected. Data exchange is a specific variant of the general data integration meta-problem, that requires the materialization of the result at the target, with the ultimate purpose of being able to subsequently pose queries to it, without the luxury of referring back to the source. Due to this inherent characteristic of the problem, we believe that the data exchange is the closest theoretical problem to ETL that we know of.

As Fagin, Kolaitis & Popa (2005) mention, several problems arise around the data exchange problem, with particular emphasis on (a) materializing the solution that reflects the source data as accurately as possible and (b) doing so in an efficient manner. A first important result comes in the identification of the best possible solutions to the problem, called *universal solutions* (Fagin, Kolaitis, Miller, & Popa, 2005). Universal solutions have the good property of having exactly the data needed for the data exchange and can be computed in polynomial time via the chase. It is interesting that if a solution exists, then a universal solution exists, too, and every other solution has a homomorphism to it. At the same time, Fagin et al (TODS 2005) deal with the problem of more than one universal solution for a problem and introduce the notion of a *core*, which is the universal solution of the smallest size. For practical cases of data exchanges, polynomial time algorithms can be used for the identification of the core. It is worth noting that the schema mappings explored are investigated for the case of tuple-generating dependencies, which assure that for each source tuple *x*, whenever a conjunctive formula applies to it, then there exists a target tuple *y*, such that a conjunctive formula over *x* and *y* applies too (in other words, we can assure that mappings and constraints are respected). To our point of view, this is a starting point for the investigation of more complex mappings that arise in ETL settings.

Further results have to do with the ability to pose queries and obtain certain answers from a data exchange setting as well as with the management of inverse mappings relationships (Fagin, 2007).

Data Cleaning

The area of data cleaning, although inherently related to the ETL process, practically constitutes a different field on its own. Covering this field adequately is well beyond the scope of this paper. The topic that has been in the center of attention of the research community in the area of data cleaning concerns record matching, with a particular emphasis on textual attributes. Record matching refers to the problem of identifying records that represent the *same* object / fact in the real world, with *different* values. Essentially, it is the case of textual fields that presents the major research challenge, since their unstructured nature allows users to perform data entry in arbitrary ways. Moreover, value discrepancies due to problems in the data entry or data processing, as well as different snapshots of the representation of the real world fact in the database contribute to making the problem harder. Typically, the identification of duplicates requires an efficient algorithm for deciding which tuples are to be compared and a distance (or, similarity) metric based on the val-

ues of the compared tuples (and possibly, some knowledge by an expert).

For recent, excellent surveys of the field, the reader is encouraged to first refer to a survey by Elmagarmid, Ipeirotis & Verykios (2007) as well as to a couple of tutorials by Koudas & Srivastava (2005) and Koudas, Sarawagi & Srivastava (2006) in the recent past.

Research Efforts Concerning Data Loading Tasks

Typically, warehouse loading tasks take place in a periodic fashion, within a particular time window during which, the system is dedicated to this purpose. Bulk loading is performed (a) during the very first construction of the warehouse and (b) in an incremental way, during its everyday maintenance. During the latter task, a set of new insertions, deletions and updates arrive at the warehouse, after being identified at the extraction phase and, subsequently transformed and cleaned. This set of data is typically called the 'delta' relation and has to be loaded to the appropriate destination table. In all occasions, loading is performed via vendor-specific bulk loaders that provide maximum performance (see Vassiliadis & Simitsis, 2009 for a discussion on the topic). Also, apart from the dimension tables and the fact tables, indexes and materialized views must also be maintained.

It is interesting that only the loading of views and indexes has been investigated by the research community; in this subsection, we give an overview of important references in the bibliography.

Maintenance of Indexes

Concerning the general setting of index maintenance, Fenk, Kawakami, Markl, Bayer & Osaki (2000) highlight the critical parameters of index bulk loading that include the minimization of random disk accesses, disk I/O, CPU load, and the optimization of data clustering and page filling. As typically happens with spatial indexes, Fenk et al., identify 3 stages in the bulk loading of a multidimensional warehouse index: (a) key calculation for each tuple of the data set, (b) sorting of the tuples on the basis of their keys and (c) loading of the sorted data into the index.

Roussopoulos, Kotidis & Roussopoulos (1997) discuss the efficient construction and bulk load of cube trees. Cube trees and their variants are based on the fundamental idea of finding an efficient data structure for all the possible aggregations of these data. Assume a relation with M attributes, out of which N, $N<M$, can act as grouping attributes for aggregate queries. The idea behind cube trees is the mapping of all the data of all these possible aggregations to a single index that can efficiently answer aggregate range queries. The packing of the empty space is crucial for the compression and efficient query answering of the cube tree. Roussopoulos et al (1997) discuss the bulk loading and maintenance of cube trees that are implemented over packed R-trees. The authors make the sharp observation that individual updates are practically impossible in terms of performance and thus, bulk updates are necessary. The approach is based on sorting the delta increment that is to be loaded and merging it with the existing cube tree. Since all possible aggregates are kept by cube trees, for every delta tuple, all its possible projections are computed and stored in the appropriate buffer. When a buffer is full, it is sorted and then it is staged for the subsequent merge that takes place once all the delta increment has been processed. The authors also highlight that as time passes, the points of all the possible cubes of the multidimensional space are covered with some values, which makes the incremental update even easier. Moreover, since the merging involves three parts (i) the old cube tree, (ii) the delta and (iii) the new cube tree, their merging can be efficiently obtained by using three disks, one for each part. Roussopoulos, Kotidis & Sismanis (1999) discuss this possibility.

Fenk et al. (2000) propose two bulk loading algorithms for the UB-Tree, one for the initial and one for the incremental bulk loading of a UB-tree. The UB-Tree is a multidimensional index, which is used along with specialized query algorithms for the sequential access to the stored data. The UB-Tree clusters data according to a space filling Z–curve. Each point of the multidimensional space is characterized by its Z-address and Z-addresses are organized in disjoined Z-regions mapped to the appropriate disk pages. This way, a tree can be formed and the location of specific points at the disk can be computed. Concerning the above-mentioned generic method for bulk loading that Fenk et al have highlighted, in the case of UB-trees, the key is computed by taking the primary key of a tuple and calculating its Z-value and the sorting is performed with external merge sorting. To achieve high page filling, the construction of the UB-tree uses the idea of organizing data in buffers twice as large as disk pages; these buffers are split in two and one of the two halves is stored as a UB-tree page. The incremental variant of the algorithm tries to identify the correct page for inserting a tuple under consideration.

Dwarfs (Sismanis, Deligiannakis, Roussopoulos & Kotidis, 2002) are indexes built by exploiting an appropriate ordering of the dimensions and the exploitation of common prefixes and suffixes in the data. A dwarf resembles a trie, with one level for each dimension of a cube and appropriate pointers among internal levels. High cardinality dimensions are placed highly in the Dwarf, to quickly reduce the branching factor. Dwarf construction exploits a single, appropriate sorting of data and proceeds in a top-down fashion. Identical sub-dwarfs (i.e., dwarfs generated from the same set of tuples of the fact table) are pinpointed and coalesced. Dwarfs constitute the state-of-the-art, both in querying and in updating sets of aggregate views and, when size and update time are considered, they significantly outperform other approaches.

Materialized View Maintenance

View maintenance is a vast area by itself; covering the topic to the full of its extent is far beyond the focus of this paper. The main idea around view maintenance is developed around the following setting: Assume a set of base tables upon which a materialized view is defined via a query. Changes (i.e., insertions, deletions and updates) occur at the base tables resulting in the need to refresh the contents of the materialized view (a) correctly and (b) as efficiently as possible. The parameters of the problem vary and include:

a.   The query class: The area started by dealing with Select-Project-Join views, but the need for aggregate views, views with nested queries in their definition, outerjoins and other more complicated components has significantly extended the field. The query class (along with several assumptions) can also determine whether the materialized view can be updated solely with the changes and its current state, without accessing the base tables.

b.   The nature of the changes: apart from simple insertions and deletions, it is an issue whether updates are treated per se or as a pair (delete old value, insert new value). Also, sets of updates as opposed to individual updates can be considered.

c.   The number of materialized views that are concurrently been updated: in the context of data warehousing, and ETL in particular, simply dealing with one view being updated is too simplistic. Typically, several materialized views (possibly related in some hierarchical fashion, where one view can be derived from the other) have to be simultaneously refreshed.

d.   The way the update is physically implemented: Typically, there are three ways to refresh views, (a) on-update, i.e., the instant a change occurs at the sources, (b) on-

demand, i.e., in a deferred way, only when someone poses a query to the view and (c), periodically, which is the typical case for data warehousing, so far.

There are several surveys that give pointers for further reading. The earliest of them was authored by Gupta & Mumick (1995). One can also refer to a note by Roussopoulos (1998) and a chapter by Kotidis (2002). Gupta & Mumick (2006) is a recent paper that discusses maintenance issues for a complicated class of views. The reader is also referred to papers by Mumick, Quass & Mumick (1997), Colby, Kawaguchi, Lieuwen, Mumick & Ross (1997), Labio, Yerneni & Garcia-Molina (1999), and Stanoi, Agrawal & El Abbadi (1999), for the update of groups of views in the presence of updates.

HOLISTIC APPROACHES

In the previous section, we have dealt with operators facilitating tasks that are located in isolation in one of the three main areas of the ETL process. In this section, we take one step back and give a holistic view to research problems that pertain to the entirety of the ETL process. First, we discuss the problems of optimization and resumption of entire ETL workflows. Second, we visit the practical problem of the lack of a reference benchmark for ETL processes. Finally, we cover the newest topic of research in the area, concerning the near real time refreshment of a data warehouse.

Optimization

The minimization of the execution time of an ETL process is of particular importance, since ETL processes have to complete their task within specific time windows. Moreover, in the unfortunate case where a failure occurs during the execution of an ETL process, there must be enough time left for the resumption of the workflow. Traditional optimization methods are not necessarily applicable to ETL scenarios. As mentioned by Tziovara, Vassiliadis & Simitsis (2007) *"ETL workflows are NOT big queries*: their structure is not a left-deep or bushy tree, black box functions are employed, there is a considerable amount of savepoints to aid faster resumption in cases of failures, and different servers and environments are possibly involved. Moreover, frequently, the objective is to meet specific time constraints with respect to both regular operation and recovery (rather than the best possible throughput)." For all these reasons, the optimization of the execution of an ETL process poses an important research problem with straightforward practical implications.

Simitsis, Vassiliadis & Sellis (ICDE 2005, TKDE 2005) handle the problem of ETL optimization as a state-space problem. Given an original ETL scenario provided by the warehouse designer, the goal of the paper is to find a scenario which is equivalent to the original and has the best execution time possible. Each state is a directed acyclic graph with relations and activities as the nodes and data provider relationships as edges. The authors propose a method that produces states that are equivalent to the original one (i.e., given the same input, they produce the same output) via transitions from one state to another. A transition involves a restructuring of the graph mainly in one of the following ways:

- *Swapping* of two consecutive activities if this is feasible, with the goal of bringing highly selective activities towards the beginning of the process (in a manner very similar to the respective query optimization heuristic in relational DBMS's),
- *Factorization* of common (or, in the paper's terminology, homologous) activities in a workflow that appear in different paths that end in a binary transformation, with the goal of applying a transformation only once, later in the workflow, possibly to fewer or sorted data,

- *Distribution* of common activities (the inverse of factorization) by pushing a transformation that appears late in the workflow towards its start, with the hope that a highly selective activity found after a binary transformation is pushed early enough in the workflow.

Two other transitions, *merge* and *split* are used for special cases. The important problem behind the proposed transitions is that a restructuring of the graph is not always possible. For example, it is important to block the swapping of activities where the operation of the second requires an attribute computed in the first. At the same time, the detection of homologous activities requires the identification of activities with common functionality over data with similar semantics. An ontological mapping of attributes to a common conceptual space facilitates this detection.

The paper uses a very simple cost model to assess the execution cost of a state and presents three algorithms to detect the best possible algorithm. Apart from the exhaustive algorithm that explores the full search space, heuristics are also employed to reduce the search space and speed up the process.

The work of Simitsis et al (ICDE 2005, TKDE 2005) for the optimization of an ETL process at the logical level was complemented with a paper on the optimization of ETL workflows at the physical level by Tziovara et al (2007). In this paper, the authors propose a method that produces an optimal physical level scenario given its logical representation as an input. Again, the input ETL workflow is considered to be a directed acyclic graph constructed as mentioned above. A logical-level activity corresponds to a *template* i.e., an abstract operation that is customized with schema and parameter information for the ETL scenario under consideration. Each logical-level template is physically implemented by a variety of implementations (much like a relational join is implemented by nested loops, merge-sort, or hash join physical-level operators). Each physical operator is sensitive to the order of the incoming stream of tuples and has a different cost and needs of system resources (e.g., memory, disk space, etc). Again, the problem is modeled as a state-space problem with states representing full implementations of all the logical level activities with their respective physical-level operators. Transitions are of two kinds: (a) replacement of a physical implementation and (b) introduction of *sorter activities* which apply on stored recordsets and sort their tuples according to the values of some, critical for the sorting, attributes. The main idea behind the introduction of sorters is that order-aware implementations can be much faster than their order-neutral equivalents and possibly outweigh the cost imposed by the sorting of data. As with classical query optimization, existing ordering in the storage of incoming data or the reuse of interesting orders in more than one operator can prove beneficial. Finally, this is the first paper where *butterflies* have been used as an experimental tool for the assessment of the proposed method (see the coming section on benchmarking for more details).

The Resumption Problem

An ETL process typically processes several MB's or GB's of data. Due to the complex nature of the process and the sheer amount of data, failures create a significant problem for warehouse administrators – mainly due to the time limits (typically referred to as the *time window*) within which the loading process must be completed. Therefore, the efficient resumption of the ETL process in the case of failures is very important.

Labio, Wiener, Garcia-Molina & Gorelik (2000) are concerned with the issue of efficiently resuming an interrupted workflow. Instead of redoing the workflow all over from the beginning, the authors propose a resumption algorithm, called *DR*, based on the fundamental observation that whenever an activity outputs data in an ordered fashion, then its resumption can start right where

it was interrupted. Activities are practically treated as black boxes (where only the input and output are of interest) and a tree of activities is used to model the workflow. Each path of the tree is characterized on the relationship of output to input tuples and on the possibility of ignoring some tuples. Each transformation in an ETL process is characterized with respect to a set of properties that concern (a) the extent to which an input tuple produces more than one output tuples (if not, this can be exploited at resumption time), (b) the extent to which a prefix or a suffix of a transformation can be produced by a prefix or a suffix of the input (in which case, resumption can start from the last tuple under process at the time of failure), (c) the order produced by the transformation (independently of the input's order) and the deterministic nature of the transformation. Combinations of these properties are also considered by the authors. Moreover, these properties are not defined only for transformations in isolation, but also, they are generalized for sequences of transformations, i.e., the whole ETL process.

The resumption algorithm has two phases: (a) *design*, where the activities of the workflow are characterized with respect to the aforementioned properties and (b) *resumption*, which is based on the previous characterization and invoked in the event of failure.

- Design constructs a workflow customized to execute the resumption of the original workflow. To this end, re-extraction procedures are assigned to extractors; these procedures regulate whether all or part of the input will be extracted from the sources. These re-extraction procedures are complemented with filters that are responsible for blocking source or intermediate tuples that have already been processed – and most importantly, stored – during the regular operation of the ETL process.
- Resume consists of the assignment of the correct values that must be assigned to the

resumption workflow's filters, so that the tuples that are already stored in the warehouse are blocked. Then, Resume performs the application of the re-extraction procedures. Subsequently, the load of the warehouse continues as in regular operation.

Benchmarking

Unfortunately, the area of ETL processes suffers from the absence of a thorough benchmark that puts tools and algorithms to the test, taking into consideration parameters like the complexity of the process, the data volume, the amount of necessary cleaning and the computational cost of individual activities of the ETL workflows.

The Transaction Processing Council has proposed two benchmarks for the area of decision support. The TPC-H benchmark (TPC-H, 2008) is a decision support benchmark that consists of a suite of business-oriented ad-hoc queries and concurrent data modifications. The database describes a sales system, keeping information for the parts and the suppliers, and data about orders and the supplier's customers. The relational schema of TPC-H is not a typical warehouse star or snowflake schema; on the contrary, apart from a set of tables that are clearly classified as dimension tables, the facts are organized in a combination of tables acting as bridges and fact tables. Concerning the ETL process, the TPC-H requires the existence of very simple insertion and deletion SQL statements that directly modify the contents of the LINEITEM and ORDERS warehouse tables. Clearly, TPC-H is not related to ETL, since there is no workflow of cleanings or transformations, no value computations and no routing of data from the sources to the appropriate targets in the warehouse.

TPC-DS is a new Decision Support (DS) workload being developed by the TPC (TPC-DS, 2005). This benchmark models the decision support system of a retail product supplier, including queries and data maintenance. The relational schema of this benchmark is more complex than the schema presented in TPC-H. TPC-DS involves six star schemata (with a large overlap of shared dimensions) standing for Sales and Returns of items purchased via three sales channels: a Store, a Catalog and the Web channel. The structure of the schemata is more natural for data warehousing than TPC-H; still, the schemata are neither pure stars, nor pure snowflakes. The dimensions follow a snowflake pattern, with a different table for each level; nevertheless, the fact table has foreign keys to all the dimension tables of interest (resulting in fast joins with the appropriate dimension level whenever necessary). TPC-DS provides a significantly more sophisticated palette of refreshment operations for the data warehouse than TPC-H. There is a variety of maintenance processes that insert or delete facts, maintain inventories and refresh dimension records, either in a history keeping or in a non-history keeping method. To capture the semantics of the refreshment functions, warehouse tables are pseudo-defined as views over the sources. The refreshment scenarios of TPC-DS require the usage of functions for transformations and computations (with date transformations and surrogate key assignments being very popular). Fact tables are also populated via a large number of inner and outer joins to dimension tables. Overall, TPC-DS is a significant improvement over TPC-H in terms of benchmarking the ETL process; nevertheless, it still lacks the notion of large workflows of activities with schema and value transformations, row routing and other typical ETL features.

A first academic effort for the benchmarking of warehouses is found in Darmont, Bentayeb, & Boussaïd (2005). Still, the benchmark explicitly mentions ETL processes as future work and does not address the abovementioned problems. A second approach towards a benchmark for ETL processes is presented in Vassiliadis, Karagiannis, Tziovara, Simitsis (2007). The authors provide a rough classification of template structures, which are called *butterflies*, due to their shape.

In the general case, a butterfly comprises three elements. First, a butterfly comprises a *left wing* where source data are successively combined (typically via join operations) towards a central point of storage (called the *body* of the butterfly). Finally, the *right wing* comprises the routing and aggregation of the tuples that arrived at the body towards materialized views (also simulating reports, spreadsheets etc.). Depending on the shape of the workflow (where one of the wings might be missing), the authors propose several template workflow structures and a concrete set of scenarios that are materializations of these templates.

Near-Real-Time ETL

Traditionally, the data warehouse refreshment process has been executed in an off-line mode, during a nightly time window. Nowadays, business needs for on-line monitoring of source side business processes drive the request for 100% data freshness at the user's reports at all times. Absolute freshness (or real time warehousing as abusively mentioned) practically contradicts with one of the fundamental reasons for separating the OLTP systems from reporting tasks for reasons of load, lock contention and efficiency (at least when large scale is concerned). Still, due to the user requests, data warehouses cannot escape their transformation to data providers for the end users with an increasing rate of incoming, fresh data. For all these reasons, a compromise is necessary and as a result, the refreshment process moves to periodic refresh operations with a period of hours or even minutes (instead of days). This brings *near real time data warehousing* in the stage. In this subsection, we will review some research efforts towards this direction.

Karakasidis, Vassiliadis & Pitoura (2005), propose a framework for the implementation of near real time warehouse (called "active" data warehousing by the authors). Several goals are taken into consideration by the authors, and specifically: (a) minimal changes in the software configuration

of the source, (b) minimal overhead on the source due to the continuity of data propagation, (c) the possibility of smoothly regulating the overall configuration of the environment in a principled way. The architecture of the system is based on pipelining: each activity behaves as a queue (and thus, it called an ETL queue) that periodically checks the contents of its queue buffers and passes a block of tuples to a subsequent queue once they are appropriately processed (i.e., filtered or transformed). The queues of an ETL workflow form a queue network and pipelining takes place. The paper explores a few other possibilities: (a) queue theory is used for the prediction of the behavior of the queue network, (b) a legacy application over ISAM files was modified with minimal software changes and (c) web services were employed at the warehouse end to accept the final blocks of tuples and load them to the warehouse. The latter performed reasonably well, although the lack of lightweightness in web service architectures poses an interesting research challenge.

The work by Luo, Naughton, Ellmann & Watzke (2006) deals with the problem of continuous maintenance of materialized views. The continuous loading of the warehouse with new or updated source data is typically performed via concurrent sessions. In this case, the existence of materialized views that are defined as joins of the source tables may cause deadlocks (practically, the term 'source tables' should be understood as referring to cleansed, integrated "replicas" of the sources within the warehouse). This is due to the fact that the maintenance of the view due to an update of source R_1 may require a lookup to source relation R_2 for the match of new delta. If R_2 is updated concurrently with R_1, then a deadlock may occur. To avoid deadlock, Luo et al. propose the reordering of transactions in the warehouse. The authors assume that the refreshment process operates over join or aggregate join materialized views. The authors suggest several rules for avoiding deadlocks. Specifically, the authors require that (a) at any time, only one of the relations of a join view is updated, (b) data coming from the sources are not randomly assigned to update sessions, but rather, all the modifications of a tuple are routed to the same refreshment session, and, (c) the traditional 2PL, tuple-level locking mechanism is replaced by some higher level protocol. Individual modifications to the same relation are grouped in transactions and a scheduling protocol for these transactions is proposed, along with some starvation avoidance heuristics. A second improvement that Luo et al. propose is the usage of "pre-aggregation" for aggregate materialized views, which practically involves the grouping of all the modifications of a certain view tuple in the same transaction to one modification with their net effect. This can easily be achieved by sorting the individual updates over their target tuple in the aggregate materialized view. The experimental assessment indicates that the throughput is significantly increased as an effect of the reordering of transactions – especially as the number of modifications per transaction increases.

Thiele, Fischer & Lehner (2007) discuss the problem of managing the workload of the warehouse in a near real time warehouse (called real time warehouse by the authors). The authors discuss a load-balancing mechanism that schedules the execution of query and update transactions according to the preferences of the users. There are two fundamental, conflicting goals that the scheduling tries to reconcile. On the one hand, users want efficient processing of their queries and low response time. This goal is referred to as Quality of Service by the authors. On the other hand, the users also want the warehouse data to be as up-to-date as possible with respect to their originating records at the sources. This goal is referred to as Quality of Data by the authors. Two queues are maintained by the algorithm, one for the queries and one for the update transactions. Since a reconciliation must be made between two conflicting requirements, the authors assume that queries are tagged with two scores, one for the requirement for freshness and another for the re-

quirement of query efficiency. To enable the near real time loading of the warehouse, Thiele et al. propose a two-level scheduling mechanism. The first level of scheduling is dedicated in deciding whether a user query or an update transaction will be executed; this decision is based on the sum of the scores of both requirements for all the queries. The winner sum determines if an update or a query will be executed. The second level of scheduling resolves which transaction will be executed. To avoid implications with data correctness and to serve both goals better, the authors resolve in two scheduling guidelines. If an update transaction is to be executed, then, it should be the one related to the data that are going to be queried by a query at the beginning of the query queue. On the other hand, if a query is to be executed (i.e., efficiency has won the first level of the scheduling contest), then the query with a higher need for Quality of Service is picked. To avoid starvation of queries with low preference to quality of service, the QoS tags of all queries that remain in the queue are increased after each execution of a query.

Thomsen, Pedersen & Lehner (2008) discuss a loader for near real time, or *right time* data warehouses. The loader tries to synchronize the loading of the warehouse with queries that require source data with a specific freshness guarantee. The idea of loading the data *when* they are needed (as opposed to *before* they are needed) produces the notion of right time warehousing. The architecture of the middleware discussed by the authors involves three tiers. The first tier concerns the data producer, at the source side. The middleware module provided for the producer captures the modification operations "insert" and "commit" for JDBC statements. The user at the source side can decide whether committed data are to become available for the warehouse (in this case, this is referred to as materialization by the authors). On insert, the new source values are cached in a source buffer and wait to be propagated to the next tier, which is called catalyst.

Apart from that, the source middleware provides callbacks for regulating its policy as steal or no steal with respect to the flushing of committed data to the hard disk at the source side, as well as a third option for regulating its policy on the basis of its current load or elapsed idle time. The catalyst side, at the same time, also buffers data for the consumer. An interesting property of the catalyst is the guarantee of freshness for the user. So, whenever a warehouse user requests data, he can set a time interval for the data he must have; then the catalyst check its own buffers and communicates with the source-side middleware to compile the necessary data. A precise synchronization of the data that must be shed from main memory via appropriate main memory indexing is also discussed by the authors. The third tier, at the warehouse side, operates in a REPEATABLE READ isolation mode and appropriately locks records (via a shared lock) so that the catalyst does not shed them during their loading to the warehouse. Finally, the authors discuss a simple programmatic facility via appropriate view definitions to allow the warehouse user retrieve the freshest data possible in a transparent way.

Polyzotis, Skiadopoulos, Vassiliadis, Simitsis & Frantzell (2007, 2008) deal with an individual operator of the near real time ETL process, namely the join of a continuous stream of updates generated at the sources with a large, disk resident relation at the warehouse side, under the assumption of limited memory. Such a join can be used in several occasions, such as surrogate key assignment, duplicate detection, simple data transformations etc. To this end, a specialized join algorithm, called MeshJoin is introduced. The main idea is that the relation is continuously brought to main memory in scans of sequential blocks that are joined with the buffered stream tuples. A precise expiration mechanism for the stream tuples guarantees the correctness of the result. The authors propose an analytic cost model that relates the stream rate and the memory budget. This way, the administrator can tune the operation of the algorithm, either in order to maximize throughput for a given memory budget, or in order to minimize the necessary memory for a given stream rate. In the case of thrashing, an approximate version of the algorithm with load shedding strategies that minimize the loss of output tuples is discussed. MeshJoin makes no assumption on the order, indexing, join condition and join relationship of the joined stream and relation; at the same time it relates the stream rate with the available memory budget and gives correctness guarantees for an exact result if this is possible, or, allows a lightweight approximate result otherwise.

SYSTEMS

Industrial systems for ETL are provided both by the major database vendors and the individual ETL-targeted vendors. Popular tools include Oracle Warehouse Builder (2008), IBM Datastage (2008), Microsoft Integration Services (2008) and Informatica PowerCenter (2008). There is an excellent survey by Barateiro & Galhardas (2005) that makes a thorough discussion and feature comparison for ETL tools both of academic and industrial origin. Friedman, Beyer & Bitterer (2007) as well as Friedman & Bitterer (2007) give two interesting surveys of the area from a marketing perspective. In this section, we will discuss only academic efforts related to ETL systems.

AJAX

The *AJAX* system (Galhardas, Florescu, Shasha & Simon, 2000) is a data cleaning tool developed at INRIA France that deals with typical data quality problems, such as duplicate identification, errors due to mistyping and data inconsistencies between matching records. This tool can be used either for a single source or for integrating multiple data sources. AJAX provides a framework wherein the logic of a data cleaning program is modeled as a directed graph of data transformations that start from some input source data. Four types of data transformations are supported:

- *Mapping transformations* standardize data formats (e.g., date format) or simply merge or split columns in order to produce more suitable formats.
- *Matching transformations* find pairs of records that most probably refer to same object. These pairs are called *matching pairs* and each such pair is assigned a similarity value.
- *Clustering transformations* group together matching pairs with a high similarity value by applying a given grouping criteria (e.g., by transitive closure).
- *Merging transformations* are applied to each individual cluster in order to eliminate duplicates or produce new records for the resulting integrated data source.

AJAX also provides a declarative language for specifying data cleaning programs, which consists of SQL statements enriched with a set of specific primitives to express mapping, matching, clustering and merging transformations. Finally, a interactive environment is supplied to the user in order to resolve errors and inconsistencies that cannot be automatically handled and support a stepwise refinement design of data cleaning programs. The linguistic aspects and the theoretic foundations of this tool can be found in Galhardas, Florescu, Shasha, Simon & Saita (2001), and Galhardas, Florescu, Shasha & Simon (1999), where apart from the presentation of a general framework for the data cleaning process, specific optimization techniques tailored for data cleaning applications are discussed.

ARKTOS

ARKTOS (Vassiliadis et al., Information Systems 2005) is an ETL tool that has prototypically been

implemented with the goal of facilitating the design, the (re-)use, and the optimization of ETL workflows. Arktos is based on the metamodel of Vassiliadis et al., (Information Systems 2005) for representing ETL activities and ETL workflows and its two key features are (a) the extensibility mechanisms for reusing transformations and (b) the close linkage to formal semantics and their representation. ARKTOS is accompanied by an ETL library that contains template code of built-in functions and maintains template code of user-defined functions. Template activities are registered in the system and they can be reused for the specification of a scenario (either graphically, or via forms and declarative languages). The customization process results in producing an ETL scenario which is a DAG of ETL activities, each specified as a parameterized software module, having instantiated input and output schemata, concrete parameters, and a special-purpose schema for problematic records. The set of templates is extensible to allow users register their own frequently used transformations.

ARKTOS also offers zoom-in/zoom-out capabilities. The designer can deal with a scenario in two levels of granularity: (a) at the *entity* or *zoom-out level*, where only the participating recordsets and activities are visible and their provider relationships are abstracted as edges between the respective entities, or (b) at the *attribute* or *zoom-in level*, where the user can see and manipulate the constituent parts of an activity, along with their respective providers at the attribute level.

Finally, it is noteworthy that the model of Vassiliadis et al., (Information Systems 2005) comes with a mechanism for expressing the semantics of activities in LDL. The expression of semantics can be done both at the template and the instance level and a macro language is discussed in the paper for this purpose. The approach is based on the fundamental observation that the LDL description can be mapped to a useful graph representation of the internals of an activity, which allows both the visualization and the measurement of interesting properties of the graph.

HumMer - Fusion

HumMer (Naumann, Bilke, Bleiholder & Weis, 2006) is a tool developed in the Hasso-Plattner Institute in Potsdam that deals with the problem of data fusion. Data fusion is the task of identifying and resolving different representations of the same object of the real world. HumMer splits the process in three steps: (a) schema alignment, (b) duplicate detection and (c) the core of the data fusion process. Schema alignment deals with the problem of schema inconsistencies. Assuming the user is in possession of different data sets representing the same entities of the real world, HumMer is equipped with a dedicated module that detects a small sample of duplicates in these data sets and tries to find schema similarities. Duplicate detection is performed via comparing tuples over a similarity threshold. Once inconsistencies at the schema and tuple level have been resolved, it is time for the resolution of value inconsistencies, which is referred to as data fusion by Naumann et al (2006). FuSem (Bleiholder, Draba & Naumann, 2007) is an extension of HumMer with the purpose of interactively facilitating the data fusion process. Assuming that the user has different data sets representing the same real world entities, FuSem allows the SQL querying of these data sources, their combination through outer join and union operations and the application of different tuple matching operators. The extension of SQL with the FYSE BY operator, proposed by Bleiholder & Naumann (2005) is also part of FuSem. FYSE BY allows both the alignment of different relations in terms of schemata and the identification of tuples representing the same real world object. An important feature of FuSem is the visualization of results, which is primarily based on different representations of Venn diagrams for the involved records and the interactive exploration of areas where two data sets overlap or differ.

Potter's Wheel

Raman & Hellerstein (2000, 2001) present the *Potter's Wheel* system, which is targeted to provide interactive data cleaning to its users. The system offers the possibility of performing several algebraic operations over an underlying data set, including *format* (application of a function), *drop, copy, add* a column, *merge* delimited columns, *split* a column on the basis of a regular expression or a position in a string, *divide* a column on the basis of a predicate (resulting in two columns, the first involving the rows satisfying the condition of the predicate and the second involving the rest), *selection* of rows on the basis of a condition, *folding* columns (where a set of attributes of a record is split into several rows) and *unfolding*. Optimization algorithms are also provided for the CPU usage for certain classes of operators. The general idea behind Potter's Wheel is that users build data transformations in iterative and interactive way. Specifically, users gradually build transformations to clean the data by adding or undoing transformations on a spreadsheet-like interface; the effect of a transformation is shown at once on records visible on screen. These transformations are specified either through simple graphical operations, or by showing the desired effects on example data values. In the background, Potter's Wheel automatically infers structures for data values in terms of user-defined domains, and accordingly checks for constraint violations. Thus, users can gradually build a transformation as discrepancies are found, and clean the data without writing complex programs or enduring long delays.

CONCLUDING REMARKS

This survey has presented the research work in the field of Extraction-Transformation-Loading (ETL) processes and tools. The main research goals around which research has been organized so far can be summarized as follows.

a. The first goal concerns the construction of commonly accepted conceptual and logical modeling tools for ETL processes, with a view to a standardized approach.

b. The second goal concerns the efficiency of individual ETL operators. To structure the discussion better, we have organized the discussion around the three main parts of the E-T-L triplet, and examined problems that fall within each of these stages. So far, research has come up with interesting solutions for the detection of differences in two snapshots of data, specific data transformations, duplicate detection mechanisms and the practical and theoretical investigation of the lineage of warehouse data.

c. A third research goal has been to devise algorithms for the efficient operation of the entire ETL process. Specifically, research has some first results for the optimization and resumption of entire ETL processes as well as some first investigations towards (near) real time ETL.

d. A fourth goal of the academic world has been the construction of tools for the facilitation of the ETL process.

Apparently, the field is quite new, and there is still too much to be done. In the sequel, we present a personal viewpoint on the possible advancements that can be made in the field.

Starting with the traditional ETL setting, there are quite a few research opportunities. Individual operators are still far from being closed as research problems. The extraction of data still remains a hard problem, mostly due to the closed nature of the sources. The loading problem is still quite unexplored with respect to its practical aspects. The optimization and resumption problems - along with the appropriate cost models - are far from maturity.

The absence of a benchmark is hindering future research (that lacks a commonly agreed way to perform experiments). The introduction of design patterns for warehouse schemata that take ETL into consideration is also open research ground.

At the same time, the presence of new heavily parallelized processors and the near certainty of disrupting effects in hardware and disk technology in the immediate future put all the database issues of efficiency back on the table. ETL cannot escape the rule and both individual transformations as well as the whole process can be reconsidered in the presence of these improvements. Most importantly, all these research opportunities should be viewed via the looking glass of near real time ETL, with the need for completeness and freshness of data to be pressing from the part of the users.

As an overall conclusion, we believe that design, algorithmic and theoretical results in the field of ETL processes are open to exploration both due to the present problems and on the basis of the changing environment of computer science, databases and user needs.

REFERENCES

Barateiro, J., & Galhardas, H. (2005). A Survey of Data Quality Tools. *Datenbank-Spektrum 14*, 15-21

Bleiholder, J., & Naumann, F. (2005). *Declarative Data Fusion - Syntax, Semantics, and Implementation*. 9th East European Conference on Advances in Databases and Information Systems (ADBIS 2005), pp.: 58-73, Tallinn, Estonia, September 12-15, 2005.

Bleiholder, J., Draba, K., & Naumann, F. (2007). *FuSem - Exploring Different Semantics of Data Fusion*. Proceedings of the 33rd International Conference on Very Large Data Bases (VLDB 2007), pp.: 1350-1353, University of Vienna, Austria, September 23-27, 2007.

Carreira P., Galhardas, H., Pereira, J., Martins, F., & Silva, M. (2007). *On the performance of one-to-many data transformations.* Proceedings of the Fifth International Workshop on Quality in Databases (QDB 2007), pp.: 39-48, in conjunction with the VLDB 2007 conference, Vienna, Austria, September 23, 2007

Carreira, P., Galhardas, H., Lopes A., & Pereira J. (2007). One-to-many data transformations through data mappers. *Data Knowledge Engineering, 62*, 3, 483-503

Carreira, P., Galhardas, H., Pereira, J., & Lopes, A. (2005). *Data Mapper: An Operator for Expressing One-to-Many Data Transformations.* 7th International Conference on Data Warehousing and Knowledge Discovery (DaWaK 2005), pp.: 136-145, Copenhagen, Denmark, August 22-26, 2005

Carreira, P., Galhardas, H., Pereira, J., & Wichert, A. (2007). *One-to-many data transformation operations - optimization and execution on an RDBMS.* Proceedings of the Ninth International Conference on Enterprise Information Systems, Volume DISI, ICEIS (1) 2007, pp.: 21-27, Funchal, Madeira, Portugal, June 12-16, 2007

Colby, L., Kawaguchi, A., Lieuwen, D., Mumick, I., & Ross, K. (1997). *Supporting Multiple View Maintenance Policies.* In Proceedings ACM SIGMOD International Conference on Management of Data (SIGMOD 1997), pp.: 405-416, May 13-15, 1997, Tucson, Arizona, USA

Cui, Y., & Widom, J. (2001). *Lineage Tracing for General Data Warehouse Transformations.* Proceedings of 27th International Conference on Very Large Data Bases (VLDB 2001), pp.: 471-480, September 11-14, 2001, Roma, Italy

Cui, Y., & Widom, J. (2003). Lineage tracing for general data warehouse transformations. *VLDB Journal 12,* 1, 41-58

Cunningham, C., Galindo-Legaria, C., & Graefe, G. (2004). *PIVOT and UNPIVOT: Optimization and Execution Strategies in an RDBMS.* Proceedings of the Thirtieth International Conference on Very Large Data Bases (VLDB 2004), pp. 998-1009, Toronto, Canada, August 31 - September 3 2004.

Darmont, J., Bentayeb, F., & Boussaïd, O. (2005). *DWEB: A Data Warehouse Engineering Benchmark.* Proceedings 7th International Conference Data Warehousing and Knowledge Discovery (DaWaK 2005), pp. 85–94, Copenhagen, Denmark, August 22-26 2005

Davidson, S., & Kosky, A. (1999). Specifying Database Transformations in WOL. *Bulletin of the Technical Committee on Data Engineering, 22,* 1, 25-30.

Elmagarmid, A., Ipeirotis, P., & Verykios, V. (2007). Duplicate Record Detection: A Survey. *IEEE Transactions on Knowledge and Data Engineering, 19,* 1, 1-16

Fagin, R. (2007). Inverting schema mappings. *ACM Transactions on Database Systems, 32,* 4, 25:1-25:53

Fagin, R., Kolaitis, P., & Popa, L. (2005). Data exchange: getting to the core. *ACM Transactions on Database Systems, 30,* 1, 174-210

Fagin, R., Kolaitis, P., Miller, R., & Popa, L. (2005). Data exchange: semantics and query answering. *Theoretical Computer Science, 336,* 1, 89-124

Fenk, R., Kawakami, A., Markl, V., Bayer, R., & Osaki, S. (2000) *Bulk Loading a Data Warehouse Built Upon a UB-Tree.* Proceedings 2000 International Database Engineering and Applications Symposium (IDEAS 2000), pp.: 179-187, September 18-20, 2000, Yokohoma, Japan

Friedman, T., & Bitterer, A. (2007). *Magic Quadrant for Data Quality Tools, 2007*. Gartner RAS Core Research Note G00149359, 29 June 2007. Retrieved 23 July, 2008 from http://mediaproducts. gartner.com/reprints/businessobjects/149359. html

Friedman, T., Beyer, M., & Bitterer, A. (2007). *Magic Quadrant for Data Integration Tools, 2007*. Gartner RAS Core Research Note G00151150, 5 October 2007. Retrieved 23 July, 2008 from http://mediaproducts.gartner.com/reprints/ oracle/151150.html

Galhardas, H., Florescu, D., Shasha, D., & Simon, E. (1999). *An Extensible Framework for Data Cleaning*. Technical Report INRIA 1999 (RR-3742).

Galhardas, H., Florescu, D., Shasha, D., & Simon, E. (2000). *Ajax: An Extensible Data Cleaning Tool*. In Proc. ACM SIGMOD International Conference on the Management of Data, pp. 590, Dallas, Texas.

Galhardas, H., Florescu, D., Shasha, D., Simon, E. & Saita, C. (2001). *Declarative Data Cleaning: Language, Model, and Algorithms*. Proceedings of 27th International Conference on Very Large Data Bases (VLDB 2001), pp.: 371-380, September 11-14, 2001, Roma, Italy

Gupta, A., & Mumick, I. (1995). Maintenance of Materialized Views: Problems, Techniques, and Applications. *IEEE Data Engineering Bulletin*, *18*, 2, 3-18

Gupta, H., & Mumick, I. (2006). Incremental maintenance of aggregate and outerjoin expressions. *Information Systems*, *31*, 6, 435-464

IBM. WebSphere DataStage. Retrieved 21 July, 2008 from http://www-306.ibm.com/software/ data/integration/datastage/

Informatica. PowerCenter. Retrieved 21 July, 2008 from http://www.informatica.com/products_ser-vices/powercenter/Pages/index.aspx

Karakasidis, A., Vassiliadis, P., & Pitoura, E. (2005). *ETL Queues for Active Data Warehousing*. In Proc. 2nd International Workshop on Information Quality in Information Systems (IQIS 2005), co-located with ACM SIGMOD/PODS 2005, June 17, 2005, Baltimore, MD, USA.

Kimbal, R., Reeves, L., Ross, M., & Thornthwaite, W. (1998). *The Data Warehouse Lifecycle Toolkit: Expert Methods for Designing, Developing, and Deploying Data Warehouses*. John Wiley & Sons.

Kimball, R., & Caserta, J. (2004). *The Data Warehouse ETL Toolkit*. Wiley Publishing, Inc.

Kotidis, Y. (2002). Aggregate View Management in Data Warehouses. In *Handbook of Massive Data Sets* (pages 711-742). *Kluwer Academic Publishers*, ISBN 1-4020-0489-3

Koudas, N., & Srivastava, D. (2005). *Approximate Joins: Concepts and Techniques*. Tutorial at the 31st International Conference on Very Large Data Bases (VLDB 2005), pp.: 1363, Trondheim, Norway, August 30 - September 2, 2005. Slides retrieved 23 July, 2008 from http://queens. db.toronto.edu/~koudas/docs/AJ.pdf

Koudas, N., Sarawagi, S., & Srivastava, D. (2006). *Record linkage: similarity measures and algorithms*. Tutorial at the ACM SIGMOD International Conference on Management of Data (SIGMOD 2006), pp.:802-803, Chicago, Illinois, USA, June 27-29, 2006. Slides Retrieved 23 July, 2008 from http://queens.db.toronto.edu/~koudas/ docs/aj.pdf

Labio, W., & Garcia-Molina, H. (1996). *Efficient Snapshot Differential Algorithms for Data Warehousing*. In Proceedings of 22nd International Conference on Very Large Data Bases (VLDB 1996), pp. 63-74, September 3-6, 1996, Mumbai (Bombay), India

Labio, W., Wiener, J., Garcia-Molina, H., & Gorelik, V. (2000). *Efficient Resumption of Interrupted Warehouse Loads*. In Proceedings of the 2000 ACM SIGMOD International Conference on Management of Data (SIGMOD 2000), pp. 46-57, Dallas, Texas, USA

Labio, W., Yerneni, R., & Garcia-Molina, H. (1999). *Shrinking the Warehouse Update Window*. Proceedings ACM SIGMOD International Conference on Management of Data, (SIGMOD 1999), pp.: 383-394, June 1-3, 1999, Philadelphia, Pennsylvania, USA

Lindsay, B., Haas, L., Mohan, C., Pirahesh, H., & Wilms, P. (1986). *A Snapshot Differential Refresh Algorithm*. Proceedings of the 1986 ACM SIGMOD International Conference on Management of Data (SIGMOD 1998), pp: 53-60, Washington, D.C., May 28-30, 1986.

Luján-Mora, S., Vassiliadis, P., & Trujillo, J. (2004). *Data Mapping Diagrams for Data Warehouse Design with UML*. In Proc. 23rd International Conference on Conceptual Modeling (ER 2004), pp. 191-204, Shanghai, China, 8-12 November 2004.

Luo, G., Naughton, J., Ellmann, C., & Watzke, M. (2006). *Transaction Reordering and Grouping for Continuous Data Loading*. First International Workshop on Business Intelligence for the Real-Time Enterprises (BIRTE 2006), pp. 34-49. Seoul, Korea, September 11, 2006

Microsoft. SQL Server Integration Services. Retrieved 21 July, 2008 from http://www.microsoft.com/sql/technologies/integration/default.mspx

Mumick, I., Quass, D., & Mumick, B. (1997) *Maintenance of Data Cubes and Summary Tables in a Warehouse*. In Proceedings ACM SIGMOD International Conference on Management of Data (SIGMOD 1997), pp.: 100-111, May 13-15, 1997, Tucson, Arizona, USA

Naumann, F., Bilke, A., Bleiholder, J., & Weis, M. (2006). Data Fusion in Three Steps: Resolving Schema, Tuple, and Value Inconsistencies. *IEEE Data Engineering Bulletin, 29,* 2, 21-31

Oracle. Oracle Warehouse Builder. Retrieved 23 July, 2008 from http://www.oracle.com/technology/products/warehouse/index.html

Polyzotis, N., Skiadopoulos, S., Vassiliadis, P., Simitsis, A., & Frantzell, N. (2007). *Supporting Streaming Updates in an Active Data Warehouse*. In Proc. 23rd International Conference on Data Engineering (ICDE 2007), pp 476-485, Constantinople, Turkey, April 16-20, 2007.

Polyzotis, N., Skiadopoulos, S., Vassiliadis, P., Simitsis, A., & Frantzell, N. (2008). Meshing Streaming Updates with Persistent Data in an Active Data Warehouse. *IEEE Transactions on Knowledge and Data Engineering, 20,* 7, 976-991

Raman, V., & Hellerstein, J. (2000). *Potters Wheel: An Interactive Framework for Data Cleaning and Transformation*. Technical Report University of California at Berkeley, Computer Science Division, 2000. Retrieved from http://www.cs.berkeley.edu/~rshankar/papers/pwheel.pdf

Raman, V., & Hellerstein, J. (2001). *Potter's Wheel: An Interactive Data Cleaning System*. In Proceedings of 27th International Conference on Very Large Data Bases (VLDB 2001), pp. 381-390, Roma, Italy.

Roth M., & Schwarz P. (1997). *Don't Scrap It, Wrap It! A Wrapper Architecture for Legacy Data Sources*. In Proceedings of 23rd International Conference on Very Large Data Bases (VLDB 1997), pp. 266-275, August 25-29, 1997, Athens, Greece

Roussopoulos, N. (1998). Materialized Views and Data Warehouses. *SIGMOD Record, 27,* 1, 21-26

Roussopoulos, N., Kotidis, Y., & Roussopoulos, M. (1997). *Cubetree: Organization of and Bulk Updates on the Data Cube*. Proceedings ACM SIGMOD International Conferenceon Management of Data (SIGMOD 1997), pp. 89-99, May 13-15, 1997, Tucson, Arizona, USA

Roussopoulos, N., Kotidis, Y., & Sismanis, Y. (1999). *The Active MultiSync Controller of the Cubetree Storage Organization*. Proceedings ACM SIGMOD International Conference on Management of Data (SIGMOD 1999), pp.: 582-583, June 1-3, 1999, Philadelphia, Pennsylvania, USA

Shu, N., Housel, B., Taylor, R., Ghosh, S., & Lum, V. (1977). EXPRESS: A Data EXtraction, Processing, and REStructuring System. *ACM Transactions on Database Systems, 2*, 2, 134-174.

Simitsis, A. (2005). *Mapping conceptual to logical models for ETL processes*. In Proceedings of ACM 8th International Workshop on Data Warehousing and OLAP (DOLAP 2005), pp.: 67-76 Bremen, Germany, November 4-5, 2005

Simitsis, A., & Vassiliadis, P. (2008). A Method for the Mapping of Conceptual Designs to Logical Blueprints for ETL Processes. *Decision Support Systems, 45*, 1, 22-40.

Simitsis, A., Vassiliadis, P., & Sellis, T. (2005). *Optimizing ETL Processes in Data Warehouses*. Proceedings 21st Int. Conference on Data Engineering (ICDE 2005), pp. 564-575, Tokyo, Japan, April 2005.

Simitsis, A., Vassiliadis, P., & Sellis, T. (2005). State-Space Optimization of ETL Workflows. *IEEE Transactions on Knowledge and Data Engineering, 17*, 10, 1404-1419

Simitsis, A., Vassiliadis, P., Terrovitis, M., & Skiadopoulos, S. (2005). *Graph-Based Modeling of ETL activities with Multi-level Transformations and Updates*. In Proc. 7th International Conference on Data Warehousing and Knowledge Discovery 2005 (DaWaK 2005), pp. 43-52, 22-26 August 2005, Copenhagen, Denmark.

Sismanis, Y., Deligiannakis, A., Roussopoulos, N., & Kotidis, Y. (2002). *Dwarf: shrinking the PetaCube*. Proceedings of the 2002 ACM SIGMOD International Conference on Management of Data (SIGMOD 2002), 464-475, Madison, Wisconsin, June 3-6, 2002

Skoutas, D., & Simitsis, A., (2006). *Designing ETL processes using semantic web technologies*. In Proceedings ACM 9th International Workshop on Data Warehousing and OLAP (DOLAP 2006), pp.:67-74, Arlington, Virginia, USA, November 10, 2006

Skoutas, D., & Simitsis, A., (2007). *Flexible and Customizable NL Representation of Requirements for ETL processes*. In Proceedings 12th International Conference on Applications of Natural Language to Information Systems (NLDB 2007), pp.: 433-439, Paris, France, June 27-29, 2007

Skoutas, D., & Simitsis, A., (2007). Ontology-Based Conceptual Design of ETL Processes for Both Structured and Semi-Structured Data. *Int. Journal of Semantic Web Information Systems (IJSWIS) 3*, 4, 1-24

Stanoi, I., Agrawal, D., & El Abbadi, A. (1999). *Modeling and Maintaining Multi-View Data Warehouses*. Proceedings 18th International Conference on Conceptual Modeling (ER 1999), pp.: 161-175, Paris, France, November, 15-18, 1999

Stöhr, T., Müller, R., & Rahm, E. (1999). *An integrative and Uniform Model for Metadata Management in Data Warehousing Environments*. In Proc. Intl. Workshop on Design and Management of Data Warehouses (DMDW 1999), pp. 12.1 – 12.16, Heidelberg, Germany, (1999).

Thiele, M., Fischer, U., & Lehner, W. (2007). *Partition-based workload scheduling in living data warehouse environments*. In Proc. ACM 10th International Workshop on Data Warehousing and OLAP (DOLAP 2007), pp. 57-64, Lisbon, Portugal, November 9, 2007.

Thomsen, C., Pedersen, T., & Lehner, W. (2008). *RiTE: Providing On-Demand Data for Right-Time Data Warehousing*. Proceedings of the 24th International Conference on Data Engineering (ICDE 2008), pp 456 – 465, April 7-12, 2008, Cancun, Mexico.

TPC. The TPC-DS benchmark. Transaction Processing Council. Retrieved 24 July, 2008 from http://www.tpc.org/tpcds/default.asp

TPC. The TPC-H benchmark. Transaction Processing Council. Available at http://www.tpc.org/ (last accessed at 24 July 2008)

Trujillo, J., & Luján-Mora, S. (2003). *A UML Based Approach for Modeling ETL Processes in Data Warehouses*. In Proceedings of 22nd International Conference on Conceptual Modeling (ER 2003), pp. 307-320, Chicago, IL, USA, October 13-16, 2003.

Tziovara, V., Vassiliadis, P., & Simitsis, A. (2007). *Deciding the Physical Implementation of ETL Workflows*. Proceedings ACM 10th International Workshop on Data Warehousing and OLAP (DOLAP 2007), pp. 49-56, Lisbon, Portugal, 9 November 2007.

Vassiliadis, P., & Simitsis, A. (2009). Extraction-Transformation-Loading. In *Encyclopedia of Database Systems*, L. Liu, T.M. Özsu (eds), Springer, 2009.

Vassiliadis, P., Karagiannis, A., Tziovara, V., & Simitsis, A. (2007). *Towards a Benchmark for ETL Workflows*. 5th International Workshop on Quality in Databases (QDB 2007), held in conjunction with VLDB 2007, Vienna, Austria, 23 September 2007.

Vassiliadis, P., Quix, C., Vassiliou, Y., & Jarke, M. (2001). Data Warehouse Process Management. *Information Systems, 26*, 3, pp. 205-236

Vassiliadis, P., Simitsis, A., & Skiadopoulos, S. (2002). *Modeling ETL activities as graphs*. In Proc. 4th International Workshop on the Design and Management of Data Warehouses (DMDW 2002), held in conjunction with the 14th Conference on Advanced Information Systems Engineering (CAiSE'02), pp. 52-61, Toronto, Canada, May 27, 2002.

Vassiliadis, P., Simitsis, A., & Skiadopoulos, S. (2002). *Conceptual Modeling for ETL Processes*. In Proc. ACM 5th International Workshop on Data Warehousing and OLAP (DOLAP 2002), McLean, VA, USA November 8, 2002.

Vassiliadis, P., Simitsis, A., Georgantas, P., & Terrovitis, M. (2003). *A Framework for the Design of ETL Scenarios*. In Proc. 15th Conference on Advanced Information Systems Engineering (CAiSE 2003), pp. 520- 535, Klagenfurt/Velden, Austria, 16 - 20 June, 2003.

Vassiliadis, P., Simitsis, A., Georgantas, P., Terrovitis, M., & Skiadopoulos, S. (2005). A generic and customizable framework for the design of ETL scenarios. *Information Systems, 30*, 7, 492-525.

Vassiliadis, P., Simitsis, A., Terrovitis, M., & Skiadopoulos, S. (2005). *Blueprints for ETL workflows*. In Proc. 24th International Conference on Conceptual Modeling (ER 2005), pp. 385-400, 24-28 October 2005, Klagenfurt, Austria. Long version retrieved 25 July, 2008 from http://www.cs.uoi.gr/~pvassil/publications/2005_ER_AG/ETL_blueprints_long.pdf

This work was previously published in the Internatinoal Journal of Data Warehousing & Mining 5(3), edited by David Taniar, pp. 1-27, copyright 2009 by IGI Publishing (an imprint of IGI Global).

Chapter 9
A State-of-the-Art in Spatio-Temporal Data Warehousing, OLAP and Mining

Leticia Gómez
Instituto Tecnológico de Buenos Aires, Argentina

Bart Kuijpers
Hasselt University and Transnational University of Limburg, Belgium

Bart Moelans
Hasselt University and Transnational University of Limburg, Belgium

Alejandro Vaisman
Universidad de la Republica, Uruguay

ABSTRACT

Geographic Information Systems (GIS) have been extensively used in various application domains, ranging from economical, ecological and demographic analysis, to city and route planning. Nowadays, organizations need sophisticated GIS-based Decision Support System (DSS) to analyze their data with respect to geographic information, represented not only as attribute data, but also in maps. Thus, vendors are increasingly integrating their products, leading to the concept of SOLAP (Spatial OLAP). Also, in the last years, and motivated by the explosive growth in the use of PDA devices, the field of moving object data has been receiving attention from the GIS community, although not much work has been done to provide moving object databases with OLAP capabilities. In the first part of this paper we survey the SOLAP literature. We then address the problem of trajectory analysis, and review recent efforts regarding trajectory data warehousing and mining. We also provide an in-depth comparative study between two proposals: the GeoPKDD project (that makes use of the Hermes system), and Piet, a proposal for SOLAP and moving objects, developed at the University of Buenos Aires, Argentina. Finally, we discuss future directions in the field, including SOLAP analysis over raster data.

DOI: 10.4018/978-1-60960-537-7.ch009

INTRODUCTION

Geographic Information Systems (GIS) have been extensively used in various application domains, ranging from economical, ecological and demographic analysis, to city and route planning (Rigaux, Scholl, & Voisard, 2001; Worboys, 1995). Spatial information in a GIS is typically stored in different so-called *thematic layers* (also called *themes*). Information in themes can be stored in data structures according to different data models, the most usual ones being the *raster model* and the *vector model*. In a thematic layer, spatial data is annotated with classical relational attribute information, of (in general) numeric or string type. While spatial data is stored in data structures suitable for these kinds of data, associated attributes are usually stored in conventional relational databases. Spatial data in the different thematic layers of a GIS system can be mapped univocally to each other using a common frame of reference, like a coordinate system. These layers can be overlapped or overlayed to obtain an integrated spatial view.

On the other hand, OLAP (On Line Analytical Processing) (Kimball, 1996; Kimball & Ross, 2002) comprises a set of tools and algorithms that allow efficiently querying multidimensional databases containing large amounts of data, usually called data warehouses. In OLAP, data is organized as a set of *dimensions* and *fact tables*. In the multidimensional model, data can be perceived as a *data cube*, where each cell contains a measure or set of (probably aggregated) measures of interest. As we discuss later, OLAP dimensions are further organized in hierarchies that favor data aggregation (Cabibbo & Torlone, 1997). Several techniques and algorithms have been developed for multidimensional query processing, most of them involving some kind of aggregate precomputation (Harinarayan, Rajaraman, & Ullman, 1996).

The Need for OLAP in GIS

Different data models have been proposed for representing objects in a GIS. ESRI (http://www.esri.com) first introduced the *Coverage* data model to bind geometric objects to non-spatial attributes that describe them. Later, they extended this model with object-oriented support, in a way that behavior can be defined for geographic features (Zeiler, 1999). The idea of the Coverage data model is also supported by the Reference Model proposed by the Open Geospatial Consortium (http://www.opengeospatial.org). Thus, in spite of the model of choice, there is always the underlying idea of binding geometric objects to objects or attributes stored in (mostly) object-relational databases (Stonebraker & Moore, 1996). In addition, query tools in commercial GIS allow users to overlap several thematic layers in order to locate objects of interest within an area, like schools or fire stations. For this, they use indexing structures based on R-trees (Gutman, 1984). GIS query support sometimes includes aggregation of geographic measures, for example, distances or areas (e.g., representing different geological zones). However, these aggregations are not the only ones that are required, as we discuss below.

Nowadays, organizations need sophisticated GIS-based Decision Support System (DSS) to analyze their data with respect to geographic information, represented not only as attribute data, but also in maps, probably in different thematic layers. In this sense, OLAP and GIS vendors are increasingly integrating their products (see, for instance, Microstrategy and MapInfo integration in http://www.microstrategy.com/, and http://www.mapinfo.com/). Thus, aggregate queries are central to DSSs. Classical aggregate OLAP queries (like "Total sales of cars in California"), and aggregation combined with complex queries involving geometric components ("Total sales in all villages crossed by the Mississippi river and within a radius of 100 km around New Orleans") must be efficiently supported. Moreover, naviga-

Figure 1. Two overlayed layers containing cities and rivers in North America

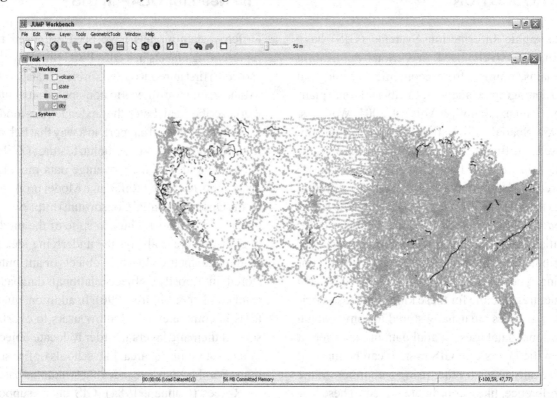

tion of the results using typical OLAP operations like roll-up or drill-down is also required. These operations are not supported by commercial GIS in a straightforward way. One of the reasons is that the GIS data models discussed above were developed with transactional queries in mind. Thus, databases storing non-spatial attributes or objects are designed to support those (non-aggregate) kinds of queries. Decision support systems need a different data model, where non-spatial data, probably consolidated from different sectors in an organization, are stored in a warehouse. Here, numerical data are stored in fact tables built along several dimensions. For instance, if we are interested in the sales of certain products in stores in a given region, we may consider that sales amounts are stored in a fact table with three dimensions Store, Time and Product. In order to guarantee summarizability (Lenz & Shoshani, 1997), dimensions are organized into aggregation

hierarchies. For example, stores can aggregate over cities which in turn can aggregate into regions and countries. Each of these aggregation levels can also hold descriptive attributes like city population, the area of a region, etc. GIS-DSS integration requires warehouse data to be linked to geographic data. For instance, a polygon representing a region must be associated to its corresponding region identifier in the warehouse. In current commercial applications, the GIS and OLAP worlds are integrated in an ad-hoc fashion, probably in a different way (and using different data models) each time an implementation is required, even when a data warehouse is available for non-spatial data.

An Introductory Example. We present now a real-world example to introduce the problem. We selected four layers with geographic and geological features obtained from the National Atlas Website (http://www.nationalatlas.gov). These layers contain the following information:

Figure 2. Two overlayed layers containing states in North America and volcanoes in the northern hemisphere

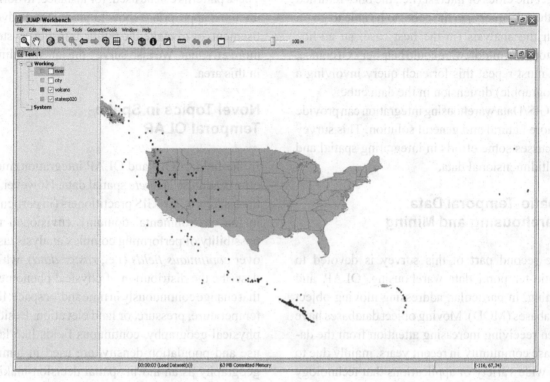

states, cities, and rivers in North America, and volcanoes in the northern hemisphere (published by the Global Volcanism Program - GVP). Figure 1 shows a detail of the layers containing cities and rivers in North America. Note the density of the points representing cities (particularly in the eastern region). Rivers are represented as polylines. Figure 2 shows a portion of two overlayed layers containing states (represented as polygons) and volcanoes (points) in the northern hemisphere. There is also non-spatial information stored in a conventional data warehouse. In this data warehouse, dimension tables contain customer, stores and product information, and a fact table contains store sales across time. Also, numerical and textual information on the geographic components exist (e.g., population, area), stored as usual as attributes of the GIS layers.

In the scenario above, conventional GIS and organizational data can be integrated for decision support analysis. Sales information could be analyzed with respect to geographical features conveniently *displayed in maps*. This analysis could benefit from the integration of both worlds in a single framework. Even though this integration could be possible with existing technologies, ad-hoc solutions are expensive because, besides requiring lots of complex coding, they are hardly portable. To make things more difficult, ad-hoc solutions require data exchange between GIS and OLAP applications to be performed. This implies that the output of a GIS query must be probably exported to become members of dimensions in a data cube, and merged for further analysis. For example, suppose that a business analyst is interested in studying the sales of nautical goods in stores located in cities crossed by rivers. She would first query the GIS, to obtain the cities of interest. She probably has stored sales in a data cube containing a dimension *Store*, with *city* as a dimension level. She would need to "manually" select the cities of interest (i.e., the ones returned by the GIS query) in the cube, to be able to go on with the analysis (in the best case, an ad-hoc customized middleware could help her). Of course, she must repeat this for each query involving a (geographic) dimension in the data cube.

GIS/Data warehousing integration can provide a more natural and general solution. This survey discusses some efforts in integrating spatial and multidimensional data.

Spatio-Temporal Data Warehousing and Mining

The second part of this survey is devoted to spatio-temporal data warehousing, OLAP, and mining, in particular, addressing moving object databases (MOD). Moving object databases have been receiving increasing attention from the database community in recent years, mainly due to the wide variety of applications that technology allows nowadays. Trajectories of moving objects like cars or pedestrians, can be reconstructed from samples describing the locations of these objects at certain points in time. Although there exist many proposals

for modeling and querying moving objects, only a small part of these proposals address the problem of aggregation of moving objects data in a GIS scenario. Many interesting applications arise, involving moving objects aggregation, mainly regarding traffic analysis, truck fleet behavior analysis, commuter traffic in a city, passenger traffic in an airport, or shopping behavior in a mall. Trajectory data warehouses have been proposed to help in the analysis of these scenarios. In this survey we review the relevant works and issues in the trajectory data warehousing problem.

Data Mining techniques are aimed at discovering hidden, non-trivial information and patterns in large databases. MOD are particularly suited for applying these techniques. For example, interesting patterns describing the movement followed by cars or pedestrians in a city can be discovered. These patterns can be used, for instance, to define the most appropriate spots to place street advertisement, or to make the public transport system more efficient. We also survey the latest findings in this area.

Novel Topics in Spatio-Temporal OLAP

In the field of GIS and OLAP integration, most efforts address *discrete* spatial data. However, in the last few years, GIS practitioners (in particular in the environmental domain), envisioned the possibility of performing complex analysis tasks over *continuous fields* (i.e., *raster data*), which describe the distribution of physical phenomena that change continuously in time and/or space, like temperature, pressure, or land elevation. Besides physical geography, continuous fields like land use and population density, are used in human geography as an aid in spatial decision-making process. Although some work has been done to support querying fields in GIS, the area of spatial multidimensional analysis of continuous data is still almost in its infancy. Here we comment on current and future steps in this topic.

The remainder of this chapter is organized as follows. We first provide a brief background on GIS, data warehousing and OLAP. Then, we review the state-of-the-art in Spatial Data Warehousing and SOLAP. After that, we discuss a recently introduced taxonomy for spatio-temporal data warehousing. We move on to the study of spatio-temporal data warehousing, OLAP and mining, including an in-depth analysis of the GeoPKDD proposal for trajectory data warehouses (TDW). Following this analysis, we provide a detailed analysis of the *Piet framework*, aimed at integrating GIS, OLAP and moving objects data. We then present recent proposals on trajectory mining. After comparing TDW and Piet, we conclude the chapter with a description of research directions in the field of spatio-temporal OLAP.

A SHORT BACKGROUND IN GIS AND OLAP

GIS

In general, information in a GIS application is stored over several *thematic layers*. Information in each layer consists of purely spatial data on the one hand, that is combined with classical alpha-numeric attribute data on the other hand (usually stored in a relational database). Two main data models are used for the representation of the spatial part of the information within one layer, the *vector model* and the *raster model*. The choice of model typically depends on the data source from which the information is imported into the GIS.

The Vector Model. The *vector model* is used the most in current GIS (Kuper & Scholl, 2000). In the vector model, infinite sets of points in space are represented as finite geometric structures, or *geometries*, like, for example, points, polylines and polygons. More concretely, vector data within a layer consists in a finite number of tuples of the form (*geometry, attributes*) where a geometry can be a point, a polyline or a polygon. There are several possible data structures to actually store these geometries (Worboys, 1995).

The Raster Model. In the *raster model,* the space is sampled into pixels or cells, each one having an associated attribute or set of attributes. Usually, these cells form a uniform grid in the plane. For each cell or pixel, the sample value of some function is computed and associated to the cell as an attribute value, *e.g.*, a numeric value or a color. In general, information represented in the raster model is organized into *zones*, where the cells of a zone have the same value for some attribute(s). The raster model has very efficient indexing structures and it is very well-suited to model continuous change but its disadvantages include its size and the cost of computing the zones.

Spatial information in the different thematic layers in a GIS is often joined or overlayed. Queries requiring map overlay are more difficult to compute in the vector model than in the raster model. On the other hand, the vector model offers a concise representation of the data, independent on the resolution. Except when we address continuous fields, we will refer to the vector model in this survey, although, indeed, conceptually, each cell is, and each pixel can be regarded as a small polygon, allowing a uniform treatment; moreover, the attribute value associated to the cell or pixel can be regarded as an attribute in the vector model.

Data Warehousing and OLAP

The importance of data analysis using OLAP tools has increased significantly in recent years as organizations in all sectors are required to improve their decision-making processes in order to maintain their competitive advantage. OLAP systems are based on a *multidimensional model*, which allows a better understanding of data for analysis purposes and provides better performance for complex analytical queries. The multidimensional model allows viewing data in an *n*-dimensional space, usually called a *data cube*. In this cube, each cell contains a measure or set of (probably aggregated) measures of interest. This factual data can be analyzed along dimensions of interest, usually organized in hierarchies (Cabibbo & Torlone, 1997). Three typical implementations of OLAP tools exist: MOLAP (standing for multidimensional OLAP), where data is stored in proprietary multidimensional structures, ROLAP (relational OLAP), where data is stored in (object) relational databases, and HOLAP (standing for hybrid OLAP, which provides both solutions. In a ROLAP environment, data is organized as a set of *dimension tables* and *fact tables*, and we assume this organization in the remainder of the paper.

There are a number of OLAP operations that allow exploiting the dimensions and their hierarchies, thus providing an interactive data analysis environment. Data warehouses are optimized for OLAP operations which, typically, imply data aggregation or de-aggregation along a dimension, called roll-up and drill-down, respectively. Other operations involve selecting parts of a cube (slice and dice) and re-orienting the multidimensional view of data (pivoting). In addition to the basic operations described above, OLAP tools provide a great variety of mathematical, statistical, and financial operators for computing ratios, variances, ranks, etc.

Temporal Data Warehouses

The relational data model as proposed by Codd (1970), is not well-suited for handling spatial and/or temporal data. Data evolution over time must be treated in this model, in the same way as ordinary data. This is not appropriate for applications that require past, present, and/or future data values to be dealt with. In real life such applications abound. Therefore, in the last decades, much research has been done in the field of temporal databases. Snodgrass (1995) describes the design of the TSQL2 Temporal Query Language, an upward compatible extension of SQL-92. The book, written as a result of a Dagstuhl seminar organized in June 1997 by Etzion, Jajodia, and Sripada (1998), contains comprehensive bibliography, glossaries for both temporal database and time granularity concepts, and summaries of work around 1998. The same author (Snodgrass, 1999), in other work, discusses practical research issues on temporal database design and implementation.

In the temporal data warehousing and OLAP field, Mendelzon and Vaisman (2000, 2003) introduce the TOLAP model, and developed a prototype and a datalog-like query language, based on a (temporal) star schema. Vaisman, Izquierdo, and Ktenas (2006) also present a Web-based implementation of this model, along with a query language, called TOLAP-QL. Along similar lines, Eder, Koncilia, and Morzy (2002) propose a data model for temporal OLAP supporting structural changes. Although these efforts, little attention has been devoted to the problem of conceptual and logical modeling for temporal data warehouses.

SPATIAL DATA WAREHOUSING AND OLAP

Spatial database systems have been studied for a long time (Buchmann, Günther, Smith, & Wang, 1990; Paredaens, Van Den Bussche, & Gucht, 1994). Rigaux et al.(2001) survey various techniques, such as spatial data models, algorithms, and indexing methods, developed to address specific features of spatial data that are not adequately handled by mainstream DBMS technology.

Although some authors have pointed out the benefits of combining GIS and OLAP, not much work has been done in this field. Vega López, Snodgrass, and Moon (2005) present a comprehensive survey on spatiotemporal aggregation that includes a section on spatial aggregation. Also, Bédard, Rivest, and Proulx (2007) present a review of the efforts for integrating OLAP and GIS.

Conceptual Modeling and SOLAP

Rivest, Bédard, and Marchand (2001) introduce the concept of SOLAP (standing for Spatial OLAP), a paradigm aimed at being able to explore spatial data by drilling on maps in an OLAP fashion. They describe the desirable features and operators a SOLAP system should have. Although they do not present a formal model for this, SOLAP concepts and operators have been implemented in a commercial tool called JMAP, developed by the Centre for Research in Geomatics and KHEOPS, see http://www.kheops-tech.com/en/jmap/solap.jsp.

Stefanovic, Han, and Koperski (2000) and Bédard, Merret, and Han (2001), classify spatial dimension hierarchies according to their spatial references in: (a) non-geometric; (b) geometric to non-geometric; and (c) fully geometric. Dimensions of type (a) can be treated as any descriptive dimension (Rivest et al., 2001). In dimensions of types (b) and (c), a geometry is associated to members of the hierarchies. Malinowski and Zimányi (2004) extend this classification to consider that even in the absence of several related spatial levels, a dimension can be considered spatial: a dimension level is *spatial* if it is represented as a spatial data type (e.g., point, region), allowing them to link spatial levels through topological relationships (e.g., contains, overlaps). Thus, a *spatial dimension* is a dimension that contains at least one spatial hierarchy. A critical point in spatial dimension modeling is the problem of multiple-dependencies, meaning that an element in one level can be related to more than one element in a level above it in the hierarchy. Jensen, Kligys, Pedersen, and Timko (2004) address this issue, and propose a multidimensional data model for mobile services, i.e., services that deliver content to users, depending on their location. This model supports different kinds of dimension hierarchies, most remarkably multiple hierarchies in the same dimension, i.e., multiple aggregation paths. Full and partial containment hierarchies are also supported. However, the model does not consider the geometry, limiting the set of queries that can be addressed. That means, spatial dimensions are standard dimensions referring to some geographical element (like cities or roads). Malinowski and Zimányi (2006) also propose a model supporting multiple aggregation paths.

Pourabbas (2003) introduces a conceptual model that uses binding attributes to bridge the gap between spatial databases and a data cube. The approach relies on the assumption that all the cells in the cube contain a value, which is not the usual case in practice, as the author expresses. Also, the approach requires modifying the structure of the spatial data to support the model. Shekhar, Lu, Tan, Chawla, & Vatsavai (2001) introduce *MapCube*, a visualization tool for spatial data cubes. Map-Cube is an operator that, given a so-called base map, cartographic preferences and an aggregation hierarchy, produces an album of maps that can be navigated via roll-up and drill-down operations.

Spatial Measures. Measures are characterized in two ways in the literature, namely: (a) measures representing a geometry, which can be aggregated along the dimensions; (b) a numerical value, using a topological or metric operator. Most proposals support option (a), either as a set of coordinates (Bédard et al., 2001; Rivest et al., 2001; Malinowski & Zimányi, 2004; Bimonte, Tchounikine, & Miquel, 2005), or a set of pointers to geometric objects (Stefanovic et al., 2000). Bimonte et al. (Bimonte et al., 2005) define measures as complex objects (a measure is thus an object containing several attributes). Malinowski and Zimányi (2004) follow a similar approach, but defining measures as attributes of an n-ary fact relationship between dimensions. Damiani and Spaccapietra (2006) propose MuSD, a model allowing defining spatial measures at different granularities. Here, a spatial measure can represent the location of a fact at multiple levels of (spatial) granularity.

Spatial Aggregation

In light of the discussion above, it should be clear that aggregation is a crucial issue in spatial OLAP. Moreover, there is not yet a consensus about a complete set of aggregate operators for spatial OLAP. We now discuss the classic approaches to spatial aggregation.

Han et al. (1998) use OLAP techniques for materializing selected spatial objects, and proposed a so-called *Spatial Data Cube*, and the set of operations that can be performed on this data cube. The model only supports aggregation of spatial objects.

Pedersen and Tryfona (2001) propose the pre-aggregation of spatial facts. First, they pre-process these facts, computing their disjoint parts in order to be able to aggregate them later. This pre-aggregation works if the spatial properties of the objects are *distributive* over some aggregate function. The paper does not address forms other than polygons, although the authors claim that other more complex forms are supported by the method, and the authors do not report experimental results.

With a different approach, Rao, Zhang, Yu, Li, and Chen (2003), and Zhang, Li, Rao, Yu, Chen, and Liu (2003) combine OLAP and GIS for querying spatial data warehouses, using R-trees for accessing data in fact tables. The data warehouse is then exploited in the usual OLAP way. Thus, they take advantage of OLAP hierarchies for locating information in the R-tree which indexes the fact table. The work assumes that some fact table containing the identifiers of spatial objects exists. These objects happen to be points, which is quite unrealistic in a GIS environment, where different types of objects appear in the different layers.

Some interesting techniques have been recently introduced to address the data aggregation problem. These techniques are based on the combined use of (R-tree-based) indexes, materialization (or pre-aggregation) of aggregate measures, and computational geometry algorithms.

Papadias, Tao, Kalnis, and Zhang (2002) introduce the *Aggregation R-tree* (aR-tree), combining indexing with pre-aggregation. The aR-tree is an R-tree that annotates each MBR (Minimal Bounding Rectangle) with the value of the aggregate function for all the objects that are enclosed by it. They extend this proposal in order to handle historic information, denoting this extension aRB-tree (Papadias, Tao, Zhang, Mamoulis, Shen, & Sun, 2002). The approach basically consists in two kinds of indexes: a host index, which is an R-tree with the summarized information, and a B-tree containing time-varying aggregate data. In the most general case, each region has a B-tree associated, with the historical information of the measures of interest in the region. This is a very efficient solution for some kinds of queries, for example, window aggregate queries (i.e., for the computation of the aggregate measure of the regions which intersect a spatio-temporal window). In addition, the method is very effective when a query is posed over a query region whose intersection with the objects in a map must be computed on-the-fly, and these objects are totally enclosed in the query region. However, problems

may appear when leaf entries partially overlap the query window. In this case, the result must be estimated, or the actual results computed using the base tables. In fact, Tao, Kollios, Considine, Li, and Papadias (2004) show that the aRB-tree can suffer from the distinct counting problem, if the object remains in the same region for several timestamps.

MOVING OBJECTS AND TRAJECTORY DATA

The field of moving object databases has been extensively studied in the last ten years, mainly regarding data modeling an indexing. Güting and Schneider (2005) provide a good reference to this large corpus of work. Moving objects, carrying location-aware devices, produce *trajectory* data in the form of a sample of (O_{id}, x, y, t)-tuples, that contain object identifier and time-space information. In this survey we will focus on the problem of building trajectory data warehouses and exploiting them through OLAP and data mining techniques. We first need to introduce some concepts about moving object data.

Wolfson, Sistla, Xu, and Chamberlain (1999) define a set of capabilities that a moving object database must have, and introduce the DOMINO system, that develops those features on top of existing database management systems (DBMS). Hornsby and Egenhofer (2002) introduce a framework for modeling moving objects, which supports viewing objects at different granularities, depending on the sampling time interval. The basic modeling element they consider is a *geospatial lifeline,* which is composed of triples of the form *<Id,location,time>*, where *Id* is the identifier of the object, *location* is given by x-y coordinates, and *time* is the timestamp of the observation. The possible positions of an object between two observations is estimated to be within two inverted half-cones that conform a *lifeline bead*, whose projection over the x-y plane is an ellipse.

Particular interest has received the topic of moving objects on road networks. Van de Weghe et al. propose a qualitative trajectory calculus for objects in a GIS (Weghe, Cohn, Tré, & Maeyer, 2005), based on the assumption that in a GIS scenario, qualitative information is necessary. Kuijpers, Moelans, and Van de Weghe (2006) show by means of experiments, the practical use of this calculus. For mining trajectories in road networks, Brakatsoulas, Pfoser, and Tryfona (2004) propose to enrich trajectories of moving objects with information about the relationships between trajectories (e.g., *intersect*, *meets*), and between a trajectory and the GIS environment (*stay within*, *bypass*, *leave*). They also proposed a data mining language denoted SML (for Spatial Mining Language). This language is oriented to traffic networks, and it is not clear how it could be extended to other scenarios.

Also in the framework of road traffic mining, Gonzalez, Han, Li, Myslinska, and Sondag (2007) use a partitioning approach for obtaining interesting driving and speed patterns from large sets of traffic data. They compute frequent path-segments at the area level with a support relative to the traffic in the area (i.e., a kind of adaptive support), and propose an algorithm to automatically partition a road network and build a hierarchy of areas.

The work of Lee, Han, and Whang (2007) is aimed at discovering common sub-trajectories using a partitioning strategy which divides a trajectory into a set of line segments, and then groups similar line segments together into a cluster.

Like in the case of spatial OLAP (and multidimensional databases, in general), from the conceptual modeling point of view, there has not been much interest from the database community. Malinowski and Zimányi (2006) propose a model to provide a graphical representation, based on the Entity/Relationship model, and on UML.

The problem of *trajectory similarity and aggregation* is a new topic in the spatio-temporal database literature. Meratnia and de By (2002) study trajectory aggregation by identifying similar trajectories, merging them in a single one, and dividing the area under study into homogeneous *spatial units*. Pelekis, Theodoridis, Vosinakis, and Panayiotopoulos (2006), and Pelekis and Theodoridis (2006) introduce a framework consisting of a set of distance operators based on parameters of trajectories like speed and direction, to determine if two trajectories can be considered similar. Frentzos, Gratsias, and Theodoridis (2007) propose an approximation method for supporting the k-most-similar-trajectory search using R-tree structures.

Finally, Kuijpers and Vaisman (2007) present a taxonomy of aggregate queries on moving object data.

Adding Semantic Information to Trajectory Data

Techniques that add semantic information to trajectory data have been recently proposed. Mouza and Rigaux (2005) present a model where trajectories are represented by a sequence of *moves*. They propose a query language based on regular expressions, aimed at obtaining so-called *mobility patterns*. Note that this language, as well as the proposals commented above, does not relate trajectories with the geographic environment where they occur, which limits the types of queries that can be addressed. Along the same lines, Damiani, Macedo, Parent, Porto, and Spaccapietra (2007) introduced the concept of *stops and moves*, in order to enrich trajectories with semantically annotated data (later in this survey we give more details about the stops and moves paradigm).

Giannotti, Nanni, Pinelli, and Pedreschi (2007) studied trajectory pattern mining, based on so-called Temporally Annotated Sequences (*TAS*), an extension of sequential patterns, where a temporal annotation between two nodes is defined. In this way, the sequence <1,2,2> defines a pattern that starts at position 1 and after 2 seconds arrives at position 2. In other words, a *trajectory pattern* is a set of trajectories that visit the same sequence of places with similar travel times between each of them. They also introduce the concept of Region of Interest (RoI), and focus on computing the RoIs dynamically from the trajectories. Similarly, Gómez, Kuijpers, and Vaisman (2008a, 2008b) propose to replace a trajectory by a sequence of its *stops and moves,* following the ideas of Alvares et al. (2007). This work differs from the one of Giannotti et al. (2007) in several ways. irst, the authors work with stops and moves instead of pre-defined regions of interest. This allows identifying which of the RoIs are really relevant to a trajectory. Second, the stops and moves are used to "encode" or compress a trajectory, which, in many practical situations turns out to be enough to identify interesting sequences very efficiently. A third difference is that in this proposal, the user defines the places of interest of an application *in advance*, and then they compute the stops and moves to perform trajectory mining. Finally, the approach of Gómez et al. (discussed later in detail) is aimed at integrating trajectories and geographic data, an issue mentioned albeit not addressed in (Giannotti et al., 2007).

A TAXONOMY FOR SPATIO-TEMPORAL DATA WAREHOUSING AND OLAP

From the previous sections, the need of a formal definition of the meaning of a "SOLAP query" or a "Spatio-temporal OLAP query" becomes clear. Comparing proposals or assessing the capabilities of different approaches becomes difficult without a precise definition of the kinds of queries they address. Vaisman and Zimáyi (2009) tackle this problem in the following way: (a) first, they define a taxonomy of classes that integrate OLAP, spatial data, and moving data types; (b) for each class in this taxonomy, they define the queries that they support. For this, they use the classic tuple relational calculus extended with aggregate functions (Klug, 1982), and incrementally extend

this calculus with spatial and moving data types, showing that each extension defines the kinds of queries in each class of the taxonomy. To address spatio-temporal scenarios they use the data types defined by Guting et. al (2000). The taxonomy, depicted in Figure 3 is defined as follows. There exist four basic classes: Temporal dimensions, OLAP, GIS, and moving data types. As a derived class, the addition of moving data types to GIS produces Spatio-Temporal data, typically allowing trajectory analysis in a geographic environment. Providing OLAP with the ability of handling temporal dimensions produces the concept of Temporal OLAP (TOLAP). The interaction of OLAP and GIS is denoted Spatial OLAP (SO-LAP). The interaction between GIS and TOLAP is called Spatial TOLAP (S-TOLAP). Adding OLAP capabilities to spatio-temporal data results in Spatio-Temporal OLAP (ST-OLAP). Finally, if the latter supports temporal dimensions, we are in the Spatio-Temporal TOLAP class (ST-TOLAP).

The authors start from the class of OLAP queries, which includes all queries expressible in Klug's relational algebra with aggregates (Klug, 1982). Extending this algebra with spatial data types leads to the class of SOLAP queries. For example, "Total population in the districts within 3KM from the district of Antwerp" is a SOLAP one, since it requires spatial types to solve the "distance" part of the query. Queries in the TOLAP class support evolution of the dimension instances in the data warehouse, a problem also referred to as slowly-changing dimensions (Kimball, 1996). Queries in the spatio-temporal OLAP (ST-OLAP) class account for the case when the spatial objects evolve over time, therefore, moving types must be included in the query. For example, the query "For each district and polluting cloud, give the duration of the passing of the cloud over the district." Finally, Spatial TOLAP (S-TOLAP) covers the case when in addition to having spatial objects and attributes in the data warehouse, the dimensions are also temporal.

Figure 3. The taxonomy for spatio-temporal OLAP, from Vaisman & Zimányi (2009)

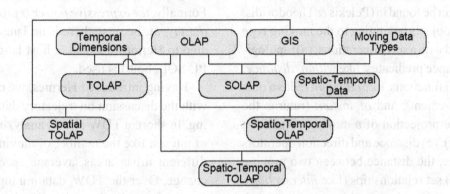

THE *GEOPKDD* APPROACH FOR TRAJECTORY DATA WAREHOUSING

Orlando, Orsini, Raffaetá, Roncato, and Silvestri (2007) were the first ones to propose a trajectory data warehouse (TDW) to analyze moving object data. This TDW is aimed at providing the infrastructure needed to deliver advanced reporting capabilities and facilitating the application of mining algorithms on aggregate data. It was devised for the GeoPKDD project (see http://www.geopkdd.eu). Since this project is based on the *Hermes architecture* for moving object data, we first give a brief overview of the Hermes system (Pelekis, N., Theodoridis, Y., Vosinakis, S., and Panayiotopoulos, T., 2006; Pelekis & Theodoridis, 2006).

The Hermes System for Location-Based Services. Hermes provides the functionality needed for handling two-dimensional objects that change location, shape and size, through four kinds of data types: (a) static base data types (b) static temporal data types; (c) static spatial types; (d) moving data types. Data of type (a) are the standard DBMS data types (integer, real, etc.). Data of type (b) are based on the so-called TAU temporal object model (Kakoudakis, 1996), and provides Hermes with temporal object-relational capabilities, through a library denoted TAU-TLL (Pelekis, 2002). The new temporal data types supported (extending the

ODMG data model) are Timepoint, Period, and Temporal Element. The spatial data types (c) are provided by the Oracle Spatial library. The object type defined in Oracle, and used by Hermes, is called *Sdo_Geometry*. The *Moving* data type (d) encapsulates semantics and functionality of different data types: moving point, linestring, circle, rectangle, polygon, and moving collection. Below these types, a class hierarchy is defined. The basic type is *moving point*, defined as a sequence of different types of simple functions. It is based on the sliced representation proposed by Güting, Böhlen, Jensen, Lorentzos, Schneider and Vazirgiannis (2000). Here, a temporal development of a moving object is decomposed in slices such that, between each slice, a simple function is defined. The idea is to decompose the definition of each moving type into several definitions, one for each function. The composition of these sub-definitions defines a moving type. This way, a *unit_function* models the case where a user is located at a point (x_i, y_i) and moves, with initial velocity v and acceleration a or a linear or circular arc route. A flag indicates the type of movement. The point (x_e, y_e) is the end point of the movement. The unit function along with the *period* object type, conforms the *moving point* data type, which is the basis for the other types. For instance, the type *moving circle* is formed by the function *unit_moving_circle* plus the *period* data type. In turn, the former is composed of three *unit_moving_point* objects. Details on these data types can be found in (Pelekis & Theodoridis, 2006). The objects belonging to the moving type are provided with a set of operations: (a) topological and distance predicates, like *within_distance*; (b) temporal functions, like *add_unit* (adds a new unit of movement), and *at_instant* (returns the union of the projection of a moving object at a time instant); (c) distance and direction operators (for instance, the distance between two moving objects); (d) set relationships (like *intersection*). Also, numeric operations on objects are supported, like area or length. In consequence, it would be easy to compute, for instance, the area of an object at a given time instant.

The Hermes architecture can be described as follows: the basic components are the TAU-TLL library, the Oracle spatial cartridge and the Hermes-MDC (Moving Data Cartridge), which includes the moving data types. PL-SQL statements, which are compiled and stored in binary form, use those cartridges and data types. Thus, the PL-SQL statements are available for interacting with Oracle 10g data structures. Applications written, for instance, in Java, can consume these data. The types of queries supported by Hermes are: (a) queries on stationary objects, like: point, range, distance-based, topological, and nearest-neighbor queries; (b) queries on moving reference objects (distance-based and similarity queries); (c) join queries; (d) queries involving unary operators (traveled distance, speed).

Actually, given that Hermes consists, essentially, in a set of data types, an application designer can define a database schema that uses these data types, and take advantage of their functionality. For example, to describe the movement of a toxic cloud, one could define a relation:

Cloud (id:integer, name: varchar, shape: moving_polygon)

Then, an application programmer could write code that uses these data structures, to find, for instance, when did the cloud arrived to California. Formally, *the expressive power is provided by the data types*, because there is no language associated to Hermes. Instead, a host language (Java, PL-SQL, both) is used.

Having introduced Hermes, we can continue with the discussion on trajectory data warehousing. In short, a TDW allows analyzing measures of interest like the number of moving objects in different urban areas, average speed, or speed change. Over the TDW, data mining techniques can also be used to discover traffic-related patterns, as we discuss later. An ETL (Extract-Transform-Load) procedure feeds a TDW with aggregate trajectory data, obtained from raw data consisting in the spatio-temporal positions of moving objects. A data cube is built from the TDW, aggregating measures for OLAP purposes. The trajectories to be analyzed present characteristics of different kinds: numeric (such as the average speed, direction, duration); spatial (geometric shape of the trajectory), and temporal (timing of the movement).

In order to support trajectory data, a spatio-temporal data cube should allow analysis along (a) temporal dimensions; (b) spatial dimensions at different levels of granularity (point, cell, road); (c) thematic dimensions, containing, for instance, demographic data. In this sense, hierarchies must take into account the fact that an element may rollup to more than one in an upper level. For instance, a road can probably cross more that one cell, yielding a relation instead of a function between a level cell to a level road. It is worth noticing that some proposals deal with this problem defining complex relationships (e.g., containment) in the dimension hierarchies (Jensen et al., 2004), which in general, lead to approximations. The Piet framework, discussed below, defines different GIS dimensions for different kinds of geometries, and the query language takes care of the problem of finding out the cells that intersect the road in the example above.

Figure 4. The trajectory warehouse architecture

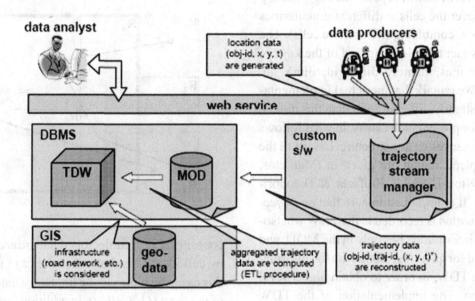

Typically, since the space is usually divided into cells, measures of interest are, among other ones: (a) The number of trajectories found in the cell (or started/ended their path in the cell, or crossed/entered/left the cell); (b) The average (or minimum or maximum) distance covered by trajectories in a cell; (c) The average (or minimum or maximum) time required to cover the distance in (b); The speed and change of speed (acceleration), direction and change of direction (turn). Finally, a TDW algebra should support typical OLAP operators like roll-up, drill-down, and slice and dice.

Figure 4, taken from Damiani, Vangenot, Frentzos, Marketos, Theodoridis, Veryklos, and Raffaeta (2007), depicts the trajectory warehouse architecture proposed in the GeoPKDD project. Initially, location data are captured, and handled by a so-called trajectory stream manager, which builds trajectories from these data (e.g., splitting the raw data according to some criteria), providing a trajectory identifier. This process is called *trajectory reconstruction*. Trajectories are stored in a relational table, denoted *RelTrajectories*, and then loaded into a moving object database (MOD),

which is in turn managed by the Hermes system introduced above. Basically, the MOD includes a relation *MODTrajectories* with schema (O_{id}, trajectory$_{id}$, trajectory), where *trajectory* is of type *Moving Point*. Actually, this results in redundancy, since trajectories are stored twice. This redundancy is a consequence of the dependency of Hermes upon Oracle (MODTrajectories provides access to the moving point data type). Finally, an ETL (Extraction, Transformation, and Loading) process feeds the TDW. Queries to this warehouse can include geographical data.

From a modeling point of view, a TDW is based on the classic star schema. It contains a standard temporal dimension, and two spatial dimensions. The former ranges over equally sized time intervals, which are aggregated according to larger intervals as we move up in the dimension hierarchy (e.g., the interval [60,120] aggregates over the interval [0,120]). The spatial dimensions, denoted DimX and DimY, range over equally sized spatial intervals (x,y, respectively), defining the cells where measures are recorded. There is a fact table containing references to the dimensions and measures of the kinds commented above.

Roll-up and drill-down are performed aggregating measures over the cells at different granularities (for instance, combining two or more cells). The key of this fact table is composed of the keys of the dimensions, namely dimX_id, dimY_id, dimT_id. We remark that the actual implementation has a slightly different form than this model, although for presentation clarity, in what follows we base ourselves on this structure. Details of the actual implementation are given in (Marketos, Frentzos, Ntousi, Pelekis, Raffaeta, & Theodoridis, 2008). It is important to note that *no trajectory information* is recorded in the TDW whatsoever. This information lies only in the MOD, and can be used for querying, along with the information in the TDW, in order to obtain higher level information. The implementation of the TDW makes use of the Oracle 10g data warehousing tools. In addition, modeling and storing trajectories is performed with *Hermes*.

The Double Counting Problem and the ETL Process. During roll-up, and due to the characteristics of the TDW, double counting may introduce errors in these operations. Figure 5 gives an example of this problem: there is a square divided in regions R1 through R6. If we perform a roll-up to aggregate the number of trajectories in regions R4, R5, and R6, we would obtain a total of six trajectories (resulting from adding three trajectories in R4, two in R5, and one in R6), while the correct number to obtain would have been three trajectories. Braz et al. (2007) address this problem.

A relevant feature of the TDW proposal is the treatment given to the ETL process, that transforms the raw location data and loads it to the trajectory data warehouse. The design of this process is aimed at minimizing the amount of memory needed to load and transform raw data into trajectory data, and also to address the double counting problem described above. Orlando et al. (2007) define a model supporting two equivalent forms of trajectory representation: (a) the standard (O_{id}, x, y, t); (b) an alternative representation where

Figure 5. The double counting problem

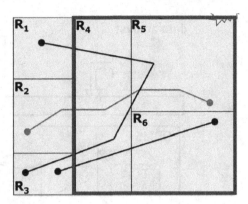

coordinates in the trajectory database are replaced by cell identifiers that cover the (x,y) points. In this case, the tuples in the trajectory database are of the form $(O_{id}, Cell_{id}, t)$. In addition, other information of interest could be recorded, like, for instance, signal strength.

Initially, *raw location data* (usually arriving as a continuous data stream) is transformed into *trajectory data*. In other words, this step is aimed at determining the starting and ending points of a trajectory. The solution consists in splitting the bulk data according to certain assumptions. For example: (a) Temporal gap (maximum time gap between two points in the same trajectory); (b) Spatial gap (maximum spatial distance between two points); (c) Maximum speed (used to detect noise); (d) Maximum noise duration (if there is a long sequence of noisy observations, a new trajectory is generated); (e) Tolerance distance D (if two observations are closer than a certain distance D, the latest one is considered redundant).

OLAP operations require aggregation of TDW measures over the set of cells. In the sequel we consider the following measures: (a) Number of trajectories in a cell, denoted *presence* ($C_{x,y}$.presence); (b) number of objects in a cell in a certain interval; (c) crossX, crossY, where crossX(Y) is the number of distinct trajectories crossing the spatial border between two cells along the horizontal (vertical) axis. The problem of *double counting* arises for some of these measures, like (a) above, not only during *aggregation* of the base data during a roll-up operation, but *also in the loading phase*. For example, suppose we have three consecutive observations 1, 2, and 3 ; further, 1 and 3 fall in the same cell, but 2 does not. When 3 arrives, the system stores a duplicate for $C_{x,y}$.presence (recall data come in a continuous input stream). The *presence* measure deserved an in-depth treatment in (Orlando et al., 2007), where the problem of multiple counting is addressed, and some strategies for approximating the results of computing the pre-aggregated facts were proposed. For instance, linear interpolation is used to prevent omitting in the result the cells crossed by a trajectory but such that no sampling occurred within them. Finally, two alternative functions for computing the aggregate *presence* are defined and compared against each other: one *algebraic*, and one *distributive*. The authors borrow from statistical methods. For example, knowing the values of presence for two cells, $C_{x,y}$ and $C_{x+1,y}$, and defining a new cell, $C_{x',y'} = C_{x,y} \cup C_{x+1,y}$, the aggregate presence over the new cell, will be:

$$C_{x',y'}.presence = C_{x,y}.presence + C_{x+1,y}.presence - C_{x,y}.crossX$$

where $C_{x,y}$.crossX is the number of distinct trajectories crossing the spatial border between $C_{x,y}$ and $C_{x+1,y}$.

Some example queries are provided in Orlando et al. (2007), and the two *presence* functions implemented (i.e., distributive and algebraic). It is reported that *algebraic presence* is more difficult to implement because it requires the combination of several aggregate functions and using non/standard SQL operations. The experiments reported showed that the distributive function (*sum*) quickly reaches large errors when the roll-up granularity increases. The *algebraic* method resulted to be more accurate.

Querying the TDW. The TDW can be exploited using OLAP techniques. The aggregated measures allow us to obtain, for example, the variable number of moving objects in different urban areas.

From the point of view of the expressive power of the TDW proposal, considerations here are similar to the ones made when discussing *Hermes*. The data types provide the functionality and clients can consume them. Of course, this allows any external data to participate in any query. However, again, the formal model is embedded in the data types, and the TDW appears as an application, such that queries are built on top of the former. This is reflected in the fact that the warehouse contains only aggregated information, and the MOD contains the moving point type. The following is an example of a query over the MOD, showing a temporal intersection, taken from the TDW demo website.

```
SELECT
m.trajectory.at_period(tau_tll.d_
period_sec(tau_tll.D_Timepoint_
Sec(2006,11,24,7,45,0),
tau_tll.D_Timepoint_
Sec(2006,11,24,7,52,0))).to_string()
as trajectory
FROM modtrajectories m where m.obj_
id=1 and m.traj_id=87
```

Here we can see that the table in the FROM clause is MODTrajectories, which includes the moving point data type. These kinds of queries could also use the fact tables that contain aggregate data. Dimensions and fact tables could also be analyzed using any OLAP viewer.

Exploiting the TDW. Leonardi et al. (2010) presented T-Warehouse, an implementation supporting the concepts explained above. T-Warehouse allows analyzing trajectory data at different levels of aggregation. Figure 6 shows an example analyzing velocity and presence for traffic in the city of Milano. A triangle's base represents the measure *presence*, while a triangle's height represents *velocity*, showing the correlation of these two

Figure 6. A T-Warehouse screen showing presence and speed

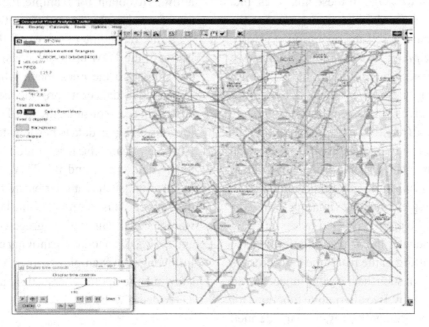

measures: when the presence is high, the speed is low (a large base and a small height).

Enhancing the TDW to Support Ad-Hoc OLAP

In Figure 4 we show that the moving object database is obtained after a reconstruction from trajectories that are given in a streamlined fashion. This reconstruction task may vary according with the trajectory analysis requirements, which can be different for different applications. For instance, there may be a considerable difference on the semantic definition of a trajectory given by a traffic analyst and a logistics manager. This way, when analyzing a fleet of trucks moving in a city and delivering goods to various locations, a logistic manager may be interested in all different trajectories between the different delivery points, while the traffic analyst may only be interested in a single trajectory for the whole day. In the first case, the reconstruction process would result in a larger number of smaller trajectories than in the second case. In later steps of the TDW process,

two different trajectory data cubes are built in order to allow users to apply OLAP techniques oriented to their purposes. Marketos & Theodoridis (2010) present an extension of the OLAP data model for TDW with the following features: (a) A flexible fact table able to answer queries considering different semantic definitions of trajectories; (b) A parameter that supports the choice of semantics for aggregation queries over trajectory data; (c) An ETL method loading raw location data in the flexible data cube; (d) OLAP techniques to support the different visions explained above. The proposal is denoted ad-hoc OLAP.

Figure 7, taken from (Marketos & Theodoridis, 2010) illustrates different possible scenarios. Figure 7a shows a raw dataset of timestamped locations. Different analytical needs may result to different set of reconstructed trajectories. Figures 7b and 7c illustrate the reconstructed trajectories for the logistic manager and for the traffic manager, respectively, while Figure 7d considers a compressed trajectory of the movement. The approach of building a TDW for each set of reconstructed trajectories, explained in the

Figure 7. Different visions of a trajectory

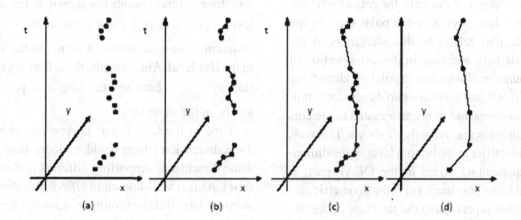

previous section, requires to repeatedly execute an ETL process to build different trajectory data cubes. The proposal of Marketos & Theodoridis is aimed at avoiding this.

THE PIET FRAMEWORK

The Piet data model (http://piet.exp.dc.uba.ar/piet) was introduced in Escribano, Gomez, Kuijpers, and Vaisman (2007) and Gómez, Haesevoets, Kuijpers, and Vaisman (2009). The core idea is the integration of spatial, spatio-temporal, and non-spatial data in a single framework, oriented to solve many of the problems discussed in Section "Data Warehousing and OLAP".

The model defines a *GIS dimension* as composed of a set of graphs, each one describing a set of geometries in a thematic layer. A GIS dimension is, as usual in databases, composed of a schema and instances. Figure 8 shows the schema of a GIS dimension: the bottom level of each hierarchy, denoted the *Algebraic part*, contains the infinite points in a layer, and could be described by means of linear algebraic equalities and inequalities (Paredaens, Kuper, & Libkin, 2000). Above this part there is the *Geometric part,* which stores the identifiers of the geometric elements

of the GIS, and is used to solve the geometric part of a query. Each point in the Algebraic part may correspond to one or more elements in the Geometric part (e.g., if more than one polylines intersect with each other). Thus, at the *GIS dimension instance* level we will have rollup *relations* (denoted $r_L^{geom1 \rightarrow geom2}$). For instance, $r_{L_{city}}^{Point \rightarrow Pg}(x, y, pg_1)$ says that, in a layer L_{city} a point (x,y) corresponds to a polygon identified by pg_1 in the Geometric part. The authors propose a mechanism to *precompute* the overlayed layers in the map, that turns these relations back into rollup functions, i.e., where a point (x,y) corresponds to *exactly* one geometry identifier. Finally, there is the *OLAP part* for storing non-spatial data. This part contains the conventional OLAP structures, as defined in (Hurtado, Mendelzon, & Vaisman, 1999). The levels in the geometric part are associated to the OLAP part via a function, denoted $\alpha_{L,D}^{\dim Level \rightarrow geom}$. For instance, $\alpha_{L_r, Rivers}^{riverId \rightarrow g_r}$ associates information about a river in the OLAP part (*riverId*) in a dimension *Rivers*, to the identifier of a polyline (g_r) in a layer denoted Lr, which represents rivers in the Geometric part.

Example 1. Figure 8 shows a GIS dimension schema with three layers, for rivers, volcanoes, and states, respectively. The schema is composed of three graphs. For example, the graph for rivers, contains edges saying that a point (*x*,*y*) in the algebraic part relates to line identifiers in the geometric part, and that, in the same portion of the dimension, lines relate to polyline identifiers. In the OLAP part there are two dimensions, representing states and rivers, associated to the corresponding graphs, as the figure shows. This way, a river identifier at the bottom layer of the dimension representing rivers in the OLAP part, is mapped to the polyline level in the geometric part in the graph representing the structure of the rivers layer.

Figure 9 shows a portion of a GIS dimension instance for the rivers layer in the dimension schema of Figure 8. We can see that an instance of a GIS dimension in the OLAP part is associated (via the α function) to the polyline pl_1 which

corresponds to the Colorado river. For clarity, only four different points are shown, at the *point* level $(x_1,y_1) \ldots (x_4,y_4)$. There is a relation $r_{L_r}^{point,line}$ containing the association of points to the lines in the *line* level. Analogously, there is also a relation $r_{L_r}^{line,polyline}$ between the line and polyline levels, in the same layer.

Time in the OLAP part is represented by a *Time* dimension (there could be more than one Time dimension, supporting different notions of time). As it is well-known in OLAP, this dimension may have different configurations that depend on the application at hand.

Measures and Facts. A key point in the Piet model is the way it accounts for measures and fact tables. Most of the proposals discussed in previous sections consider *spatial* measures, and apply OLAP operators over them. Piet is capable

Figure 8. An example of a GIS dimension schema

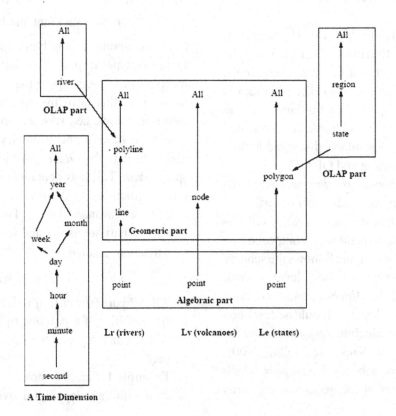

of working in this way, operating over the GIS dimensions (the authors define the concept of *spatial aggregation* for this), but also to use facts defined in the OLAP part, to support spatial DSS queries. Thus, elements in the geometric part are associated with *facts*, each fact being quantified by one or more *measures*, not necessarily a numeric value. The following example gives the intuition of a so-called GIS fact table. For details, we refer the reader to (Gómez et al., 2009).

Example 2. Consider a fact table containing state populations. Also assume that this information is stored at the polygon level. In this case, the fact table schema would be (*polyId*, L_s, *population*) where *polyId* is the polygon identifier, represents the states layer, and population is the measure. If information about, for example, temperature data, is stored at the *point* level, we would have a base fact table with schema (*point*, L_e, *temperature*), with instances of the form $(x_1, y_1, L_e, 25)$ Note that temporal information could be also stored in these fact tables, by simply adding the *time* dimension to the fact table. This would allow storing temperature information across time. □

Example 2 shows that a GIS fact table is basically a standard OLAP fact table where one of the dimensions is composed of geometric objects in a layer. Classical fact tables in the OLAP part, defined in terms of the OLAP dimension schemas can also exist. For instance, instead of storing the population associated to a polygon identifier, as in Example2, this information may reside in a data warehouse, with schema (*state*, *population*).

Geometric Aggregation

Based on the data model described above, the notion of *geometric aggregation* is defined in Piet. In general, geometric aggregation queries are hard to evaluate because they require the computation of a double integral representing the area where some condition is satisfied. Thus, Piet addresses a class of queries denoted *summable*, of the form: $\sum_{g \in s} h(g)$, where h is a function (represented, for instance, by a fact table), and the sum is performed over all the identifiers of the objects that satisfy a condition. For example, the query "total population of the cities crossed by the Colorado

Figure 9. A GIS dimension instance for Figure 4

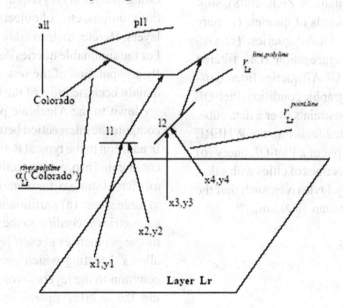

River" would read (here we assume there is a layer for cities):

$$Q \sum_{g_{\mathrm{id}} \in C} ft_{pop}(g_{\mathrm{id}}, L_c)$$

$$C = \{g_{id} \mid (\exists x)(\exists y)(\exists pl_1)(\exists c \in dom(Ci))$$
$$(\alpha_{L_r,Rivers}^{Ri \to Pl}(\text{'Colorado'}) = (pl_1) \wedge r_{L_r}^{Pt \to Pl}(x, y, pl_1) \wedge$$
$$\alpha_{L_c,Districts}^{Ci \to Pg}(c) = g_{id} \wedge r_{L_c}^{Pt \to Pg}(x, y, g_{id}))\}$$

The meaning of the query is: $\alpha_{L_r,Rivers}^{Ri \to Pl}(\text{'Colorado'})$ maps the identifier of the Colorado river to a polyline in layer Lr (representing rivers). The relation $r_{L_r}^{Pt \to Pl}(x, y, pl_1)$ contains the mapping between the points and the polylines representing the rivers that satisfy the condition. The other functions are analogous. Thus, the identifiers of the geometric elements that satisfy both conditions can be retrieved, and the sum of ft_{pop} (which represents the population associated to a polygon) over these objects can be performed.

Piet-QL

Piet comes equipped with a query language, Piet-QL (Gómez, Vaisman, & Zich, 2008), supporting the following kinds of queries: (a) pure GIS queries; (b) pure OLAP queries; (c) GIS queries filtered with aggregation (i.e., filtered using a data cube); (d) OLAP queries filtered using a geometric or geographic condition. Piet-QL also allows to place constraints over a data cube, including pre-aggregated facts into the WHERE clause. A typical example of a Piet-QL query (of the class C above) is: "Names of cities with sales, in provinces crossed by Dyle river, such that the cities had sales greater than 5000 units."

```
SELECT GIS lc1.name
FROM bel_city lc1, bel_prov lp2, bel_
river lr2
```

```
WHERE contains(lp2, lc1) AND
intersects(lp2, lr2) AND lr2.
name="Dijle"
AND lc1 IN(
    SELECT CUBE
    filter([Store].[Store City].Mem-
bers, [Measures].[Unit Sales]>5000)
    FROM [Sales])
    AND lp2 IN(
        SELECT CUBE
        filter([Store].[Store City].
Members, [Measures].[Unit Sales]>0)
        FROM [Sales]))
```

If we consider the classification proposed by Pelekis et.al. (2004), attribute, point, range, distance-based, nearest neighbor and topological queries are supported by Piet-QL. Note that these queries could be used to build the other ones, that include aggregation and OLAP capabilities. According with the classification of Vaisman and Zimányi (2009), Piet-QL falls in the SOLAP class.

Figure 10 shows a screen of the Piet implementation. We can see a Piet-QL query of type (c), and the result represented as a map layer, with the districts satisfying the query represented in green.

Overlay Pre-computation in Piet. Many interesting queries in GIS require computing intersections, unions, etc., of objects that are in different layers. Hereto, their overlay has to be computed. For the summable queries defined above, on-the-fly computation of the sets "C" would be costly, mainly because most of the time we will need to go down to the Algebraic part of the system to compute the intersection between the geometries. In addition to the typical R-tree-based techniques commented in previous sections, Piet implements a different strategy for materialization, consisting in three steps: (a) partitioning each layer in sub-geometries according to the carrier lines defined by the geometries in each layer (see below); this allows detecting which geographic regions are common to the layers involved; (b) pre-computing the overlay operation; (c) evaluating the

Figure 10. The carrier sets of a point, a polyline and a polygon are the dotted lines

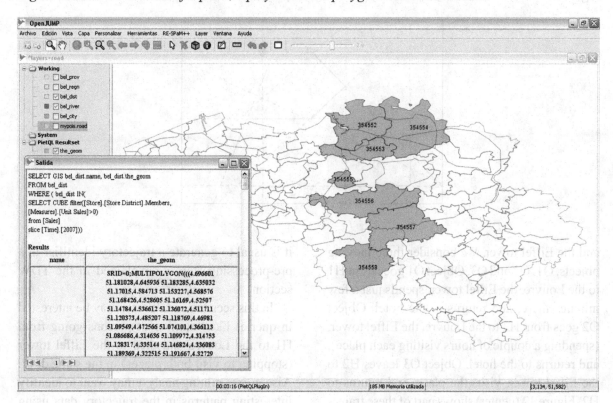

queries using the layer containing all the pre-computed sub-geometries.

The carrier set of a layer (denoted C_L) induces a partition of the plane into open convex polygons, open line segments and points. Thus, the rollup relations r will turn into functions (given that no two points can map to the same open convex polygon). Given C_L and a bounding box, we denote the *convex polygonization of L*, the set of open convex polygons, open line segments, and points induced by C_L that are strictly inside the bounding box. Given two layers L_1 and L_2, and their carrier sets C_{L1} and C_{L2}, the *common sub-polygonization of L_1 according to L_2*, denoted CSP(L_1,L_2) is a refinement of the convex polygonization of L_1, computed by partitioning each open convex polygon and each open line segment in it along the carriers of C_{L2}. This can be generalized for more than two layers. Figure 11 illustrates the carrier sets of a point, a polyline and a polygon.

Experimental evaluation showed that overlay pre-computation (i.e., pre-computing the common sub-polygonization) in general can perform better that R-trees, and also be competitive with aR-trees, except when the query region must be computed in running time, because computing the intersection between the query region and the common sub-polygonization, turns out to be expensive in some situations (Escribano et al., 2007).

QUERYING AND MINING TRAJECTORY DATA

Moving objects can be integrated in the Piet framework, by means of a distinguished fact table that we denote *Moving Object Fact Table* (MOFT).

Figure 12 (left) shows a (very) simplified map of Paris, containing two hotels, denoted Hotel 1 and Hotel 2 (H1 and H2 from here on), the Louvre

Figure 11. The carrier sets of a point, a polyline and a polygon are the dotted lines

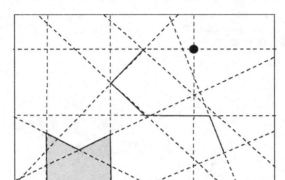

and the Eiffel tower. We consider three moving objects, O1, O2 and O3. Object O1 goes from H1 to the Louvre, the Eiffel tower, spends just a few minutes there, and returns to the hotel. Object O2 goes from H2 to the Louvre, the Eiffel tower, (spending a couple of hours visiting each place), and returns to the hotel. Object O3 leaves H2 to the Eiffel tower, visits the place, and returns to H2. Figure 12 (center) shows part of these trajectory samples. All points of the same trajectory are temporally ordered and stored together (i.e., the raw trajectories table is sorted by O_{id} and t). In what follows, we will use the object identifier as the trajectory identifier, unless specified, although

it is usual to generate a trajectory identifier in a pre-processing step, as explained in the TDW section.

In this scenario, a GIS user may be interested in queries like "number of persons going from H1 to the Louvre and then to the Eiffel tower (stopping to visit both places) in the same day". Also, a data mining analyst may want to identify interesting patterns in the trajectory data using association rule mining or sequential patterns algorithms, like "people do not visit two museums in the same day". Complex queries that aggregate non-spatial information, and also involve GIS and moving object data, must also be addressed. For

Figure 12. Three trajectories (left), the MOFT (center), and the SM-MOFT (right)

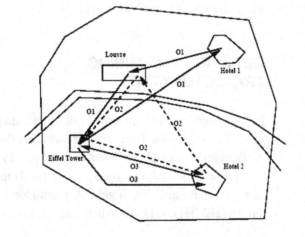

O_{id}	t	x	y
O_1	1	x_1	y_1
O_1	2	x_2	y_2
O_1	3	x_3	y_3
O_1	4	x_4	y_4
...	...	...	...
O_2	5	x_5	y_5
O_2	6	x_6	y_6
O_2	7	x_7	y_7
...	...	...	...
O_3	4	x_5	y_5
O_3	5	x_8	y_8
O_3	6	x_9	y_9
...	...	...	...

O_{id}	g_{id}	t_s	t_f
O_1	H_1	1	10
O_1	L	20	30
O_1	H_1	100	140
O_2	H_2	5	20
O_2	L	25	40
O_2	E	50	80
O_2	H_2	120	140
O_3	H_2	4	10
O_3	E	10	40
O_3	H_2	60	140

instance, "total sales in museum shops, for museums located on the left bank of the Seine, such that people visit them before going to the Eiffel Tower in the same day".

A moving object fact table (MOFT for short, see the table in the center of Figure 12), contains a finite number of identified trajectories. Definition 1 formalizes this.

Definition 1 (Moving Object Fact Table) Given a finite set T of trajectories, a *Moving Object Fact Table* (MOFT) for T is a relation with schema $<O_{id}, T, X, Y>$, where O_{id} is the identifier of the moving object, T represents time instants, and X and Y represent the spatial coordinates of the objects. An instance M of the above schema contains a finite number of tuples of the form $<O_{id}, t, x, y>$ that represent the position (x,y) of the object O_{id} at instant t, for the trajectories in T.

In practice, the MOFTs can contain huge amounts of data. For instance, suppose a GPS takes observations of daily movements of one thousand people, every ten seconds, during one month. This gives a MOFT of $1000 \times 360 \times 24 \times 30 = 259,200,000$ records. In this scenario, querying trajectory data may become extremely expensive. Note that a MOFT only provides the position of objects at a given instant. Sometimes we are not interested in such level of detail, but we look for more aggregated information instead. For example, we may want to know how many people go from a hotel to a museum on weekdays. Or, we can even want to perform data mining tasks like inferring trajectory patterns that are hidden in the MOFT. These tasks require semantic information, not present in the MOFT. In the best case, obtaining this information from that table will be expensive, because it would imply a join between this table and the spatial data.

Gómez, Kuijpers, & Vaisman (2008b) present an in-depth study on how moving object data analysis can benefit from replacing raw trajectory data by a sequence of *stops and moves*. The authors propose to use the notion of *stops and moves* in order to obtain a concise MOFT, that

can represent the trajectory in terms of places of interest, characterized as *stops*. This table cannot replace the whole information provided by the MOFT, but allows to quickly obtain information of interest without accessing the complete data set. In this sense, this concise MOFT, which we will denote SM-MOFT, behaves like a summarized materialized view of the MOFT. The SM-MOFT will contain the object identifier, the identifier of the geometries representing the Stops, and the interval $[t_s, t_f]$ of the stop duration. Obviously, we do not need to store the information about the moves, which remains implicit, because we know that between two stops there could only be a move. Definition 2 formalizes the above.

Definition 2 (SM-MOFT) Let the set
$$\mathcal{P}_A = \{C_1 = (R_{C_1}, \Delta_{C_1}), ..., C_N = (R_{C_N}, \Delta_{C_N})\}$$
be the PoIs of an application, and let M be a MOFT. The *SM-MOFT M^{sm} of M with respect to* P_A consists of the tuples $(O_{id}, g_{id}, t_s, t_f)$ such that (a) O_{id} is the identifier of a trajectory in M; (b) g_{id} is the identifier of the geometry of a PoI $C_k = (R_{C_k}, \Delta_{C_k})$ in P_A, such that the trajectory with identifier O_{id} in M has a stop in this PoI during the time interval $[t_s, t_f]$. This interval is called the *stop interval* of this stop.

The table in Figure 12 (right) shows the SM-MOFT for our example of the beginning of this section. Note that we only need to represent stops, since between two stops, a move is implicitly represented. For example, object O1 is at H1 between instants 1 and 10, and at L between 20 and 30. That means, in the interval [11,19] a *move* is assumed. Also note that since O1 just spent some minutes at E, the Eiffel tower is not a stop for O1. □

The SM-MOFT is a way of implementing the notion of *semantic similarity of trajectories*, which can be used to discover trajectory patterns in an efficient way, as we show below. Figure 13 shows three trajectories that, although different if we consider the positions of the three objects, from the point of view of an application could be considered similar, since the three objects traverse

Figure 13. Three semantically similar trajectories

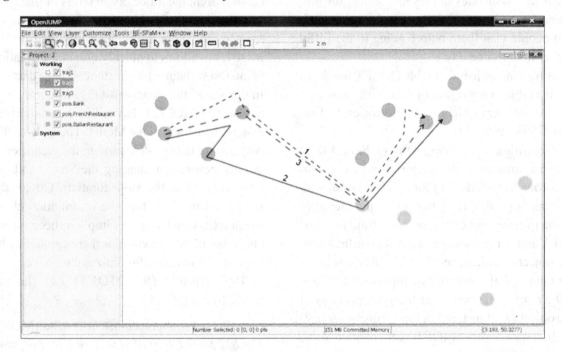

the same kinds of places (identified by coloured circles).

Trajectory Mining with RE-SPaM

Gómez and Vaisman (2009) introduce a pattern language, denoted RE-SPaM, based on regular expressions, and aimed at obtaining sequential patterns in trajectory databases using the notion of semantic trajectory. Four key features characterize RE-SPaM:

1. The items to be mined are not only composed of identifiers of stops, but are also *complex objects, composed of attributes that can be organized in hierarchies.* This allows adding *OLAP capabilities to the language* in a very natural way, and is a clear difference of classic sequential pattern mining algorithms, like SPIRIT, introduced by Garofalakis et al. (1999).

2. The support of rollup functions allows performing *mining at different levels of ag-*

gregation. Thus, complex sequential patterns can be found, at different granularity levels.

3. It can be proved that RE-SPaM is actually a subset of the first-order language introduced in Section "Geometric Aggregation" extended to support moving objects.

4. As a consequence of the above, not only semantic trajectories are supported, but also, if necessary, one can *go back to the base data, in order to support any kind of queries,* for instance, most of the ten queries in the benchmark proposed by Theodoridis (2003) (in fact, aggregation is not considered in such benchmark).

RE-SPaM could be used as a query language over a trajectory database, or to prune the patterns obtained during the mining process. Used in the latter way, a RE-SPaM expression is used during the typical sequential pattern discovery technique to indicate which are the patterns that the user wants to obtain. Therefore, during min-

Figure 14. Category instances

Category	Instance
hotels	$[(ID, H1), (categoryName, hotel), (geom, pol1), (star, 3)]$ $[(ID, H2), (categoryName, hotel), (geom, pol2), (star, 5)]$
restaurants	$[(ID, R1), (categoryName, restaurant), (geom, pol3), (typeOfFood, French), (price, cheap)]$ $[(ID, R2), (categoryName, restaurant), (geom, pol4), (typeOfFood, French), (price, expensive)]$ $[(ID, R3), (categoryName, restaurant), (geom, pol5), (typeOfFood, Italian), (price, cheap)]$
airports	$[(ID, A1), (categoryName, airport), (geom, pol6), (type, International)]$ $[(ID, A2), (categoryName, airport), (geom, pol7), (type, Local)]$ $[(ID, A3), (categoryName, airport), (geom, pol8), (type, International)]$
attractions	$[(ID, C1), (categoryName, touristattraction), (geom, pol9), (name, CathedralofO.L.), (price, free)]$ $[(ID, C2), (categoryName, touristattraction), (geom, pol10), (name, CastleofG.theD.), (price, free)]$

Figure 15. A normalized ToI

OID	Items
O_1	$([[(ts, 04/08/2008\ 14:05), (tf, 04/08/2008\ 14:33), (ID, R2)]])$ $([[(ts, 04/08/2008\ 17:30), (tf, 04/08/2008\ 18:48), (ID, R3)]])$ $([[(ts, 08/08/2008\ 06:22), (tf, 08/08/2008\ 07:05), (ID, R1)]])$ $([[(ts, 08/08/2008\ 17:10), (tf, 08/08/2008\ 18:17), (ID, R1)]])$
O_2	$([[(ts, 19/08/2008\ 09:00), (tf, 19/08/2008\ 10:20), (ID, R1)]])$ $([[(ts, 19/08/2008\ 17:00), (tf, 19/08/2008\ 18:12), (ID, R2)]])$

ing, all candidates that do not verify the pattern are pruned early in the process.

The RE-SPaM data model is basically composed of category schemas, category occurrences, category instances, and the table of items (ToI). For example, our tourist application above can include four category schemas, namely hotels, restaurants, airports and tourist attractions. Each category schema is composed of a set of attributes that describe it. An element in a category is denoted a category occurrence, and the set of all occurrences in all categories in an application is denoted a category instance. A set of category instances for our running example is shown in Figure 14, where, for example, the category hotels has two occurrences. A value of the attribute *geom* represents the geometric extension of the corresponding category occurrence (e.g., in the first tuple, pol1 can be Point(10 20)). Adding a time interval to a category occurrence, produces an *item*. The time interval of an item is described by its initial and final instants, and denoted [ts, tf]. A pair (Oid,

item) is a tuple in the ToI. For the same Oid the time-ordered sequence of items represent the semantic trajectory of the object. Figure 15 shows a normalized instance of the ToI corresponding to the category instances of Figure 14. Normalization arises from the fact that the table contains only the Oid of the objects, plus their the category occurrence identifier, and the temporal attributes. All other attributes are stored elsewhere. The figure shows two moving objects, *O*1 and *O*2; Over this model, a pattern language based on regular expressions is built. The atoms in RE-SPaM are constraints expressed as formulas over attributes of the complex items defined above. Constraints consist in conjunctions of expressions, enclosed in squared brackets. The regular expression language is built in the usual way, supporting the standard operators ('()','*','+','?','.','|'). The language also supports variables (strings preceded by '@'). A pattern expressing trajectories of tourists who visit hotel H1 and then a place characterized as 'cheap' or that serves French food, reads:

[ID="H1"].([price="'heap'"]|[typeOfFood="Fr ench'"])

Note that the second constraint does not mention any ID, only categorical attributes. The disjunction is evaluated as follows: 'cheap' places are restaurants R1 and R3. Places that serve French food are R1 and R2. During the mining process, the items which satisfy these conditions are computed, without the need of explicit enumeration of all the possibilities, allowing writing concise expressions.

Functions in RE-SPaM can be defined ad-hoc, and are of the forms functionName(attr,...) = 'constant', and functionName(attr,...) = @variable. Syntactically, the first parameter can be an attribute of a category occurrence (for example, typeOfFood in the tourist application example), or a temporal attribute. All other parameters must be literals, and the function also returns a literal. For example, a function *compares* (*price, c*), compares the attribute price with a literal, and returns 'equal', 'less', or 'greater than'; the first parameter is an attribute of the category occurrences of restaurants and tourist attractions, and the second one is a constant. The function can be invoked as *compares* (*price,* "100"). Also rollup functions à la OLAP can be defined to return ranges of time for a temporal attribute of an item (e.g., "Early Morning", "Morning",..). Below we show other examples of RE-SPaM queries.

Q1. "Trajectories of tourists who visit hotel H1, then optionally stop at restaurant R3 and the Zoo, and either end at H1 or visiting the Eiffel Tower"

[ID="H1"].([ID="R3"].[ID="Z"])*. ([ID="E"]|[ID="H1"])

Q2. "Trajectories that visit hotel H1, then, optionally visit different places, and finish at the Eiffel Tower or going back to H1."

[ID="H1"].[]*.([ID="E"]|[ID="H1"])

Here, the empty condition allows avoiding enumeration of the items. The next queries show the use of variables.

Q3. "Trajectories that start at a place characterized by price, then stop either at the zoo or the Eiffel Tower, and end up going to a place that serves French food, and has the same price range as the initial stop."

[price=@x].([ID="Z"] | [ID="E"]). [typeOfFood="French" **and** price=@x]

Finally, Q4 below shows the use of a rollup function in a constraint.

Q4. "Trajectories that stopped at two places (the second one having cheap prices), at the same part of the day (e.g., both of them during the morning), on 10/10/2008"

[rollup(ts_time, "range", "Time")=@z **and** ts_date="10/10/2008"].[rollup(ts_time, "range", "Time")=@z **and** ts_date="10/10/2008" **and** price="cheap"]

RE-SPAM++: Extending RE-SPaM to Support Geographic Information

Since objects move in a geographic environment, it is important to allow geometric conditions to be included in the patterns. Therefore, RE-SPAM was extended with this capability by Gardella et al. (Gardella, Gómez & Vaisman, 2010). This extension is denoted RE-SPaM++. The language includes SOLAP conditions in RE-SPaM constraints using Piet-QL, the query language supporting Piet, accomplishing the goal of integrating SOLAP and moving object data in a single framework. Syntactically, the extension is very simple: a WITH statement is added to the Piet-QL SELECT clause. This statement generates a sort of materialized view that is used in a RE-SPaM expression. Thus, the language allows not only single statements but also programs comprising sequences of Piet-QL and RE-SPaM statements. Next, we show an example of a RE-SPaM++ query.

Q5. "Trajectories that stop at a place which belongs to a region that contains a river, and whose next stop is an airport or a tourist attraction." The query reads in RE-SPaM++:

```
WITH TABLE regRiver(the_geom) AS
SELECT GIS DISTINCT(bel_regn.the_
geom)
FROM bel_regn, bel_river

WHERE contains(bel_regn.the_geom,bel_
river.the_geom);

[containedBy(geom,regRiver.the_
geom)='true'].([categoryName='Airpo
rt']|[categoryName='Tourist Attrac-
tion'])
```

The Piet-QL part of the query returns a set of geometric objects (polygons) representing regions containing rivers, in the cursor regRiver(the_

geom). In the RE-SPaM part of the query, the first constraint checks if the PoI is contained in one of the regions in the set. In other words, when an item in the Table of Items is being evaluated (e.g., during the mining process or just using RE-SPaM++ as a query language), the corresponding PoI geometry (represented by the attribute geom) is compared against each one of the geometric elements in the cursor.

Figure 16 shows a screenshot of the implementation of RE-SPaM++, and Figure 17 depicts the result, where we can see trajectories of lengths 1 to 4 satisfying the pattern. Figure 18 shows in more detail a trajectory of length two over real trajectories verifying a pattern.

HERMES AND PIET: SIMILARITIES AND DIFFERENCES

We now compare the two proposals that, in our opinion, more comprehensively address the issue of spatio-temporal OLAP: *Hermes-GeoPKDD*,

Figure 16. The RE-SPaM query interface

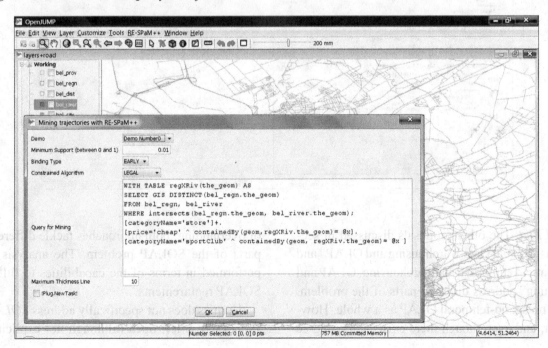

Figure 17. Showing query result

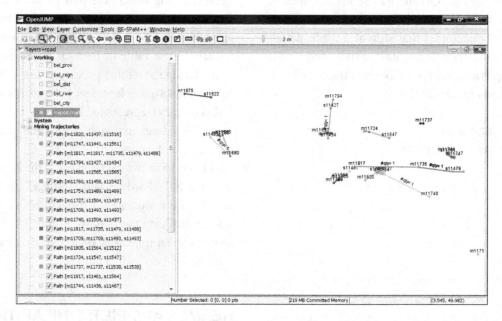

Figure 18. A detail of the query result: a pattern of length two

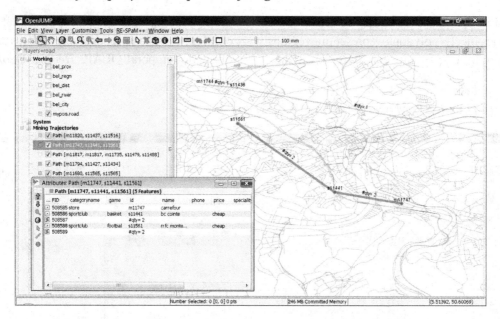

and Piet. The other proposals discussed in sections "Spatial Data Warehousing and OLAP" and "Spatio-Temporal Data Warehousing, OLAP and Mining" address different parts of the problem, but no spatio-temporal OLAP as a whole. However, and even though there exists some degree of overlapping, both approaches tackle different parts of the SOLAP problem. The analysis is performed in terms of the capabilities to fulfill SOLAP requirements.

Hermes does not specifically address *SOLAP support.* It is left open (although not explicitly stated) as a possible application of the general framework, but no formal model supports spatial data aggregation, probably because Hermes has been designed as an architecture to support spatio-temporal data, not as a model for *spatio-temporal decision support*. On the other hand, Piet focuses on GIS-OLAP integration, and is oriented specifically toward aggregate queries and spatial decision-support, although, as showed, standard spatial queries are also supported.

Integrating geographic data and warehouse data is not built into the Hermes model, while Piet handles this integration through the "α" function. A tool to semi-automatically match geometric elements in the GIS layers to non-spatial objects in the warehouse was implemented for Piet. On the Hermes side, integration of an external warehouse would require defining, in an ad-hoc fashion, how geographic objects will be mapped to warehouse objects.

Being conceived as a SOLAP system, the Piet formal data model also integrates naturally into the SOLAP framework the problem of modeling and analyzing trajectory data, either using the whole trajectory data (i.e., the MOFT), or the semantic trajectory represented via the SM-MOFT.

Probably the strongest point of the Hermes proposal is the analysis and implementations of the ETL process for *trajectory data* analysis. On the other hand, Piet does not have similar automatic data loading machinery, and assumes that data has already been loaded into a (continuous) trajectory file.

The approaches of Hermes and Piet for building a *trajectory data warehouse* (TDW) are quite different. Hermes loads *only aggregate measures* into a fact table, and dimensions conform cells in a three-dimensional space (x,y,t). The main achievement, in this sense, is the treatment of *double counting* for some of the measures. Trajectory data in the GeoPKDD proposal is stored in the moving object database (MOD), and it is used to extract higher level knowledge that may also be used to feed

the TDW. In this sense, the TDW could be considered an application, developed over the underlying architecture that uses the traditional star schema. Instead, in the Piet/RE-SpaM (Piet's regular query language for trajectories) approach, the MOFT and SM-MOFT *do not store aggregated measures* (actually, the "facts" here are represented by the existence of the trajectory in the database), but just the base trajectories (or the "semantic" trajectories, in the SM-MOFT). Actually, the MOFT is, basically, the *RELTrajectories* table in the TDW approach. Aggregation over the 'cells' hierarchy could be supported by RE-SPaM, although the language is mainly oriented to trajectory pattern mining. Further, aggregation is performed over trajectories that satisfy a certain pattern – see the work by Gómez, Kuijpers, & Vaisman (2008a) for details on the different aggregate operators and their arguments. In summary, implementing aggregation over cells in Piet in the way proposed in GeoPKDD would not be trivial.

Hermes-MDC is based on moving objects that can change shape or position over time, while *Piet assumes that the regions and geometric objects, in general, are static*, and that traceable objects (e.g., representing pedestrians, buses, cars) move through the geographic space. In other words, Piet does not provide temporal support for the GIS part of the model, only for the moving objects whose trajectories are being analyzed. However, a temporal extension for Piet has been proposed (Gómez, Kuijpers & Vaisman, 2010), and it is being implemented at the time this survey is written (see below).

In summary, using the taxonomy proposed by Vaisman and Zimányi, Hermes fall in the Spatio-Temporal class, while Piet falls in the SOLAP class. Piet and RE-SPaM together would fall in the Spatio-Temporal OLAP class, and the TDW proposal also belongs to this class.

Finally, while all Piet software components are open source: the database, postgres, and its GIS extension postGIS (http://postgis.refractions.

net), the Mondrian OLAP server (http://www. mondrian.sourceforge.net), and Java. On the other hand, Hermes is built as an extension of Oracle 10g. Table 1 summarizes the comparison between Hermes, the TDW, and Piet/ RE-SPaM.

FUTURE DIRECTIONS IN SPATIO-TEMPORAL OLAP

An Emerging Topic: SOLAP for Continuous Fields

Continuous fields describe the distribution of physical phenomena that change continuously in time and/or space. Examples of such phenomena are temperature, pressure, and land elevation. Besides physical geography, continuous fields

(from now on, fields), like land use and population density, are used in human geography as an aid in spatial decision making process. Some work has been done to support querying fields in GIS, although the area of spatial multidimensional analysis of continuous data is still almost unexplored. Integrating spatiotemporal continuity within multidimensional structures poses numerous challenges. Further, existing multidimensional structures and models dealing with discrete data, are not adequate for the analysis of continuous phenomena. Multidimensional models and associated query languages are thus needed, to support continuous data.

In a seminal work on the topic, Tomlin(1990} proposes an algebra for fields, denoted map algebra, based on the notion that a map is used to represent a continuous variable (e.g., tempera-

Table 1. Comparing Hermes, TDW, Piet and RE-SpaM

	Hermes	Trajectory DW	Piet	RE-SPaM
GIS-OLAP integration	No	Through Hermes-MDC	Yes	Yes
SOLAP Formal model	No	N/A	Yes	N/A
Fact table	N/A (can be defined ad-hoc)	Pre-aggregated measures	External, defined in the OLAP part	MOFT,SM MOFT (no pre-aggregation)
Dimensions	N/A (can be defined ad-hoc)	Spatial dimensions, Time dimension	GIS dimension, regular OLAP dimensions	OLAP hierarchies integrated in the query language
Support for spatial aggregation	Ad-hoc	Yes	Yes	Partially
Support of querying an external DW	Ad-hoc	Ad-hoc	Provided by model & query language	Provided by model & query language
Spatial Queries	Point,Range, distance, nearest-neighbor	Point,Range, distance, nearest-neighbor	Point,Range, distance, nearest-neighbor	Point,Range, distance, nearest-neighbor
Mining capabilities	No	Through external functionality	No	Yes
Support of changing geometric objects	Yes	Through Hermes-MDC	No	No
Temporal support	Yes	Through Hermes-MDC	No	Only for moving points
ETL Support and tools	N/A	Yes	No	No
Semantic trajectory support	N/A	Through external functionality	N/A	Built-in
Open Source Architecture	No	No	Yes	Yes
Needs non-standard data libraries for querying?	Yes	Yes	No	No

ture). There are three types of functions in Map algebra: *local*, *focal*, and *zonal*. Local functions compute a value at a certain location as a function of the value(s) at this location in other map layer(s), allowing queries like "Total desert land in a country, where a region is classified as desert if the annual rain is less than 500 mm per year". Focal functions compute each location's value as a function of existing values in the neighboring locations of existing layers, allowing aggregate queries like "Local altitude in clay soil regions, in a map containing soils distribution in some portion of land". Zonal functions compute a location's new value from one layer (containing the values for a variable), associated to the zone (in another map) containing the location, supporting queries like "Total area in a province, with elevation greater than 1000 m above sea level". Cámara et al (2005) and Cordeiro et. al. (2005) formalize and extend these functions, supporting more topological predicates. Mennis et al. (2005) extend map algebra operators to support time-varying fields.

In spite of the above, regarding fields and multidimensional models, the joint contribution of the GIS and OLAP has been limited.

Shanmugasundaram et. al (1999) propose a data cube representation that deals with continuous dimensions not needing a predefined discrete hierarchy. They focus on using the known data density to calculate aggregate queries without accessing the data. The representation reduces the storage requirements, but continuity is addressed in a limited way. Ahmed and Miquel. (2005) use interpolation methods to estimate (continuous) values for dimension levels and measures, based on existing sample data values. Continuous cube cells are computed on-the-fly, producing a continuous representation of the discrete cube. A sequel of this proposal introduces SOLAP concepts, and a SOLAP application supporting some form of continuous data (Ahmed,2008). These works are based on a data model devised for OLAP, not

for spatial OLAP, leading to a representation of spatial dimensions which is not the best one. The approach of Vaisman and Zimányi (2009) is based on the Multidim conceptual model discussed above (Malinowski & Zimányi, 2008), which is extended in a natural way to support this new data type. The authors characterize multidimensional queries over fields using the taxonomy described above in this survey, denoting this class of queries SOLAP-CF (standing for SOLAP with Continuous Fields). Along the lines of their previous work, they make use of the relational calculus supporting aggregate functions, extending it with a *field data type*. They also analyze the operators that this data type must include to support and extend map algebra. They also discuss different implementation choices for the abstract model, using regular gridded digital elevation models (DEM), and triangulated irregular networks (TIN) as data structures. Finally, recently Gómez et. al. (2010) presented an implementation of this model over a gridded structure.

Extending Piet with Temporal Capabilities

We commented above that Piet does not support for querying the history of spatial objects, that is geometric objects are assumed to be static. This is a limitation in real-world applications, which are temporal in nature. For example, in a cadastral system, parcels can change shape, and be merged or split. That is, not only alphanumeric attributes can change, but also geometric ones. Therefore, queries like "Total production by year per square mile for each parcel of land, for the parcels in Antwerp" cannot be answered in Piet. In another scenario, a pollution stain can move forward or backward, grow and/or shrink (or even disappear), split into two or more, or be merged with other ones. Environmental control agencies monitor these changes in order to keep the situation within certain limits. Interesting information can be obtained in this scenario, as long as we have a data model and query language allowing to represent a dynamic setting. For instance, the evolution of the stain across time, how far from a school it had passed, or how many people were exposed to its effect.

Addressing situations like the ones above requires extending non-temporal SOLAP data models and query languages with temporal capabilities. Gómez et al. (2010) extended the Piet data model to support spatio-temporal OLAP. The work presents a formal data model, based on the timestamp temporal model, and proposes a query language, extending Piet-QL. This model would fall into the Spatio-Temporal OLAP class in the Vaisman-Zimányi taxonomy.

ACKNOWLEDGMENT

This research has been partially funded by the European Union under the FP6-IST-FET program, Project n. FP6-14915, "GeoPKDD: Geographic Privacy-Aware Knowledge Discovery and Delivery", (www.geopkdd.eu) and by the Research Foundation Flanders (FWO-Vlaanderen), Research Project G.0344.05, and the Argentinian National Scientific Agency, project PICT 2004 11-21.350.

REFERENCES

Ahmed, T. O. (2008). Continuous Spatial Data Warehousing. In *Proceedings 9th International Arab Conference on Information Technology*.

Ahmed, T. O., & Miquel, M. (2005). Multidimensional Structures Dedicated to Continuous Spatiotemporal Phenomena. In *Proceedings of BNCOD* (p. 29-40).

Alvares, L. O., Bogorny, V., Kuijpers, B., de Macedo, J. A. F., Moelans, B., & Vaisman, A. (2007). *A model for enriching trajectories with semantic geographical information.* ACM-GIS.

Bédard, Y., Merret, T., & Han, J. (2001). Fundamentals of spatial data warehousing for geographic knowledge discovery. In *Geographic data mining and knowledge discovery* (pp. 53–73). Taylor & Francis. doi:10.4324/9780203468029_chapter_3

Bédard, Y., Rivest, S., & Proulx, M.-J. (2007). Spatial online analytical processing (SOLAP): Concepts, architectures, and solutions from a geomatics engineering perspective. In *Data warehouses and OLAP: Concepts, architectures and solutions* (p. 298 – 319). IGI Global.

Bimonte, S., Tchounikine, A., & Miquel, M. (2005). *Towards a spatial multidimensional model* (pp. 39–46). DOLAP.

Brakatsoulas, S., Pfoser, D., & Tryfona, N. (2004). Pre-aggregation in spatial data warehouses. In [Washington D.C, USA.]. *Proceedings of IDEAS, 04*, 68–77.

Braz, F., Orlando, S., Orsini, R., Raffaetá, A., Roncato, A., & Silvestri, C. (2007). Approximate Aggregations in Trajectory Data Warehouses. In *Proceedings of STDM* (p. 536-545).

Buchmann, A. P., Günther, O., Smith, T. R., & Wang, Y.-F. (1990). Design and implementation of large spatial databases. In *First symposium (SSD)* (Vol. 409). Springer.

Cabibbo, L., & Torlone, R. (1997). Querying multidimensional databases. In *Database programming languages, LCNS* (1369) (p. 319–335).

Cámara, G., Palomo, D., de Souza, R. C. M., & de Oliveira, D. (2005). *Towards a Generalized Map Algebra: Principles and Data Types* (pp. 66–81). GeoInfo.

Codd, E. F. (1970). A relational model of data for large shared data banks. *Communications of the ACM,13*(6),377–387.doi:10.1145/362384.362685

Cordeiro, J. P., Cámara, G., Moura, U. F., Barbosa, C. C., & Almeida, F. (2005). *Algebraic Formalism over Maps* (pp. 49–65). GeoInfo.

Damiani, M., & Spaccapietra, S. (2006). Spatial data warehouse modelling. In *Processing and managing complex data for decision support* (pp. 21–27). Idea Group. doi:10.4018/9781591406556. ch001

Damiani, M.L., Macedo, J. A.F. de, Parent, C., Porto, F., & Spaccapietra, S. (2007). A conceptual view of trajectories. *Technical Report, Ecole Polythecnique Federal de Lausanne, April 2007*.

Damiani, M. L., Vangenot, C., Frentzos, E., Marketos, G., Theodoridis, Y., Veryklos, V., & Raffaeta, A. (2007). Design of the trajectory warehouse architecture. *Technical Report D1.3, GeoPKDD project*.

de Weghe, N. V., Cohn, A., Tré, G. D., & Maeyer, P. D. (2005). *A qualitative trajectory calculus as a basis for representing moving objects in geographical information systems*. Control and Cybernetics.

Eder, J., Koncilia, C., & Morzy, T. (2002). *The COMET metamodel for temporal data warehouses* (pp. 83–99). Caise.

Escribano, A., Gomez, L., Kuijpers, B., & Vaisman, A. A. (2007). Piet: a GIS-OLAO implementation. In *ACM 10th international workshop on data warehousing and OLAP (DOLAP)* (p. 73–80). ACM.

Etzion, O., Jajodia, S., & Sripada, S. M. (Eds.). (1998). *Temporal databases: Research and practice*. Springer. doi:10.1007/BFb0053695

Frentzos, E., Gratsias, K., & Theodoridis, Y. (2007). Index-based Most Similar Trajectory Search. In proceedings of ICDE (p.816-825).

Gardella, J. P., Gómez, L., & Vaisman, A. (2010). Trajectory Sequential Patterns with Regular Expression Constraints Including Spatial Queries. In *Proceedings of AMW*.

Garofalakis, M., Rastogi, R., & Shim, K. (1999). SPIRIT: Sequential Pattern Mining with Regular Expression Constraints. *In proceedings of VLDB* (p. 223-234).

Giannotti, F., Nanni, M., Pinelli, F., & Pedreschi, D. (2007). *Trajectory pattern mining* (pp. 330–339). KDD.

Gómez, L., Haesevoets, S., Kuijpers, B., & Vaisman, A. A. (2009). Spatial aggregation: Data model and implementation. *Information Systems(34)* (6) (p. 551-576).

Gómez, L., Kuijpers, B., & Vaisman, A. A. (2008a). Aggregation languages for moving object and places of interest. In *SAC 2008 - ASIIS track*.

Gómez, L., Kuijpers, B., & Vaisman, A. A. (2008b). Querying and mining trajectory databases using places of interest. *Annals of Information Systems*.

Gómez, L., Kuijpers, B., & Vaisman, A. A. (2010). A data model and query language for spatio-temporal decision support. *GeoInformatica*, 1–47. http://dx.doi.org/10.1007/ s10707-010-0110-7.

Gómez, L., & Vaisman, A. (2009). Efficient constraint evaluation in categorical sequential pattern mining for trajectory databases. In *Proceedings of EDBT* (p. 541-552).

Gómez, L., Vaisman, A., & Zich, S. (2008). Piet-QL: a query language for GIS-OLAP integration. In *Proceedings of ACM-GIS* (27).

Gómez, L., Vaisman, A., & Zimányi, E. (2010). Physical Design and Implementation of Spatial Data WarehousesSupporting Continuous Fields. In *Proceedings of DaWaK* (p. 25-39).

Gonzalez, H., Han, J., Li, X., Myslinska, M., & Sondag, J. P. (2007). *Adaptive fastest path computation on a road network: A traffic mining approach* (pp. 794–805). VLDB.

Güting, R. H., Böhlen, M., Jensen, C., Lorentzos, N., Schneider, M., & Vazirgiannis, M. (2000). A foundation for representing and quering moving objects. In *ACM Transactions Database Systems, 25*(1), (p. 1-42

Güting, R. H., & Schneider, M. (2005). *Moving objects databases*. Morgan Kaufman.

Gutman, A. (1984). R-trees: A dynamic index structure for spatial searching. In. *Proceedings of SIGMOD, 84*, 47–57.

Han, J., Stefanovic, N., & Koperski, K. (1998). Selective materialization: An efficient method for spatial data cube construction. In *Research and development in knowledge discovery and data mining (PAKDD)* (Vol. 1394) (p. 144-158). Springer.

Harinarayan, V., Rajaraman, A., & Ullman, J. D. (1996). Implementing data cubes efficiently. In *SIGMOD conference* (pp. 205–216). ACM Press.

Hornsby, K., & Egenhofer, M. J. (2002). Modeling moving objects over multiple granularities. *Annals of Mathematics and Artificial Intelligence, 36*(1-2), 177–194. doi:10.1023/A:1015812206586

Hurtado, C., Mendelzon, A., & Vaisman, A. (1999). Maintaining data cubes under dimension updates. In *Proceedings of ICDE* (p. 346-355).

In *Data warehousing and knowledge discovery (DaWak)* (Vol. 2737, p. 35–44). Springer.

Jensen, C. S., Kligys, A., Pedersen, T. B., & Timko, I. (2004). Multidimensional data modeling for location-based services. *VLDB, 13*(1), 1–21. doi:10.1007/s00778-003-0091-3

Kakoudakis, I. (1996). The TAU Temporal Object Model. *M.Ph. Thesis*.UMIST, Department of Computation.

Kimball, R. (1996). *The data warehouse toolkit.* J.Wiley and Sons, Inc.

Kimball, R., & Ross, M. (2002). *The data warehouse toolkit: The complete guide to dimensional modeling* (2nd ed.). J.Wiley and Sons, Inc.

Klug, A. (1982). Equivalence of relational algebra and relational calculus query languages having aggregate functions. *Journal of the ACM, {29}* (3) (p. 699—717).

Kuijpers, B., Moelans, B., & Van de Weghe, N. (2006). Qualitative polyline similarity testing with applications to query-by-sketch, indexing and classification. I*n proceedings of ACM-GIS* (p.11-18).

Kuijpers, B., & Vaisman, A. (2007). A data model for moving objects supporting aggregation. In *Proceedings of STDM*.

Lee, J.-G., Han, J., & Whang, K.-Y. (2007). Trajectory clustering: a partition-and-group framework. In *SIGMOD conference* (p.593-604).

Lenz, H., & Shoshani, A. (1997). Summarizability in olap and statistical data bases. In *Ninth international conference on scientific and statistical database management, proceedings, august 11-13, 1997, olympia, washington, usa* (p. 132-143). IEEE Computer Society.

Leonardi, L., Marketos, G., Frentzos, E., Giatrakos, N., Orlando, S., Pelekis, N., et al. T-Warehouse: Visual OLAP analysis on trajectory data (2010). In Proceedings of ICDE (p. 1141-1144).

López, I. F. V., Snodgrass, R., & Moon, B. (2005). Spatiotemporal aggregate computation: A survey. *IEEE Transactions on Knowledge and Data Engineering, 17*(2), 271–286. doi:10.1109/TKDE.2005.34

Malinowski, E., & Zimányi, E. (2004). *Representing spatiality in a conceptual multidimensional model* (pp. 12–22). GIS.

Malinowski, E., & Zimányi, E. (2006). Hierarchies in a multidimensional model: From conceptual modeling to logical representation. *Data & Knowledge Engineering, 59*(2), 348–377. doi:10.1016/j.datak.2005.08.003

Malinowski, E., & Zimányi, E. (2008). *Advanced Data Warehouse Design: From Conventional to Spatial and Temporal Applications.* Springer, 2008.

Marketos, G., Frentzos, E., Ntousi, I., Pelekis, N., Raffaeta, A., & Theodoridis, Y. (2008). *Building real-world trajectory data warehouses* (*Vol. 08*). Mobi, DE.

Marketos, G., & Theodoridis, Y. (2010). Ad-hoc OLAP on Trajectory Data. In *MDM 2010* (p. 189,198).

Mendelzon, A. O., & Vaisman, A. A. (2000). *Temporal queries in OLAP* (pp. 242–253). VLDB.

Mendelzon, A. O., & Vaisman, A. A. (2003). Time in multidimensional databases. In *Multidimensional databases* (p. 166-199).

Mennis, J., Viger, R., & Tomlin, C.D. (2005). Cubic map algebra functions for spatio-temporal analysis. *Cartography and Geographic Information Science* (32)(1) (p. 17-32).

Meratnia, N., & de By, R. A. (2002). *Aggregation and comparison of trajectories* (pp. 49–54). ACM-GIS.

Mouza, C., & Rigaux, P. (2005). Mobility patterns. *GeoInformatica, 9*(23), 297–319. doi:10.1007/s10707-005-4574-9

Orlando, S., Orsini, R., Raffaetà, A., Roncato, A., & Silvestri, C. (2007). Spatio-temporal aggregations in trajectory data warehouses. In *DaWaK* (p. 66-77).

Papadias, D., Tao, Y., Kalnis, P., & Zhang, J. (2002). Indexing spatio-temporal data warehouses. In *International conference on data engineering (ICDE)* (p. 166–175). IEEE Computer Society.

Papadias, D., Tao, Y., Zhang, J., Mamoulis, N., Shen, Q., & Sun, J. (2002). Indexing and retrieval of historical aggregate information about moving objects. *IEEE Data Eng. Bull., 25*(2), 10–17.

Paredaens, J., Kuper, G., & Libkin, L. (Eds.). (2000). *Constraint databases.* Springer-Verlag.

Paredaens, J., Van Den Bussche, J., & Gucht, D. V. (1994). Towards a theory of spatial database queries. In *Thirteenth ACM SIGACT-SIGMOD-SIGART symposium on principles of database systems, (PODS)* (p. 279–288). ACM Press.

Pedersen, T. B., & Tryfona, N. (2001). Pre-aggregation in spatial data warehouses. In *Advances in spatial and temporal databases* (pp. 460–480). SSTD.

Pelekis, N. (2002). Stau: A spatio-temporal extension to ORACLE DBMS. *Ph.D Thesis, UMIST Department of Computation.*

Pelekis, N., & Theodoridis, Y. (2006). *Boosting location-based services with a moving object database engine* (pp. 3–10). Mobide.

Pelekis, N., Theodoridis, Y., Vosinakis, S., & Panayiotopoulos, T. (2006). *Hermes - a framework for location-based data management* (pp. 1130–1134). EDBT.

Pelekis, N., Theodoulidis, B., Kopanakis, Y., & Theodoridis, Y. (2004). Literature Review of Spatio-Temporal Database Models. In *The Knowledge Engineering Review journal*, 19(3) (p. 235-274).

Pourabbas, E. (2003). Cooperation with geographic databases. In *Multidimensional databases: Problems and solutions* (pp. 393–432). Idea group. doi:10.4018/9781591400530.ch013

Rao, F., Zhang, L., Yu, X., Li, Y., & Chen, Y. (2003). Spatial hierarchy and OLAP-favored search in spatial data warehouse. In *ACM sixth international workshop on data warehousing and OLAP (DOLAP)* (p. 48–55). ACM.

Rigaux, P., Scholl, M., & Voisard, A. (2001). *Spatial databases: With application to GIS*. Morgan Kaufmann.

Rivest, S., Bédard, Y., & Marchand, P. (2001). Towards better support for spatial decision making: Defining the characteristics of spatial on-line analytical processing (SOLAP). *Geomatica, 55*(4), 539–555.

Rizzi, S., & Golfarelli, M. (2000). *Date warehouse design* (pp. 39–42). ICEIS.

Shekhar, S., Lu, C.-T., Tan, X., Chawla, S., & Vatsavai, R. R. (2001). Map cube: A visualization tool for spatial data warehouses. In *Geographic data mining and knowledge discovery* (pp. 73–108). Taylor and Francis. doi:10.4324/9780203468029_chapter_4

Snodgrass, R. T. (Ed.). (1995). *The TSQL2 temporal query language*. Kluwer.

Snodgrass, R. T. (Ed.). (1999). *Developing time-oriented database applications in SQL*. Morgan Kaufmann.

Stefanovic, N., Han, J., & Koperski, K. (2000). Object-based selective materialization for efficient implementation of spatial data cubes. *IEEE Transactions on Knowledge and Data Engineering, 12*(6), 938–958. doi:10.1109/69.895803

Stonebraker, M., & Moore, D. (1996). *Object-relational DBMSs: The next great wave*. Morgan Kaufmann.

Tao, Y., Kollios, G., Considine, J., Li, F., & Papadias, D. (2004). *Spatio-temporal aggregation using sketches* (pp. 214–226). ICDE.

Theodoridis, Y. (2003). Ten benchmark database queries for location-based services. *The Computer Journal, 46*(6), 713–725. doi:10.1093/comjnl/46.6.713

Tomlin, D. C. (1990). *Geographic Information Systems and Cartographic Modelling*. Prentice-Hall.

Vaisman, A., Izquierdo, A., & Ktenas, M. (2006). Web-enabled Temporal OLAP. In *Proceedings of LA_WEB '06,* 220-229, Puebla, Mexico.

Vaisman, A., & Zimányi, E. (2009). A Multidimensional Model Representing Continuous Fields in Spatial Data Warehouses. In *Proceedings of GIS* (p.168-177).

Wolfson, O., Sistla, P., Xu, B., & Chamberlain, S. (1999). Domino: Databases fOr MovINg Objects tracking. In *Proceedings of SIGMOD* (p. 547 - 549).

Worboys, M. F. (1995). *Gis: A computing perspective*. Taylor&Francis.

Zeiler, M. (1999). *Modeling our world: The ESRI guide to geodatabase design*. ESRI Press.

Zhang, L., Li, Y., Rao, F., Yu, X., Chen, Y., & Liu, D. (2003). An approach to enabling spatial OLAP by aggregating on spatial hierarchy.

Chapter 10
A Survey of Open Source Tools for Business Intelligence

Christian Thomsen
Aalborg University, Denmark

Torben Bach Pedersen
Aalborg University, Denmark

ABSTRACT

The industrial use of open source Business Intelligence (BI) tools is becoming more common, but is still not as widespread as for other types of software. It is therefore of interest to explore which possibilities are available for open source BI and compare the tools. In this survey article, we consider the capabilities of a number of open source tools for BI. In the article, we consider a number of Extract-Transform-Load (ETL) tools, database management systems (DBMSs), On-Line Analytical Processing (OLAP) servers, and OLAP clients. We find that, unlike the situation a few years ago, there now exist mature and powerful tools in all these categories. However, the functionality still falls somewhat short of that found in commercial tools.

INTRODUCTION

The use of Business Intelligence (BI) tools is popular in industry. However, the use of open source tools for BI is still quite limited compared to other types of software. The dominating tools are closed source and commercial. Only for database management systems (DBMSs), there seems to be a sizeable market where open source products are used in industry, including business-critical sys-

tems such as online travel booking, management of subscriber inventories for telecommunications, etc. (Yuhanna, 2006). Thus, the situation is quite different from, for example, the web server market where open source tools as Linux and Apache are very popular.

To understand the limited use of open source BI tools better, it is of interest to consider which tools are available and what they are capable of. This is the purpose of this article.

In the survey, we will consider products for making a complete solution with an Extract-Transform-Load (ETL) tool that loads data into a database managed by a DBMS. On top of the DBMS, an On-Line Analytical Processing (OLAP) server providing for fast aggregate queries will be running. The user will be communicating with the OLAP server by means of an OLAP client. We limit ourselves to these kinds of tools and do not consider, for example, data mining tools or Enterprise Application Integration (EAI) tools. Use of data mining tools is also of relevance in many BI settings, but open-source data mining tools have been considered in a recent survey (Chen, Ye, Williams, & Xu, 2007). EAI tools may have some similarities with ETL tools, but are more often used in online transactional processing (OLTP) systems. We focus on the individual components such that a "customized" solution is built, not the integrated BI suites – but the integrated BI suites are briefly described later.

The article is an updated version of a previous survey done in late 2004 (Thomsen & Pedersen, 2005). In comparison with the status in 2004, there are now mature and powerful open source tools available in all four categories (in 2004, only the DBMS category had sufficiently mature tools), so it is now for the first time possible to make a complete BI solution using only open source tools. More detailed findings are reported in the sections for each tool category.

The rest of the article is structured as follows. First, the method for conducting the survey is described. Second, the ETL category is described. Third, the DBMS category is described. Fourth, the OLAP server category is treated. Fifth, the OLAP client category is surveyed. Finally, the article describes the available integrated BI suites, before concluding remarks are offered.

CONDUCT OF THE SURVEY

To collect data about the tools, the Internet was searched for open source tools in each category. Some projects were left out of the survey if they only stated goals for *future* development and did not provide any working code at the moment. Also, projects for which no activity had taken place for years were left out. The presented data was found by inspecting the products' official homepages as well as their documentation (if any), mailing lists and forums. Finally, the source code was also inspected in some cases to clarify questions. For time reasons, the tools were, however, not evaluated by configuring and running each of them. The findings were collected from mid May to mid June 2008 with smaller updates in July 2008.

The data about the tools was collected carefully but nevertheless it is possible that certain information about products was misunderstood or not found and thus not considered correctly in this survey. The authors therefore disclaim any liability arising from omissions or errors and do not give any guarantees about completeness or accuracy. It should be emphasized that the authors are not involved in developing any of the described tools or any of their competitors and that the authors do not have any interests in recommending certain tools instead of other tools.

In the following, the criteria used for the evaluations of the considered products are described. Some general criteria are of relevance to all the categories of tools. Other more technical criteria are only of relevance to a specific product category.

Criteria for All Tool Categories

There exist many different open source *licenses* (Open Source Initiative, 2006), for example the GNU Public License and the Mozilla Public License. The different licenses vary widely with respect to what they allow and how modified source code can or must be distributed. Although it is outside the scope of this article to describe the different open source licenses, it is of interest to see which licenses are used for the particular products.

For a potential user, it is important if a certain tool can be used with her existing *platform*. It is thus of interest to consider with which hardware and software platforms the tools can be used.

For many professional users, it is important to know whether *commercial support, training, and consulting services* are available for a product, and the survey therefore considers these aspects. A related considered issue is the type and amount of *documentation* available. Many open source projects have strong user communities using *forums and/or mailing lists*. The survey therefore also considers if such active forums or mailing lists exist for the products.

Criteria for Extract-Transform-Load Tools

For an ETL tool, it is investigated if the tool is for *relational OLAP* (ROLAP) where relational database tables are loaded or if it is for *multidimensional OLAP* (MOLAP) where multidimensional cubes are loaded. The supported data sources and targets are obviously also of interest.

In many DW environments, it is of great practical interest to be able to load only the changes made to the source data since the previous load. The survey therefore considers the possibilities for doing such an *incremental load*. The survey also considers *how an ETL job is specified*, for example by means of a graphical user interface (GUI) or an Extensible Markup Language (XML) file. Also the possibilities for doing *transformations* and *data cleansing* are considered – both with respect to predefined transformations and user-defined transformations.

Due to the large data volumes in data warehousing, *parallel job execution* is also of great practical interest and it is investigated if the tools support parallelism.

Criteria for Database Management Systems

For DBMSs there are many interesting things to consider. In this article, the scope is limited to investigate features and possibilities that are relevant to data warehousing. This includes investigating whether the DBMS can handle *large datasets* of many gigabytes. Related issues to consider for the DBMSs are their support for *materialized views, bitmap indices,* and *star joins* which all can improve performance for DW applications.

Possibilities for *replication* and *partitioning* are also of interest for many DW environments and the survey also considers if the tools support these features. Finally, it is considered which *programming languages* are supported for stored procedures/user-defined functions.

Criteria for On-Line Analytical Processing Servers

For an OLAP server, the survey investigates whether it is a *ROLAP* or a *MOLAP* server. It is also considered which *data sizes* it aims at handling and which underlying *data sources* it can be used with if any (for example a specific DBMS like MySQL). For performance reasons it can be very beneficial for an OLAP server to use precomputed *aggregate tables*, and the possibilities for this are also investigated here.

It is also investigated how the user performs the *specification of cubes*, for example by means of a GUI or an XML file. Finally, it is considered what *application programming interface (API)* and *query language* the OLAP server offers.

Criteria for On-Line Analytical Processing Clients

For an OLAP client, the survey considers which *OLAP server(s)* the client can be used with and which *query language* it uses/generates. Further, the types of supported *reports* are investigated.

239

EXTRACT-TRANSFORM-LOAD TOOLS

This section presents the ETL tools that were found in the survey. In previous work (Thomsen & Pedersen, 2005), the category of ETL tools only had few possibilities and was considered to be the least mature and most difficult to use. At the time of this writing, many more tools are available and some of these are quite mature. All of the described tools but Pequel are implemented in Java and can thus be used on many different hardware and software platforms. In this and the following sections, the tools are presented in alphabetical order.

Apatar

Apatar (Apatar, 2008) is a data integration and ETL tool developed by the company also bearing the name Apatar. This survey considers Apatar version 1.1.9 from May 2008. Apatar seems to have a very fast release cycle as version 1.1.0 was released in October 2007 and version 1.1.10 in June 2008. Apatar is released under a dual-licensing scheme and is available under the GNU General Public License (GPL) or under a commercial license, if desired. The development company offers training, support, and consulting. The documentation exists in four PDF files (around 40 pages in total) as well as in some wikis. Further, some user forums exist.

Apatar is ROLAP-oriented and has direct support for a wide selection of relational DBMSs (as well as generic JDBC support). Further it supports file formats such a comma separated values (CSV) and Excel and ERP and CRM systems (Compiere ERP, SalesForce.com, and SugarCRM). The specification of a job is done in a GUI. However, it is not possible to do an incremental load. It is not possible to run jobs in parallel yet.

Apatar has built-in data quality tools for verification of US addresses, phone numbers and email addresses. It is possible for the user to define transformations in Java, although this is not as simple as in some of the other tools. To make her own transformation available in Apatar, the user must define two classes (both inheriting from provided base classes) and edit an XML file describing the available plug-ins.

Clover.ETL

Clover.ETL (*Clover.ETL*, 2008) is developed by OpenSys and Javlin and is offered under either a GNU Library General Public License (LGPL) or a commercial license. Support and consulting can be bought from the above-mentioned companies. Here, version 2.4.6 of Clover.ETL is considered (2.4 was released in Feb. 2008, 2.4.7 was released in June 2008). Unlike the previously described ETL tool, Clover.ETL does not have an open source GUI. A closed source GUI exists, but is only free of charge if not used commercially. So, for a solution fully based on open source, the user has to specify the ETL job in XML when using Clover.ETL. A free 181-page manual exists for the GUI, but for Clover.ETL itself, the user has to settle with the wiki-documentation and a User's Guide consisting of 104 slides from a presentation. Further, two forums exist.

Clover.ETL is a ROLAP tool and transfers structured data from different DBMSs and file formats. The user can create transformations in Java (together with XML descriptions of them) or in Clover.ETL's own *TL* language. Clover.ETL supports parallel execution and, for some DBMSs, also bulk-loading, while no support for incremental load was found.

ETL Integrator

ETL Integrator (*JBIWiki: ETLSE*, 2008) is an ETL tool developed by Sun Microsystems. It has a service engine that makes ETL operations available as web services and further it has an ETL editor which is integrated into the Netbeans integrated development environment (IDE) version 6.1. It is released under the Common Development and Distribution License (CDDL). No information about commercial support specific for ETL Integrator was found. But Sun will provide commercial support for its upcoming integration platform GlassFish ESB (Sun, 2008) which is built on the OpenESB project which ETL Integrator is part of. The documentation found consists of design documents, wikis, and video tutorials. Also, the User Guide is a tutorial. Further, forums for the OpenESB project exist, but only few postings are related to ETL Integrator.

ETL Integrator is a ROLAP tool outputting to relations. It supports different relational DBMSs as sources as well as different file formats and OpenESB components for connecting to ERP/CRM systems. The tool is integrated into the Netbeans IDE and ETL jobs can be specified graphically from there. ETL Integrator supports incremental load as well as parallel execution of parts. Also bulk loading is supported. In the descriptions of ETL Integrator it is said that its editor "has many predefined transformations as well as cleansing operators/functions" and further that it is possible to add user defined functions. ETL Integrator offers parsing and normalization of names and addresses but these operations depend on SQL calls to the database except for flat files for which an internal engine is used.

KETL

KETL (Kinetic Networks, 2008) – not to be mistaken for Kettle described below – is developed by Kinetic Networks from which support can also purchased. The latest version of KETL is 2.1.24 from April 2008. The oldest generally available release in the 2.1 series is 2.1.12 from April 2007. KETL is partly released under the GPL license and partly under the LGPL license. The homepage for KETL states that the documentation currently is being overhauled and that only the Installation Guide has already been updated. Older versions of the documentation are still available in the mean

time. However, these (37 pages Administration Guide and 24 slides in a Training Presentation) fail to describe how ETL jobs are defined in the used XML language. More than 60 example XML files are available but they also lack documentation.

KETL is ROLAP oriented and can be used with JDBC sources (KETL has special support for three DBMSs) and flat files as well as XML files. The user must specify the ETL jobs in an XML file. Transformations are apparently possible, but due to the missing documentation it is not clear how to create them. Likewise, it is unclear if incremental loads are supported. KETL is capable of executing parts in parallel.

Kettle / Pentaho Data Integration

Kettle (Pentaho, 2008c) started as an independent open source ETL project, but was in 2006 acquired by Pentaho to be included in the Pentaho BI suite (Pentaho, 2008b). Thus Kettle is now also branded under the name Pentaho Data Integration. This survey considers version 3.0 of Kettle (3.0.0 was released in Nov. 2007, 3.0.4 in June 2008), but version 3.1 is expected to be released soon. Kettle is released under the LGPL. Kettle has a graphical designer for jobs and transformations. This designer has a manual of 274 pages and also 40 pages with frequently asked questions (FAQs) and answers. Further, very active forums exist (more than 22,000 posts in 5,000 threads in the last 2½ years). Pentaho offers support, training and consulting, but many Pentaho partners also offer such services.

Kettle is ROLAP oriented but another open source project (Gimenez & Lopez, 2007) provides a plug-in that enables Kettle to output data to the Palo MOLAP server. Kettle supports around 35 different DBMSs (also generic JDBC and ODBC) as well as a variety of flat files. A 3rd party SAP connector is also available, but it is not yet ready for version 3.0 and it is commercial. Incremental load is possible in the sense that Kettle logs when a job was executed and it is possible to use this timestamp in the queries to only select new data. Further, an "insert or update" step is available. ETL jobs are specified in a GUI. Kettle is shipped with more than 80 predefined transformations, and further the user can implement transformations in Java and JavaScript. Kettle also supports debugging of transformations with breakpoints etc. It is possible to use "clustering" where a transformation step can be split into parts that are executed on distinct servers. Apart from that, parallel jobs are not supported in version 3.0, but planned for the up-coming 3.1 release. Junk dimensions and slowly changing dimensions of type 1 and 2 (Kimball & Ross, 2002) are supported by Kettle and for some DBMSs (experimental) bulk loading can be applied.

Octopus

Octopus (Together Teamlösungen, 2007) is an ETL tool from Enhydra.org with the LGPL license. Here version 3.6-5 from Oct. 2007 is considered (3.6-1 was released in June 2006). A manual of 122 pages exists for Octopus and further a mailing list exists. The latter is, however, not very active and has had 2 posts in the first half of 2008 and 25 in all of 2007. Commercial support for Enhydra.org's products is available from Together Teamlösungen and other commercial vendors.

Octopus is also ROLAP oriented and uses JDBC to connect to data sources and targets. ETL jobs are specified in XML files (a GUI for generating skeletons for these XML files as well as file dumps of the database content exists, though). Octopus can update values, but does not support incremental loads in more advanced ways. It is possible to implement transformations in Java and JavaScript. Further, Octopus has a few predefined transformations for setting a default value, ensuring a maximum length of a string, and for correction of foreign key values. Parallel job parts and bulk loading are apparently not supported.

Palo ETL Server

Palo ETL Server (Jedox, 2008a) is developed by Jedox AG from which commercial support and training options are also available. Palo ETL Server is released under the GPL. Version 1.0 was released in April 2008 and followed by 1.1 in July 2008. A manual with 56 pages is freely available. A forum with some activity also exists.

Palo ETL Server is the only considered ETL tool that is MOLAP oriented as it is made for loading data into the Palo MOLAP server also created by Jedox AG (described later). It loads data from JDBC sources and CSV files, LDAP servers, and MOLAP cubes/dimensions. Jobs are specified in XML (a GUI is planned for a future release), and transformations can be implemented in Java. The jobs can be parameterized such that incremental loads to some degree can be supported. Parallel jobs are not supported.

Pequel

Pequel (Gaffiero, 2007) is the only considered ETL tool that is not written in Java. It is implemented in Perl and runs on UNIX-like platforms and on Windows using Cygwin. Pequel's license is GPL. Version 3.0.94 of Pequel is considered here, but as the documentation is not complete, documentation for version 2.4.6 has also been used. The documentation for version 3.0 consists of a Programmer's Reference (30 pages) and a Pequel Type Catalog (54 pages) which are both quite technical and serve as documentation for the Pequel source code. For version 2.4, a User Guide (72 pages) also exists but with many sections that have been left empty. Forums exist, but the traffic is low (no posts from Sep. 2007 to June 2008). No commercial support offerings were found in this survey.

Pequel generates Perl and C code for the load job. It is mainly targeted at processing files to generate other files. However, support for relations using Perl's DBI module also exists. A job is specified either by means of function calls or by means of an XML file. Data conversion and rejection of records (based on regular expressions) are possible. Further, the user can use Perl's functions and operators. It is possible to distribute read data records to different Pequel processes and merge them again and in this way execute parts in parallel.

Scriptella

Scriptella (Kupolov, 2008) is an ETL and script execution tool. It is released under the Apache License. Here, version 1.0beta is considered. A manual of 23 pages exists as well as a forum. The developer offers commercial support and consulting.

Scriptella is intended for ROLAP-use (as well as output to files) and JDBC drivers for different DBMSs are included together with JDBC drivers for different flat files, XML files, and LDAP servers (but any other JDBC driver can also be used). ETL jobs are specified in an XML file where Java or any scripting language compatible with the JSR-223 standard can be used directly. In a Scriptella script, data rows can be fetched from multiple connections by queries. In the script it is specified what to do for each row in the query result (e.g., perform an SQL statement using the values from the result of the outer query, or apply certain transformations). It is possible to nest queries and scripts written in different languages while still sharing variables. Scriptella's focus is on simplicity and it does not have out-of-the-box transformations available or incremental load support. On the other hand, the simplicity of using code for user-defined transformations and logic should be noted.

Talend Open Studio / JasperETL

Talend Open Studio (Talend, 2008) is developed by Talend that also offers support, training and consulting. The GPL-licensed Talend Open Studio is also included in the open source BI package

from JasperSoft (JasperSoft, 2008), there under the name JasperETL. The survey considers version 2.3 of Talend Open Studio (2.3.0 was released in Feb. 2008, 2.3.3 in May 2008), but since the data was collected, version 2.4.0 has been released. Compared to the other open source ETL tools, it has a large printable documentation with a User's Guide (161 pages) and a Reference Guide (550 pages). However, personal information, like name and email, must be given to access this documentation.

Talend Open Studio is primarily ROLAP oriented, but output to the Palo MOLAP server is also supported. Talend claims to support more than 100 different source systems. These include different DBMSs, files, and web services, Subversion logs etc. Further CRM systems like SugarCRM, CentricCRM, SalesForce.com, and VtigerCRM are supported. The ETL jobs are specified in a GUI. Like Pequel, Talend Open Studio generates code for a standalone ETL application. The generated code is Java or Perl. It is possible for the user to specify transformations (also in Java or Perl). Further, Talend Open Studio comes with a set of predefined transformations, including six for data quality (matching, replacing, etc.) and from version 2.4 also name and address parsing (but only when Perl code is generated). The generated code can execute parts in parallel, but the parallelism support in Talend is still being extended. Talend supports slowly changing dimensions and bulk load, while incremental load is done by use of look-ups possibly followed by inserts or updates.

Summary

Compared to the previous survey (Thomsen & Pedersen, 2005), many more open source ETL tools are available today. Also, the quality of the existing tools seems to have increased a lot in the meantime. Four out of the ten tools include GUIs where ETL jobs are specified and for one of the remaining tools, a closed source (but free for non-commercial use) GUI exists.

Nine out of the ten described tools are implemented in Java and the remaining one in Perl and all the tools thus run on many different platforms. The tools are primarily targeted at ROLAP (Palo ETL Server being the exception) and in general support a variety of relational DBMSs as well as generic JDBC, common file formats like Excel and XML. Some of the tools can also extract data from ERP and CRM systems, but not all of these connectors are for free.

The most notable tools are Kettle and Talend which both have large user communities, comprehensive documentation, and many features and are included in BI suites.

DATABASE MANAGEMENT SYSTEMS

In previous work (Thomsen & Pedersen, 2005), the category of DBMSs was considered to be the most mature of the considered categories. Also, for the current survey many mature DBMSs have been found. More open source DBMSs than those described below exist, but they have a low visibility compared to the described ones and/or are mainly for use-cases that are less relevant for BI usage, e.g., for embedded usage with smaller data sets.

Firebird

Firebird (Firebird Project, 2008) is based on the code base for the commercial DBMS InterBase version 6.0. The current version of Firebird is 2.1 (from April 2008). Firebird uses two licenses which are both similar to the Mozilla Public License (MPL). Firebird runs on Windows, Linux, FreeBSD, and MacOS X. Binary releases for Solaris and HP-UX are not yet available for version 2.1, but are available for the 2.0 series from November 2006. Firebird is a commercially independent project, but a large part of the development is done by the company IBPhoenix which also offers support, training, and consulting. The

documentation for Firebird is still not complete. On the homepage it is stated that the project is working on full user's and reference guides, but that the current documentation still consists of the manuals for InterBase 6.0 combined with the Firebird release notes that describe changes made to the Firebird code. All changes between InterBase 6.0 and Firebird 1.5 are documented, but updates for 2.0 and 2.1 are still in preparation. Apart from this documentation, different (rather short) guides and manuals exist in PDF and HTML format. Active mailing lists exist for the project (the support list has had around 95,000 posts since November 2000).

On-disk bitmap indexes are not supported, but Firebird can combine indexes and form bitmaps in memory. Firebird does not support materialized views, star joins or partitioning. Replication is not available in the Firebird distribution itself, but (both commercial and open source) 3rd party tools provide this. With respect to data sizes, it should be noted that tables are limited to 2 billion rows in Firebird, but that there is no limit on the byte-size of databases (the largest known database has more than 11TB data). It is reported that the current Firebird has problems with scalability on computers with multiple CPUs, but these problems will be solved in the coming Firebird version 3.0.

The user can implement stored procedures (SPs) in Firebird's procedural language PSQL. Further user-defined functions (UDFs) can be loaded from external shared object libraries and, thus, the user can implement in C, C++, Delphi, etc.

Ingres Database

Ingres Database (Ingres, 2008) developed by Ingres is available under a commercial license (this is the "Enterprise Edition" of Ingres Database) or under the GPL (the "Community Edition"). The current version is Ingres 2006 Release 2 but Release 3 is available in a beta version. Ingres supports its products for 15 years, but support and maintenance from Ingres is only available for the

Enterprise Edition (however other independent companies also provide support and training). Ingres Database runs on Windows and a variety of different UNIX-like platforms. Active community forums exist and Ingres also offers 25 free manuals with close to 8,000 pages in total.

Materialized views, bitmap indexes, and star joins are not supported. Multi-master replication and partitioning (based on range, value, or hash) including sub-partitioning are supported out-of-the-box in Ingres Database. With respect to scalability, Ingres claims that Ingres Database is capable of handling many terabytes of data easily.

SQL can be used for stored procedures and further user-defined functions can be implemented in C.

LucidDB

LucidDB (*LucidDB*, 2008) is developed by the software company LucidEra and the non-profit organization The Eigenbase Project. The LucidDB server is licensed under the GPL while the LucidDB client is licensed under the LGPL. The newest version of LucidDB is version 0.7.3 from March 2008. On LucidDB's homepage, it is stated that LucidDB is "purpose-built entirely for data warehousing and business intelligence". This is in contrast to the other considered tools apart from MonetDB (see below). LucidDB and MonetDB are also the only considered column-stores (Abadi, Madden, & Hachem, 2008). In a column-store, all data tables are split vertically at the physical layer such that each column is stored on-disk independently of other columns. This is different from traditional row-stores where data from different columns is stored together in rows.

LucidDB runs on 32 and 64 bit Linux and on 32 bit Windows (using Cygwin). LucidEra does explicitly not intend to sell support or commercial licenses for LucidDB. The documentation consists of relatively short wiki manuals and tutorials. Further, there is a mailing list but this has had less than 100 posts from May 2007 to May 2008.

LucidDB supports B-tree and bitmap indexes. LucidDB chooses itself which indexes to create and can also combine the two types. Star joins are also supported, while partitioning and replication is not supported. Support for materialized views is planned for a future release. It is reported that LucidDB has been tested with 10GB TPC-H data, but the performance results have not been found during this survey. User-defined functions can be created in Java. It is also possible to wrap external data sources like files or tables from another DBMS and use them as traditional tables from LucidDB.

While LucidDB offers many features relevant for data warehousing, it should be noted that it is still not a mature DBMS. For example, foreign keys, sub-queries, transaction handling, and support for altering table definitions are still missing.

MonetDB

MonetDB (CWI, 2008) is the second column-store considered in this survey. Like LucidDB, it is not a DBMS made for on-line transactional processing (OLTP) with highly concurrent workloads. Instead the focus is on efficient handling of query-intensive access patterns. MonetDB is developed by the research institute CWI and has a license similar to the MPL. It runs on Windows and different UNIX-like operating systems. In the implementation, care has been taken to use the hardware very efficiently. In this survey the "Feb2008" release of MonetDB is considered (the "Jun2008" release became available at the end of June 2008). A manual with 260 pages is provided for MonetDB. Further, a manual of 113 pages exist for the SQL part of MonetDB. A commercial spin-off that offered support existed but this has been acquired by another company and no commercial support for the current MonetDB has been found during this survey. An active mailing list also exists.

Like LucidDB, MonetDB itself picks which indexes to create. However, bitmap indexes seem to be unsupported. Partitioning, replication, and materialized views are also currently unsupported, but future additions are planned for these areas. The user can define stored procedures in SQL as well as external functions in MonetDB's proprietary MAL language and in C.

MySQL

MySQL (MySQL, 2008), developed by MySQL (now owned by Sun Microsystems), is available under a commercial license or under the GPL. It can be downloaded in two versions: The "Community Server" which is free and the "MySQL Enterprise" edition which is not free, but for which extra features and commercial services exist. The latest production release of the community server is 5.0.51 from April 2008 (the first production release from the 5.0 series was from October 2005), and version 5.1 is available as a release candidate. Sun offers a wide range of commercial support, consulting, and training. It is reported that MySQL-based data warehouses larger than 30 terabytes exist. MySQL runs on Windows and a large collection of UNIX-like systems. The manual has 2071 pages and further very active forums exist.

There is no support for star joins or materialized views. Also partitioning is not supported in the 5.0 series, but is available in the upcoming 5.1 series where range, list, hash, and key partitioning are supported. Statement-based master-slave asynchronous replication has been available in MySQL since version 3.23, but from release 5.1, row-based replication is also available. Synchronous replication is also possible using MySQL Cluster but it is stated in the manual that "all live data storage is done in memory" then (from version 5.1 non-indexed columns can be saved on-disk). On-disk bitmap indexes are not supported in MySQL, but MySQL can perform an index merge where a bitmap is built in-memory. The user can implement stored procedures in SQL and user-defined functions in C/C++.

PostgreSQL

PostgreSQL (PostgreSQL Global Development Group, 2008) is released under the BSD license. The newest version is 8.3.3 from June 2008 (8.3.0 was released in February 2008). PostgreSQL runs on Windows and on a large collection of UNIX-like operating systems. PostgreSQL's development is led by its community and not by a single company. Due to its non-restrictive BSD license, several (open source and commercial) derivatives exist. For example, Netezza (Netezza, 2008), EnterpriseDB (EnterpriseDB, 2008), and Greenplum (Greenplum, 2008) offer PostgreSQL-based products. Several companies also offer commercial support, training and consulting. The PostgreSQL manual consists of 1908 pages and very active mailing lists also exist as well as Internet Relay Chats (IRCs) in more languages. It is reported that databases larger than 4 terabytes are used in production environments.

Materialized views and star joins are not supported in PostgreSQL. On-disk bitmaps are not supported yet but they are planned for inclusion in a future version. PostgreSQL does already support creation of an in-memory bitmap when combining other, existing indexes. Partitioning is to some degree supported by means of PostgreSQL's table inheritance features. The user has to create each partition manually and to create logic for redirecting inserts to the correct partition. The solution does not work well with parameterized queries and enforcement of integrity constraints. In the current PostgreSQL distribution, replication is not supported out-of-the-box as this deliberately has been left to let 3rd party tools offer competing solutions. As this standpoint is now considered to hinder acceptance of PostgreSQL, it has been decided to include simple asynchronous replication in the future standard distributions. But for the current PostgreSQL and for more advanced use-cases in the future, existing 3rd party tools (for example, Slony-I (Slony Development Group, 2008) and Pgpool-II (Ishii et al., 2007)) already offer replication.

PostgreSQL offers several languages for user-defined functions: PL/pgSQL, PL/Tcl, and PL/Python. Further, it is possible to add new language support (for example, Java is supported this way). The user can also create external functions in C libraries.

Summary

Many open source DBMSs are available and overall they have reached a high maturity, also with respect to commercial support etc. Some features offered by leading commercial DBMSs are, however, still missing from the open source DBMSs. For example, none of the considered DBMSs support materialized views and most of them do not support on-disk bitmaps, star joins, and partitioning. Nevertheless, the open source DBMSs provide sufficient functionality for many BI projects and they are being used for large BI projects in industry. Ingres Database, MySQL, and PostgreSQL are notable for their documentation, large user communities and rich feature sets.

ON-LINE ANALYTICAL PROCESSING SERVERS

Not many open source on-line analytical processing (OLAP) servers are available. For this survey, only two open source OLAP servers with running code were found. This might be due to the success of the first of them, Mondrian. This server is included in the leading open source BI packages and uses de-facto standards and is a very popular choice for ROLAP usage.

Mondrian / Pentaho Analysis Services

Mondrian (Pentaho, 2008a) started as an independent open source project developing an OLAP server in 2002. In late 2005, Mondrian joined forces with Pentaho and is now being developed as part of Pentaho's BI package (Mondrian can be downloaded and used without the rest of the Pentaho software). Mondrian is a relational OLAP (ROLAP) server. The most recent version of Mondrian is 3.0.3 from May 2008 (the 3.0 series was released in March 2008). It is released under the Common Public License (CPL). As Mondrian is implemented in Java, it runs on many platforms and uses JDBC such that it can be used with most DBMSs. The documentation consists of HTML pages with relatively large contents – close to 200 pages of text in printing. Further, active forums exist. Commercial support, consulting, and training are available from Pentaho and its partners.

The Mondrian project is involved in the standardization work for the olap4j specification which is intended to become a common API for OLAP servers (a kind of JDBC for multidimensional data). The primary API to Mondrian is olap4j. Further, Mondrian is shipped with support for XML for Analysis (XMLA) (Microsoft & Hyperion Solutions, 2002). Queries to Mondrian are expressed in the de-facto standard in industry, MultiDimensional eXpressions (MDX) (Spofford, Harinath, Webb, Huang, & Civardi, 2008). Cubes are specified by means of an XML file. GUIs for creating these XML files do exist, but they are still described as incubator projects and have version numbers starting with 0.

With respect to scalability, it is stated in the FAQ for Mondrian, that large data sets can be handled if the underlying RDBMS can handle them, since all aggregation is delegated to the DBMS. Mondrian does have support for use of pre-computed aggregate tables. Users are reporting that Mondrian performance is good even when handling hundreds of gigabytes data with hundreds of millions rows in industrial settings.

Palo

Palo (Jedox, 2008b) is a multidimensional OLAP (MOLAP) server developed by Jedox AG. It is available under a commercial license or under the GPL. Windows and Linux are the primarily supported platforms. Commercial support and consulting is available from Jedox. A manual of around 376 pages exist but costs €29.50. Active forums for Palo also exist. For this survey, version 2.0 was considered but version 2.5 was released in early July 2008.

Palo loads its data set completely into memory and thus the memory on the host computer limits the supported data sets. Proprietary programming interfaces to communicate with Palo exist for Java, .NET, PHP, and C. There is also a free, but closed-source add-in for Microsoft Excel – the manual for Palo even states that "Palo was developed for Microsoft Excel". Using the plug-in, Palo-specific constructs like PALO.DATAC(...) can be used in formulas. The Excel add-in can also be used to specify cubes.

Summary

Only two open source OLAP servers with running code were found. They are targeting different segments as Mondrian is a ROLAP server which can handle large data volumes while Palo is a memory-based (and thus also memory-limited) MOLAP server. The Mondrian OLAP server seems very popular as it is not only included in the developer company's (i.e., Pentaho's) BI suite, but also in other open source BI suites. Both of the OLAP servers are used in industry for BI projects.

ON-LINE ANALYTICAL PROCESSING CLIENTS

Compared to the previous survey (Thomsen & Pedersen, 2005) where only two open source OLAP clients were found, many more products are available at the time of this writing. From the previous survey, JPivot is still actively developed and parts of it are also used in other products.

FreeAnalysis

FreeAnalysis (BPM Conseil, 2008) is developed by BPM Conseil from which commercial support, training, and consulting also can be bought. From the downloadable code, the license is not clear. Previously the MPL and a license derived from the MPL have been used. A (currently empty) project created for FreeAnalysis on Google Code also states that the license is MPL. Version 1.14 from June 2008 is considered here. FreeAnalysis is implemented in Java and can be used as a standalone application or as a web application. A manual of 13 pages is available in French and another two-page document with an example of a connection specification is also available. It is, however, said that a URL to a manual will be given to those who subscribe to FreeAnalysis's mailing list.

FreeAnalysis works with Mondrian and servers that use XMLA and FreeAnalysis generates MDX queries. Reports in FreeAnalysis consist of pivot tables and graphs (the JFreeChart package (Object Refinery Limited, 2008) is included in the distribution). FreeAnalysis does also support generation of cube definitions for the Mondrian OLAP server (described above).

JPalo Client and JPalo Web Client

JPalo Client (Tensegrity Software, 2008) is a standalone application while JPalo Web Client is an Ajax-based web application. Both products are developed by Tensegrity Software and available under a commercial license or the GPL. The most recent version for both is 2.0 from June 2008. JPalo is here used to refer generically to JPalo Client and JPalo Web Client. As suggested by the name, JPalo works with the Palo server. It offers modeling and administration for the Palo server as well as tabular exploration of the data (in JPalo Client the data can also be represented in charts). But JPalo can also be used with XMLA-enabled sources. In any case, the user can explore the data in the GUI without typing queries manually. JPalo is implemented in Java and JPalo Web Client does not require any installation on the end-user's computer. During this survey, no manual for JPalo was found. Forums for JPalo exist and have some activity.

JMagallanes Olap & Reports

JMagallanes Olap & Reports is an open source component of Grupo Calipso's JMagallanes suite (Grupo Calypso, 2006) where other components are closed source. The latest version is 1.0 from May 2006. The development company sells support and installation services. The documentation consists of videos and some rather short HTML documents. Forums do exist, but have had little activity lately. JMagallanes Olap & Reports is distributed under the BSD license.

The open source part of JMagallanes reads data from JDBC sources as well as XML and Microsoft Excel. Apart from static reports based on JasperReports, the user can explore the data in pivot tables and with charts based on JFreeCharts. Data can be exported to PDF, XML, Excel, CVS and HTML. It is possible to schedule reports and have them sent by email.

JPivot

JPivot (Tonbeller, 2008), developed by Tonbeller, is among the first open source OLAP clients and parts of its code are also used in some of the more recent clients. JPivot is also included in BI suites like those from Pentaho and JasperSoft. JPivot is licensed under the CPL. The newest version of JPivot is version 1.8 from March 2008. It is a web application implemented in Java and JavaServer Pages (JSP) and thus the end-user uses a normal web browser to explore the data. Some HTML documentation exists for the JSP tags and for the Java source code. Apart from this, active forums exist for JPivot (and for the BI suites that include it).

JPivot was originally developed to be used with Mondrian, but it can now be used with other XMLA-enabled servers as well (the JPivot project is also involved in the olap4j specification). JPivot generates MDX queries. The user explores data by means of pivot tables and graphs (the latter are based on JFreeChart) and can choose to enter MDX queries manually. Support for exporting data to Excel format and PDF is present.

JRubik

JRubik (*Introduction to JRubik*, 2005) is an OLAP client which is based on JPivot components. JRubik is, however, a standalone Java application while JPivot is a web application. It is licensed under the CPL. The documentation is in HTML format and is relatively short. A forum with some activity exists. Version 0.9.4 was released in December 2006. That version only worked with Mondrian. In May, 2008, a new version of JRubik using the new olap4j definition was released (with version number 0.0.0). In both versions, the tool generates MDX queries.

The user explores data by means of pivot tables, charts (again from JFreeChart), or in a map component. Tabular data can be exported to PDF, XML, HTML, and Excel. Chart data can be exported to XML and HTML.

OpenI

OpenI (OpenI.Org, 2008) was developed by the company Loyalty Matrix from which commercial support was also available. The company has now been acquired by another company and its technology is being integrated into a closed source application. It is therefore not known if the OpenI project will continue. The existing source code is available under a license similar to the MPL. The documentation is in HTML and rather short. Forums exist and have been active. Lately the activity has been limited, though.

OpenI is implemented in Java and thus runs on different platforms. OpenI connects to XMLA sources and generates MDX queries. The user explores data in tables and charts which are based on components from JPivot and JFreeChart, respectively.

REX

REX (*SourceForge.net: REX*, 2007) is an – untraditional – abbreviation of "wa*r*ehouse *explorer*". The latest release is 0.7 from November 2007. It is released under the LGPL. The documentation consists of a tutorial. Some forums do exist, but they are not very active with less than 60 messages in three years. No commercial support offerings for REX were found during this survey.

REX is implemented in Java and runs on many different platforms. It works with XMLA sources and generates MDX queries. Data is browsed in pivot tables and charts using JPivot and JFreeChart components, respectively.

Summary

All the considered OLAP clients are implemented in Java. Six of the eight tools run directly on the client while the two remaining run on a web server. JPivot is widely spread since it is included in different BI suites. JPivot components are also used in four of the other OLAP clients. While many more clients are available compared to the previous survey (Thomsen & Pedersen, 2005), it is still the case that the OLAP client category leaves some room for improvements. The available documentation is limited and in some cases also the available support possibilities.

INTEGRATED BUSINESS INTELLIGENCE SUITES

The focus of this survey is not on pre-packed, integrated BI suites, but instead on the individual tools that can be used at the different layers in a full BI solution. This provides flexibility for a completely customized solution. Integrated open source BI packages do, however, also exist. In this section integrated packages are briefly described.

JasperSoft Business Intelligence Suite

JasperSoft Business Intelligence Suite (JasperSoft, 2008) from JasperSoft ships with MySQL and the web server Tomcat (The Apache Software Foundation, 2008) such that it can be used out-of-the-box. Further, it includes JasperServer for ad-hoc queries, reports, charts, crosstabs and dashboards. It is also possible to schedule, share, and interact with reports using JasperServer. JasperSoft Business Intelligence Suite also includes JasperAnalysis for OLAP and JasperETL. These are based on Mondrian/JPivot and Talend, respectively. Finally, the JasperReports reporting tool is included in the suite.

Pentaho Open BI Suite

Pentaho Open BI Suite (Pentaho, 2008b) from Pentaho does not have a DBMS in the package. Pre-configured setups that use Firebird or MySQL do exist for easy testing, though. The suite includes Pentaho Data Integration, also known as Kettle. It also includes Pentaho Analysis with Mondrian and JPivot as well as Pentaho Dashboards. A reporting tool (based on JFreeReports which are now developed as part of the Pentaho suite) and the data mining tool Weka (Pentaho, 2008d) are also included.

SpagoBI

SpagoBI (Engineering Ingegneria Informatica, 2008) from OW2 Consortium is an integration platform. As it is an integration platform, and not a product platform, it is not made to use a certain tool set. Instead different "engines" (closed or open source) can be used, even at the same time. Thus, SpagoBI has drivers that integrate other tools into the platform such that, for example, Talend can be used as ETL tool and Mondrian as OLAP server in a SpagoBI project. SpagoBI's behavioral model regulates visibility of data and documents. Also, administration tools for scheduling, configuration, etc. are included. A tool for designing and maintaining analytical documents and module for metadata management are also included in SpagoBI.

CONCLUSION

Compared to the findings in the last survey of open source BI tools from 2005 (Thomsen & Pedersen, 2005), there has been a strong development. Many more tools are available and their maturity has improved. In the current survey, ten ETL tools, six DBMSs, two OLAP servers, and seven OLAP clients were considered. As in the previous survey, the DBMS category is the most mature. The DBMSs have many advanced features, and good commercial support and documentation are available. The ETL tool category has improved a lot compared to the previous survey. ETL tools with advanced features and GUIs now exist. The OLAP servers are still dominated by the ROLAP server Mondrian which has been developed further and now offers better and faster functionality. For the OLAP clients, there are also many tools available, but this category seems to lack a little behind and leave room for new "killer applications".

While this survey considers many pre-defined general criteria for the different categories, there are other factors to consider for the specific cases. Issues like stability and performance are also important for BI projects. As the tools were not configured and run in this survey, it was not possible to investigate these issues.

Future work includes building two full BI solutions for the same purpose and data sets. One of them will be built using open source tools while the other will be built with commercially licensed tools. For such two solutions, it is interesting to investigate the possible differences in development time, ease-of-use, features and problems.

ACKNOWLEDGMENT

This work was supported by the Agile & Open Business Intelligence (AOBI) project co-funded by the Regional ICT Initiative under the Danish Council for Technology and Innovation.

REFERENCES

Abadi, D. J., Madden, S. R., & Hachem, N. (2008). Column-Stores vs. Row-Stores: How Different Are They Really? In Wang, J. T.-L. (Ed.), *Proceedings of the ACM SIGMOD International Conference on Management of Data, SIGMOD 2008* (pp. 967-980). New York: ACM.

BPM Conseil (2008). *http://freeanalysis.org.* Retrieved August 7, 2008 from http://freeanalysis.org/.

Chen, X., Ye, Y., Williams, G., Xu, X. (2007). A Survey of Open Source Data Mining Systems. In Washio, T., et al., *Proceedings of Emerging Technologies in Knowledge Discovery and Data Mining, PAKDD 2007, International Workshops* (pp. 3-14). Berlin Heidelberg: Springer.

Clover.ETL – open source data integration tool (2008). Retrieved August 7, 2008 from http://cloveretl.org/.

CWI (2008). *Query Processing at Light Speed.* Retrieved August 7, 2008 from http://monetdb.cwi.nl/.

Engineering Ingegneria Informatica (2008). *Spago Solutions – SpagoBI.* Retrieved August 7, 2008 from http://spagobi.org/.

EnterpriseDB (2008). *Postgres Plus – Open Source Database | EnterpriseDB.* Retrieved August 7, 2008 from http://www.enterprisedb.com/.

Firebird Project (2008). *Firebird – The RDBMS that's going where you're going.* Retrieved August 7, 2008 from http://firebirdsql.org/.

Gaffiero, M. (2007). *SourceForge.net: Pequel ETL Data Transformation Engine.* Retrieved August 7, 2008 from http://sourceforge.net/projects/pequel/.

Gimenez, J. & Lopez, J. (2007). *SourceForge.net: PaloKettlePlugin.* Retrieved August 7, 2008 from http://sourceforge.net/palokettleplug/.

Greenplum (2008). *Greenplum database redefines data warehousing, the bi database, and the data warehouse appliance.* Retrieved August 7, 2008 from http://greenplum.com/.

Grupo Calypso (2006). *JMagallanes.* Retrieved August 7, 2008 from http://jmagallanes.sourceforge.net/en/.

Ingres (2008). *Enterprise Open Source Database – Ingres.* Retrieved August 7, 2008 from http://ingres.com/.

Introduction to JRubik (2005). Retrieved August 7, 2008 from http://rubik.sourceforge.net/jrubik/intro.html.

Ishii, T., et al. (2007). *pgpool-II README.* Retrieved August 7, 2008 from http://pgpool.projects.postgresql.org/.

JasperSoft (2008). *JasperSoft – Open Source Business Intelligence.* Retrieved August 7, 2008 from http://jaspersoft.com/.

Jedox (2008a). *Introduction to ETL | Jedox-Enterprise Spreadsheets für Excel.* Retrieved August 7, 2008 from http://www.jedox.com/en/enterprise-spreadsheet-server/etl-server/introduction.html.

Jedox (2008b). *Palo Open-Source OLAP for Excel – Multidimensional Database for Budgeting, Forecasting, Planning, Reporting, MOLAP, Analysis Software - Business Performance Management (Excel-friendly OLAP) | Jedox - Enterprise Spreadsheets für Excel.* Retrieved August 7, 2008 from http://www.jedox.com/en/enterprise-spreadsheet-server/excel-olap-server/palo-server.html.

JBIWiki: ETLSE (2008). Retrieved August 7, 2008 from http://wiki.open-esb.java.net/Wiki.jsp?page=ETLSE.

Kimball, R. & Ross, M. (2002). *The Data Warehouse Toolkit* (2nd ed.). New York: John Wiley & Sons.

Kinetic Networks (2008). *KETL.org – Designed to support the community that uses the KETL™ open source ETL product.* Retrieved August 7, 2008 from http://ketl.org/.

Kupolov, F. (2008). *Welcome to Scriptella ETL Project.* Retrieved August 7, 2008 from http://scriptella.javaforge.com/.

LucidDB Home Page (2008). Retrieved August 7, 2008 from http://luciddb.org/.

Microsoft, & Hyperion Solutions (2002). *XML for Analysis Specification.* Retrieved from http://www.xmlforanalysis.com/xmla1.1.doc.

MySQL (2008). *MySQL :: The world's most popular open source database.* Retrieved August 7, 2008 from http://mysql.com/.

Netezza (2008). *Data warehouse appliances, data warehousing, Netezza, Netezza.com.* Retrieved August 7, 2008 from http://netezza.com/.

Object Refinery Limited (2008). *JFreeChart.* Retrieved August 7, 2008 from http://www.jfree.org/jfreechart/.

Open Source Initiative (2006). *Open Source Licenses*. Retrieved from http://opensource.org/licenses.

OpenI.Org (2008). *openi.org - Open Source Web Application for OLAP Reporting*. Retrieved August 7, 2008 from http://openi.sourceforge.net/.

Pentaho (2008a). *Pentaho Analysis Services: Mondrian Project*. Retrieved August 7, 2008 from http://mondrian.pentaho.org/.

Pentaho (2008b). *Pentaho Commercial Open Source Business Intelligence: Home*. Retrieved August 7, 2008 from http://pentaho.org/.

Pentaho (2008c). *Pentaho Commercial Open Source Business Intelligence: Kettle Project*. Retrieved August 7, 2008 from http://kettle.pentaho.org/.

Pentaho (2008d). *Pentaho Commercial Open Source Business Intelligence: Weka Project*. Retrieved August 7, 2008 from http://weka.pentaho.org/.

PostgreSQL Global Development Group (2008). *PostgreSQL: The world's most advanced open source database*. Retrieved from http://postgresql.org/.

Slony Development Group (2008). *Slony-I*. Retrieved August 7, 2008 from http://www.slony.info/.

SourceForge.net: REX – waRehouse Explorer (2007). Retrieved August 7, 2008 from http://sourceforge.net/projects/whex/.

Spofford, G., Harinath, S., Webb, C., Huang, D. H., & Civardi, F. (2006). *MDX Solutions* (2nd ed.). New York: John Wiley & Sons.

Sun (2008). *GlassFish ESB*. Retrieved August 7, 2008 from http://glassfishesb.org/.

Talend (2008). *Talend – first provider of open source data integration software*. Retrieved August 7, 2008 from http://talend.com/.

Tensegrity Software (2008). *JPalo – Palo Java World – Business Intelligence Reporting*. Retrieved August 7, 2008 from http://www.jpalo.com/en/products/start_products.html.

The Apache Software Foundation (2008). *Apache Tomcat – Apache Tomcat*. Retrieved August 7, 2008 from http://tomcat.apache.org/.

Thomsen, C. & Pedersen, T. B. (2005). A Survey of Open Source Tools for Business Intelligence. In Tjoa, A. M. & Trujillo, J. (Eds.), *Proceedings of the 7th International Conference on Data Warehousing and Knowledge Discovery* (pp. 74-84). Berlin Heidelberg: Springer.

Together Teamlösungen (2007). *JDBC Data Transformations*. Retrieved August 7, 2008 from http://www.enhydra.org/tech/octopus/.

Tonbeller (2008). *JPivot – Home*. Retrieved August 7, 2008 from http://jpivot.sourceforge.net/.

Yuhanna, N. (2006). *The Forrester Wave™: Open Source Databases, Q2, 2006*. Cambridge, MA, USA: Forrester.

APPENDIX: TABULAR SUMMARY

ETL tools / *Criteria*	Apatar	Clover.ETL	ETL Integrator	KETL	Kettle
License	GPL or commercial	LGPL or commercial	CDDL	GPL	LGPL
Platform	Java	Java	Java	Java	Java
Support	Yes	Yes	Not found	Yes	Yes
Documentation and forums	~40 pages PDF	181 pages for GUI, wiki and slides	Design doc.s, videos, tutorials.	Deprecated	274 + 40 pages
Category	ROLAP	ROLAP	ROLAP	ROLAP	ROLAP
Sources	DBMSs, files, ERP, CRM	DBMSs, files	DBMSs, files, ERP, CRM	DBMSs, files	DBMSs, files
Targets	Same	Same	DBMSs	Same	DBMS, files
Inc. load	No	No	Yes	?	Yes via timestamp
Job spec.	GUI	XML (commercial GUI avail.)	GUI	XML	GUI
Own transformations	Java	Java and TL	Java	?	Java, JavaScript
Parallel jobs	No	Yes	Yes	Yes	From next version

ETL tools / *Criteria*	Octopus	Palo ETL Server	Pequel	Scriptella	Talend
License	LGPL	GPL	GPL	Apache	GPL
Platform	Java	Java	Perl	Java	Java
Support	Yes	Yes	?	Yes	Yes
Documentation and forums	122 pages	56 pages	72 pages User's guide (deprecated)	23 pages	161 + 550 pages
Category	ROLAP	MOLAP	Files and ROLAP	ROLAP	ROLAP
Sources	JDBC	JDBC, CSV, Palo, LDAP	Files and DBMSs	DBMSs, files	DBMSs, files, CRM, Palo
Targets	JDBC	Palo	Same	Same	Same
Inc. load	Can update	Not directly	No	No	Can update
Job spec.	XML	XML	XML	XML	GUI
Own transformations	Java, JavaScript	Java	Perl	Scripting lang.s	Java, Perl
Parallel jobs	No	No	Yes	No	Yes

DBMSs / Criteria	Firebird	Ingres	LucidDB
License	MPL-like	GPL or commercial	GPL + LGPL
Platform	Windows, Linux, MacOS X, FreeBSD, Solaris, HP-UX	UNIX-like, Windows	Linux, Windows (Cygwin)
Support	Yes	Yes	No
Documentation	Deprecated	~8000 pages	Wikis and tutorials
Mat. views	No	No	No (but planned)
Bitmap indexes	In-memory when combining indexes	No	Yes
Star joins	No	No	Yes
Partitioning	No	Yes	No
Replication	3rd party tools	Yes	No
Stored procedures and user-defined functions	PSQL, C, Delphi	SQL, C	Java

DBMSs / Criteria	MonetDB	MySQL	PostgreSQL
License	MPL-like	GPL or commercial	BSD
Platform	UNIX-like, Windows	UNIX-like, Windows	UNIX-like, Windows
Support	No	Yes	Yes
Documentation	260 + 113 pages	2071 pages	1908 pages
Mat. views	No	No	No
Bitmap indexes	No	In-memory when combining indexes	In-memory when combining indexes, on-disk planned
Star joins	No	No	No
Partitioning	No	From next version	Partly supported
Replication	No	Yes	3rd party tools
Stored procedures and user-defined functions	SQL, MAL, C	SQL, C	PL/pgSQL,PL/Tcl, PL/Python (and extensible to other lang.s), C

OLAP servers *Criteria*	Mondrian	Palo
License	CPL	GPL or commercial
Platform	Java	Primarily Linux and Windows
Support	Yes	Yes
Documentation	HTML (~200 pages of text)	~376 pages
Category	ROLAP (uses underlying DBMS)	MOLAP (memory-based)
DBMS	Any JDBC-compliant	n/a
Specification of cube	XML	Via Excel add-in or via API
Aggregate tables	Yes	No
API + query language	Olap4j, XMLA, MDX	Proprietary

OLAP clients *Criteria*	FreeAnalysis	JPalo Client and Web Client	JMagallanes Olap & Reports	JPivot
License	MPL	GPL or commercial	BSD	CPL
Platform	Web	Java and Web (Java), respectively	Java	Web (Java)
Support	Yes	Yes	Yes	Yes
Documentation	?	Not found	Videos and short HTML documents	Short HTML documents
OLAP servers / API	XMLA	Palo and XMLA	No OLAP server support. Connects to DBMSs, XML, and Excel	XMLA, olap4j
Reports	Tables and charts	Tables and charts (only tables in JPalo Web Client)	Tables and charts.	Tables and charts

OLAP clients *Criteria*	JRubik	OpenI	REX
License	CPL	MPL-like	LGPL
Platform	Java	Java	Java
Support	No	No	No
Documentation	Short HTML documents	Short HTML documents	Tutorial as HTML document
OLAP servers / API	Mondrian and exp. olap4j support	XMLA	XMLA
Reports	Tables, charts, and maps	Tables and charts	Tables and charts

This work was previously published in the International Journal of Data Warehousing & Mining 5(3), edited by David Taniar, pp. 56-75, copyright 2009 by IGI Publishing (an imprint of IGI Global).

Section 4

Chapter 11
Primary and Referential Horizontal Partitioning Selection Problems:
Concepts, Algorithms and Advisor Tool

Ladjel Bellatreche
University of Poitiers, France

Kamel Boukhalfa
University of Poitiers, France

Pascal Richard
University of Poitiers, France

ABSTRACT

Horizontal partitioning has evolved significantly in recent years and widely advocated by the academic and industrial communities. Horizontal Partitioning affects positively query performance, database manageability and availability. Two types of horizontal partitioning are supported: primary and referential. Horizontal fragmentation in the context of relational data warehouses is to partition dimension tables by primary fragmentation then fragmenting the fact table by referential fragmentation. This fragmentation can generate a very large number of fragments which may make the maintenance task very complicated. In this paper, we first focus on the evolution of horizontal partitioning in commercial DBMS motivated by decision support applications. Secondly, we give a formalization of the referential fragmentation schema selection problem in the data warehouse and we study its hardness to select an optimal solution. Due to its high complexity, we develop two algorithms: hill climbing and simulated annealing with several variants to select a near optimal partitioning schema. We present ParAdmin, an advisor tool assisting administrators to use primary and referential partitioning during the physical design of their data warehouses. Finally, extensive experimental studies are conducted using the data set of APB1 benchmark to compare the quality the proposed algorithms using a mathematical cost model. Based on these experiments, some recommendations are given to ensure the well use of horizontal partitioning.

DOI: 10.4018/978-1-60960-537-7.ch011

INTRODUCTION

Data warehouses store large volumes of data mainly in relational models such as star or snowflake schemas. A star schema contains a large fact table and various dimension tables. A star schema is usually queried in various combinations involving many tables. The most used operations are joins, aggregations and selections (Papadomanolakis & Ailamaki, 2004). Joins are well known to be expensive operations, especially when the involved relations are substantially larger than the size of the main memory (Lei & Ross, 1999) which is usually the case of business intelligence applications. The typical queries defined on the star schema are commonly referred to as star join queries, and exhibit the following two characteristics: (1) there is a multi-table join among the large fact table and multiple smaller dimension tables, and (2) each of the dimension tables involved in the join operation has multiple selection predicates on its descriptive attributes. To speed up star join queries, many optimization techniques were proposed. In (Bellatreche, Moussaoui, Necir & Drias, 2008), we classified them into two main categories: *redundant techniques* such as materialized views, advanced index schemes, vertical partitioning, parallel processing with replication and *non redundant techniques* like ad-hoc joins, where joins are performed without additional data structures like indexes (hash join, nested loop, sort merge, etc.), horizontal partitioning, parallel processing without replication. In this paper, we concentrate only on *horizontal partitioning,* since it is more adapted to reduce the cost of star join queries.

Horizontal partitioning has been mainly used in logical distributed and parallel databases design in last decades (Özsu & Valduriez, 1999; Sacca & Wiederhold, 1985). Recently, it becomes a crucial part of physical database design (Sanjay, Narasayya & Yang, 2004; Papadomanolakis & Ailamaki, 2004; Eadon et al., 2008; Tzoumas, Deshpande & Jensen, 2010; Bellatreche, Cuzzocrea & Benkrid, 2009), where most of today's commercial DBMS offer native DDL (data definition language) support for defining horizontal partitions (fragments) of a table (Sanjay et al., 2004). In context of relational warehouses, horizontal partitioning allows tables, indexes and materialised views to be partitioned into *disjoint sets* of rows that are physically stored and accessed separately. Contrary to materialised views and indexes, horizontal data partitioning does not replicate data, thereby reducing space requirements and minimising the update overhead. The main characteristic of data partitioning is its ability to be combined with some redundant optimization techniques such as indexes and materialized views. It also affects positively query performance, database manageability and availability. Query performance, is guaranteed by performing *partition elimination*. If a query includes a partition key as a predicate in the WHERE clause, the query optimizer will automatically route the query to only relevant partitions. Partitioning can also improve the performance of multi-table joins, by using a technique known as *partition-wise joins*. It can be applied when two tables are being joined together, and at least one of these tables is partitioned on the join key. *Partition-wise joins* break a large join into smaller joins. With partitioning, maintenance operations can be focused on particular portions of tables. For maintenance operations across an entire database object, it is possible to perform these operations on a per-partition basis, thus dividing the maintenance process into more manageable chunks. The Administrator can also allocating partitions in different machines (Stöhr, Märtens & Rahm, 2000; Bellatreche, Cuzzocrea & Benkrid, 2010). Another advantage of using partitioning is when it is time to remove data, an entire partition can be dropped which is very efficient and fast, compared to deleting each row individually. Partitioned database objects provide *partition independence*. This characteristic of partition independence can be an important part of a high-availability strategy. For example, if one partition of a partitioned table is unavailable, all of the other partitions of the table remain online and available. The application can continue to execute queries and transactions against this partitioned table, and these database operations will run successfully if they do not need to access the unavailable partition.

Two versions of horizontal partitioning exist (Ceri, Negri & Pelagatti, 1982; Özsu & Valduriez, 1999): primary and derived (known as referential partitioning in Oracle 11g (Eadon et al., 2008)). Primary horizontal partitioning of a table is performed using attributes defined on that table. Derived horizontal partitioning, on the other hand, is the fragmentation of a table using attribute(s) defined on another table(s). In other word, the derived horizontal partitioning of a table is based on the fragmentation schema of another table (the fragmentation schema is the result of the partitioning process of a given table). The derived partitioning of a table R according a fragmentation schema of S is feasible if and only if there is a join link between R and S (R contains a foreigner key of S). It has been used to optimize data transfer when executing queries in the distributed database environment.

In traditional databases (relational and object oriented), tables/classes are horizontally partitioned in isolation. Consequently, the problem of selecting horizontal fragments of a given table *T* of a database may be formulated as follows:

Given a representative workload *W* defined on the table *T*, find a partitioning schema *FS* of *T*, such that the overall query processing cost ($\sum_{Q \in W} f_Q \times Cost(Q, FS)$, where f_Q represents the access frequency of the query *Q*) is minimized. According this formalization, database administrator (DBA) *does not have any control* on the generated fragments of table *T*. Since each table is fragmented in an isolation way, it is difficult to measure the impact of generated fragments on the rest of tables of database schema.

In relational data warehouses, horizontal partitioning is more challenging compared to that in traditional databases. This challenge is due to the different choices to partition a star schema:

1. Partition only the dimension tables using *simple predicates* defined on these tables (a simple predicate p is defined by: $p: A_i \theta$ *Value*, where A_i is an attribute of a dimension table, $\theta \in \{=, <, >, \leq, \geq\}$, and *Value* $\in Dom(A_i)$). This scenario is not suitable for OLAP queries, because the size of dimension tables is generally smaller than the size of fact table and any star query accesses the fact table. Therefore, any horizontal partitioning that does not take into account the fact table is *discarded*.

2. Partition only the fact table using simple predicates defined on this table if there exist, since it is very large. Usually, restriction (selection) predicates are defined on dimension tables and not on fact table. The raw data of the fact table usually never contain descriptive (textual) attributes because the fact relation is designed to perform arithmetic operations such as summarization, aggregation, average and so forth on such data. Recall that star join queries access dimension tables first and after that fact table. This choice is also *discarded*.

3. Partition some/all dimension tables using their predicates, and then partition the fact table based on the fragmentation schemas of dimension tables using referential partitioning mode. This approach is more adapted to partition relational data warehouses, since it takes into consideration the star join query requirements and the relationship between the fact table and dimension tables. In our study, we adopt this scenario. To illustrate it, we consider the following example.

Example 1

Let us consider a star schema with three dimension tables (*Customer*, *Time* and *Product)* and one fact table *Sales*. Suppose that the dimension table *Customer* is partitioned into two fragments $Cust_{Female}$ and $Cust_{Male}$ using *Gender* attribute and table *Time* into two fragments $Time_{Half1}$ and $Time_{Half2}$ using *Month* attribute, as follows:

```
Cust_Female = σ_(Gender = 'F')  (Customer)
Cust_Male   = σ_(Gender = 'M')  (Customer)
Time_Half1  = σ_(Month< = 6)  (Time)
Time_Half2  = σ_(Month>6)  (Time)
```

⋈Following the third scenario, the fact table *Sales* is then fragmented based on the partitioning schema of *Customer* and *Time* into four fragments $Sales_1$, $Sales_2$, $Sales_3$ and $Sales_4$ such as:

```
Sales_1 = Sales ⋈ Cust_Female ⋈ Time-
Half1 Sales_2 = Sales ⋈ Cust_Female ⋈ Time-
Half2
Sales_3 = Sales ⋈ Cust_Male ⋈ Time_Half1
Sales_4 = Sales ⋈ Cust_Male ⋈ Time_Half2
```

The initial star schema *(Sales, Customer, Product, Time)* may be represented as the juxtaposition of four sub star schemas S_1, S_2, S_3 and S_4 such as: S_1: *(Sales$_1$, Cust$_{Female}$, Time$_{Half1}$, Product)* (sales activities for only female customers during the first half), S_2: *(Sales$_2$, Cust$_{Female}$, Time$_{Half2}$, Product)* (sales activities for only female customers during the second half), S_3: *(Sales$_3$, Cust$_{Male}$, Time$_{Half1}$, Product)* (sales activities for only male customers during the first half) and S_4: *(Sales$_4$, Cust$_{Male}$, Time$_{Half2}$, Product)* (sales activities for only male customers during the second half).

The generated number of fragments (*N*) of the fact table is given by:

$$N = \prod_{i=1}^{g} m_i,$$

where m_i and g represent the number of fragments of the dimension table D_i and the number of dimension tables participating in the fragmentation

process, respectively. This number may be very large. For example, suppose we have: *Customer* table partitioned into 50 fragments using the *State* attribute (case of 50 states in the U.S.A.), *Time* into 36 fragments using the *Month* attribute (if the sale analysis is done based on the three last years), and *Product* into 80 fragments using *Package_type* attribute. Therefore, the fact table is decomposed into *144 000* fragments (50 * 36 * 80) using *referential partitioning mode*. Consequently, instead to manage one star schema, the DBA will manage 144 000 sub star schemas. It will be very hard for her/him to maintain all these sub-star schemas (Bellatreche, Boukhalfa & Richard, 2008). To avoid the explosion of the number of fact table fragments, we formalize the problem of selecting horizontal partitioning schema as an optimization problem:

Given a representative workload *W* defined on a relational data warehouse schema with *n* dimension tables $\{D_1,..., D_n\}$ and one fact table *F* and a constraint (called *maintenance bound B*) representing the number of fact fragments, identify dimension table(s) that could be used to derived partition the fact table *F*, such that ($\sum_{Q \in W} f_Q \times Cost(Q, FS)$) is minimized and maintenance constraint is satisfied ($N \leq B$). The number *B* may be given by the DBA.

We present in this paper a comprehensive study of horizontal partitioning problem including primary and referential modes based on five aspects: (1) proposition of a methodology for horizontal partitioning in relational data warehouses guided by the total number of fragments. (2) Study of complexity of referential data horizontal partitioning problem, (3) proposition of two selection algorithms ensuring simultaneously primary and referential partitionings, (4) proposition of tool assisting data warehouse administrators to use different concepts related to data partitioning and (5) experimental study to show the benefit and limitations of horizontal partitioning.

The rest of the paper is organized as follows: Section 2 presents the state of the art and related work. Section 3 is devoted to the presentation of our horizontal partitioning approach. In section 4 we study the complexity of the horizontal partitioning selection problem and we show its hardness. Section 5 presents two selection algorithms: simulated annealing and hill climbing to select near optimal fragmentation schemes. Section 6 describes in details our tool, baptised *ParAdmin* to assist administrator during her/his tasks. In Section 7 we present the experiments that we conducted using the most popular benchmark APB-1. Section 8 concludes the paper by summarizing the main results and discussing the future works.

BACKGROUND AND RELATED WORK

Horizontal partitioning has been largely studied in the literature, where several algorithms were proposed that we propose to classify them into two main categories: *unconstrained approaches* and *Threshold-based approaches* (Figure 1.). Early work on the horizontal fragmentation can be found in the first category. They select a partitioning schema for a database without worrying about the number of generated fragments. We have shown that this number may be very important that greatly complicates their manageability. We can find three classes in this category of approaches, *minterm generation-based approaches* and *affinity-based approaches*.

Minterm generation-based (Özsu & Valduriez, 1999) approach starts with a table T and a set of predicates $\{p_1, ..., p_n\}$ of most frequently asked queries defined on relation T and outputs a set of horizontal fragments of the table T. The main steps of mimterm generation-based approach are: (1) generation of minterm predicates $M = \{m \mid m = \wedge_{(1 \leq k \leq n)} p_k^*\}$, where p_k^* is either p_k or $\neg p_k$, (2) simplification minterms in M and elimination of useless ones and (3) generation of fragments: each

Figure 1. Classification of HP approaches

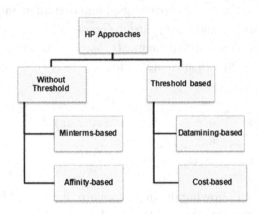

minterm m generates a fragment defined as $\sigma_m(R)$ (σ is a selection operation). This approach is simple, but it has a high complexity. For n simple predicates, this algorithm generates 2^n minterms. It can be used for a reasonable number of simple predicates.

In order to reduce this complexity, another approach was proposed which adapts the vertical partitioning algorithm of (Navathe & Ra, 1989). Predicates having a high affinity are grouped together. An affinity between two predicate p_i and p_j is computed as the sum of frequencies of queries accessing simultaneously these two predicates. Each group gives a horizontal fragment defined as a conjunction of its predicates. This algorithm has a low complexity (Karlapalem, Navathe & Ammar, 1996), but it takes into account only access frequencies to generate horizontal fragments and ignores parameters like size of tables, selectivity factors of predicates, etc.

Given the need to have a reasonable and controled number of fragments, new *threshold-based approaches* are proposed. This threshold represents the maximum number of fragments that the administrator wants to have. The main objective of *threshold-based approaches* is to partition a table into B fragments such that B is less than or equal to the threshold (*constraint bound*). Thus, in addition to set of selection predicates, these approaches require that the administrator sets the threshold value. Two major classes of works exist in this category: *data mining-based approaches* and *cost-based approaches*.

Data mining-based approach was proposed in the context of XML data warehouses (Hadj Mahboubi & Jérôme Darmont, 2009). It uses the *K-Means* clustering algorithm to group selection predicates that can fragment the data warehouse. The threshold *B* (number of fragments) is given as input parameter for the *K-means* algorithm. *K-means* is used to group the predicates in *B* groups. The proposed approach consists in three main steps, (1) coding of selection predicates, (2) classification of predicates and (3) generating fragments. The coding of predicate is to assign each predicate to the query in which it is referenced to build the extraction context. The classification of predicates uses the clustering algorithm K-Means (Pham, Dimov & Nguyen 2004) to create B classes of predicates. The construction of fragments is based on classes of predicates identified in classification stage. Each class of predicates is used to generate a horizontal partition. The approach proposes to partition the dimension document by horizontal primary partitioning and the facts document by horizontal derived fragmentation. To ensure complementarity of fragmentation, a fragment ELSE is added. It is the negation of all conjunctions of predicates. This approach controls the number of generated fragments but does not guarantee performance of the generated fragmentation schema.

Cost-based approach starts with a set of potential fragmentation schemes of relation *R* and using a cost model measuring the number of inputs outputs required for executing a set of queries; it computes the goodness of each schema (Bellatreche *et al.*, 2000). The schema with a low cost is considered as the final solution. DBA may quantify the benefit obtained by this solution. Its main drawback is that DBA does not have control the number of generated fragments.

All the work we cited has proposed approaches for horizontal partitioning of isolated selection.

Several works proposed to combine the horizontal partitioning with other optimization techniques. (Sanjay et al. 2004), proposed an integration of horizontal and vertical fragmentation in the physical design of databases. (Stohr et al, 2000) proposed the combination of horizontal partitioning with parallel processing in parallel data warehouses. The approach exploits hierarchies of dimensions to fragment data warehouses modeled by a star schema. The approach exploits parallelism within and between queries to reduce the cost of query execution. The approach also proposes the use of bitmap join indexes defined on attributes not used to partition the data warehouse. In (Bellatreche et al. 2009) we proposed HP&BJI approach that combines horizontal partitioning and bitmap join indexes in physical design of relational data warehouses. HP&BJI start with selecting horizontal partitioning schema then identify the set of not profit queries after partitioning and set of attributes not used to partition the data warehouse. In the second step, HP&BJI select a configuration of join indexes based on the two sets of attributes and queries identified in the last stage. The main particularity of this approach is that it prunes the search space of an optimization technique (indexes) using another optimization technique (horizontal partitioning). Recently (Benkrid et al, 2010) proposed a combination design approach of parallel data warehouses using horizontal partitioning. Unlike existing works that consider the problems of fragmentation and allocation independently, the proposed approach considers a combined problem of fragmentation and allocation.

Actually, horizontal fragmentation is an integral part of physical design of most important DBMS editors: Oracle (Oracle Corporation, 2010), DB2 (International Business Machines Corporation. 2006), SQL Server (Microsoft Corporation, 2005), PostgreSQL (PostgreSQL, n.d.) and MySQL (MySQL, n.d.). To show this interest, we consider an example of one of the most popular DBMS which is *Oracle*.

Figure 2. Horizontal Partitioning Modes

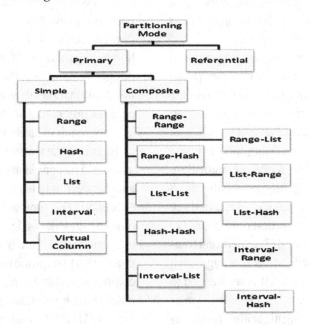

Figure 2 show the main partitioning modes on Oracle. The first horizontal partitioning mode supported by Oracle was *Range partitioning* (in Oracle 8). It is defined by a tuple *(c, V)*, where *c* is a column type and *V* is an ordered sequence of values from the domain of *c*. In this partitioning, an access path (table, materialized view and index) is split according to a range of values of a given set of columns. Oracle 9 and 9i added others modes like *Hash* and *List* and *Composite* (*Range-Hash, Range-List*). *Hash* mode decomposes the data according to a hash function (provided by the system) applied to the values of the partitioning columns. *List* partitioning splits a table according list values of a column. Composite partitioning is supposed by using *PARTITION - SUBPARTITION* statement. Note that these modes are also supported by other commercial databases like SQL Server, Sybase, DB2, etc. These partitioning modes are considered as basic modes of any partitioning tool supported by commercial DBMS. *Oracle 11g* proposes several fragmentation modes. The *Composite partitioning* method has been enriched to include all possible combinations

of basic methods (except those that begin with hash mode): *List-List, Range-Range, List-Range, List-Hash*, etc. Recently, a new composite mode Hash-Hash is supported by Oracle 11g Release 2 (Oracle Corporation, 2010). Another interesting mode called *Column partitioning* is proposed which allows a table to be decomposed using a virtual attribute defined by an expression, using one or more existing columns of a table, and storing this expression as *Meta data* only. Oracle supports another partitioning mode, *Interval Partitioning*. This mode extends the capabilities of the range mode to define equi-partitioned ranges using an interval definition. Rather than specifying individual ranges explicitly, Oracle will create any partition automatically as-needed whenever data for a partition is inserted for the very first time. Recently, in Oracle 11g Release 2, the *interval composite mode* is introduced. Three interval composites are supported: *interval-range, interval-list and interval-hash*. Note that all these modes concern only the primary horizontal partitioning, where a table is partitioned using its attribute(s). The *Referential partitioning mode* allows partitioning a table by

Box 1.

```
ALTER TABLE <table_name>
MERGE PARTITIONS <first_partition>,<second_partition>
INTO PARTITION <partition_name>
 TABLESPACE <tablespace_name>;
ALTER TABLE <table_name>
SPLIT PARTITION <partition_name>
AT <range_definition>
INTO (PARTITION <first_partition>, PARTITION <second_partition>)
```

leveraging an existing parent-child relationship. This partitioning is *similar to derived horizontal partitioning* (Ceri et al., 1982). Unfortunately, a table may be partitioned based only one table.

Oracle and several commercial DBMS provide DDL for managing partitions. Two main functions are provided: *merge partitions* and *slip partition*. The first function consists in merging two partitions into one. The second function splits a partition into two partitions. The syntax of the use of these functions is given in Box 1.

Note that other functions are available such as deleting a partition, add a new partition, move partition, rename a partition, etc.

Oracle also allows index fragmentation. An index created on a table is either coupled or uncoupled with the underlying partitioning mode of this table. Two kinds of partitioned indexes are supported in Oracle, local and global partitioned indexes. A local index is created on a partitioned table that is coupled with the partitioning strategy of this table (attributes, mode and number of fragments). Consequently, each partition of a local index corresponds to one and only one partition of the underlying table. A local index enables optimized performance and partition maintenance. When a query references one partition only its local index is loaded instead of the entire index. When a partition is dropped/updated only its local index will be removed/updated. Local indexes are very suitable for OLAP applications. A global partitioned index is defined on a partitioned or on non-partitioned table. It is partitioned using a different partitioning strategy than the indexed

Figure 3. domain decomposition approaches classification

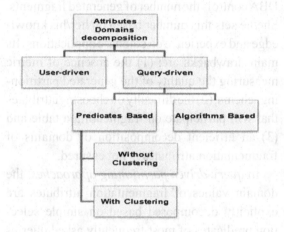

table. For example, table *Customer* could be rage-partitioned by Attribute *Age*, while a global index is range-partitioned by attribute Salary. This kind of indexes is suitable for OLTP applications.

By exploring most of academic and industrial works, we figure out that most of approaches of selecting horizontal partitioning schema suppose a decomposition of domain values of attributes participating in the fragmentation process. We can classify these approaches into two main categories (see figure 3): (1) *user-driven approaches* and (2) *query-driven approaches*.

In the first category, DBA decomposes domain values of each partitioning attribute based on her/ his knowledge of database applications and *a priori* imposes the number of generated horizontal fragments. For example, the statement in Box

Box 2.

```
CREATE TABLE Customer (CID NUMBER(5), Name VARCHAR2(30), State VARCHAR2(20), City Var-
char2(20))
PARTITION BY LIST(State) (
PARTITION Customer _west VALUES('California', 'Hawaii'),
PARTITION Customer _east VALUES ('New York', 'Virginia', 'Florida'),
PARTITION Customer _central VALUES('Texas', 'Illinois'),
PARTITION Customer _other VALUES(DEFAULT));
```

2 allows partitioning the table *Sales* using *Customer* attribute using *List* mode into 4 fragments.

The main characteristic of this category is that DBA controls the number of generated fragments. She/he sets this number based on her/his knowledge and experience on database applications. Its main drawbacks are: (1) the absence of metric measuring the quality of the generated partitioning schema, (2) the difficulty on choosing attributes that will participate on fragmenting a table and (3) an efficient decomposition of domains of fragmentation attributes is not ensured.

In *query-driven partitioning approaches*, the domain values of fragmentation attributes are explicitly decomposed based on simple selection predicates of most frequently asked queries defined on relation T. We can classify these approaches into two categories, those which use predicates to generate the final decomposition of domains and those which use algorithms to do so. We can distinguish two trends in the first category, approaches without predicates clustering and approaches with predicates clustering. The first trend uses directly selection predicates for generating minterms (Özsu & Valduriez, 1999). Minterms are used to generate the domains decomposition. Predicates clustering approaches begins with a step of grouping predicates into multiple partitions. These partitions are used to generate domains decomposition. Clustering is based on either the affinities (Karlapalem, Navathe & Ammar, 1996) or clustering algorithm like *k-means* (Hadj Mahboubi & Jérôme Darmont, 2009). All the approaches we have presented do not guarantee the quality of the final domain decomposition.

To overcome this problem, greedy approaches have been proposed. Their idea is to start by initial decomposition (random or issued from a different approach we have cited), then iteratively improve decomposition by merging or splitting subdomains. Improving the initial decomposition is guided by a cost model, which estimates the execution cost of frequently queries on partitioned schema generated by domain decomposition.

We present in the next section our fragmentation methodology and two selection algorithms that we proposed.

FRAGMENTATION METHODOLOGY

As for redundant technique (materialized views, indexes) selection problems, horizontal selection schema selection is done based a set of most frequently asked queries ($\{Q_1, ..., Q_w\}$), where each query Q_j has an access frequency f_{Qj}. Note that each star join query Q_j is defined by a set of selection predicates and a set of join predicates. The selection predicates are essential for the partitioning process. Note that each selection predicate has a selectivity factor. To partition a relational data warehouse, we present the following methodology:

1. Extraction of all selection predicates used by the queries,
2. Assignment to each dimension table D_i ($1 \le i \le n$) its set of selection predicates, denoted by $SSPD_i$.

Figure 4. An example of decomposition of domains in sub domains

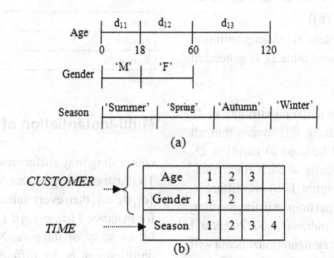

3. Ignorance of dimension tables having an empty *SSPD* (i.e., they will not participate in fragmenting the fact table). Let $D^{candidate}$ be the set of all dimension tables having a non-empty SSPD. Let g be the cardinality of $D^{candidate}$ ($g \leq n$).

4. Identification of the set fragmentation attributes *SFAC* candidate. A fragmentation attribute is an attribute of dimension table participating in the partitioning process.

5. A decomposition of domain values of each fragmentation attribute into sub domains. This decomposition may be done either intuitively by DBA using her/his knowledge of warehouse applications or guided by simple predicates defined on each fragmentation attribute. Each sub domain may be represented by a simple predicate and it has a selectivity factor defined on the fact table.

6. Selection of final fragmentation schema using an algorithm that exploits the decomposition of all domains of fragmentation attributes. Such algorithm shall reduce query processing cost and satisfy the maintenance constraint.

In order to illustrate this methodology, let us consider the following example.

Example 2

Suppose that *SFAC* contains three attributes (*Age, Gender, Season*), where *Age* and *Gender* belong to *Customer* dimension table, whereas *Season* belongs to *Time* ($D^{candidate}$ ={Customer, Time}). The domain of these attributes are: Dom(*Age*) = [0, 120], Dom(*Gender*) = {'M', 'F'}, and Dom(*Season*)= {'Summer', 'Spring', 'Autumn', 'Winter'}. We assume that DBA splits domains of these attributes into sub domains as follows: Dom(*Age*) = $d_{11} \cup d_{12} \cup d_{13}$, with d_{11} = [0, 18], d_{12} =]18, 60[, d_{13} = [60, 120]. Dom(*Gender*) = $d_{21} \cup d_{22}$, with d_{21} = {'M'}, d_{22} = {'F'}. Dom(*Season*) = $d_{31} \cup d_{32} \cup d_{33} \cup d_{34}$, where d_{31} = {'Summer'}, d_{32} = {'Spring'}, d_{33} = {'Autumn'}, and d_{34} = {'Winter'}. Sub domains of all three fragmentation attributes are represented in Figure 4(a).

Domain partitioning of different fragmentation attributes may be represented by *multidimensional arrays*, where each array represents the domain partitioning of a fragmentation attribute. The value of each cell of a given array representing an attribute A_i^k belongs to (1..n_i), where n_i

represents the number of sub domain of the attribute A_i^k (see Figure 4 (b)).

Based on this representation, fragmentation schema of each dimension table D_j is generated as follows:

1. All cells of a fragmentation attribute of D_j have different values: this means that all sub domains will be used to partition D_j. For instance, the cells of each fragmentation attribute in Figure 1 (b) are different. Therefore, they all participate in fragmenting their corresponding tables (*CUSTOMER* and *TIME*). The final fragmentation schema will generate 24 fragments of the fact table.

2. All cells of a fragmentation attribute have the same value: this means that it will not participate in the fragmentation process. Table 1 gives an example of a fragmentation schema, where all sub domains of *Season* (of dimension table *TIME*) have the same value; consequently, it will not participate in fragmenting the warehouse schema.

3. Some cells have the same value: their corresponding sub domains will be merged into one. In Table 1, the first ([0, 18]) and the second (]18, 60[) sub domains of *Age* will be merged to form only one sub domain which is the union of the merged sub domains ([0, 60[). The final fragmentation attributes are: *Gender* and *Age* of dimension table *CUSTOMER*.

The coding in Table 1 may be used by DBA to partition the dimension table *CUSTOMER* and the fact table *SALES* using the primary partitioning (*Range* on *Age* and *List* on *Gender*) and referential partitioning modes, respectively (see Box 3).

Since, the *CUSTOMER* was partitioned into 4 fragments; the fact table is also partitioned into 4 partitions as shown in Box 4.

Table 1. An example of partitioning schema

Age	1	1	2	
Gender	1	2		
Season	1	1	1	1

Multi-Instantiation of our Coding

Our coding may suffer from multi-instantiation. To illustrate this problem, we consider a set $D = \{d_1, d_2, d_3\}$, then every subset in the partition of D, for instance $\{\{d_1, d_3\}, \{d_2\}\}$, can be represented by an array of integers. Nevertheless, a given partition can be by different arrays of integers (see Table 2).

Clearly arrays 1 and 2 only differ by integers used for representing these subsets: in both solutions d1 and d3 belong to the same subset and d2 is in the other subset. Such a problem can solve this problem using Restricted Growth Functions:

Let [n] be a set $\{1, ..., n\}$, a restricted growth function is a function f such as:

```
F: [n] → [n] such that:
    f(1) = 0
    f(i + 1) ≤ max{f(1), ...,
f(i)} + 1,
```

where $f(i)$ defines the subset index where the item i belongs to. For instance, the partition $\{\{1, 3, 5\}, \{2, 6\}, \{4\}\}$ is represented by the restricted growth function [0, 1, 0, 2, 0, 1], where 0 is the index of the first subset. There is a one-to-one equivalence between set partitions and restricted growth functions. In our previous example, only array 1 respects the lexicographic order induced by restricted growth functions while array 2 will never be considered during the set partitioning.

Theorem 1: There is a one-to-one correspondence between the set of [n] and the set of restricted growth functions.

Box 3.

```
CREATE TABLE CUSTOMER
(CID NUMBER, Name Varchar2(20), Gender CHAR, Age Number)
PARTITION BY RANGE (Age)
SUBPARTITION BY LIST (Gender)
SUBPARTITION TEMPLATE (SUBPARTITION Female VALUES ('F'),
SUBPARTITION Male VALUES ('M'))
(PARTITION Cust_0_60 VALUES LESS THAN (61),
PARTITION Cust_60_120 VALUES LESS THAN (MAXVALUE));
```

Box 4.

```
CREATE TABLE SALES (customer_id NUMBER NOT NULL, product_id NUMBER NOT NULL,
time_id Number NOT NULL, price NUMBER, quantity NUMBER,
constraint Sales_customer_fk foreign key(customer_id) references CUSTOMER(CID))
PARTITION BY REFERENCE (Sales_customer_fk);
```

Table 2. Two ways to represent the same individual

Sub Domain	d_1	d_2	d_3
Array 1	0	1	0
Array 2	1	0	1

Several algorithms are known for generating all partitions of a set D in lexicographic order (see (Er., 1988) for instance).

Example 3

To show the contribution of the restricted growth function in eliminating multi-instantiation, let us consider the following example. The two top coding of Figure 5 represent the same fragmentation schema. The application of the restricted growth function gives only one schema (the bottom one).

HARDNESS STUDY

We consider the horizontal partitioning of data warehouse through a simplified decision problem that considers the derived horizontal partitioning of the fact table based on partitioning schema of one dimension table using only one attribute. The corresponding optimization problem consists in computing a partition of the fact table so that the number of partitions is bounded by a constant B and the maximum number of Input/Output operations is minimized. We state the decision problem as follows:

Figure 5. An example of using restricted growth function

Gender	1	2		
Season	1	3	2	2
Age	2	2	1	

Gender	2	1		
Season	2	1	3	3
Age	3	3	1	

Gender	1	2		
Season	1	2	3	3
Age	1	1	2	

Problem One-Domain Horizontal Partitioning

- **Instance:** A set D of disjoint sub domains $\{d_1, \ldots, d_n\}$ of the fragmentation attribute of the partitioned dimension table and the number of Input/Output operations in order to read data corresponding to the sub domain d_i in the fact table, denoted

$l(d_i)$, $1 \leq i \leq n$.

A set of queries $\{q_1, ..., q_m\}$, where each query q_j has a list $f(q_j) \subseteq D$ of used sub domains until the query completion: $\{d_{j1}, ..., d_{jn_j}\}$, where n_j is the number of sub domains used in the fact table to run q_j.

Two positive integers K and L, representing respectively the maximum number of partitions that can be created and the maximum number of Input/Output operations allowed for each query, $L \geq \sum_{d \in f(qj)} l(d)$

Question: Can D be partitioned in at most K subsets, $D_1, ..., D_K$ such that every query requires at most L Input/Output operations.

The optimal number of Input/Output operations required by a query q_j is: $\sum_{d \in f(qj)} l(d)$. It assumes that only required data are loaded in memory to run q_j. According to a given partition, the number of Input/Output operations increases since all data of a partition are loaded when used by a given query, even if that query do not requires all data of the partition (i.e., a subset of domains in the partition). Thus, the number of Input/Output operations required by a query after partitioning does not depend on the used sub domains but only on used partitions. The number of Input/Output operations while loading a partition D is defined by:

$$l(D) \geq \sum_{d \in D} l(d).$$

As a consequence the number of Input/Output operations required by running a query can be defined as:

$$l(q_j) = \sum_{D \in F(q_j)} l(D),$$

where $F(q_j)$ is the list of partitions used by a query q_j.

The objective is to perform a derived horizontal partitioning of the fact table such that the number of partitions is limited to K and the number of Input/Output operations is bounded by L for every query. Obviously, if $K \leq n$, the optimal horizontal partitioning is achieved by defining exactly one partition to every d_i ($d_i \in D$). In that way, every query only loads required data during its execution. We shall see that our simplified decision problem becomes hard when $K < n$. We also assume $L \geq \sum_{d \in f(qj)} l(d)$ since otherwise the answer of the One-Domain Horizontal Partitioning is always *false*.

Theorem 1: One-Domain horizontal partitioning is NP-Complete in the strong sense.

Proof: One-Domain horizontal partitioning clearly belongs to NP since if one guesses a partition of D, then a polynomial time algorithm can check that at most K partitions are used and that every query requires at most L Input/Output operations.

We now prove that One-Domain horizontal partitioning is NP-Complete in the strong sense. We shall use 3-Partition that is strongly NP-Complete (Garey & Johnson, 1990).

Problem: 3-Partition

Instance: Set A of $3m$ elements, a bound $B \in Z^+$, and a size $s(a) \in Z^+$, for each $a \in A$ such that $B/4 < s(a) < B/2$ and such that $\sum_{a \in A} s(a) = mB$

Question: Can A be partitioned into m disjoint sets $A_1, ..., A_m$ such that, for $1 \leq i \leq m$, $\sum_{a \in A_i} s(a) = B$ (note that each Ai must therefore contain exactly three elements from A)?

To prove the NP-Completeness of One-Domain horizontal partitioning, we reduce from 3-Partition. To every 3-Partition instance, an instance of One-Domain horizontal partitioning is defined as follows:

- to every $a_i \in A$, a sub domain d_i is created so that $l(d_i) = s(a_i)$, $1 \leq i \leq 3m$;
- $3m$ queries are created such that every query uses exactly one sub domain: $f(q_i) = \{d_i\}$, $1 \leq i \leq 3m$;
- $K = L = B$.

Clearly the transformation is performed in polynomial time since it consists in a one-to-one mapping of 3-partition elements into sub domains and queries. We now prove that we have a solution to the 3-partition instance if, and only if, we have a solution to the One-Domain horizontal partitioning instance.

Necessary condition: Assume that we have a solution of the One-Domain horizontal partitioning, and then it satisfies the following conditions:

- Since $B/4 < l(d) < B/2$, every subset of D will be define with exactly 3 sub domains (as in every 3-Partition instance).
- Since we have a feasible solution of the One-Domain Horizontal Partitioning, then no query requires more than Input/Output operations. By construction we verify that: $\sum_{d \in D} l(d) = mB$ As a consequence, every query requires exactly B Input/Output in the fact tables (otherwise it is not a solution). Using a one-to-one mapping of sub domains into elements of 3-Partition, a feasible solution of the 3-partition instance is obtained.

Sufficient condition: Assume that we have a solution to the 3-Partition instance. Then, every subset A_i as a total size of B and is composed of exactly 3 elements of A. Starting from A_1, we define a sub domain partition using sub domains with same indexes of elements belonging to A_1. Since every query is associated to exactly one sub domain and three sub domains are grouped in every partition, then exactly three queries use a given partition. As a consequence, the number of Input/Output associated to these 3 corresponding queries is exactly B. Repeating this process for every remaining subset A_i, and then a feasible solution of the *One-Dimension horizontal partitioning Problem* is obtained.

Every sub domain can be used to define a horizontal partitioning of the fact table. As a consequence, the number of solutions (i.e., the number of ways to partition the fact table) is defined by the number of partitions of the set D. For a set of size k, this number is defined by the Bell number. Even if the number of solutions is limited when k is small, it vastly becomes intractable (e.g., if $k = 10$, then the number of different partitions is 115 975).

PROPOSED SELECTION ALGORITHMS

Due to the high complexity of horizontal partitioning selection problem, development of heuristics selecting near optimal solutions is recommended. In this section, we present a hill climbing and simulated annealing algorithms with several variants.

Hill Climbing Algorithm

Hill climbing heuristic consists of the following two steps:

1. Find an initial solution.
2. Iteratively improve the initial schema solution by using the hill climbing operations until no further reduction in total query processing time can be achieved and the maintenance bound B is satisfied. Since there is finite number of fragmentation schemes,

the heuristic algorithm will complete its execution.

Choices of the Initial Solution

Theoretically, the choice of the initial solution of hill climbing has an impact on the quality of the final solution. We propose three initial solutions: (1) a uniform distribution, (2) a *Zipf* distribution and (3) a random distribution. Let C be the cardinal of set of fragmentation attributes *SFAC*, where each attribute A_k has n_k sub domains.

Uniform distribution: in this solution, each cell i of fragmentation attribute (A_k) is filled using the following formula:

$$Array[i]_k = \left\lfloor \frac{i}{n} \right\rfloor,$$

where n is an integer ($1 \leq n \leq \max_{1 \leq j \leq C}(n_j)$).

To illustrate this distribution, let us consider three fragmentation attributes: *Gender*, *Season* and *Age*, where $n_{gender} = 2$, $n_{Season} = 4$ and $n_{Age} = 3$ (see Example 2). The coding in Figure 6 represents uniform distribution with $n = 2$ (n_{gender}), $n = 3$ (n_{Age}) and $n = 4$ (n_{Season}). The generated fragments of partitioning schema corresponding to n = 2, n = 3 and n = 4 are 12, 4 and 2 respectively. If DBA wants an initial fragmentation schema with a large number of fragments, she/he considers n with a low value. In this case, all initial sub domains (proposed by DBA) have the same probability to participate on the fragmentation process.

Zipf Distribution: This distribution is largely used in database physical design (Das, Gunopulos, Koudas, & Tsirogiannis, 2006) and Web access documents (Breslau, Cao, Fan, Phillips, & Shenker, 1999), where it is used as follows: the relative probability of a request for a document is inversely proportional to its popularity rank I ($1 \leq i \leq N$). The probability $P(i)$ of a request for the ith

Figure 6. An example of generation of initial solution with uniform distribution

Gender	0	1		
Season	0	1	1	2
Age	0	1	2	

n = 2

Gender	0	0		
Season	0	0	1	1
Age	0	0	1	

n = 3

Gender	0	0		
Season	0	0	0	1
Age	0	0	0	

n = 4

popular document is proportional to $\frac{1}{i^\alpha}$ ($0 < \alpha \leq 1$).

In our context, we claim that it is appropriate to model the sub domains access using this *Zipf*-like distribution. Let N_1 be the number of sub domains of the first partition of domain of fragmentation attribute A_k. Each cell of A_k is filled as follows:

$$Array[i]_k = \left\lfloor \frac{N_1}{i} \right\rfloor,$$

where N_1 is obtained by dividing the number total of sub domains of A_k per 2 and incrementing the result per p (p an integer $1 \leq p \leq \max_{1 \leq j \leq C}(n_j)$).

This distribution is called *direct (simple) Zipf* (see Figure 7). We can imagine two other distributions: *random Zipf* and *inverse Zipf*. In the random *Zipf* distribution, cells of each fragmentation attribute are filled randomly following the direct *Zipf* law. The final coding is reorganized by applying the restricted grow function. An example of this coding is given by the following Figure 8.

Inverse *Zipf* distribution is similar to the simple *Zipf* distribution; the only difference is that the first partition of each domain has a smaller number of sub domains. An example of this coding is illustrated by the Figure 9.

We notice that all *Zipf* variants generate the same number of fragments.

Random distribution: In this distribution, multidimensional arrays representing fragmentation is filled randomly. Two variants of this distribution are considered: random with renumbering using restricted grows functions and random without renumbering.

Improvement of the Initial Solution

In order to improve the initial solution, two operations, namely merge and split are applied to reduce the total query processing cost. They have the same semantic of those used by commercial DBMS (see background and related work Section).

Merge: This function has the following signature:

Merge(P_i^k, P_j^k, A^k, SF) → SF'

It takes two partitions P_i^k and P_j^k of the fragmentation attribute A^k of fragmentation schema *SF* and gives another schema *SF'*, where P_i^k and P_j^k are merged. The merging process consists in assigning the same number of their respective cells. This operation reduces the number of fragments. This operation is used when the number of generated fragments is greater than the maintenance constraint *B*.

Split: This function has the following signature:

Split(P_i^k, A^k, SF) → SF'

It takes one partition P_i^k of the fragmentation attribute A^k of fragmentation schema *SF* and gives another schema *SF'*, where P_i^k is splited into two partitions. This operation increases the number of fragments.

Figure 7. An example of generation of initial solution with direct Zipf distribution

p = 0

Gender	1	2		
Season	1	1	2	3
Age	1	1	2	

p = 1

Gender	1	1		
Season	1	1	1	2
Age	1	1	1	

Figure 8. An example of generation of initial solution with random Zipf distribution

p = 0

Gender	1	2		
Season	1	2	3	1
Age	1	2	1	

p = 1

Gender	1	1		
Season	1	2	1	1
Age	1	1	1	

Figure 9. An example of generation of initial solution with inverse Zipf distribution

p = 0

Gender	1	2		
Season	1	2	3	3
Age	1	2	2	

p = 1

Gender	1	1		
Season	1	2	2	2
Age	1	1	1	

Example 4

Figure 10 presents a coding of a fragmentation schema SF generating 12 fragments of the fact table: 2 (fragments generated by *Age*) * 2 (fragments generated by *Gender*) * 3 (fragments generated by *Season*). On this schema, we first apply merge function on attribute *Gender* using where

Figure 10. Applying merge and split operations

Gender	1	2		
Season	1	2	3	3
Age	1	2	1	

SF

Gender	1	1		
Season	1	2	3	3
Age	1	2	1	

SF'

Gender	1	2		
Season	1	2	3	3
Age	1	2	1	

SF''

sub domains 1 and 2 are merged. We obtain another fragmentation schema *SF'* generating 6 fragments; since the attribute *Gender* will not participate on fragmenting *CUSTOMER* table. We can apply the split function (which is a dual operation of merge) on the fragmentation schema *SF'* on the *Gender* attribute, where we get the fragmentation schema *SF''* which is identical to *SF*.

Problems when Using Merge and Split Operations

When applying these two functions, we have identified three main problems: (1) the order of applying merge and split functions, (2) the choice of starting attributes for merge and split functions and (3) the choice of sub domains.

1. *The order of applying merge and split functions:* To solve this problem, we have used a feasibility criterion for each solution. A fragmentation schema is *feasible if it* does not violate the maintenance constraint (the generated fragments should satisfy the maintenance bound B). Therefore, if a solution is feasible, the split function is first applied in order to generate a solution with more fragments than the current one. Otherwise, if the current solution is not feasible, then

the merge function is applied in order to reduce the number of generated fragments.

2. *Choice of starting attributes:* Recall that each fragmentation schema solution is coded using multidimensional arrays, where each row represents a fragmentation attribute. In order to apply merge and split, fragmentation attributes are *sorted* using their access frequencies. The frequency of each attribute is calculated as the sum of query frequencies using that attribute. Merge function is applied on least frequently used attributes in order to reduce their use on the fragmentation process. Whereas the split function is used on most frequently used attributes in order to increase their participation on fragmenting the data warehouse schema.

3. *Choice of sub domains participating on merge and split operations*: If an attribute is chosen, all its cells are candidate for merge and split functions. Our choices are realized as follows:

    a. *Merge function*: to apply the merge function on attribute A_k, we do all pair wise sub domain merges. The quality of each merge operation is evaluated using a cost model. If attribute A_k has m_k sub domains, $\frac{m_k * (m_k - 1)}{2}$ merge operations are possible. In order to select the best merge, we define a function, called, *BestMerge* with the following signature: *BestMerge(A_k, SF)* → *SF*. It takes an attribute A_k and a fragmentation schema SF and gives the best merge among all possible merges.

    b. *Split Function:* Generating all possible splits is more complicated compared to merges. In our study, we propose to split sub domains having a high selectivity factor. This choice reduces the size of generated fragments. In order to select

Figure 11. Hill Climbing algorithm description

```
Hill climbing algorithm
Inputs:
        Set of most frequently asked queries W, B
Output:
        Fragmentation schema SF
Variables:
N: number of fragmentation attributes
        Use[]: array containing N attributes sorted using their access
        frequencies
Begin
            FS ← intial_solution();
            If (( ¬IsFeasible(FS)) Or (NS = W)) Then
            i ← 0;
            While ( ¬IsFeasible(FS) AND (I < N)) Do
                Attrib ← USE[i] ;
                If (¬SF.CanMerge(attrib)) Then
                    i ← i+1;
                End If
                If ((SF.CanMerge(attrib)) And (¬SF.IsFeasible()))
                Then SF.BestMerge(attrib);
                End If
            End While
            Else
            j ← N-1;
            While ((SF.IsFeasible()) And (j ≥ 0)) Do
                attrib1 ← USE[j];
                If (¬SF.CanSplit(attrib1)) Then
                    j ← j-1;
                Endif
                If ((SF.CanSplit(attrib1) And (SF.IsFeasible()))
                Then
                    SF.BestSplit(attrib1);
                    j ← j-1;
                End If
            End While
            End If
            Return (SF);
End.
```

the best split, we define a function, called, *BestSplit* with the following signature: *BestSplit(A$_k$ SF)* → *SF*.

Evaluation of the Quality of Generated Solution

The application of these operations is controlled by a cost model computing the number of inputs and outputs required for executing a set of queries on the selected horizontal partitioning schema. A particularity of this model is that it considers buffer size when executing a query. For lack of space it cannot be presented in this paper. For more details see (Boukhalfa, Bellatreche, & Richard, 2008).

Now we have all ingredients to present our hill climbing algorithm (see Figure 11).

Simulated Annealing Algorithm

It is well known that one of the main weaknesses of the hill climbing approach is that it suffers of the problem of local optima. To overcome such a problem, a simulating annealing approach can be applied instead. It is a randomised technique for finding a near-optimal solution of difficult combinatorial optimisation problems (Kirkpatrick, Gelatt, & Vecchi, 1983). It starts with a randomly solution candidate, then it repeatedly attempts to find a better solution by moving to a neighbour with higher fitness, until it finds a solution where none of its neighbours has a higher fitness. To avoid getting trapped in poor local optima, simulated annealing allows occasionally uphill moves to solutions with lower fitness by using a temperature parameter to control the acceptance of the moves but also uphill moves with some probability that depends on a number of parameters.

In our context, simulated annealing has an input an initial fragmentation schema as for hill climbing algorithm (random, uniform and *Zipf*). It uses a function called *RandomTransform* which takes a fragmentation schema *FS* and returns a schema *FS'* with better quality. This function applies random changes on the initial schema using the two functions *merge* and *split* (see hill climbing algorithm), but the choice of attributes and sub domains is done randomly. The main structure of this algorithm is described in Figure 12.

HORIZONTAL PARTITIONING ADVISOR

To assist the administrator in physical design of his/her data warehouse, we propose the tool *ParAdmin*. This tool support primary and derived partitioning and bitmap join indexes. In this paper, we pres-

Figure 12. Simulated annealing algorithm description

```
Simulated Annealing Algorithm
Inputs: Set of most frequently asked queries W, B
Output: Fragmentation schema SF
Variables:
Fragmentation schema SFinitial, SFfinal, tempo
TEMPR: initial temperature which will be decreased during execution of algorithm
STOP: stopping condition of algorithm
Equilibrium: number of iterations to each value of temperature
coefDecr: temperature decrease's coefficient
Begin
    SFinitial ← initial_solution();
    Temperature ← TEMPR;
    J ← 1;
    While (j < STOP) DO
        i ← 1;
        While (i < Equilibrium) Do
            tempo ← RandomTransform(SFinitial);
            If (tempo.Score() > SFinitial.Score()) Then
                SFinitial ← tempo;
                If (SFinitial.Cost() < SFfinal.Cost()) Then
                    SFfinal ← SFinitial;
                End If
            Else
                delta ← (tempo.Score() − SFinitial.Score());
                Deterioration ← exp((delta) / Temperature));
                If (deterioration > RandomFunction()) Then
                    SFinitial ← tempo;
                    If (SFinitial.Cost()<SFfinal.Cost()) Then
                        SFfinal ← SFinitial;
                    End If
            End If
            i ← i + 1;
        End While
        Temperature ← (Temperature * coefDecr);
        j ← j + 1;
    End While
    Return (SFfinal);
End
```

ent only the features on horizontal partitioning. *ParAdmin* accepts as inputs a data warehouse schema, a workload of queries Q and the maintenance constraint (the maintenance bound B) and outputs all the scripts necessary to partition the data warehouse. We develop our tool under C++ as modular application. *ParAdmin* consists of a set of five modules (see Figure 13): (1) meta-base querying module, (2) Managing queries module, (3) Horizontal partitioning selection module (HPSM) and (4) Horizontal partitioning module and (5) Query rewriting module.

The meta-base querying module is a very important module which allows the tool to work with any type of DBMS. From a type of DBMS, user name and password the module allows to connect to that account and collect some information from the meta-base. These information concerns logical and physical levels of the data warehouse. Information of logical level includes tables and attributes in these tables. Information

of physical level includes optimization techniques used and a set of statistics on tables and attributes of the data warehouse (number of tuples, cardinality, etc.). The Managing queries module help administrator to define the workload of queries (W) on which the selection is based. The module allows manual editing of a query or import from external files. It may also manage the workload, giving the possibility to add, delete or update queries. This module integrates parser that identifies syntax errors as well as tables and attributes used by each query. Horizontal Partitioning Selection Module (HPSM) requires as inputs a schema of data warehouse, a workload and a threshold B. Using these data; HPSM selects a partitioning schema (PS) to minimize the cost of the workload and generating a number of fragments not exceeding B. Our tool supports three selection algorithms: Genetic Algorithm (Boukhalfa, Bellatreche & Mohania 2005), Simulated Annealing algorithm and Hill Climbing algorithm (see previous sec-

Figure 13. Architecture of ParAdmin

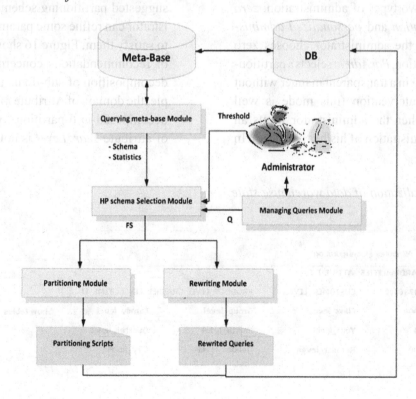

277

tion). Horizontal partitioning module fragments physically the data warehouse using partitioning schema obtained from HPSM. From the partitioning schema, this module determines the dimension table(s) to partition by horizontal primary partitioning and attributes used to perform this fragmentation. The module is also used to partition the fact table by horizontal derived partitioning mode using fragments of dimension tables. Query Rewriting Module rewrite queries on fragmented schema. It starts with identifying valid fragments for each query; rewrite the query on each of these fragments and finally performing union of the obtained results.

The main features of *ParAdmin* are:

1. Displaying the current state of the database (the schema, attributes, size of each table, definition of each attribute, etc.) and the workload (description of queries, number of selection operations, selection predicates, etc.). Figure 14 show the displaying information interface of *ParAdmin*.

2. Offering two types of administration: *zero administration* and *personalized administration*. If the administrator chooses zero administration, *ParAdmin* selects a partitioning schema in a transparent manner without designer intervention (this mode is well adapted when the administrator wants an auto-administration of his/her database). In

the personalized administration, the administrator chooses candidate dimension tables, candidate attributes and selection algorithms and sets different parameters that she/he considers important. In Figure 15, the administrator chose a personalized administration, where three dimension tables participate in partitioning process (*Chanlevel, ProdLevel* and *TimeLevel*) and only table *Custlevel* is not a candidate for partitioning. Among 12 attributes, the administrator has chosen two attributes of the table *Prodlevel*, two attributes of the table *TimeLevel* and one attribute of the table *ChanLevel*.

3. Improving iteratively the selected partitioning schema based on the proposed recommendation based on feedback. *ParAdmin* displays the quality of final partitioning schema. This quality is based on a cost model estimating the number of inputs outputs required for executing each query (Boukhalfa, Bellatreche & Richard, 2008). Therefore, if some queries do not get benefit from the suggested partitioning schema, the administrator can refine some parameters in order to satisfy them. Figure 16 show an example of recommendations concerning the final decomposition of sub-domains. For example, the domain of Attribute *Month_Level* is decomposed in 6 partitions, when domain of attribute *Year_Level* is not decomposed

Figure 14. Visualization of data warehouse state

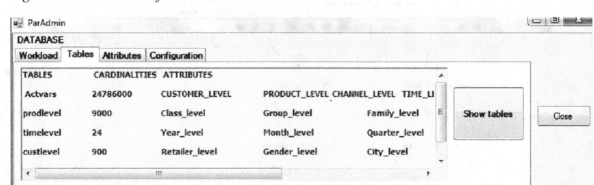

(it does not participate in data warehouse partitioning)

4. Generating scripts for primary and derived horizontal partitioning. They can be directly executed on the data warehouse to partition it physically, in the case, where the administrator is satisfied with the suggested recommendations.

EXPERIMENTAL STUDIES

We have conducted many experimental studies in order to evaluate and to compare the proposed algorithms: hill climbing and simulated annealing with their variants. We first evaluate each algorithm and then we jointly study them.

Dataset: We use the dataset from the APB1 benchmark (APB1, 1998). The star schema of this benchmark has one fact table *Actvars* (33 324 000 tuples) and four dimension tables: *Prodlevel* (99 000 tuples), *Custlevel* (990 tuples), *Timelevel* (24 tuples) and *Chanlevel* (10 tuples). This schema is implemented using Oracle 11G.

Workload: We have considered a workload of 55 single block queries (i.e., no nested subqueries) with 40 selection predicates defined on ten different attributes: *Class_Level, Group_Level, Family_Level, Line_Level, Division_Level, Year_Level, Month_Level, Quarter_Level, Retailer_Level, All_Level*. The domains of these attributes are split into: 4, 2, 5, 2, 4, 2, 12, 4, 4, 5 sub domains, respectively. We did not consider update and delete queries. Note that each selec-

Figure 15. Personnalized Administration

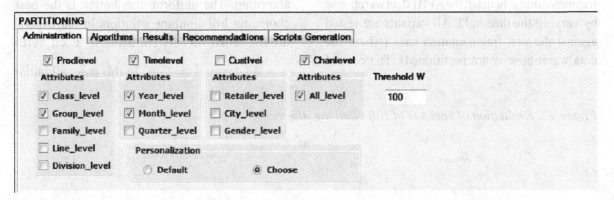

Figure 16. Final Domains Decomposition

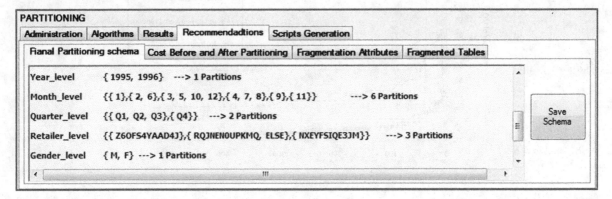

tion predicate has a selectivity factor computed using SQL query executed on the data set of APB 1 benchmark. In our coding, cells representing sub domains are arranged in ascended sorted order based on their selectivity factors.

Our algorithms have been implemented using Visual C++ performed under Intel Pentium Centrino with a memory of 3 Go.

Evaluation of Hill Climbing Algorithm

Figure 17 compares the performance in terms of number of inputs outputs of our hill climbing algorithm and its variants by varying the threshold. This variation is given in Table 3.

Six variants of hill climbing heuristic are evaluated: *uniform, direct Zipf, inverse Zipf, random Zipf, not renumbered random* and *renumbered random* (using restricted grow function). Each variant is executed in order to generate the fragmentation schema of the APB1 data warehouse by varying the threshold. All variants are tested against the non fragmentation case (where the data warehouse is not partitioned). The cost of

the 55 queries is estimated using our cost model that uses the size of dimension and fact tables, selectivity factors, buffer size, etc over each fragmentation schema generated by each variant. The first observation is that fragmentation schema obtained by all variants of hill climbing algorithm out performs the non fragmentation case, especially when the threshold becomes large. The second observation concerns the maintenance constraint (threshold) on its effect on performance of queries. When the threshold increases, hill climbing gives better results compare to the non fragmented case. From a threshold varying from 280 and 500, we get fragmentation schemas with same quality. This result is very interesting since it allows DBA to choose his/her maintenance constraint from this range to ensure a high performance of her/his queries. Another observation concerns the impact of the initial solution on the quality of generated solution by hill climbing algorithm. The uniform distribution is the best choice for hill climbing solution. In our experiments, uniform distribution is used with $n = 4$ $\left(Array[i]_k = \left\lfloor \dfrac{i}{n} \right\rfloor \right)$. In this case, all initial

Figure 17. Evaluation of Variants of Hill climbing Algorithm

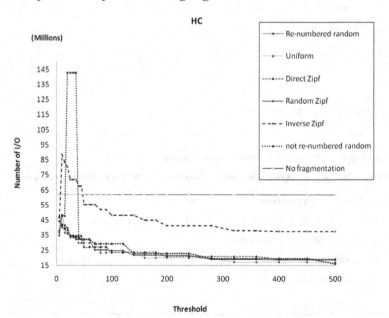

sub domains have the same probability to participate on fragmenting tables. *Zipf inverse* distribution has less performance compared to the other variants, since sub domains of each fragmentation attribute are sorted, merge operations are usually done on sub domains with high selectivity. This generates fragments with large population.

In Figure 18, we study the effect of buffer size on performance of queries. To do so, we vary the buffer size from 0 to 15 000 pages and we execute the hill climbing with uniform variant (since it is the best variant) and we compute the cost of execution all queries. The threshold is fixed at 50. This experiment shows the impact of buffer on query performance, especially, when we increase its size. When buffer size is around 900 pages, the behaviour of hill climbing algorithm is stable.

Evaluation of Simulated Annealing Algorithm

Figure 19 shows the performance of simulated annealing (SA) and its variants *(random renumbered, random Zipf, uniform, random not renumbered* and *simple Zipf)*. We conduct same experiments as for hill climbing. All variants of simulated annealing outperform largely the non fragmentation case, contrary to hill climbing algorithm. We found that uniform distribution out performs the other variants for all variations of the threshold. We note a stability of performance of simulated annealing when the threshold reaches 200. Augmenting the threshold does not means improving performance of queries. Therefore, the threshold should be chosen carefully by database administrator. Even for small threshold, simulated

Table 3. Variation of the threshold

5	10	15	20	25	30	35	40	45
50	60	70	80	90	100	120	140	160
180	200	240	280	320	360	400	450	500

Figure 18. Effect of the buffer on hill climbing performance

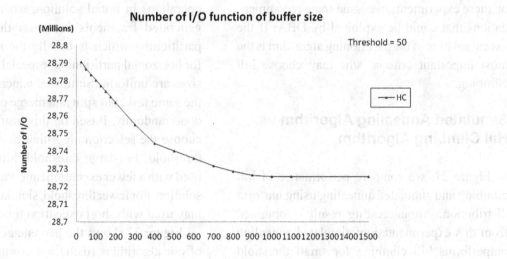

Number of I/O function of buffer size

(Millions)

Threshold = 50

HC

Buffer

Figure 19. Performance of simulated annealing and its variants

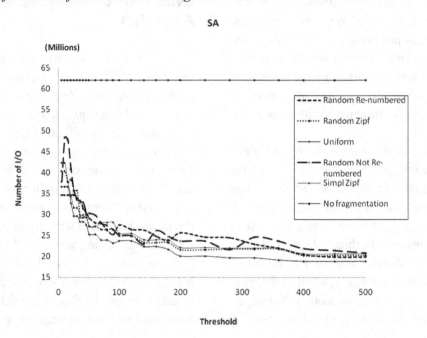

annealing gives interesting results compared to the no fragmentation case.

Figure 20 gives the running time required by simulated annealing. Note that hill climbing execution is very fast (a most 3 seconds). In this experiment, the threshold value is set from 10 and 200. Simulating annealing is time consuming compared to hill climbing. When threshold is very large, the execution time increases rapidly. Based on these experiments, we issue some recommendations that could be exploited by DBA: If the execution time of the partitioning algorithm is the most important criteria, s/he may choose hill climbing.

Simulated Annealing Algorithm vs. Hill Climbing Algorithm

In Figure 21, we compare performance of hill climbing and simulated annealing using uniform distribution. An interesting result is obtained from this experimentation: simulated annealing outperforms hill climbing for small threshold (when it varies from 5 till 160), whereas hill climbing gives better performance for large number of threshold (when it varies from 300 till 500). For small thresholds, hill climbing performs more merge operations on initial solution which usually increase sizes of generated fragments. Consequently, horizontal partitioning does not perform well in this situation. For large number of threshold, hill climbing performs split operations in initial solution, where number of generated fragments increases the horizontal partitioning which is usually the best scenario for horizontal partitioning, especially when their sizes are uniform. Simulated annealing is doing the same task, but split and merge operations are done randomly. Based on this result, DBA may choose the selection algorithm based on her/his threshold. For large threshold, hill climbing is used with a fewer execution time and high quality solution. For fewer threshold, simulated annealing may used with short execution time.

Figure 22 shows the percentage of reduction of our algorithms (using a uniform distribution

Figure 20. Execution time required for simulated annealing and its variants

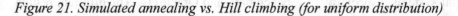

Figure 21. Simulated annealing vs. Hill climbing (for uniform distribution)

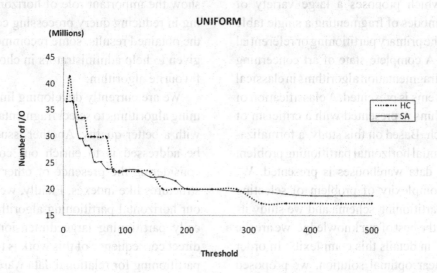

as an initial solution) computed against the non fragmentation case. The results show the benefit of partitioning in reducing query processing cost. This reduction is almost stable when varying the maintenance cost (threshold). That's why commercial DBMS advocated massively horizontal partitioning.

CONCLUSION AND PERSPECTIVES

Horizontal data partitioning has been largely studied by academic community in last decades and recently massively advocated by most of commercial database systems (Oracle, SQL Server, IBM DB2, MySQL and PostgreSQL), where they offer native data definition language support for defining horizontal partitions of a table using sev-

Figure 22. Gain in percent obtained by simulated annealing and Hill climbing algorithms

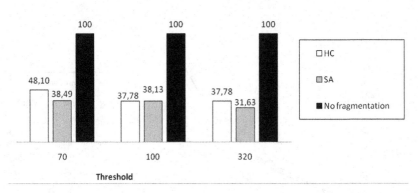

eral modes. This adoption has been motivated by business intelligence applications. In this paper, we showed the spectacular evolution of horizontal partitioning on commercial systems, especially in Oracle, which proposes a large variety of partitioning modes of fragmenting a single table using either the primary partitioning or referential partitioning. A complete state of art concerning the different fragmentation algorithms in classical database systems is presented. A classification of these algorithms is presented with a criticism of each approach. Based on this study, a formalization of referential horizontal partitioning problem in relational data warehouses is presented. We derive the complexity of problem of selecting an optimal partitioning schema and we study its hardness. To the best of our knowledge, we are the first to study in details this complexity. In order to select a near optimal solution, we proposed two algorithms: hill climbing and simulated annealing with various variants. The main characteristic of these algorithms is that they partition simultaneously dimension and fact tables. Due the complexity of using fragmentation algorithms involving several parameters: threshold, nature of distribution of initial solution, etc. we propose a tool (*ParAdmin*) assisting administrators during their tasks. It gives recommendations for each workload and the quality of the generated partitioning schemes. Administrators have the possibility to tune algorithms and their parameters to get best solutions. Intensive experimental studies have been presented using data set of ABP 1 benchmark and Oracle 11g. The different results show the important role of horizontal partitioning in reducing query processing cost. Based on the obtained results, some recommendations are given to help administrators in choosing her/his favourite algorithm.

We are currently developing linear programming algorithms to select fragmentation schemes with a better quality. Another issue that should be addressed is to enrich our cost model by considering the presence of other optimization structures like indexes. Finally, we are adapting our horizontal partitioning algorithms for vertically partitioning large dimension tables. The direct consequence of this work is to offer mixed partitioning for relational data warehouses.

REFERENCES

Bellatreche, L., & Boukhalfa, K. (2005): An Evolutionary Approach to Schema Partitioning Selection in a Data Warehouse. 7th International Conference on Data Warehousing and Knowledge Discovery (DAWAK'05), pp. 115-125, August, Springer-Verlag.

Bellatreche, L., Boukhalfa, K., & Richard, P. (2008). Horizontal Partitioning in Data Warehouse: Hardness Study, Selection Algorithms and Validation on ORACLE10G. *10th International Conference on Data Warehousing and Knowledge Discovery (DAWAK)*, pp. 87-96, September, Springer-Verlag.

Bellatreche, L., Cuzzocrea, A., & Benkrid, S. (2009) Query Optimization over Parallel Relational Data Warehouses in Distributed Environments by Simultaneous Fragmentation and Allocation, *The 10th International Conference on Algorithms and Architectures for Parallel Processing* (ICA3PP), pp. 124–135, May, Springer-Verlag.

Bellatreche, L., Karlapalem, K., & Simonet, A. (2000). Algorithms and Support for Horizontal Class Partitioning in Object-Oriented Databases. *Distributed and Parallel Databases, 8*(2), 155–179. doi:10.1023/A:1008745624048

Bellatreche, L., Moussaoui, R., Necir, H., & Drias, H. (2008). A Data Mining Approach for Selecting Bitmap Join Indices. *Journal of Computing Science and Engineering, 2*(1), 206–223.

Boukhalfa, K., Bellatreche, L., & Richard, P. (2008). Fragmentation Primaire et Dérivée: Étude de Complexité, Algorithmes de Sélection et Validation sous Oracle10g. (Report No. 01 -2008), LISI/ENSMA, available at: http://www. lisi.ensma.fr/ members/bellatreche

Breslau, L., Cao, P., Fan, L., Phillips, G., & Shenker, S. (1999). Web Caching and Zipf-like Distributions: Evidence and Implications. Eighteenth Annual Joint Conference of the IEEE Computer and Communications Societies (IEEE INFOCOM), pp. 126-134.

Ceri, S., Negri, M., & Pelagatti, G. (1982). Horizontal data partitioning in database design, Proceedings of the International Conference on Management of Data (SIGMOD), pp. 128-136.

Das, G., Gunopulos, D., Koudas, N., & Tsirogiannis, D. (2006). Answering Top-k Queries Using Views. Proceedings of 32th International Conference on Very Large Data Bases (VLDB'2006), pp. 451-462

Eadon, G., Chong, E. I., Shankar, S., Raghavan, A., Srinivasan, J., & Das, S. (2008). Supporting Table Partitioning by Reference in Oracle. Proceedings of the International Conference on *Management of Data (SIGMOD)*, pp. 1111-1122.

Er, M. C. (1988). A Fast Algorithm for Generating Set Partitions. *The Computer Journal, 31*(3), 283–284. doi:10.1093/comjnl/31.3.283

Garey, M. R., & Johnson, D. S. (1990). *Computers and Intractability; A Guide to the Theory of NP-Completeness*. New York, NY, USA: W. H. Freeman & Co.

Holland, J. H. (1975). *Adaptation in Natural and Artificial Systems*. Ann Arbor, MI: University of Michigan Press.

International Business Machines Corporation. (2006), DB2 partitioning features, An overview for data warehouses. Retrieved from http://www.ibm. com/developerworks /data/library/techarticle/ dm-0608mcinerney/

Ioannidis, Y., & Kang, Y. (1990). Randomized algorithms for optimizing large join queries. *Proceedings of the International Conference on Management of Data (SIGMOD)*, pp. 9-22.

Karlapalem, K., Navathe, S. B., & Ammar, M. (1996). Optimal Redesign Policies to Support Dynamic *Processing of Applications on a Distributed Database System. Information Systems, 21*(4), 353–367. doi:10.1016/0306-4379(96)00018-X

Kirkpatrick, S., Gelatt, C. D., & Vecchi, M. P. (1983). Optimization by simulated annealing. *Science, 220*(4598), 671–680. doi:10.1126/science.220.4598.671

Lei, H., & Ross, K. A. (1999). Faster Joins Using Join Indices. *The VLDB Journal, 8*(1), 1–24. doi:10.1007/s007780050071

Mahboubi, H., & Darmont, J. (2009) Enhancing XML Data Warehouse Query Performance by Fragmentation, 24th Annual ACM Symposium on Applied Computing (SAC 09), Hawaii, USA, 2009, pp. 1555-1562

Microsoft Corporation. (2005). Partitioned Tables and Indexes in SQL Server 2005. Retrieved from http://msdn.microsoft.com/ en-us/library/ms345146.aspx

MySQL, n.d., Partition Types, Retrieved from http://dev.mysql.com/doc/ refman/5.1/en/ partitioning-types.html.

Navathe, S. B., & Ra, M. (1989). Vertical Partitioning for Database Design: A Graphical Algorithm. *Proceedings of the International Conference on Management of Data (SIGMOD)*, pp. 440-450.

OLAP Council. (1998) APB-1 OLAP Benchmark, Release II. Retrieved from http://www.olapcouncil.org/ research/resrchly.htm

Oracle Corporation. (2010). Partitioning with Oracle Database 11g Release 2. An oracle White Paper. Retrieved from www.oracle.com/technetwork/ middleware/bi-foundation/ twp-partitioning-11gr2-2009-09- 130569.pdf

Ozsu, T. M., & Valduriez, P. (1999). *Principles of Distributed Database Systems* (2nd ed.). Prentice Hall.

Papadomanolakis, S., & Ailamaki, A. (2004). Autopart: Automating Schema Design for Large Scientific Databases using Data Partitioning. *Proceedings of the 16th International Conference on Scientific and Statistical Database Management*, pp. 383–392.

Pham, D., Dimov, S., & Nguyen, C. (2004). An incremental k-means algorithm. *Journal of Mechanical Engineering Science, 218*(7), 783–795.

Postgres, S. Q. L. n.d., Partitioning, Retrieved from http://www.postgresql.org/docs /8.1/static/ddl-partitioning.html.

Sacca, D., & Wiederhold, G. (1985). Database Partitioning in a Cluster of Processors. [TODS]. *ACM Transactions on Database Systems, 10*(1), 29–56. doi:10.1145/3148.3161

Sanjay, A., Chaudhuri, S., & Narasayya, V. R. (2000). Automated selection of materialized views and indexes in Microsoft SQL server. *Proceedings of 26th International Conference on Very Large Data Bases (VLDB'2000)*, pp. 496-505.

Sanjay, A., Narasayya, V. R., & Yang, B. (2004). Integrating vertical and horizontal partitioning into automated physical database design. *Proceedings of the International Conference on Management of Data (SIGMOD)*, pp. 359–370.

Stöhr, T., Märtens, H., & Rahm, E. (2000). Multidimensional database allocation for parallel data warehouses. *Proceedings of the International Conference on Very Large Databases (VLDB)*, pp. 273–284.

Tzoumas, K., Deshpande, A., & Jensen, C. (2010). Sharing-Aware Horizontal Partitioning for Exploiting Correlations During Query Processing, Proceedings of 36th International Conference on Very Large Data Bases, 3(1), pp. 542-553.

Chapter 12
What–If Application Design Using UML

Matteo Golfarelli
University of Bologna, Italy

Stefano Rizzi
University of Bologna, Italy

ABSTRACT

Optimizing decisions has become a vital factor for companies. In order to be able to evaluate beforehand the impact of a decision, managers need reliable previsional systems. Though data warehouses enable analysis of past data, they are not capable of giving anticipations of future trends. What-if analysis fills this gap by enabling users to simulate and inspect the behavior of a complex system under some given hypotheses. A crucial issue in the design of what-if applications is to find an adequate formalism to conceptually express the underlying simulation model. In this paper we report on how, within the framework of a comprehensive design methodology, this can be accomplished by extending UML 2 with a set of stereotypes. Our proposal is centered on the use of activity diagrams enriched with object flows, aimed at expressing functional, dynamic, and static aspects in an integrated fashion. The paper is completed by examples taken from a real case study in the commercial area.

INTRODUCTION

Market conditions increasingly force companies to reduce waste and optimize decisions. This has become not only a critical, but a vital factor for companies. In this direction, *business intelligence* (BI) provides a set of tools and techniques that

DOI: 10.4018/978-1-60960-537-7.ch012

enable a company to transform its business data into timely and accurate information for the decisional process. BI platforms are used by decision makers to get a comprehensive knowledge of the business and of the factors that affect it, as well as to define and support their business strategies. The goal is to enable data-based decisions aimed at gaining competitive advantage, improving operative performance, responding more quickly

Figure 1. The business intelligence pyramid

to changes, increasing profitability and creating added value for a company (Rizzi, 2009a).

As summarized by the so-called *BI pyramid* shown in Figure 1, BI platforms make it possible for companies to extract and process their own business *data* and then transform those data into *information* useful for the decision-making process. The information obtained in this way is then contextualized and enhanced by the decision-makers' own skills and experience, generating *knowledge* that is used to make conscious and well-informed decisions (Golfarelli & Rizzi, in press).

The BI pyramid demonstrates that data warehouses, that have been playing a lead role within BI platforms in supporting the decision process over the last decade, are no more than the starting point for the application of more advanced techniques that aim at building a bridge to the real decision-making process. This is because data warehouses are aimed at enabling analysis of past data, but they are not capable of giving anticipations of future trends. Indeed, in order to be able to evaluate beforehand the impact of a strategic or tactical move, decision makers need reliable previsional systems. So, almost at the top of the BI pyramid, what-if analysis comes into play.

What-if analysis is a data-intensive simulation whose goal is to inspect the behavior of a complex system (i.e., the enterprise business or a part of it) under some given hypotheses called *scenarios*. More pragmatically, what-if analysis measures how changes in a set of independent variables impact on a set of dependent variables with reference to a *simulation model* offering a simplified representation of the business, designed to display significant features of the business and tuned according to the historical enterprise data (Kellern et al., 1999).

Example 1. A simple example of what-if query in the marketing domain is: How would my profits change if I run a 3×2 (pay 2, take 3) promotion for one week on all audio products on sale? Answering this query requires a simulation model to be built. This model, that must be capable of expressing the complex relationships between the business variables that determine the impact of promotions on product sales, is then run against the historical sale data in order to determine a reliable forecast for future sales.

Among the killer applications for what-if analysis, it is worth mentioning profitability analysis in commerce, hazard analysis in finance, promotion analysis in marketing, and effectiveness analysis in production planning (Rizzi, 2009b). Less traditional, yet interesting applications described in the literature are urban and regional planning supported by spatial databases, index selection in relational databases, and ETL maintenance in data warehousing systems.

Surprisingly, though a few commercial tools are already capable of performing forecasting and what-if analysis, very few attempts have been made so far outside the simulation community to address methodological and modeling issues in this field (Golfarelli et al., 2006). On the other hand, facing a what-if project without the support of a design methodology is very time-consuming, and does not adequately protect designers and customers against the risk of failure.

From this point of view, a crucial issue is to find an adequate formalism to conceptually express simulation models. Such formalism, by providing a set of diagrams that can be discussed and agreed upon with the users, could facilitate the transition from the requirements informally expressed by users to their implementation on the chosen platform. Besides, as stated by Balci (1995), it could positively affect the accuracy in formulating simulation problems and help the designer to detect errors as early as possible in the life-cycle of the project. Unfortunately, no suggestion to this end is given in the literature, and commercial tools do not offer any general modeling support.

In this paper we show how, in the light of our experience with real case studies, an effective conceptual description of the simulation model for a what-if application in the context of BI can be accomplished by extending UML 2 with a set of stereotypes. As concerns static aspects we adopt as a reference the multidimensional model, used to describe both the source historical data and the prediction; the YAM^2 (Abelló et al., 2006) UML extension for modeling multidimensional cubes is adopted to this end. From the functional and dynamic point of view, our proposal is centered on the use of activity diagrams enriched with object flows. In particular, while control flows allow sequential, concurrent, and alternative computations to be effectively represented, object flows are used to describe how business variables and cubes

are transformed during simulation. The approach to simulation modeling proposed integrates and completes the design methodology presented by Golfarelli et al. (2006).

The paper is structured as follows. In the second section we survey the literature on modeling and design for what-if analysis. In the third section we outline the methodological framework that provides the context for our proposal. The fourth section enunciates a wish list for a conceptual formalism to support simulation modeling. The fifth section discusses how we employed UML 2 for simulation modeling. The sixth section proposes some examples taken from a case study concerning branch profitability and explains how we built the simulation model. Finally, the seventh section draws the conclusion.

RELATED WORKS AND TOOLS

There are a number of papers related to what-if analysis in the literature. In several cases, they just describe its applications in different fields such as e-commerce (Bhargava et al., 1997) hazard analysis (Baybutt, 2003), spatial databases (Klosterman, 1999; Lee & Gahegan, 2000), and index selection for relational databases (Chaudhuri & Narasayya, 1998). Other papers, such as the one by Fossett et al. (1991), are focused on the design of simulation experiments and the validation of simulation models. In (1999), Armstrong & Brodie survey a set of alternative approaches to forecasting, and give useful guidelines for selecting the best ones according to the availability and reliability of knowledge.

In the literature about simulation, different formalisms for describing simulation models are used, ranging from colored Petri nets (Lee et al., 2006) to event graphs (Kotz et al., 1994) and flow charts (Atkinson & Shorrocks, 1981). The common trait of these formalisms is that they mainly represent the dynamic aspects of the simulation, almost completely neglecting the functional (how are data transformed during the simulation?) and static (what data are involved and how are they structured?) aspects that are so relevant for data-intensive simulations like those at the core of what-if analysis in BI.

A few related works can be found in the database literature. Dang & Embury (2004) use constraint formulae to create hypothetical scenarios for what-if analysis, while Koutsoukis et al. (1999) explore the relationships between what-if analysis and multidimensional modeling. Balmin et al. (2000) present the SESAME system for formulating and efficiently evaluating what-if queries on data warehouses; here, scenarios are defined as ordered sets of hypothetical modifications on multidimensional data. In all these papers, no emphasis is placed on modeling and design issues.

In the context of data warehousing, there are relevant similarities between simulation modeling for what-if analysis and the modeling of ETL (*Extraction, Transformation and Loading*) applications; in fact, both ETL and what-if analysis can be seen as a combination of elemental processes each transforming an input data flow into an output. Vassiliadis et al. (2002) propose an ad hoc graphical formalism for conceptual modeling of ETL processes. While such proposal is not based on any standard formalisms, other proposals extend UML by explicitly modeling the typical ETL mechanisms. For example, Trujillo & Lujan-Mora (2003) represent ETL processes by a class diagram where each operation (e.g., conversion, log, loader, merge) is modeled as a stereotyped class. All these proposals cannot be considered as feasible alternatives to ours, since the expressiveness they introduce is specifically oriented to ETL modeling. An approach compatible with ours is the one by Pardillo et al. (2009), who propose a UML-based framework for uniformly modeling data flows in all data warehosue related applications (e.g., OLAP, ETL, data mining, and what-if analysis). The authors argue that designers would greatly benefit from such a framework due to the importance and complexity of data flows in this domain. Although both the framework and the UML profile for extending activity diagrams in OLAP application are discussed in the paper, no specific catalogue (i.e., set of application-specific actions) for what-if analysis is provided.

All the previous approaches strengthen our claim that extending UML is a promising direction for achieving a better support to the design activities in the area of BI. We finally mention two relevant approaches for UML-based multidimensional modeling (Abelló et al., 2006;, Lujan-Mora et al., 2006). Both define a UML profile for multidimensional modeling based on a set of specific stereotypes, and represent cubes at three different abstraction levels. However, the approach by Abelló et al. (2006) is preferred to the one by Lujan-Mora et al. (2006) for the purpose of this work since it allows for easily modeling different aggregation levels over the base cube, which is essential in simulation modeling for what-if analysis.

Recently, what-if analysis has been gaining wide attention from vendors of business intelligence tools. For instance, both SAP SEM-BPS (Strategic Enterprise Management - Business Planning and Simulation) and SAS Forecast Server enable users to make assumptions on the enterprise state or future behavior, as well as to analyze the effects of such assumptions by relying on a wide set of forecasting models. Also Microsoft Analysis Services provides some limited support for what-if analysis. Other commercial tools that can be used for what-if analysis to some extent are Applix TM1, Powersim Studio and QlikView.

Also spreadsheets and OLAP tools are often used to support what-if analysis. Spreadsheets offer an interactive and flexible environment for specifying scenarios, but lack seamless integration with the bulk of historical data. Conversely, OLAP tools lack the analytical capabilities of spreadsheets and are not optimized for scenario evaluation.

METHODOLOGICAL FRAMEWORK

As summarized in Figure 2, a what-if application is centered on a *simulation model*. The simulation model establishes a set of complex relationships between some *business variables* corresponding to significant entities in the business domain (e.g., products, branches, customers, costs, revenues, etc.). In order to simplify the specification of the simulation model and encourage its understanding by users, we functionally decompose it into *scenarios*, each describing one or more alternative ways to construct a *prediction* of interest for the user. The prediction typically takes the form of a multidimensional cube, meant as a set of cells of a given type, whose dimensions and measures correspond to business variables, to be interactively explored by the user by means of an OLAP front-end. A scenario is characterized by a subset of business variables, called *source variables*, and by a set of additional parameters, called *scenario parameters*, whose value the user has to enter in order to execute the simulation model and obtain the prediction. While business variables are related to the business domain, scenario parameters convey information technically related to the simulation, such as the type of regression adopted for forecasting and the number of past years to be considered for regression. Distinguishing source variables among business variables is important since it enables the user to understand which are the "levers" that she can independently adjust to drive the simulation; also non-source business variables are involved in scenarios, where they can be used to store simulation results. Each scenario may give rise to different simulations, one for each assignment of values to the source variables and to the scenario parameters.

Example 2. In the promotion domain of Example 1, the source variables for the scenario are the type of promotion, its duration, and the product category it is applied to; possible scenario parameters are the forecasting algorithm and its tuning parameters. The specific simulation ex-

Figure 2. What-if analysis at a glance

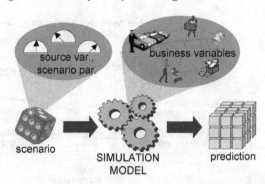

pressed by the what-if query reported in the text is determined by giving values "3×2", "one week" and "audio", respectively, to the three source variables. The prediction is a sales cube with dimensions Week and Product and measures Revenue, Cost and Profit, which the user could effectively analyze by means of any OLAP front-end.

Designing a what-if application requires a methodological framework; the one we consider, presented by Golfarelli et al. (2006) and sketched in Figure 3, relies on the seven phases sketched in the following:

1. *Goal analysis* aims at determining which business phenomena are to be simulated, and how they will be characterized. The goals are expressed by (i) identifying the set of business variables users want to monitor and their granularity; and (ii) outlining the relevant scenarios in terms of source variables users want to control.

2. *Business modeling* builds a simplified model of the application domain in order to help the designer understand the business phenomenon, enable her to refine scenarios, and give her some preliminary indications about which aspects can be neglected or simplified for simulation.

3. *Data source analysis* aims at understanding what information is available to drive the simulation, how it is structured and how it

Figure 3. A methodology for what-if analysis application design

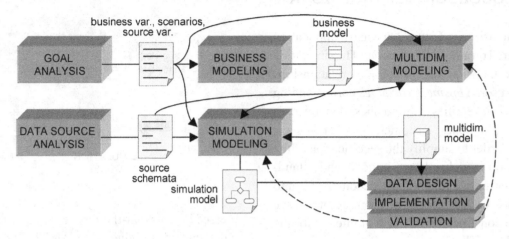

has been physically deployed, with particular regard to the cube(s) that store historical data.

4. *Multidimensional modeling* structurally describes the prediction by taking into account the static part of the business model produced at phase 2 and respecting the requirements expressed at phase 5. Very often, the structure of the prediction is a coarse-grain view of the historical cube(s).

5. *Simulation modeling* defines, based on the business model, the simulation model allowing the prediction to be constructed, for each given scenario, from the source data available.

6. *Data design and implementation*, during which the cube type of the prediction and the simulation model are implemented on the chosen platform, to create a prototype for testing.

7. *Validation* evaluates, together with the users, how faithful the simulation model is to the real business model and how reliable the prediction is. If the approximation introduced by the simulation model is considered to be unacceptable, phases 4 to 7 are iterated to produce a new prototype.

The five analysis/modeling phases (1 to 5) require a supporting formalism. Standard UML can be used for phases 1 (use case diagrams), 2 (a class diagram coupled with activity and state diagrams) and 3 (class, component and deployment diagrams), while any formalism for conceptual modeling of multidimensional databases can be effectively adopted for phase 4 (e.g., (Abelló et al., 2006) or (Lujan-Mora et al., 2006)). On the other hand, finding in the literature a suitable formalism to give broad conceptual support to phase 5 is much harder.

A WISH LIST FOR SIMULATION

Phase 5, simulation modeling, is the core phase of design. In the light of our experience with real case studies of what-if analysis in the BI context, we enunciate a wish list for a conceptual formalism to support it:

1. The formalism should be capable of coherently expressing the simulation model according to three perspectives: functional, that describes how business variables are transformed and derived from each other during simulation; dynamic, required to define the simulation workflow in terms of

sequential, concurrent and alternative tasks; static, to explicitly represent how business variables are aggregated during simulation.

2. It should provide constructs for expressing the specific concepts of what-if analysis, such as business variables, scenario parameters, predictions, etc.

3. It should support hierarchical decomposition, in order to provide multiple views of the simulation model at different levels of abstraction.

4. It should be extensible so that designers can effectively model the peculiarities of the specific application domain they are describing.

5. It should be easy to understand, to encourage the dialogue between designers and final users.

6. It should rely on a standard notation to minimize the learning effort.

UML perfectly fits requirements #4 and #6, and requirement #5 to some extent. In particular, it is well known that the stereotyping mechanism allows UML to be easily extended. As to requirements #1 and #3, the UML diagrams that best achieve integration of functional, dynamic and static aspects while allowing hierarchical decomposition are *activity diagrams*. Within UML 2, activity diagrams take a new semantics inspired by Petri nets, which makes them more flexible and precise than in UML 1 (OMG, 2008). Their most relevant features for the purpose of this work are summarized below:

*   An *activity* is a graph of *activity nodes* (that can be action, control or object nodes) connected by *activity edges* (either control flows or object flows).

*   An *action node* represents a task within an activity; it can be decorated by the rake symbol to denote that the action is described by a more detailed activity diagram.

*   A *control node* manages the control flow within an activity; control nodes for modeling decision points, fork and synchronization points are provided.

*   An *object node* denotes that one or more instances of a given class are available within an activity, possibly in a given state. Input and output objects for activities are denoted by overlapping them to the activity borderline.

*   *Control flows* connect action nodes and control nodes; they are used to denote the flow of control within the activity.

*   *Object flows* connect action nodes to object nodes and vice versa; they are used to denote that objects are produced or consumed by tasks.

*   *Selection* and *transformation* behaviors can be applied to object nodes and flows to express selection and projection queries on object flows.

Though activity diagrams are a nice starting point for simulation modeling since they already support advanced functional and dynamic modeling, some extensions are required in order to attain the desired expressiveness as suggested by requirement #2. In particular, it is necessary to define an extension allowing basic multidimensional modeling of objects in order to express how simulation activities are performed on data at different levels of aggregation.

With regard to this we recall that, as stated by OMG (2008), it is expected that the UML 2 Diagram Interchange specification will support a form of integration between activity and class diagrams, by allowing an object node to be linked to a class diagram that shows the classifier for that object and its relations to other elements. In this way, while activities provide a functional view of processes, associated class diagrams can be used to show static details. This argument has a relevant weight in our approach, since we associate activity diagrams with class diagrams to basically model the structure of cubes and their relationships with business variables.

EXPRESSING SIMULATION MODELS IN UML 2

In our proposal, the core of simulation modeling is a set of UML 2 diagrams organized as follows:

1. A use case diagram that reports a what-if analysis use case including one or more scenario use cases.
2. One or more class diagrams that statically represent scenarios and multidimensional cubes. A scenario is a class whose attributes are scenario parameters; it is related via an aggregation to the business variables that act as source variables for the scenario. Cubes are represented in terms of their dimensions, levels and measures.
3. An activity diagram (called *scenario diagram*) for each scenario use case. Each scenario diagram is hierarchically exploded into activity diagrams at increasing level of detail. All activity diagrams represent, as object nodes, the business variables, the scenario parameters and the cubes that are produced and consumed by tasks.

Static Modeling

Representation of cubes is supported by YAM[2] (Abelló et al., 2006), a UML extension for conceptual multidimensional modeling. YAM[2] models concepts at three different detail levels: *upper*, *intermediate*, and *lower*. At the upper level, *stars* are described in terms of *facts* and *dimensions*. At the intermediate level, a fact is exploded into *cells* at different aggregation granularities, and the aggregation *levels* for each dimension are shown. Finally, at the lower level, *measures* of cells and *descriptors* of levels are represented.

In our approach, the intermediate and lower levels are considered. The intermediate level is used to model, through the «cell» stereotype (represented by the C icon), the aggregation granularities at which data are processed by activities, and to show the combinations of dimension levels («level» stereotype, represented by the L icon) that define those granularities. The lower level allows single measures of cells to be described as attributes of cells, and their type to be separately modeled through the «KindOfMeasure» stereotype.

In order to effectively use YAM[2] for simulation modeling, three additional stereotypes are introduced for modeling, respectively, scenarios, business variables and scenario parameters (see Table 1).

Dynamic Modeling

As already mentioned, activity diagrams at different levels of detail are used to dynamically model how simulation is carried out. The main features of this representation are summarized below:

- The rake symbol denotes the actions that will be further detailed in subdiagrams.
- Object nodes that represent cubes of class <Class> cells are named as Cube of <Class>. The state in the object node is used to express the current state of the cubes being processed.
- Other object nodes represent business variables and scenario parameters used by activities.
- The «datastore» stereotype is used to represent an object node that stores non-transient information, such as a cube storing historical data.
- Selection operations on cubes are represented by decorating object flows with a selection behavior («selection» stereotype). Projection operations on cubes (i.e., restricting the set of measures to be processed) are represented by decorating ob-

Table 1.

name:	scenario
base class:	class
icon:	S
description:	classes of this stereotype represent scenarios
constraints:	a scenario class is an aggregation of business variable classes (that represent its source variables)
name:	business variable
base class:	class
icon:	B
description:	classes of this stereotype represent business variables
tagged values:	isNumerical (type Boolean, indicates whether the business variable can be used as a measure) isDiscrete (type Boolean, indicates whether the business variable can be used as a dimensions)
name:	scenario parameter
icon:	SP
base class:	attribute
description:	attributes of this stereotype represent parameters that model user settings concerning scenarios
constraints:	a scenario parameter attribute belongs to a scenario class

·   ject flows with a transformation behavior («transformation» stereotype).

Based on the characteristics of each specific application domain, some ad hoc stereotypes can be defined to model recurrent types of actions. The action stereotypes we defined based on our experience are listed in Table 2.

A CASE STUDY

Orogel S.p.A. is a large Italian company in the area of deep-frozen food. It has a number of branches scattered on the national territory, each typically entrusted with selling and/or distribution of products. Its data warehouse includes a number of data marts, one of which dedicated to commercial analysis and centered on a sales cube with dimensions Month, Product, Customer, and Branch.

The managers of Orogel are willing to carry out an in-depth analysis on the *profitability* (i.e., the net revenue) of branches. More precisely, they wish to know if, and to what extent, it is convenient for a given branch to invest on either selling or distribution, with particular regard to the possibility of taking new customers or new products. Thus, the four scenarios chosen for prototyping are: (i) analyze profitability during next 12 months in case one or more new products were taken/dropped by a branch; and (ii) analyze profitability during next 12 months in case one or more new customers were taken/dropped by a branch. Decision makers ask for analyzing profitability at different levels of detail; the finest granularity required for the prediction is the same of the sales cube.

The main issue in simulation modeling is to achieve a good compromise between reliability and complexity. To this end, in constructing the simulation model we adopted a two-step approach that consists in first forecasting past data, then

Table 2.

name:	olap
base class:	action
description:	actions of this stereotype transform cubes by applying OLAP operators; mainly, they aggregate, select and project cube cells
constraints:	at least one input and one output object flow must connect an olap action to Cube of <Class> object nodes
name:	regression
base class:	action
description:	actions of this stereotype carry out regression to extrapolate future data from past data
constraints:	at least one input object flow and one output object flow must connect a regression action to Cube of <Class> object nodes
name:	apportion
base class:	action
description:	actions of this stereotype apportion values of aggregate cube cells among a set of finer cube cells according to a given driver
constraints:	at least one input object flow and one output object flow must connect a regression action to Cube of <Class> object nodes
name:	user input
base class:	action
description:	actions of this stereotype allow manual input of data
constraints:	at least one output object flow must exit a user input action

"stirring" the forecasted data according to the event (new product or new customer) expressed by the scenarios. We mainly adopted statistical techniques for both the forecasting and the stirring steps; in particular, linear regression is employed to forecast unit prices, quantities and costs starting from historical data taken from the commercial data mart and from the profit and loss account during a past period taken as a reference. Based on the decision makers' experience, and aimed at avoiding irrelevant statistical fluctuations while capturing significant trends, we adopted different granularities for forecasting the different measures of the prediction cube (Golfarelli, 2006).

Representing the Simulation Model: Static Aspects

The four what-if use cases (one for each scenario) are part of a use case diagram that, as suggested by List et al. (2000), expresses how the different organization roles take advantage of BI in the context of sales analysis. Figure 4 shows a part of the use-case diagram for our case study. For space reasons, in this paper we will discuss only the Add product use case.

The class diagram shown in Figure 5 gives a (partial) specification of the multidimensional structure of the cubes involved. Sale is the base cell of the sales cube; its measures are quantitySold, unitPrice, fixedCosts, variableCosts and

Figure 4. Use-case diagram

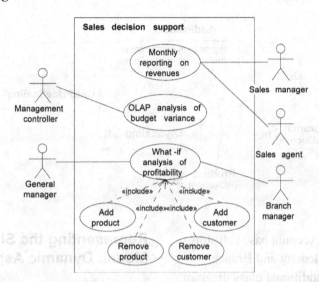

Figure 5. Multidimensional class diagram

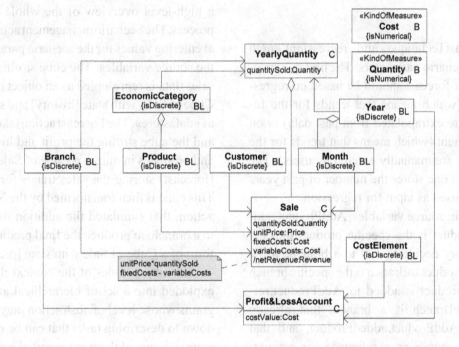

netRevenue (the latter is derived from the others), while the dimensions are Product, Customer, Month and Branch. Aggregations from one level to another represent roll-up hierarchies (e.g., products roll up to economic categories). Both dimension levels and measure types are further

stereotyped as business variables. YearlyQuantity is a cell derived from Sale by aggregating by EconomicCategory, Year and Branch and projecting on quantitySold; it will be used in activity diagrams to model aggregated data for regression.

Figure 6. Scenario class diagram

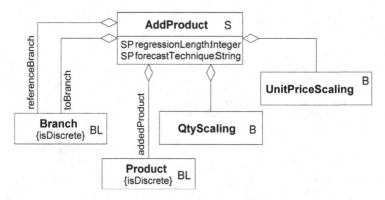

Finally, the Profit&LossAccount base cell stores the costs by Year, CostElement and Branch.

Figure 6 reports an additional class diagram that statically represents the AddProduct scenario in terms of its parameters and source variables:

*   forecastTechnique and regressionLength are scenario parameters. The first one specifies if forecast should be based on regression (which means that trends for the future are extrapolated from past data) or on judgment (which means that trends for the future are manually entered by users). The second one stores the number of past years to be used as input for regression.
*   Among source variables, AddProduct.addedProduct is the specific product that users may decide to add to a branch, while AddProduct.toBranch is the specific branch that product is added to. AddProduct.referenceBranch is a branch, that already sells AddProduct.addedProduct, and that users choose as a reference for estimating quantities and unit prices for selling AddProduct.addedProduct in AddProduct.toBranch. Finally, UnitPriceScaling and QtyScaling store the percentage change in unit price and quantity sold that users expect in AddProduct.toBranch with reference to AddProduct.referenceBranch.

Representing the Simulation Model: Dynamic Aspects

The Add product use case is expanded in the scenario diagram reported in Figure 7, that provides a high-level overview of the whole simulation process. The Scenario management action is aimed at entering values for the scenario parameters and the source variables. The cube storing historical sales data is represented as an object node called Cube of Sale, with state [history] and stereotyped as «datastore». The Forecast action takes this cube and the cube storing the profit and loss account, and produces in output a Cube of Sale with state [forecast] storing the sales trends for next year. This cube is then transformed by the Stir product action, that simulated the addition of a product to a branch, to produce the final prediction in the form of a Cube of Sale with state [prediction].

The action nodes of the context diagram are exploded into a set of hierarchical activity diagrams whose level of abstraction may be pushed down to describing tasks that can be regarded as atomic. Some of them are reported here in a simplified form and briefly discussed below:

*   Activity Scenario management (Figure 8) enables users to set all source variables and scenario parameters. This is represented by decorating actions with the «user input» stereotype.

Figure 7. Scenario diagram

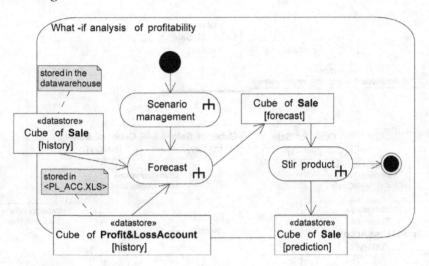

Figure 8. Activity diagram for Scenario management

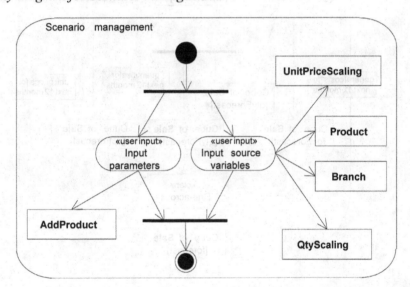

- Activity Forecast (Figure 9) is aimed at extrapolating sale data for the next twelve months, represented by the Cube of Sale object node with state [forecast]. This is done separately for each single measure of the Sale cell. In particular, forecasting general costs requires to extrapolate the future fixed and variable costs from the past profit and loss accounts, and scale variable costs based on the forecasted quantities. Input and output objects nodes for Forecast are emphasized by placing them on the activity borderline. The «selection» and «transformation» stereotypes are used to express, respectively, that only the sales data of the last few years have to be selected (as defined by the regressionLength scenario parameter) and which measure(s) from cube cells are to be processed. States [gcForecast], [qtyForecast] and [upFore-

Figure 9. Activity diagram for Forecast

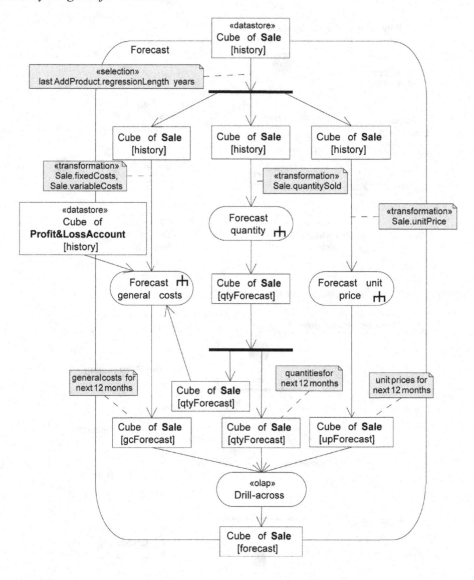

cast] denote forecast cubes where only cost, quantity and price measures have been calculated, respectively. These three cubes are then joined together through the Drill-across action.

- The quantity forecast granularity suggested by users is Year, Branch, EconomicCategory. The forecast for next year (Figure 10) can be done, depending on the value taken by the forecastTechnique scenario parameter, either by judgment (the yearly quantities for next year are directly entered by the user) or by regression (based on the yearly quantities sold during the last regressionLength years, stored in a Cube of YearlyQuantity with state [history]). In both cases, the total quantities by branch and economic category are stored in a Cube of YearlyQuantity with state [forecast]. This cube is then apportioned on the single months, products and customers proportionally to the quantities sold

Figure 10. Activity diagram for Forecast quantity

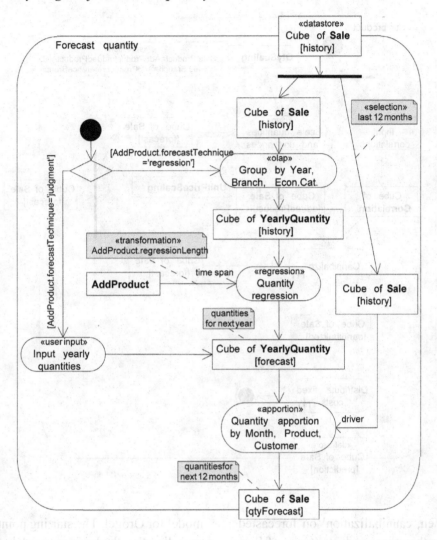

during the last 12 months. Note the use of names to express specific roles of object flows within actions. For instance, the time span object flow in input to Quantity regression carries the temporal span used for regression; the driver object flow in input to Quantity apportion denotes the flow carrying the cube whose cells provide the historical data used as a driver to proportionally distribute yearly quantities among months, products and customers.

• Finally, Figure 11 explodes the Stir product activity, that simulates the effects of adding

a new product (AddProduct.addedProduct) to a branch (AddProduct.toBranch) by reproducing the sales of that product in a different branch (AddProduct.referenceBranch) where that product is already sold. First, the past sales of the product are scaled according to the user-specified percentages stored in the qtyScaling and unitPriceScaling source variables (action Scale quantities and unit prices), and they are ascribed to the AddProduct.toBranch branch. This action produces a Cube of Sale object node with state [addedProd-

Figure 11. Activity diagram for Stir product

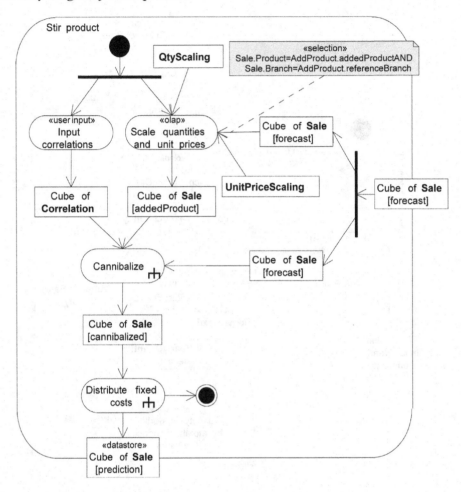

uct]. Then, cannibalization[1] on forecasted sales for the other products (Cube of Sale with state [forecast]) is simulated by applying a product correlation matrix (Cube of Correlation) built by judgmental techniques, i.e., by user input. Finally, fixed costs are properly redistributed on the single forecasted sales, changing the state of the Cube of Sale object node from [cannibalized] to [prediction].

Building the Simulation Model

In this section we give an overview of the approach we pursued to build the UML simulation model for Orogel. The starting points are the use case diagram, the business model and the multidimensional model obtained, respectively, from phases 1, 2 and 4 of the methodology outlined in the third section. For simplicity, we assume that the multidimensional model is already coded in YAM[2].

1. The class diagram is created first, by extending the multidimensional model that describes the prediction with the static specification of scenarios, source variables and scenario parameters.

2. For each scenario reported in the use case diagram, a high-level scenario diagram

is created. This diagram should show the macro-phases of simulation, the main data sources and the prediction. The object nodes should be named consistently with the classes diagram.

3. Each activity in each scenario diagram is iteratively exploded and refined into additional activity diagrams. As new, more detailed activities emerge, business variables and scenario parameters from the class diagram may be included in activity diagrams. Relevant aggregation levels for processing business variables within activities may be identified, in which case they are increasingly reported on the class diagram. Refinement goes on until the activities are found that are elemental enough to be understood by an executive designer/programmer.

We chose to build activity diagrams in a top-down fashion since, in our experience, this approach provides a stronger thread for reasoning with users, especially in the very common case that, in the beginning, users have little or no idea about how the basic laws that rule their business world should be coded.

In order to validate the simulation model, we used 2003 and 2004 data to forecast the profitability for 2005. A comparison with the actual data for 2005 yielded an average error of about 18% on the total profitability of the single branches, which decision makers judged to be very promising. The error on the total profitability for 2005 was significantly lower (about 7%) due to a compensation effect.

CONCLUSION

To sum up, our approach to simulation modeling fulfills the wish list proposed in the fourth section as follows: (#1) Static, functional and dynamic aspects are modeled in an integrated fashion by combining use case, class and activity diagrams;

(#2) Specific constructs of what-if analysis are modeled through the UML stereotyping mechanism; (#3) Multiple levels of abstraction are provided by both activity diagrams, through hierarchical decomposition, and class diagrams, through the three detail levels provided by YAM^2; (#4) Extensibility is provided by applying the stereotyping mechanism; (#5) Though completely understanding the implications of a UML diagram is not always easy for business users, the precision and methodological rigor encouraged by UML let them more fruitfully interact with designers, thus allowing solutions to simulation problems to emerge easily and clearly during analysis even when, in the beginning, users have little or no idea about how the basic laws that rule their business world should be coded; (#6) UML is a standard.

In practice, the approach proved successful in making the design process fast, well-structured and transparent. A critical evaluation of the proposed approach against its possible alternatives unveils that the decisive factor is the choice of adopting UML as the modeling language rather than devising an ad hoc formalism. Indeed, adopting UML poses some constraints in the syntax of diagrams (for instance, the difficulty of directly showing on activity diagrams the aggregation level at which cells are processed); on the other hand it brings some undoubted advantages to the designer, namely, the fact of relying on a standard and widespread formalism. Besides, using hierarchical decomposition of activity diagrams to break down the complexity of modeling increases the scalability of the approach.

A possible extension to our work goes in the direction proposed by Pardillo et al. (2009). In particular, we could evaluate to which extent our stereotypes fit the visual framework proposed in that paper, and we could develop the catalogue of actions specific to what-if analysis.

The simulation model designed has been prototyped in C#. Oracle 9i is the platform chosen for hosting the predictions and as a repository for business variables and model parameters. Business

Figure 12. Scenario management window for defining hypotheses on general costs

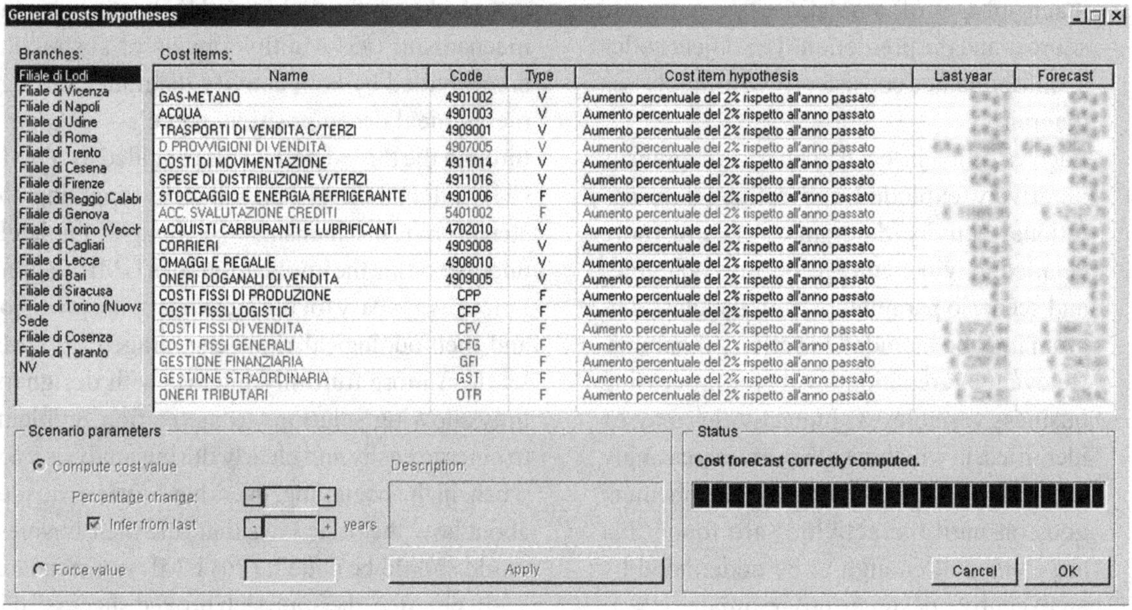

Objects is used for OLAP analysis of predictions. A screenshot of the GUI used to input business variables and scenario parameters is reported in Figure 12; in particular, the form used to formulate hypotheses about general costs is shown.

We conclude by remarking that the proposed formalism is oriented to support simulation modeling at the *conceptual* level, which in our opinion will play a crucial role in reducing the overall effort for design and in simplifying its reuse and maintenance. Devising a formalism capable of adequately expressing the simulation model at the *logical* level, so that it can be directly translated into an implementation, is a subject for our future work.

REFERENCES

Abelló, A., Samos, J., & Saltor, F. (2006). YAM²: a multidimensional conceptual model extending UML. *Information Systems*, *31*(6), 541–567. doi:10.1016/j.is.2004.12.002

Armstrong, S., & Brodie, R. (1999). Forecasting for marketing. In Hooley, G., & Hussey, M. (Eds.), *Quantitative methods in marketing* (pp. 92–119). Int. Thompson Business Press.

Atkinson, W. D., & Shorrocks, B. (1981). Competition on a Divided and Ephemeral Resource: A Simulation Model. *Journal of Animal Ecology*, *50*, 461–471. doi:10.2307/4067

Balci, O. (1995). Principles and Techniques of Simulation Validation, Verification, and Testing. In *Proceedings Winter Simulation Conference* (pp. 147-154). Arlington, USA.

Balmin, A., Papadimitriou, T., & Papakonstantinou, Y. (2000). Hypothetical Queries in an OLAP Environment. In *Proceedings Conference on Very Large Data Bases* (pp. 242-253). Cairo, Egypt.

Baybutt, P. (2003). Major hazards analysis – An improved process hazard analysis method. *Process Safety Progress*, *22*(1), 21–26. doi:10.1002/prs.680220103

Bhargava, H. K., Krishnan, R., & Muller, R. (1997). Electronic Commerce in Decision Technologies: A Business Cycle Analysis. *International Journal of Electronic Commerce, 1*(4), 109–127.

Chaudhuri, S., & Narasayya, V. (1998). AutoAdmin what-if index analysis utility. *SIGMOD Record, 27*(2), 367–378. doi:10.1145/276305.276337

Dang, L., & Embury, S. M. (2004). What-If Analysis with Constraint Databases. In *Proceedings British National Conference on Databases*. Edinburgh, Scotland.

Fossett, C., Harrison, D., & Weintrob, H. (1991). An assessment procedure for simulation models: a case study. *Operations Research, 39*(5), 710–723. doi:10.1287/opre.39.5.710

Golfarelli, M., & Rizzi, S. (in press). Data warehouse design: Modern principles & methodology. *McGraw-Hill Professional.*

Golfarelli, M., Rizzi, S., & Proli, A. (2006). Designing What-if Analysis: Towards a Methodology. In *Proceedings International Workshop on Data Warehousing and OLAP* (pp. 51-58). Arlington, USA.

Kellner, M., Madachy, R., & Raffo, D. (1999). Software process simulation modeling: Why? What? How? *Journal of Systems and Software, 46*(2-3), 91–105. doi:10.1016/S0164-1212(99)00003-5

Klosterman, R. (1999). The What if? collaborative support system. *Environment and Planning. B, Planning & Design, 26*, 393–408. doi:10.1068/b260393

Kotz, D., Toh, S. B., & Radhakrishnan, S. (1994). *A Detailed Simulation Model of the HP 97560 Disk Drive (Tech. Rep.)*. Hanover, USA: Dartmouth College.

Koutsoukis, N. S., Mitra, G., & Lucas, C. (1999). Adapting on-line analytical processing for decision modelling: the interaction of information and decision technologies. *Decision Support Systems, 26*(1), 1–30. doi:10.1016/S0167-9236(99)00021-4

Lee, C., Huang, H. C., Liu, B., & Xu, Z. (2006). Development of timed colour Petri net simulation models for air cargo terminal operations. *Computers & Industrial Engineering, 51*(1), 102–110. doi:10.1016/j.cie.2006.07.002

Lee, I., & Gahegan, M. (2000). What-if Analysis for Point Data Sets Using Generalised Voronoi Diagrams. In *Proceedings International Conference on GeoComputation*. Greenwich, UK.

List, B., Schiefer, J., & Tjoa, A. M. (2000). Process-Oriented Requirement Analysis Supporting the Data Warehouse Design Process – A Use Case Driven Approach. *Proceedings 11th International Conference Database and Expert Systems Applications* (pp. 593-603). London, UK.

Lujan-Mora, S., Trujillo, J., & Song, I.-Y. (2006). A UML profile for multidimensional modeling in data warehouses. *Data & Knowledge Engineering, 59*(3), 725–769. doi:10.1016/j.datak.2005.11.004

OMG. (2008). UML: Superstructure, version 2.0. Retrieved December 10, 2008, from http://www.omg.org.

Pardillo, J., Golfarelli, M., Rizzi, S., & Trujillo, J. (2009). Visual Modelling of Data Warehousing Flows with UML Profiles. In *Proceedings International Conference on Data Warehousing and Knowledge Discovery* (pp. 36-47). Linz, Austria.

Rizzi, S. (2009a). Business Intelligence. In Liu, L., & Özsu, T. (Eds.), *Encyclopedia of Database Systems*. Springer.

Rizzi, S. (2009b). What-if analysis. In L. Liu and T. Özsu (Eds.), *Encyclopedia of Database Systems*. Springer. Trujillo, J., & Lujan-Mora, S. (2003). A UML based approach for modelling ETL processes in data warehouses. In *Proceedings International Conference on Conceptual Modeling* (pp. 307-320). Chicago, USA.

Vassiliadis, P., Simitsis, A., & Skiadopoulos, S. (2002). Conceptual modeling for ETL processes. In *Proceedings International Workshop on Data Warehousing and OLAP* (pp. 14-21). McLean, USA.

ENDNOTE

[1] *Cannibalization* is the process by which a new product gains sales by diverting sales from existing products, which may deeply impact the overall profitability.

Chapter 13
A Dynamic and Semantically–Aware Technique for Document Clustering in Biomedical Literature

Min Song
New Jersey Institute of Technology, USA

Xiaohua Hu
Drexel University, USA

Illhoi Yoo
University of Missouri, USA

Eric Koppel
New Jersey Institute of Technology, USA

ABSTRACT

As an unsupervised learning process, document clustering has been used to improve information re-trieval performance by grouping similar documents and to help text mining approaches by providing a high-quality input for them. In this paper, the authors propose a novel hybrid clustering technique that incorporates semantic smoothing of document models into a neural network framework. Recently, it has been reported that the semantic smoothing model enhances the retrieval quality in Information Retrieval (IR). Inspired by that, the authors developed and applied a context-sensitive semantic smoothing model to boost accuracy of clustering that is generated by a dynamic growing cell structure algorithm, a varia-tion of the neural network technique. They evaluated the proposed technique on biomedical article sets from MEDLINE, the largest biomedical digital library in the world. Their experimental evaluations show that the proposed algorithm significantly improves the clustering quality over the traditional clustering techniques including k-means and self-organizing map (SOM).

DOI: 10.4018/978-1-60960-537-7.ch013

INTRODUCTION

Document clustering, unlike document classification, is an unsupervised learning process meaning that there is no known information about documents including the number of document groups (usually called k). Document clustering organizes textual documents into meaningful groups that represent topics in document collections without any known information about a document set. As a result, the documents in a document cluster are similar to one another while documents from different clusters are dissimilar.

Document clustering was originally studied to enhance the performance of information retrieval (IR) because similar documents tend to be relevant to the same user queries (Wang et al., 2002; Zamir & Etzioni, 1998). Document clustering has been used to facilitate nearest-neighbor search (Buckley & Lewit, 1985), to support an interactive document browsing paradigm (Cutting et al., 1992; Gruber, 1993; Koller & Sahami, 1997; Gruber, 1993), and to construct hierarchical topic structures (van Rijsbergen, 1979). Thus, document clustering plays a more important role for IR and text mining communities since the most natural form for storing information is text, and text information has increased exponentially.

In the biomedical domain, document clustering technologies have been used to facilitate the practice of evidence-based medicine. This is because document clustering enhances biomedical literature searching (e.g., MEDLINE searching) in several ways and literature searches are one of the core skills required for the practice of evidence-based medicine (Evidence-based Medicine Working Group, 1992). For example, Pratt and her colleagues (Pratt et al., 1999; Pratt & Fagan, 2000), and Lin and Demner-Fushman (2007) introduced interesting semantic document clustering approaches that automatically cluster biomedical literature (MEDLINE) search results into document groups for the better understanding of literature search results.

Current information technologies allow us to acquire, store, archive, and retrieve documents electronically. To this end, document clustering has been given focal attention because document clustering assists users in discovering hidden similarities and key concepts in documents. One of most serious problems making document clustering difficult to deal with text information is that the size of text collections in digital libraries are increasing rapidly. To handle the increasing size of document collections, a clustering algorithm has to not only solve the incremental problem but it must also have high efficiency in a large dataset.

Most document clustering algorithms require a form of data pre-processing including stop-word removal and feature selection. Through the data pre-processing, unimportant features are eliminated and the original dimension is reduced to a more manageable size. However, the data pre-processing has two problems. First, although the data pre-processing can reduce the original dimension size, the reduced dimension is still sparse, which is called "the curse of dimensionality". As the result, clustering results are often low quality. Second, the reduction of dimensionality by the data-preprocessing may disturb the preservation of the original topological structure of the input data.

To solve these problems, we propose a context-sensitive semantic smoothing of a document model and incorporate it into Dynamic Growing Cell Structure (DynGCS). The effect of model smoothing has not been extensively studied in the context of document clustering (Zhang et al., 2006). Most model-based clustering approaches simply use Laplacian smoothing to prevent zero probability (Nigam & McCallum, 1998; Zhong & Ghosh, 2005), while most similarity-based clustering approaches employ the heuristic TF*IDF scheme to discount the effect of general words (Steinbach et al., 2000). As showed in (Zhong & Ghosh, 2005), model-based clustering has several advantages over discriminative based approaches. One of the advantages of model-based approaches is that it learns generative models from the documents, with each model representing one particular document set. Due to the promising results reported in model-based clustering approaches, we propose a novel semantic smoothing technique to improve clustering quality.

DynGCS is an adaptive variant of an artificial neural network model, Self-Organizing Map (SOM), which is well suited for mapping high-dimensional data into a 2-dimensional representation space. The training process is based on weight vector adaptation with respect to the input vectors. SOM has shown to be a highly effective tool for document clustering (Kohonen et al, 1999). One of the disadvantages of SOM in document clustering is its fixed size in terms of the number of units and their particular arrangement, which must be defined prior to the start of the training process. Without knowing the type and the organization of documents, it is difficult to get satisfying results without multiple training runs using different parameter settings. This is extremely time consuming, given the high-dimensional data representation. DynGCS solves the problem of fixed-sized structure by dynamically generating multiple layers of SOM.

The organization of this paper is as follows: Section 2 describes semantic smoothing of document model. Section 3 denotes the DynGCS algorithm. Section 4 presents results. We conclude our paper in Section 5.

RELATED WORK

In this section, we highlight work done on document clustering. Jain et al. (1999) provided an extensive survey of various clustering techniques. Zamir and Etioni (1998) provided a survey on applying hierarchical clustering algorithms into clustering documents. Hierarchical clustering algorithm has been widely used among the numerous document clustering algorithms. Several variants from this algorithm include single-link, group-average and complete-link. Recently, partitional

clustering algorithms were proposed to cluster large document datasets due to their relatively low computational requirements (Eissen & Potthast, 2005; Larsen & Aone, 1999; Aggarwal et al., 1999; Allen & Littman, 1993).

Cutting et al. (1992) adapted two partition-based clustering algorithms, Buckshot and Fractionation, to clustering documents. Buckshot selects a small sample of documents to pre-cluster them using a standard clustering algorithm and assigns the rest of the documents to the clusters formed. Fractionation splits the N documents into 'm' buckets where each bucket contains N/m documents.

Zamir et al. introduce the notion of phrase-based document clustering. They use a generalized suffix-tree to obtain information about the phrases and use them to cluster the documents (Zamir et al., 1997).

According to Allen and Littman, the two cluster selection methods of BiSecting K-means that are used to select the cluster to be bisected, do not significantly affect clustering quality; the two methods are selecting the largest cluster and the cluster with the least overall similarity (Allen & Littman, 1993). We believe the choice of the cluster selection methods does affect the clustering quality because the choice may lead to different document clustering results. Allen and Littman (1993) and Beil et al (2002) show BiSecting K-means is better than K-means while Pantel and Lin (2002) shows K-means is superior to Bisecting K-means.

Suffix tree document model was firstly proposed in 1997 (Nigam & McCallum, 1998; Zamir et al., 1997). Different from document models, which treat a document as a set of words and ignores the sequence order of the words, suffix tree document model considers a document to be a set of suffix substrings such that common prefixes of the suffix substrings are selected as phrases to label the edges of a suffix tree. The STC algorithm is based on this model and works well in clustering Web document snippets returned from several search engines. However, the properties of the suffix tree model and STC have not been analyzed in their papers (Zamir et al., 1997). Eissen et al. continued their work and pointed out that the STC algorithm is a fusion heuristic that efficiently evaluates the graph-based similarity measure for large document collections (Eissen et al., 2005). Furthermore, they also proposed several new graph-based similarity measures to compute document similarities. Their experimental evaluation results showed that the similarity measures, especially the hybrid similarity measure had achieved significant performance improvements in the MajorClust algorithm and the GAHC algorithm.

According to Zamir et al., Suffix Tree Clustering (STC) provides better clustering quality for web documents than K-means in terms of precision (Zamir et al., 1997). On the other hand, STC showed poor clustering results for Eissen et al. (2005). Larsen and Aone (1999) claim hierarchical clustering is better than K-means based on the experiments where one document set is used, while Zhao and Karypis (2002) and Steinbach et al (2000) indicate BiSecting K-means and K-means are better than hierarchical clustering.

Most document clustering studies (Beil et al, 2002; Cutting et al, 1992; Hotho et al, 2002; Larsen & Aone, 1999; Pantel & Lin, 2002; Steinbach et al., 2000; Eissen et al., 2005) uses only 1000 to 20,000 documents in their experiments. To test the scalability of document clustering approaches, much larger document sets are required. Hotho et al (2002) claim the use of ontology may improve document clustering. However, the authors used their own manually modeled ontology for tourism domain for document clustering.

SEMANTIC SMOOTHING OF DOCUMENT MODELS

In document clustering, a TF*IDF score is often used as the dimension values of document vectors. In the context of language model, a TF*IDF

scheme is roughly equivalent to the background model smoothing. Since TF*IDF is a pure probabilistic scheme, it does not convey semantics of content represented by terms and phrases. As an alternative, (Lafferty & Zhai, 2001) proposes semantic smoothing where context and sense information are incorporated into the model. Latent Semantic Indexing (LSI) is an early attempt at semantic smoothing which projects documents in a corpus into a reduced space where document semantics becomes clear. LSI explores the structure of term co-occurrence with Singular Value Decomposition (SVD). However, the problem of LSI is that it increases noise while reducing the dimensionality because it is unable to recognize polysemy. In practice, it is also criticized for the lack of scalability and ability to interpret.

Our semantic smoothing technique is similar to the one proposed in (Zhang et al., 2006). Their approach utilizes multi-word phrases (e.g. "star war", "movie star") as topic signatures. Using multi-word phrases has several advantages: 1) a multi-word phrase is often unambiguous: 2) multi-word phrases can be extracted from a corpus by existing statistical approaches without human knowledge: and 3) documents are often full of multi-word phrases; thus, it is robust to smooth a document model through statistical translation of multi-word phrases in a document to individual terms. Unlike (Zhang et al., 2006), we employ an information gain-based keyphrase extraction technique (Song et al, 2003) to generate a set of phrases in documents that achieves competitive performance in biomedical data collections

Our keyphrase extraction procedure consists of two stages: building an extraction model and extracting keyphrases. The extraction model is trained for keyphrases before the keyphrase extraction technique is applied. Keyphrases are extracted by referencing the keyphrase model, which was built based on a decision tree technique (Song et al., 2003). Both training and test data are processed by the following three components: 1) Data Cleaning, 2) Data Tokenizing, and 3) Data

Figure 1. Phrase/Term and Document Relation

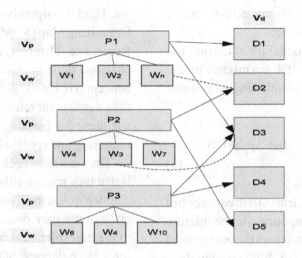

Discretizing. After that, there are three features to calculate information gain: 1) TF-IDF, 2) Part-Of-Speech (POS), and 3) First Occurrence of Phrases. Based on these features, we build a discretization table and rank the candidate keyphrases based on its information gain measure. We compared information gain with other techniques such as Naïve Bayesian used in KEA (Willett et al, 1999) and found that information gain gave us the best performance in our previous experiments. In addition, we adopted the Mahalanobis Distance to measure distance among models. Mahalanobis distance takes into account the covariance among the variables in calculating distances (Pearson, 2005). Suppose we have indexed all documents in a given collection C with terms and phrases as illustrated in Figure 1. Note that Vp denotes phrase vector, Vw denotes word vector, and Vd denotes document vector. The translation probabilities from a keyphrase t_k to any individual term w, denoted as $p(w|t_k)$, are also given. Then we can easily obtain a document model below:

$$p_t(w \mid d) = \sum_k p(w \mid t_k)p_{ml}(t_k \mid d) \qquad (1)$$

The likelihood of a given document generating the keyphrase t_k can be estimated with

$$p_{ml}(t_k \mid d) = \frac{c(t_k, d)}{\sum_i c(t_i, d)} \qquad (2)$$

where $c(t_i, d)$ is the frequency of the keyphrase t_i in a given document d.

We refer to the above model as translation model indicated in (Lafferty & Zhai, 2001). As we discussed in the introduction, the translation from multi-word phrases to individual terms would be very specific. Thus, the translation model not only weakens the effect of "general" words, but also relieves the sparseness of class-specific "core" words. However, not all topics in a document can be expressed by key phrases. If only the translation model is used, there will be serious information loss. A natural extension is to interpolate the translation model with a unigram language model below:

$$p_b(w \mid d) = (1 - \alpha)p_{ml}(w \mid d) + \alpha p(w \mid C) \qquad (3)$$

$P_{ml}(w|d)$ is a maximum likelihood estimator. We refer to this unigram model as simple language model or baseline language model. We use Jelinek-

Mercer smoothing on the purpose of further discounting "general" words that do not convey the high discriminated power.

The final document model for clustering use is described in equation (4). It is a mixture model with two components: a simple language model and a translation model.

$$p_{bt}(w \mid d) = (1 - \lambda)p_b(w \mid d) + \lambda p_t(w \mid d)$$

$$(4)$$

The translation coefficient (λ) is used to control the influence of two components in the mixture model. In our experiment, we set the background translation coefficient to 0.5. With training data, the translation coefficient can be trained by optimizing the clustering quality. After estimating a language model for each document in the corpus with context-sensitive semantic smoothing, we use the Mahalanobis Distance of two language models as the distance measure of the corresponding two documents. Given two probabilistic document models $p(w|d_x)$ and $p(w|d_y)$, the Mahalanobis Distance of $p(w|d_x)$ to $p(w|d_y)$ is defined as:

$$d(\overrightarrow{p_x}, \overrightarrow{p_y}) = \sqrt{\sum_{i=1}^{p} \frac{(p_y - p_x)^2}{\sigma_i^2}}$$

$$(5)$$

where σ_i is the standard deviation of the p_x over the sample set.

DYNGCS

DynGCS is a self-organizing neural network model that incrementally builds a Dirichlet Voronoi tessellation of input space while automatically finding its structure and size. DynGCCs are used in artificial neural network (ANN) architectures. ANN can allow clusters to search and reduce search time. Unsupervised ANN learning for document clustering offers a number of advantages. Most

commonly unsupervised ANN learning methods are Hard Competitive Learning (HCL), Self-Organizing Map (SOM) algorithm, and Adaptive Resonance Theory (ART). All these methods have one thing in common: the winner-takes-all concept. HCL and SOM are dependent on input data density, therefore it would not be wise to use these for purpose of improved information clustering and retrieval.

The main drawback of the existing algorithms is that they require either pre-specification of the number of clusters (K-means clustering and SOM), or have the user decide the number of clusters to the user (hierarchical clustering). Particularly for a large dataset, SOM suffers from its fixed network architecture, which has motivated the development of a number of adaptive variants (Zhong & Ghosh, 2005).

In this paper, we introduce an adaptive variant of SOM to resolve the aforementioned issue. DynGCC is an unsupervised clustering method that adaptively decides on the best architecture for the self-organizing map. This stems from Growing Cell Structure (GCS), introduced by Fritzke (1994, 1995). Fritzke introduced an incremental self-organizing network with variable topology, known as GCS based on SOM and Hebbian learning. The GCS has three main advantages over the SOM: first, the network structure is determined automatically by the input pattern. Second, the network size needs not to be predefined. Third, all parameters of the model are constant. Therefore, a "cooling schedule" is not required which is a contrast to the conventional SOM. The problem with GCS, however, is that it tends to overspill as the map grows larger.

To tackle the problem of overspill, we combine GCS with the Growing Hierarchical Self-Organizing Map (GH-SOM). GH-SOM adopts a hierarchical structure with multiple layers, where each layer consists of a set of independent self-organizing maps (Dittenbach et al, 2000). With the probability of adding every cell in a SOM from one layer to the next layer of the hierarchy, it shares the sample adaptation steps with GCS. There is, however, one exception that uses a decreasing learning rate and a decreasing neighborhood radius. The mean quantization error of the map is used to decide whether a new level of the hierarchy needs to be created. For instance, at level 0, the single SOM unit is assigned a weight vector m_0, such that $m_0 = [\mu 0_1, \mu 0_2, ..., \mu 0_n]^T$ is computed as the average of all input data. The mean quantization error of this single unit is computed as the following with d representing the number of input data x:

$$mqe_0 = \frac{1}{d} \| m_0 - x \| \qquad (6)$$

DynGCS produces distribution-preserving mappings as other SOM related algorithms. DynGCS operates on the following principle of GCS (Bruske & Sommer, 1995):

1. During the training stage, the number of clusters and the connections among them are dynamically assigned.
2. Adaptation strength is constant over time.
3. Adaptation occurs only in the best-matching cell (BMU) and its neighborhood.
4. Adaptation increments the signal counter for BMU and decrements the remaining cells.
5. For the adaptation of the output map to the distribution of the input vectors, insertion of new cells and deletion of existing cells occur.

The DynGCS hierarchy is constructed from and superimposed onto the standard GCS algorithm detailed above (Figure 2). DynGCS starts with the small architecture. The DynGCS is a hierarchical self-organizing neural network designed to preserve topological structure of input data based on GCS and Growing Hierarchical Self-Organizing Map. DynGCS grows dynamically. In each growth, the DynGCS adds two children to the leaf whose

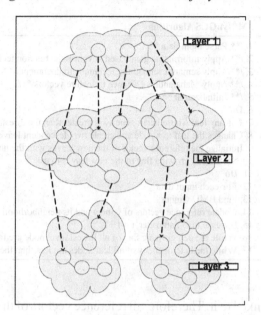

Figure 2. Hierarchical Structure of DynGSC

heterogeneity exceeds a threshold and turns it to a node. This process goes on until the heterogeneity of all cells is less than the threshold. A learning process similar to GCS is adopted.

The DynGCS algorithm is shown in Table 1. Initially there is only one root node. All the input data is linked to the root. The reference vector of the root node is initialized with the centroid of the data. In growth mode, two child nodes are appended to the root node. All input data linked to the root node is distributed between these child nodes by employing a learning process. Once the learning process is finished, the heterogeneities of the leaf nodes are scrutinized to decide whether expansion to another level is necessary. If another expansion is needed, then a new growth step is invoked. Two child nodes are appended to the leaf nodes if the level of heterogeneity is greater than the threshold. All input data is distributed again with the learning process and a new growth begins. This process continues until the heterogeneity of all the leaves is less than the threshold. In DynGCS, each leaf represents a cluster that includes all data linked to it. The reference vector of a leaf is the centroid of all data

Table 1. SM/DynGCS Algorithm

SM/DynGCS Algorithm
1. /** Parse input data **/
2. /** Apply information gain based keyphrase extraction techniques to input data **/
3. /** Apply semantic smoothing technique to documents **/
4. /** Apply Mahalanobis Distance to feature vectors **/
5. /** Initialization **/
6. **Do**
7. **For** any leaf whose heterogeneity is greater than the threshold
8. Changes the leaf to a node and create two descendent leaves.
9. Initialize the reference vector of the new leaves with the node's reference vector
10. Set the cell growing flag of the new leaves to true
11. **Do**
12. **For** each input data
13. Find BMU winner
14. Update reference vectors of winner and its neighborhood
15. Increase time parameter, t = t +1.
16. **While** the cell growing flag of all lowest level node are false
17. **While** the heterogeneity of all leaf nodes are less than the threshold

linked to it. Therefore, all reference vectors of the leaves form a Voronoi set of the original dataset. Each internal node represents a cluster that includes all data linked to its leaf descendants. The reference vector of an internal node is the centroid of all data linked to its leaf descendants.

The height of DynGCC is $\log_d M$, where d is the branch factor and M is the number of nodes in the hierarchy. M is $O(N)$ where N is the number of data. Let J be the average number of learning iterations for each learning process. Thus, the time complexity factor for DynGCC will be $O[\log_d N * (J * N + d * J * N)]$. Since J and d are constants, the complexity will be. $O(cN * \log_d) \sim O(N * \log_d N)$

EXPERIMENTS

In this section, we report our evaluation method, data collection, and experiment results.

Evaluation Method

We evaluated the proposed algorithm by comparing clustering output with known classes as answer keys. There have been a number of comparison metrics, such as mutual information metric, misclassification index (MI), purity, confusion matrix, F-measure, and Entropy. In our experiment we used misclassification index, purity, and Entropy as clustering evaluation metrics. MI is the ratio of the number of misclassified objects to the size of the whole dataset; thus, MI with 0% means the perfect clustering.

$$MI = \frac{no\_misclassified\_objects}{total\_no\_of\_objects}$$

The cluster purity indicates the percentage of the dominant class members in a given cluster; the percentage is nothing more than the maximum precision over the classes.

$$Purity = \sum_j \frac{n_i}{n} \max_i \{precision(i,j)\},$$

where n is the number of documents.

The entropy of a cluster implies how the members of the k classes are distributed within each cluster. We use weight average entropy as an overall clustering metric as shown below:

$$Entropy = -\sum_{j} \frac{n_j}{n} \sum_{i} P(i,j) * \log_2 P(i,j),$$

where $p(i,j)$ is $precision(i,j)$ and n is the number of documents

Note that the smaller MI and Entropy imply the better clustering quality while the larger purity indicates the better clustering quality.

Data Collections

We used public MEDLINE data for the experiments by collecting document sets related to various diseases. We use the "MajorTopic" tag along with the MeSH disease terms as queries to MEDLINE. Table 2 shows the document sets used in our experiments.

Each corpus name in Table 3 indicates the number of document sets (i.e. k) used for the corpus generation, as well as what document sets are used (document set IDs (see Table 2) are delimited by "-"). The format of the corpus ID is [Ck.n], where k is the number of document sets (classes) and n is a sequence number.

Once we retrieve the datasets, we generate various document combinations by randomly mixing the document sets whose numbers of classes are 2 to 12 (Table 3).

The document sets used for generating the combinations are later used as answer keys on the performance measure. Refer to (Yoo et al, 2007) for details on data collections and test data sets.

Experiment Results

In this section, we will report experiment results with average (μ) and standard deviation (σ). In our experiments, we compared our method, SM/DynGCS with three other algorithms such as TF*IDF/DynGCS, K-means, and SOM.

TF*IDF/DynGCS: TF*IDF, which is widely used in information retrieval, was implemented for feature vectors. It is a measure of importance

Table 2. Document Collections and Their Size

Document Sets	ID	No. of Docs
Otitis	Ot	5,233
Osteoarthritis	OA	8,987
Osteoporosis	Ost	8,754
Migraine	Mg	4,174
Coronary Heart Disease	CHD	53,664
Breast Neoplasm	Bre	56,075
Depressive Disorder	Dep	19,926
AIDS	AIDS	19,671
Alzheimer Disease	Alz	18,033
Diabetes Type 2	Diab	18,726
Age-related Macular Degeneration	AMD	3,277
Parkinson Disease	Pk	9,933

Table 3. Overview of Test Data

Corpus Name	ID	Size
2_Bre-CHD	C2.1	110k
4_Dep-AIDS-Alz-Diab	C4.2	76k
2_Mg-Alz	C2.3	22k
3_OA-Ost-Pk	C3.3	28k
4_Alz-AMD-Ot-Ost	C4.1	35k

for a term in a document or class. As indicated by formula 7, TF*IDF is a term frequency in a document or class, relative to overall frequency. The TF*IDF feature is a well-known weighting scheme in information retrieval.

$$W_{ij} = tf_{ij} * \log_2 \frac{N}{n} \tag{7}$$

W_{ij} weight of term t_i in document D_j and tf_{ij} is frequency of term t_j in document D_j. N is the number of documents in a collection and n is the number of documents where term t_j occurs at least once.

SOM: Self-Organizing Map (SOM) is a well accepted neural network technique in document clustering. In this experiment, we used 10,000

Table 4. Comparison of Evaluation Metrics

	MI	**Entropy**	**Purity**
Tf*idf/DynGCS	μ:0.23 σ: 0.13	μ:0.26 σ:0.21	μ:0.92 σ:0.16
SM/DynGCS	μ:0.35 σ: 0.17	μ:0.31 σ:0.23	μ:0.93 σ:0.21
K-means	μ:0.19 σ:0.12	μ:0.17 σ:0.14	μ:0.79 σ:0.12
SOM	μ:0.28 σ:0.13	μ:0.27 σ:0.15	μ:0.88 σ:0.15

Figure 3. Performance Comparison on Different Datasets by Purity

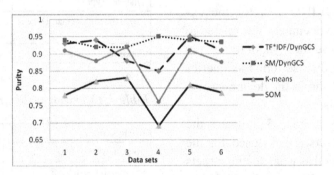

iterations and set the initial learning rate to 0.1. The 10 x 10 SOM is trained to cluster and the final number of cells is 250.

K-Means: K-Means is a simple but powerful unsupervised learning algorithm that solves the well known clustering problem. Because K-Means may produce different clustering results every time due to its random initializations, we ran it five times and averaged the values of clustering evaluation metrics.

Table 4 shows the comparison of the overall clustering quality of SM/DynGCS, TF*IDF/DynGCS, K-means, and SOM. The clustering results are from 5 datasets from which the averages and standard deviations are calculated. We notice that SM/DynGCS is superior to the hierarchical algorithms.

Comparing miscalculation indexes, SM/DynGCS outperforms the other three. Compared to K-means, it is 0.16% better in terms of μ.

In terms of entropy, the best performance was made by SM/DynGCS. SM/DynGCS improves accuracy by about 0.14% when compared to K-means. TF*IDF/DynGCS and SOM perform almost at the same level. With purity, the results show that SM/DynGCS performs 0.14% better than K-means. As indicated by the results, integrating semantic smoothing into clustering algorithm improves accuracy more than DynGCS with TF*IDF does.

Figure 3 shows how four different clustering techniques perform on five different datasets. Unlike the other three techniques, TF*IDF/DynGCS, K-means, and SOM, the performance of semantic smoothing-based DynGCS is stable across five datasets.

Figure 4 also indicates that the semantic smoothing-based DynGCS outperforms the other three techniques, TF*IDF/DynGCS, K-means, and SOM in terms of entropy measure. The superior performance of our semantic smoothing-

Figure 4. Performance Comparison on Different Datasets by Entropy

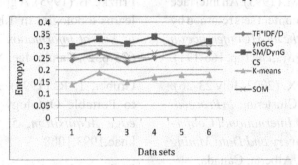

Figure 5. Performance Comparison on Different Datasets by MI

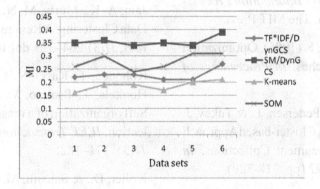

based DynGCS is observed by MI measure (Figure 5).

CONCLUSION

In this paper, we proposed a hybrid clustering algorithm that combines semantic smoothing of document model and dynamic growing cell structure. We developed a context-sensitive smoothing method for document models and used Mahalanobis distance for smoothed probabilistic models as a document similarity measure for clustering. These feature vectors were used as input for document clustering. Our document clustering technique combined GCS with the Growing Hierarchical Self-Organizing Map (GH-SOM). GH-SOM adopts a hierarchical structure with multiple layers, where each layer consists of a set of independent self-organizing maps.

We performed a comparison study of SM/DynGCS with the other three techniques: TF*IDF/DynGCS, K-means, and SOM on 5 MEDLINE corpora. The experimental results indicated that our SM/DynGCS is superior to the other three approaches in terms of μ and σ. For future work, we will conduct more comprehensive experiments including other model-based partitional approaches. We also plan to apply our technique to dynamic document clustering, i.e. clustering search results.

REFERENCES

Aggarwal, C. C., Wolf, J. L., Yu, P. S., Procopiuc, C., & Park, J. S. (1999). Fast algorithms for projected clustering. *Proceedings of the 1999 ACM SIGMOD International Conference on Management of data* (pp. 61-72).

Allen, P. O. R., & Littman, M. (1993). An interface for navigating clustered document sets returned by queries. *In Proceedings of the ACM Conference on Organizational Computing Systems* (pp. 166-171).

Beil, F., Ester, M., & Xu, X. (2002, July 23-26). Frequent Term-Based Text Clustering. *In Proceedings of 8th ACM SIGKDD International Conference on Knowledge Discovery and Data Mining* (pp. 436-442). Edmonton, Alberta, Canada.

Bruske, J., & Sommer, G. (1995). Dynamic cell structures. In G. Tesauro, D. Touretzky, & T. Leen (Eds.), *Advances in Neural Information Processing Systems, 7*, 497–504. The MIT Press.

Buckley, C., & Lewit, A. F. (1985). Optimization of inverted vector searches. *In Proceedings of SIGIR-85* (pp. 97-110).

Cutting, D., Karger, D., Pedersen, J., & Tukey, J. (1992). Scatter/Gather: A Cluster-based Approach to Browsing Large Document Collections. *In Proceedings of SIGIR '92* (pp. 318-329).

Dittenbach, M., Merkl, D., & Rauber, A. (2000). The Growing Hierarchical Self-Organizing Map. *In Proc. Intl. Joint Conf. on Neural Networks (IJCNN'00)*.

Eissen, S. M., Stein, B., & Potthast, M. (2005). The Suffix Tree Document Model Revisited. *In Proceedings of the 5th International Conference on Knowledge Management* (pp. 596-603).

Evidence-Based Medicine Working Group. (1992). Evidence-based medicine. A new approach to teaching the practice of medicine. *Journal of the American Medical Association, 268*, 2420–2425. doi:10.1001/jama.268.17.2420

Fritzke, B. (1994). Growing cell structures - a self-organizing network for unsupervised and supervised learning. *Neural Networks, 7*(9), 1441–1460. doi:10.1016/0893-6080(94)90091-4

Fritzke, B. (1995). A growing neural gas network learns topologies. In T.K. Lean (Ed.), *Advances in Neural Information Processing Systems* (pp. 625-632). Cambridge, MA: MIT Press.

Gruber, T. R. (1993). A Translation Approach to Portable Ontology Specifications. *Knowledge Acquisition, 5*, 199–220. doi:10.1006/knac.1993.1008

Hotho, A., Maedche, A., & Staab, S. (2002). Text Clustering Based on Good Aggregations. [KI]. *Künstliche Intelligenz, 16*(4), 48–54.

Jain, A. K., Murty, M. N., & Flynn, P. J. (1999). Data Clustering: A Review. *ACM Computing Surveys, 31*(3), 264–323. doi:10.1145/331499.331504

Kohonen, T., Kaski, S., Lagus, K., Salojärvi, J., Honkela, J., Paatero, V., & Saarela, A. (1999). Self organization of a massive text document collection. *IEEE Transactions on Neural Networks, 11*(3), 171–182.

Koller, D., & Sahami, M. (1997). Hierarchically classifying documents using very few words. *In Proceedings of ICML-97* (pp. 170–176).

Lafferty, J., & Zhai, C. (2001). Document Language Models, Query Models, and Risk Minimization for Information Retrieval. *In Proceedings of the 24th ACM SIGIR Conference on Research and Development in IR* (pp. 111-119).

Larsen, B., & Aone, C. (1999). [San Diego, California.]. *Fast and Effective Text Mining Using Linear-time Document Clustering., KDD-99*, 16–22.

Lin, J., & Demner-Fushman, D. (2007). Semantic Clustering of Answers to Clinical Questions. *Proceedings of the 2007 Annual Symposium of the American Medical Informatics Association (AMIA 2007)* (pp. 458-462). Chicago, Illinois.

Nigam, K., & McCallum, A. (1998). Text Classification from Labeled and Unlabeled Document Using EM. *Machine Learning, 39*(2-3), 103–134.

Pantel, P., & Lin, D. (2002). Document clustering with committees. *In Proceedings of the 2002 ACM SIGMOD International Conference on Management of data* (pp. 199-206).

Pearson, R. K. (2005). Mining imperfect data; dealing with contamination and incomplete records. *SIAM 2005.*

Pratt, W., & Fagan, L. (2000). The Usefulness of Dynamically Categorizing Search Results. *Journal of the American Medical Informatics Association, 7*(6), 605–617.

Pratt, W., Hearst, M., & Fagan, L. (1999). A knowledge-based approach to organizing retrieved documents. *AAAI '99: Proceedings of the 16th National Conference on Artificial Intelligence* (pp. 80-85). Orlando, Florida.

Song, M., Song, I.-Y., & Hu, X. (2003). KPSpotter: a flexible information gain-based keyphrase extraction system. *The 5th ACM international workshop on web information and data management* (pp. 50-53).

Steinbach, M., Karypis, G., & Kumar, V. (2000). *A Comparison of Document Clustering Techniques*. Department of Computer Science and Engineering, University of Minnesota.

van Rijsbergen, C. J. (1979). Information Retrieval (2nd ed). London: Butterworths.

Wang, B. B., McKay, R. I., Abbass, H. A., & Barlow, M. (2002). Learning Text Classifier using the Domain Concept Hierarchy. *In Proceedings of International Conference on Communications, Circuits and Systems*. China.

Willett, P. (1988). Recent trends in hierarchic document clustering: a critical review. *Information Processing & Management, 24*(5), 577–597. doi:10.1016/0306-4573(88)90027-1

Witten, I. H., Paynter, G. W., Frank, E., Gutwin, C., & Nevill-Manning, C. G. (1999). KEA: Practical automatic keyphrase extraction. *Proc. DL '99* (pp. 254-256).

Yoo, I., Hu, X., & Song, I.-Y. (2007). A Coherent Graph-based Semantic Clustering and Summarization Approach for Biomedical Literature and a New Summarization Evaluation Methods. *BMC Bioinformatics, 8*(Suppl 9), S4. doi:10.1186/1471-2105-8-S9-S4

Zamir, O., & Etzioni, O. (1998). Web Document Clustering: A Feasibility Demonstration. *In Proceedings of SIGIR 98* (pp. 46-54).

Zamir, O., Etzioni, O., & Karp, R. M. (1997). Fast and intuitive clustering of web documents. *In Proceedings of the 3rd International Conference on Knowledge Discovery and Data Mining*.

Zhang, X., Zhou, X., & Hu, X. (2006, Dec. 18-22). Semantic Smoothing for Model-based Document Clustering. *The 2006 IEEE International Conference on Data Mining (IEEE ICDM06*. HongKong.

Zhao, Y., & Karypis, G. (2002). *Criterion functions for document clustering: Experiments and Analysis*. Department of Computer Science, University of Minnesota.

Zhong, S., & Ghosh, J. (2005). Generative Model-based Document Clustering: a Comparative Study. *Knowledge and Information Systems, 8*(3), 374–384. doi:10.1007/s10115-004-0194-1

This work was previously published in the International Journal of Data Warehousing and Mining 5(4), edited by David Taniar, pp. 44-57, copyright 2009 by IGI Publishing (an imprint of IGI Global).

Chapter 14
Reliability Estimates for Regression Predictions:
Performance Analysis

Zoran Bosnić
University of Ljubljana, Slovenia

Igor Kononenko
University of Ljubljana, Slovenia

ABSTRACT

In machine learning, the reliability estimates for individual predictions provide more information about individual prediction error than the average accuracy of predictive model (e.g. relative mean squared error). Such reliability estimates may represent decisive information in the risk-sensitive applications of machine learning (e.g. medicine, engineering, and business), where they enable the users to distinguish between more and less reliable predictions. In the atuhors' previous work they proposed eight reliability estimates for individual examples in regression and evaluated their performance. The results showed that the performance of each estimate strongly varies depending on the domain and regression model properties. In this paper they empirically analyze the dependence of reliability estimates' performance on the data set and model properties. They present the results which show that the reliability estimates perform better when used with more accurate regression models, in domains with greater number of examples and in domains with less noisy data.

1. INTRODUCTION

When using supervised learning for modeling data, we aim to achieve the best possible prediction accuracy for the unseen examples which were not included in the learning process (Kononenko & Kukar, 2007). For evaluation of the prediction accuracies, the *averaged accuracy measures* (e.g. the relative mean squared error). However, such measures provide no information about the

DOI: 10.4018/978-1-60960-537-7.ch014

expected error of an *individual prediction* for an unseen example.

Examples of areas, where such reliability estimates for the individual predictions present an important benefit (Crowder, Kimber, Smith, & Sweeting, 1991), are the risk-sensitive areas, where acting upon predictions may have financial or medical consequences (e.g. medical diagnosis, stock market, navigation, control applications). For example, in the medical diagnosis, the use of individual prediction reliability estimates allows the physicians to decide more easily whether to trust the automatically predicted patient's diagnosis or not.

In our previous work we proposed and compared eight reliability estimates (based on five approaches) for the model-independent reliability estimation for individual examples in regression (Bosnić & Kononenko, 2008b). We evaluated performance of the proposed reliability estimates using 5 regression models (regression trees, linear regression, neural networks, support vector machines and locally weighted regression) and on 15 testing domains. The empirical evaluation of our approach showed that our approaches provide good estimation of the prediction error for individual examples. As such, they offer a tool which improves the safety of implementing the automatically generated decisions in the risk-sensitive areas.

In this paper we extend the previous evaluation with the sixth regression model (random forests) and larger number of testing datasets (27). Additionally, we perform experiments using artificial data sets and empirically analyze the dependence of reliability estimates' performance on the data set and model properties (noise in data, number of examples, model accuracy).

The paper is organized as follows. First, we introduce reliability estimates that were proposed and empirically evaluated in our previous work. After describing their evaluation protocol and presenting their performance on regression models and 27 testing domains, we empirically analyze the dependence of their performance on the domain and regression model properties. We focus on analyzing impacts of three factors: the accuracy of the regression model, the number of examples in the training set, and the training data noise level. We finish by providing conclusions and ideas for the further work.

2. RELATED WORK

In order to enable users of classification and regression models to gain more insight into the reliability of individual predictions, various methods aiming at this task were developed in the past. Some of these methods were focused on *extending formalizations of the existing predictive models*, enabling them to make predictions with their adjoined reliability estimates. The other group of methods focused on the *development of model-independent approaches*, which are more general, but harder to analytically evaluate with individual models. In the following, we present the related work from the both groups of approaches. For detailed field review of reliability estimation for individual predictions, see (Bosnić & Kononenko, 2009).

The idea of reliability estimation for individual predictions originated in statistics, where confidence values and intervals are used to express the reliability of estimates. In machine learning, the statistical properties of predictive models were utilized to extend the predictions with adjoined reliability estimates, e.g. with support vector machines (Gammerman, Vovk, & Vapnik, 1998; Saunders, Gammerman, & Vovk, 1999), ridge regression (Nouretdinov, Melluish, & Vovk, 2001), and multilayer perceptron (Weigend & Nix, 1994). Since these approaches are bound to a particular model formalism, their reliability estimates can be probabilistically interpretable, thus being the *confidence measures* (*0* represents the confidence of the most inaccurate prediction and *1* the confidence of the most accurate one).

However, since not all approaches offer probabilistic interpretation, we use more general term, *the reliability estimate*, to name the measure that provides information about the trust in accuracy of the individual prediction.

In contrast to the previous group of methods, the second group is more general and model-independent (not bound to particular model). These methods utilize the model-independent approaches to find their reliability estimates, e.g. local modeling of prediction error based on input space properties and local learning (Birattari, Bontempi, & Bersini, 1998; Giacinto & Roli, 2001), using the variance of bagged models (Heskes, 1997), or by meta-predicting the leave-one-out error of a single example (Tsuda, Rätsch, Mika, & Müller, 2001). Inspired by transductive reasoning (Vapnik, 1995), Kukar and Kononenko (2002) proposed a method for estimation of the classification reliability. Their work introduced a set of reliability measures which successfully separate correct and incorrect classifications and are independent of the learning algorithm. We later adapted this approach to regression (Bosnić & Kononenko, 2007; Bosnić, Kononenko, Robnik-Šikonja, & Kukar, 2003).

The work presented here extends the work of Bosnić and Kononenko (2008b) and empirically analyzes the performance properties of eight reliability estimates (based on five approaches). The approaches and reliability estimates are summarized in the following section.

3. RELIABILITY ESTIMATES

3.1. Sensitivity Analysis-Based Reliability Estimates

In our previous work (Bosnić & Kononenko, 2007) we used the sensitivity analysis approach to develop two reliability estimates, which measure the local variance and the local bias for the prediction of an individual example, *SAvar* (Sensitivity Analysis variance) and *SAbias* (Sensitivity Analysis bias).

Let us briefly summarize the concept behind the sensitivity analysis approach. Both estimates are based on observing the change in the output prediction if a small and controlled change is induced in the learning set, i.e. by expanding the initial learning set with an additional learning example. The predictions of the *sensitivity models* (i.e. models which are generated on the modified learning sets) are afterwards used to compose the reliability estimates, which are defined as:

$$SAvar = \frac{\sum_{\varepsilon \in E} (K_\varepsilon - K_{-\varepsilon})}{|E|} \quad (1)$$

and

$$SAbias = \frac{\sum_{\varepsilon \in E} (K_\varepsilon - K) + (K_{-\varepsilon} - K)}{2|E|} \quad (2)$$

In both of the above estimates, K represents the prediction of the initial regression model, whereas K_ε and $K_{-\varepsilon}$ denote predictions of two sensitivity models which are obtained using positive and negative value of parameter ε (chosen in advance). The chosen ε determines the label value of the additional learning example (which equals K, modified by some $f(\varepsilon)$) and therefore indirectly defines the magnitude of the induced change in the initial learning set. It is defined relative to the interval of the learning examples' label values, hence its values are domain-independent. To widen the observation windows in the local problem space and make the measures robust to local anomalies, the reliability measures use predictions from sensitivity models, gained and averaged using various values of parameter $\varepsilon \in E$.

3.2. Variance of a Bagged Model

In related work, the variance of predictions in the bagged aggregate (Breiman, 1996) of artificial neural networks has been used to indirectly estimate the reliability of the aggregated prediction (Heskes, 1997). Since an arbitrary regression model can be used with the bagging technique, we evaluate the proposed reliability estimate in combination with other learning algorithms.

Given a bagged aggregate of m predictive models, where each of the models yields a prediction Km, the prediction of an example is therefore computed by averaging the individual predictions:

$$K = \frac{\sum_{i=1}^{m} K_i}{m} \qquad (3)$$

and reliability estimate *BAGV* as the prediction variance

$$BAGV = \frac{1}{N} \sum_{i=1}^{m} (K_i - K)^2 \qquad (4)$$

In our experimental work the testing bagged aggregates contained $m=50$ model instances.

3.3. Local Cross-Validation Reliability Estimate

Approaches in the related work have demonstrated a potential for applying the general cross-validation procedure locally (Birattari et al., 1998; Giacinto & Roli, 2001; Schaal & Atkeson, 1994) and to use it for the local estimation of prediction reliability. Analogously, we implemented the *LCV* (Local Cross-Validation) reliability estimate, which is computed using the local leave-one-out (LOO) procedure. For a given unlabeled example, in each iteration (for every nearest neighbor) we generate a leave-one-out (LOO) model, excluding one of the neighbors. By making the LOO predic-

tion K_i for each of the neighbors $i = 1,..., k$ and using its true label C_i, we then compute absolute LOO prediction error $|C_i - K_i|$. The reliability of the unlabeled example x is therefore defined as the weighted average of the absolute LOO prediction errors of its nearest neighbors x_i (weighted by distance $d(x_i, x)$):

$$LCV = \frac{\sum_{(x_i, C_i) \in N} d(x_i, x) \cdot |C_i - K_i|}{\sum_{(x_i, C_i) \in N} d(x_i, x)} \qquad (5)$$

Here N denotes the set of k nearest neighbors $N = \{(x_1, C_1),..., (x_k, C_k)\}$ of the unlabeled example $(x, \_)$, $d()$ denotes a distance function, and K_i denotes a LOO prediction for the neighbor (x_i, C_i) computed on the local learning set $N \backslash (x_i, C_i)$. In our work, we implemented the *LCV* algorithm to be adaptive to the size of the neighborhood with respect to the number of examples in the learning set. The parameter k was therefore dynamically assigned as $\left\lceil \frac{1}{20} \times |L| \right\rceil$, where L denotes the training set.

3.4. Density-Based Reliability Estimate

One of the traditional approaches to estimation of the prediction reliability is based on the distribution of learning examples in the input space. The density-based estimation of the prediction error assumes that the error is lower for predictions which are made in *denser* problem subspaces (a local part of the input space with larger number of learning examples), and higher for predictions which are made in *sparser* subspaces (a local part of the input space with fewer learning examples).

A typical use of this approach is, for example, with decision and regression trees, where we trust each prediction according to the proportion of learning examples that fall in the same leaf of a tree as the predicted example. But although this approach considers the quantity of available information, it also has a disadvantage that it does not consider the learning examples' labels. This causes the method to perform poorly in noisy data in cases and when the distinct examples are dense but not clearly separable. Namely, although it is obvious that such cases present a modeling challenge, the density estimate would characterize such regions of the input space as highly reliable.

We define the reliability estimate *DENS* as the value of the estimated probability density function for a given unlabeled example. To estimate density we use the Parzen windows (Silverman, 1986) with the Gaussian kernel. We reduced the problem of calculating the multidimensional Gaussian kernel to the calculation of two-dimensional kernel using a distance function applied to the pairs of example vectors. Given the learning set $L = ((x_1, y_1),..., (x_n, y_n))$, the density estimate for an unlabeled example $(x, \_)$ is therefore defined as:

$$p(x) = \frac{\sum_{i=1}^{n} \kappa(d(x, x_i))}{n} \qquad (6)$$

where $d()$ denotes a distance function and κ a kernel function (in our case the Gaussian). Since we expect the prediction error to be higher in the cases where the value of density is lower, this means that $p(x)$ would correlate negatively with the prediction error. To establish the positive correlation with prediction error as with other reliability estimates (to improve the comparability), we need to invert $p(x)$, defining *DENS* as:

$$DENS(X) = \max_{i=1...n}(p(x_i)) - p(x) \qquad (7)$$

3.5. Local Modeling of Prediction Error

For the comparison with previous reliability estimates we also propose an approach to local estimation of the prediction reliability using the nearest neighbors' labels. If we are given a set of nearest neighbors $N = \{(x_1, C_1),..., (x_k, C_k)\}$, we define the estimate *CNK* $(C_{Neighbors} - K)$ for an unlabeled example $(x, \_)$ as a difference between the average label of the nearest neighbors and the example's prediction K (using the model that was generated on all learning examples):

$$CNK = \frac{\sum_{i=1}^{k} C_i}{k} - K = C_{Neighbors} - K \qquad (8)$$

In our experiments we computed the estimate *CNK* using 5 nearest neighbors.

4. PERFORMANCE OF RELIABILITY ESTIMATES

We measured the performance of the presented reliability estimates in terms of computing their correlation coefficients to the prediction error of the individual examples. By computing the correlation coefficient and its statistical significance for each reliability estimate, we were able to measure the strength of the estimate's association to prediction error for examples of each testing domain. Testing therefore consisted of two phases. In the first phase, the prediction errors and reliability estimates based on the five described approaches (*SAvar, SAbias, BAGV, LCV, DENS, and CNK*) were computed for every example, computing them using the leave-one-out cross-validation procedure. In the second, the evaluation phase of testing, the correlation coefficients between the errors and each estimate were computed and their significance was statistically evaluated using the t-test for correlation coefficients with significance level $\alpha = 0.05$.

Note that all of the estimates were expected to correlate positively with the prediction error. This means that all the estimates are designed so that their higher absolute values represent less reliable predictions and their lower absolute values represent more reliable predictions (the value *0* represents the reliability of the most reliable prediction). Also note that all of the estimates, except *SAbias* and *CNK*, can take only positive values. Besides the absolute magnitude of these two estimates, which we interpret as the prediction reliability, these two estimates provide the additional information about the error direction (whether the value of prediction was too high or too low). This carries a potential for the further work, for correcting the initial predictions using these two estimates. We therefore performed the experiments by correlating only the magnitudes of estimates (absolute values of *SAbias* and *CNK*) to the absolute prediction error of test examples. For estimates *SAbias* and *CNK*, we also correlated their signed values to the signed prediction error of test examples. In this way we actually tested the performance of eight estimates: *SAvar*, *SAbias-s* (signed), *SAbias-a* (absolute), *BAGV*, *LCV*, *DENS*, *CNK-s* (signed) and *CNK-a* (absolute).

The performance of reliability estimates was tested using six regression models, implemented in the statistical package R (2006). The models are listed below and feature the following key properties:

- regression trees (RT): trees (Breiman, Friedman, Olshen, & Stone, 1984), with the mean squared error used as the splitting criterion, the values in leaves represent the average label of corresponding training examples,
- linear regression (LR): no explicit parameters,
- neural networks (NN): three-layered perceptron (Rumelhart, Hinton, & Williams, 1986) with 5 hidden neurons, *tanh* activation function, the backpropagation learning algorithm uses the adaptive gradient descent,
- support vector machines (SVM): a version of regression SVM (Vapnik, 1995; Smola

& Schölkopf, 1998) implemented in the LIBSVM library (Christiannini & Shawe-Taylor, 2000; Chang & Lin, 2001),
- locally weighted regression (LWR): local regression with Gaussian kernel,
- random forests (RF): random forests (Breiman, 2001) with 100 trees in each forest.

For testing, 27 standard benchmark data sets were used, each data set representing a regression problem. The application domains varied from medical, ecological, technical to mathematical and physical. Most of the data sets are available from the UCI Machine Learning Repository (Asuncion & Newman, 2007) and from the StatLib DataSets Archive (StatLib, 2005). A brief description of data sets is given in Table 1.

Performance of the tested estimates is shown in Figure 1. Graphs in the figure depict the percent of domains with the significant positive/negative correlations between the reliability estimates and the prediction error. Bars in each graph denote the performance of each regression model individually and the bar below each graph shows the average performance of each estimate (i.e. the average number of positive and negative correlations across all regression models). As the charts are displayed in the decreasing order of estimates' average performance, we can see that the best results were achieved using the estimates *BAGV*, *CNK-a*, *LCV* and *SAvar*. The estimate *SAbias-a* achieved the worst average results.

The results show that the reliability estimates mostly positively correlate with the prediction error, as expected. Namely, we can see that the number of positive correlations (desired correlations, depicted by light grey bars) dominates the number of negative correlations (non-desired correlations, depicted by dark grey bars) in all regression model/reliability estimate pairs. By observing the detailed results we can see that the

Table 1. Basic characteristics of testing data sets.

	Dataset	Number of examples	Number of discrete attributes	Number of continuous attributes
1	autoprice	159	1	14
2	auto93	93	6	16
3	autohorse	203	8	17
4	baskball	96	0	4
5	bodyfat	252	0	14
6	brainsize	20	0	8
7	breasttumor	286	1	8
8	cloud	108	2	4
9	cpu	209	0	6
10	diabetes	43	0	2
11	echomonths	130	3	6
12	elusage	55	1	1
13	fishcatch	158	2	5
14	fruitfly	125	2	2
15	grv	123	0	3
16	hungarian	294	7	6
17	lowbwt	189	7	2
18	mbagrade	61	1	1
19	pharynx	195	4	7
20	pollution	60	0	15
21	pwlinear	200	0	10
22	servo	167	2	2
23	sleep	58	0	7
24	transplant	131	0	2
25	triazines	186	0	60
26	tumor	86	0	4
27	wpbc	198	0	32

performance of the following estimates attracts the most attention:

- *CNK-s* with regression trees (the estimate achieved significant positive correlation with the prediction error in 80% of experiments and did not negatively correlate with the prediction error in any experiment).
- *SAbias-s* with regression trees (the estimate positively correlated with the predic-

tion error in 73% of tests and negatively in none of tests).

In the following sections, we analyze the dependence of reliability estimates' performance on various model-dependent and domain-dependent properties.

Figure 1. Performance (percentage of testing domains where estimates achieved significant correlation) of reliability estimates, shown for each tested regression model. The bars below each graph depict the average performance across all six used regression models

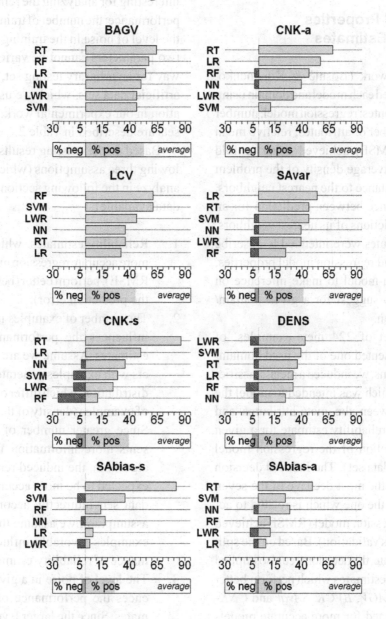

5. DEPENDENCE OF RELIABILITY ESTIMATES' PERFORMANCE ON MODEL AND DOMAIN PROPERTIES

The empirical results on 27 domains showed that the reliability estimates achieved different performances using different regression models and on different data sets. Based on this finding, in our previous work (Bosnić & Kononenko, 2008a) we focused on automatically selecting the best performing reliability estimate for a given domain and regression model. After scratching the surface, in this paper we aim at going deeper and analyze which model and domain properties cause good or bad performance of the reliability estimates.

5.1. Influential Properties on Reliability Estimates

In our previous work (Bosnić & Kononenko, 2008a) we described each model and domain using several meta-attributes: regression model, number of examples, number of attributes, relative mean squared error (RMSE) achieved using tenfold cross validation, average density of the problem space, average distance to the nearest neighbors, and average distance between prediction for an example and predictions of its nearest neighbors. These meta-attributes were intended to describe the key domain and regression model properties, enabling the meta-model to make inference on which estimate to suggest for a given domain/ model combination.

On the dataset of 224 meta-examples, of which each represented one of the used domain/ model combinations, we induced a meta-classifier (decision tree), which was intended to model the dependences between the meta-attributes and the most suitable reliability estimate for a given problem (combination of the regression model and the problem data set). The induced decision tree revealed that the most decisive of the seven meta-attributes is the one which is related to accuracy of the regression model (RMSE achieved using tenfold cross validation). Based on the split of that meta-attribute, the decision tree also implied that the reliability estimates which perform better on the average (*BAGV, BVCK, SAvar* and *CNK-a*) should be selected for more accurate models (lower RMSE) and the reliability estimates which perform worse on the average (*DENS, CNK-s, SAbias-s*) should be selected for less accurate models (higher RMSE). Besides suggesting the most suitable estimate to be selected, this result implies the dependence between model accuracy and the performance of reliability estimate on that model, as well.

Besides the model accuracy, there are two more domain properties which may intuitively be interesting for analyzing the reliability estimates' performance: the number of training examples and the level of noise in the training data. Since these two parameters cannot be varied in a controlled way for an arbitrary testing set, we created three artificial data sets, which we used for the evaluation in our experimental work. These three data sets are described in Table 2.

Based on the existing results we state the following three assumptions (which we empirically analyze in the following section given the testing data available):

1. Reliability estimates, which are used with more accurate regression models (with lower RMSE), perform better (better correlate with the prediction error).

2. The number of examples in a given domain influences the performance of reliability estimates. Assume we are given two datasets with examples generated from the same distribution, which differ only in the number of examples (density of the problem space). Since greater number of examples represents more information for the modeling algorithm, the induced regression model is expected to be more accurate on the denser data set. Indirectly, according to the first assumption, we assume that the number of examples favorably influences the performance of reliability estimates.

3. The level of noise in a given domain influences the performance of reliability estimates. Since the larger level of noise in data is expected to negatively influence the model accuracy, with respect to the first assumption we assume that greater noise deteriorates the performance of estimates, as well.

In the following sections we validate our assumptions on the testing data sets and on artificial data sets.

Table 2. A brief description of the artificial data sets. Each data set contains examples with label Y, 5 relevant attributes A_1, A_2, A_3, A_4, A_5 and two irrelevant (noise) attributes A_6, A_7.

LIN
linear function $Y = A_1 + 2 \cdot A_2 + 3 \cdot A_3 + 4 \cdot A_4 + 5 \cdot A_5$
TRI
trigonometric function $Y = 10 \cdot \sin(A_1 \cdot A_2) + 20 \cdot \cos(A_3 + A_4) + A_5$
SPH
two spheres $Y = \begin{cases} A_2^2 + A_3^2 + A_4^2 & A_1 > 0 \\ A_3^2 + A_4^2 + A_5^2 & else \end{cases}$

5.2. Dependence on Regression Model's Accuracy

Since some regression models can more accurately model data than the others, we analyze the dependence of reliability estimates' performance on the accuracy of regression models, achieved on a particular data set. Given 27 testing data sets, 6 regression models and 8 reliability estimates, we therefore accumulated the performance data (i.e. the relative mean squared error of the model and the correlation coefficients between used reliability estimate and prediction errors) for 1296 experiments (i.e. combinations of selected domain/model/reliability estimates).

The dependence of reliability estimate's performance on the model accuracy for all 1296 experiments is shown in Figure 2. The regression line through the dots shows that the correlation between the reliability estimate and the prediction error has a decreasing trend for the models with greater RMSE (less accurate models). Since variance of the points forming the regression line is seemingly too large to make any definite conclusions, in the following we analyze the same dependence with respect to combinations of different regression models and reliability estimates.

The dependence of estimate's performance on the model accuracy for combinations of used models/estimates is shown in Figure 3. We can see that the same trend as in the aggregated chart (Figure 2) is present also in the majority of combinations (in 42 out of 48 model combinations). However, the graphs show that the contrary association between the model's performance and the reliability estimate's performance is present for estimate *CNK-s* (using random forests, support vector machines and linear regression), and for estimate *SAbias-s* (using random forests, neural networks and locally weighted regression). Interesting point is that the regression line in the chart of these two estimates is the steepest for random forests, which is also the best performing regression model (it achieved the lowest average RMSE) on all 27 testing data sets (the average performance results of regression models are shown in Table 3 and in Figure 4). In addition, support vector machines and neural networks, which were also in the list of the top performing regression models, stand out as exceptions to our above observations, as well.

To conclude, the empirical results generally indicate that the reliability estimates perform better (strongly correlate to prediction error) when used with more accurate models (models with

Figure 2. The dependence of reliability estimate's performance (its correlation to prediction errors) on the accuracy of the model. The dots represent data accumulated in 1296 experiments and the line represents the least squares fit (regression line) through the given dots

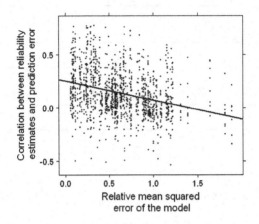

Figure 3. The dependence of reliability estimate's performance (its correlation to prediction errors) on the accuracy of the model, visualized for each separate used regression model. The line represents the least squares fit (regression line) through the given dots

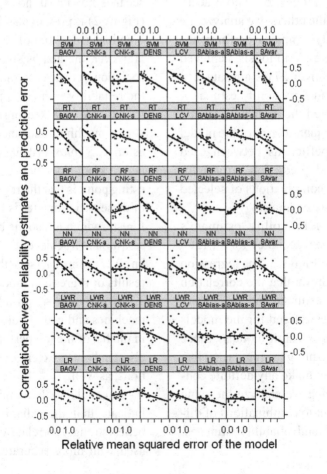

Table 3. Average relative mean squared error (RMSE) of used regression models, averaged across all experiments using 8 reliability estimates and 27 data sets.

Regression model	RMSE
random forests	0.5415
support vector machines	0.5848
neural networks	0.6393
linear regression	0.6518
locally weighted regression	0.6534
regression trees	0.6733

lower RMSE). The results also indicate that two signed reliability estimates (*CNK-s* and *SAbias-s*) when used with regression models that performed best on testing data (random forests, neural networks, support vector machines) are the exception to this rule and on our testing data sets perform better when the error of the model is larger. This finding is beneficial, since it enables the user to select a good performing reliability estimate for cases when he either did or did not have an opportunity of inducing an accurate regression model. Namely, in cases when the estimated accuracy of the above listed models is low, the results indicate that the user may improve the reliability estimation by using estimates *CNK-s* and *SAbias-s*.

5.3. Dependence on the Number of Training Examples

To evaluate the dependence of reliability estimates' performance on the number of training examples, we evaluated the reliability estimates, computed on various versions of data sets, consisting of different numbers of examples. Since we are not familiar with the original distribution of 27 used data sets, we were therefore unable to produce these data sets replicas of different sizes. Instead, we constructed three artificial data sets, for which

Figure 4. Average relative mean squared error of used regression models, averaged on 27 data sets and using 8 reliability estimates (216 experiments)

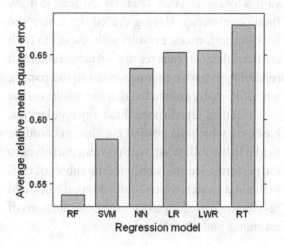

we were able to generate data in a consistent and controlled way.

The description of three data sets is shown in Table 2. All three of them contain 7 attributes (out of which two are random) and represent a mathematical dependence between five relevant attributes $A_1,..., A_5$ and label Y. For each of the three data sets we generated training sets of five different sizes, containing 100, 150, 200, 250 and 300 examples. Each data set version of larger size was generated incrementally, i.e. besides 50 new additional examples it included all examples from the dataset of the smaller size. We generated new examples by uniformly picking the attribute values from interval *(-1, 1)*. In addition to generating training sets of different sizes we also generated five versions of each data set (of each data set size), having various levels of random noise applied to examples' labels (described in the next subsection), altogether producing therefore 75 data sets (3 domains * 5 sizes * 5 noise levels).

Performance of reliability estimates with respect to the data set size for 75 artificially generated data sets is shown in Figure 5. Although the whisker plots at the first glance show that the performance of the estimates slightly decreases with the additional examples, we can also see that the variance of the correlation coefficients' values for each test set size is far too great to draw final conclusions. Having drilled down into the detailed performance results with respect to each artificial data set, each regression model and each reliability estimate (not presented in the paper), we additionally concluded that the results on the artificial data sets do not exhibit any regularities, based on which the general conclusion could be made. In the following, we thus limit ourselves to the performance study only for the subset of estimates and models which achieved good empirical results when used together. Such combinations of estimates and models are:

- *SAbias-s* with regression trees (significantly positively correlated with the prediction error in 82% of tests),
- *CNK-s* with regression trees (significantly positively correlated with the prediction error in 86% of tests),

- *BAGV* with regression trees (significantly positively correlated with the prediction error in 64% of tests),
- *CNK-a* with regression trees (significantly positively correlated with the prediction error in 68% of tests),
- *LCV* with random forests and support vector machines (significantly positively correlated with the prediction error in 61% of tests; additionally, random forests and support vector machines achieved the lowest average RMSE on 27 testing sets).

The dependency of reliability estimate on the data set size for the best performing combinations of regression models and reliability estimates is shown in Figure 6. We can see that all of the observed estimates, when used with the selected models, follow the assumed rule, except for the *LCV* estimate when used with support vector machines. The chart namely shows that the performance of reliability estimates increases when the problem domain contains more examples.

Figure 5. Dependency of reliability estimates' performance on the data set size (depicted for 75 artificial data sets)

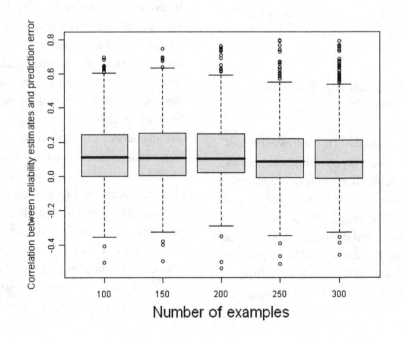

The intuitive explanation of this phenomenon could be that the additional training examples provide the learning algorithm with additional information which assists the regression model to describe problem space more accurately. Since the results from Section 5.2 showed that the performance of reliability estimates benefits when used with more accurate regression models, their performance therefore improves also with the number of training examples. To verify this indirect reasoning, we analyzed the dependence of the regression models' performance based on the number of training examples. The results for each of the artificial domains are shown in Figure 7. Results indeed support our assumption that the model accuracy improves with the number of training examples.

5.4. Dependence on the Level of Noise

In addition to generating artificial data sets of different sizes, we also varied the level of additive Gaussian noise applied to the training examples' labels. We used five different values of noise parameter and applied it to the labels as follows. The labels Y in each domain were modified according to the rule

$$Y_{new} = Y + (Y_{max} - Y_{min}) \cdot random(\sigma) \quad (9)$$

where Y_{max} and Y_{min} denote known upper and lower label bounds, and $random(\sigma)$ denotes a random number, generated from the normal distribution $N(0,\sigma)$. For applying various noise levels, we se-

Figure 6. Dependency of reliability estimates' performance on the data set size, analyzed for better performing combinations of regression models and reliability estimates

Figure 7. Performance of regression models with respect to the number of training examples (shown for artificial domains LIN, SPH and TRI)

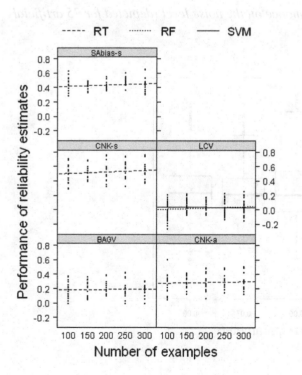

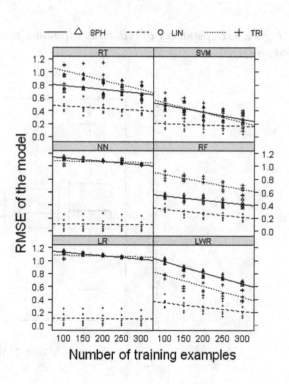

lected five different values of σ: *0.01, 0.03, 0.05, 0.07, 0.09*. Such values were selected based on the shape of the corresponding Gaussian. Namely, when generating random numbers from distribution *N(0,0.09)*, the probability of randomly generating a number around ±0.3 (which corresponds to 30% change of the label) becomes close to zero. In our experiments we therefore chose ~30% change as the maximally allowed change of the labels and gradually increased the value of σ to attain five levels of noise.

The performance of reliability estimates with respect to the level of noise for the 75 artificially generated data sets is shown in Figure 8. The figure at the first glance shows that the performance of the estimates slightly decreases with greater noise levels. By observing boxes and whiskers in the plot it is also interesting to note that the variance of the reliability estimates' correlation coefficients to the prediction errors seems to decrease when used with data sets containing higher noise levels. If the observation is correct in general, this means that all of the reliability estimates tend to become more and more similar in terms of their performance when used with increasingly noisy data (this shall be investigated in our further work).

Similarly as in the previous section, we thus limit our study to the subset of estimates and models which achieved good empirical results when used together. The dependency of reliability estimate on the noise level for the best performing combinations of regression models and reliability estimates is shown in Figure 9. We can see that all of the observed estimates, when used with the selected models, follow the assumed rule, except for the *LCV* estimate when used with random forests. The chart namely shows that the performance of reliability estimates decreases when the higher level of noise has been introduced into the training data.

Analogously to the explanation of why the performance of reliability estimates generally increases with greater number of examples, one may try to argue the last phenomenon as follows.

Figure 8. Dependency of reliability estimates' perfomance on the noise level (depicted for 75 artificial data sets)

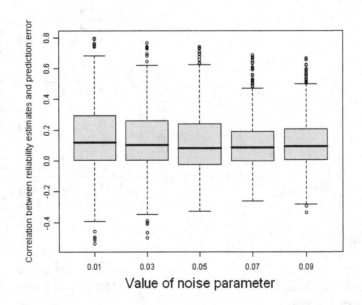

It can be said that higher noise in data set blurs the information which is available to the learning algorithm when modeling data, thus reducing its performance in terms of inducing the greater prediction error. Since the results from our previous sections indicate that the reliability estimates perform better with more accurate regression models, this therefore implies that the absence of noise causes the performance of reliability estimates to increase as well, since in those cases regression algorithms fit data more accurately. The dependence of model accuracy on the level of noise for individual artificial domains is depicted in Figure 10. The results in the figure support our latter assumption, since they show that the model accuracy decreases (RMSE increases) with the higher level of noise.

Figure 9. Dependency of reliability estimates' performance on the noise level, analyzed for selected combinations of regression models and reliability estimates

6. CONCLUSION AND FURTHER WORK

In this paper we analyzed the dependence of performance of eight reliability estimates on the selected domain and model properties. By analyzing the estimates' performance on 27 testing and 3 artificial data sets we stated assumptions about their impacting factor and concluded the following:

Based on the existing results we stated the following three assumptions, which we empirically confirmed in this study:

1. The reliability estimates, which are used with more accurate regression models (lower RMSE), generally perform better (better correlate with the prediction error).

Figure 10. Performance of regression models with respect to applied level of noise to the labels of training examples (shown for artificial domains LIN, SPH and TRI)

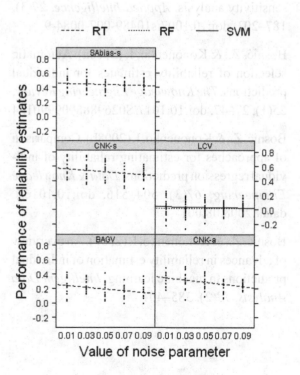

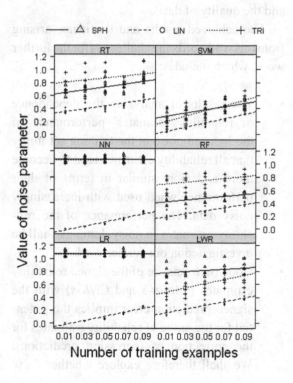

2. The number of examples in a given domain favorably influences the performance of reliability estimates.
3. The level of noise in a given domain decreases the performance of reliability estimates.

The experimental results of the first conclusion above reveal that the signed estimates *SAbias-s* and *CNK-s* are the exception to the rule when used with two top performing regression models, i.e. random forests and support vector machines. Since these two estimates performed better with less accurate regression models, they show the potential of providing the mechanisms of reliability estimation even when the induced models are not fit perfectly to the data.

The last two conclusions provide more general guidelines that it is more likely to expect good reliability estimates' performance in problem domains with greater number of examples and lower level of noise in data. In practice, this can therefore enable a user to decide in advance whether the proposed approach of reliability estimation would be productive (knowing the size and the quality of data).

The achieved results and the ideas, arising from this work, offer the challenges for the further work, which includes:

- The results of analyzing the dependence of reliability estimates' performance of the induced noise in the training set imply that all reliability estimates tend to become more and more similar in terms of their performance when used with increasingly noisy data. The performance of the reliability estimates in noisy domains shall be investigated in our further work.
- Good performance of the signed reliability estimates (*SAbias-s* and *CNK-s*) with the signed prediction error implies the potential for the usage of reliability estimates for the correction of regression predictions. We shall therefore explore whether these

two reliability estimates can be utilized to significantly reduce the error of regression predictions.
- Since different estimates perform with different success in different domain-model pairs, the approach for selection of the best performing reliability estimate for a given domain and model shall be developed.

REFERENCES

Asuncion, A., & Newman, D. J. (2007). *UCI Machine Learning Repository*. Irvine, CA: University of California, School of Information and Computer Science.

Birattari, M., Bontempi, H., & Bersini, H. (1998). Local learning for data analysis. In *Proceedings of the 8th Belgian-Dutch conference on Machine Learning* (pp. 55–61).

Bosnić, Z., & Kononenko, I. (2007). Estimation of individual prediction reliability using the local sensitivity analysis. *Applied Intelligence*, *29*(3), 187–203. doi:10.1007/s10489-007-0084-9

Bosnić, Z., & Kononenko, I. (2008a). Automatic selection of reliability estimates for individual predictions. *The Knowledge Engineering Review*, *25*(1), 27–47. doi:10.1017/S0269888909990154

Bosnić, Z., & Kononenko, I. (2008b). Comparison of approaches for estimating reliability of individual regression predictions. *Data & Knowledge Engineering*, *67*(3), 504–516. doi:10.1016/j.datak.2008.08.001

Bosnić, Z., & Kononenko, I. (2009). An overview of advances in reliability estimation of individual predictions in machine learning. *Intelligent Data Analysis*, *13*(2), 385–401.

Bosnić, Z., Kononenko, I., Robnik-Šikonja, M., & Kukar, M. (2003). Evaluation of prediction reliability in regression using the transduction principle. In B. Zajc & M. Tkalčič (Eds.), *Proceedings of EUROCON 2003* (pp. 99–103). Ljubljana.

Breiman, L. (1996). Bagging predictors. *Machine Learning, 24*(2), 123–140. doi:10.1007/BF00058655

Breiman, L. (2001). Random forests. *Machine Learning, 45*(1), 5–32. doi:10.1023/A:1010933404324

Breiman, L., Friedman, J. H., Olshen, R. A., & Stone, C. J. (1984). *Classification and Regression Trees.* Belmont, CA: Wadsworth International Group.

Chang, C., & Lin, C. (2001). *LIBSVM: a Library for Support Vector Machines* (software available at http://www.csie.ntu.edu.tw/ ~cjlin/libsvm).

Christiannini, N., & Shawe-Taylor, J. (2000). *Support Vector Machines and Other Kernel-based Learning Methods.* Cambridge University Press.

Crowder, M. J., Kimber, A. C., Smith, R. L., & Sweeting, T. J. (1991). *Statistical Concepts in Reliability. Statistical Analysis of Reliability Data.* London, UK: Chapman & Hall.

Department of Statistics at Carnegie Mellon University. (2005). *Statlib – Data, Software and News from the Statistics Community.* http://lib.stat.cmu.edu/.

Gammerman, A., Vovk, V., & Vapnik, V. (1998). Learning by transduction. In *Proceedings of the 14th Conference on Uncertainty in Artificial Intelligence* (pp. 148–155). Madison, Wisconsin.

Giacinto, G., & Roli, F. (2001). Dynamic classifier selection based on multiple classifier behaviour. *Pattern Recognition, 34*(9), 1879–1881. doi:10.1016/S0031-3203(00)00150-3

Heskes, T. (1997). Practical confidence and prediction intervals. In M. C. Mozer, M. I. Jordan, & T. Petsche (Eds.), *Advances in Neural Information Processing Systems, 9,* 176–182. The MIT Press.

Kononenko, I., & Kukar, M. (2007). *Machine Learning and Data Mining: Introduction to Principles and Algorithms.* UK: Horwood Publishing Limited.

Kukar, M., & Kononenko, I. (2002). Reliable classifications with machine learning. In Elomaa, T., Manilla, H., & Toivonen, H. (Eds.), *Proc. Machine Learning: ECML-2002* (pp. 219–231). Helsinki, Finland: Springer Verlag. doi:10.1007/3-540-36755-1_19

Nouretdinov, I., Melluish, T., & Vovk, V. (2001). Ridge regressioon confidence machine. In *Proceedings of the 18th Iinternational Conference on Machine Learning* (pp. 385–392). San Francisco, CA: Morgan Kaufmann.

R Development Core Team. (2006). *A Language and Environment for Statistical Computing.* Vienna, Austria: R Foundation for Statistical Computing.

Rumelhart, D., Hinton, G., & Williams, R. (1986). Learning internal representations by error propagation. In *Parallel Distributed Processing: Explorations in the Microstructure of Cognition, vol. 1: Foundations* (pp. 318–362). Cambridge MA, USA: MIT Press.

Saunders, C., Gammerman, A., & Vovk, V. (1999). Transduction with confidence and credibility. In *Proceedings of IJCAI'99, 2,* 722–726.

Schaal, S., & Atkeson, C. G. (1994). Assessing the quality of learned local models. In *J. D. Cowan, G. Tesauro, & J. Alspector (Eds.), Advances in Neural Information Processing Systems*, (6), 160–167. Morgan Kaufmann Publishers, Inc.

Silverman, B. W. (1986). *Density Estimation for Statistics and Data Analysis. Monographs on Statistics and Applied Probability*. London: Chapman and Hall.

Smola, A. J., & Schölkopf, B. (1998). A Tutorial on Support Vector Regression. *NeuroCOLT2 Technical Report NC2-TR-1998-030*.

Tsuda, K., Rätsch, G., Mika, S., & Müller, K. (2001). Learning to predict the leave-one-out error of kernel based classifiers. In *Lecture Notes in Computer Science* (pp. 331–338). Berlin, Heidelberg: Springer.

Vapnik, V. (1995). *The Nature of Statistical Learning Theory*. Springer.

Weigend, A., & Nix, D. (1994). Predictions with confidence intervals (local error bars). In *Proceedings of the International Conference on Neural Information Processing (ICONIP '94)* (pp. 847–852). Seoul, Korea.

Compilation of References

Abdessalem, T., & Jomier, G. (1997). VQL: A query language for multiversion databases. In *Proc. of Int. Workshop on Database Programming Languages (DBPL)* (pp. 103-122). LNCS 1369.

Abelló, A., Samos, J., & Saltor, F. (2006). YAM²: a multidimensional conceptual model extending UML. *Information Systems, 31*(6), 541–567. doi:10.1016/j.is.2004.12.002

Abelló, A., & Martín, C. (2003). A Bi-temporal Storage Structure for a Corporate Data Warehouse. *Proceedings International Conference on Enterprise Information Systems*, Angers, France, 177-183.

Abelló, A., & Romero, O. (2010). Using Ontologies to Discover Fact IDs. In I. Song, C. Ordoñez (Eds.), *Proceedings of ACM 13th International Workshop on Data Warehousing and OLAP*; pp 1-8, Toronto, Canada: ACM Press.

Abiteboul, S., & Santos, C. S. (1995). IQL(2): A model with ubiquitous objects. In *Proc. of Int. Workshop on Database Programming Languages (DBPL)* (p. 10).

Aggarwal, C. C., Wolf, J. L., Yu, P. S., Procopiuc, C., & Park, J. S. (1999). Fast algorithms for projected clustering. *Proceedings of the 1999 ACM SIGMOD International Conference on Management of data* (pp. 61-72).

Agrawal, R., Buroff, S., Gehani, N., & Shasha, D. (1991). Object versioning in ODE. In *Proc. of Int. Conference on Data Engineering (ICDE)* (pp. 446-455).

Ahmed, T. O. (2008). Continuous Spatial Data Warehousing. In *Proceedings 9th International Arab Conference on Information Technology.*

Ahmed, T. O., & Miquel, M. (2005). Multidimensional Structures Dedicated to Continuous Spatiotemporal Phenomena. In *Proceedings of BNCOD* (p. 29-40).

Allen, P. O. R., & Littman, M. (1993). An interface for navigating clustered document sets returned by queries. In *Proceedings of the ACM Conference on Organizational Computing Systems* (pp. 166-171).

Alvares, L. O., Bogorny, V., Kuijpers, B., de Macedo, J. A. F., Moelans, B., & Vaisman, A. (2007). *A model for enriching trajectories with semantic geographical information.* ACM-GIS.

Andonoff, E., Hubert, G., & Le Parc, A. (1998). A database interface integrating a querying language for versions. In *Proc. of East European Conference Advances in Databases and Information Systems (ADBIS)* (pp. 200-211). LNCS 1475.

Andonoff, E., Hubert, G., Le Parc, A., & Zurfluh, G. (1995). Modelling inheritance, composition and relationship links between objects, object versions and class versions. In *Proc. of Conference on Advanced Information Systems Engineering (CAiSE)* (pp. 96-111). LNCS 932.

Andzic, J., Fiore, V., & Sisto, L. (2007). Extraction, transformation, and loading processes. In Wrembel, R., & Koncilia, C. (Eds.), *Data Warehouses and OLAP: Concepts, Architectures and Solutions* (pp. 88–110). Idea Group Inc.

Annoni, E., Ravat, F., Teste, O., & Zurfluh, G. (2006). Towards Multidimensional Requirements Design. *Proceedings of 8th International Conference on Data Warehousing and Knowledge Discovery; Vol. 4081, Lecture Notes of Computer Science* (pp. 75-84). Krakow, Poland: Springer.

Armstrong, S., & Brodie, R. (1999). Forecasting for marketing. In Hooley, G., & Hussey, M. (Eds.), *Quantitative methods in marketing* (pp. 92–119). Int. Thompson Business Press.

Asuncion, A., & Newman, D. J. (2007). *UCI Machine Learning Repository*. Irvine, CA: University of California, School of Information and Computer Science.

Atkinson, W. D., & Shorrocks, B. (1981). Competition on a Divided and Ephemeral Resource: A Simulation Model. *Journal of Animal Ecology*, *50*, 461–471. doi:10.2307/4067

Balci, O. (1995). Principles and Techniques of Simulation Validation, Verification, and Testing. In *Proceedings Winter Simulation Conference* (pp. 147-154). Arlington, USA.

Balmin, A., Papadimitriou, T., & Papakonstanitnou, Y. (2000a). Hypothetical queries in an OLAP environment. In *Proc. of Int. Conference on Very Large Data Bases (VLDB)* (pp. 220-231).

Balmin, A., Papadimitriou, T., & Papakonstanitnou, Y. (2000b). Optimization of hypothetical queries in an OLAP environment. In *Proc. of Int. Conference on Data Engineering (ICDE)* (p. 311).

Balmin, A., Papadimitriou, T., & Papakonstantinou, Y. (2000). Hypothetical Queries in an OLAP Environment. In *Proceedings Conference on Very Large Data Bases* (pp. 242-253). Cairo, Egypt.

Baybutt, P. (2003). Major hazards analysis – An improved process hazard analysis method. *Process Safety Progress*, *22*(1), 21–26. doi:10.1002/prs.680220103

Bębel, B., Eder, J., Koncilia, C., Morzy, T., & Wrembel, R. (2004). Creation and management of versions in multiversion data warehouse. In *Proc. of ACM Symposium on Applied Computing (SAC)* (pp. 717-723).

Bębel, B., Królikowski, Z., & Wrembel, R. (2006). Managing evolution of data warehouses by means of nested transactions. In *Proc. of Int. Conference on Advances in Information Systems (ADVIS)* (pp. 119-128). LNCS 4243.

Becker, B., Gschwind, S., Ohler, T., Seeger, B., & Widmayer, P. (1996). An asymptotically optimal multiversion B-tree. *The VLDB Journal*, *5*(4), 264–275. doi:10.1007/s007780050028

Bédard, Y., Merret, T., & Han, J. (2001). Fundamentals of spatial data warehousing for geographic knowledge discovery. In *Geographic data mining and knowledge discovery* (pp. 53–73). Taylor & Francis. doi:10.4324/9780203468029_chapter_3

Bédard, Y., Rivest, S., & Proulx, M.-J. (2007). Spatial online analytical processing (SOLAP): Concepts, architectures, and solutions from a geomatics engineering perspective. In *Data warehouses and OLAP: Concepts, architectures and solutions* (p. 298 – 319). IGI Global.

Beil, F., Ester, M., & Xu, X. (2002, July 23-26). Frequent Term-Based Text Clustering. *In Proceedings of 8th ACM SIGKDD International Conference on Knowledge Discovery and Data Mining* (pp. 436-442). Edmonton, Alberta, Canada.

Bellahsene, Z. (2002). Schema Evolution in Data Warehouses. *Knowledge and Information Systems*, *4*(3), 283–304. doi:10.1007/s101150200008

Bellahsene, Z. (2002). Schema evolution in data warehouses. [KAIS]. *Knowledge and Information Systems*, *4*(3), 283–304. doi:10.1007/s101150200008

Bellahsene, Z. (1998). View Adaptation in Data Warehousing Systems. *Proceedings International Conference on Database and Expert Systems Applications*, Vienna, Austria, 300-309.

Bellahsene, Z. (1998). View adaptation in data warehousing systems. In *Proc. of Int. Conference on Database and Expert Systems Applications (DEXA)* (pp. 300-309). LNCS 1460.

Bellatreche, L., Karlapalem, K., & Simonet, A. (2000). Algorithms and Support for Horizontal Class Partitioning in Object-Oriented Databases. *Distributed and Parallel Databases*, *8*(2), 155–179. doi:10.1023/A:1008745624048

Bellatreche, L., Moussaoui, R., Necir, H., & Drias, H. (2008). A Data Mining Approach for Selecting Bitmap Join Indices. *Journal of Computing Science and Engineering*, *2*(1), 206–223.

Bellatreche, L., & Boukhalfa, K. (2005): An Evolutionary Approach to Schema Partitioning Selection in a Data Warehouse. 7th International Conference on Data Warehousing and Knowledge Discovery (DAWAK'05), pp. 115-125, August, Springer-Verlag.

Bellatreche, L., Boukhalfa, K., & Richard, P. (2008). Horizontal Partitioning in Data Warehouse: Hardness Study, Selection Algorithms and Validation on ORACLE10G. *10th International Conference on Data Warehousing and Knowledge Discovery (DAWAK)*, pp. 87-96, September, Springer-Verlag.

Bellatreche, L., Cuzzocrea, A., & Benkrid, S. (2009) Query Optimization over Parallel Relational Data Warehouses in Distributed Environments by Simultaneous Fragmentation and Allocation, *The 10th International Conference on Algorithms and Architectures for Parallel Processing* (ICA3PP), pp. 124–135, May, Springer-Verlag.

Bellosta, M. J., Wrembel, R., & Jomier, G. (1995). *Management of schema versions and versions of a schema instance in a multiversion database. Research report. Project VERSO.* Paris, France: INRIA Rocquencourt.

Berners-Lee, T., Hendler, J. & Lassila, O. (2001). The Semantic Web. *Scientific American.*

Beyer, K. S., & Ramakrishnan, R. (1999). Bottom-up computation of sparse and iceberg cubes. In Delis, A., Faloutsos, C., and Ghandeharizadeh, S., editors, *SIGMOD Conference*, pages 359–370. ACM Press.

Bhargava, H. K., Krishnan, R., & Muller, R. (1997). Electronic Commerce in Decision Technologies: A Business Cycle Analysis. *International Journal of Electronic Commerce, 1*(4), 109–127.

Bimonte, S., Tchounikine, A., & Miquel, M. (2005). *Towards a spatial multidimensional model* (pp. 39–46). DOLAP.

Birattari, M., Bontempi, H., & Bersini, H. (1998). Local learning for data analysis. In *Proceedings of the 8th Belgian-Dutch conference on Machine Learning* (pp. 55–61).

Birkhoff, G. (1970). *Lattice Theory*, volume XXV of *AMS Colloquium Publications.* American Mathematical Society, third (new) edition.

Blaschka, M. (2000). *FIESTA - A Framework for Schema Evolution in Multidimensional Databases.* PhD Thesis, Technische Universitat Munchen, Germany.

Blaschka, M., Sapia, C., & Höfling, G. (1999). On Schema Evolution in Multidimensional Databases. *Proceedings International Conference on Data Warehousing and Knowledge Discovery*, Florence, Italy, 153-164.

Bliujute, R., Saltenis, S., Slivinskas, G., & Jensen, C. S. (1998). Systematic Change Management in Dimensional Data Warehousing. *Proceedings International Baltic Workshop on Databases and Information Systems*, Riga, Latvia, 27–41.

Body, M., Miquel, M., Bédard, Y., & Tchounikine, A. (2003). Handling Evolutions in Multidimensional Structures. *Proceedings International Conference on Data Engineering*, Bangalore, India, 581-591.

Body, M., Miquel, M., Bédard, Y., & Tchounikine, A. (2002). A multidimensional and multiversion structure for OLAP applications. In *Proc. of ACM Int. Workshop on Data Warehousing and OLAP (DOLAP)* (pp. 1-6).

Böehnlein, M., & Ulbrich-vom Ende, A. (1999). Deriving Initial Data Warehouse Structures from the Conceptual Data Models of the Underlying Operational Information Systems. In I. Song, T. J. Teorey (Eds.), *Proceedings of 2nd International Workshop on Data Warehousing and OLAP;* pp, 15-21. Kansas City, USA: ACM Press.

Bonifati, A., Cattaneo, F., Ceri, S., Fuggetta, A., & Paraboschi, S. (2001). Designing Data Marts for Data Warehouses. *ACM Transactions on Software Engineering and Methodology, 10*(4), 452–483. doi:10.1145/384189.384190

Bosnić, Z., & Kononenko, I. (2007). Estimation of individual prediction reliability using the local sensitivity analysis. *Applied Intelligence, 29*(3), 187–203. doi:10.1007/s10489-007-0084-9

Bosnić, Z., & Kononenko, I. (2008a). Automatic selection of reliability estimates for individual predictions. *The Knowledge Engineering Review, 25*(1), 27–47. doi:10.1017/S0269888909990154

Bosnić, Z., & Kononenko, I. (2008b). Comparison of approaches for estimating reliability of individual regression predictions. *Data & Knowledge Engineering, 67*(3), 504–516. doi:10.1016/j.datak.2008.08.001

Bosnić, Z., & Kononenko, I. (2009). An overview of advances in reliability estimation of individual predictions in machine learning. *Intelligent Data Analysis, 13*(2), 385–401.

Bosnić, Z., Kononenko, I., Robnik-Šikonja, M., & Kukar, M. (2003). Evaluation of prediction reliability in regression using the transduction principle. In B. Zajc & M. Tkalčič (Eds.), *Proceedings of EUROCON 2003* (pp. 99–103). Ljubljana.

Boukhalfa, K., Bellatreche, L., & Richard, P. (2008). Fragmentation Primaire et Dérivée: Étude de Complexité, Algorithmes de Sélection et Validation sous Oracle10g. (Report No. 01 -2008), LISI/ENSMA, available at: http://www.lisi.ensma.fr/ members/bellatreche

Brakatsoulas, S., Pfoser, D., & Tryfona, N. (2004). Pre-aggregation in spatial data warehouses. In [Washington D.C, USA.]. *Proceedings of IDEAS, 04*, 68–77.

Braz, F., Orlando, S., Orsini, R., Raffaetá, A., Roncato, A., & Silvestri, C. (2007). Approximate Aggregations in Trajectory Data Warehouses. In *Proceedings of STDM* (p. 536-545).

Breiman, L. (1996). Bagging predictors. *Machine Learning, 24*(2), 123–140. doi:10.1007/BF00058655

Breiman, L. (2001). Random forests. *Machine Learning, 45*(1), 5–32. doi:10.1023/A:1010933404324

Breiman, L., Friedman, J. H., Olshen, R. A., & Stone, C. J. (1984). *Classification and Regression Trees*. Belmont, CA: Wadsworth International Group.

Breslau, L., Cao, P., Fan, L., Phillips, G., & Shenker, S. (1999). Web Caching and Zipf-like Distributions: Evidence and Implications. Eighteenth Annual Joint Conference of the IEEE Computer and Communications Societies (IEEE INFOCOM), pp. 126-134.

Bruckner, R., & Tjoa, A. (2002). Capturing Delays and Valid Times in Data Warehouses - Towards Timely Consistent Analyses. *Journal of Intelligent Information Systems, 19*(2), 169–190. doi:10.1023/A:1016555410197

Bruske, J., & Sommer, G. (1995). Dynamic cell structures. In G. Tesauro, D. Touretzky, & T. Leen (Eds.), *Advances in Neural Information Processing Systems, 7*, 497–504. The MIT Press.

Buchmann, A. P., Günther, O., Smith, T. R., & Wang, Y.-F. (1990). Design and implementation of large spatial databases. In *First symposium (SSD)* (Vol. 409). Springer.

Buckley, C., & Lewit, A. F. (1985). Optimization of inverted vector searches. *In Proceedings of SIGIR-85* (pp. 97-110).

Cabibbo, L., & Torlone, R. (1998). A Logical Approach to Multidimensional Databases. In H. Schek, F. Saltor, I. Ramos, G. Alonso (Eds.), *Proceedings of 6th International Conference on Extending Database Technology; Vol. 1377, Lecture Notes of Computer Science* (pp, 183-197). Valencia, Spain: Springer.

Cabibbo, L., & Torlone, R. (1997). Querying multidimensional databases. In *Database programming languages, LCNS* (1369) (p. 319–335).

Cámara, G., Palomo, D., de Souza, R. C. M., & de Oliveira, D. (2005). *Towards a Generalized Map Algebra: Principles and Data Types* (pp. 66–81). GeoInfo.

Carmè, A., Mazón, J. N., & Rizzi, S. (2010). A Model-Driven Heuristic Approach for Detecting Multidimensional Facts in Relational Data Sources. *Proceedings of 12th International Conference on Data Warehousing and Knowledge Discovery; Vol. 6263, Lecture Notes of Computer Science* (pp, 13-24). Bilbao, Spain: Springer.

Casali, A., Nedjar, S., Cicchetti, R., & Lakhal, L. (2009a). Closed cube lattices. [New Trends in Data Warehousing and Data Analysis.]. *Annals of Information Systems, 3*(1), 145–164.

Casali, A., Nedjar, S., Cicchetti, R., Lakhal, L., & Novelli, N. (2009b). Lossless reduction of datacubes using partitions. *International Journal of Data Warehousing and Mining, 5*(1), 18–35. doi:10.4018/jdwm.2009010102

Casali, A., Cicchetti, R., & Lakhal, L. (2003a). Cube lattices: A framework for multidimensional data mining. In Barbará, D., & Kamath, C. (Eds.), *SDM. SIAM*.

Casali, A., Cicchetti, R., & Lakhal, L. (2003b). Extracting semantics from data cubes using cube transversals and closures. In Getoor, L., Senator, T. E., Domingos, P., & Faloutsos, C. (Eds.), *KDD* (pp. 69–78). ACM.

Castro, C. D., Grandi, F., & Scalas, R. R. (1997). Schema versioning for multitemporal relational databases. *Information Systems, 22*(5), 249–290. doi:10.1016/S0306-4379(97)00017-3

Cellary, W., & Jomier, G. (1990). Consistency of versions in object-oriented databases. In *Proc. of Int. Conference on Very Large Data Bases (VLDB)* (pp. 432-441).

Cellary, W., Jomier, G., & Koszlajda, T. (1991). Formal model of an object-oriented database with versioned objects and schema. In *Proc. of Int. Conference on Database and Expert Systems Applications (DEXA)* (pp. 239-244).

Ceri, S., Negri, M., & Pelagatti, G. (1982). Horizontal data partitioning in database design, Proceedings of the International Conference on Management of Data (SIGMOD), pp. 128-136.

Chamoni, P., & Stock, S. (1999). Temporal Structures in Data Warehousing. *Proceedings International Conference on Data Warehousing and Knowledge Discovery*, Florence, Italy, 353-358.

Chang, C., & Lin, C. (2001). *LIBSVM: a Library for Support Vector Machines* (software available at http://www.csie.ntu.edu.tw/ ~cjlin/libsvm).

Chaudhuri, S., & Dayal, U. (1997). An overview of data warehousing and olap technology. *SIGMOD Record*, 26(1), 65–74. doi:10.1145/248603.248616

Chaudhuri, S., & Narasayya, V. (1998). AutoAdmin what-if index analysis utility. *SIGMOD Record*, 27(2), 367–378. doi:10.1145/276305.276337

Chen, S., Zhang, X., & Rundensteiner, E. (2006). A Compensation-Based Approach for View Maintenance in Distributed Environments. *IEEE Transactions on Knowledge and Data Engineering*, 18(8), 1068–1081. doi:10.1109/TKDE.2006.117

Chen, J., Chen, S., & Rundensteiner, E. (2002). A transactional model for data warehouse maintenance. In *Proc. of Int. Conference on Conceptual Modeling (ER)* (pp. 247-262). LNCS 2503.

Chen, J., Chen, S., Zhang, X., & Rundensteiner, E. (2004). Detection and correction of conflicting source updates for view maintenance. In *Proc. of Int. Conference on Data Engineering (ICDE)* (pp. 436-448).

Chien, S. Y., Tsotras, V., & Zaniolo, C. (2001). XML document versioning. *SIGMOD Record Web Edition*, 30(3). (Retrieved November 29, 2006 from http://www.sigmod.org/record/issues/0109/).

Chien, S. Y., Tsotras, V. J., Zaniolo, C., & Zhang, D. (2002). Efficient complex query support for multiversion XML documents. In *Proc. of Int. Conference on Extending Database Technology (EDBT)* (pp. 161-178). LNCS 2287.

Chmiel, J., Morzy, T., & Wrembel, R. (2009). Multiversion join index for multiversion data warehouse. *Information and Software Technology*, 51(1), 98–108. doi:10.1016/j.infsof.2008.01.003

Chmiel, J., & Wrembel, R. (2007). Storing and sharing versions of data in multiversion data warehouse - implementation and experimental evaluation. *Foundations of Computing and Decision Sciences Journal*, 32(2), 87–109.

Chmiel, J. (2010). Indexing Multiversion Data Warehouse: From ROWID-Based Multiversion Join Index to Bitmap-Based Multiversion Join Index. In Proc. of ADBIS Workshops (pp. 71-78). LNCS 5968.

Chou, H. T., & Kim, W. (1988). Versions and Change Notification in an Object-Oriented Database System. In proc. of *ACM/IEEE Design Automation Conference* (pp. 275-281).

Christiannini, N., & Shawe-Taylor, J. (2000). *Support Vector Machines and Other Kernel-based Learning Methods*. Cambridge University Press.

Codd, E. F., Codd, S. B., & Salley, C. T. (1993). *Providing OLAP (On Line Analytical Processing) to Users-Analysts: an IT Mandate*. E. F. Codd and Associates.

Codd, E. F. (1970). A relational model of data for large shared data banks. *Communications of the ACM*, 13(6), 377–387. doi:10.1145/362384.362685

Combi, C., & Oliboni, B. (2007). Temporal semistructured data models and data warehouses. In Wrembel, R., & Koncilia, C. (Eds.), *Data Warehouses and OLAP: Concepts, Architectures and Solutions* (pp. 277–297). Idea Group Inc.

Combi, C., & Oliboni, B. (2007). Temporal semistructured data models and data warehouses. In *Data Warehouses and OLAP: Concepts, Architectures and Solutions*, Wrembel & Koncilia (Eds.), IRM Press, 277-297.

Cordeiro, J. P., Cámara, G., Moura, U. F., Barbosa, C. C., & Almeida, F. (2005). *Algebraic Formalism over Maps* (pp. 49–65). GeoInfo.

Crowder, M. J., Kimber, A. C., Smith, R. L., & Sweeting, T. J. (1991). *Statistical Concepts in Reliability. Statistical Analysis of Reliability Data*. London, UK: Chapman & Hall.

Curino, C. A., Moon, H. J., & Zaniolo, C. (2008a). Graceful database schema evolution: the PRISM workbench. In *Proc. of Int. Conference on Very Large Data Bases (VLDB)* (pp.761-772).

Curino, C. A., Moon, H. J., & Zaniolo, C. (2008b). Managing the history of metadata in support for DB archiving and schema evolution. *In Proc. of the ER 2008 Workshops* (pp. 78-88). LNCS 5232.

Cutting, D., Karger, D., Pedersen, J., & Tukey, J. (1992). Scatter/Gather: A Cluster-based Approach to Browsing Large Document Collections. *In Proceedings of SIGIR '92* (pp. 318-329).

Czejdo, B., Messa, K., Morzy, T., & Putonti, C. (2000). Design of data warehouses with dynamically changing data sources. In *Proc. of Southern Conference on Computing* (pp. 1-15).

Damiani, M., & Spaccapietra, S. (2006). Spatial data warehouse modelling. In *Processing and managing complex data for decision support* (pp. 21–27). Idea Group. doi:10.4018/9781591406556.ch001

Damiani, M. L., Vangenot, C., Frentzos, E., Marketos, G., Theodoridis, Y., Veryklos, V., & Raffaeta, A. (2007). Design of the trajectory warehouse architecture. *Technical Report D1.3, GeoPKDD project*.

Damiani, M.L., Macedo, J. A.F. de, Parent, C., Porto, F., & Spaccapietra, S. (2007). A conceptual view of trajectories. *Technical Report, Ecole Polythecnique Federal de Lausanne, April 2007*.

Dang, L., & Embury, S. M. (2004). What-If Analysis with Constraint Databases. In *Proceedings British National Conference on Databases*. Edinburgh, Scotland.

Das, G., Gunopulos, D., Koudas, N., & Tsirogiannis, D. (2006). Answering Top-k Queries Using Views. Proceedings of 32th International Conference on Very Large Data Bases (VLDB'2006), pp. 451-462

De Amo, S., & Halfeld Ferrari Alves, M. (2000). Efficient Maintenance of Temporal Data Warehouses. *Proceedings International Database Engineering and Applications Symposium*, Yokohoma, Japan 188-196.

de Matos Galante, R., dos Santos, C. S., Edelweiss, N., & Moreira, A. F. (2005). Temporal and versioning model for schema evolution in object-oriented databases. [DKE]. *Data & Knowledge Engineering, 53*(2), 99–128. doi:10.1016/j.datak.2004.07.001

de Weghe, N. V., Cohn, A., Tré, G. D., & Maeyer, P. D. (2005). *A qualitative trajectory calculus as a basis for representing moving objects in geographical information systems*. Control and Cybernetics.

Department of Statistics at Carnegie Mellon University. (2005). *Statlib – Data, Software and News from the Statistics Community*. http://lib.stat.cmu.edu/.

Devlin, B. (1997). Managing Time In The Data Warehouse. *InfoDB, 11*(1), 7–12.

Dittenbach, M., Merkl, D., & Rauber, A. (2000). The Growing Hierarchical Self-Organizing Map. *In Proc. Intl. Joint Conf. on Neural Networks (IJCNN'00)*.

Eadon, G., Chong, E. I., Shankar, S., Raghavan, A., Srinivasan, J., & Das, S. (2008). Supporting Table Partitioning by Reference in Oracle. Proceedings of the International Conference on *Management of Data (SIGMOD)*, pp. 1111-1122.

Easton, M. (1986). Key-sequence data sets on indelible storage. *IBM Journal of Research and Development, 30*(3), 230–241. doi:10.1147/rd.303.0230

Eder, J., & Wiggisser, K. (2010). Data Warehouse Maintenance, Evolution and Versioning. In *Bellatreche, L. (2010). Data Warehousing Design and Advanced Engineering Applications*. IGI Global. doi:10.4018/978-1-60566-756-0.ch010

Eder, J., Koncilia, C., & Morzy, T. (2002). *The COMET metamodel for temporal data warehouses* (pp. 83–99). Caise.

Eder, J., & Koncilia, C. (2001). Changes of Dimension Data in Temporal Data Warehouses. *Proceedings International Conference on Data Warehousing and Knowledge Discovery*, Munich, Germany, 284-293.

Eder, J., & Koncilia, C. (2001). Changes of dimension data in temporal data warehouses. In *Proc. of Int. Conference on Data Warehousing and Knowledge Discovery (DaWaK)* (pp. 284-293). LNCS 2114.

Eder, J., Koncilia, C., & Morzy, T. (2002). The COMET Metamodel For Temporal Data Warehouses. *Proceedings International Conference on Advanced Information Systems Engineering*, Toronto, Canada, 83-99.

Eder, J., Koncilia, C., & Mitsche, D. (2003). Automatic detection of structural changes in data warehouses. In *Proc. of Int. Conference on Data Warehousing and Knowledge Discovery (DaWaK)* (pp. 119-128). LNCS 2737.

Eder, J., Koncilia, C., & Mitsche, D. (2004). Analysing slices of data warehouses to detect structural modifications. In *Proc. of Conference on Advanced Information Systems Engineering (CAiSE)* (pp. 492-505). LNCS 3084.

Eder, J., Koncilia, C., & Morzy, T. (2001). A model for a temporal data warehouse. In *Int. Workshop on Open Enterprise Solutions: Systems, Experiences, and Organizations (OESSEO)*. (Electronic edition. Retrieved December 20, 2006, from http://cersi.luiss.it/oesseo2001/papers/papers.htm).

Eissen, S. M., Stein, B., & Potthast, M. (2005). The Suffix Tree Document Model Revisited. *In Proceedings of the 5th International Conference on Knowledge Management* (pp. 596-603).

El Akkaoui, Z., & Zimányi, E. (2009). Defining ETL workflows using BPMN and BPEL. In *Proc. of the ACM Int. Workshop on Data Warehousing and OLAP (DOLAP)* (pp. 41-48).

Elmasri, R., & Navathe, S. B. (2000). *Fundamentals of Database Systems* (3rd ed.). Addison-Wesley.

Elmasri, R., Wuu, G., & Kim, Y. J. (1991). Efficient implementation of techniques for the time index. In *Proc. of Int. Conference on Data Engineering (ICDE)* (pp. 102-111).

Er, M. C. (1988). A Fast Algorithm for Generating Set Partitions. *The Computer Journal, 31*(3), 283–284. doi:10.1093/comjnl/31.3.283

Escribano, A., Gomez, L., Kuijpers, B., & Vaisman, A. A. (2007). Piet: a GIS-OLAO implementation. In *ACM 10th international workshop on data warehousing and OLAP (DOLAP)* (p. 73–80). ACM.

Etzion, O., Jajoda, S., & Sripada, S. (Eds.). (1998). *Temporal databases: Research and practice*. Springer Verlag, LNCS 1399.

Evidence-Based Medicine Working Group. (1992). Evidence-based medicine. A new approach to teaching the practice of medicine. *Journal of the American Medical Association, 268*, 2420–2425. doi:10.1001/jama.268.17.2420

Fan, H., & Poulovassilis, A. (2004). Schema Evolution in Data Warehousing Environments - A Schema Transformation-Based Approach. *Proceedings International Conference on Conceptual Modeling*, Shanghai, China, 639-653.

Favre, C., Bentayeb, F., & Boussaid, O. (2007). Evolution of Data Warehouses' Optimization: A Workload Perspective. In Proc. of Int. Conference on Data Warehousing and Knowledge Discovery (*DaWaK*)(pp. 13-22). LNCS 4654.

Feng, Y., Li, H.-G., Agrawal, D., & El Abbadi, A. (2005). Exploiting Temporal Correlation in Temporal Data Warehouses. *Proceedings International Conference on Database Systems for Advanced Applications*, Beijing, China, 662-674.

Ferrandina, F., Meyer, T., Zicari, R., Ferran, G., & Madec, J. (1995). Schema and database evolution in the O2 object database system. In *Proc. of Int. Conference on Very Large Data Bases (VLDB)* (pp. 170-181).

Fossett, C., Harrison, D., & Weintrob, H. (1991). An assessment procedure for simulation models: a case study. *Operations Research, 39*(5), 710–723. doi:10.1287/opre.39.5.710

Frentzos, E., Gratsias, K., & Theodoridis, Y. (2007). Index-based Most Similar Trajectory Search. In proceedings of ICDE (p.816-825).

Fritzke, B. (1994). Growing cell structures - a self-organizing network for unsupervised and supervised learning. *Neural Networks, 7*(9), 1441–1460. doi:10.1016/0893-6080(94)90091-4

Fritzke, B. (1995). A growing neural gas network learns topologies.In T.K. Lean (Ed.), *Advances in Neural Information Processing Systems* (pp. 625-632). Cambridge, MA: MIT Press.

Galhardas, H., Florescu, D., Shasha, D., & Simon, E. (2000). Ajax: An extensible data cleaning tool. In *Proc. of ACM SIGMOD Int. Conference on Management of Data* (p. 590).

Gammerman, A., Vovk, V., & Vapnik, V. (1998). Learning by transduction. In *Proceedings of the 14th Conference on Uncertainty in Artificial Intelligence* (pp. 148–155). Madison, Wisconsin.

Gançarski, S., & Jomier, G. (2001). A framework for programming multiversion databases. *Data & Knowledge Engineering*, *1*(27), 29–53. doi:10.1016/S0169-023X(00)00033-1

Ganter, B., & Wille, R. (1999). *Formal Concept Analysis: Mathematical Foundations*. Springer.

Gao, D., Jensen, C. S., Snodgrass, R. T., & Soo, D. M. (2005). Join operations in temporal databases. *The VLDB Journal*, *14*(1), 2–29. doi:10.1007/s00778-003-0111-3

Gardella, J. P., Gómez, L., & Vaisman, A. (2010). Trajectory Sequential Patterns with Regular Expression Constraints Including Spatial Queries. In *Proceedings of AMW*.

Garey, M. R., & Johnson, D. S. (1990). *Computers and Intractability; A Guide to the Theory of NP-Completeness*. New York, NY, USA: W. H. Freeman & Co.

Garofalakis, M., Rastogi, R., & Shim, K. (1999). SPIRIT: Sequential Pattern Mining with Regular Expression Constraints. *In proceedings of VLDB* (p. 223-234).

Giacinto, G., & Roli, F. (2001). Dynamic classifier selection based on multiple classifier behaviour. *Pattern Recognition*, *34*(9), 1879–1881. doi:10.1016/S0031-3203(00)00150-3

Giannotti, F., Nanni, M., Pinelli, F., & Pedreschi, D. (2007). *Trajectory pattern mining* (pp. 330–339). KDD.

Giorgini, P., Rizzi, S., & Garzetti, M. (2005). Goal-oriented Requirement Analysis for Data Warehouse Design. In I. Song, J. Trujillo (Eds.), *Proceedings of 8th International Workshop on Data Warehousing and OLAP*; pp, 47-56. Bremen, Germany: ACM Press.

Golfarelli, M., Lechtenbörger, J., Rizzi, S., & Vossen, G. (2006). Schema Versioning in Data Warehouses: Enabling Cross-Version Querying via Schema Augmentation. *Data & Knowledge Engineering*, *59*(2), 435–459. doi:10.1016/j.datak.2005.09.004

Golfarelli, M., & Rizzi, S. (1999). Designing the data warehouse: key steps and crucial issues. *Journal of Computer Science and Information Management*, *2*(1), 1–14.

Golfarelli, M., & Rizzi, S. (2007b). Managing late measurements in data warehouses. *International Journal of Data Warehousing and Mining*, *3*(4), 51–67. doi:10.4018/jdwm.2007100103

Golfarelli, M., Maio, D., & Rizzi, S. (1998a). The Dimensional Fact Model: A Conceptual Model for Data Warehouses. *International Journal of Cooperative Information Systems*, *7*(2-3), 215–247. doi:10.1142/S0218843098000118

Golfarelli, M., & Rizzi, S. (2009). *Data Warehouse Design. Modern Principles and Methodologies*. McGraw Hill.

Golfarelli, M., & Rizzi, S. (in press). Data warehouse design: Modern principles & methodology. *McGraw-Hill Professional*.

Golfarelli, M., & Rizzi, S. (2007a). X-Time: Schema Versioning and Cross-Version Querying in Data Warehouses. *Proceedings International Conference on Data Engineering*, Istanbul, Turkey, 1471-147.

Golfarelli, M., & Rizzi, S. (1998b). Methodological Framework for Data Warehouse Design. In In I. Song, T. J. Teorey (Eds.), *Proceedings of 1st ACM International Workshop on Data Warehousing and OLAP*; pp, 3-9. Bethesda, USA: ACM Press.

Golfarelli, M., Lechtenbörger, J., Rizzi, S., & Vossen, G. (2004). Schema versioning in data warehouses. In *Proc. of ER Workshops* (pp. 415-428). LNCS 3289.

Golfarelli, M., Rizzi, S., & Proli, A. (2006). Designing What-if Analysis: Towards a Methodology. In *Proceedings International Workshop on Data Warehousing and OLAP* (pp. 51-58). Arlington, USA.

Gómez, L., Kuijpers, B., & Vaisman, A. A. (2010). A data model and query language for spatio-temporal decision support. *GeoInformatica*, 1–47. http://dx.doi.org/10.1007/s10707-010-0110-7.

Gómez, L., & Vaisman, A. (2009). Efficient constraint evaluation in categorical sequential pattern mining for trajectory databases. In *Proceedings of EDBT* (p. 541-552).

Gómez, L., Haesevoets, S., Kuijpers, B., & Vaisman, A. A. (2009). Spatial aggregation: Data model and implementation. *Information Systems(34)* (6) (p. 551-576).

Gómez, L., Kuijpers, B., & Vaisman, A. A. (2008a). Aggregation languages for moving object and places of interest. In *SAC 2008 - ASIIS track.*

Gómez, L., Kuijpers, B., & Vaisman, A.A. (2008b). Querying and mining trajectory databases using places of interest. *Annals of Information Systems.*

Gómez, L., Vaisman, A., & Zich, S. (2008). Piet-QL: a query language for GIS-OLAP integration. In *Proceedings of ACM-GIS* (27).

Gómez, L., Vaisman, A., & Zimányi, E. (2010).Physical Design and Implementation of Spatial Data Warehouses-Supporting Continuous Fields. In *Proceedings of DaWaK* (p. 25-39).

Gonzalez, H., Han, J., Li, X., Myslinska, M., & Sondag, J. P. (2007). *Adaptive fastest path computation on a road network: A traffic mining approach* (pp. 794–805). VLDB.

Google. (2010). Google Scholar. Retrieved October, 15th, 2010, from http://scholar.google.com/.

Grandi, F. (2002). A Relational Multi-Schema Data Model and Query Language for full Support of Schema Versioning. *Proceedings SEBD*, Portoferraio, Italy, 323-336.

Grandi, F. (2004). Svmgr: A tool for the management of schema versioning. In *Proc. of Int. Conference on Conceptual Modeling (ER)* (pp. 860-861). LNCS 3288.

Gray, J., Chaudhuri, S., Bosworth, A., Layman, A., Reichart, D., & Venkatrao, M. (1997). Data cube: A relational aggregation operator generalizing group-by, cross-tab, and sub totals. *Data Mining and Knowledge Discovery, 1*(1), 29–53. doi:10.1023/A:1009726021843

Gruber, T. R. (1993). A Translation Approach to Portable Ontology Specifications. *Knowledge Acquisition, 5*, 199–220. doi:10.1006/knac.1993.1008

Gupta, A., & Mumick, I. S. (1995). Maintenance of materialized views: problems, techniques, and applications. *Data Engineering Bulletin, 18*(2), 3–18.

Gupta, A., & Mumick, I. S. (Eds.). (1999). *Materialized Views: Techniques, Implementations, and Applications.* MIT Press.

Güting, R. H., & Schneider, M. (2005). *Moving objects databases.* Morgan Kaufman.

Güting, R. H., Böhlen, M., Jensen, C., Lorentzos, N., Schneider, M., & Vazirgiannis, M. (2000). A foundation for representing and quering moving objects. In *ACM Transactions Database Systems, 25*(1), (p. 1-42

Gutman, A. (1984). R-trees: A dynamic index structure for spatial searching. In. *Proceedings of SIGMOD, 84*, 47–57.

Gyssens, M., & Lakshmanan, L. V. S. (1997). A foundation for multidimensional databases. In Proc. of *Int. Conference on Very Large Data Bases (VLDB)* (pp. 106-115).

Han, J., & Kamber, M. (2006). *Data Mining: Concepts and Techniques.* Morgan Kaufmann.

Han, J., Pei, J., Dong, G., & Wang, K. (2001). Efficient computation of iceberg cubes with complex measures. In *SIGMOD Conference*, pages 1–12.

Han, J., Stefanovic, N., & Koperski, K. (1998). Selective materialization: An efficient method for spatial data cube construction. In *Research and development in knowledge discovery and data mining (PAKDD)* (Vol. 1394) (p. 144-158). Springer.

Harinarayan, V., Rajaraman, A., & Ullman, J. D. (1996). Implementing data cubes efficiently. In *SIGMOD conference* (pp. 205–216). ACM Press.

Harzing (2010). Publish or Perish. Retrieved October, 15th, 2010, from http://www.harzing.com/pop.htm

Heskes, T. (1997). Practical confidence and prediction intervals. In M. C. Mozer, M. I. Jordan, & T. Petsche (Eds.), *Advances in Neural Information Processing Systems, 9*, 176–182. The MIT Press.

Holland, J. H. (1975). *Adaptation in Natural and Artificial Systems.* Ann Arbor, MI: University of Michigan Press.

Hornsby, K., & Egenhofer, M. J. (2002). Modeling moving objects over multiple granularities. *Annals of Mathematics and Artificial Intelligence, 36*(1-2), 177–194. doi:10.1023/A:1015812206586

Hotho, A., Maedche, A., & Staab, S. (2002). Text Clustering Based on Good Aggregations. [KI]. *Künstliche Intelligenz, 16*(4), 48–54.

Hurtado, C. A., & Mendelzon, A. O. (2002). Olap dimension constraints. In Popa, L. (Ed.), *PODS* (pp. 169–179). ACM.

Hurtado, C., Mendelzon, A., & Vaisman, A. (1999a). Maintaining Data Cubes under Dimension Updates. *Proceedings International Conference on Data Engineering*, Sydney, Austrialia, 346-355.

Hurtado, C., Mendelzon, A., & Vaisman, A. (1999b). Updating OLAP Dimensions. *Proceedings International Workshop on Data Warehousing and OLAP*, Kansas City, USA, 60-66.

Hüsemann, B., Lechtenbörger, J., & Vossen, G. (2000). Conceptual Data Warehouse Modeling. In M. A. Jeusfeld, H. Shu, M. Staudt, G. Vossen (Eds.), *Proceedings of 2nd International Workshop on Design and Management of Data Warehouses*; pp 6. Stockholm, Sweden: CEUR-WS.org.

In *Data warehousing and knowledge discovery (DaWak)* (Vol. 2737, p. 35–44). Springer.

Inmon, W. (1996). *Building the data warehouse*. John Wiley & Sons.

Inmon, W. H., Strauss, D., & Neushloss, G. (2008). *DW 2.0: The Architecture for the Next Generation of Data Warehousing*. Morgan Kauffman.

Institute, S. A. P. (2000). *Multi-dimensional Modeling with SAP BW*. SAP America Inc. and SAP AG.

International Business Machines Corporation. (2006), DB2 partitioning features, An overview for data warehouses. Retrieved from http://www.ibm.com/developerworks/data/library/techarticle/ dm-0608mcinerney/

Ioannidis, Y., & Kang, Y. (1990). Randomized algorithms for optimizing large join queries. *Proceedings of the International Conference on Management of Data (SIGMOD)*, pp. 9-22.

Jain, A. K., Murty, M. N., & Flynn, P. J. (1999). Data Clustering: A Review. *ACM Computing Surveys*, *31*(3), 264–323. doi:10.1145/331499.331504

Jarke, M., Jeusfeld, M., Quix, C., & Vassiliadis, P. (1999). Architecture and Quality in Data Warehouses: An Extended Repository Approach. *Information Systems*, *24*(3), 229–253. doi:10.1016/S0306-4379(99)00017-4

Jarke, M., Quix, C., Blees, G., Lehmann, D., Michalk, G., & Stierl, S. (1999). Improving OLTP data quality using data warehouse mechanisms. In *Proc. of ACM SIGMOD Int. Conference on Management of Data* (pp. 536-537).

Jensen, C., Clifford, J., Elmasri, R., Gadia, S. K., Hayes, P. J., & Jajodia, S. (1994). A Consensus Glossary of Temporal Database Concepts. *SIGMOD Record*, *23*(1), 52–64. doi:10.1145/181550.181560

Jensen, C. S., Kligys, A., Pedersen, T. B., & Timko, I. (2004). Multidimensional data modeling for location-based services. *VLDB*, *13*(1), 1–21. doi:10.1007/s00778-003-0091-3

Jensen, M. R., Holmgren, T., & Pedersen, T. B. (2004). Discovering Multidimensional Structure in Relational Data. In Y. Kambayashi, M. K. Mohania, W. Wöß (Eds.), Proceedings of 6th International Conference on Data Warehousing and Knowledge Discovery; Vol. 3181, Lecture Notes of Computer Science (pp 138-148). Zaragoza, Spain: Springer.

Jensen, O. G., & Böhlen, M. H. (2004). Multitemporal conditional schema evolution. In *Int. Workshop on Evolution and Change in Data Management (ECDM)* (pp. 441-456). LNCS 3289.

Jiang, L., Salzberg, B., Lomet, D. B., & Barrena, M. (2000). The BT-tree: a branched and temporal access method. In *Proc. of Int. Conference on Very Large Data Bases (VLDB)* (pp. 451-460).

Jouini, K., & Jomier, G. (2008). Design and analysis of index structures in multiversion data warehouses. In Kozielski, S., & Wrembel, R. (Eds.), *New trends in data warehousing and data analysis* (pp. 169–185). Springer Verlag.

Jouini, K., & Jomier, G. (2007). Indexing multiversion databases. In *Proc. of ACM Conference on Information and Knowledge Management (CIKM)* (pp. 915-918).

Kaas, C., Pedersen, T. B., & Rasmussen, B. (2004). Schema Evolution for Stars and Snowflakes. *Proceedings International Conference on Enterprise Information Systems*, Porto, Portugal, 425-433.

Kakoudakis, I. (1996). The TAU Temporal Object Model. *M.Ph. Thesis*.UMIST, Department of Computation.

Kang, H. G., & Chung, C. W. (2002). Exploiting versions for on-line data warehouse maintenance in MOLAP servers. In *Proc. of Int. Conference on Very Large Data Bases (VLDB)* (pp. 742-753).

Karlapalem, K., Navathe, S. B., & Ammar, M. (1996). Optimal Redesign Policies to Support Dynamic *Processing of Applications on a Distributed Database System. Information Systems, 21*(4), 353–367. doi:10.1016/0306-4379(96)00018-X

Kellner, M., Madachy, R., & Raffo, D. (1999). Software process simulation modeling: Why? What? How? *Journal of Systems and Software, 46*(2-3), 91–105. doi:10.1016/S0164-1212(99)00003-5

Kim, W., & Chou, H. T. (1988). Versions of schema for object-oriented databases. In Proc. of *Int. Conference on Very Large Data Bases (VLDB)* (pp. 148-159).

Kimball, R. (1996). *The Data Warehouse Toolkit: Practical Techniques for Building Dimensional Data Warehouses.* John Wiley & Sons, Inc.

Kimball, R., Reeves, L., Thornthwaite, W., & Ross, M. (1998). *The Data Warehouse Lifecycle Toolkit: Expert Methods for Designing, Developing and Deploying Data Warehouses.* John Wiley & Sons, Inc.

Kimball, R., & Caserta, J. (2004). *The data warehouse ETL toolkit.* John Wiley & Sons Inc.

Kimball, R. (1996). *The data warehouse toolkit.* J.Wiley and Sons, Inc.

Kimball, R., & Ross, M. (2002). *The data warehouse toolkit: The complete guide to dimensional modeling* (2nd ed.). J.Wiley and Sons, Inc.

Kimball, R. (2000). Backward in Time. *Intelligent Enterprise Magazine, 3*(15).

Kirkpatrick, S., Gelatt, C. D., & Vecchi, M. P. (1983). Optimization by simulated annealing. *Science, 220*(4598), 671–680. doi:10.1126/science.220.4598.671

Klosterman, R. (1999). The What if? collaborative support system. *Environment and Planning. B, Planning & Design, 26*, 393–408. doi:10.1068/b260393

Klug, A. (1982). Equivalence of relational algebra and relational calculus query languages having aggregate functions. *Journal of the ACM, {29}*(3) (p. 699—717).

Kohonen, T., Kaski, S., Lagus, K., Salojärvi, J., Honkela, J., Paatero, V., & Saarela, A. (1999). Self organization of a massive text document collection. *IEEE Transactions on Neural Networks, 11*(3), 171–182.

Koller, D., & Sahami, M. (1997). Hierarchically classifying documents using very few words. *In Proceedings of ICML-97* (pp. 170–176).

Kolovson, C., & Stonebreaker, M. (1989). Indexing techniques for historical databases. In *Proc. of Int. Conference on Data Engineering (ICDE)* (pp. 127-137).

Koncilia, C. (2003). A Bi-Temporal Data Warehouse Model. *Short Paper Proceedings Conference on Advanced Information Systems Engineering*, Klagenfurt/Velden, Austria.

Kononenko, I., & Kukar, M. (2007). *Machine Learning and Data Mining: Introduction to Principles and Algorithms.* UK: Horwood Publishing Limited.

Kotz, D., Toh, S. B., & Radhakrishnan, S. (1994). *A Detailed Simulation Model of the HP 97560 Disk Drive (Tech. Rep.).* Hanover, USA: Dartmouth College.

Koutsoukis, N. S., Mitra, G., & Lucas, C. (1999). Adapting on-line analytical processing for decision modelling: the interaction of information and decision technologies. *Decision Support Systems, 26*(1), 1–30. doi:10.1016/S0167-9236(99)00021-4

Kuijpers, B., & Vaisman, A. (2007). A data model for moving objects supporting aggregation. In *Proceedings of STDM.*

Kuijpers, B., Moelans, B., & Van de Weghe, N. (2006). Qualitative polyline similarity testing with applications to query-by-sketch, indexing and classification. In *proceedings of ACM-GIS* (p.11-18).

Kukar, M., & Kononenko, I. (2002). Reliable classifications with machine learning. In Elomaa, T., Manilla, H., & Toivonen, H. (Eds.), *Proc. Machine Learning: ECML-2002* (pp. 219–231). Helsinki, Finland: Springer Verlag. doi:10.1007/3-540-36755-1_19

Kulkarni, S., & Mohania, M. (1999). Concurrent maintenance of views using multiple versions. In *Proc. of Int. Database Engineering and Application Symposium (IDEAS)* (pp. 254-259).

Lafferty, J., & Zhai, C. (2001). Document Language Models, Query Models, and Risk Minimization for Information Retrieval. *In Proceedings of the 24th ACM SIGIR Conference on Research and Development in IR* (pp. 111-119).

Lakshmanan, L. V. S., Pei, J., & Han, J. (2002). Quotient cube: How to summarize the semantics of a data cube. In Lochovsky, F. H. and Shan, W., editors, *VLDB*, pages 778–789. Morgan Kaufmann.

Lakshmanan, L. V. S., Sadri, F., & Subramanian, I. N. (1993). On the logical foundation of schema integration and evolution in heterogeneous database systems. In *Proc. of Int. Conference on Deductive and Object-Oriented Databases (DOOD)* (pp. 81-100). LNCS 760.

Lanka, S., & Mays, E. (1991). Fully persistent B⁺-trees. In *Proc. of ACM SIGMOD Int. Conference on Management of Data* (pp. 426-435).

Laporte, M., Novelli, N., Cicchetti, R., & Lakhal, L. (2002). Computing full and iceberg datacubes using partitions. In Hacid, M.-S., Ras, Z. W., Zighed, D. A., and Kodratoff, Y., editors, *ISMIS*, volume 2366 of *Lecture Notes in Computer Science*, pages 244–254. Springer.

Larsen, B., & Aone, C. (1999). [San Diego, California.]. *Fast and Effective Text Mining Using Linear-time Document Clustering., KDD-99*, 16–22.

Lee, A., Nica, A., & Rundensteiner, E. (2002). The EVE Approach: View Synchronization in Dynamic Distributed Environments. *IEEE Transactions on Knowledge and Data Engineering, 14*(5), 931–954. doi:10.1109/TKDE.2002.1033766

Lee, C., Huang, H. C., Liu, B., & Xu, Z. (2006). Development of timed colour Petri net simulation models for air cargo terminal operations. *Computers & Industrial Engineering, 51*(1), 102–110. doi:10.1016/j.cie.2006.07.002

Lee, I., & Gahegan, M. (2000). What-if Analysis for Point Data Sets Using Generalised Voronoi Diagrams. In *Proceedings International Conference on GeoComputation*. Greenwich, UK.

Lee, J.-G., Han, J., & Whang, K.-Y. (2007). Trajectory clustering: a partition-and-group framework. In *SIGMOD conference* (p.593-604).

Lehner, W., Albrecht, J., & Wedekind, H. (1998). Normal Forms for Multidimensional Databases. In M. Rafanelli, M. Jarke (Eds.), *Proceedings of 10th International Conference on Statistical and Scientific Database Management*; pp 63-72, Capri, Italy: IEEE.

Lei, H., & Ross, K. A. (1999). Faster Joins Using Join Indices. *The VLDB Journal, 8*(1), 1–24. doi:10.1007/s007780050071

Leja, W., Wrembel, R., & Ziembicki, R. (2010). On Querying Data and Metadata in Multiversion Data Warehouse. In *Bellatreche, L. (2010). Data Warehousing Design and Advanced Engineering Applications*. IGI Global. doi:10.4018/978-1-60566-756-0.ch012

Lenz, H. J., & Shoshani, A. (1997). Summarizability in OLAP and Statistical Databases. *Proceedings Statistical and Scientific Database Management Conference*, Olympia, US, 132-143.

Lenz, H., & Shoshani, A. (1997). Summarizability in olap and statistical data bases. In *Ninth international conference on scientific and statistical database management, proceedings, august 11-13, 1997, olympia, washington, usa* (p. 132-143). IEEE Computer Society.

Leonardi, L., Marketos, G., Frentzos, E., Giatrakos, N., Orlando, S., Pelekis, N., et al. T-Warehouse: Visual OLAP analysis on trajectory data (2010). In Proceedings of ICDE (p. 1141-1144).

Letz, C., Henn, E., & Vossen, G. (2002). Consistency in Data Warehouse Dimensions. *Proceedings International Database Engineering and Application Symposium*, Edmonton, Canada, 224-232.

Leung, T., & Muntz, R. (1993). Stream processing: Temporal query processing and optimization. In Tansel, A., Clifford, J., Gadia, S., Jajodia, S., Segev, A., & Snodgrass, R. (Eds.), *Temporal databases: Theory, design, and implementation* (pp. 329–355). Benjamin/Cummings.

Lin, J., & Demner-Fushman, D. (2007). Semantic Clustering of Answers to Clinical Questions. *Proceedings of the 2007 Annual Symposium of the American Medical Informatics Association (AMIA 2007)* (pp. 458-462). Chicago, Illinois.

List, B., Bruckner, R. M., Machaczek, K., & Schiefer, J. (2002). A Comparison of Data Warehouse Development Methods Case Study of the Process Warehouse. In A. Hameurlain, R. Cicchetti, R. Traunmüller (Eds.) *Proceedings of 13th International Conference on Database and Expert Systems Applications; Vol. 2453, Lecture Notes in Computer Science (pp 203-215)*. Aix-en-Provence, France: Springer.

List, B., Schiefer, J., & Tjoa, A. M. (2000). Process-Oriented Requirement Analysis Supporting the Data Warehouse Design Process – A Use Case Driven Approach. *Proceedings 11th International Conference Database and Expert Systems Applications* (pp. 593-603). London, UK.

Liu, L., Zicari, R., Hürsch, W. L., & Lieberherr, K. J. (1997). The role of polymorphic reuse mechanisms in schema evolution in an object-oriented database. [TKDE]. *IEEE Transactions on Knowledge and Data Engineering*, *9*(1), 50–67. doi:10.1109/69.567047

Liu, X., Nelson, D., Stobart, S., & Stirk, S. (2005). Managing schema versions in object-oriented databases. In *Proc. of East European Conference Advances in Databases and Information Systems (ADBIS)* (pp. 97-108). LNCS 3631.

Lomet, D., & Barga, R. (2005). *Microsoft ImmortalDB*. (Retrieved November 25, 2005, from http://research.microsoft.com /db/ImmortalDB/).

Lomet, D., & Salzberg, B. (1989). Access methods for multiversion data. In *Proc. of ACM SIGMOD Int. Conference on Management of Data* (pp. 315-324).

Lopes, S., Petit, J.-M., & Lakhal, L. (2002). Functional and approximate dependency mining: database and fca points of view. *Journal of Experimental & Theoretical Artificial Intelligence*, *14*(2-3), 93–114. doi:10.1080/09528130210164143

López, I. F. V., Snodgrass, R., & Moon, B. (2005). Spatiotemporal aggregate computation: A survey. *IEEE Transactions on Knowledge and Data Engineering*, *17*(2), 271–286. doi:10.1109/TKDE.2005.34

Lu, H., Ooi, B. C., & Tan, K. L. (1994). On Spatially Partitioned Temporal Join. In *Proc. of Int. Conference on Very Large Data Bases (VLDB)* (pp. 546-557).

Lujan-Mora, S., Trujillo, J., & Song, I.-Y. (2006). A UML profile for multidimensional modeling in data warehouses. *Data & Knowledge Engineering*, *59*(3), 725–769. doi:10.1016/j.datak.2005.11.004

Machado, R., Moreira, A. F., & de Matos Galante, R. (2006). Type-safe versioned object query language. *Journal of Universal Computer Science*, 12 (7). (Retrieved January 3, 2007, from http://www.jucs.org/jucs 12 7).

Mahboubi, H., & Darmont, J. (2009) Enhancing XML Data Warehouse Query Performance by Fragmentation, 24th Annual ACM Symposium on Applied Computing (SAC 09), Hawaii, USA, 2009, pp. 1555-1562

Malinowski, E., & Zimányi, E. (2008). A conceptual model for temporal data warehouses and its transformation to the ER and the object-relational models. *Data & Knowledge Engineering*, *64*, 101–133. doi:10.1016/j.datak.2007.06.020

Malinowski, E., & Zimányi, E. (2008). *Advanced data warehouse design: from conventional to spatial and temporal applications*. Springer Publishing Company, Inc.

Malinowski, E., & Zimányi, E. (2004). *Representing spatiality in a conceptual multidimensional model* (pp. 12–22). GIS.

Malinowski, E., & Zimányi, E. (2006). Hierarchies in a multidimensional model: From conceptual modeling to logical representation. *Data & Knowledge Engineering*, *59*(2), 348–377. doi:10.1016/j.datak.2005.08.003

Malinowski, E., & Zimányi, E. (2008). *Advanced Data Warehouse Design: From Conventional to Spatial and Temporal Applications*. Springer, 2008.

Mannila, H., & Toivonen, H. (1996). *Multiple uses of frequent sets and condensed representations (extended abstract)* (pp. 189–194). KDD.

Manolopoulos, Y., & Kapetanakis, G. (1990). Overlapping B⁺-trees for temporal data. In *Proc. of Jerusalem Conference on Information Technology (JCIT)* (pp. 491–498).

Marketos, G., Frentzos, E., Ntousi, I., Pelekis, N., Raffaeta, A., & Theodoridis, Y. (2008). *Building real-world trajectory data warehouses (Vol. 08)*. Mobi, DE.

Marketos, G., & Theodoridis, Y. (2010). Ad-hoc OLAP on Trajectory Data. In *MDM 2010* (p. 189,198).

Mazón, J. N., Trujillo, J., & Lechtenborger, J. (2007). Reconciling Requirement-Driven Data Warehouses with Data Sources Via Multidimensional Normal Forms. *Data & Knowledge Engineering, 23*(3), 725–751. doi:10.1016/j.datak.2007.04.004

McBrien, P., & Poulovassilis, A. (2002). Schema evolution in heterogeneous database architectures, a schema transformation approach. In *Proc. of Conference on Advanced Information Systems Engineering (CAiSE)* (pp. 484-499). LNCS 2348.

McKenzie, E., & Snodgrass, R. (1990). Schema Evolution and the Relational Algebra. *Information Systems, 15*(2), 207–232. doi:10.1016/0306-4379(90)90036-O

Mendelzon, A. O., & Vaisman, A. A. (2000). *Temporal queries in OLAP* (pp. 242–253). VLDB.

Mendelzon, A. O., & Vaisman, A. A. (2003). Time in multidimensional databases. In *Multidimensional databases* (p. 166-199).

Mendelzon, A. O., Rizzolo, F., & Vaisman, A. (2004). Indexing temporal XML documents. In *Proc. of Int. Conference on Very Large Data Bases (VLDB)* (pp. 216-227).

Mendelzon, A., & Vaisman, A. (2000). Temporal queries in OLAP. *Proceedings Conference on Very Large Data Bases*, Cairo, Egypt, 242-253.

Mennis, J., Viger, R., & Tomlin, C.D. (2005). Cubic map algebra functions for spatio-temporal analysis. *Cartography and Geographic Information Science* (32)(1) (p. 17-32).

Meratnia, N., & de By, R. A. (2002). *Aggregation and comparison of trajectories* (pp. 49–54). ACM-GIS.

Microsoft Corporation. (2005). Partitioned Tables and Indexes in SQL Server 2005. Retrieved from http://msdn.microsoft.com/ en-us/library/ ms345146.aspx

Microsoft, B. O. L. (2007). *Slowly changing dimension.* (Retrieved February 25, 2007, from http://msdn2.microsoft.com/ enus/library/ms141715.aspx).

Moody, D. L., & Kortink, M. A. (2000). From Enterprise Models to Dimensional Models: A Method for Data Warehouse and Data Mart Design. In M. A. Jeusfeld, H. Shu, M. Staudt, G. Vossen (Eds.), *Proceedings of 2nd International Workshop on Design and Management of Data Warehouses*; pp 6. Stockholm, Sweden: CEUR-WS.org.

Moon, H. J., Curino, C. A., Deutsch, A., Hou, C.-Y., & Zaniolo, C. (2008). Managing and querying transaction-time databases under schema evolution. In *Proc. of Int. Conference on Very Large Data Bases (VLDB)* (pp. 882-895).

Moreno, F., Fileto, R., & Arango, F. (2010). Season queries on a temporal multidimensional model for OLAP. *Mathematical and Computer Modelling, 52*(7-8), 1103–1109. doi:10.1016/j.mcm.2010.02.007

Morfonios, K., Konakas, S., Ioannidis, Y. E., & Kotsis, N. (2007). Rolap implementations of the data cube. *ACM Computing Surveys, 39*(4). doi:10.1145/1287620.1287623

Morfonios, K., & Ioannidis, Y. E. (2006). Cure for cubes: Cubing using a rolap engine. In Dayal, U., Whang, K.-Y., Lomet, D. B., Alonso, G., Lohman, G. M., & Kersten, M. L. (Eds.), *VLDB* (pp. 379–390). ACM.

Morzy, T., & Wrembel, R. (2004). On querying versions of multiversion data warehouse. *Proceedings International Workshop on Data Warehousing and OLAP*, Washington, DC, 92-101.

Morzy, T., & Wrembel, R. (2004). On querying versions of multiversion data warehouse. In *Proc. of ACM Int. Workshop on Data Warehousing and OLAP (DOLAP)* (pp. 92-101).

Mouza, C., & Rigaux, P. (2005). Mobility patterns. *GeoInformatica, 9*(23), 297–319. doi:10.1007/s10707-005-4574-9

Muñoz, L., Mazón, J.-N., & Trujillo, J. (2009). Automatic generation of ETL processes from conceptual models. *In Proc. of the ACM Int. Workshop on Data Warehousing and OLAP (DOLAP)* (pp. 33-40).

MySQL, n.d., Partition Types, Retrieved from http://dev.mysql.com/doc/ refman/5.1/en/ partitioning-types.html.

Nascimento, M. A., & Dunham, M. H. (1999). Indexing valid time databases via B⁺-trees. [TKDE]. *IEEE Transactions on Knowledge and Data Engineering, 11*(6), 929–947. doi:10.1109/69.824609

Nascimento, M. A., & Dunham, M. H. (1996). Indexing a transaction decision time database. In *Proc. of ACM Symposium on Applied Computing (SAC)* (pp. 166-172).

Nascimento, M. A., & Dunham, M. H. (1997). A proposal for indexing bitemporal databases via cooperative B$^+$-trees. In *Proc. of Int. Database Engineering and Application Symposium (IDEAS)* (p. 349).

Nascimento, M. A., & Silva, J. R. O. (1998). Towards historical R-trees. In *Proc. of ACM Symposium on Applied Computing (SAC)* (pp. 235-240).

Navathe, S. B., & Ra, M. (1989). Vertical Partitioning for Database Design: A Graphical Algorithm. *Proceedings of the International Conference on Management of Data (SIGMOD)*, pp. 440-450.

Nebot, V., Berlanga, R., Pérez-Martínez, J.M., Aramburu, M.J. & Pedersen, T.B. (2009). Multidimensional Integrated Ontologies: A Framework for Designing Semantic Data Warehouses. *Journal of Data Semantics XIII, Vol. 5530, Lecture Notes of Computer Science* (pp, 1-36). Springer.

Nedjar, S., Casali, A., Cicchetti, R., & Lakhal, L. (2009). Emerging cubes: Borders, size estimations and lossless reductions. *Information Systems, 34*(6), 536–550. doi:10.1016/j.is.2009.03.001

Nedjar, S., Cicchetti, R., & Lakhal, L. (2010). *Constrained Closed and Quotient Cubes*, volume 2 of *Studies in Computational Intelligence*, chapter 5. Springer-Verlag.

Nica, A., Lee, A. J., & Rundensteiner, E. (1998). The CVS algorithm for view synchronization in evolvable large-scale information systems. In *Proc. of Int. Conference on Extending Database Technology (EDBT)* (pp. 359-373). LNCS 1377.

Nigam, K., & McCallum, A. (1998). Text Classification from Labeled and Unlabeled Document Using EM. *Machine Learning, 39*(2-3), 103–134.

Nouretdinov, I., Melluish, T., & Vovk, V. (2001). Ridge regressioon confidence machine. In *Proceedings of the 18th Iinternational Conference on Machine Learning* (pp. 385–392). San Francisco, CA: Morgan Kaufmann.

O'Neil, P. (1987). Model 204 architecture and performance. In *Int. Workshop on High Performance Transactions Systems* (pp. 40-59). LNCS 359.

OLAP Council. (1998) APB-1 OLAP Benchmark, Release II. Retrieved from http://www.olapcouncil.org/ research/ resrchly.htm

OMG. (2008). UML: Superstructure, version 2.0. Retrieved December 10, 2008, from http://www.omg.org.

Oracle Corporation. (2010). Partitioning with Oracle Database 11g Release 2. An oracle White Paper. Retrieved from www.oracle.com/technetwork/ middleware/bi-foundation/ twp-partitioning-11gr2-2009-09- 130569.pdf

Orlando, S., Orsini, R., Raffaetà, A., Roncato, A., & Silvestri, C. (2007). Spatio-temporal aggregations in trajectory data warehouses. In *DaWaK* (p. 66-77).

Ozsu, T. M., & Valduriez, P. (1999). *Principles of Distributed Database Systems* (2nd ed.). Prentice Hall.

Pantel, P., & Lin, D. (2002). Document clustering with committees. *In Proceedings of the 2002 ACM SIGMOD International Conference on Management of data* (pp. 199-206).

Papadias, D., Tao, Y., Zhang, J., Mamoulis, N., Shen, Q., & Sun, J. (2002). Indexing and retrieval of historical aggregate information about moving objects. *IEEE Data Eng. Bull., 25*(2), 10–17.

Papadias, D., Tao, Y., Kalnis, P., & Zhang, J. (2002). Indexing spatio-temporal data warehouses. In *International conference on data engineering (ICDE)* (p. 166–175). IEEE Computer Society.

Papadomanolakis, S., & Ailamaki, A. (2004). Autopart: Automating Schema Design for Large Scientific Databases using Data Partitioning. *Proceedings of the 16th International Conference on Scientific and Statistical Database Management*, pp. 383–392.

Papastefanatos, G., Vassiliadis, P., Simitsis, A., Sellis, T., & Vassiliou, Y. (2009). HECATAEUS: Regulating schema evolution. Proceedings 26th International Conference on Data Engineering, Long Beach, California, 1181-1184.

Papastefanatos, G., Vassiliadis, P., Simitsis, A., Sellis, T., & Vassiliou, Y. (2009). Rule-based management of schema changes at ETL sources. In *ADBIS Workshop on Managing Evolution of Data Warehouses (MEDWa)* (pp. 55-62). LNCS 5968.

Papastefanatos, G., Vassiliadis, P., Simitsis, A., & Vassiliou, Y. (2007). What-if analysis for data warehouse evolution. In *Proc. of Int. Conference on Data Warehousing and Knowledge Discovery (DaWaK)* (pp. 23-33). LNCS 4654.

Papastefanatos, G., Vassiliadis, P., Simitsis, A., & Vassiliou, Y. (2008). Design Metrics for Data Warehouse Evolution. In Proc. of Int. Conference on Conceptual Modeling (*ER*) (pp. 440-454). LNCS 5231.

Pardillo, J., Golfarelli, M., Rizzi, S., & Trujillo, J. (2009). Visual Modelling of Data Warehousing Flows with UML Profiles. In *Proceedings International Conference on Data Warehousing and Knowledge Discovery* (pp. 36-47). Linz, Austria.

Pardillo, J., Mazón, J. N., & Trujillo, J. (2008). Model-Driven Metadata for OLAP Cubes from the Conceptual Modelling of Data Warehouses. *Proceedings of 10th International Conference on Data Warehousing and Knowledge Discovery; Vol. 5182, Lecture Notes of Computer Science* (pp, 13-22). Turin, Italy: Springer.

Paredaens, J., Kuper, G., & Libkin, L. (Eds.). (2000). *Constraint databases*. Springer-Verlag.

Paredaens, J., Van Den Bussche, J., & Gucht, D. V. (1994). Towards a theory of spatial database queries. In *Thirteenth ACM SIGACT-SIGMOD-SIGART symposium on principles of database systems, (PODS)* (p. 279–288). ACM Press.

Pasquier, N., Bastide, Y., Taouil, R., & Lakhal, L. (1999). Efficient mining of association rules using closed itemset lattices. *Information Systems, 24*(1), 25–46. doi:10.1016/S0306-4379(99)00003-4

Pearson, R. K. (2005). Mining imperfect data; dealing with contamination and incomplete records. *SIAM 2005.*

Pedersen, T. B., & Tryfona, N. (2001). Pre-aggregation in spatial data warehouses. In *Advances in spatial and temporal databases* (pp. 460–480). SSTD.

Pedersen, T. B., & Jensen, C. (1998). Research Issues in Clinical Data Warehousing. *Proceedings Statistical and Scientific Database Management Conference*, Capri, Italy, 43-52.

Pedersen, T. B., & Jensen, C. (1999). Multidimensional Data Modeling for Complex Data. *Proceedings International Conference on Data Engineering*, Sydney, Austrialia, 336-345.

Pelekis, N., & Theodoridis, Y. (2006). *Boosting location-based services with a moving object database engine* (pp. 3–10). Mobide.

Pelekis, N., Theodoridis, Y., Vosinakis, S., & Panayiotopoulos, T. (2006). *Hermes - a framework for location-based data management* (pp. 1130–1134). EDBT.

Pelekis, N. (2002). Stau: A spatio-temporal extension to ORACLE DBMS. *Ph.D Thesis, UMIST Department of Computation.*

Pelekis, N., Theodoulidis, B., Kopanakis, Y., & Theodoridis, Y. (2004). Literature Review of Spatio-Temporal Database Models. In *The Knowledge Engineering Review journal, 19*(3) (p. 235-274).

Peters, R. J., & Özsu, M. T. (1997). An axiomatic model of dynamic schema evolution in object base systems. *ACM Transactions on Database Systems, 22*(1), 75–114. doi:10.1145/244810.244813

Pham, D., Dimov, S., & Nguyen, C. (2004). An incremental k-means algorithm. *Journal of Mechanical Engineering Science, 218*(7), 783–795.

Phipps, C., & Davis, K. C. (2002). Automating Data Warehouse Conceptual Schema Design and Evaluation. In L. V. S. Lakshmanan (Ed.), *Proceedings of 4th International Workshop on Design and Management of Data Warehouses*; pp 23-32, Toronto, Canada: CEUR-WS.org.

Postgres, S. Q. L. n.d., Partitioning, Retrieved from http://www.postgresql.org/docs /8.1/static/ddl-partitioning. html.

Pourabbas, E. (2003). Cooperation with geographic databases. In *Multidimensional databases: Problems and solutions* (pp. 393–432). Idea group. doi:10.4018/9781591400530.ch013

Prat, N., Akoka, J., & Comyn-Wattiau, I. (2006). A UML-based Data Warehouse Design Method. *Decision Support Systems, 42*(3), 1449–1473. doi:10.1016/j.dss.2005.12.001

Pratt, W., & Fagan, L. (2000). The Usefulness of Dynamically Categorizing Search Results. *Journal of the American Medical Informatics Association, 7*(6), 605–617.

Pratt, W., Hearst, M., & Fagan, L. (1999). A knowledge-based approach to organizing retrieved documents. *AAAI '99: Proceedings of the 16th National Conference on Artificial Intelligence* (pp. 80-85). Orlando, Florida.

Quass, D., & Widom, J. (1997). On-line warehouse view maintenance. In *Proc. of ACM SIGMOD Int. Conference on Management of Data* (pp. 393-404).

Quix, C. (1999). Repository Support for Data Warehouse Evolution. *Proceedings International Workshop on Design and Management of Data Warehouses*, Heidelberg, Germany.

R Development Core Team. (2006). *A Language and Environment for Statistical Computing*. Vienna, Austria: R Foundation for Statistical Computing.

Rahm, E., & Hai Do, H. (2000). Data cleaning: Problems and current approaches. *IEEE Technical Bulletin on Data Engineering, 23*(4), 3–13.

Raman, V., & Hellerstein, J. M. (2001). Potter's wheel: An interactive data cleaning system. In *Proc. of Int. Conference on Very Large Data Bases (VLDB)* (pp. 381-390).

Rana, S. P., & Fotouhi, F. (1993). Efficient processing of time-joins in temporal data bases. In *Proc. of Int. Conference on Database Systems for Advanced Applications (DASFAA)* (pp. 427-432).

Rao, F., Zhang, L., Yu, X., Li, Y., & Chen, Y. (2003). Spatial hierarchy and OLAP-favored search in spatial data warehouse. In *ACM sixth international workshop on data warehousing and OLAP (DOLAP)* (p. 48–55). ACM.

Ravat, F., Teste, O., & Zurfluh, G. (2006). A Multiversion-Based Multidimensional Model. *Proceedings International Conference on Data Warehousing and Knowledge Discovery*, 65-74.

Ravat, F., Teste, O., & Zurfluh, G. (2006). A multiversion-based multidimensional model. In *Proc. of Int. Conference on Data Warehousing and Knowledge Discovery (DaWaK)* (pp. 65-74). LNCS 4081.

Rechy-Ramírez, E.-J., & Benítez-Guerrero, E. (2006). A Model and Language for Bi-temporal Schema Versioning in Data Warehouses. *Proceedings International Conference on Computing*, Mexico City, Mexico.

Riedewald, M., Agrawal, D., & El Abbadi, A. (2002). Efficient integration and aggregation of historical information. *Proceedings SIGMOD Conference*, Madison, Wisconsin, 13-24.

Rigaux, P., Scholl, M., & Voisard, A. (2001). *Spatial databases: With application to GIS*. Morgan Kaufmann.

Rivest, S., Bédard, Y., & Marchand, P. (2001). Towards better support for spatial decision making: Defining the characteristics of spatial on-line analytical processing (SOLAP). *Geomatica, 55*(4), 539–555.

Rizzi, S., & Golfarelli, M. (2000). *Date warehouse design* (pp. 39–42). ICEIS.

Rizzi, S. (2009a). Business Intelligence. In Liu, L., & Özsu, T. (Eds.), *Encyclopedia of Database Systems*. Springer.

Rizzi, S. (2009b). What-if analysis. In L. Liu and T. Özsu (Eds.), *Encyclopedia of Database Systems*. Springer. Trujillo, J., & Lujan-Mora, S. (2003). A UML based approach for modelling ETL processes in data warehouses. In *Proceedings International Conference on Conceptual Modeling* (pp. 307-320). Chicago, USA.

Rizzi, S., & Golfarelli, M. (2007). X-time: Schema versioning and cross-version querying in data warehouses. In *Proc. of Int. Conference on Data Engineering (ICDE)* (pp. 1471-1472).

Rizzi, S., Abelló, A., Lechtenbörger, J., & Trujillo, J. (2006). Research in Data Warehouse Modeling and Design: Dead or Alive? *Proceedings International Workshop on Data Warehousing and OLAP*, Arlington, USA, 3-10.

Roddick, J. (1995). A Survey of Schema Versioning Issues for Database Systems. *Information and Software Technology, 37*(7), 383–393. doi:10.1016/0950-5849(95)91494-K

Roddick, J. F. (1992). SQL/SE - a query language extension for databases supporting schema evolution. *SIGMOD Record, 21*(3), 10–16. doi:10.1145/140979.140985

Rodic, J., & Baranovic, M. (2009). Generating data quality rules and integration into ETL process. In *Proc. of the ACM Int. Workshop on Data warehousing and OLAP (DOLAP)* (pp. 65-72).

Romero, O., & Abelló, A. (2010a). Automatic Validation of Requirements to Support Multidimensional Design. *Data & Knowledge Engineering, 69*(9), 917–942. doi:10.1016/j.datak.2010.03.006

Romero, O., & Abelló, A. (2010b). A Framework for Multidimensional Design of Data Warehouses from Ontologies. *Data & Knowledge Engineering, 69*(11), 1138–1157. doi:10.1016/j.datak.2010.07.007

Romero, O., & Abelló, A. (2006). Multidimensional Design by Examples. In A. M. Tjoa, J. Trujillo (Eds.), *Proceedings of 8th International Conference on Data Warehousing and Knowledge Discovery; Vol. Lecture Notes of Computer Science (pp 85-94)*. Krakow, Poland: Springer.

Romero, O., & Abelló, A. (2007). Automating Multidimensional Design from Ontologies. In I. Song, T. B. Pedersen (Eds.), *Proceedings of ACM 10th International Workshop on Data Warehousing and OLAP*; pp 1-8, Lisbon, Portugal: ACM Press.

Rose, R., & Segev, A. (1993). TOOSQL - A Temporal Object-Oriented Query Language. In Proc. of Int. Conference on Conceptual Modeling (ER) (pp. 122-136). LNCS 823.

Ross, K. A., & Srivastava, D. (1997). Fast computation of sparse datacubes. In Jarke, M., Carey, M. J., Dittrich, K. R., Lochovsky, F. H., Loucopoulos, P., & Jeusfeld, M. A. (Eds.), *VLDB* (pp. 116–125). Morgan Kaufmann.

Rumelhart, D., Hinton, G., & Williams, R. (1986). Learning internal representations by error propagation. In *Parallel Distributed Processing: Explorations in the Microstructure of Cognition, vol. 1: Foundations* (pp. 318–362). Cambridge MA, USA: MIT Press.

Rundensteiner, E., Koeller, A., & Zhang, X. (2000). Maintaining data warehouses over changing information sources. *Communications of the ACM, 43*(6), 57–62. doi:10.1145/336460.336475

Rundensteiner, E. A., Koeller, A., Zhang, X., Lee, A. J., Nica, A., Van Wyk, A., & Lee, Y. (1999). Evolvable view environment (EVE): non-equivalent view maintenance under schema changes. In *Proc. of ACM SIGMOD Int. Conference on Management of Data* (pp. 553-555).

Rundensteiner, E. A., Lee, A. J., & Nica, A. (1997). On preserving views in evolving environments. In *Proc. of Int. Workshop on Knowledge Representation Meets Databases* (pp. 1-11).

Sacca, D., & Wiederhold, G. (1985). Database Partitioning in a Cluster of Processors. [TODS]. *ACM Transactions on Database Systems, 10*(1), 29–56. doi:10.1145/3148.3161

Salzberg, B., & Tsotras, V. J. (1999). Comparison of access methods for time-evolving data. *ACM Computing Surveys, 31*(2), 158–221. doi:10.1145/319806.319816

Salzberg, B., Jiang, L., Lomet, D., Barrena, M., Shan, J., & Kanoulas, E. (2004). A framework for access methods for versioned data. In *Proc. of Int. Conference on Extending Database Technology (EDBT)* (pp. 730-747). LNCS 2992.

Sanjay, A., Chaudhuri, S., & Narasayya, V. R. (2000). Automated selection of materialized views and indexes in Microsoft SQL server. *Proceedings of 26th International Conference on Very Large Data Bases (VLDB'2000)*, pp. 496-505.

Sanjay, A., Narasayya, V. R., & Yang, B. (2004). Integrating vertical and horizontal partitioning into automated physical database design. *Proceedings of the International Conference on Management of Data (SIGMOD)*, pp. 359–370.

Sarda, N. L. (1999). Temporal Issues in Data Warehouse Systems. *Proceedings International Symposium on Database Applications in Non-Traditional Environments*, Kyoto, Japan, 27-34.

Saunders, C., Gammerman, A., & Vovk, V. (1999). Transduction with confidence and credibility. In *Proceedings of IJCAI'99, 2*, 722–726.

Schaal, S., & Atkeson, C. G. (1994). Assessing the quality of learned local models. In *J. D. Cowan, G. Tesauro, & J. Alspector (Eds.), Advances in Neural Information Processing Systems*, (6), 160–167. Morgan Kaufmann Publishers, Inc.

Schlesinger, L., Bauer, A., Lehner, W., Ediberidze, G., & Gutzman, M. (2001). Efficiently synchronizing multidimensional schema data. In *Proc. of ACM Int. Workshop on Data Warehousing and OLAP (DOLAP)* (pp. 69-76).

Sciore, E. (1994). Versioning and configuration management in an object-oriented data model. *The VLDB Journal, 3*(1), 77–106. doi:10.1007/BF01231359

Shahzad, M. K. (2010). From Conventional to Multiversion Data Warehouse: Practical Issues. In Furtado, P. (Ed.), *Evolving Application Domains of Data Warehousing and Mining*. IGI Global. doi:10.4018/978-1-60566-816-1.ch003

Shahzad, K., Nasir, J. A., & Pasha, M. A. (2007). Intermingling evolutionary and versioning approach for data warehouse by Versioning Algebra. In Sobh, T. (Ed.), *Innovations and Advanced Techniques in Computer and Information Sciences and Engineering* (pp. 295–300). Springer Verlag. doi:10.1007/978-1-4020-6268-1_53

Shekhar, S., Lu, C.-T., Tan, X., Chawla, S., & Vatsavai, R. R. (2001). Map cube: A visualization tool for spatial data warehouses. In *Geographic data mining and knowledge discovery* (pp. 73–108). Taylor and Francis. doi:10.4324/9780203468029_chapter_4

Shen, H., Ooi, B. C., & Lu, H. (1994). The TP-index: A dynamic and efficient indexing mechanism for temporal databases. In *Proc. of Int. Conference on Data Engineering (ICDE)* (pp. 274-281).

Shoshani, A. (1997). Olap and statistical databases: Similarities and differences. In Mendelzon, A. and Özsoyoglu, Z. M., editors, *PODS*, pages 185–196, New York, NY, USA. ACM. Chairman-Mendelzon, Alberto and Chairman-Özsoyoglu, Z. Meral.

Silverman, B. W. (1986). *Density Estimation for Statistics and Data Analysis. Monographs on Statistics and Applied Probability*. London: Chapman and Hall.

Simitsis, A., Vassiliadis, P., & Sellis, T. (2005b). State-space optimization of ETL workflows. [TKDE]. *IEEE Transactions on Knowledge and Data Engineering*, *17*(10), 1404–1419. doi:10.1109/TKDE.2005.169

Simitsis, A., Vassiliadis, P., & Sellis, T. (2005a). Optimizing ETL processes in data warehouses. In *Proc. of Int. Conference on Data Engineering (ICDE)* (pp. 564-575).

Sismanis, Y., Deligiannakis, A., Roussopoulos, N., & Kotidis, Y. (2002). Dwarf: shrinking the petacube. In *SIGMOD Conference*, pages 464–475.

Sjøberg, D. (1993). Quantifying schema evolution. *Information and Software Technology*, *35*(1), 35–54. doi:10.1016/0950-5849(93)90027-Z

Smola, A. J., & Schölkopf, B. (1998). A Tutorial on Support Vector Regression. *NeuroCOLT2 Technical Report NC2-TR-1998-030*.

Snodgrass, R. T. (1995). *The TSQL2 Temporal Query Language*. Kluwer Academic Publishers.

Snodgrass, R. (Ed.). (1995). *The TSQL2 temporal query language*. Kluwer Academic Publishers.

Snodgrass, R. T. (Ed.). (1999). *Developing time-oriented database applications in SQL*. Morgan Kaufmann.

Son, D., & Elmasri, R. (1996). Efficient temporal join processing using time index. In *Proc. of Int. Conference on Scientific and Statistical Database Management (SSDBM)* (pp. 252-261).

Song, I., Khare, R., & Dai, B. (2007). SAMSTAR: A Semi-Automated Lexical Method for Generating STAR Schemas from an ER Diagram In I. Song, T. B. Pedersen (Eds.), *Proceedings of ACM 10th International Workshop on Data Warehousing and OLAP;* pp 9-16, Lisbon, Portugal: ACM Press.

Song, M., Song, I.-Y., & Hu, X. (2003). KPSpotter: a flexible information gain-based keyphrase extraction system. *The 5th ACM international workshop on web information and data management* (pp. 50-53).

Soo, M. D., Snodgrass, R. T., & Jensen, C. J. (1994). Efficient evaluation of the valid-time natural join. In *Proc. of Int. Conference on Data Engineering (ICDE)* (pp. 282-292).

Spyratos, N. (1987). The partition model: A deductive database model. *ACM Transactions on Database Systems*, *12*(1), 1–37. doi:10.1145/12047.22718

Stefanovic, N., Han, J., & Koperski, K. (2000). Object-based selective materialization for efficient implementation of spatial data cubes. *IEEE Transactions on Knowledge and Data Engineering*, *12*(6), 938–958. doi:10.1109/69.895803

Steinbach, M., Karypis, G., & Kumar, V. (2000). *A Comparison of Document Clustering Techniques*. Department of Computer Science and Engineering, University of Minnesota.

Stockinger, K., & Wu, K. (2007). Bitmap Indices for Data Warehouses. In Wrembel, R., & Koncilia, C. (Eds.), *Data Warehouses and OLAP: Concepts, Architectures and Solutions* (pp. 157–178). Idea Group Inc.

Stöhr, T., Märtens, H., & Rahm, E. (2000). Multi-dimensional database allocation for parallel data warehouses. *Proceedings of the International Conference on Very Large Databases (VLDB)*, pp. 273–284.

Stonebraker, M., & Moore, D. (1996). *Object-relational DBMSs: The next great wave.* Morgan Kaufmann.

Stumme, G., Taouil, R., Bastide, Y., Pasquier, N., & Lakhal, L. (2002). Computing iceberg concept lattices with titanic. *Data & Knowledge Engineering, 42*(2), 189–222. doi:10.1016/S0169-023X(02)00057-5

Talens, G., Oussalah, C., & Colinas, M. F. (1993). Versions of simple and composite objects. In *Proc. of Int. Conference on Very Large Data Bases (VLDB)* (pp. 62-72).

Tansel, A. U., Clifford, J., Gadia, S. K., Jajodia, S., Segev, A., & Snodgrass, R. T. (1993). *Temporal databases: theory, design and implementation.* Benjamin Cummings.

Tansel, A., Clifford, J., Gadia, S., Jajodia, S., Segev, A., & Snodgrass, R. (Eds.). (1993). *Temporal databases: Theory, design, and implementation.* Benjamin/Cummings.

Tao, Y., Papadias, D., & Zhang, J. (2002). Cost models for overlapping and multi-version structures. [TODS]. *ACM Transactions on Database Systems, 27*(3), 299–342. doi:10.1145/581751.581754

Tao, Y., Kollios, G., Considine, J., Li, F., & Papadias, D. (2004). *Spatio-temporal aggregation using sketches* (pp. 214–226). ICDE.

Tao, Y., & Papadias, D. (2001a). Efficient historical R-trees. In *Proc. of Int. Conference on Scientific and Statistical Database Management (SSDBM)* (pp. 223-232).

Tao, Y., & Papadias, D. (2001b). MV3R-tree: A spatio-temporal access method for timestamp and interval queries. In *Proc. of Int. Conference on Very Large Data Bases (VLDB)* (pp. 431-440).

Tao, Y., Papadias, D., & Faloutsos, C. (2004). Approximate Temporal Aggregation. *Proceedings International Conference on Data Engineering*, Boston, Massachusetts, 190-201.

Teschke, M., & Ulbrich, A. (1998). Concurrent warehouse maintenance without compromising session consistency. In *Proc. of Int. Conference on Database and Expert Systems Applications (DEXA)* (pp. 776-785). LNCS 1460.

Theodoridis, Y. (2003). Ten benchmark database queries for location-based services. *The Computer Journal, 46*(6), 713–725. doi:10.1093/comjnl/46.6.713

Thiele, M., Fischer, U., & Lehner, W. (2009). Partition-based workload scheduling in living data warehouse environments. *Information Systems, 34*(4-5), 382–399. doi:10.1016/j.is.2008.06.001

Thomsen, C., & Pedersen, T. B. (2009). pygrametl: a powerful programming framework for extract-transform-load programmers. In *Proc. of the ACM Int. Workshop on Data Warehousing and OLAP (DOLAP)* (pp. 49-56).

Tomlin, D. C. (1990). *Geographic Information Systems and Cartographic Modelling.* Prentice-Hall.

Tresh, M. T. (1991). A framework for schema evolution by meta object manipulation. In *Int. Workshop on Foundations of Models and Languages for Data and Objects* (pp. 1-13).

Trujillo, J., & Luján-Mora, S. (2003). A UML based approach for modeling ETL processes in data warehouses. In *Proc. of Int. Conference on Conceptual Modeling (ER)* (pp. 307-320). LNCS 2813.

Tsuda, K., Rätsch, G., Mika, S., & Müller, K. (2001). Learning to predict the leave-one-out error of kernel based classifiers. In *Lecture Notes in Computer Science* (pp. 331–338). Berlin, Heidelberg: Springer.

Tzoumas, K., Deshpande, A., & Jensen, C. (2010). Sharing-Aware Horizontal Partitioning for Exploiting Correlations During Query Processing, Proceedings of 36th International Conference on Very Large Data Bases, 3(1), pp. 542-553.

Tzouramanis, T., Manolopoulos, Y., & Lorentzos, N. A. (1999). Overlapping B+-trees: an implementation of a transaction time access method. [DKE]. *Data & Knowledge Engineering, 29*(3), 381–404. doi:10.1016/S0169-023X(98)00046-9

Tzouramanis, T., Vassilakopoulos, M., & Manolopoulos, Y. (1998). Overlapping linear quadtrees: a spatio-temporal access method. In *Proc. of ACM Int. Symposium on Advances in Geographic Information Systems* (pp. 1-7).

Vaisman, A., Mendelzon, A., Ruaro, W., & Cymerman, S. (2004). Supporting Dimension Updates in an OLAP Server. *Information Systems, 29*, 165–185. doi:10.1016/S0306-4379(03)00049-8

Vaisman, A., & Mendelzon, A. (2001). A Temporal Query Language for OLAP: Implementation and a Case Study. *Proceedings DBPL.*

Vaisman, A., & Mendelzon, A. (2001). A temporal query language for OLAP: implementation and case study. In *Proc. of Int. Workshop on Database Programming Languages (DBPL)* (pp. 78-96). LNCS 2397.

Vaisman, A., & Zimányi, E. (2009). A Multidimensional Model Representing Continuous Fields in Spatial Data Warehouses. In *Proceedings of GIS* (p.168-177).

Vaisman, A., Izquierdo, A., & Ktenas, M. (2006). Web-enabled Temporal OLAP. In *Proceedings of LA_WEB '06*, 220-229, Puebla, Mexico.

Valduriez, P. (1987). Join indices. [TODS]. *ACM Transactions on Database Systems, 12*(2), 218–246. doi:10.1145/22952.22955

van Rijsbergen, C. J. (1979). Information Retrieval (2nd ed). London: Butterworths.

Vapnik, V. (1995). *The Nature of Statistical Learning Theory.* Springer.

Varman, P., & Verma, R. (1997). An efficient multi-version access structure. [TKDE]. *IEEE Transactions on Knowledge and Data Engineering, 3*(9), 391–409. doi:10.1109/69.599929

Vassiliadis, P., Simitsis, A., Georgantas, P., Terrovitis, M., & Skiadopoulos, S. (2005). A generic and customizable framework for the design of ETL scenarios. *Information Systems, 30*(7), 492–525. doi:10.1016/j.is.2004.11.002

Vassiliadis, P., & Simitsis, A. (2009). Near real time ETL. In Kozielski, S., & Wrembel, R. (Eds.), *New Trends in Data Warehousing and Data Analysis* (pp. 19–49). Springer Verlag. doi:10.1007/978-0-387-87431-9_2

Vassiliadis, P., Simitsis, A., & Skiadopoulos, S. (2002). Conceptual modeling for ETL processes. In *Proceedings International Workshop on Data Warehousing and OLAP* (pp. 14-21). McLean, USA.

Velegrakis, Y., Miller, R. J., & Popa, L. (2003). Mapping adaptation under evolving schemas. In *Proc. of Int. Conference on Very Large Data Bases (VLDB)* (pp. 584-595).

Vrdoljak, B., Banek, M., & Rizzi, S. (2003). Designing Web Warehouses from XML Schemas. In In Y. Kambayashi, M. K. Mohania, W. Wöß (Eds.), *Proceedings of 5th International Conference on Data Warehousing and Knowledge Discovery; Vol. 2737, Lecture Notes of Computer Science* (pp 89-98). Prague, Czech Republic: Springer.

Wang, B. B., McKay, R. I., Abbass, H. A., & Barlow, M. (2002). Learning Text Classifier using the Domain Concept Hierarchy. *In Proceedings of International Conference on Communications, Circuits and Systems.* China.

Wei, W., Lu, H., Feng, J., & Yu, J. X. (2002). *Condensed cube: An efficient approach to reducing data cube size* (pp. 155–165). ICDE.

Weigend, A., & Nix, D. (1994). Predictions with confidence intervals (local error bars). In *Proceedings of the International Conference on Neural Information Processing (ICONIP'94)* (pp. 847–852). Seoul, Korea.

Willett, P. (1988). Recent trends in hierarchic document clustering: a critical review. *Information Processing & Management, 24*(5), 577–597. doi:10.1016/0306-4573(88)90027-1

Winter, R., & Strauch, B. (2003). A Method for Demand-Driven Information Requirements Analysis in DW Projects. *In Proceedings of 36th Annual Hawaii International Conference on System Sciences*; pp 231-239. Hawaii, USA: IEEE.

Witten, I. H., Paynter, G. W., Frank, E., Gutwin, C., & Nevill-Manning, C. G. (1999). KEA: Practical automatic keyphrase extraction. *Proc. DL '99* (pp. 254-256).

Wolfson, O., Sistla, P., Xu, B., & Chamberlain, S. (1999). Domino: Databases fOr MovINg Objects tracking. In *Proceedings of SIGMOD* (p. 547 - 549).

Worboys, M. F. (1995). *Gis: A computing perspective.* Taylor&Francis.

Wrembel, R. (2009). A Survey of Managing the Evolution of Data Warehouses. *International Journal of Data Warehousing and Mining*, 5(2), 24–56. doi:10.4018/jdwm.2009040102

Wrembel, R., Bębel, B., & Królikowski, Z. (2005). The framework for detecting and propagating changes from data sources structure into a data warehouse. *Foundations of Computing and Decision Sciences Journal*, 30(4), 361–372.

Wrembel, R., & Bębel, B. (2005). Metadata management in a multiversion data warehouse. In *Proc. of Ontologies, Databases, and Applications of Semantics (ODBASE)*, (pp. 1347-1364). LNCS 3761.

Wrembel, R., & Bębel, B. (2007). Metadata management in a multiversion data warehouse. *Journal on Data Semantics (JODS)*, 8, 118-157. LNCS 4380.

Wrembel, R., & Morzy, T. (2006). Managing and querying versions of multiversion data warehouse. In *Proc. of Int. Conference on Extending Database Technology (EDBT)* (pp. 1121-1124). LNCS 3896.

Wuu, G. T. J., & Dayal, U. (1992). A Uniform Model for Temporal Object-Oriented Databases. In Proc. of Int. Conference on Data Engineering (ICDE) (pp. 584-593).

Xin, D., Han, J., Li, X., Shao, Z., & Wah, B. W. (2007). Computing iceberg cubes by top-down and bottom-up integration: The starcubing approach. *IEEE Transactions on Knowledge and Data Engineering*, 19(1), 111–126. doi:10.1109/TKDE.2007.250589

Xin, D., Shao, Z., Han, J., & Liu, H. (2006). C-cubing: Efficient computation of closed cubes by aggregation-based checking. In Liu, L., Reuter, A., Whang, K.-Y., & Zhang, J. (Eds.), *ICDE* (p. 4). IEEE Computer Society.

Xu, X., Han, J., & Lu, W. (1990). RT-tree: An improved R-tree index structure for spatiotemporal databases. In *Proc. of Int. Symposium on Spatial Data Handling* (pp. 1040-1049).

Yang, J., & Widom, J. (1998). Maintaining Temporal Views over Non-Temporal Information Sources for Data Warehousing. *Proceedings International Conference on Extending Database Technology*, Valencia, Spain, 389-403.

Yang, J., & Widom, J. (2001). Incremental Computation and Maintenance of Temporal Aggregates. *Proceedings International Conference on Data Engineering*, Heidelberg, Germany, 51-60.

Yoo, I., Hu, X., & Song, I.-Y. (2007). A Coherent Graph-based Semantic Clustering and Summarization Approach for Biomedical Literature and a New Summarization Evaluation Methods. *BMC Bioinformatics*, 8(Suppl 9), S4. doi:10.1186/1471-2105-8-S9-S4

Zamir, O., & Etzioni, O. (1998). Web Document Clustering: A Feasibility Demonstration. *In Proceedings of SIGIR 98* (pp. 46-54).

Zamir, O., Etzioni, O., & Karp, R. M. (1997). Fast and intuitive clustering of web documents. *In Proceedings of the 3rd International Conference on Knowledge Discovery and Data Mining*.

Zeiler, M. (1999). *Modeling our world: The ESRI guide to geodatabase design*. ESRI Press.

Zhang, X., & Rundensteiner, E. (2002). Integrating the maintenance and synchronization of data warehouses using a cooperative framework. *Information Systems*, 27, 219–243. doi:10.1016/S0306-4379(01)00049-7

Zhang, D., Tsotras, V., & Seeger, B. (2002). Efficient temporal join processing using indices. In *Proc. of Int. Conference on Data Engineering (ICDE)* (pp. 103-116).

Zhang, L., Li, Y., Rao, F., Yu, X., Chen, Y., & Liu, D. (2003). An approach to enabling spatial OLAP by aggregating on spatial hierarchy.

Zhang, X., Zhou, X., & Hu, X. (2006, Dec. 18-22). Semantic Smoothing for Model-based Document Clustering. *The 2006 IEEE International Conference on Data Mining (IEEE ICDM06*. HongKong.

Zhao, Y., & Karypis, G. (2002). *Criterion functions for document clustering: Experiments and Analysis*. Department of Computer Science, University of Minnesota.

Zhong, S., & Ghosh, J. (2005). Generative Model-based Document Clustering: a Comparative Study. *Knowledge and Information Systems*, 8(3), 374–384. doi:10.1007/s10115-004-0194-1

About the Contributors

David Taniar holds Bachelor, Master, and PhD degrees - all in Computer Science, with a particular specialty in Databases. His current research is applying data management techniques to various domains, including mobile and geography information systems, parallel and grid computing, web engineering, and data mining. Every year he publishes extensively, including his recent co-authored book: High Performance Parallel Database Processing and Grid Databases (John Wiley & Sons, 2008). His list of publications can be viewed at the DBLP server (http://www.informatik.uni-trier.de/~ley/db/indices/a-tree/t/Taniar:David.html). He is a founding editor-in-chief of three SCI-E journals: Intl. J. of Data Warehousing and Mining, Mobile Information Systems, and Intl. J. of Web and Grid Services. He is currently an Associate Professor at the Faculty of Information Technology, Monash University, Australia.

Li Chen obtained a Masters degree in Computer Science from La Trobe University, Australia, in 2008. Her thesis was in the area of near real-time data warehousing. Currently, she is pursuing a PhD degree at the Department of Computer Science, La Trobe University. Her research interests include near-real time data warehousing, temporal data warehousing and spatial temporal data warehousing.

* * *

Matteo Golfarelli received his Ph.D. for his work on autonomous agents in 1998. Since 2005 he is Associate Professor, teaching Information Systems, Database Systems, and Data Mining. He has published about 70 papers in refereed journals and international conferences in the fields of pattern recognition, mobile robotics, multi-agent systems, and business intelligence that is now his main research field, and he is co-author of a book on data warehouse design. He is co-chair of the MiproBIS Conference and member of the editorial board of the Int. Jour. of Data Mining, Modeling, and Management and of the Int. Jour. of Knowledge-Based Organizations. His current research interests include distributed and semantic data warehouse systems, what-if analysis, and Business Performance Monitoring.

Stefano Rizzi received his Ph.D. in 1996 from the University of Bologna, Italy. Since 2005 he is Full Professor at the University of Bologna, where he is the head of the Data Warehousing Laboratory and teaches Business Intelligence and Software Engineering. He has published about 100 papers in refereed journals and international conferences mainly in the fields of data warehousing, pattern recognition, and mobile robotics, and a research book on data warehouse design. He joined several research projects on the above areas and has been involved in the PANDA thematic network of the European Union concerning pattern-base management systems. He is member of the steering committee of DOLAP. His current research interests include data warehouse design and business intelligence, in particular multidimensional modeling, OLAP preferences, and what-if analysis.

Sébastien Nedjar obtained the Phd degree in computer science from the University of Aix-Marseille (France) in 2009. He is an assistant professor at the University of Aix-Marseille II - IUT of Aix en Provence and is a member of the LIF laboratory. His research work concerns OLAP Mining, Data Warehousing and Multidimensional Skylines.

Rosine Cicchetti is a full professor at the University of Aix-Marseilles (France) and responsible of the database and machine learning research team at the Laboratory of Fundamental Computer Science (LIF) of Marseilles. She obtained the PhD in 1990 (University of Nice, France) and the Habilitation for Research Direction in 1996 (University of Aix-Marseilles). Her research topics encompass Databases, Data Mining, Data Warehousing, Statistical databases and Multidimensional Skylines.

Lotfi Lakhal received the Phd degree in computer science and the Habilitation for Research Direction from the University of Nice-Sophia-Antipolis (France) respectively in 1986 and in 1991.He is a full professor at the University of Aix-Marseille II - IUT of Aix en Provence and member of the laboratory LIF. His research interest includes Databases, Formal Concept Analysis, Data Mining, Data Warehousing and Multidimensional Skylines.

Noel Novelli received the Phd degree in computer science from the University of Aix-Marseille (France) in 2001.He is a assistant professor at the University of Aix-Marseille II and member of the laboratory LIF. His research interest includes Databases, Formal Concept Analysis, Data Mining, Data Warehousing.

Alain Casali obtained the Phd degree in computer science from the University of Aix-Marseilles (France) in 2005. He is an assistant professor at the University of Aix-Marseille II - IUT of Aix en Provence and is a member of the LIF laboratory.

Vasudha Bhatnagar did her Masters in Computer Applications from University of Delhi, Delhi, India in 1985. She completed her doctoral studies from Jamia Millia Islamia, New Delhi, India in 2001. She worked in C-Dot from 1985 - 1989 as a software engineer. Thereafter she taught in Moti Lal Nehru College, University of Delhi (1989 - 2002). She is currently a reader in Department of Computer Science, University of Delhi, Delhi, India. Her broad area of interest is Intelligent Data Analysis. She is particularly interested in developing process models for Knowledge Discovery in Databases and data mining algorithms, problems pertaining to modeling of changes in discovered knowledge in evolving (streaming) data sets, handling user subjectivity in KDD, projected clustering, outlier detection.

Sharanjit Kaur received her Masters Degree in Computer Applications in 1994 and Bachelor degree in Computer Science in 1991. She started teaching in 1995. Currently she is pursuing her doctoral studies in the area of 'Data Mining' from Department of Computer Science, University of Delhi, Delhi, India. Her research interest spans the area of Data Mining, Databases and Operating System.

Laurent Mignet received his MS in Computer Science (1997) from Paris VI/CNAM/ENST and PhD in Database (2001) from INRIA/CNAM. He then spent two years at the Department of Computer Science of University of Toronto with an INRIA fellowship the first year. Since February 2004 he joined IBM research in Delhi. His research works resulted to international publications in journals and top conferences as well as patents filled in USPTO. Some of his work has been transferred to the industry in a 2 startup during his PhD and now in IBM products. He is DB2 Subject Matter Expert as well as IBM Advocate for the Information Management brand for some IBM customers.

Guangzhu Yu received his master's degree in computer science from the Yangtze University, Jingzhou, China in 2002. He is currently a doctoral student at the Donghua University (formerly China Textile University), Shanghai, China. His research interests include data mining and network security.

Shihuang Shao received his bachelor's degree in electrical engineering from Southeast University, Nanjin, China, in 1960. He was a Visiting Scientist at the University of Maryland, College Park, from 1986 to 1988, and was the Chairman of Donghua University, Shanghai, China, from 1994 to 2001. He is currently a Professor of the same university. His research interests include fuzzy control, neural networks, genetic algorithms, chaos control, and data mining.

Bing Luo, male, was born in April 1966. He got his master's degree from Jianghan Petroleum Institute in 1996 and doctor's degree from Guangdong University of Technology in 2007. Now he is working in Guangdong University of Technology as an associate professor. His research interests include data mining, information acquisition and processing.

Xianhui Zeng received his master's degree from the Donghua University, Shanghai, China, in 1999. He is currently an associate professor and a doctoral student at the same University. His research interests include data mining, decision support system and intelligent information processing.

Alberto Abelló (aabello@lsi.upc.edu) has a MSc and a PhD in computer science from the Universitat Politècnica de Catalunya (Polytechnical University of Catalonia). He is associate professor at the Facultat d'Informàtica de Barcelona (Computer Science School of Barcelona). He is a member of the GESSI research group (Grup de recerca en Enginyeria del Software per als Sistemes d?Informació) at the same university, specializing in software engineering, databases and information systems. His research interests are database design, data warehousing, OLAP tools, ontologies and reasoning. He is the author of articles and papers in national and international conferences and journals on these subjects.

Oscar Romero (oromero@lsi.upc.edu) has a MSc in computer science from the Universitat Politècnica de Catalunya (Polytechnical University of Catalonia). Currently, he is a PhD student at the same university and an assistant professor at the Escola Tècnica Superior d'Enginyeria Industrial i Aeronàutica de Terrassa (Industrial and Aeronautical Engineering School of Terrassa). He is a member of the GESSI research group (Grup de recerca en Enginyeria del Software per als Sistemes d'Informació) at the same university, specializing in software engineering, databases and information systems. His research interests are database design, data warehousing, OLAP tools, ontologies and reasoning. He is the author of articles and papers in national and international conferences on these subjects.

Robert Wrembel (PhD, DSc) works in the Institute of Computing Science, at the Poznań University of Technology, Poland. In 2008 he received the post-doctoral degree (habilitation) in computer science, specializing in database systems and data warehouses. In 2008 he was elected a deputy dean of the Faculty of Computing, at the Poznań University of Technology for the period of 2008 - 2012. In 2010 he received the IBM Faculty Award for highly competitive research project. Since 1996 he has been actively involved in numerous projects in the field of information technologies, including 6 research, 5 industrial and 1 educational project. He has paid a number of visits to research and education centers, including: Université Lyon 2 (France), Université de Poitiers (France), University of Maribor (Slovenia), the INRIA Paris-Rocquencourt (France), Université Paris Dauphine (France), the Klagenfurt University (Austria), and the Loyola University (USA). His main research interests encompass data warehouse technologies (temporal, multiversion, object-relational) and object-oriented systems (views, data access optimization, methods and views materialization).

Pedro Furtado is an assistant professor of Computer Sciences at the University of Coimbra, where he teaches both undergraduate and postgraduate curricula, mostly in data management related areas. He is also an active researcher in the databases group of the CISUC research laboratory. His research interests include data warehousing, approximate query answering, parallel and distributed database systems, with a focus on performance and scalability and data management in distributed data intensive systems. He received a PhD in computer science from the University of Coimbra - Portugal in 2000.

Panos Vassiliadis received the PhD degree from the National Technical University of Athens in 2000. Since 2002, he has been with the Department of Computer Science, University of Ioannina, Greece, where he is also a member of the Distributed Management of Data (DMOD) Laboratory (http://www.dmod.cs.uoi.gr). His research activity and published work concerns the area of data warehousing, with particular emphasis on metadata, OLAP, and ETL, as well as the areas of database evolution and web services. He is a member of the ACM, the IEEE, and the IEEE Computer Society. More information is available at http://www.cs.uoi.gr/~pvassil.

Leticia Gomez was born in Buenos Aires, Argentina. She has received a bachelor degree in Computer Science from the University of Buenos Aires. She is a PhD candidate at the Instituto Tecnológico de Buenos Aires. Her research interests are in the field of databases, particularly in OLAP and data mining, and their use in the field of spatio-temporal databases, and Geographic Information Systems (GIS). She has several publications in referred international conferences and journals. She is currently a professor with the Software Engineering Departament at Instituto Tecnólogico de Buenos Aires.

Bart Kuijpers is a professor in the Theoretical Computer Science group at Hasselt University and the Transnational University of Limburg in Belgium. He has a Master degree in Mathematics from the University of Leuven and a Doctoral degree in Computer Science from the University of Antwerp. His PhD dissertation won the IBM-Belgium Prize for Computer Science awarded by the Research Foundation of Flanders and IBM. He was Researcher at the Universities of Leuven and Antwerp and was a Post-Doctoral Researcher of the Research Foundation of Flanders before becoming professor of Theoretical Computer Science at Hasselt University. He has several publications on database theory and GIS in leading journals and conference proceedings. He has organized, among others, the 1st International

Symposium on Constraint Databases in 2004 and the Dagstuhl seminar "Constraint Databases, Geometric Elimination and Geographic Information Systems" in 2007. He studies query evaluation and the expressive power of database query languages for (possibly infinite) database systems that are described by constraints. The main motivation for constraint databases and their most important application domain are spatial databases and geographic information systems (GIS). His interests also include data models and query languages for spatio-temporal data. More recently he also studies spatial and spatio-temporal data mining. He is participating in national and European research projects and in a research collaboration between Argentina and Belgium.

Bart Moelans is a teaching assistant in the Theoretical Computer Science group at Hasselt University and the Transnational University of Limburg in Belgium. He is preparing a Ph.D on spatial and spatio-temporal data mining. In particular, he studies qualitative similarity measures of trajectories and data mining query for trajectory data. He has published several papers in international conferences and workshops on GIS and data mining and has contributed to a book on spatio-temporal data mining.

Alejandro Vaisman was born in Buenos Aires (UBA), Argentina. He received a BA degree in Civil Engineering, a BA in Computer Science, and a PhD in Computer Science from UBA, and he has been a post-doctoral researcher at the University of Toronto. He is a Professor at the UBA since 1994. He was an invited professor at the Universidad Politecnica de Madrid in 1997. In 2001 he was appointed Vice-Dean of the School of Engineering and Information Technology at the University of Belgrano, in Argentina. He was a visiting researcher at the University of Toronto, University of Hasselt and Universidad de Chile. His research interests are in the field of databases, particularly in OLAP, Datawarehousing, Data Mining, P2P databases, XML, the Semantic Web, and Geographic Information Systems In 2004 he was appointed Vice-Head of the Department of Computer Science, and Chair of the Graduate Program in Data Mining at the Computer Science Department, UBA. He is the main responsible of the project "Using OLAP Techniques in Geographical Information Systems", funded by the Argentinian Scientific Agency. He is currently on leave from UBA, in the Theoretical Computer Science Group, University Of Hasselt, Beligum.

Torben Bach Pedersen is a full professor at the Center for Data-Intensive Systems (Daisy) at the Department of Computer Science, Aalborg University, Denmark. In 2000, he received his PhD in Computer Science from Aalborg University. His research interests generally concern business intelligence with a special focus on complex application areas and include multidimensional databases, data warehousing, right-time data warehousing, on-line analytical processing, federated databases, and location-based services. Among other projects, he manages the Agile & Open Business Intelligence (AOBI) project where the possibilities for using agile development methods and open source tools for business intelligence projects are explored in cooperation with industrial partners.

Christian Thomsen is a postdoctoral fellow at the Center for Data-Intensive Systems (Daisy) at the Department of Computer Science, Aalborg University, Denmark. In 2008, he received his PhD in Computer Science from Aalborg University. His research interests concern business intelligence and include multidimensional databases, data warehousing, right-time data warehousing, and on-line analytical processing. He currently works on the Agile & Open Business Intelligence (AOBI) project where the possibilities for using agile development methods and open source tools for business intelligence projects are explored in cooperation with industrial partners. Further, he is involved in projects where open source data warehouse technologies are used for analyzing web data.

Kamel Boukhalfa received his engineer diploma and master degree in Computer Science from Bab Ezzouare University Algeria in 1997 and 2002, respectively. He joined, in 2002, the advanced technology development research center for the development of Telehealth projects. He is currently doing his Ph.D in Bab Ezzouare and Poitiers Universities. His main research interests are data warehousing and optimization.

Ladjel Bellatreche received his Ph.D. in Computer Science from the Clermont Ferrand University – France in 2000. He is an assistant professor in Computer Science at Poitiers University – France since 2002. Before joining Poitiers University, he has been a visiting researcher at Hong Kong University of Science and Technology from 1997 to 1999 and also been a visiting researcher in Computer Science Department at Purdue University - USA during summer 2001. He has worked extensively in the areas: distributed databases, data warehousing, data mining, and heterogeneous data integration using formal ontologies. He has published more than 75 research papers in these areas in leading international journal and conferences. Ladjel has been associated with many conferences and journals as program committee members.

Pascal Richard is a professor in computer science at the University of Poitiers, France. He received the PhD degree in computer science from the University of Tours (France) in 1997. His research interests include real-time systems, scheduling theory, database systems, on-line algorithms and combinatorial optimization.

Min Song is an assistant professor of Department of Information Systems at NJIT. He received his M.S. in School of Information Science from Indiana University in 1996 and received Ph.D. degree in Information Systems from Drexel University in 2005. Min has a background in Text Mining, Bioinfomatics, Information Retrieval and Information Visualization. Min received the Drexel Dissertation Award in 2005. In 2006, Min's work received an honorable mention award in the 2006 Greater Philadelphia Bioinformatics Symposium. In addition, The paper entitled "Extracting and Mining Protein-protein interaction Network from Biomedical Literature" has received the best paper award from 2004 IEEE Symposium on Computational Intelligence in Bioinformatics and Computational Biology, which was held in San Diego, USA, Oct. 7-8, 2004. In addition, another paper entitled "Ontology-based Scalable and Portable Information Extraction System to Extract Biological Knowledge from Huge Collection of Biomedical Web Documents" was nominated as the best paper at 2004 IEEE/ACM Web Intelligence Conference, which was held in Beijing, China, Sept, 20-24, 2004.

Xiaohua (Tony) Hu is currently an associate professor (early tenured in 2007) and the founding director of the data mining and bioinformatics lab at the College of Information Science and Technology. He is the now also serving as the IEEE Computer Society Bioinformatics and Biomedicine Steering Committee Chair, and the IEEE Computational Intelligence Society Granular Computing Technical Committee Chair (2007-2008). Tony is a scientist, teacher and entrepreneur. He joined Drexel University in 2002, founded the International Journal of Data Mining and Bioinformatics (SCI indexed) in 2006, International Journal of Granular Computing, Rough Sets and Intelligent Systems in 2008. Earlier, he worked as a research scientist in the world-leading R&D centers such as Nortel Research Center, GTE labs and HP Labs. In 2001, he founded the DMW Software in Silicon Valley, California. His research ideas have been integrated into many commercial products and applications.

Illhoi Yoo is an assistant professor of the department of Health Management and Informatics, University of Missouri School of Medicine. He gained his M.S. degree in information science from University of Pittsburgh and his Ph.D. in information science and technology from Drexel University. His research interest is in semantic-oriented MEDLINE search and biomedical literature mining using biomedical ontologies. He has published 35 peer reviewed papers in various journals, conferences and book chapters. He won the best paper award as the co-author of a paper published in the Proceedings of the 2004 IEEE Symposium on Computational Intelligence in Bioinformatics and Computational Biology on Oct. 7, 2004.

Eric Koppel is an undergraduate at the New Jersey Institute of Technology, working toward a B.S. in Computer Science. His research interests include knowledge discovery, pattern mining and Web 2.0 technologies.

Zoran Bosnić obtained his Master and Doctor degrees in Computer Science at University of Ljubljana (Slovenia) in 2003 and 2007, respectively. Since 2006 he has been employed at Faculty of Computer and Information Science and currently works as an assistant professor in the Laboratory of Cognitive Modelling. His research interests include artificial intelligence, machine learning, regression, and reliability estimation for individual predictions, as well as applications in these areas.

Igor Kononenko received his PhD in 1990 from University of Ljubljana, Slovenia. He is a professor at the Faculty of Computer and Information Science in Ljubljana and the head of the Laboratory for Cognitive Modeling. His research interests include artificial intelligence, machine learning, neural networks and cognitive modeling. He is a member of the editorial board of Applied Intelligence Journal and Informatica Journal. He is a (co)author of 180 papers and 10 textbooks. Recently he co-authored the book "Machine Learning and Data Mining: Introduction to Principles and Algorithms" (Hoorwood, 2007).

Index